Leveraging LLMs for Business Innovation:

Practical Solutions and Future Trends

Sherif Mohamed A. Ismail
https://orcid.org/0009-0000-0852-873X
American University in Cairo, Egypt

IGI Global
Scientific Publishing
Publishing Tomorrow's Research Today

Published in the United States of America by
IGI Global Scientific Publishing
701 East Chocolate Avenue
Hershey, PA, 17033, USA
Tel: 717-533-8845 | Fax: 717-533-7115
Website: https://www.igi-global.com E-mail: cust@igi-global.com

Library of Congress Cataloging-in-Publication Data

Names: Ismail, Sherif Mohamed A., 1973- editor
Title: Leveraging LLMs for business innovation : practical solutions and future trends / [edited by] Sherif Mohamed A. Ismail.
Description: Hershey, PA : IGI Global Scientific Publishing, [2026] | Includes bibliographical references and index. | Summary: "This book aims to provide a thorough understanding of how LLMs can be leveraged for business innovation"-- Provided by publisher.
Identifiers: LCCN 2025021017 (print) | LCCN 2025021018 (ebook) | ISBN 9798337339122 hardcover | ISBN 9798337339139 paperback | ISBN 9798337339146 ebook
Subjects: LCSH: Technological innovations--Management | Natural language processing (Computer science) | Artificial intelligence--Business applications
Classification: LCC HD45 .L43685 2026 (print) | LCC HD45 (ebook) | DDC 658.5/14--dc23/eng/20250710
LC record available at https://lccn.loc.gov/2025021017
LC ebook record available at https://lccn.loc.gov/2025021018

British Cataloguing in Publication Data
A Cataloguing in Publication record for this book is available from the British Library.

Table of Contents

Detailed Table of Contents

This chapter delves into the intricate world of Large Language Models (LLMs), exploring their foundational architecture, evolution, and practical applications. The purpose is to provide a comprehensive understanding of how LLMs function, from the groundbreaking Transformer architecture to advanced techniques like prompt engineering and fine-tuning. Key concepts such as attention mechanisms, multi-head attention, and positional encodings are explained to reveal the inner workings of these models. The chapter examines the progression of LLM families, including GPT, BERT, and Gemini, highlighting innovations in scalability, efficiency, and multimodal capabilities. Techniques for optimizing LLM performance, such as quantization, distillation, and retrieval-augmented generation, are discussed alongside ethical considerations and evaluation methodologies. Through detailed explanations and practical examples, the chapter aims to equip readers with the knowledge needed to effectively interact with and leverage the power of LLMs

As large language models (LLMs) transition from research projects to enterprise workflows, this chapter aims to be a practical guide to implementing them through the solution lifecycle, from exploration through deployment and monitoring. There are considerations regarding architecture decisions, such as whether to use an API or self-hosted model, level of integration in the system, and trade-offs between costs, performance, and scalability. Also examined are application approaches, such as fine-tuning, prompt engineering, and RAG, to name a few, in addition to cloud and open-source platforms, MLOps practices, and real-world examples and case studies, to ultimately support technical and business leaders in capitalizing on the potential for LLMs to create sustained impact.

The integration of Large Language Models (LLMs) into key domains like finance and healthcare is transforming intelligent automation and decision-making. This chapter examines LLM applications in fraud detection and financial forecasting, as well as in clinical support and patient interaction. In finance, LLMs analyze transaction data, user behavior, and financial texts to detect fraud and enhance predictive insights from news, reports, and sentiment. In healthcare, they support diagnosis, treatment planning, and patient communication by processing and generating human-like medical language. The chapter outlines practical implementation frameworks, highlights challenges in data governance and compliance, and addresses concerns around model transparency and fairness. By presenting cross-industry use cases, this work illustrates how LLMs can generate actionable insights and drive innovation while upholding ethical and operational standards.

This chapter explores how Large Language Models (LLMs) integrated within Enterprise Resource Planning (ERP) systems are transforming financial reporting. Traditional ERP systems automate business processes but often struggle with providing real-time insights or handling vast datasets and unstructured data. LLMs, powered by Natural Language Processing (NLP), offer a promising solution by enabling ERP systems to generate accurate, real-time financial reports, while incorporating external data sources such as financial news, market sentiment, and economic indicators. The chapter delves into the benefits and challenges of integrating LLMs into ERP systems for financial reporting, showcasing leading ERP platforms that have already adopted LLM capabilities. Furthermore, it discusses how this integration enhances report generation, improves forecasting, ensures compliance, and ultimately provides actionable insights for businesses. The chapter also explores the future potential of LLMs in revolutionizing financial reporting within ERP systems.

The Large Language Model (LLM) has great potential for Islamic finance, a sector that is grounded in Sharia principles that emphasizes ethics, transparency, and risk sharing, but its application is still underexplored. This study examines how LLM improves transparency, risk management, and customer experience in Islamic finance using a qualitative method approach. A systematic literature review was conducted through the Scopus database, selecting peer-reviewed articles relevant to LLM, Islamic finance, as well as tasks such as sentiment analysis and risk assessment. Articles are filtered by title/abstract, full text, with data extracted for research purposes, methodology, findings, and limitations, organized into themes. Thematic and quantitative analyses synthesize findings to propose an LLM integration framework, addressing challenges such as hallucinations and data privacy with techniques such as Labeled Guide Prompting and DP-LoRA. The findings show LLMs such as ChatGPT-4o, TAT-LLM, and FinQAPT automate audits, improve risk management through predictive analytics for profit-sharing contracts, and provide culturally sensitive financial advice, outperforming traditional methods in efficiency and objectivity. The framework offers practical implications for financial institutions, advancing ethical AI in the Sharia financial system while emphasizing human oversight for reliability and compliance.

Direct selling is a business model rooted in personal trust and human interaction. While sales enablement strategies aim to support independent sellers, they often fall short in scaling personalized communication an area where manual efforts become inefficient. This paper explores the potential of generative AI, particularly LLMs like Claude by Anthropic, deployed via Amazon Bedrock, to automate personalized outreach including emails, social messages, and product recommendations. A real-world case is examined where a legacy, template-based system was upgraded to an AI-powered platform capable of tailoring messages using customer history and preferences. Cost and ROI analysis reveal improved efficiency, higher repeat purchases, and stronger customer relationships. The study also explores how LLMs analyze unstructured data for hyper-personalized journeys and addresses key implementation concerns such as CRM integration, data privacy, training, and bias. The paper concludes that genAI, when used ethically and strategically, enhances rather than replaces the human role in direct selling.

Preface

INTRODUCTION

Over the past several years, the rapid evolution of Large Language Models (LLMs) has transformed the global technological landscape, reshaping how organizations operate, innovate, and compete. What was once an area dominated by research and experimental prototypes has quickly matured into a critical driver of business transformation across sectors. Today, LLMs power intelligent automation, enhance data-driven decision-making, and enable new forms of human–machine interaction that were previously unimaginable. As enterprises strive to navigate uncertainty and volatility, the strategic deployment of LLMs has become essential not only for efficiency but for long-term competitiveness and growth.

This edited volume, *Leveraging LLMs for Business Innovation: Practical Solutions and Future Trends*, was developed to bring together a diverse set of perspectives, methodologies, and use cases that illuminate the true breadth of LLM capabilities. Our goal as editors is to provide a comprehensive yet practical resource that bridges the gap between theoretical advances in AI and their application in real-world business environments. Each chapter offers insights from scholars and practitioners across disciplines—including engineering, management, finance, information systems, and applied AI—collectively illustrating how LLMs are reshaping contemporary organizational landscapes.

At the heart of this book is the recognition that LLM adoption is not merely a technological shift but a strategic and cultural one. Effective integration requires rethinking processes, workforce dynamics, governance structures, and ethical frameworks. The authors featured in this volume emphasize not only technical implementation but also issues of transparency, accountability, fairness, and human-centered design. As LLM-driven systems become increasingly embedded in daily operations, these considerations are essential for ensuring responsible and sustainable innovation. This book aims to support students, researchers, managers, and policymakers in understanding both the opportunities and complexities that accompany LLM-enabled transformation.

CHAPTER OVERVIEW

Chapter 1 introduces readers to the foundational concepts behind LLMs, tracing their evolution from Transformer architectures to modern multimodal systems. It offers essential grounding in attention mechanisms, model scaling, training strategies, and optimization techniques.

Chapter 2 shifts to practical implementation, outlining how organizations can build LLM-enabled solutions through prompt engineering, fine-tuning, architectural decision-making, and MLOps practices. Case studies illustrate common deployment challenges and success strategies.

Chapter 3 examines Retrieval-Augmented Generation (RAG) as a bridge between static model knowledge and dynamic enterprise data. The authors explore its architectures, retriever technologies, and applications across industry functions such as marketing, HR, and finance.

Chapter 4 focuses on fine-tuning LLMs for domain-specific business environments, covering instruction tuning, RLHF, LoRA, data preparation, compliance, and real-world applications in sectors including healthcare, finance, and legal services.

Chapter 5 highlights how LLMs are transforming intelligent enterprise functions, including decision-making, forecasting, ROI assessment, and human–AI collaborative workflows. Organizational readiness and ethical compliance are core themes.

Chapter 6 analyzes the economic implications of AI adoption, addressing productivity gains, labor market disruptions, wage inequality, and policy frameworks required to balance innovation with economic sustainability.

Chapter 7 explores cross-industry applications of LLMs in finance and healthcare, particularly in fraud detection, financial forecasting, clinical support, and patient interaction. The chapter emphasizes governance, transparency, and implementation risks.

Chapter 8 examines the integration of LLMs in ERP systems, showing how they enhance financial reporting, real-time analytics, compliance processes, and decision support in modern enterprise environments.

Chapter 9 presents a qualitative study of LLM adoption in Islamic finance, proposing a structured framework for transparency, risk management, and customer engagement aligned with Sharia principles.

Chapter 10 offers a real-world case study from the direct selling industry, demonstrating how LLMs automate personalized customer outreach, increase scalability, and improve seller support through ethical and human-centered generative AI.

Chapter 11 explores the transition from compliance-focused AI governance to proactive ethical stewardship, aligning LLM governance with ESG principles, organizational culture, and global human-centered standards.

Chapter 12 analyzes emerging trends in collaborative technologies powered by LLMs—including multilingual communication, knowledge sharing, and AI-enabled teamwork—while addressing ethical considerations around trust, privacy, and dependency.

Chapter 13 concludes the volume by presenting the Enterprise LLM Deployment Lifecycle (ELDL), a strategic framework for planning, deploying, governing, and scaling LLM solutions responsibly across industries.

CONCLUSION

As editors, we recognize that the integration of LLMs into modern business environments represents a defining moment in technological and organizational evolution. This book underscores that the value of LLMs extends far beyond automation: they are reshaping how knowledge is created, how decisions are made, and how organizations understand and serve their customers. The contributions in this volume collectively reflect a growing global effort to harness these technologies ethically, strategically, and inclusively.

The insights presented here reveal that effective LLM adoption demands a holistic approach. Technical sophistication must be matched with robust governance frameworks, ethical leadership, talent development, and an unwavering commitment to transparency and fairness. The chapters demonstrate that organizations able to balance these dimensions will be best positioned to thrive in increasingly data-driven and AI-augmented environments. The future of business innovation belongs to those who view LLMs not only as tools but as catalysts for new forms of collaboration, creativity, and strategic transformation.

We extend our sincere appreciation to the authors who contributed their expertise, research, and practical experience to this volume. Their work demonstrates the breadth of global perspectives and the interdisciplinary nature required for meaningful progress in AI-driven business innovation. We hope this book serves as a valuable resource for readers seeking to understand, apply, and shape the future of LLM-enabled enterprise transformation. It is our belief that by fostering informed, responsible, and forward-looking adoption of LLM technologies, organizations can unlock profound opportunities for economic growth, social impact, and sustainable development.

Chapter 1
Diving Deep Into the World of LLMs

Mohamad Saleh
https://orcid.org/0009-0005-6283-4187
University of Colorado, USA

ABSTRACT

This chapter delves into the intricate world of Large Language Models (LLMs), exploring their foundational architecture, evolution, and practical applications. The purpose is to provide a comprehensive understanding of how LLMs function, from the groundbreaking Transformer architecture to advanced techniques like prompt engineering and fine-tuning. Key concepts such as attention mechanisms, multi-head attention, and positional encodings are explained to reveal the inner workings of these models. The chapter examines the progression of LLM families, including GPT, BERT, and Gemini, highlighting innovations in scalability, efficiency, and multimodal capabilities. Techniques for optimizing LLM performance, such as quantization, distillation, and retrieval-augmented generation, are discussed alongside ethical considerations and evaluation methodologies. Through detailed explanations and practical examples, the chapter aims to equip readers with the knowledge needed to effectively interact with and leverage the power of LLMs

DIVING DEEP INTO THE WORLD OF LLMS

Alright, buckle up, everyone, and welcome to the deep dive! Today, we're plunging headfirst into the fascinating – and frankly, enormous – world of Large Language Models (LLMs). These aren't just the buzzwords of the moment; they're foundational technologies that are rapidly reshaping everything around us. From

DOI: 10.4018/979-8-3373-3912-2.ch001

the way we write code to the stories we tell, LLMs are popping up everywhere, and their influence is only growing.

But here's the thing: LLMs are only as good as the instructions we give them. That's where the art and science of prompt engineering comes in. Think of it as learning to speak the language of AI – crafting the perfect prompts to unlock the full potential of these powerful models. We're not just talking about asking simple questions; we're talking about using techniques like Chain-of-Thought prompting to guide the LLM through complex reasoning, or Few-Shot prompting to teach it new tasks with just a handful of examples. We'll even explore how Role Prompting can shape the LLM's personality and style.

The pace of advancement in this field is absolutely breathtaking. To give you an idea, we're pushing right up to the edge of what's known as of February 2025 – seriously cutting-edge stuff! So, our mission in this chapter is to distill this complex landscape, to get to the heart of what LLMs are: what they're made of, how they evolve, and, crucially, how they learn. And, of course, we'll tackle the big question: how do we even measure how good they are? We'll even peek under the hood at some of the clever tricks used to make these powerhouses run faster. It's a lot to cover, but hopefully, we can make it a fun ride. Let's jump in, and let's learn how to *talk* to these amazing machines!

THE TRANSFORMER: OUR LAUNCHPAD

The starting point for understanding modern LLMs is the Transformer architecture. It's almost humorous to consider that this revolutionary design originated from a Google project focused on language translation, dating back to 2017 (Vaswani et al., 2017).

The original Transformer, as you might recall, comprised two key components: an encoder and a decoder. Envision it as a system that receives a sentence in one language and transforms it into another.

The encoder takes the input—for instance, a sentence in French—and generates a representation of it, essentially a summary of its meaning. Subsequently, the decoder utilizes this representation to produce the output, such as the English translation, incrementally. Each of these increments is termed a token. A token can be a complete word, like "Cat," or a segment of a word, such as "pre" in "prefix." However, the true ingenuity lies in the processes occurring within each layer of this Transformer architecture. Let's delve into that magic.

INSIDE A TRANSFORMER LAYER: UNVEILING THE INNER WORKINGS

So, what's the secret sauce that makes a Transformer layer so powerful? Let's peel back the layers and see what's going on:

1. Preparing the Text: From Words to Building Blocks

Initially, the raw text must be converted into a format that the model can interpret. We dissect the text into smaller units known as tokens, utilizing a specific vocabulary that the model recognizes. Each token is then transformed into a dense vector, referred to as an embedding. This embedding functions as a digital fingerprint, encapsulating the meaning of the token (Mikolov et al., 2013).

Analogy: Think of it like building with LEGOs. The words are like complex structures, but we need to break them down into individual LEGO bricks (tokens) that the model can manipulate. The embedding is like the unique shape and color of each brick, representing its properties.

2. The Order Matters: Adding Context with Positional Encodings

Here's a crucial point: Transformers process all the tokens in a sentence simultaneously. This is incredibly efficient, but it means we initially lose the information about the order of the words. To compensate, we add something called positional encodings. These encodings inject information about the position of each word within the sentence (Vaswani et al., 2017).

Analogy: Imagine a band playing a song. Each instrument (word) plays its part, but the order in which they play is crucial to the melody. Positional encodings are like musical notation, telling the model when each instrument should play.

3. Multi-Head Attention: The Relationship Detective

Now we arrive at what is arguably the most famous and crucial part: multi-head attention. This is where the model starts to understand the relationships between words in the sentence (Vaswani et al., 2017).

Let's use the "thirsty tiger" example to illustrate this. Consider the sentence: "The thirsty tiger jumped out of the tree to get a drink because it was thirsty." Self-attention is what allows the model to connect the pronoun "it" back to the "tiger."

It achieves this by creating three vectors for each word:

- **Query:** Represents the word's need for information.
- **Key:** Represents the word's relevance to other words.
- **Value:** Represents the actual information the word carries.

Analogy: Think of it like a detective investigating a crime scene. Each word is a suspect, and the query, key, and value vectors are like the detective's questions, clues, and evidence.

The model then compares each word's query to all the other words' keys, calculating a score that represents how relevant they are to each other. These scores are then normalized to create attention weights. These weights tell the model how much attention each word should pay to the others. Finally, the model uses these weights to create a weighted sum of all the value vectors, resulting in a rich representation of each word that takes into account its relationships with all the other words in the sentence.

The truly remarkable aspect is that all of this comparison and calculation happens in parallel, using matrices for the query (Q), key (K), and value (V) of all the tokens.

This ability to process all these relationships concurrently is a major reason why Transformers excel at capturing the subtle nuances of language, a task that previous sequential models struggled with, especially when dealing with longer sentences.

4. Multi-Head: Seeing the Whole Picture

Think of "multi-head" as performing the self-attention process multiple times simultaneously, each time using a different set of query, key, and value matrices (Vaswani et al., 2017).

Each "head," or parallel self-attention process, learns to focus on different types of relationships. One head might concentrate on grammatical structure, while another might focus on semantic connections between words. By combining these diverse perspectives, the model gains a much deeper and more comprehensive understanding of the text.

Analogy: Imagine a group of art critics analyzing a painting. Each critic has their own perspective and expertise, focusing on different aspects of the artwork. By combining their insights, they create a richer and more complete understanding of the painting.

In essence, multi-head attention is like having a team of experts working together to analyze the text from multiple angles, resulting in a more nuanced and accurate understanding. It's incredibly powerful stuff!

5. Keeping Things Stable: Layer Normalization and Residual Connections

You might also come across terms like Layer Normalization (Ba et al., 2016) and Residual Connections (He et al., 2016). These are crucial for keeping the training process stable, especially when dealing with the really deep networks that LLMs are. They're absolutely essential for successful training.

- **Layer Normalization:** Helps maintain a consistent activity level within each layer. It ensures that the activations (the signals passing through the network) stay within a healthy range, which speeds up training and improves results.

Analogy: Think of it like regulating the voltage in an electrical circuit. If the voltage is too high or too low, the circuit can malfunction. Layer normalization ensures that the "voltage" (activation) stays within the optimal range.

- **Residual Connections:** Act like shortcuts within the network. They allow the original input of a layer to bypass the main processing path and be added directly to the output. This helps the network remember what it learned earlier, even after passing through many layers.

Analogy: Imagine you're trying to learn a complex skill. Residual connections are like having a cheat sheet that reminds you of the basic principles, even as you delve into more advanced techniques.

Residual connections are particularly important because they help prevent the "vanishing gradient problem." This is where the signal gets weaker and weaker as it passes through deeper layers of the network, making it difficult for the earlier layers to learn. Residual connections provide a direct path for the signal to flow, preventing it from fading away.

6. The Final Touch: The Feed Forward Layer

After all the attention mechanisms, we have the Feed Forward Layer. This is a feed forward network that's applied to each token's representation separately, after all the attention calculations.

Analogy: Think of the attention mechanism as highlighting the important parts of a document. The Feed Forward Layer is like a skilled editor who takes those highlighted parts and refines them, adding clarity and depth.

This layer gives the model even more power to represent information and learn complex functions of the input. It's the final step in processing each token within a Transformer layer, preparing it for the next layer or for generating the final output.

BEYOND THE ORIGINAL: DECODER-ONLY ARCHITECTURES AND MIXTURE OF EXPERTS

So, we've discussed the encoder-decoder structure of the original Transformer (Vaswani et al., 2017). However, you might notice that many of the newer LLMs are opting for a decoder-only architecture. What's the advantage of ditching the encoder?

Well, if your primary goal is generating text, like writing stories or engaging in conversations, you don't always need the encoder. The encoder's main task is to create a comprehensive representation of the entire input sequence upfront. Decoder-only models skip this step and directly generate the output token by token (Radford et al., 2018).

They achieve this using a special type of self-attention called Masked Self-Attention. This ensures that when the model is predicting the next token, it can only "see" the tokens that came before it, just like when we write or speak. This simpler design is particularly well-suited for generating text.

Before we move on from the topic of architecture, there's one more fascinating technique to discuss: Mixture of Experts (MOE). This is a clever way to make these already massive models even bigger without sacrificing speed (Shazeer et al., 2017).

How do you make these classical models more efficient? MOE seems to be a key part of the solution. In MOE, you have specialized submodels, called "experts," all residing within a single, large model. The trick is that there's a "gating network" that decides which experts are best suited to process each input.

Analogy: Imagine you have a team of highly specialized professionals, each with expertise in a different area. Instead of having one generalist handle every task, you have a system that routes each task to the most qualified specialist.

So, you might have a model with billions of parameters, but for any given input, only a small fraction of those parameters (the active experts) are actually engaged. It's like having a team of specialists, and you only call in the ones you need for the specific job. This allows for massive models that are still surprisingly efficient

THE LLM FAMILY TREE: CHARTING A COURSE THROUGH INNOVATION

Efficiency is paramount, and it's now beneficial to take a broader perspective: how have LLMs progressed over time? The Transformer architecture (Vaswani et al., 2017) served as the initial catalyst, but subsequent developments truly ignited the field. A rich lineage of LLMs has emerged, so where did this journey begin after the introduction of the original Transformer paper?

- **GPT-1 (OpenAI, 2018):** This marked a significant turning point (Radford et al., 2018). GPT-1 employed a decoder-only design and underwent training in an unsupervised manner, leveraging a vast collection of books known as BooksCorpus. This unsupervised pre-training proved crucial, enabling the model to acquire general language patterns from the extensive raw text. Subsequently, it was adapted for specific tasks. While GPT-1 exhibited limitations, such as a tendency to repeat phrases and challenges in sustaining lengthy conversations, it nonetheless represented a substantial advancement.
- **BERT (Google, 2018):** In the same year, Google introduced BERT, which adopted a contrasting strategy (Devlin et al., 2018). BERT utilized an encoder-only architecture and prioritized comprehending language, rather than generating it. Its training involved tasks like masked language modeling and next sentence prediction, all geared towards deciphering the meaning of text.

Consequently, GPT-1 possessed conversational abilities but occasionally faltered, whereas BERT excelled at understanding but struggled to engage in dialogue.

- **GPT-2 (OpenAI, 2019):** GPT-2 expanded upon the foundation laid by GPT-1, employing more data from a dataset known as WebText (sourced from Reddit) and increasing the model's parameter count (Radford et al., 2019). This resulted in enhanced coherence, improved handling of long-range dependencies between words, and, notably, the capacity to acquire new skills without explicit training. This phenomenon is termed zero-shot learning, where the model can often deduce how to perform a task simply by being presented with an example in the prompt. This represented a considerable stride forward!
- **The GPT-3 Lineage (OpenAI, 2020 onwards):** Beginning in 2020, the GPT-3 family emerged (Brown et al., 2020). These models underwent continuous scaling, incorporating ever-increasing numbers of parameters. GPT-3, boasting 175 billion parameters, was immense and demonstrated improved few-shot learning, acquiring knowledge from limited examples. Furthermore, we

witnessed the emergence of instruction-tuned models, such as InstructGPT (Ouyang et al., 2022), specifically trained to adhere to instructions articulated in natural language. Subsequently, models like GPT-3.5, renowned for their proficiency in understanding and generating code, and GPT-4, a transformative innovation, were developed. GPT-4 was a genuinely multimodal model, capable of processing both images and text, and its context window expanded dramatically, enabling it to consider far more extensive text segments.

- **LaMDA (Google, 2021):** Google also actively pursued innovation. LaMDA, their conversational AI, was a noteworthy development (Thoppilan et al., 2022). It was meticulously crafted for natural-sounding conversations.

While the GPT models were becoming more versatile, LaMDA concentrated on dialogue, and its capabilities in this area were evident.

- **Gopher (DeepMind, 2021):** DeepMind entered the arena with Gopher (Rae et al., 2021). What distinguished Gopher? It was another decoder-only model, but DeepMind prioritized the use of high-quality data for training, assembling a dataset known as Massive Text. They also implemented sophisticated optimization techniques. Gopher performed well on knowledge-intensive tasks but encountered difficulties with more intricate reasoning challenges. An intriguing discovery was that simply enlarging the model by adding more parameters does not invariably enhance performance across all tasks. Certain tasks necessitate alternative strategies; sheer size is not the sole determinant of success.
- **PaLM (Google):** Then there was PaLM from Google, which leveraged the MOE concept we previously discussed (Chowdhery et al., 2022), enabling these massive models to operate more efficiently. PaLM demonstrated that it was possible to attain comparable or even superior performance to a dense model like GPT-3 while consuming significantly less computational power. This represented a substantial gain in efficiency.
- **Chinchilla (DeepMind, 2022):** Chinchilla challenged established scaling principles, specifically the notion that larger models are invariably superior (Hoffmann et al., 2022). They determined that, for a given parameter count, training on a considerably larger dataset than was previously customary yielded better results. Their 70 billion parameter model outperformed significantly larger models due to its training on an extensive dataset. This prompted a reevaluation of scaling strategies; model size is not the only critical factor, the quantity of training data is also paramount.
- **PaLM 2 (Google):** Google introduced PaLM and PaLM 2. PaLM debuted in 2022 and exhibited impressive performance across a range of benchmarks,

attributable in part to Google's pathway system, which facilitated efficient model scaling. PaLM 2 was released in 2023 and demonstrated even greater proficiency in areas such as reasoning, coding, and mathematics, despite having fewer parameters than its predecessor. PaLM 2 now serves as the foundation for much of Google's GenAI initiatives within Google Cloud.

- **Gemini (Google):** Gemini represents Google's latest family of models, designed from the outset to be multimodal. Gemini is pushing the boundaries of what's possible, engineered to process not only text but also images, audio, and video. They have been refining architectural designs to enable these models to scale significantly and optimizing Gemini to operate rapidly on their Tensor Processing Units (TPUs). MOE is also incorporated into some Gemini models. A range of sizes, from ultra to pro to nano to flash, cater to diverse requirements. Gemini 1.5 Pro, with its expansive context window, has been particularly noteworthy, capable of handling millions of tokens, a truly remarkable feat.
- **The Rise of Open Source LLMs:** What about the contributions from the open-source community? The open-source LLM landscape is experiencing rapid growth. Google unveiled Gemma and Gemma 2 in 2024, which are lightweight yet potent open models built upon their Gemini research.

Gemma boasts an extensive vocabulary, and a 2 billion parameter variant is available that can run on a single GPU, enhancing accessibility. Gemma 2's performance is comparable to that of considerably larger models, such as Meta's Llama 3 70B. Meta's Llama series has been highly influential, commencing with Llama 1, followed by Llama 2 (Touvron et al., 2023) (which is subject to a commercial use license), and subsequently Llama 3. These models have undergone continuous refinement in areas like reasoning, coding, general knowledge, and safety, and multilingual and vision capabilities have been incorporated in the Llama 3.2 release. Mistral AI's Mixtral employs a sparse mixture of experts architecture, utilizing eight experts but activating only two at any given time. It excels in mathematics, coding, and multilingual tasks, and many of its models are open source.

- **Advanced Reasoning at OpenAI:** OpenAI's O1 models are dedicated to complex reasoning tasks. They are achieving top-tier results on demanding scientific reasoning benchmarks.
- **DeepSeek's Approach:** DeepSeek is also pursuing compelling research in reasoning, employing a novel reinforcement learning technique known as group relative policy optimization. Their DeepSeek R1 model exhibits performance comparable to OpenAI's O1 on numerous tasks, although it remains closed source despite releasing model weights.

Beyond these examples, a multitude of other open models are under development, demonstrating the remarkable pace of innovation in this field.

UNLOCKING THE POWER OF LLMS: FINE-TUNING AND PROMPT ENGINEERING

- **The Foundation:** Before we delve into fine-tuning, it's important to understand the initial step: **pre-training**. LLMs are first trained on massive datasets of text and code, learning general language patterns, grammar, and world knowledge. This pre-training phase is computationally intensive and lays the groundwork for subsequent fine-tuning (Devlin et al., 2018; Radford et al., 2018).
- **What is Fine-Tuning?** Fine-tuning is the process of taking a pre-trained LLM (trained on a massive dataset) and further training it on a smaller, task-specific dataset. This adapts the model to perform better on specific tasks, improve its style, or incorporate new knowledge.
- **Why Fine-Tune?**
    - **Improved Performance:** Fine-tuning significantly boosts performance on target tasks compared to using the pre-trained model directly.
    - **Task Specialization:** Tailors the model to specific domains (e.g., legal, medical, customer service).
    - **Style Adaptation:** Adjusts the model's writing style to match a desired tone or brand voice.
    - **Knowledge Injection:** Incorporates new information not presented in the original training data.
- **Fine-Tuning Techniques**
    - **Full Fine-Tuning:** Training *all* the parameters of the pre-trained model. This is computationally expensive and requires a large amount of task-specific data.
    - **Parameter-Efficient Fine-Tuning (PEFT):** Training only a *small portion* of the model's parameters, leaving the majority of the pre-trained weights frozen. This significantly reduces computational cost and data requirements (Houlsby et al., 2019).
        - **Adapter-Based Fine-Tuning:**
        - Adds small, task-specific modules called "Adapters" into the pre-trained model's architecture (Houlsby et al., 2019).
        - Only the parameters within these Adapters are trained, while the original pre-trained weights remain unchanged.

        - Simple to implement and allows for modularity (different adapters for different tasks).
        - **Low-Rank Adaptation (LoRA):**
        - Approximates the weight updates that would be made during full fine-tuning using low-rank matrices (Hu et al., 2021).
        - This drastically reduces the number of trainable parameters.
        - **QLoRA:** An even more efficient variant of LoRA that uses quantized weights to further reduce memory footprint (Dettmers et al., 2023).
        - **Soft Prompting:**
        - Learns a small, continuous vector called a "soft prompt" that is added to the input (Lester et al., 2021).
        - This soft prompt guides the model to perform the desired task without modifying the original pre-trained weights.
- **Key Considerations for Fine-Tuning:**
    - **Data Quality:** The quality and relevance of the fine-tuning data are crucial for achieving good results.
    - **Hyperparameter Tuning:** Experimenting with different learning rates, batch sizes, and other hyperparameters is essential for optimizing performance.
    - **Overfitting:** Carefully monitor the model for overfitting (memorizing the training data instead of generalizing to new data). Techniques like regularization and early stopping can help prevent overfitting.

Prompt Engineering

Imagine you have a super-smart AI assistant, ready to help with anything from coding to creative writing. But here's the catch: it only understands you if you ask the right way. That's where prompt engineering comes in!

Prompt engineering is the art and science of crafting effective prompts – the instructions you give to AI models like Large Language Models (LLMs) – to get the results you want. It's about understanding how LLMs work and using that knowledge to guide them toward the best possible output. Think of it as learning how to "speak AI."

Why is this important for you?

- **Boost your skills:** Whether you're a computer science major, a marketing student, or an aspiring writer, prompt engineering can enhance your abilities and open up new possibilities.

- **Solve real-world problems:** Use LLMs to automate tasks, generate creative content, analyze data, and more.
- **Stand out in the job market:** As AI becomes more prevalent, prompt engineering skills will be highly valued by employers.

UNDERSTANDING LLM OUTPUTS: SHAPING WHAT COMES OUT

Before diving into specific techniques, let's understand how LLMs generate responses. It's not just about what you put in, but how you shape what comes out. You have more control than you think!

Output Length: Tokens and Cost

LLMs generate text by predicting the next word in a sequence. The length of the output is measured in "tokens," which can be words, parts of words, or even punctuation marks. Keep in mind that the number of tokens directly impacts processing time and cost, especially when using cloud-based LLMs.

Sampling Controls: Temperature, Top K, and Top P

These parameters control the randomness and creativity of the LLM's output.

- **Temperature:** Think of this as a "creativity dial."
  - **Low temperature (e.g., 0.2):** Produces more predictable, deterministic outputs. Good for tasks requiring accuracy and precision, like generating code with correct syntax.
  - **High temperature (e.g., 0.9):** Introduces more randomness, leading to diverse and unexpected results. Useful for brainstorming and exploring new ideas.
- **Top K:** Limits the LLM to considering only the K most likely next words.
  - **Low K (e.g., 1):** Very focused and deterministic.
  - **High K (e.g., 40):** More variety in the output.
- **Top P (Nucleus Sampling):** Selects the smallest set of words whose probabilities add up to at least the value of P.
  - **Low P (e.g., 0.1):** Restrictive, focuses on the most probable words.
  - **High P (e.g., 0.99):** Considers almost all possible words.

How to Adjust These Values:

The specific method for adjusting these parameters depends on the LLM you're using. Here are a few common examples:

General Setup (Assumed)

I'm assuming you're using Google Colab with Python and likely one of these libraries:

- **Hugging Face Transformers:** For working with pre-trained language models like GPT-2, BERT, etc.
- **OpenAI API:** If you're using models like GPT-3, GPT-4, etc.

1. Hugging Face Transformers

Figure 1. This is a very common scenario in Colab

```python
from transformers import pipeline

# Load a text generation pipeline (e.g., GPT-2)
generator = pipeline('text-generation', model='gpt2')

# Generate text with adjusted parameters
prompt = "The quick brown fox"
response = generator(prompt,
                     max_length=50,  # Adjust as needed
                     temperature=0.7,  # Adjust for creativity
                     top_k=50,         # Adjust for diversity
                     top_p=0.95,       # Adjust for probability mass
                     num_return_sequences=1) # How many different sequences to generate

print(response[0]['generated_text'])
```

Explanation:

- temperature: Controls the randomness of the output. Lower values (e.g., 0.2) make the output more deterministic, while higher values (e.g., 1.0) make it more creative.
- top_k: The model will only consider the top_k most likely next words.

- top_p: The model will consider the smallest set of words whose cumulative probability exceeds top_p. Also known as "nucleus sampling."
- num_return_sequences: If you want to generate multiple different outputs based on the same prompt and parameters, increase this value

2. OpenAI API

If you're using the OpenAI API (e.g., for GPT-3, GPT-4), you'll use the openai Python library.

Figure 2.

```python
import openai

openai.api_key = "YOUR_OPENAI_API_KEY"  # Replace with your API key

response = openai.Completion.create(
  engine="text-davinci-003",  # Or another engine
  prompt="Write a haiku about autumn.",
  temperature=0.7,
  max_tokens=60,
  top_p=0.9,
  frequency_penalty=0.0,
  presence_penalty=0.0
)

print(response.choices[0].text)
```

- **Explanation:**
    - You set your OpenAI API key.
    - The openai.Completion.create() method is used to generate text.
    - temperature, max_tokens, and top_p are parameters that control the generation process.
    - frequency_penalty and presence_penalty are other parameters that can influence the output.

Important Notes and Best Practices

- **Experimentation:** The best values for temperature, top_k, and top_p depend heavily on the specific task and the model you're using. Experiment to find what works best.

- **Model-Specific Ranges:** Check the documentation for the specific model you're using to see the recommended ranges for these parameters. Some models might have different scales or limitations.
- **top_k vs. top_p:** It's generally recommended to use either top_k or top_p, but not both at the same time. They control the sampling process in slightly different ways. top_p is often preferred because it's more adaptive.
- **Zero Temperature:** Setting temperature to 0 is often used for deterministic outputs, but it can sometimes lead to repetitive or boring results.
- **Error Handling:** Always include error handling in your code to catch potential exceptions from the API calls.
- **API Keys:** Never hardcode your API keys directly into your Colab notebooks. Use environment variables or a secure configuration method.
- **Colab Pro:** If you're doing a lot of LLM work in Colab, consider Colab Pro for increased resources and longer runtimes.

Example: Finding the Right Temperature

Figure 3. Run this code and compare the outputs for different temperatures. You'll see how the creativity and randomness of the story change.

```python
import openai

openai.api_key = "YOUR_OPENAI_API_KEY"

prompt = "Write a short story about a cat who goes on an adventure."

temperatures = [0.2, 0.7, 1.2]

for temp in temperatures:
    print(f"--- Temperature: {temp} ---")
    response = openai.Completion.create(
        engine="text-davinci-003",
        prompt=prompt,
        temperature=temp,
        max_tokens=150
    )
    print(response.choices[0].text)
    print("\n")
```

PROMPT ENGINEERING TECHNIQUES: YOUR TOOLKIT FOR SUCCESS

Now, let's explore some powerful prompt engineering techniques.

1. General/Zero-Shot Prompting

- **Concept:** Provide a task description and input without any examples.
- **Example:**

Figure 4.

```text
Prompt: "Write a Python function to calculate the factorial of a number."
```

2. One-Shot and Few-Shot Prompting

- **Concept:** Provide one or a few examples to guide the LLM.
- **Example:**

Figure 5.

```text
Prompt:
"Example 1:
Input: 5
Output: 120

Example 2:
Input: 3
Output: 6

Now, calculate the factorial of 7."
```

3. System Contextual Prompting

- **Concept:** Set the overall context and purpose for the LLM.

- **Example:**

Figure 6.

```text
Prompt:
"You are a helpful and efficient coding assistant for a college student.
Write a Python function to calculate the factorial of a number."
```

4. Role Prompting

- **Concept:** Give the LLM a specific persona or identity.
- **Example:**

Figure 7.

```text
Prompt:
"You are a Senior Software Engineer explaining a code snippet to a junior developer.
Explain the following Python function:

def factorial(n):
    if n == 0:
        return 1
    else:
        return n * factorial(n-1)"
```

5. Step-Back Prompting

- **Concept:** Ask the LLM a broader related question before the specific task.
- **Example:**

Figure 8.

```text
Prompt:
"First, explain the concept of recursion.
Now, write a Python function to calculate the factorial of a number using recursion."
```

6. Chain of Thought (COT) Prompting

- **Concept:** Prompt the LLM to explicitly generate intermediate reasoning steps.
- **Example:**

Figure 9.

```text
Prompt:
"First, break down the steps to calculate the factorial of a number.
Then, write a Python function to implement those steps."
```

7. Self-Consistency

- **Concept:** Generate multiple reasoning paths and choose the most consistent answer.
- **How to implement:** Run the same COT prompt multiple times and compare the results.

8. Tree-of-Thoughts (TOT) Prompting

- **Concept:** Explore multiple reasoning paths simultaneously.
- **Note:** This is a more advanced technique that requires careful planning and execution.

9. React Prompting

- **Concept:** Combine the LLM's reasoning capabilities with external tools.
- **Example:** (Requires external libraries and APIs)

Figure 10.

```python
# This is a conceptual example and requires setup with LangChain or similar
prompt = "Use a search engine to find the current price of Bitcoin. Then, write a short analysis of the price trend."
```

10. Automatic Prompt Engineering (APE)

- **Concept:** Use the LLM to generate and evaluate prompt variations.
- **Note:** This is an advanced technique that requires careful setup and evaluation.

11. Code Prompting

- **Concept:** Use prompts to generate, explain, translate, debug, and review code.
- **Examples:**
  - **Generating Code:** "Write a Python function to sort a list of numbers."
  - **Explaining Code:** "Explain what this Python function does: [code snippet]"
  - **Translating Code:** "Translate this Python code to JavaScript: [code snippet]"
  - **Debugging Code:** "Find the error in this Python code: [code snippet] [error message]"

Best Practices: Tips for Effective Prompting

- **Provide Examples:** Use one-shot and few-shot prompting to guide the LLM. Demonstrating the desired input-output relationship is often far more effective than simply describing it.
  - **Example:** Instead of saying "Translate this sentence into French," provide an example: "English: Hello, how are you? French: Bonjour, comment allez-vous? Now translate: Good morning, have a nice day."
- **Design with Simplicity:** Keep your prompts clear, concise, and easy to understand. Avoid jargon, ambiguity, and overly complex sentence structures. The LLM needs to understand your intent quickly and accurately.
  - **Example:** Instead of "Given the current market conditions and considering the prevailing economic indicators, generate a report outlining potential investment strategies," try "Write a short report on investment strategies, considering the current market."
- **Be Specific:** Clearly state your desired output format and constraints. This is crucial for getting structured and predictable results.
  - **Example:**
    - **Bad:** "Summarize this article." (The LLM might summarize in any way it chooses.)
    - **Good:** "Summarize this article in three bullet points, each no more than 20 words." (This provides clear constraints on the output.)

        - **Even Better (for structured data):** “Extract the following information from this article and output it as a JSON object: title, author, publication date, summary (max 50 words).”

- **Use Positive Language:** Focus on what you *want* the LLM to do, rather than what you *don't* want it to do. Positive instructions are generally more effective.
    - **Example:**
        - **Negative:** “Don't include any personal opinions in your summary.”
        - **Positive:** “Write an objective summary of the article.”
- **Specify the Tone and Style:** If the tone or style of the output is important, explicitly state it in your prompt.
    - **Example:** “Write a formal email to a client,” or “Write a humorous blog post about the benefits of exercise.”
- **Iterate and Refine:** Prompt engineering is an iterative process. Don't expect to get perfect results on your first try. Experiment with different prompts, analyze the outputs, and refine your prompts based on the results.
- **Consider the Model's Knowledge:** Be aware of the LLM's training data and capabilities. Don't ask it to perform tasks that are outside its scope of knowledge or abilities.
- **Use Delimiters:** Use clear delimiters (e.g., triple quotes “"""”, backticks `, or XML-style tags) to separate different parts of your prompt, such as instructions, context, and input data. This helps the LLM understand the structure of your prompt.
    - **Example:**

Figure 11.

```text
"""
Instructions: Summarize the following article.
Article:
[Article Text Here]
"""
```

- **Test for Bias:** Be mindful of potential biases in the LLM's training data and test your prompts to ensure they don't produce biased or discriminatory outputs.

- **Document Your Prompts:** Keep a record of the prompts you've used, the results you've obtained, and any changes you've made. This will help you track your progress and learn from your experiments.
- **Use System Prompts Effectively:** If the LLM supports system prompts (instructions given at the beginning of the conversation that set the overall context), use them to define the LLM's role, personality, and general guidelines.
    - o **Example:** "You are a helpful and unbiased AI assistant. Your goal is to provide accurate and informative answers to user questions."
- **Break Down Complex Tasks:** If you're trying to solve a complex problem, break it down into smaller, more manageable subtasks and use separate prompts for each subtask.
- **Check for Hallucinations:** LLMs can sometimes "hallucinate" or make up facts. Always verify the accuracy of the information they provide, especially for critical tasks.
- **Monitor Token Usage:** Be aware of the token limits and pricing of the LLM you're using. Optimize your prompts to minimize token usage and avoid unnecessary costs.

By following these best practices, you can significantly improve the effectiveness of your prompts and unlock the full potential of LLMs. Remember that prompt engineering is a skill that improves with practice, so keep experimenting and learning.

Democratizing LLMs

PEFT techniques and effective prompt engineering are making LLMs more accessible to a wider range of users and organizations. By reducing the computational cost and data requirements for fine-tuning, and by enabling users to control the model's output through carefully crafted prompts, these techniques are democratizing the power of LLMs.

How Do We Know If LLMs Are Actually Good?

- **The Evaluation Headaches:** So, you've built this amazing new language model. But how do you really know if it's any good? It's not like traditional machine learning where you can just look at a number and say, "Okay, it's 95% accurate!" With LLMs, it's much more nuanced. How do you measure something as subjective as the quality of generated text? It's a tough problem, especially when you want to move beyond simple demos and into real-world applications.
- **Building a Better Yardstick: Key Evaluation Principles:**

- **Look at the Whole Picture:** Evaluation needs to be more than just one number. We need to look at the whole picture and consider different aspects of the model's performance.
- **Use the Right Data:** The data you use to test the model should be relevant to the specific task you're evaluating. It should be representative of what the model will encounter in the real world, and it should include both real user interactions and synthetic data to cover a wide range of scenarios.
- **Consider the System:** Don't just evaluate the model in isolation. Think about the whole system it's part of. Is it using retrieval-augmented generation (RAG) (Lewis et al., 2020)? Is it controlling an agent? All of these things can affect the overall performance.
- **Define "Good" for Your Use Case:** What does "good" actually mean for your specific application? Is it accuracy, helpfulness, creativity, or something else entirely? You need to tailor your evaluation to the specific application.

- **The Tools of the Trade: Evaluation Methods:**
    - **Quantitative Metrics:** We still use traditional quantitative methods like BLEU (Papineni et al., 2002) and ROUGE (Lin, 2004) to compare the model's output to ground truth answers. But these metrics don't always tell the whole story. Sometimes a creative or unexpected response might be just as good, or even better, than the expected one.
    - **Human Judgment:** That's why human evaluation is so important. Human reviewers can provide more nuanced judgments on things like fluency, coherence, and overall quality. But, let's be honest, human evaluation is expensive and time-consuming.
    - **AI Judging AI:** So, people have started using LLMs to evaluate other LLMs (Zheng et al., 2023). It's like using AI to judge AI! You give the evaluator model the task, the evaluation criteria, and the responses generated by the model you're testing. The evaluator then gives you a score, often with a reason for its judgment. There are different types of these evaluators, like generative models, reward models, and discriminative models.
        - **Calibrating the AI Judge:** One crucial thing is that you need to calibrate these AI evaluators. This means comparing their judgments to human judgments to make sure they're actually measuring what you want them to measure. And you always need to be aware of the limitations of the evaluator model itself.
    - **More Advanced Approaches:** There are even more advanced approaches being developed, like breaking down tasks into sub-tasks and using

rubrics with multiple criteria to make the evaluation more interpretable. This is especially useful for evaluating multimodal generation, where you need to assess the quality of the text, images, or videos separately.

Supercharging LLMs: Making Them Respond in a Flash!

- **Why Speed Matters:** How can we make these brainy models think faster? As LLMs grow bigger and more intricate, they often become slower and more demanding on resources. Optimizing the process of generating responses (what we call "inference") is absolutely essential, especially for applications where every millisecond counts. So, what are the secret ingredients for accelerating inference?
- **The Art of Compromise: Balancing Speed and Quality:** There's a whole range of strategies, but it often boils down to a delicate balancing act: how do you juggle the quality of the output with the speed and cost of producing it? Sometimes, you might be willing to accept a tiny dip in accuracy to achieve a significant leap in speed. You also need to weigh the trade-offs between how quickly you get a single response (latency) and how many requests the system can handle simultaneously (throughput). The ideal approach really hinges on the specific application you have in mind.
- **Two Main Paths to Faster LLMs:** We can generally group these techniques into two broad categories:
    - **"Good Enough" Methods (Output-Approximating):** These are the techniques where we're okay with the output being slightly different if it means we get a big boost in efficiency.
    - **"No Compromises" Methods (Output-Preserving):** These are the techniques where we insist on the output being exactly the same, but we try to make the calculations more efficient under the hood.
- **"Good Enough" Methods: When Close is Good Enough:**
    - **Quantization: Shrinking the Numbers:** Let's start with quantization (Jacob et al., 2018). Think of it as simplifying the numbers the model uses. Instead of using super-precise numbers (like 32-bit floating-point), we use smaller, less precise numbers (like 8-bit or even 4-bit integers). This is like using rounded numbers instead of exact decimals. It saves a ton of memory and makes the calculations much faster, often with only a minor impact on accuracy. There are also clever techniques like quantization-aware training (QAT) that help minimize any accuracy loss, and you can even fine-tune how the quantization works.
    - **Distillation: Learning from the Master:** What about distillation (Hinton et al., 2015)? Isn't that like training a smaller model to be a

mini-version of a bigger one? Exactly! Distillation is another way to boost efficiency. You have a large, super-accurate "teacher" model, and you train a smaller "student" model to mimic its behavior. The student model is usually much faster and more efficient, and it can still do a pretty darn good job. There are different flavors of distillation, like data distillation, knowledge distillation, and on-policy distillation. These are the techniques that might tweak the output a little bit.

- **"No Compromises" Methods: Speed Without Sacrificing Quality:**
  - **FlashAttention: Turbocharging Attention:** What if we want to keep the output exactly the same? That's where techniques like FlashAttention come in (Dao et al., 2022). FlashAttention is specifically designed to optimize those self-attention calculations inside the Transformer. It basically cuts down on the amount of data that needs to be moved around during those calculations, which can be a major bottleneck. The awesome thing about FlashAttention is that it doesn't change the results of the attention calculations, just how they're done, so the output remains perfect.
  - **Prefix Caching: Remembering What You Already Know:** Prefix caching is a smart trick, especially for conversational applications. It's all about saving time when you have parts of the input that keep repeating. Think about a conversation where each turn builds on what was said before. With prefix caching, you remember the results of the attention calculations for the initial part of the conversation, so you don't have to recalculate them every time. It's like remembering what you already figured out so you don't have to do it all over again.
  - **Speculative Decoding: Guessing the Future:** What about speculative decoding (Chen et al., 2023)? This is a pretty ingenious idea. You use a smaller, faster "draft" model to guess what the next few words (tokens) will be. Then, the main model quickly checks those guesses in parallel. If the draft model is right, you can just accept those words and skip the full calculations, which speeds things up considerably. The trick is to have a draft model that's pretty good and usually agrees with the main model.
- **The Optimization Toolkit: A Comprehensive Arsenal of Techniques for Enhanced Model Performance**
  - In the realm of machine learning and deep learning, optimizing models is a critical step to ensure they run faster, more efficiently, and with greater scalability. To achieve this, researchers and practitioners have developed a rich collection of techniques, often referred to as an "optimization toolkit" or "bag of tricks." These methods encompass a wide

range of strategies designed to improve various aspects of model training and inference, including computational efficiency, memory usage, convergence speed, and overall performance.

- Some of these techniques focus on hardware acceleration, such as leveraging GPUs or TPUs to parallelize computations and reduce processing time. Others involve algorithmic improvements, like advanced optimization algorithms (e.g., AdamW, SGD with momentum) that help models converge more quickly and avoid suboptimal solutions. Additionally, there are model-specific optimizations, such as pruning redundant parameters, quantizing weights to lower precision, or employing knowledge distillation to compress large models into smaller, more efficient ones.
- Beyond these, data-centric optimizations play a crucial role. For instance, preprocessing pipelines can be streamlined, and data augmentation techniques can be tailored to maximize the utility of available datasets. Moreover, distributed training strategies allow models to be trained across multiple devices or nodes, further accelerating the process for large-scale applications.
- Each of these techniques, while powerful on its own, becomes even more effective when combined with others. Together, they form a versatile toolkit that empowers developers to fine-tune their models for specific use cases, whether the goal is to deploy a lightweight model on edge devices or to train a state-of-the-art system on massive datasets. By strategically applying these methods, we can unlock the full potential of modern machine learning frameworks, ensuring that our models are not only accurate but also practical and sustainable in real-world scenarios

ETHICAL CONSIDERATIONS

As Large Language Models (LLMs) continue to evolve and permeate various aspects of society, their ethical implications have become a critical area of concern. While these models offer immense potential for innovation and efficiency, they also pose significant risks that must be addressed to ensure responsible deployment. Below are two key ethical considerations related to prompt engineering and LLMs:

1. Bias in Outputs

One of the most pressing ethical challenges is the propagation of biases present in the training data. LLMs learn from vast corpora of text sourced from the internet, books, and other repositories, which often contain implicit or explicit biases related to race, gender, socioeconomic status, and other sensitive attributes. These biases can manifest in the outputs generated by the model, leading to harmful stereotypes, discriminatory language, or unfair treatment of certain groups.

For example:

- A poorly designed prompt might inadvertently reinforce societal prejudices. For instance, asking an LLM to "describe the typical CEO" could result in stereotypical portrayals based on outdated or biased data.
- Similarly, prompts that lack diversity in examples or context might lead to outputs that exclude underrepresented groups.

Mitigation Strategies:

- Bias-Aware Prompt Design: Incorporate diverse and inclusive examples in prompts to guide the model toward equitable responses. For instance, explicitly instructing the model to consider multiple perspectives or demographics can help mitigate bias.
- Data Audits: Regularly audit training datasets and fine-tuning processes to identify and address sources of bias.
- Post-Processing Filters: Implement mechanisms to review and filter outputs for biased or harmful content before they reach end users.

2. Misinformation and Harmful Content

LLMs have the capability to generate highly convincing yet entirely fabricated information, commonly referred to as "hallucinations." This poses a significant risk when the models are used in contexts where accuracy is paramount, such as journalism, scientific research, or legal documentation. Moreover, malicious actors could exploit LLMs to generate disinformation campaigns, phishing emails, or propaganda tailored to manipulate public opinion.

For example:

- An LLM could be prompted to write persuasive but false narratives about historical events, misleading readers and spreading misinformation.
- Similarly, bad actors might use role prompting to simulate authoritative voices (e.g., pretending to be a doctor or lawyer) to deceive individuals.

Mitigation Strategies:

- Fact-Checking Mechanisms: Integrate external knowledge bases or retrieval-augmented generation (RAG) systems to ground the model's responses in verified facts.
- Guardrails in Prompt Engineering: Use system contextual prompts to define boundaries, such as prohibiting the generation of harmful, illegal, or unethical content.
- Transparency and Accountability: Clearly communicate to users when content is AI-generated and provide avenues for reporting erroneous or harmful outputs.

3. Privacy Concerns

The training data for LLMs often includes personal information scraped from online sources, raising concerns about privacy violations. Additionally, improperly designed prompts could inadvertently reveal sensitive user data stored within the model's memory during inference.

Mitigation Strategies:

- Data Anonymization: Ensure that training datasets are anonymized to remove personally identifiable information (PII).
- Prompt Restrictions: Avoid designing prompts that encourage the model to recall private or confidential details unless absolutely necessary.

By proactively addressing these ethical considerations through thoughtful prompt engineering, robust safeguards, and ongoing monitoring, we can harness the power of LLMs while minimizing their potential for harm.

FUTURE DIRECTIONS

The field of Large Language Models (LLMs) and prompt engineering is advancing at an unprecedented pace, opening up exciting possibilities for future research and development. Below are some promising directions that hold significant potential to shape the next generation of AI technologies:

1. Enhancing Interpretability and Explainability

One of the major limitations of current LLMs is their "black-box" nature, making it difficult to understand how they arrive at specific decisions or outputs. As these models become increasingly integral to decision-making processes in fields like healthcare, law, and finance, there is a growing demand for transparency and explainability.

Future Research Opportunities:

- Explainable Prompt Engineering: Develop techniques to make the reasoning process behind LLM outputs more interpretable. For instance, combining Chain-of-Thought (COT) prompting with visualizations or step-by-step breakdowns could help users trace the logic behind complex responses.
- Model-Specific Insights: Investigate methods to extract insights into the inner workings of attention mechanisms and token representations without compromising performance.

2. Multimodal Integration

While text-based LLMs dominate the current landscape, the integration of multiple modalities—such as images, audio, and video—is poised to unlock new capabilities. Models like Gemini already showcase the potential of multimodal architectures, but further advancements in this area will expand their applicability across industries.

Future Applications:

- AI-Assisted Creativity: Enable LLMs to collaborate seamlessly with designers, filmmakers, and musicians by generating ideas, scripts, or compositions based on visual or auditory inputs.
- Accessibility Tools: Develop multimodal assistants capable of interpreting sign language, reading handwritten notes, or summarizing videos for visually impaired users.

3. Sustainable and Efficient Scaling

As LLMs grow larger and more complex, their environmental impact and computational costs become increasingly unsustainable. Future innovations must focus on creating lightweight, energy-efficient models without sacrificing performance.

Emerging Trends:

- Parameter-Efficient Fine-Tuning (PEFT): Continue refining techniques like LoRA, QLoRA, and Adapter-Based Fine-Tuning to minimize resource consumption during model customization.
- Sparse Architectures: Explore sparse mixture-of-experts (MoE) designs and other parameter-sharing strategies to achieve scalability while reducing redundancy.

4. Democratizing Access to AI

The high cost and technical expertise required to develop and deploy LLMs currently limit their accessibility to large organizations and well-funded institutions. Efforts to democratize access will empower smaller businesses, educators, and individual creators to leverage these tools effectively.

Potential Initiatives:

- Open-Source Ecosystems: Encourage the release of open-source models, tools, and benchmarks to foster innovation at all levels.
- User-Friendly Interfaces: Create intuitive platforms that allow non-experts to experiment with prompt engineering and deploy AI solutions without extensive coding knowledge.

5. Human-AI Collaboration

Rather than replacing human expertise, the future of LLMs lies in augmenting human capabilities through seamless collaboration. By designing systems that complement human strengths—such as creativity, empathy, and judgment—AI can serve as a powerful co-pilot in problem-solving and decision-making.

Examples of Collaborative Systems:

• Code Assistance: Platforms like GitHub Copilot demonstrate how LLMs can assist developers by suggesting code snippets, debugging errors, and optimizing algorithms.

• Educational Support: Develop intelligent tutoring systems that adapt to individual learning styles and provide personalized feedback to students.

6. Addressing Ethical Challenges Proactively

Ethical considerations will remain a cornerstone of LLM development. Future work should prioritize building frameworks that embed fairness, accountability, and transparency into every stage of the AI lifecycle—from dataset curation to real-world deployment.

Key Areas of Focus:

- Bias Detection Tools: Automate the identification and mitigation of biases in both training data and model outputs using advanced statistical techniques.
- Regulatory Compliance: Collaborate with policymakers to establish guidelines and standards for the ethical use of LLMs in sensitive domains.

By pursuing these future directions, researchers and practitioners can ensure that LLMs not only continue to push the boundaries of what is technically possible but also contribute positively to society in meaningful and sustainable ways.

END-OF-CHAPTER QUESTIONS AND PROJECT: PROMPT ENGINEERING

Conceptual Understanding:

1. **Define Prompt Engineering:** In your own words, explain what prompt engineering is and why it's important in the context of Large Language Models (LLMs).
2. **The LLM Black Box:** Explain why understanding the inner workings of LLMs is helpful, but not strictly necessary, for effective prompt engineering. What's more important?
3. **Ethical Considerations:** Discuss at least two ethical considerations related to prompt engineering. How can prompts be used to create harmful or biased outputs, and what steps can be taken to mitigate these risks?
4. **The Iterative Process:** Why is prompt engineering considered an iterative process? What steps are involved in refining a prompt to achieve the desired results?

Prompt Engineering Techniques:

5. **Technique Comparison:** Briefly describe the following prompt engineering techniques and provide a scenario where each would be most appropriate:
   - Zero-Shot Prompting
   - Few-Shot Prompting
   - System Contextual Prompting
   - Role Prompting
   - Chain-of-Thought (COT) Prompting
6. **Scenario-Based Prompting:** You need to generate a Python function that calculates the nth Fibonacci number. Design prompts using *three* different prompt engineering techniques (from the list above) to achieve this. Compare the results and discuss which technique was most effective and why.
7. **Combining Techniques:** Explain how you might combine System Contextual Prompting with Chain-of-Thought Prompting to improve the accuracy and clarity of an LLM's response. Provide an example.

8. **Code Prompting Applications:** Describe three different ways you could use code prompting in a software development project. Provide specific examples of prompts you might use.
9. **Real-World Application:** Choose a real-world problem (e.g., summarizing customer reviews, generating marketing copy, writing code documentation). Describe how you would use prompt engineering to address this problem, specifying the techniques you would employ and why.

Temperature, Top K, and Top P:

10. **Sampling Parameters Explained:** Explain the purpose of each of the following sampling parameters in LLMs:
    - Temperature
    - Top K
    - Top P (Nucleus Sampling)
11. **Creativity vs. Accuracy:** How does adjusting the temperature parameter affect the balance between creativity and accuracy in an LLM's output? Provide examples of scenarios where you would prioritize creativity and scenarios where you would prioritize accuracy.
12. **Top K and Top P Trade-offs:** What are the trade-offs between using Top K and Top P sampling? In what situations might you prefer one over the other?
13. **Parameter Tuning:** You're using an LLM to generate creative writing prompts. The outputs are either too predictable or nonsensical. How would you adjust the temperature, Top K, and Top P parameters to improve the quality of the prompts? Explain your reasoning.
14. **The Repetition Loop:** Describe the “repetition loop” problem in LLMs. How can adjusting temperature, Top K, and Top P help to mitigate this issue?
15. **Practical Application:** You want to use an LLM to generate highly accurate and factual summaries of scientific research papers. What values would you choose for temperature, Top K, and Top P? Explain your choices.

Advanced Questions (Optional):

16. **Automatic Prompt Engineering (APE):** Research and explain the concept of Automatic Prompt Engineering (APE). How does it work, and what are its potential benefits and limitations?
17. **Bias Mitigation:** Research and discuss techniques for mitigating bias in LLM outputs through prompt engineering. Provide examples of prompts that could be used to reduce bias.

18. **The Future of Prompt Engineering:** In your opinion, what are the most promising future directions for prompt engineering research and development?

PROJECT TITLE: AI-POWERED MARKET RESEARCH AND CONTENT CREATION FOR A NEW PRODUCT LAUNCH

Project Overview:

Your team is a marketing consultancy hired by a fictional company, "InnovateTech," to assist with the launch of their new product: "SmartScribe," an AI-powered writing assistant designed for business professionals. InnovateTech wants to create a comprehensive marketing strategy, including market research, target audience identification, content creation, and social media engagement. Your team will leverage LLMs and prompt engineering techniques to accomplish these tasks.

Project Goals:

- Conduct market research to understand the competitive landscape and identify potential customer needs.
- Define the target audience for SmartScribe, including their demographics, psychographics, and pain points.
- Generate compelling marketing content, including website copy, blog posts, email campaigns, and social media posts.
- Develop a social media engagement strategy to build brand awareness and generate leads.
- Evaluate the effectiveness of different prompt engineering techniques in achieving the project goals.

Project Deliverables:

1. **Market Research Report:** A detailed report summarizing the market research findings, including competitor analysis, market trends, and customer needs.
2. **Target Audience Profile:** A comprehensive profile of the target audience, including demographics, psychographics, pain points, and preferred communication channels.
3. **Marketing Content Portfolio:** A collection of marketing content generated using LLMs, including:
    - Website copy (homepage, product page, pricing page)
    - Blog posts (at least 3)

- Email campaign (at least 3 emails)
- Social media posts (at least 10, across different platforms)

4. **Social Media Engagement Strategy:** A detailed plan for engaging with the target audience on social media, including content calendar, posting schedule, and engagement tactics.
5. **Prompt Engineering Analysis:** A report analyzing the effectiveness of different prompt engineering techniques used throughout the project, including:
   - Comparison of different techniques for specific tasks (e.g., Zero-Shot vs. Few-Shot for content generation)
   - Analysis of the impact of temperature, Top K, and Top P on the quality and creativity of the generated content
   - Recommendations for best practices in prompt engineering for marketing applications.
6. **Presentation:** A presentation summarizing the project findings, deliverables, and key insights.

PROJECT STAGES AND PROMPT ENGINEERING TECHNIQUES

Stage 1: Market Research (Using LLMs for Data Gathering and Analysis)

- **Techniques:**
  - **Zero-Shot Prompting:** Use LLMs to generate questions for market research surveys and interviews.
    - *Example Prompt:* "Generate 5 open-ended questions to understand the needs of business professionals regarding writing assistance tools."
  - **Few-Shot Prompting:** Provide examples of well-structured market research reports and ask the LLM to summarize competitor websites or analyze market trends.
    - *Example Prompt:* "Here's an example of a market research report: [Report Text]. Now, summarize the key findings from this competitor website: [Competitor Website Text]."
  - **System Contextual Prompting:** Define the LLM's role as a market research analyst.
    - *Example Prompt:* "You are a market research analyst. Summarize the key trends in the AI-powered writing assistant market."
- **Deliverable:** Market Research Report

Stage 2: Target Audience Identification (Defining the Ideal Customer)

- **Techniques:**
    - o **Role Prompting:** Ask the LLM to create a persona of the ideal SmartScribe user.
        - ■ *Example Prompt:* "You are a marketing expert. Create a detailed persona of the ideal SmartScribe user, including their demographics, psychographics, pain points, and goals."
    - o **Chain-of-Thought Prompting:** Guide the LLM to break down the process of identifying the target audience into smaller steps.
        - ■ *Example Prompt:* "First, identify the key characteristics of business professionals who would benefit from a writing assistant. Then, create a detailed profile of the ideal SmartScribe user based on those characteristics."
- **Deliverable:** Target Audience Profile

Stage 3: Content Creation (Generating Marketing Materials)

- **Techniques:**
    - o **Few-Shot Prompting:** Provide examples of effective website copy, blog posts, and email campaigns, and ask the LLM to generate similar content for SmartScribe.
        - ■ *Example Prompt:* "Here's an example of effective website copy: [Website Copy Text]. Now, write website copy for the SmartScribe homepage, highlighting its key features and benefits."
    - o **Role Prompting:** Assign the LLM different roles, such as a copywriter, a blogger, or an email marketing specialist.
        - ■ *Example Prompt:* "You are a copywriter. Write a compelling headline for the SmartScribe website."
    - o **Temperature, Top K, and Top P Tuning:** Experiment with different values for these parameters to control the creativity and quality of the generated content.
        - ■ *Example Task:* Generate 5 different versions of a blog post introduction using different temperature settings (0.2, 0.5, 0.8). Analyze the impact of temperature on the creativity and coherence of the introductions.
- **Deliverable:** Marketing Content Portfolio

Stage 4: Social Media Engagement Strategy (Planning and Generating Content)

- **Techniques:**
  - **Zero-Shot Prompting:** Ask the LLM to generate ideas for social media posts and engagement tactics.
    - *Example Prompt:* "Generate 10 ideas for social media posts to promote SmartScribe on LinkedIn."
  - **Few-Shot Prompting:** Provide examples of successful social media campaigns and ask the LLM to create a content calendar for SmartScribe.
    - *Example Prompt:* "Here's an example of a successful social media campaign: [Campaign Description]. Now, create a content calendar for SmartScribe on Twitter for the next month."
  - **Role Prompting:** Assign the LLM the role of a social media manager.
    - *Example Prompt:* "You are a social media manager. Write a tweet to announce the launch of SmartScribe."
- **Deliverable:** Social Media Engagement Strategy

Stage 5: Prompt Engineering Analysis (Evaluating and Optimizing Techniques)

- **Techniques:**
  - **Comparative Analysis:** Compare the effectiveness of different prompt engineering techniques for specific tasks.
    - *Example Task:* Compare the quality of website copy generated using Zero-Shot Prompting, Few-Shot Prompting, and Role Prompting.
  - **Parameter Tuning Analysis:** Analyze the impact of temperature, Top K, and Top P on the quality and creativity of the generated content.
    - *Example Task:* Generate multiple versions of a blog post introduction using different combinations of temperature, Top K, and Top P. Analyze the impact of these parameters on the creativity and coherence of the introductions.
  - **Best Practices Recommendations:** Develop a set of best practices for prompt engineering in marketing applications based on the project findings.
- **Deliverable:** Prompt Engineering Analysis Report

Assessment Criteria:

- **Quality of Market Research:** Thoroughness, accuracy, and relevance of the market research findings.
- **Clarity of Target Audience Profile:** Completeness, accuracy, and insightsfulness of the target audience profile.
- **Effectiveness of Marketing Content:** Compellingness, clarity, and persuasiveness of the marketing content.
- **Feasibility of Social Media Engagement Strategy:** Practicality, creativity, and alignment with the target audience.
- **Depth of Prompt Engineering Analysis:** Thoroughness, accuracy, and insightsfulness of the prompt engineering analysis.
- **Presentation Quality:** Clarity, organization, and persuasiveness of the presentation.
- **Teamwork and Collaboration:** Effective collaboration and communication within the team.

Additional Notes:

- Students should use a variety of LLMs (e.g., GPT-3.5, GPT-4, Llama 2) to compare their performance.
- Students should document all prompts used throughout the project.
- Students should cite all sources used in their reports and presentations.
- This project can be adapted to fit different course lengths and learning objectives.

SUMMARY

This chapter has taken us on an extensive journey through the fascinating realm of Large Language Models (LLMs), exploring their architecture, evolution, and practical applications. We began by understanding the foundational Transformer architecture, which revolutionized natural language processing with its innovative attention mechanisms and parallel processing capabilities.

We delved into the inner workings of Transformer layers, examining key components such as tokenization, positional encodings, multi-head attention, and various normalization techniques. These elements collectively enable LLMs to capture complex relationships within text and process information efficiently.

The chapter then traced the evolutionary path of LLMs, highlighting significant milestones from GPT-1 to the latest multimodal models like Gemini. We explored how architectural innovations, training methodologies, and scaling strategies have continuously pushed the boundaries of what these models can achieve.

A crucial section focused on fine-tuning and prompt engineering, emphasizing their importance in adapting pre-trained models to specific tasks and domains. We examined various fine-tuning techniques, including parameter-efficient methods like LoRA and adapter-based approaches, which make LLMs more accessible and practical for diverse applications.

The discussion on prompt engineering revealed it as both an art and a science, showcasing numerous techniques to effectively communicate with LLMs. From zero-shot and few-shot prompting to advanced methods like chain-of-thought reasoning and role prompting, we explored how carefully crafted instructions can significantly influence model outputs.

Evaluation of LLMs emerged as a complex but essential topic, requiring a multifaceted approach that combines quantitative metrics with human judgment and AI-assisted evaluation. We also examined various optimization techniques that balance speed and quality, making LLMs more efficient for real-world applications.

Finally, the chapter concluded with practical considerations for implementing LLMs in marketing applications, demonstrating how theoretical knowledge translates into tangible business solutions. Through a comprehensive project outline, we saw how prompt engineering techniques could be systematically applied to market research, content creation, and social media strategy development.

As we've seen throughout this chapter, LLMs represent a rapidly evolving field with immense potential to transform numerous industries. However, their successful implementation requires not just technical expertise but also careful consideration of ethical implications and continuous refinement of our interaction methods. The journey through LLMs is far from over, and future developments promise even more exciting possibilities in this dynamic landscape.

REFERENCES

Ba, J. L., Kiros, J. R., & Hinton, G. E. (2016). Layer normalization. *arXiv preprint arXiv:1607.06450.*

Brown, T. B., Mann, B., Ryder, N., Subbiah, M., Kaplan, J., Dhariwal, P., & Amodei, D. (2020). Language models are few-shot learners. *Advances in Neural Information Processing Systems*, *33*, 1877–1901.

Chen, Y., Kong, L., Cheng, N., & Kumar, S. (2023). Accelerating large language model decoding through speculative sampling. *arXiv preprint arXiv:2302.01318*

Chowdhery, A., Narang, S., Devlin, J., Gale, O., Song, K., Liu, F., . . . Thoppilan, R. (2022). Palm: Scaling language modeling with pathways. *arXiv preprint arXiv:2204.02311.*

Dao, T., Fu, D. K., Ermon, S., Rudra, A., & Ré, C. (2022). Flashattention: Fast and memory-efficient exact attention with io-awareness. *Advances in Neural Information Processing Systems*, *35*, 16344–16357.

Dettmers, T., Pagnoni, G., Holtzman, A., & Zettlemoyer, L. (2023). QLoRA: Efficient finetuning of quantized LLMs. *arXiv preprint arXiv:2305.14314*

Devlin, J., Chang, M. W., Lee, K., & Toutanova, K. (2018). Bert: Pre-training of deep bidirectional transformers for language understanding. *arXiv preprint arXiv:1810.04805.*

He, K., Zhang, X., Ren, S., & Sun, J. (2016). Deep residual learning for image recognition. In *Proceedings of the IEEE conference on computer vision and pattern recognition* (pp. 770-778).

Hinton, G., Vinyals, O., & Dean, J. (2015). Distilling the knowledge in a neural network. *arXiv preprint arXiv:1503.02531*

Hoffmann, J., Borgeaud, S., Mensch, A., Buchholtz, M., Casajus, D., Mudrakarta, E., . . . De Las Casas, D. (2022). Training compute-optimal large language models. *arXiv preprint arXiv:2203.15556.*

Houlsby, N., Jastrzebski, S., Hessel, J., Strub, F., Gorniak, V., Morrone, R. R., . . . De Freitas, N. (2019). Parameter-efficient transfer learning for NLP. *arXiv preprint arXiv:1902.00751*

Hu, E. J., Shen, Y., Wallis, P., Allen-Zhu, Z., Li, Y., Wang, S., . . . Chen, W. (2021). LoRA: Low-rank adaptation of large language models. *arXiv preprint arXiv:2106.09685.*

Jacob, B., Kligerman, Y., Krishna, B., Zhu, S., Chen, H., Howard, A., & Kalenichenko, D. (2018). Quantization and training of neural networks for efficient integer-arithmetic-only inference. In *Proceedings of the IEEE conference on computer vision and pattern recognition* (pp. 2765-2774)

Lester, B., Al-Rfou, R., & Constant, N. (2021). Power efficient management of large language models via parameter-efficient transfer learning. *arXiv preprint arXiv:2104.08691*

Lewis, P., Perez, E., Piktus, A., Petroni, F., Karpukhin, V., Goyal, N., . . . Kiela, D. *(*2020*)*. Retrieval-Augmented Generation for Knowledge-Intensive NLP Tasks. *Advances in Neural Information Processing Systems (NeurIPS), 33.*

Lin, C. Y. (2004). ROUGE: a package for automatic evaluation of summaries. In *Text summarization branches out: Proceedings of the ACL-04 workshop* (pp. 1-8)

Mikolov, T., Chen, K., Corrado, G., & Dean, J. (2013). Efficient estimation of word representations in vector space. *arXiv preprint arXiv:1301.3781.*

Papineni, K., Roukos, S., Ward, T., & Zhu, W. J. (2002). BLEU: a method for automatic evaluation of machine translation. In *Proceedings of the 40th annual meeting on association for computational linguistics* (pp. 311-318).

. Radford, A., Narasimhan, K., Salimans, T., & Sutskever, I. (2018). Improving language understanding by generative pre-training.

Shazeer, N., Mirhoseini, A., Maziarz, K., Davis, A., Le, Q., Hinton, G., & Dean, J. (2017). Outrageously large neural networks: The sparsely-gated mixture-of-experts layer. *arXiv preprint arXiv:1701.06538.*

Vaswani, A., Shazeer, N., Parmar, N., Uszkoreit, J., Jones, L., Gomez, A. N., . . . Polosukhin, I. (2017). Attention is all you need. In *Advances in neural information processing systems* (pp. 5998-6008).

Zheng, L., Chiang, W. L., Zhang, H., Wu, S., Zhuang, J., Fan, L., . . . Gonzalez, J. E. (2023). Judging LLM-as-a-judge with MT-Bench and Chatbot Arena. *arXiv preprint arXiv:2306.05685*

Chapter 2
Building With LLMs: Strategies for Real-World Business Implementation

Charvi Sanjay Suri
https://orcid.org/0009-0007-4451-6059
Yeshwantrao Chavan College of Engineering, India

Isha Sanjay Suri
https://orcid.org/0009-0006-9979-7751
St. Vincent Pallotti College of Engineering and Technology, India

Gaurav M. Divtelwar
Ramdeobaba University, India

ABSTRACT

As large language models (LLMs) transition from research projects to enterprise workflows, this chapter aims to be a practical guide to implementing them through the solution lifecycle, from exploration through deployment and monitoring. There are considerations regarding architecture decisions, such as whether to use an API or self-hosted model, level of integration in the system, and trade-offs between costs, performance, and scalability. Also examined are application approaches, such as fine-tuning, prompt engineering, and RAG, to name a few, in addition to cloud and open-source platforms, MLOps practices, and real-world examples and case studies, to ultimately support technical and business leaders in capitalizing on the potential for LLMs to create sustained impact.

DOI: 10.4018/979-8-3373-3912-2.ch002

1. INTRODUCTION

1.1 Background on the evolution of enterprise systems

Enterprise systems have undergone a significant transformation over the past few decades, evolving from rigid, monolithic software solutions to agile, integrated platforms capable of supporting real-time decision-making and complex business operations. Initially centered on Enterprise Resource Planning (ERP), systems expanded to include modules for Supply Chain Management (SCM), Customer Relationship Management (CRM), and Business Intelligence (BI). These systems laid the groundwork for digitization but were limited in their ability to adapt dynamically to fast-changing business environments (Yammanur, 2025).

With the advent of cloud computing, big data, and IoT, enterprises began rearchitecting their systems for scalability, interoperability, and data-centric operations. However, these transformations reached a turning point with the integration of artificial intelligence (AI), enabling systems not only to automate but also to learn, predict, and optimize autonomously (Moreno et al., 2019; Oloruntoba, 2025).

The shift from traditional on-premises solutions to cloud-based platforms such as Software-as-a-Service (SaaS), Platform-as-a-Service (PaaS), and Infrastructure-as-a-Service (IaaS) marked a fundamental change in how businesses approached IT. Cloud technology enabled organizations to rapidly scale infrastructure, lower total cost of ownership, and ensure continuous availability and disaster recovery. It also promoted decentralized access, making enterprise systems accessible to global teams in real time. These advancements significantly reduced the latency of decision-making and allowed businesses to become more responsive to market changes.

In parallel, the rise of big data analytics transformed enterprise systems from transactional engines into strategic assets. Organizations began collecting massive volumes of structured and unstructured data from various sources, including internal systems, social media, customer interactions, IoT devices, and external market feeds. By integrating data lakes and advanced analytics capabilities into enterprise systems, businesses were able to uncover hidden patterns, forecast demand, optimize operations, and personalize customer experiences at scale.

The incorporation of IoT further revolutionized enterprise systems by bridging the digital and physical worlds. In industries such as manufacturing, logistics, and energy, IoT-enabled devices and sensors began feeding real-time data into enterprise platforms. This allowed for predictive maintenance, improved asset utilization, and real-time supply chain visibility. For example, a smart factory integrated with ERP and IoT could automatically adjust production schedules based on machine performance data and real-time demand.

Artificial intelligence took these capabilities to a new level. Machine learning models embedded within enterprise systems began handling complex tasks such as fraud detection, dynamic pricing, inventory forecasting, and customer segmentation. Natural language processing enabled conversational interfaces, allowing users to interact with systems via chatbots and voice assistants. AI-powered robotic process automation (RPA) began automating repetitive back-office processes, freeing up human capital for higher-value tasks.

Moreover, modern enterprise systems are increasingly built with modular, microservices-based architectures. This composable approach allows organizations to integrate best-of-breed applications rather than being locked into a single vendor's monolithic suite. APIs and integration platforms as a service (iPaaS) play a crucial role in facilitating seamless data exchange and process orchestration across disparate systems.

Cybersecurity and compliance have also become integral to enterprise system design, especially with the rise of data privacy regulations such as GDPR and industry-specific standards. Modern platforms incorporate real-time threat detection, identity and access management, and end-to-end encryption to safeguard sensitive data and maintain compliance.

In summary, enterprise systems have evolved from static data repositories to dynamic, intelligent ecosystems. The convergence of cloud, data, IoT, and AI has empowered organizations to operate with unprecedented agility, efficiency, and customer centricity. As digital transformation continues, future enterprise systems are expected to become even more autonomous, predictive, and adaptive, supporting not just operational excellence but continuous innovation.

1.2 The transformative role of AI in modern enterprises

Artificial intelligence is now a strategic asset, reshaping how enterprises manage knowledge, make decisions, and engage with stakeholders. AI technologies—including machine learning, natural language processing, and large language models (LLMs)—have transitioned from experimental deployments to core components of enterprise architecture (Fu et al., 2025; Mustafa & Zeebaree, 2025).

Enterprises are leveraging AI for a wide range of applications: intelligent automation of workflows, predictive decision-making, real-time customer support using LLMs, and trust-based knowledge retrieval using semantic models like knowledge graphs (Sequeda et al., 2025; Su et al., 2025). This transformation signals a shift from process-oriented computing to cognition-oriented enterprise systems (Bellomarini et al., 2019).

1.3 Objectives and scope of the chapter

This chapter aims to explore the **strategic integration** of AI within enterprise systems by synthesizing recent technological advances, enterprise-level use cases, and theoretical frameworks. Specifically, it focuses on:

- The strategic imperatives driving AI adoption in enterprises
- Architectural frameworks that enable AI integration
- Innovations in enterprise operations through AI-driven intelligence
- The enabling role of knowledge graphs and LLMs in enterprise applications
- Sustainable, ethical, and trust-centered AI practices
- Future directions for enterprise AI aligned with organizational goals

The chapter is grounded in contemporary scholarly and industry research (e.g., Bashir, 2025; Dash, 2025; Mackenzie et al., 2025), ensuring relevance to both academic and practitioner audiences.

2. STRATEGIC IMPERATIVES FOR AI ADOPTION IN ENTERPRISES

2.1 Drivers of AI integration: Competitiveness, agility, innovation (Żmijowska, 2024; Mustafa & Zeebaree)

The integration of AI into enterprise systems is propelled by a strategic need to enhance competitiveness, organizational agility, and continuous innovation. In today's hyperconnected, data-saturated global marketplace, traditional enterprise systems—built around static business logic—struggle to deliver the flexibility and intelligence required to adapt and grow. AI fills this gap by enabling intelligent automation, predictive analytics, and dynamic decision-making capabilities that respond in real-time to internal and external stimuli (Żmijowska, 2024; Mustafa & Zeebaree, 2025).

Competitiveness is a major driving force. As digital-native startups and technology-savvy competitors redefine customer experiences and operational efficiency through AI, traditional enterprises are under pressure to modernize or risk obsolescence. AI technologies allow firms to extract actionable insights from enterprise data lakes, detect patterns in customer behavior, optimize supply chain flows, and manage risk proactively—creating clear competitive advantages across sectors.

Agility—defined as the enterprise's ability to adapt quickly to market changes—is another key motivator. AI supports operational agility by enabling enterprises to pivot faster, reconfigure resources dynamically, and automate decision cycles. For example, AI-powered demand forecasting tools can help adjust inventory in real time based on weather, consumer sentiment, or geopolitical risks, ensuring faster response and lower wastage.

Innovation, both incremental and disruptive, is catalyzed by AI's ability to uncover unseen opportunities within enterprise data. From intelligent product design based on usage data to hyper-personalized customer services driven by behavioral analysis, AI helps organizations move beyond reactive strategies toward anticipatory innovation (Mustafa & Zeebaree, 2025). Furthermore, AI's capacity for continual learning creates a feedback loop that accelerates innovation cycles across the enterprise.

2.2 Challenges in legacy systems and digital transformation

While the drivers for AI integration are compelling, enterprises often face considerable resistance and complexity in implementation—primarily due to the inertia of legacy systems and the fragmented nature of digital transformation efforts.

Many enterprises still rely on monolithic or siloed information systems that were not designed to support the scale, flexibility, or data integration requirements of modern AI applications. These systems may use outdated programming languages, store data in incompatible formats, and lack APIs or modular architecture—all of which hinder seamless AI integration (Moreno et al., 2019). Attempts to layer AI capabilities on top of such infrastructure frequently result in inefficiencies, performance issues, or outright failure.

In parallel, digital transformation efforts are often fragmented across departments or business units, with inconsistent goals, mismatched technologies, and poorly defined KPIs. While AI is frequently viewed as a silver bullet, its success is highly dependent on the maturity and alignment of broader digital transformation initiatives. A successful AI strategy requires harmonization of data governance, IT modernization, process reengineering, and change management (Dash, 2025).

Additionally, legacy enterprise systems tend to produce data silos, where information is stored in isolated systems without a unified view. These silos complicate data pre-processing, training of AI models, and real-time decision-making. Integrating AI into such environments necessitates significant investment in data integration pipelines, cloud migration, and enterprise-wide data models.

Lastly, technical debt and high costs of transformation often delay AI adoption. Enterprises must balance the short-term cost of AI integration with its long-term strategic value, a calculation that many struggle to justify without a clear ROI model or successful pilot initiatives.

2.3 Organizational readiness and leadership strategies (Bashir, J.)

The successful integration of AI in enterprise settings depends heavily on organizational readiness, which goes far beyond having the right technology stack. It encompasses strategic vision, cultural alignment, leadership commitment, and workforce capability (Bashir, 2025).

At the heart of readiness is executive leadership. C-level champions must not only sponsor AI initiatives but also articulate a compelling vision that connects AI efforts to business objectives such as customer satisfaction, revenue growth, or sustainability. Without executive support and cross-functional alignment, AI projects risk remaining isolated proofs of concept with no enterprise-wide impact.

Strategic alignment is also essential. AI strategies must align with the broader organizational roadmap, ensuring that projects are prioritized based on business value rather than technical novelty. This includes establishing metrics that measure AI's contribution to core KPIs—such as reduced churn, improved forecast accuracy, or lower operational costs.

Another pillar of readiness is AI talent and capability development. Enterprises need to foster cross-disciplinary teams that blend domain knowledge with data science, MLOps, and AI governance expertise. A key trend is the rise of "AI translators"—professionals who bridge the gap between technical teams and business units to ensure relevant and responsible AI deployment (Fan, 2025).

Furthermore, organizational culture must evolve to embrace experimentation, data-driven thinking, and ethical responsibility. This includes establishing guardrails for responsible AI use, such as ethics committees, bias detection protocols, and transparent decision-making frameworks (Balayn et al., 2025).

Finally, enterprises must adopt iterative implementation strategies, starting with pilot projects that validate feasibility and ROI. These pilots should be used to build organizational confidence, improve stakeholder buy-in, and establish internal best practices before scaling AI initiatives enterprise-wide.

3. ARCHITECTURES AND FRAMEWORKS FOR ENTERPRISE AI

3.1 Conceptual models: Big data, cloud, and AI integration (Moreno et al., 2019)

The integration of big data platforms, cloud computing, and AI technologies forms the core of the modern enterprise architecture. Traditional centralized systems lack the flexibility and computational power to handle today's high-volume, high-velocity, and high-variety enterprise data. A shift toward **data-centric architectures** has given rise to models where AI is embedded within cloud-native, elastic environments capable of supporting advanced analytics at scale (Moreno et al., 2019).

In their conceptual enterprise AI model, Moreno et al. (2019) propose a cloud-based big data architecture that integrates data ingestion, distributed processing, AI-powered analytics, and business services. This architecture enables continuous learning and intelligence delivery through a feedback loop that connects front-end applications with back-end analytical engines. The framework is particularly effective for market-oriented organizations where real-time customer insights and predictive modeling are essential for competitiveness.

Key features of such architectures include:

- **Data lakes and warehouses**: Storing structured and unstructured data for AI processing.
- **Distributed computing frameworks**: Such as Apache Spark or Hadoop to process massive datasets in parallel.
- **AI/ML pipelines**: Deployed through MLOps tools for training, testing, and versioning models.
- **API gateways and service buses**: To facilitate real-time communication between AI components and enterprise applications.

This model underscores that AI is not a stand-alone layer but an embedded service across the enterprise infrastructure—making scalability, interoperability, and continuous integration essential design principles.

3.2 Integrated enterprise systems: ERP, EDI, and AI (Yammanur, 2025)

Modern enterprise systems are evolving toward intelligent integration, where traditional operational platforms like ERP and EDI are enhanced with AI capabilities. Enterprise Resource Planning (ERP) systems, which historically managed data around finance, logistics, and HR, now increasingly incorporate AI for functions such as demand forecasting, anomaly detection, predictive maintenance, and decision support (Yammanur, 2025).

According to Yammanur (2025), integrating AI with ERP and Electronic Data Interchange (EDI) platforms helps enterprises synchronize internal operations with external ecosystems. For example:

- **AI-enhanced ERP** can dynamically adjust procurement schedules based on predictive inventory models.

- **AI in EDI systems** can intelligently route invoices and shipping confirmations, detect fraudulent transactions, or optimize partner selection.

This integration enables:

- **Cognitive automation**: Automating not just repetitive tasks but decision-making processes using AI insights.
- **Real-time enterprise response**: Using AI models to anticipate supply chain disruptions and adjust planning instantly.
- **Enhanced interoperability**: Standardizing formats and communication protocols using AI to bridge heterogeneous systems.

Furthermore, such integrated systems support **enterprise-wide visibility**, ensuring that decisions made in one domain (e.g., logistics) are informed by insights from another (e.g., customer sentiment analysis).

3.3 AI-driven enterprise architecture and scalability

As enterprises scale their operations globally and across digital channels, scalability becomes a defining factor for AI success. AI-driven enterprise architectures are designed to be modular, extensible, and loosely coupled, enabling organizations to scale horizontally (across departments) and vertically (across complexity levels of intelligence).

A scalable AI-driven architecture typically features the following:

- **Microservices architecture**: Each AI component (e.g., recommender engine, fraud detection model) is deployed as a standalone service that can scale independently.
- **Containerization and orchestration**: Using technologies like Docker and Kubernetes to manage the deployment, scaling, and monitoring of AI services.
- **Multi-cloud or hybrid deployment**: Distributing workloads across cloud vendors or combining on-premise systems with cloud services for flexibility.
- **Federated learning and edge AI**: Allowing AI models to train on decentralized data (e.g., from IoT devices), improving privacy and reducing latency.

This approach is particularly relevant in sectors such as manufacturing, logistics, and finance, where real-time inference and large-scale data processing are critical.

Crucially, AI scalability also depends on governance frameworks and model lifecycle management. Without tools for versioning, monitoring, and retraining models, enterprises risk deploying outdated or biased models at scale—undermining trust and performance. Therefore, AI-driven architectures must integrate MLOps pipelines that support continuous monitoring, drift detection, and retraining (Dash, 2025; Oloruntoba, 2025).

4. AI-DRIVEN INNOVATIONS IN ENTERPRISE OPERATIONS

Artificial intelligence has transcended the traditional role of a decision-support tool to become an operational core of modern enterprise systems. Through intelligent automation, predictive modeling, and adaptive learning, AI enables enterprises to enhance efficiency, reduce risk, optimize processes, and deliver personalized customer experiences. Innovations in this space are transforming enterprise operations across sectors—from finance to supply chains, customer service to IT infrastructure—through increasingly autonomous and intelligent systems.

4.1 Decision intelligence and optimization (Natta, 2025)

At the heart of AI innovation lies decision intelligence, a discipline that combines data science, AI, and decision theory to optimize strategic, tactical, and operational decisions. Enterprises are increasingly embedding decision intelligence into their systems to support complex, high-stakes decisions with real-time insights and simulations (Natta, 2025).

According to Natta (2025), AI-powered decision intelligence systems integrate structured enterprise data with unstructured external data to build context-aware models that evaluate various scenarios, anticipate outcomes, and recommend the most effective actions. For instance, AI can support supply chain managers in selecting optimal vendors under fluctuating market conditions or assist CFOs in scenario-based financial forecasting during economic uncertainty.

Some examples of enterprise-level applications include:

- **Revenue optimization models** in retail and e-commerce using real-time customer behavior data.
- **Dynamic pricing algorithms** that adjust rates based on demand forecasts, competitor behavior, and seasonal trends.
- **Portfolio optimization tools** in finance that manage investment decisions based on market volatility and predictive risk assessments.

The strategic advantage lies in proactive decision-making, where enterprises can simulate multiple outcomes, factor in uncertainty, and make decisions that optimize for long-term value rather than short-term reactivity.

4.2 Autonomous systems: Self-tuning DBMS, predictive analytics (Oloruntoba, 2025)

Another significant innovation in enterprise operations is the shift toward autonomous systems—AI-powered solutions that can configure, monitor, and optimize themselves with minimal human intervention. In enterprise IT, autonomous database management systems (DBMS) represent a major leap forward. These systems can automatically manage indexing, performance tuning, and query optimization based on system workload and usage patterns (Oloruntoba, 2025).

As Oloruntoba (2025) notes, such systems rely on predictive analytics, reinforcement learning, and adaptive control algorithms to achieve:

- **Self-tuning queries** that adjust execution plans for optimal performance.
- **Predictive indexing**, where the system creates, modifies, or deletes indexes based on observed query behavior.
- **Fault tolerance** and anomaly detection, allowing systems to preemptively mitigate outages or slowdowns.

Beyond databases, autonomous AI is also applied to:

- **IT operations (AIOps)**: Monitoring and diagnosing issues in real-time across complex IT environments.
- **Predictive maintenance**: In manufacturing or logistics, AI models analyze sensor data to predict equipment failures before they occur.
- **Autonomous agents**: Such as chatbots and virtual assistants that operate independently within enterprise environments, handling customer support or internal service requests.

The evolution toward autonomous enterprise systems reflects a broader vision of self-managing, self-optimizing platforms capable of reducing operational overhead, improving service reliability, and freeing up human capital for more strategic tasks.

4.3 Cross-application innovation and pattern evolution (Fan, X.)

One of the most compelling impacts of AI in enterprise settings is its ability to drive cross-application innovation—enabling intelligent systems to identify patterns across domains and repurpose them in novel contexts. This capability breaks down traditional silos between departments, tools, and workflows, fostering innovation at the intersections of enterprise functions (Fan, X., 2025).

Fan (2025) emphasizes that enterprises can use AI not only to optimize individual applications but also to create composite intelligence—where insights from one domain inform strategies in another. Examples include:

- Using **customer service interactions** to improve product design through sentiment analysis and issue clustering.
- Leveraging **HR analytics** to enhance project team formation by identifying skill synergies and predicting collaboration effectiveness.
- Integrating **marketing and sales data** to detect emerging customer behavior patterns and inform demand forecasting models.

Moreover, AI enables pattern innovation—the ability to spot non-obvious trends, correlations, or operational anomalies that were previously invisible to human analysts. These patterns can fuel new product ideas, process redesigns, or even strategic pivots.

Such innovation is particularly evident in the use of multi-modal AI, which integrates text, voice, image, and sensor data to create rich, cross-contextual models. For example, combining visual inspection data from manufacturing lines with predictive maintenance models improves production quality and minimizes downtime.

Cross-application AI also benefits from continuous learning loops, where every operational outcome refines future predictions across multiple systems. This capability fosters what Fan (2025) refers to as "pattern evolution"—an enterprise-wide intelligence that continuously adapts and innovates.

5. THE ROLE OF KNOWLEDGE GRAPHS AND SEMANTIC TECHNOLOGIES

As enterprises embrace increasingly complex AI systems, the need for structured, interpretable, and trustworthy knowledge representation becomes critical. Traditional databases and keyword-based search systems often fail to deliver meaningful insights in enterprise settings due to disconnected data silos and semantic ambiguity. To overcome these limitations, enterprises are turning to knowledge graphs (KGs) and semantic technologies—tools that organize information around meaning, relationships, and context rather than isolated records.

Knowledge graphs provide a way to model, store, and query domain knowledge in a machine-understandable format, enabling reasoning, transparency, and rich interconnections between enterprise data sources. Their integration into enterprise AI systems enhances not only operational intelligence but also decision traceability, compliance, and explainability.

5.1 Enterprise knowledge representation and trust (Sequeda et al., 2025)

One of the most urgent challenges in enterprise AI is the trustworthiness of automated decision systems. AI models, particularly large language models (LLMs), often function as opaque black boxes. Without interpretability or traceability, they can erode trust—especially in high-stakes environments like finance, healthcare, or legal services. Knowledge graphs address this problem by introducing structured, explainable knowledge into AI pipelines (Sequeda et al., 2025).

Sequeda et al. (2025) argue that knowledge graphs act as sources of trust by grounding LLM outputs in verified, curated enterprise knowledge. This is achieved through:

- **Contextual grounding**: Aligning LLM responses with structured domain knowledge, reducing hallucinations.
- **Provenance tracking**: Providing a record of where, how, and when data was generated or modified.
- **Semantic disambiguation**: Clarifying entity relationships and resolving conflicting data points.

In enterprise settings, trust is not only a technical concern but also a regulatory and strategic one. For instance, in financial services or pharmaceuticals, AI decisions must be auditable and justifiable to regulators. Knowledge graphs enable transparent inference chains, where each recommendation or prediction can be traced back to its source—thereby increasing stakeholder confidence and compliance readiness.

5.2 Knowledge graphs as a foundation for enterprise AI (Bellomarini et al., 2019)

Beyond trust, knowledge graphs serve as a foundational layer for enterprise AI—enabling more intelligent, context-aware, and interoperable applications. Unlike relational databases, which store data in rigid schemas, knowledge graphs offer flexible, graph-based models that reflect real-world relationships between entities (Bellomarini et al., 2019).

Bellomarini et al. (2019) emphasize that knowledge graphs are essential to bridging the gap between symbolic reasoning and machine learning. This hybrid approach allows enterprises to combine:

- **Logic-based inference** (e.g., deducing rules or relationships from existing data),
- With **pattern recognition** (e.g., ML models discovering correlations),
- Within a **shared semantic context**.

This integration supports several enterprise functions:

- **Semantic search**: Users can query data not by keyword, but by intent (e.g., "Find customers at risk of churn who also reduced purchases in Q2").
- **Personalization**: Product or content recommendations can be enriched with semantic similarity and contextual understanding.
- **Process automation**: AI agents can navigate enterprise workflows using ontology-based rules and entity relationships.

In essence, knowledge graphs provide the scaffolding upon which enterprise AI systems can reason, generalize, and explain outcomes—bridging raw data and high-level decision-making in a coherent, scalable manner.

5.3 Use cases in customer support, Q&A, and internal data management (Su et al., 2025)

Practical applications of knowledge graphs and semantic technologies span a wide range of enterprise operations, particularly in areas where intelligent information retrieval, contextualization, and interaction are required.

Su et al. (2025) highlight several enterprise use cases where knowledge graphs enhance the performance of large language models and conversational AI, including:

Customer Support and Virtual Agents

By integrating knowledge graphs into customer service chatbots, enterprises can:

- Deliver **faster and more accurate responses** by grounding answers in structured knowledge.
- Improve **consistency** across channels by using a centralized knowledge base.

- Enable **context-aware escalation**, where queries requiring human intervention are prioritized intelligently based on semantic complexity.

Enterprise Question Answering (QA) Systems

In large organizations, retrieving answers from scattered internal documents is time-consuming. LLMs paired with KGs can interpret complex natural language queries and return semantically relevant results, citing sources and providing links to associated documents (Su et al., 2025). This is particularly effective in:

- **Legal and policy research**
- **Compliance auditing**
- **Product documentation retrieval**

Internal Data Management and Discovery

Knowledge graphs also support enterprise data discovery, allowing users to explore relationships between datasets, systems, and processes. For example, a knowledge graph can map the relationships between customer complaints, support tickets, product defects, and warranty claims—enabling root cause analysis and strategic interventions.

Moreover, KGs facilitate metadata enrichment and data cataloging, which are essential for data governance, lineage tracking, and compliance with regulations like GDPR.

6. LARGE LANGUAGE MODELS (LLMS) IN ENTERPRISE ENVIRONMENTS

The integration of Large Language Models (LLMs) into enterprise systems is redefining the interface between human decision-making and automated intelligence. Once reserved for research and consumer-facing applications, LLMs such as GPT-4, Claude, and domain-specific transformers are now being embedded into enterprise tools, dashboards, and workflows—offering context-aware, natural language interaction, intelligent summarization, and task automation.

Their deployment across enterprise ecosystems is rapidly growing due to their ability to understand unstructured data, generate human-like text, and provide real-time assistance at scale. As enterprises aim to balance efficiency with accountability, the fusion of LLMs with traditional enterprise systems also raises critical concerns around trust, explainability, and control, which are being addressed through human-in-the-loop (HITL) systems and design frameworks.

6.1 LLM-enhanced enterprise tools (Power BI, CRM, etc.) (Mohammed et al.)

LLMs are increasingly being embedded into enterprise productivity and decision-support platforms to enhance data accessibility, reduce manual effort, and facilitate natural-language interactions with structured systems. One of the most visible applications of this integration is in business intelligence and CRM tools.

For instance, Microsoft Power BI now integrates LLMs to allow users to query data using conversational language, generate visual summaries, and even suggest patterns or anomalies in datasets. Similarly, Salesforce and HubSpot are embedding LLM-powered agents that offer real-time email generation, sentiment analysis, and sales recommendations directly within CRM workflows (Mohammed et al.).

According to Mohammed et al., LLMs in enterprise tools help achieve the following:

- **Democratization of data access**: Non-technical users can query enterprise data using plain language.
- **Enhanced productivity**: LLMs automate routine tasks like drafting reports, analyzing customer interactions, and generating executive summaries.
- **Improved customer engagement**: By analyzing historical communication, LLMs can suggest personalized outreach strategies or flag potential churn risks.

This marks a shift from static dashboards to interactive, adaptive intelligence layers that evolve with user needs and organizational goals.

6.2 Trust, explainability, and human-in-the-loop systems (Balayn et al., 2025)

While the benefits of LLMs in enterprise contexts are substantial, concerns about reliability, hallucinations, and bias pose significant risks, particularly in regulated industries. Balayn et al. (2025) argue that to operationalize LLMs responsibly, enterprises must adopt trust-centered design principles and incorporate human-in-the-loop (HITL) systems to oversee, validate, and contextualize LLM outputs.

Balayn et al. (2025) identify three pillars of trust in enterprise AI:

1. **Explainability**: Users must be able to understand why an LLM made a specific recommendation or decision.
2. **Control**: Humans should remain in charge, especially in scenarios involving sensitive data or high-impact decisions.
3. **Auditability**: All interactions and outputs must be traceable for regulatory and compliance purposes.

HITL systems are instrumental in this process. They allow:

- Experts to review or edit LLM-generated content before it is published or acted upon.
- Feedback loops that help fine-tune the model based on enterprise-specific constraints.
- Guardrails to prevent the propagation of misinformation or unintended actions.

The shift toward augmented intelligence—where LLMs act as copilots rather than autonomous agents—ensures both scalability and accountability in enterprise AI deployments.

6.3 Gamified and domain-specific AI agents (Costa, 2025; Liang & Tong, 2025)

The next frontier in enterprise LLM applications involves the emergence of gamified and domain-specific AI agents—LLMs trained or fine-tuned on narrow, high-value domains such as legal documentation, scientific research, HR onboarding, or procurement processes.

Costa (2025) illustrates the growing use of gamified AI agents in enterprise training and knowledge dissemination. These agents turn learning modules or SOP familiarization into interactive, narrative-driven experiences, increasing employee engagement and retention. For example:

- An AI-powered onboarding agent may use a "choose-your-own-adventure" format to train new hires.
- Cybersecurity awareness programs may employ LLMs to simulate phishing scenarios and assess response behavior dynamically.

Meanwhile, Liang and Tong (2025) emphasize the utility of domain-specific LLMs—models that outperform general-purpose LLMs by being deeply tuned to the language, constraints, and logic of a particular field. These agents:

- Reduce hallucination rates by grounding outputs in verified corpora or enterprise knowledge graphs.
- Accelerate task completion by understanding specialized terminology and workflows.
- Increase relevance in customer service, legal documentation, and healthcare records analysis.

For instance, a legal assistant agent trained on enterprise contracts and compliance documents can draft clauses, summarize changes, or flag risky language with high contextual accuracy.

7. SUSTAINABLE AND RESPONSIBLE ENTERPRISE AI

As enterprises increasingly integrate artificial intelligence (AI) into their core operations, concerns related to sustainability, ethics, and regulatory compliance have become critical. While AI delivers significant operational and strategic advantages, it also raises new challenges: energy consumption of large models, opaque decision-making processes, data privacy risks, and potential regulatory breaches. Thus, a future-oriented enterprise AI strategy must embrace both technological innovation and social responsibility to align with organizational values, stakeholder expectations, and environmental goals.

This section explores how enterprises can operationalize Green AI, ensure ethical AI deployment, and build systems that are both trustworthy and compliant.

7.1 Green AI and energy-efficient systems (Dash, 2025)

The environmental impact of AI—especially large-scale machine learning models and inference engines—is now a pressing concern. Dash (2025) notes that the computational costs of training large AI models have grown exponentially, contributing significantly to energy consumption and carbon emissions. For example, training a state-of-the-art LLM can consume more electricity than 100 U.S. homes use in a year.

To address this, enterprises are adopting Green AI practices that focus on efficiency over raw performance. This involves:

- **Model optimization** techniques such as quantization, pruning, and knowledge distillation to reduce model size and inference time.
- **Edge AI** and **on-device processing**, reducing the reliance on energy-intensive cloud infrastructure.

- Selecting **data centers powered by renewable energy** and using intelligent workload scheduling to balance computational loads.

Furthermore, enterprise architects are increasingly designing energy-aware AI workflows, which monitor and manage resource usage dynamically. These efforts help align AI deployments with broader corporate ESG (Environmental, Social, and Governance) goals and global sustainability standards (Dash, 2025).

7.2 Ethical and responsible AI use in enterprise decision-making

Beyond environmental considerations, enterprises face ethical imperatives when deploying AI in domains such as HR, finance, healthcare, and public services. Ethical concerns include algorithmic bias, data misuse, surveillance, and lack of consent—any of which can undermine public trust and legal compliance.

To mitigate these risks, enterprises must embed responsible AI governance into every stage of the AI lifecycle:

- **Data ethics**: Ensuring datasets are representative, anonymized, and used with consent.
- **Bias audits**: Regular testing of models for disparate impacts across gender, ethnicity, age, or geography.
- **Transparent algorithms**: Favoring interpretable models or using explainability techniques (e.g., SHAP, LIME) in black-box systems.

This shift towards ethical AI is not purely reactive. It enhances brand integrity, promotes inclusive decision-making, and helps enterprises build AI systems that are socially acceptable and legally defensible.

Several global initiatives such as the OECD AI Principles, the EU AI Act, and ISO/IEC 42001 provide frameworks and standards to support enterprise AI ethics. Adhering to such standards reflects an enterprise's maturity and accountability in the digital era.

7.3 Trust dynamics and regulatory frameworks (Mackenzie et al., 2025)

Trust is foundational to enterprise AI adoption. Without trust, AI systems—no matter how accurate or efficient—will face resistance from users, regulators, and consumers. Mackenzie et al. (2025) emphasize that enterprise trust in AI involves transparency, explainability, security, and compliance, all of which must be continuously monitored and enforced.

Building trust in enterprise AI systems involves multiple dimensions:

- **Explainability**: Users need to understand how AI decisions are made and how outcomes are derived.
- **Security and privacy**: Strong controls must be in place to prevent data leaks, adversarial attacks, or unauthorized access.
- **Compliance readiness**: Enterprises must prepare for emerging legal frameworks such as the **EU AI Act**, **GDPR**, and **industry-specific AI regulations**.

Mackenzie et al. (2025) argue that "compliance by design" is essential—meaning AI systems should be designed with auditability, documentation, and policy constraints embedded from the outset. For instance, model cards and datasheets for datasets can help document model assumptions, risks, and intended uses.

In addition, enterprises are beginning to adopt AI ethics boards and automated compliance tools to systematically review AI deployments. These governance structures ensure that enterprise AI remains aligned with evolving legal standards and public expectations.

8. FUTURE DIRECTIONS AND RESEARCH OPPORTUNITIES

The evolution of enterprise artificial intelligence (AI) continues at an accelerating pace, driven by breakthroughs in computing power, data availability, algorithmic efficiency, and strategic business imperatives. As organizations seek to scale AI deployment beyond isolated use cases into enterprise-wide transformation, the next decade will witness a fundamental shift in how AI is delivered, aligned, and studied. This section highlights emerging paradigms, strategic realignments, and the need for collaborative, cross-disciplinary research to fully harness the potential of enterprise AI.

8.1 Emerging paradigms: AI-as-a-service (AIaaS), federated AI, industry-specific LLMs (Yan & Zhu, 2025)

A major direction shaping the future of enterprise AI is the transition to modular, scalable, and service-based delivery models. In particular, AI-as-a-Service (AIaaS) is gaining traction, allowing businesses to access pre-built AI tools, platforms, and models without the need for extensive infrastructure or in-house expertise. This model democratizes AI by offering flexible, cost-effective access to sophisticated capabilities such as natural language processing, vision, or predictive analytics through APIs or low-code platforms.

Alongside AIaaS, federated AI is emerging as a solution to the growing tension between data privacy and model performance. Rather than centralizing sensitive data, federated AI allows multiple enterprises or departments to collaboratively train models on decentralized data—enhancing security while maintaining model efficacy. This is particularly valuable in sectors like healthcare, finance, and legal services where data sharing is heavily restricted (Yan & Zhu, 2025).

Moreover, the development of domain-specific large language models (LLMs) marks a significant advance in tailoring AI to enterprise needs. Unlike general-purpose models, these specialized LLMs are fine-tuned on curated datasets within domains such as finance, legal compliance, customer service, or logistics. This improves accuracy, relevance, and interpretability in decision-making, enabling LLM-powered agents to provide expert-level insights and automation across industry verticals (Yan & Zhu, 2025).

These paradigms—AIaaS, federated AI, and verticalized LLMs—will redefine enterprise AI from a toolset into a dynamic ecosystem of services and agents embedded across business functions.

8.2 Strategic alignment of AI with corporate goals and innovation (Fu et al., 2025)

As enterprises mature in their AI capabilities, the next challenge lies in strategically aligning AI initiatives with broader corporate visions and goals. Fu et al. (2025) emphasize that AI should not be treated as an isolated IT innovation, but as a strategic asset integrated into enterprise planning, innovation pipelines, and competitive positioning.

This alignment involves:

- **Embedding AI in innovation strategy**, where AI becomes a co-creator in product development, customer experience, and business model innovation.
- Ensuring **AI governance supports strategic KPIs**, not just operational efficiency.
- Aligning AI with **corporate digital transformation roadmaps**, sustainability targets, and industry disruptions.

Moreover, AI can act as a strategic radar, helping enterprises detect emerging market signals, simulate strategic scenarios, and adapt dynamically. In this role, AI becomes not just a tool, but a cognitive partner in shaping and executing long-term vision (Fu et al., 2025).

To achieve this, enterprises must foster closer integration between data science teams, strategic planners, domain experts, and executive leadership. This convergence will ensure that AI outcomes are measurable, explainable, and directionally consistent with enterprise goals.

8.3 Open questions and potential for cross-disciplinary research

Despite its rapid progress, enterprise AI still presents many unanswered questions and research frontiers, many of which require input from multiple disciplines:

- **Human-AI collaboration**: How can enterprises design interfaces and workflows that balance automation with human judgment?
- **Trust calibration**: How do users develop or lose trust in AI systems over time? What role do organizational culture and transparency play?
- **Regulatory compliance and explainability**: How can AI be both high-performing and compliant with emerging laws and ethical standards?
- **Economic and labor impacts**: How should businesses reimagine roles, skills, and workflows in AI-augmented enterprises?
- **Resilience and failure modes**: How can enterprises anticipate, detect, and recover from failures in AI-driven systems?

Cross-disciplinary research—combining computer science, organizational psychology, strategy, ethics, and law—will be critical to answering these questions. For instance, designing effective human-in-the-loop systems requires insights from HCI and cognitive science, while evaluating the economic impact of AI on workforce structures requires input from labor economists and sociologists.

Finally, future research must also consider the global diversity of enterprise environments, adapting AI strategies for small and medium enterprises (SMEs), emerging economies, and resource-constrained contexts.

CONCLUSION

This chapter has examined the rapidly transforming landscape of enterprise systems, emphasizing the strategic integration of artificial intelligence (AI) into organizational processes, architectures, and decision-making frameworks. We began by tracing the evolution of enterprise systems from static ERP platforms to dynamic, AI-enabled ecosystems that support agility, innovation, and data-driven intelligence (Mustafa & Zeebaree, 2025; Żmijowska, 2024).

The drivers for AI adoption—competitiveness, adaptability, and the pursuit of innovation—have been explored in parallel with the organizational and technological challenges posed by legacy systems and digital inertia. We then examined the critical role of leadership, change management, and organizational readiness in enabling successful AI integration (Bashir, 2025).

Architectural advancements, including cloud-based platforms, ERP-AI convergence, and scalable models for AI deployment, are reshaping enterprise infrastructure (Moreno et al., 2019; Yammanur, 2025). Simultaneously, AI-driven innovations are transforming operational intelligence through optimization algorithms, autonomous analytics, and cross-domain applications (Natta, 2025; Oloruntoba, 2025; Fan, 2025).

Beyond infrastructure and automation, the chapter explored the semantic layer of enterprise AI—highlighting the role of knowledge graphs in representing trustable, interconnected enterprise knowledge (Sequeda et al., 2025; Bellomarini et al., 2019), as well as the expanding use of large language models (LLMs) in enhancing CRM, business analytics, and internal enterprise tools (Mohammed et al., 2025; Balayn et al., 2025).

We emphasized the importance of responsible and sustainable AI practices, with particular attention to energy-efficient computation, ethical governance, and regulatory alignment (Dash, 2025; Mackenzie et al., 2025). Finally, we identified future research opportunities around AI-as-a-Service (AIaaS), federated AI, strategic alignment, and human-AI collaboration (Yan & Zhu, 2025; Fu et al., 2025).

Enterprise AI is no longer a futuristic concept; it is an ongoing reality that demands a thoughtful, systemic approach to design, deployment, and governance. As AI continues to permeate every layer of enterprise systems—from infrastructure to strategic planning—it is essential to approach its integration not just with technological rigor but with a deep sensitivity to human, ethical, and institutional dimensions.

Organizations that embrace AI as a strategic collaborator, rather than a mere tool, will be best positioned to thrive in an increasingly complex, data-driven world. Meanwhile, academia and industry must jointly champion research and standards that ensure this transformation remains equitable, transparent, and sustainable.

The enterprise of the future is not just intelligent—it is responsible, adaptive, and deeply human-centric.

In addition, the role of explainability in enterprise AI must not be understated. As decisions increasingly rely on algorithmic insights, organizations must prioritize transparent AI models that can be interpreted by diverse stakeholders—especially in high-stakes sectors such as finance, healthcare, and law. Investing in explainable AI (XAI) frameworks not only builds internal trust but also ensures regulatory compliance and mitigates operational risks.

Furthermore, the success of AI in enterprise systems hinges on a robust data foundation. Data quality, interoperability, privacy, and lineage are core prerequisites for unlocking AI's full potential. Enterprises must establish strong data governance frameworks that align with their AI ambitions, enabling seamless integration across departments and ensuring that insights are derived from reliable, contextualized information.

Lastly, continuous education and workforce transformation are critical for sustaining enterprise AI initiatives. Organizations must proactively reskill their employees, embedding AI literacy and digital competencies across all levels of the enterprise. By fostering a culture of experimentation, inclusivity, and lifelong learning, enterprises can not only navigate AI disruption but also harness it as a catalyst for sustainable competitive advantage.

REFERENCES

Balayn, A., Yurrita, M., Rancourt, F., Casati, F., & Gadiraju, U. (2025, April). Unpacking Trust Dynamics in the LLM Supply Chain: An Empirical Exploration to Foster Trustworthy LLM Production & Use. In *Proceedings of the 2025 CHI Conference on Human Factors in Computing Systems* (pp. 1-20).

. Bashir, J. (2025). Strategic enterprise artificial intelligence.

Bellomarini, L., Fakhoury, D., Gottlob, G., & Sallinger, E. (2019, April). Knowledge graphs and enterprise AI: the promise of an enabling technology. In *2019 IEEE 35th international conference on data engineering (ICDE)* (pp. 26-37). IEEE.

Costa, C. J. (2025). Integrating LLM usage in gamified systems. *WSEAS Transactions on Mathematics, 24*, 258–267.

Dash, S. (2025). Green AI: Enhancing Sustainability and Energy Efficiency in AI-Integrated Enterprise Systems. *IEEE Access : Practical Innovations, Open Solutions.*

. Fan, X. (2025). Research on Cross-Application and Pattern Innovation of Artificial Intelligence Technology in Enterprise Management.

Fu, Y., Ni, J., & Fang, M. (2025). The impact of artificial intelligence on digital enterprise innovation. *Journal of Strategy & Innovation, 36*(1), 200538.

Liang, G., & Tong, Q. (2025). LLM-Powered AI Agent Systems and Their Applications in Industry. *arXiv preprint arXiv:2505.16120.*

Mackenzie, T., Radeljic, B., Salgado, L., Paul, A., Khan, R., Tursunbayeva, A., . . . Bhaduri, S. (2025). What We Do Not Know: GPT Use in Business and Management. *arXiv preprint arXiv:2504.05273.*

. Mohammed, A. K., Ansari, S. F., Ahmed, M. I., & Mohammed, Z. A. Boosting Decision-Making with LLM-Powered Prompts in PowerBI.

. Moreno, C., Carrasco, R. A., & Herrera Viedma, E. (2019). Data and artificial intelligence strategy: A conceptual enterprise big data cloud architecture to enable market-oriented organisations.\

. Mustafa, B. S., & Zeebaree, S. R. (2025). AI-Driven Innovations in Enterprise Systems.

Natta, P. K. (2025). AI-Driven Decision Intelligence: Optimizing Enterprise Strategy with AI-Augmented Insights. *Journal of Computer Science and Technology Studies, 7*(2), 146–152.

Oloruntoba, N. O. (2025). AI-Driven autonomous database management: Self-tuning, predictive query optimization, and intelligent indexing in enterprise it environments. *World Journal of Advanced Research and Reviews, 25*(2), 1558–1580.

Sequeda, J., Allemang, D., & Jacob, B. (2025). Knowledge Graphs as a source of trust for LLM-powered enterprise question answering. *Journal of Web Semantics, 85*, 100858.

Su, H., Luo, W., Mehdad, Y., Han, W., Liu, E., Zhang, W., & Zhang, J. (2025, January). LLM-Friendly Knowledge Representation for Customer Support. In *Proceedings of the 31st International Conference on Computational Linguistics: Industry Track* (pp. 496-504).

Yammanur, V. (2025). INTEGRATED ENTERPRISE SYSTEMS: LEVERAGING ERP, EDI, AND AI FOR ENHANCED US BUSINESS COMPETITIVENESS. *INTERNATIONAL JOURNAL OF COMPUTER ENGINEERING AND TECHNOLOGY, 16*, 454–466.

Yan, S., & Zhu, T. (2025, January). CreditLLM: Constructing Financial AI Assistant for Credit Products using Financial LLM and Few Data. In *Proceedings of the Joint Workshop of the 9th Financial Technology and Natural Language Processing (FinNLP), the 6th Financial Narrative Processing (FNP), and the 1st Workshop on Large Language Models for Finance and Legal (LLMFinLegal)* (pp. 141-152).

. ŻMIJOWSKA, P. (2024). AREAS OF USE OF ARTIFICIAL INTELLIGENCE IN ENTERPRISE STRATEGY. SELECTED ISSUES. *Scientific Papers of Silesian University of Technology. Organization & Management/Zeszyty Naukowe Politechniki Slaskiej. Seria Organizacji i Zarzadzanie*, (204).

ADDITIONAL READING

Berman, S. J., & Marshall, A. (2014). The next digital transformation: From an individual-centered to an everyone-to-everyone economy. *Strategy and Leadership, 42*(5), 9–17. DOI: 10.1108/SL-07-2014-0048

Brynjolfsson, E., & McAfee, A. (2017). *Machine, Platform, Crowd: Harnessing Our Digital Future.* W.W. Norton & Company.

Davenport, T. H., & Ronanki, R. (2018). Artificial intelligence for the real world. *Harvard Business Review, 96*(1), 108–116.

Gentsch, P. (2018). *AI in Marketing, Sales and Service: How Marketers Without a Data Science Degree Can Use AI, Big Data and Bots*. Palgrave Macmillan.

. IBM Institute for Business Value. (2020). *The Enterprise Guide to Closing the Skills Gap*.

Marr, B. (2020). *Artificial Intelligence in Practice: How 50 Successful Companies Used AI and Machine Learning to Solve Problems*. Wiley.

Russell, S., & Norvig, P. (2021). *Artificial Intelligence: A Modern Approach* (4th ed.). Pearson.

Shrestha, Y. R., Ben-Menahem, S. M., & von Krogh, G. (2019). Organizational decision-making structures in the age of artificial intelligence. *California Management Review*, *61*(4), 66–83.

Vial, G. (2019). Understanding digital transformation: A review and a research agenda. *The Journal of Strategic Information Systems*, *28*(2), 118–144.

Westerman, G., Bonnet, D., & McAfee, A. (2014). *Leading Digital: Turning Technology into Business Transformation*. Harvard Business Review Press.

KEY TERMS AND DEFINITIONS

AI-as-a-Service (AIaaS): A cloud-based service model where AI capabilities—such as machine learning, computer vision, or NLP—are provided on demand, enabling enterprises to scale AI without deep technical infrastructure.

Decision Intelligence: An interdisciplinary framework combining data science, social science, and managerial science to support better decision-making through AI-driven analytics and simulations.

Digital Transformation: The fundamental shift in business operations and models enabled by the adoption of digital technologies, including cloud computing, data analytics, AI, and automation tools.

Enterprise AI: The strategic application of artificial intelligence technologies to automate, optimize, and augment business processes, decision-making, and organizational operations at scale.

Green AI: A set of practices and technologies focused on reducing the environmental impact of AI systems by improving energy efficiency, optimizing resource use, and supporting sustainability goals.

Human-in-the-Loop (HITL): An AI system design approach where human oversight and decision-making are incorporated into automated processes to ensure accountability, explainability, and contextual relevance.

Knowledge Graph: A structured data representation that captures relationships between concepts and entities, enabling machines to understand, reason, and generate insights across enterprise domains.

Large Language Models (LLMs): Advanced AI models trained on vast textual data to understand, generate, and manipulate natural language, increasingly used for enterprise tasks such as summarization, support, and analytics.

Organizational Readiness: The extent to which an enterprise is culturally, technically, and strategically prepared to adopt and integrate emerging technologies such as AI into core business processes.

Semantic Technologies: Tools and frameworks that enable machines to interpret the meaning of data, often using ontologies and metadata, to improve knowledge management and contextual AI applications.

Chapter 3
Retrieval-Augmented Generation (RAG) for Enterprise Intelligence:
Architectures, Applications, and Future Trends

Shubhamkumar Pandit
Marwadi University, Rajkot, India

R. N. Ravikumar
https://orcid.org/0009-0009-3705-1681
Marwadi University, Rajkot, India

Neeharika Joshi
Marwadi University, Rajkot, India

Sonukumar Pandit
Marwadi University, Rajkot, India

Satwik Kishore
Marwadi University, Rajkot, India

S. Aarthi
https://orcid.org/0009-0006-9064-2091
Marwadi University, Rajkot, India

ABSTRACT

In today's data-driven world, traditional BI platforms fall short in providing real-time, context-aware insights. Large Language Models (LLMs) like GPT-3 and LLaMA excel in natural language tasks but struggle with outdated knowledge and hallucinations. Retrieval-Augmented Generation (RAG) bridges this gap by integrating LLMs with external data sources such as databases, APIs, or vector stores. This chapter explores RAG's architecture, combining retrievers (e.g., FAISS, Elasticsearch) with generators (e.g., GPT, Claude) and its enterprise applications in finance, marketing, HR, and supply chain. Key challenges like data governance, latency, and ethical considerations are discussed, offering a roadmap for deploying RAG to enhance real-time decision-making.

DOI: 10.4018/979-8-3373-3912-2.ch003

1. INTRODUCTION

In this high-velocity, digitalized economy, organizations have to quickly determine the correct course of action using fast-changing volumes of data. Although Large Language Models (LLMs) such as GPT-3 and LLaMA have revolutionized the process of natural language processing, certain shortcomings, including its inability to adapt to changing business circumstances due to their inability to obtain access to business-specific data, hallucinations, and ability to only use static knowledge also negatively affect their practical utility. Retrieval-Augmented Generation (RAG) is an effective remedy as it unites generative capabilities of LLMs with real-time, context-sensitive information retrieval against both structured and unstructured endpoints. This chapter discusses the design, uses and advantages of RAG systems in business intelligence and decision support. RAG can be used to provide fact-based, explainable, scalable enterprise solutions, such as personalized marketing, real-time supply chain visibility and many more. It provides a revolutionizing twist in the way organizations access and make use of data and enables them with the timely and domain specific intelligence by empowering the decision-makers. Technical implementations, efficient deployment plans, and prospects of RAG in enterprise ecosystems are also described in the chapter.

1.1 Rise Of Data-Aware and Real-Time Enterprise Demands

Modern companies are more and more active in the conditions, where huge amounts of dynamic and continuous data exist. In this regard, there are three essential principles that the decision-making should follow in these contexts. One is that it must be timely based upon the current information that is available and up to date. Second, the choices made must be situation- based and never go against the organizational objectives, emerging customer needs and the external market environments. Third, decision making should be justifiable and decision makers can audit their actions, thus, making decisions based on the data attached to reliable and transparent sources (Arslan & Cruz, 2024). However, these needs are making the accustomed business intelligence (BI) systems hard to come up with these needs. Such legacy tools, usually based on static dashboards, scheduled batch reports and SQL-based queries carried out manually and manually, not only cannot handle the quick decision cycles common today, but also lead to serious consequences during the maintenance process. They are not responsive enough, to make informed and specific, real-time questions to unstudied, non-technical stakeholders, or provide responsive strategies in fluid situations.

Such shortcoming has made data-sensitive AI systems that intelligently read what is produced and transform it into the meaningful and timely information, with an understanding of the natural language and knowledge of sources, that provide personalized and contextualized insights available at the right time and in real-time, an apparent and pressing need. RAG systems have developed as one of the solutions that make a lot of sense to this issue. These systems have a combination of LLMs and their ability to retrieve accurate data so that they provide a contextually relevant and factually accurate response (Emelia et al., n.d.). The path taken towards such systems is a tremendous development in the field of enterprise decision support. Businesses are placed in a situation where they require AI tools that can not only understand the context of an organization but also utilize new and reliable information in informing action, without yielding the accuracy and explainability. Such development indicates that the future is here where business-related insights powered by the AI become a common trend and an element integrated as part of the business process supporting fast, strategic, and decisive decision-making.

1.2 Retrieval-Augmented Generation (RAG)

RAG refers to an area of rapidly developing AI architecture, aiming to boost the potential of standalone LLMs by teaming them with complementary outside sources of information. RAG also differs with traditional models that generate responses guided by pre-trained internal parameters only (Chen et al., 2025). The initial level is the retriever, and this task retrieves relevant pieces of information on multiple external sources, e.g., vector databases (e.g., FAISS, Vespa) and keyword-based search engines (e.g., Elasticsearch), various databases (structured or unstructured) internal, and even real-time streams APIs. The second step involves a generator, which is most often a language model, such as GPT, LLaMA or Cohere, to automatically generate the retrieved data into a coherent, context-aware response (Khan et al., 2024).

Such design makes RAG-based systems such that they produce facts-based writings, which is much more likely to end hallucinations, as that way, it ties generation to something verifiable (Niu et al., 2024). What is more, RAG models can be calibrated with an enterprise-specific knowledge to provide a customized intelligence solution. Their outputs are also explainable and auditable which means they are particularly applicable to high stakes compliance-based environments. Steadily, RAG is thus a paradigm change in business intelligence and decision support- The means of delivering real-time, scalable, and reliable AI-driven analytics in present-day enterprises.

2. THE ARCHITECTURE OF RAG

RAG is an intermediate architecture that is built to improve on the weaknesses of standalone LLMs, by making them contextually grounded by incorporating an external source of knowledge. The innermost aspect of RAG is a split in the knowledge storage and the language generation processes allowing flexible access at run time to the appropriate data. This enables the outputs thus generated to be linguistically natural as well as factually correct and contextually contented to what the user intends.

2.1 Components: Retriever + Generator

RAG is an intermediate AI structure that supplements the shortcomings of independent LLMs, which entails a method of contextual grounding through the use of outside sources of knowledge. Fundamentally, RAG decouples the storage of the knowledge with the language generation process so that it is dynamic in the sense that given information can be accessed during run-time. This enables the outputs produced could not just be linguistically fluent but also factually accurate and contextually appropriate towards the intention of the user.

2.2 Typical pipeline: Query → Retrieve → Generate

Retriever: The retriever indicates the happiest fragments of data, that a big collection (e.g. in- house company files, structured databases, or indexed consumer responses) contains. It typically does so by using a dense representation (embeddings) of both the user query, as well as the documents and determining similarity between those representations. Retrieval Techniques:

- Dense retrieval: Vector similarity (e.g. FAISS, Vespa)
- Sparse retrieval: Keyword based search (e.g. Elasticsearch)
- Retrieval range: It is possible to retrieve structured data (SQL-databases) as well as unstructured information (PDFs, emails, and reports and etc).
- Top-k retrieval: It usually returns k most relevant results of the similarity scores.

Generator: The generator is a Large Language Model (LLM) that with query and the retrieved documents as inputs, is able to provide a rational, contextually explanatory answer.

- Function: Makes a synthesis of the known knowledge retrieved and makes a total answer.
- Models applied: GPT (OpenAI), Claude (Anthropic), LLaMA (Meta), Mistral, Cohere Command R, and so on. [8]
- Input parameter: Query + Retrieved Context = Generated Answer
- Positive: Limited hallucination, increased relevancy by basing creation on real facts which are retrieved.

Figure 1. Pipeline Flowchart of Retrieval-Augmented Generation (RAG)

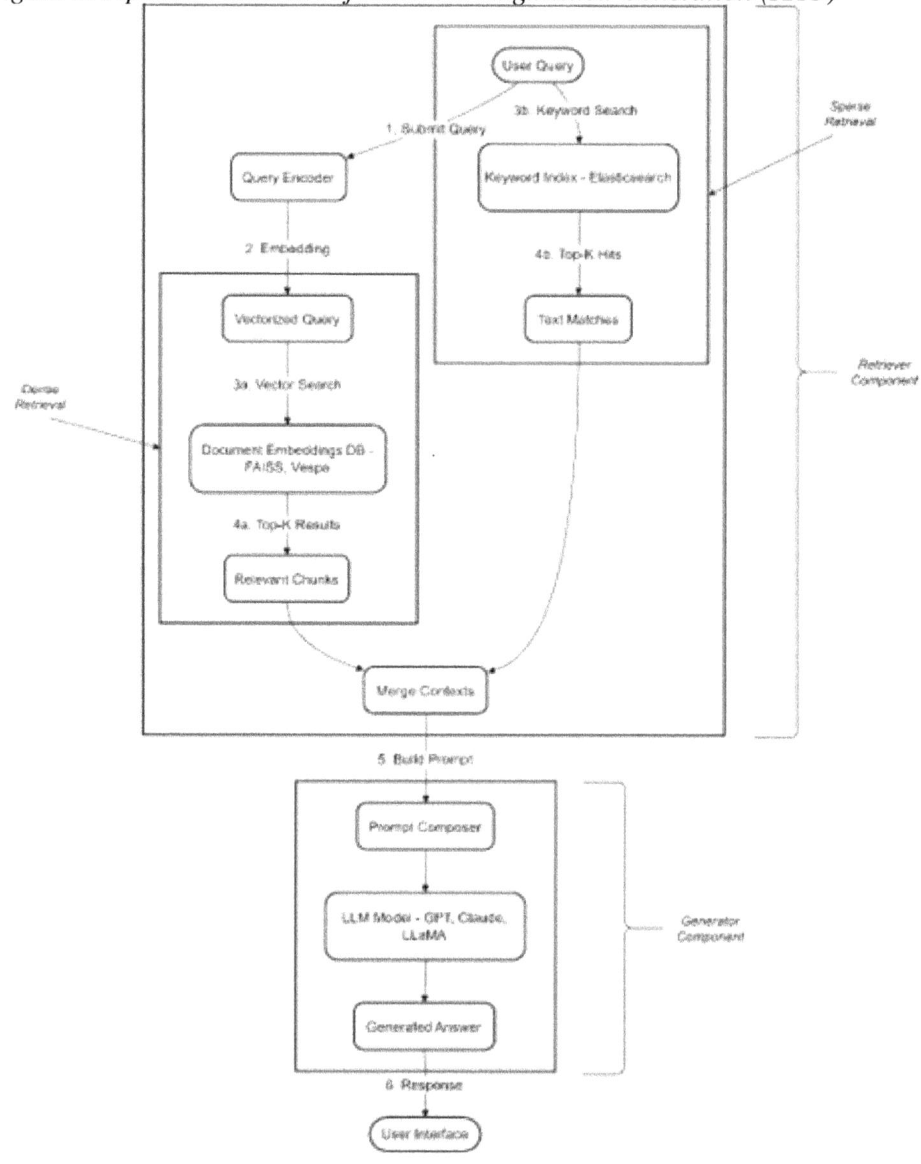

The RAG scheme adopts a modular workflow pipeline Figure 1 matching between user intentions and applicable knowledge and translating them into useful smart output. It describes each of the stages in full detail, combining the dense (semantic) and sparse (keywords-based) retrieval strategies, and demonstrates them operating alongside a Large Language Model (LLM). To help drive this point home we use business example as follows: A territory sales person shares a query “What were the top-selling products in South Asia in Q2?" into the enterprise RAG-powered dashboard.

Step 1: Submission of Queries

- The user poses his or her question through a dashboard or conversational interface.
- The query is then given to a query encoder, which is usually based on transformers (e.g. BERT or Sentence Transformers).
- This encoder changes a plain text query into a dense vector - the numerical representation that reflects the piece of the semantic meaning of the question.

In our case:

The question under analysis is, "What were the top-selling products in South Asia in Q2?" is reinterpreted as a vector of intent (top product performance request) and context (regional and time specific constraints).

Step 2: Finding Information

A. Dense Retrieval (Semantic matching)

The user query is initially converted to a vector form, and is indexed against a vector database, e.g.: FAISS, Vespa, etc. which has already computed the embeddings of enterprise documents, e.g.: sales reports, product reviews, and CRM (Han et al., 2024). This process enables the system to understand the query on the semantical level as opposed to being based on matching keywords. This causes the retriever to retrieve the Top-K most semantically nearby documents even in those cases where the documents themselves contain different keywords than the ones used on the query. This semantic search guarantees that context and meaning of the query is retained for further downstream generation of more precise and relevant information (Khan et al., 2024).

Example Output:

Internal quarter 2 sales report that reads: "The revenue of South Asia was up by 14% due to the growth of Product X and Product Y." in the Figure 2

Figure 2. South Asia Monthly Sales Trends 2

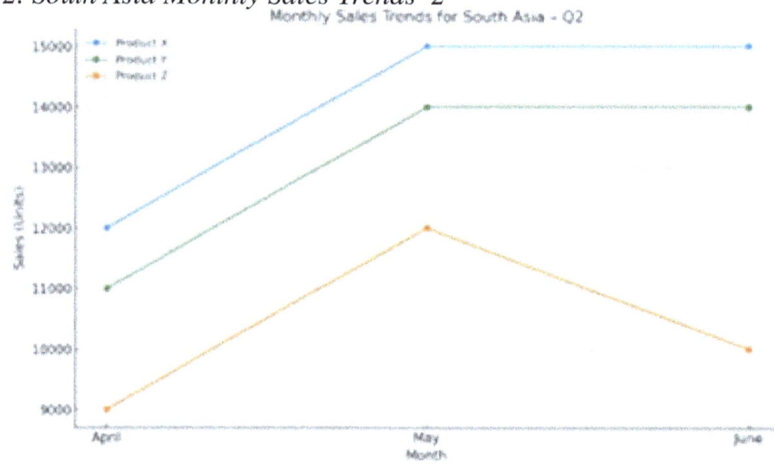

B. Sparse Search (Keyword Matching)

At the same time, the original query is also directed to such a sparse one as Elasticsearch. This module leverages the classic information retrieval methods such as BM25 or TF-IDF to find the documents having a full or partial matching of the keywords (Han et al., 2024)(Li et al., 2024). Compared to semantic search, the technique pays attention to lexical similarity and, therefore, could be used to locate documents where the sought-after terms are explicitly stated. Namely, when given the query of product catalogs or marketing summaries with keywords like Q2, South Asia, top-selling, and Product X, the system can give concise results that are based on textual matches. This will make sure strictly keyword like content will not be lost during the retrieval process (Khan et al., 2024).

C. Context Converging

It then combines the results of the two the dense (semantic) and sparse (keyword) retrievers to achieve a balanced system with both an emphasis on the semantic relevancy of the user query and an emphasis on keyword matching as used in IR. This mixed retrieval technique makes retrieved information to be completer and more correct. In the process, redundant documents will be eliminated, and the context windows will be either cut or clipped to fit within the word limitations of the LLM. The step is essential as it is needed to optimize the length of the input and keep the most relevant and high-quality content that can be generated (Khan et al., 2024).

Step 3: Prompt Construction and Generation

The combined and screened contextual data is formed into a well-rounded query that encompasses the actual user query along with the derived context i.e., derived sales data, product names, bullet points, and regional performance data. This orderly information is then forwarded to Large Language Model (LLM) such as GPT, Claude, or LLaMA, which uses it to come up with an expressive, situationally-aware, and enterprise-ready reply (Shao et al., 2023). As an illustration, one example of using a user query is as follows: what were the best-selling products in South Asia in Q2? The system enhances this query with corresponding retrieved information e.g.:

- Product X and Y contributed to the South Asian 14 percent number growth in revenues.
- In May, the performance of the product Z was good and it decreased in June.
- The performance of the South Asia sales team represented 8 percent higher sales than the target was on a quarterly basis.

Upon command, this set makes the LLM produce a sensible answer such as:

In South Asia, the results during the Q2 were the most popular in terms of Product X and Product Y, where revenue went up by 14 percent. Product Z was good in the month of May and was down in the month of June. In general, the South Asian team has surpassed its share of the quarterly target by eight percent." This case demonstrates how RAG could provide such business intelligence as unstructured data is converted into knowledge in action by means of structured contextual prompting and natural language generation.

Step 4: Delivery of Response

The last leg of the RAG pipeline is the user interface, and here the sales manager/business stakeholder gets the AI insights in consumable mediums, on which he/she can act. The response can be in the form of:

- Abridged sentence responses, giving accurate description of material in a short story form.
- Visual display that can be in the form of charts, graphs, or dashboards that enables the user to keep trend and pattern easily.
- Insight reports in downloadable formats (e.g. PDF or Excel) can be archived, shown in presentation or used in additional analysis.

This is immediate and multiple mode of delivering information that helps the manager make real-time decisions- shifting inventory in one region to another region based on its sales figures, the creation of executive briefs in record time or planning a product campaign that has a limited focus and meets the demand and growth of its market. The RAG system, therefore, connects the raw data about the enterprise and direct response-based action in the table 1.

Table 1. Fundamental Elements of a Retrieval-Augmented Generation (RAG) System

Component	Function	Common Tools/Examples
Query Encoder	Converts user query to embedding or tokens	Sentence-BERT, OpenAI Embeddings
Retriever	Searches for relevant chunks/documents	FAISS, Elasticsearch, Vespa
Generator	Uses context to produce a natural language response	GPT-4, Claude, LLaMA
Prompt Composer	Builds the final input for the LLM	LangChain, Haystack Templates

2.3 The RAG Pipeline Business Relevance

Rather good business intelligence benefits come with the combination of retrieval and generation in this pipeline. First, it enables decision-makers to access data-supported reactions in real time without involving complicated technical knowledge and SQL proficiency. Second, it minimizes the reliance on data analysts or IT-based users to produce the periodic report since it will be on-demand and AI-powered. Third, this is an important aspect of the grounding of LLM outputs in verified, retrieved data, which decreases hallucinations and other factual errors, and makes one believe more in automatic responses. Lastly, System architecture is scalable and the enterprises can roll out this functionality to more departments, business units and geographies with significantly less reconfiguration (Niu et al., 2024) (Emelia et al., n.d.).

3. TOOLS AND FRAMEWORKS: LANGCHAIN, HAYSTACK, FAISS, VESPA

In order to practically implement RAG states in businesses, scalable modular tools should be provided. There are a number of frameworks (both open source and commercial) that aim to support production quality RAG pipelines. LangChain, a Python library, allows creating multi-step applications that can easily work with

LLMs (Xu et al., 2024). It has prompts, retriever, database modules, and connects to vector stores such as FAISS and Pinecone. Another strong framework that can be used on both extractive and generative question answering is Haystack. It is compatible with models of OpenAI, Cohere, and Hugging Face and has features that allow logging and performance monitoring. FAISS (Facebook AI Similarity Search) is heavily tailored to searching dense vectors similarity, which allows ANN algorithms to scale to millions of vectors, creating high-quality retrieval results (Kim & Mahajan, 2025). Vespa is an enterprise-grade search engine, which also supports dense and sparse retrieval system and is at its best in high-performance systems such as large-scale recommendation systems. When these tools are combined, they provide the foundation of enterprise RAG systems, which are scalable RAG systems, responsive, and domain-specific AI solutions (Gan et al., 2025).

3.1 Advantages of RAG in Business Decision-Making

With more and more enterprises using data-driven strategies, the capacity of retrieving, interpreting, and operating on information in real time will become necessary. RAG is an important step in the manner in which businesses interact with their knowledge and data systems. RAG, a combination of the LLMs and dynamic information retrieval, opens the doors to a wide range of possibilities in business intelligence and strategic decision-making.

3.2 Real-Time Data Access and Reasoning

Traditional LLMs are not dynamic in nature since they are purely based on information that is pre-trained. This shortcoming causes slow response in business conditions that are changing at rapid rates. The above constraint is addressed by RAG, which can retrieve and update models with the most up-to-date and relevant enterprise data, during querying. Take the example of a financial analyst who wants to obtain the recent trend of revenue of Product X- Q2. Real-time data A RAG-enabled system can access live information as well, pulling actual sales data using live databases, business dashboards, or document repositories to inform the current or past few hours or days. This will make sure that the decisions will be determined by information relevant in the current business environment, and not row forecasts, or the old figures of the day before. In addition, RAG improves the multi-source reasoning- the models can refer and compare information between product documentation, regional performance, and historical trends. The ability to quickly interpret a message is especially important in the fields of finance and e- commerce, supply chains, and healthcare, where any hitch in the interpretation can cause big losses, or operational threats (Zhao et al., 2023)(Kostopoulos et al., 2024).

3.3 Factual Grounding and Reduced Hallucinations

Hallucination, that is, producing factually incorrect or fictitious material is one of the serious threats with standalone Large Language Models (LLMs) and therefore is a significant business risk. These errors may result in impaired decision making, mistrust among the stakeholders, and regulatory violations particularly in the industries where accuracy on information and subsequent traceability is important. RAG solves this problem by basing deliverables on validated enterprise particular data. In contrast with regular LLMs, RAG accesses facts that are taken directly trusted sources e.g. CRM logs, audit report or policy documents, which limits the risk of hallucination. Additionally, RAG guarantees traceability and auditability whereby response can be traced back to original documents which is very important in regulated sectors such as finance and healthcare sectors. As an example, a RAG system can even give evidence-based outcomes when asking why regional sales fell, e.g., supply chain delay or market saturation, instead of guesswork. Incorporating a solid factual basis and transparency, RAG produces trust in AI-created products and provides more trustful data-driven choices within the context of real-life business operations in the table 2.

Table 2. Usage of Retrieval-Augmented Generation (RAG) in Business Functions

Business Function	What RAG Enables
Finance	Instant summaries of market activity, fraud detection, compliance draft generation
Supply Chain	On-demand queries for logistics, warehouse, and inventory systems
Marketing	Retrieval of persona data, campaign insights, customer behaviour summaries
HR	Dynamic policy reference, candidate evaluation, personalized onboarding
Legal	Accurate clause search, live regulation interpretation, contract comparison

3.4 Better User Interaction with Natural Language User Interface

Among the most groundbreaking benefits of Retrieval Augmented Generation (RAG) systems is the consideration that makes complex enterprise information simpler by means of, and in a natural tongue. RAG systems allow people to interact with data through a casual conversational language, unlike traditional business intelligence (BI) tools where one needs advanced skills in writing SQL queries or cooking their way on occasion complex dashboards. This drastically reduces the data-driven skill threshold of the non-technical staff at every level of the organization including managers, human resource specialists, customer service managers and marketing analysts. As an example, a human resource head can ask the question, what is our staff turnover trend in the first quarter of the year, by department or a customer support head may ask, give me the number of customer complaints related to late delivery over the past 30 days. In the two scenarios, RAG returns the most topical and up-to-date documents/datasets before converting them into a compact and precise answer (Arslan & Cruz, 2024). The fact that the user may ask the business-related questions in their own words in a RAG system makes it more accessible, fosters the use of AI throughout the enterprise by removing the training overhead that is often required to use analytics tools. This leads to the more efficient operations and data literacy, and accelerated decision response time in everyday decisions in the table 3.

Table 3. Business Benefits of Retrieval-Augmented Generation (RAG)

Advantage	Business Value
Real-Time Data Access	Enables fast, informed decision-making based on the latest enterprise data
Factual Grounding	Reduces hallucinations, improves trust in LLM responses
Domain-Specific Adaptability	Aligns AI responses with industry- and company-specific knowledge
Natural Language Access	Empowers non-technical users with intuitive, conversational interfaces

4. BUSINESS APPLICATIONS OF RAG

The Retrieval-Augmented Generation (RAG) systems are very flexible and may be adjusted to any great percentage of business needs. With powerful state-interpolated language models coupled to the latest, multitemporal data retrieval, RAG supports enterprises to automate decision-making, personalize communication, and increase department-wide operational intelligence.

4.1 Finance: Market Reports, Fraud Alerts, Investment Summaries

RAG allows real-time intelligence to be created dynamically instead of viewing stagnant analytics dashboards and historical business intelligence pipelines that are present in fluctuating financial services (Krause, 2023). RAG systems can also make financial professionals more responsive and data-driven in their decisions by interacting with enterprise data in natural language because it can accept live data feeds like stock market APIs, financial news, and the internal transaction records

(Wang et al., 2025). The below Figure 3 illustrates a RAG-enabled financial intelligence pipeline where real-time data from stock feeds and transactions is merged, processed via a GPT-style LLM, and used to generate investment summaries and fraud alerts for dashboards and alerting systems.

Figure 3. Workflow of RAG-Driven Financial Intelligence and Fraud Detection

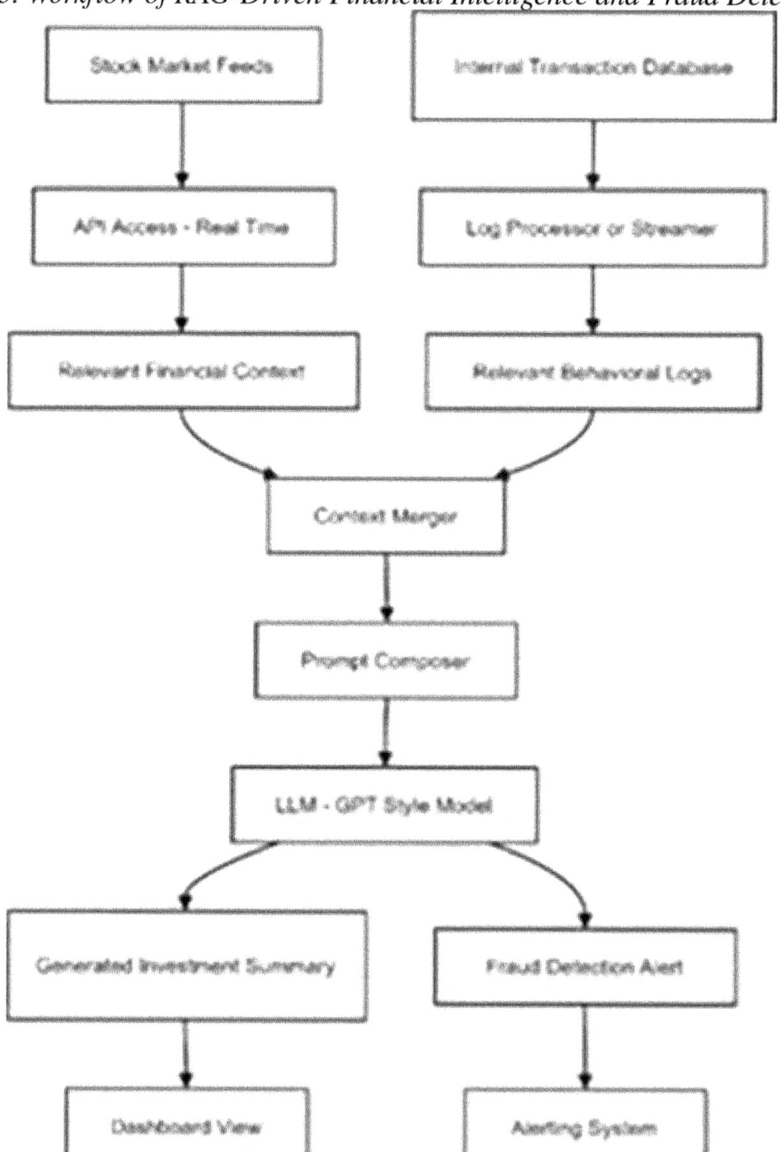

The RAG systems provide revolutionary potentials in the financial sphere as they also provide real-time and intelligent analysis. Instantaneous market summarization the important usage is an on-demand market summarization, in which RAG creates a live summary of stock prices and financial news based on an investor portfolio (Krause, 2023). Another important application is the fraud detection warnings, which have the system constantly review transaction records to detect unusual patterns, anomalous or criminal habits, and activate immediate alerts to aid in the regulatory compliance and managing the risk. Also, RAG enables personalized investment analysis whereby an investor will query the trends in the performance, assets, and summaries on time. The insights are generated on a real-time basis, and their decisions on portfolio optimization are data-driven and timely (Wang et al., 2025).

The RAG pipeline, in return, will access the portfolio data of the user, compare the current performance to the historical trends, and provide a risk-conscious report that is personalized and finished within several seconds. An example of such intelligent pipeline is presented in Figure 3 that shows samples of the working process in a financial intelligence program powered by RAG. The figure highlights the process through which real-time data streams are consumed and processed using a retriever and a generator and then returned in form of useful actionable insights as a response to the query that was presented by the user. This end-to-end procedure is the bright example of how RAG manages to transfer financial analysis to the agile interactive and reliable support system.

4.2 Marketing: Personalized Campaign Generation

On incorporation of RAG into the marketing processes, it enables organizations to create hyper-personalized textual content using user engagement, campaign history, and customer segmentation insights. RAG, unlike other traditional rule- based systems has the ability to dynamically access and restructure pertinent data across any enterprise system (ex: CRM databases, A/B testing results, and demographic analytics) to generate marketing content that is not only contextually accurate, but specific to the target audience. The below Figure 4 illustrates a RAG-powered personalized marketing workflow, where campaign data, CRM records, and demographics are merged to generate engagement-aware email and ad copy through an LLM-driven message generator.

Figure 4. Personalized marketing content generation workflow using RAG

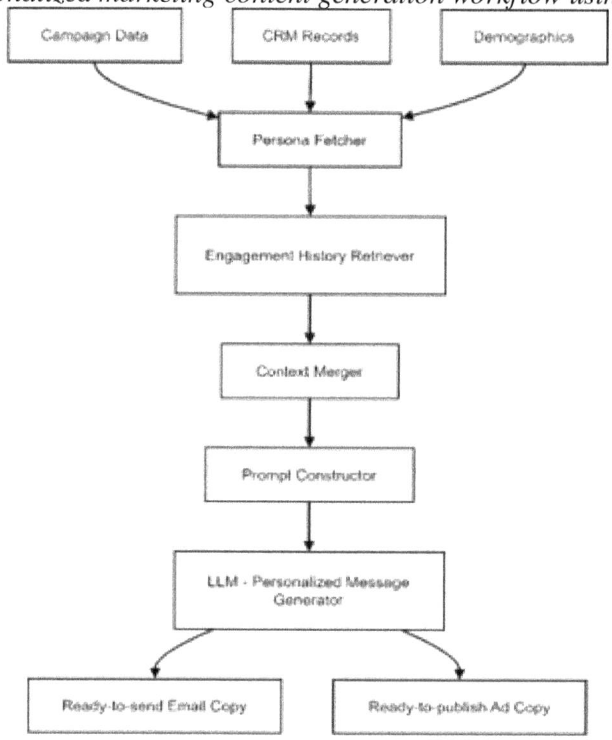

RAG will then extract the pertinent CRM records, records the success rates on the marketing campaign when it comes to that demographic group and then creates a tailored marketing email that will be captivating and tailored. It shows the graph of this smartly developed content creation pipeline, and the personalized marketing process, driven by RAG. It also illumines the way in which input request are carried out by using retrieval and generation stages with the help of the enterprise knowledge to provide relevant timely and conversions directed message. With these implementations, not only does a business increase levels of engagement, but it also maximizes its marketing ROI via parts and personalization.

4.3 Customer Service: Context-Aware Chatbot Responses

RAG is a new generation of chatbots and is revolutionizing customer service with contextual, personalized and live assistance. In contrast to traditional bots which are limited by limited, rule-based answers, RAG-enhanced systems could dynamically retrieve most recent support tickets, product manuals, FAQs, and, best of all, individual customer history to learn the most precise and understanding answers.

Figure 5. Flow of Customer Service Interaction RAG-Enhanced

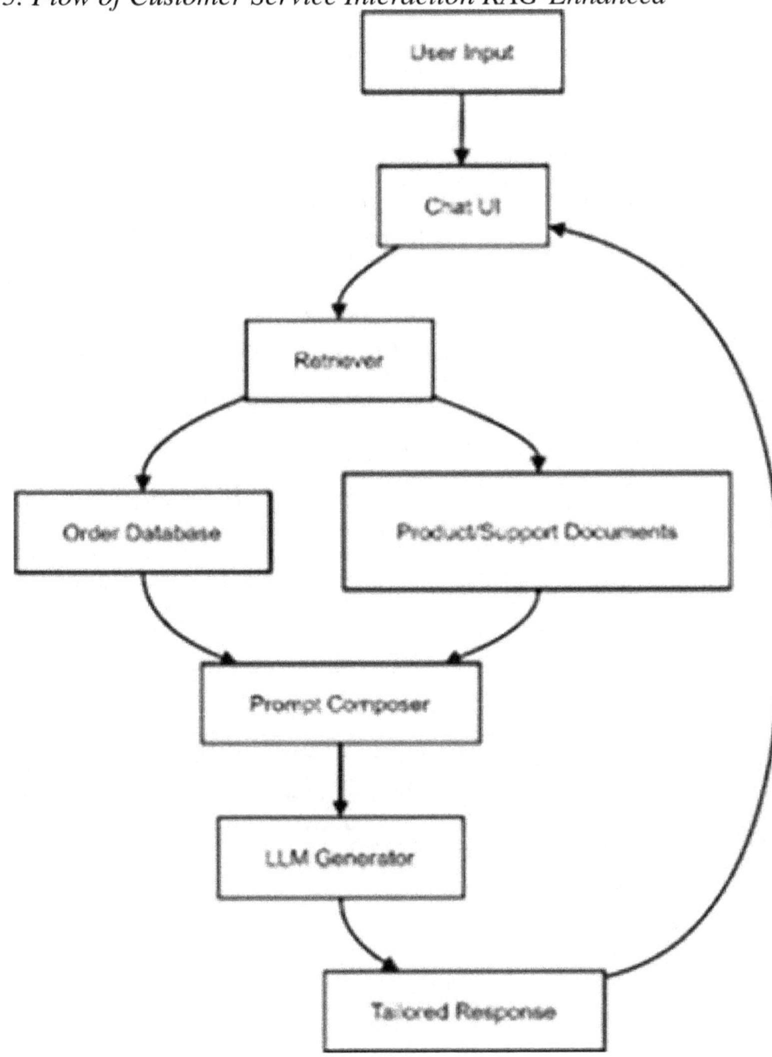

The Figure 5 shows Flow of Customer service interaction RAG-Enhanced displays that the user query passes through a two-step retrieval and generation pipeline that draws data (customer-specific and policy-related) and constructs a logical and actionable response. This results through improved resolution times as well as a decreased agent workload and a more personalized customer experience which fuels greater satisfaction and loyalty.

4.4 Supply Chain: Real-Time Inventory and Logistics Q&A

Amidst the world of supply chain management, where time and accuracy is of essence, the RAG systems promise a revolutionary means of managing natural language queries. Manual files are frequently extracted by using traditional systems, which are isolated audit data and logistics dashboards or supplier portals in a warehouse. Quite conversely, RAG systems accelerate this process by linking with these backend engines and providing quick, context specific responses in real time (Gaddala & Sharma Gaddala, 2023). The below Figure 6 This diagram represents a RAG-based supply chain query resolution system where a user query is processed through retrieval from warehouse, transport, and supplier data sources, synthesized by a prompt composer, and answered via an LLM to deliver a final, actionable response.

Figure 6. RAG-Powered Query Resolution Flow in the supply chain

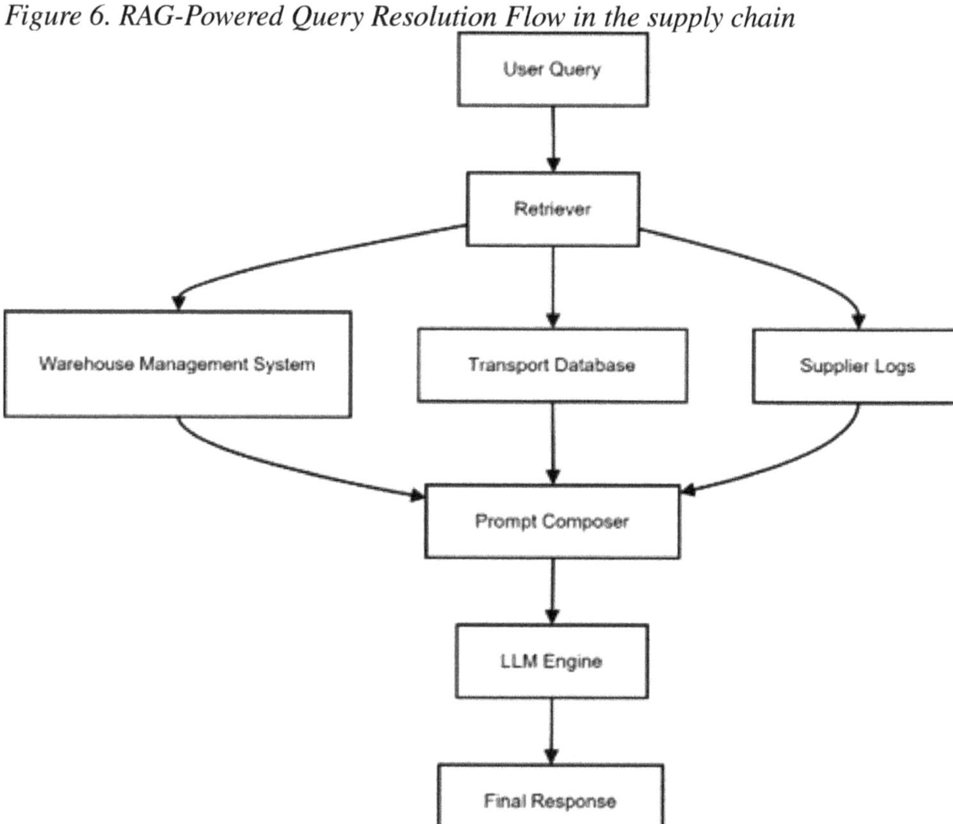

Once a query such as; How many units of Product Z do we have on stock currently in Mumbai and when is the next batch arriving has been keyed in the RAG system goes into a multi-stage process. It retrieves live inventory information on the Warehouse Management System (WMS), queries delivery and logistical services (e.g. ERP or SCM APIs) and consolidates the information to produce a human-readable response. The answer may be: Product Z quantity in Mumbai warehouse is 320 units. The other one will come on June 22 by Supplier A. The ability saves time as well but more importantly avoids human error so that decision-makers are able to take some immediate actions. An example has been noted where the stocks are low and there is no shipment that is expected to be received in days to come; the insights that can be made known by the system may prompt an immediate decision of procurement, which may avoid the disruptions.

Examples of where RAG will be an applicable strategy in the supply chain include:

- Giving stock-availability in real-time in various warehouses.
- Reporting delay in delivery, distributes or customs assessments.
- corps production of supplier performance summaries and identification of possible risks.

The workflow of the system will be incorporated effectively with the APIs and operational databases so that the responses given by the system will be precise and timely as is shown in RAG-Powered Query Resolution Flow in the Supply Chain (Wu et al., 2025). Such an architecture can add considerable value in terms of efficiency, responsiveness, operational intelligence throughout the supply-chain enterprise (Gaddala & Sharma Gaddala, 2023).

5. HR AND LEGAL: POLICY GENERATION, COMPLIANCE SUMMARIES

Human Resources and Legal teams regularly have too much documentation to process, e.g. policy manual, regulatory requirements, compliance requirements, contracts and internal processes. Browsing and interpreting this information manually is cumbersome not only because it is time consuming but also subjected to missing out. To counter this, Retrieval- Augmented Generation (RAG) systems solve this problem by ensuring that such material is searchable, readable and actionable via simple natural language queries, on-demand contextual answers.

Figure 7. HR and Legal Query Resolution Process RAG-Based

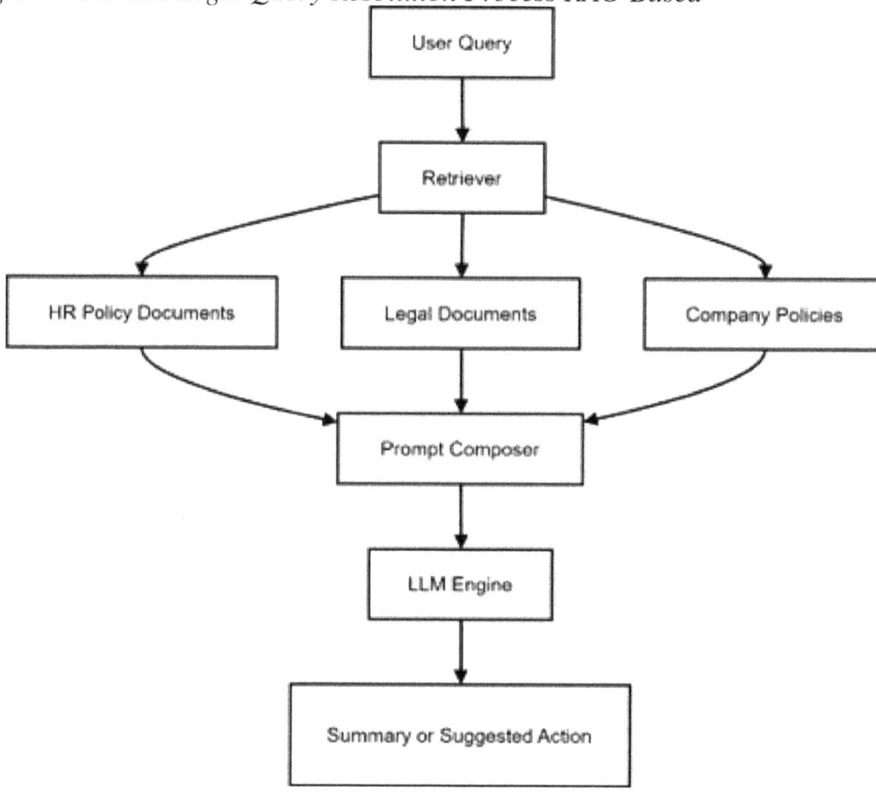

The above Figure 7 represents a RAG-based supply chain query resolution system where a user query is processed through retrieval from warehouse, transport, and supplier data sources, synthesized by a prompt composer, and answered via an LLM to deliver a final, actionable response. These types of systems can effectively address both HR and legal inquiries by accessing both structured and unstructured enterprise data resources as indicated in HR and Legal Query Resolution Process RAG-Based. On the HR side, some of the common use cases are summarizing a policy on leave, benefits or onboarding, outputting a job description or internal communications, and answering contextual questions like, what is our policy on remote working on contract employees?

Legally, RAG can be applied to extract and interpret the provisions of regulatory documents or contracts, author compliance reports and even monitor any change of policy over time. To give an example, when the question is presented, such as: Provide an overview of the key changes to our policy of data privacy since the last quarter, the RAG system would retrieve potentially relevant documents out of the repository of the policies, use vector-based similarity (semantic diff) to compare the current and previous policy versions, and generate a clear answer, like: In the policy update of the previous quarter, the terms of employee consent have been extended and control on data sharing with third-parties is added (Li, 2024). This kind of functionality significantly enhances the effectiveness, precision, and appurtenance of HR and legal operations so that an organization can answer timely to any internal requests, be compliant, and make wise decisions having verified contents to support them all. The table 5 as follows.

Table 5. Real-world Applications of Retrieval-Augmented Generation (RAG) the business functions

Domain	Application	Example Query
Finance	Risk summary, investment reports	"Summarize top 3 market risks this week"
Marketing	Campaign optimization, customer persona building	"What worked best in last 2 ad campaigns?"
Supply Chain	Inventory tracking, logistics Q&A	"Where are delays occurring this week?"
HR & Legal	Policy insights, compliance checks	"What are leave policy changes post-2023?"

5.1 Data Sources and Index Management

A working RAG system has its basis by ensuring that reliable and pertinent information is extracted out of enterprise data stores. They may include:

Figure 8. Data Sources for Retrieval-Augmented Generation (RAG) Systems

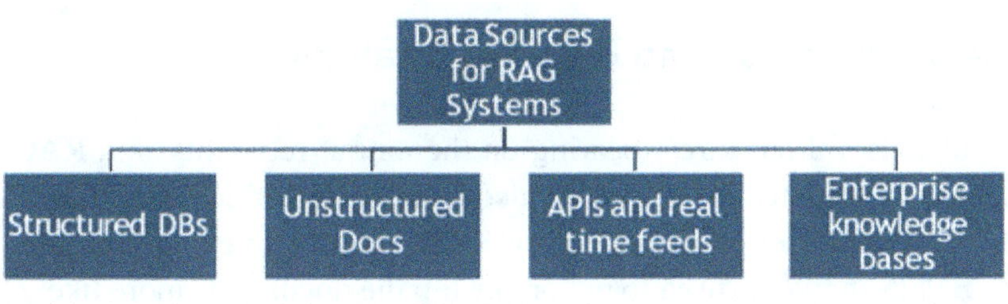

a. Structured databases (PostgreSQL, Snowflake, Big Query)
b. Unstructured documents (PDFs, word files, email, internal reports)

c. APIs and real time feeds (ERP, CRM, IoT systems)
d. Enterprise knowledge bases (on Confluence, Notion, SharePoint)

The Figure 8 categorizes the primary data sources for RAG systems into four types: Structured Databases, Unstructured Documents, APIs and Real-Time Feeds, and Enterprise Knowledge Bases each contributing essential context for generating accurate, data-grounded responses. Preprocessing of information and structuring is a technique that is needed to make sure that efficient and accurate retrieval can be done in a RAG system. The initial process is to divide raw data into semantically rich segments, paragraphs, sections or tables and so on, depending on the type and scenario of the document. This contributes towards logical consistency and retrievability. These text blocks are segmented, and then they are fed into complex embedding models, and the most common are Sentence-BERT or OpenAI Embeddings to get the vector representation (Kim & Mahajan, 2025). The semantic meaning of such texts, as defined by these embeddings, is then stored and indexed efficiently by utilizing such tools as FAISS, Vespa, or We aviate, which are optimized to efficiently and consistently retrieve similarity search in large collections.

Also, in the case of an environment where there is a constant shift in the data the utilization of automated daily indexing and synchronization pipelines is imperative, e.g., sales reports or HR regulations (Macdonald et al., 2025). The processes make sure that the state of the vector database is not outdated and always has the newest content thereof, thus keeping the responses generated accurate. One such best practice in the implementation of RAG is the parallel use of dense indexing (in support of semantic search) and sparse indexing (in support of precision in keyword search). The hybrid method goes even further, being able to provide the system with results that are not only contextual but also match certain terms within the query presented by the user, thereby improving the memory and the amount of precision with information finding.

5.2 Retrieval Precision and Ranking Strategies

Quality of retrieval has direct bearing on the output reliability in a RAG system. Irrelevant or outdated results could also be retrieved which would turn even the well-formed responses containing error. Ranking techniques such as similarity (cosine) or BM25 should be used to put on the top the documents more likely to be interesting. Reduce the search space using filters and metadata tags (e.g., department, time frame) and rewritten queries was used to improve short or vague queries. To make the precision more accurate, apply multi-stage retrieval pipeline: the initial stage retrieves broadly relevant documents by performing a vector search, and the second stage re- ranks them by employing task-specific models such as BERT-based cross encoders. This will cause only the most relevant content to reach the LLM, making responses of higher quality in general.

5.3 Latency, Scalability, and Cost Optimization

As RAG systems are dependent on a number of stages, retrieval, prompt building, and generation, the response latency may be an issue (particularly where real-time response is required, such as chatbots or decision dashboards) (Kim & Mahajan, 2025). The below Figure 9 outlines key challenges faced by RAG systems latency, scalability, and cost and presents targeted optimizations for each. It highlights solutions such as ANN-based vector search, distributed retrieval, and the use of open-source LLMs to enhance performance and efficiency.

Figure 9. Typical Example of RAG use cases in business areas

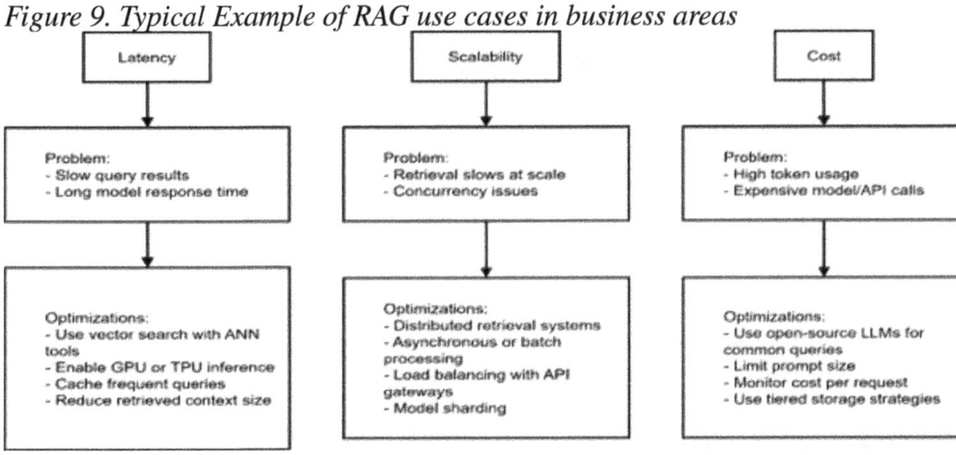

Enterprises that want to reduce latency in their RAG systems should implement low-latency vector databases with approximate nearest neighbor (ANN) search, perform LLM inference at low-latency GPUs or APIs such as OpenAI or vLLM and cache common queries and answers. To scale horizontally and vertically, to allow retrievers and generators to be containerized and to support high throughput with non-blocking async responses, microservices can be considered. Size reduction can be achieved by local optimization using reduction/condensing of records and there can be several tiers of embeddings (summary and detailed) that can be saved. In house deployment of open-source LLMs such as LLaMA can also reduce API cost.

5.4 Performance Measuring and Evaluation

After implementation, evaluation of RAG systems should be conducted continuously with the help of quantitative indicators and qualitative feedbacks. This is done by monitoring the performance; this keeps retrieval and generation precise, quick, and current to business performance.

However, Key Evaluation Metrics are planned as follows:

a. Top- k Accuracy (Hit Rate): Indicates the top k retrieved documents in order to determine whether the correct document is retrieved (Maksim, 2024).

$$Top - k\ Accuracy =$$
$$Number\ of\ correct\ queries\ with\ relevant\ document\ in\ top - k$$
$$Total\ number\ of\ queries$$

b. Precision@ K: Proportion of the retrieved documents by the top K which are relevant (Maksim, 2024).

$$Precision@K =$$
$$Number\ of\ relevant\ documents\ in\ Top - K$$
$$K$$

c. Mean Reciprocal Rank (MRR): Measures the quality of ranking through the average of the reciprocal rank of the first relevant document (Maksim, 2024).

$$MRR = N1_{\Sigma}Ni=11\text{rank}_i$$

Where $rank_i$ denotes the rank of the first relevant document retrieved for the ith query.

d. Latency (Time per Query): The grand total time of user query processing including retrieval through generation.
e. The Score of user feedback was: Summarized Thumbs-up/Downs or Likelert rating by user on an output.

Determined decline in MRR or Top-k Accuracy will possibly be evidence of index drift or inadequate chunking of documents.

6. TEMPLATING TACTICS AND PROMPT ENGINEERING

Although the responsiveness of documents retrieval may be right, the overall performance of any RAG system can only rely on good prompt formulation. Prompt engineering is a practice of creating a scaffolded template that nudges the Large Language Model (LLM) with regards to tone, scope, and reasoning. A number of methods augment this: template prompts are pre-programmed messages on frequent tasks such as summaries or reports; chain-of-thought prompts train the model to describe its reasoning step-by-step; and role-based instructions assign a particular role (e.g., Act as a financial analyst) to render responses in the desired manner; and metadata-based prompts implement metadata such as titles or timestamps to clarify context. Designed prompts do not only lower the number of hallucinations but augment specificity of the domains and clarity of response (Krause, 2023).

6.1 Preprocessing and Chunking of Documents

Successful RAG systems rely on the quality of division of source documents into meaningful chunks in order to embed. What constitutes best practices in chunking is the optimal 200-500 token size of the chunk and a sliding window approach to enable 20-50 percent contextual overlap between the previous and the next chunk. Arbitrary divisions are undesirable but NLP can be used to guide semantic splitting according to headings, punctuation marks, or any other section titles. Preprocessing is also significant-this includes eliminating the header, footer, and the boilerplate text, use of OCR on a scanned image, and maintenance of important business entities made by means of Named/Entity Recognition (NER). Properly engineered, eliminating-noise chunks are much more accurate in retrieving and lead to more consistent and contextually relevant LLM outputs.

6.2 Logging, Monitoring and Observability

RAG systems to be reliable, auditable, and easily debug gable, robust observability in production is essential. Key elements to log include user queries, retrieved documents, LLM responses, source identifiers, confidence scores, embedding versions, latency, token usage, and failure reasons. Monitoring tools play a critical role: Grafana and Prometheus help track latency, error rates, and API performance; Open Telemetry supports distributed tracing across LLMs, retrievers, and databases; and the ELK Stack (Elasticsearch, Logstash, Kibana) enables efficient log storage, search, and visualization. These logs are vital for auditing, troubleshooting, and tracing the exact data sources used in decision-making, ensuring transparency and accountability.

6.3 Feedback Loop and Integration at the User Experiences (UX) Level

No matter how well designed a RAG model is, it is not guaranteed to work, especially when the end-users do not trust the results of the report or simply cannot understand it. User-friendly interface, the visibility of sources, and sensitive feedback lines are important (Chen et al., 2025). The below Figure 10 highlights key UI elements cited sources, confidence indicators, editable responses, and feedback buttons that enhance user trust, explainability, and interaction quality in RAG-powered applications. UX To Include Features:

Figure 10. User Interface Features for RAG System Transparency and Feedback

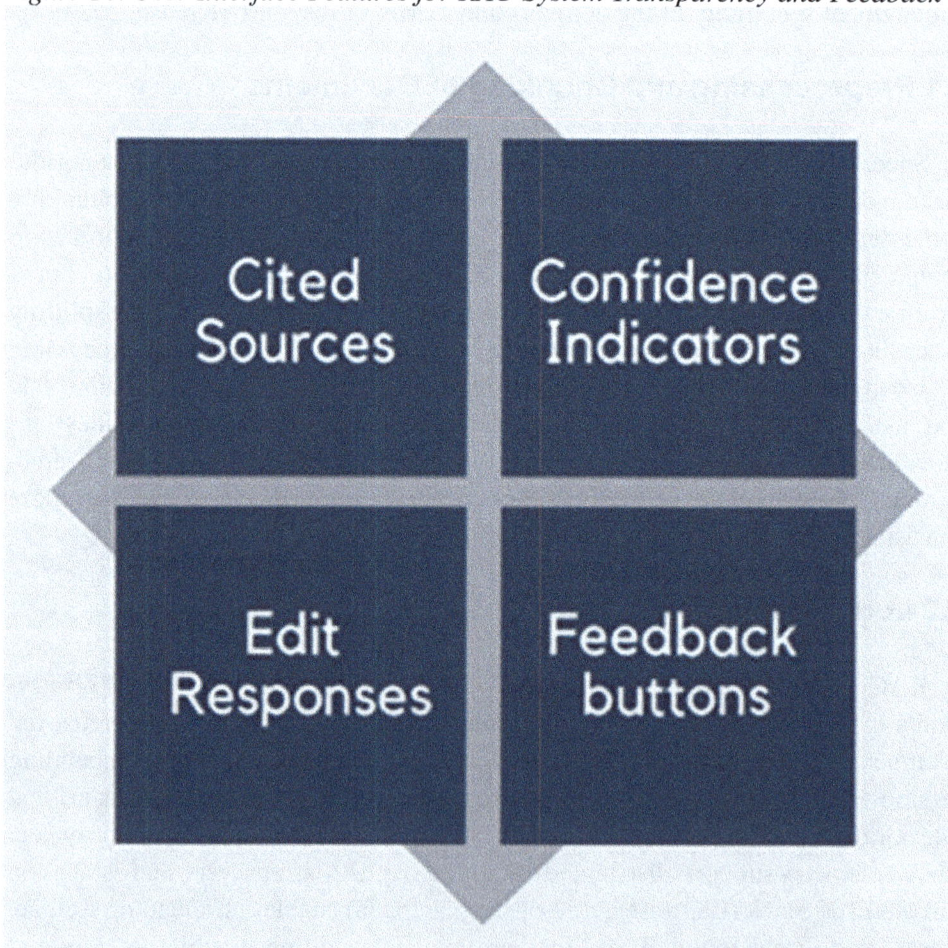

User-friendly interface is a critical success factor of RAG systems and introducing interactive elements to the interface should improve usability and overall system polishing. The most important UX features are cited sources as they show names of documents, links, and timestamps with corresponding response; confidence indicators, which reflect the trustworthiness of answers using scores or color codes; editable responses, where a user can edit or re-render the same information in a different context; and feedback buttons such as Helpful or Not Helpful with an ability to add optional commentary (Roychowdhury et al., 2024). The feedback loops are important to improve system because it improves prompt templates, advances retrieval or chunking strategies, and determines frequently asked questions to cover them better. To give an example, when the user will give out a response as unhelpful and choose the explanation like: "Outdated Info" or "Wrong Source," the system will adjust itself accordingly and over time will be able to learn and perform better continuously.

7. SECURITY, PRIVACY, AND ETHICAL ISSUES

Since companies are implementing RAG systems to communicate with sensitive internal information, it is urgent to examine the issues of data protection, clarity, regulatory compliance, and ethical AI. The RAG systems Unlike the traditional language models-RAG systems touch the real business documents-creating new vectors of risk unless handled properly. This segment describes the fundamental areas that organizations have to put into consideration so as to maintain the RAG implementations as reliable and as lawful.

7.1 Data Sensitivity and Access Control

RAG systems frequently access confidential business information, such as employee records, legal agreements, customer profiles or financial statements (Joshi, n.d.). Without the right number of limitations, the user might end up reading sensitive material not meant to him or her, worse still an LLM in such case can hallucinate access to confidential data in case such data has found its way into a retrievable source (Fleischer et al., 2024). As countermeasures against security and privacy threats in RAG systems, the organizations need to install multi-layered access controls at data retrieving and user interaction levels. RBAC is also necessary, as it will guarantee limited access to certain categories of data by such users as the HR department or the financial team. On top of that, document-level authorization ought to then categorize content according to level of confidentiality or business unit, and so on the access is further limited. Additional layer of protection is provided by secure authentication in enterprise identity systems like OAuth2, Single Sign-On (SSO) or LDAP. e.g., customer service agent is not supposed to suspect legal contracts except they are allowed to do so. Such controls guarantee availability of sensitive information to only those privileged to do so, and keep the enterprise data in line with the regulations and internal policies.

7.2 Auditability and Explainability in RAG Pipelines

The success of AI systems greatly depends on trust among their users, which is related to transparency, particularly toward the more controlled fields of finance, healthcare, and legal services. In contrast to conventional black-boxes LLMs, RAG systems have better traceability, by revealing which specific documents each response is based on. Central actions of retrieving logs to record what documents were accessed by whom and when, citing the sources in responses to show document names, timestamps, or other metadata, and offering retrieval confidence scores to reflect reliability of the information, are among the key ones. This explainability is important to internal audits, regulatory compliance, user trust especially when AI decisions have any bearing on the generation of a vital decision on hiring a person, making an investment, or deciphering a law (Kostopoulos et al., 2024).

7.3 Regulatory Compliance (e.g., GDPR, HIPAA)

Where RAG systems are dealing with individual or controlled information, the local and international data protection legislation must be considered vital, in order to prevent any legal charges as well as maintain consumer/user assurance of privacy. Other important regulations are GDPR (EU) with requirements of the right to be forgotten, processing data based on consent and auditability; HIPAA (US) with its requirements to protections of health data through encryption and audit trail; and DPDP Act of India that enforces purpose limitation and user consent on processing of personal data. The actions to be taken, through which adherence may be assured, include data masking or anonymization of personal identifiers, geo-specific deployment models (such as deployment of GDPR-compliant systems in the EU), and extensive data access, processing and retention logs. Moreover, RAG systems must have processes that require the consent of the user prior to operating information, which is identifiable. An example of how a GDPR system would store mission-critical data about its users is that the retriever database would not include or pseudonymize the identity fields to maintain the privacy of individuals within the legal limits of the GDPR (Maddali, 2024).

7.4 Biasness, Equity and Liable Output Production

Although using factual sources, RAG-based responses may have biases that are present in society or dataset-levels, especially when the retriever gives access to archaic or prejudiced papers. This becomes a big threat in areas that matter like in HR, finance or in the policy area where AI-based decisions may have direct impact on individuals. To alleviate these kinds of problems organizations will have to embrace ideas of Responsible AI. These steps include creating balanced and diverse corpora to train and search through as well as performing an audit on them regularly to identify possible patterns of prejudice or hurtful language and using post-editing filters to weed out stereotyping, hate, or exclusionary terms and phrases (Emelia et al., n.d.). Also, the incorporation of human in loop processes makes sure that AI is assistive and will not substitute human judgment when making critical decisions. As an example, when developing a profiling system to select candidates, it should not reproduce historical discrimination by advancing and discriminating against a certain group of people. These would contribute to ensuring fairness accountability, and ethical integrity within RAG enabled enterprise systems.

8. FUTURE TRENDS AND OPPORTUNITIES

The liability of RAG systems is rapidly developing to the next generation as businesses proceed to implement intelligence and decision support on the existence of RAG support. These systems are no longer being simple text-based Q&A, but are becoming dynamic, multi modal and adaptive. These areas of future development will indicate six of the most essential future directions that will define how enterprises will use RAG in the upcoming years.

8.1 Multimodal RAG (text + image + video)

The RAG systems that have been in prominence allow only textual documents to be used and therefore cannot cater to rich information, visual or auditory information that exists within enterprise knowledge (Mei et al., 2025). Nevertheless, valuable data in the digital enterprise context are not just in format as PDFs or policy document, the data could also be in images of products, recorded meetings, infographics, scanned forms, training videos and so forth. To fill that gap, multimodal RAG tries to combine all these modalities, the text, the image, the audio and the video, in one coherent retrieval and generation pipeline. (Chen et al., 2022)Within a multimodal RAG structure, the embeddings produced are based on both text and visual or acoustical information which enables the retriever to bring up the most pertinent content without mattering on the structure (Mei et al., 2025). Then the LLM can combine responses that take into consideration several kinds of context (Zhao et al., 2023).

Multimodal RAG systems have great values in that they go beyond the text to include other types of data which are images, diagrams and multimedia information. A major advantage is that of cross-modal perception to allow generation of response given visual data such as annotated diagrams or product catalogs based on an image. This significantly increases coverage of knowledge, as the system is able to access and provide meaning on valuable information which is not textual and in other formats, otherwise, unable to be utilized in conventional RAG pipelines. In addition, the accessibility is enhanced because it is now possible to respond based on a larger pool of documentation, such as scanned forms, infographics, and videos, which makes the system more accommodative and sensible to different business use cases.

8.2 Integration with Business Knowledge Graphs

Although conventional RAG systems conduct semantic search in flat document databases, with the addition of business knowledge graphs, they offer a more structured overlay that can better understand and interpret context, precision and reasoning. A knowledge graph is an entity and relationship model whose entities (e.g., customers, suppliers, departments) and relationship (e.g., orders) reflect the business logic and structure of an organization (Zhu et al., 2025). Integrating RAG and knowledge graphs with the retriever enables it to filter or pre-sort search with regard to semantic relations. This information can then be used by the generator in a manner that enables the generation of responses that are contextually correct and are relevant with the internal logic of the organization. Knowledge graphs have extremely effective benefits with respect to enterprise applications when they are integrated into RAG systems. To begin with, it facilitates fact checking and constraint-based querying of the responses made on fact based, verified relationships. This will particularly come in handy where data accuracy is important in the regulated industries. Second, it enables more efficient processing of complex queries across the enterprise, especially queries over hierarchies, or related data elements e.g. organizational charts, or data dependencies in a supply chain. Finally, knowledge graphs increase explainability through visual and semantic representation of the relationship of entities involved in production of a response. This not only will make this more transparent but also generate trust in the decision-making process of the AI.

8.3 Self-Improving Enterprise Assistants with Continuous Learning

The further development of RAG systems will be along adaptive and self-improving assistants that learn through the history of interaction, feedbacks by users, and continuous changes in the data (Shukla, n.d.). Instead of remaining fixed tools, these assistants will develop as time goes by to meet the expectations of the user and enterprise objectives better (Asai et al., 2023). Through these systems, users will interact with responses and see their beliefs and uncertainties in their interaction, using their frustrations to adjust ranking or prompt, or generative behavior. They are also able to survey the documents that are most accessed and update the embeddings when new information is entered. Its main highlights are optimization of queries depending on previous activity and feedback, dynamic prompt optimization with the focus on relevance and tone. Moreover, the re-indexation and document refresh is applied to continuously ensure that responses are kept up to date with the most up-to-date environment.

9. RAG + TASK EXECUTABLE AGENTS (AUTONOMOUS)

Although RAG is good at responding to questions, making it behave on information would be the next step. RAG systems, combined with AI agents, are able to drive workflows, schedule tasks or communicate with people creating automated action out of insights (Roychowdhury et al., 2024). RAG can act as memory or context provider to autonomous agents such as those created with LangChain Agents, AutoGen, or CrewAI. The agent, based on the documents retrieved, takes informed actions of drafting a message, updating a record, or calling an API. The RAG systems augmented with self-administered task fulfillment agents develop to become active (and eventually active) digital assistants who can perform real business logics.

These systems are able to prepare and send performance summaries to departmental heads, automatically initiate recommended orders of the supply chain in case of critical shortage of stocks and intelligently propose useful insights by analyzing meeting notes or reports. To use a real example, a RAG-enabled finance assistant can access monthly expense reports and policy documents, make a compliant email proposal to the CFO related to changes in the budget, and add relevant summaries, all without the influence of a human being. This transition is a major upgrade in automation of enterprise, and can result in intelligent, situationally aware action.

9.1 Streaming Data Real-Time RAG Integration

Static document repositories are a common feature used by traditional RAG pipelines but are not applicable to modern enterprise-paced business such as financial environments, logistics, and operations based on IoTs. The gaps addressed by real-time RAG integration with live streams of data (e.g., Kafka, AWS Kinesis, MQTT), and make intelligence dynamic and event based. Such ability enables the organization to instantly respond to the emerging situations. The application in the real world includes providing customer support in real-time, tracking movement of goods and services using GPS and traffic API as well as detecting fraud based on transactional anomalies. As another example, a logistic manager who wants to know about late deliveries gets an insight in real-time, supported by real time sensors on the ground, and delivery history, timelines and trends. Such responsiveness necessitates the use of high-performance retrieval engines such as Vespa and low latency LLMs with short efficient prompts. (Gan et al., 2025)

9.2 Privacy-Preserving and Federated RAG

An increase in data privacy laws including GDPR, HIPAA, and the DPDP Act in India continuously restricts the possibility to centralize enterprise data (Li, 2024). Federated RAG enables enterprises to query data on many secure sources without any copying or centralization. With this arrangement, every department or region will have its own retriever and index whereas one central LLM index will query each one separately as well as generate the eventual result (Macdonald et al., 2025). The architecture secures sensitive information, allows compliance, and honors data sovereignty. A privacy-preserving solution, which places retrieval nodes on the remote site runs on the Federated RAG systems and makes data on a local index to keep data in a regional scope, so it is not transmitted outside the region. Important features are implementation of local retrieval infrastructure, introduce privacy-preserving techniques that will protect the identity of the users, and use encryption on the queries as well as document transfer. As an example, an international business that has customers in the EU and APAC will be able to run the customer satisfaction queries by region and produce no more than generalized information without exporting the raw data to other jurisdictions. This strategy will help to comply with data protection laws such as GDPR, HIPAA, etc., and thus will help the company serve industries dealing with data (medicine, finance, law, and others) where central storage of data can be a legal and business liability and the table 6 as follows.

Table 6. Retrieval-Augmented Generation Future Improvements of Enterprise Applications

Trend	Capability Added	Tool or Technique
Multimodal RAG	Handles images, videos, PDFs	CLIP, Donut, LayoutLM
Knowledge Graph Integration	Relationship-aware search & prompts	Neo4j, RDF, SPARQL
Self-learning Assistants	Learns from feedback and logs	LangChain Agents, Reinforcement Learning
Real-time Streaming RAG	Uses live data feeds	Kafka, AWS Kinesis, Vespa with API layer

10. CONCLUSION

Retrieval-Augmented Generation (RAG) is a paradigm-changing method in the field of business intelligence and decision support as it is possible to create competitive advantages in an era of timely, accurate and situation-appropriate insight. Conventionally, language models (LLMs) are tremendously amazing when it comes to generation but lacking dynamic knowledge, dangerous to hallucination and can only access business proprietary data when it

is already in the market. These shortcomings are directly solved by RAG which integrates the fresh language fluency of LLMs with factual accuracy and current context of dynamic retrieval methods. Based on the chapter, we learned about the technical structure of RAG systems, which is broken down into retrievers, generators, and orchestrating frameworks such as LangChain and Haystack and illustrated that they combine in a typical pipeline of: RAG systems can supply a founded output whose verisimilitude in business can be traced by accessing related chunks in structured databases, unstructured documents, APIs, or other vector search engines.

RAG is most applicable in business terms including real time financial reporting, individualized marketing, supply chain diagnostics and HR/legal compliance. Such systems do not only automate what has been manual before but also provide instant, personalized, and explainable information to decision-makers. In addition, the fine-tuning potential of RAG enables organizations to incorporate company-specific jargon, processes, and compliance- related logic into its AI system, turning it scalable, highly customized to in-house objectives, and deeply integrated with company dynamics. A variety of practical concerns should be taken into account to use RAG successfully in data preprocessing and chunking, prompt engineering, retrieval performance, latency, cost optimization, observability, user experience. As it was emphasized, security, ethical compliance, and privacy (e.g., GDPR, HIPAA, DPDP) should be an essential part of any enterprise-level RAG system development.

Looking into the future, RAG is ready to develop even more. The future trends are multimodal integration (text + image + video), increase in the knowledge graph, real time streaming support, Federated deployment with privacy-preserving intelligence application, and adaptive assistants that learn over time. Such innovations are a promise of a future where RAG systems not only inform decisions, but also make them, explain them and learn their consequences. To sum up, the Retrieval-Augmented Generation is not only a technical improvement but a strategic tool of contemporary business. As an intermediary between the generative intelligence and real-life business information, RAG enables organizations to make smarter, faster and more transparent decisions. Thus, it is the future of AI-enabled business change with a viable and futuristic basis of businesses to prosper in a data-intensive fast-paced business environment.

REFERENCES

Arslan, M., & Cruz, C. (2024). Business-RAG: Information extraction for business insights. In *Proceedings of the 21st International Conference on Smart Business Technologies (ICSBT 2024)* (pp. 88–94). Science and Technology Publications, Lda. https://doi.org/10.5220/0012812800003764

Asai, A., Wu, Z., Wang, Y., Sil, A., & Hajishirzi, H. (2023). *Self-RAG: Learning to retrieve, generate, and critique through self-reflection.* arXiv. https://arxiv.org/abs/2310.11511

Chen, J., Ye, J., & Wang, G. (2025). *From standalone LLMs to integrated intelligence: A survey of compound AI systems.* arXiv. https://arxiv.org/abs/2506.04565

Chen, W., Hu, H., Chen, X., Verga, P., & Cohen, W. W. (2022). *MuRAG: Multimodal retrieval-augmented generator for open question answering over images and text.* arXiv. https://arxiv.org/abs/2210.02928

Emelia, C., Genesis, J., & Nickolas, B. (n.d.). *Unifying retrieval and generation: A survey on retrieval-augmented generation in NLP.*

Fleischer, D., Berchansky, M., Wasserblat, M., & Izsak, P. (2024). *RAG Foundry: A framework for enhancing LLMs for retrieval augmented generation.* arXiv. https://arxiv.org/abs/2408.02545

Gaddala, V., & Sharma Gaddala, V. (2023). *Unleashing the power of generative AI and RAG agents in supply chain management: A futuristic perspective.* ResearchGate. https://www.researchgate.net/publication/391917883

Gan, A., ... (2025). *Retrieval augmented generation evaluation in the era of large language models: A comprehensive survey.* arXiv. https://arxiv.org/abs/2504.14891

Han, B., Susnjak, T., & Mathrani, A. (2024). Automating systematic literature reviews with retrieval-augmented generation: A comprehensive overview. *Applied Sciences (Basel, Switzerland), 14*(19), 9103. Advance online publication. https://doi.org/10.3390/app14199103

Joshi, S. (n.d.). *The synergy of generative AI and big data for financial risk: Review of recent developments.* International Journal of Formal Methods and Research. https://www.ijfmr.com

Khan, A. A., Hasan, M. T., Kemell, K. K., Rasku, J., & Abrahamsson, P. (2024). *Developing retrieval augmented generation (RAG) based LLM systems from PDFs: An experience report.* arXiv. https://arxiv.org/abs/2410.15944

Kim, J., & Mahajan, D. (2025). *An adaptive vector index partitioning scheme for low-latency RAG pipeline*. arXiv. https://arxiv.org/abs/2504.08930

Kostopoulos, G., Davrazos, G., & Kotsiantis, S. (2024). Explainable artificial intelligence-based decision support systems: A recent review. *Electronics (Basel)*, *13*(14), 2842. Advance online publication. https://doi.org/10.3390/electronics13142842

Krause, D. S. (2023). *Mitigating risks for financial firms using generative AI tools. SSRN*. https://ssrn.com/abstract=4452600

Li, D., Li, Z., Yang, Y., Sun, L., An, D., & Yang, Q. (2024). Knowledge graph-enhanced large language model for domain-specific question answering systems. *Authorea Preprints*.

Li, Z. (2024). Leveraging AI automated emergency response with natural language processing: Enhancing real-time decision making and communication. *Applied and Computational Engineering*, *71*(1), 1–6. https://doi.org/10.54254/2755-2721/71/20241629

Macdonald, C., Fang, J., Parry, A., & Meng, Z. (2025). Constructing and evaluating declarative RAG pipelines in PyTerrier. *Proceedings of the ...*, Article 3726302. https://doi.org/10.1145/3726302.3730150

Maddali, R. (2024). AI-powered data security frameworks for regulatory compliance (GDPR, CCPA, HIPAA) [Preprint]. *Zenodo*. https://doi.org/10.5281/zenodo.15072096

Mei, L., Mo, S., Yang, Z., & Chen, C. (2025). *A survey of multimodal retrieval-augmented generation*. arXiv. https://arxiv.org/abs/2504.08748

Niu, C., ... (2024). *RAGTruth: A hallucination corpus for developing trustworthy retrieval-augmented language models*. arXiv. https://arxiv.org/abs/2401.00396

Roychowdhury, S., Soman, S., Ranjani, H. G., Gunda, N., Chhabra, V., & Bala, S. K. (2024). *Evaluation of RAG metrics for question answering in the telecom domain*. arXiv. https://arxiv.org/abs/2407.12873

Shao, Z., Gong, Y., Shen, Y., Huang, M., Duan, N., & Chen, W. (2023). *Enhancing retrieval-augmented large language models with iterative retrieval-generation synergy*. arXiv. https://arxiv.org/abs/2305.15294

Shukla, A. (n.d.). *From AI agents to self-driving organizations: Technological foundations, applications, and ethical considerations in autonomous AI systems* [Preprint]. ResearchGate., https://doi.org/10.13140/RG.2.2.20847.34729

Wang, J., Ding, W., & Zhu, X. (2025). Financial analysis: Intelligent financial data analysis system based on llm-rag. arXiv preprint arXiv:2504.06279.

Wu, S., ... (2025). *Retrieval-augmented generation for natural language processing: A survey*. arXiv. https://arxiv.org/abs/2407.13193

Xu, Z.. (2024). Retrieval-augmented generation with knowledge graphs for customer service question answering. In *Proceedings of the 47th International ACM SIGIR Conference on Research and Development in Information Retrieval (SIGIR '24)* (pp. 2905–2909). Association for Computing Machinery. https://doi.org/10.1145/3626772.3661370

Zhao, R., ... (2023). *Retrieving multimodal information for augmented generation: A survey*. arXiv. https://arxiv.org/abs/2303.10868

Zhu, X., Xie, Y., Liu, Y., Li, Y., & Hu, W. (2025). *Knowledge graph-guided retrieval augmented generation*. arXiv. https://arxiv.org/abs/2502.06864

Chapter 4
Fine-Tuning Large Language Models for Domain-Specific Business Applications

R. N. Ravikumar
https://orcid.org/0009-0009-3705-1681
Marwadi University, Rajkot, India

S. Aarthi
https://orcid.org/0009-0006-9064-2091
Marwadi University, Rajkot, India

ABSTRACT

Large Language Models (LLMs) like GPT, LLaMA, and Claude are powerful tools for understanding and generating human language. However, their real value in business lies in domain-specific fine-tuning, allowing them to align with unique industry needs, terminologies, and workflows. This chapter explores how fine-tuning through techniques like instruction tuning, RLHF, LoRA, and PEFT enables the creation of highly accurate, efficient, and context-aware systems in sectors such as finance, healthcare, legal, and retail. It also addresses practical aspects such as data preparation, model selection, and evaluation, along with considerations for privacy, governance, and compliance (e.g., GDPR, HIPAA). Real-world case studies demonstrate the success of fine-tuned LLMs in applications like contract review, fraud detection, and personalized customer service. The chapter concludes with guidance on building robust domain-specific LLM pipelines, tackling challenges like data scarcity, domain drift, and hallucination.

DOI: 10.4018/979-8-3373-3912-2.ch004

1. INTRODUCTION TO DOMAIN-SPECIFIC LLMS

Large Models like GPT, LLaMA, and Claude have made a revolution in business processes and language generation. Their cross ability to do is very powerful and they cannot do anything industry related very accurately. Such models can be trained to comprehend some automotive words and vocabularies, regulation, and workers operations procedures due to specialized training based on specialized data. This personalization enhances precision and pragmatism in the working applications like a legal overview of documents, or medical examination or even in fiscal forecasts. Not only do fine-tuned LLMs enhance decision-making and automation, but also assist in complying with the industry-specific legislation, including GDPR and HIPAA (Ragab and Altahhan, 2024). Particularly with the increasing number of personal AI applications in business, domain-specific LLM is emerging as a crucial instrument in improving competitive advantage, originality, and scale through digital transformations in the modern business setting.

1.1 The Rise of Large Language Models in Business

Large Language Models (LLM) usage, including GPT, LLaMA, Claude, and many others, have gained the reputation of being core tools in the digitalization of businesses. Developed on a diversity and abundance of internet-based information, they are capable of reading natural language, answering questions and they can also summarise and generate meaningful writing. Digital businesses that include the financial, health care, retail and legal establishments are coming to the realization that they can run an automated process, enhance their decision-making process, and offer their customers a unique room experience. Since APIs allow making LLMs popular, non-technical companies finally receive an opportunity to implement conversational AI, document generation, and analytics in their practice (Bora & Cuayáhuitl, 2024). However, the fun is about turning the common sense about generalized intelligence, and proceed towards the applications that represent the depth and the specificity of the individual industries. Since business have become interested in extracting still more value out of internal data, LLMs are no longer confined in their usability to mere language-generation tools, but are already developing to be the strategic assets that will drive compliance, innovation, and customer-centricity in an extensive number of domains of operation.

1.2 Limitations of Generic LLMs for Industry-Specific Needs

Although General-purpose LLMs have impressive language understanding powers, they are usually ineffective when used in instructional spaces. These models are then trained using general, mixed datasets and they do not provide the depth and precision of jargon, workflows or regulatory needs specific to the industry. To use an example, a generic LLM might simply fail at recognizing an abbreviation on a medical chart, or not comprehend the specific meaning of a specific phrase on financial earnings statements (Peng et al., 2024). In addition, such models can produce hallucinated responses that appear to be actually true when in reality they contain false information when they are presented with niche questions. In such areas as law, medicine or even finance where trust and accuracy are vital, this can be very hazardous. Moreover, the generic models would not fit the data privacy requirements, including HIPAA or GDPR, or be functional in particular tasks, including contract language extraction, fraud detection, or one-to-one support. These shortcomings also point to the necessity of special fine-tuning solutions, which will both increase in domain relevance and make them safe, compliant, and efficient in their operations.

1.3 Opportunities and Business Value of Domain-Specific Fine-Tuning

Domain fine-tuning of LLMs enables companies to realize performance improvement and develop value-added AI solutions that fit the particularity of the industry. Training LLMs on company or even industry-specific data, organizations can greatly increase the relevance, accuracy and contextual knowledge of the model (Agarwal et al., 2025). Tightly-tuned models can be used to accelerate the workflow, such as smart contract analysis, individualized sales copy, or identification of anomalous activities in financial transactions. They also make mistakes and enhance reliability of automation and satisfaction of customers. Fine-tuning can be done through cost-effective mechanism such as LoRA, PEFT, and prompt-based since it does not have to be only big firms. In addition, to a larger degree as data privacy and regulatory requirements increase, organizations can regain control over the entire AI lifecycle by local training and governance. Generally speaking, domain-specific fine-tuning is more than a technical optimisation. It is a strategic innovation and differentiation tool and source of resilience in the AI-enabled future of business.

2. FOUNDATIONS OF FINE-TUNING LLMS

Fine-tuning is a method of adapting a pre-trained Large Language Model (LLM) to a particular task or domain by further training it on a smaller, domain-specific training set. This helps the model to learn more on the contextual nuances, industry jargon and the processes structured in a specific industry. Compared to training a model which starts with no knowledge of the language however, fine-tuning shares the knowledge of language already built on the model but focuses on specific behaviour, this allows the strategy to be more cost effective and efficient. The most important are supervised fine-tuning, instruction tuning, and Reinforcement Learning with Human Feedback (RLHF), and even more recently Low-Rank Adaptation (LoRA) and Parameter-Efficient Fine-Tuning (PEFT). Instead of counting on the computers, they reduce the computational demands in favour of the quality of the models (Bakker et al., 2025). Fine-tuned binds make sure that LLams operate with higher accuracy, fewer mistakes, and with respect to more business goals involvement in situations of work in domain-critical jobs. The Figure 1 illustrates the core process of fine-tuning a pre-trained Large Language Model (LLM) for domain-specific tasks. It highlights key techniques such as supervised fine-tuning, instruction tuning, RLHF, and parameter-efficient methods like LoRA and PEFT.

Figure 1. Foundations of Fine-Tuning LLMs

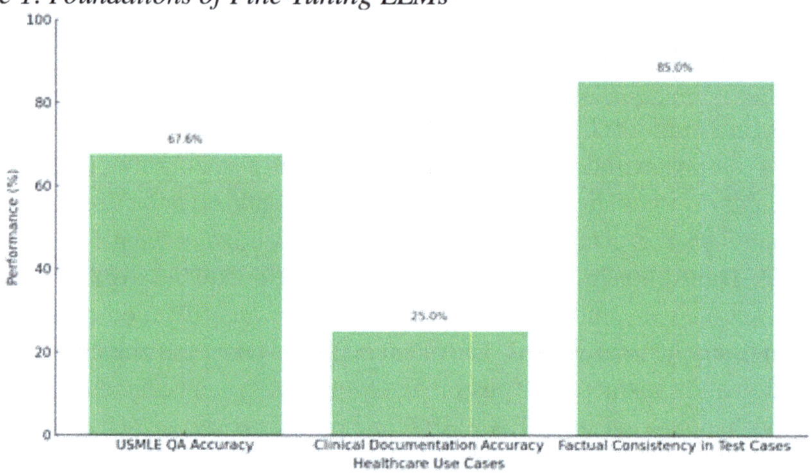

2.1 Overview of Fine-Tuning Techniques (Full vs. Partial Fine-Tuning)

Fine-tuning an LLM consists of training an already trained system on domain-specific data to customize their outputs to perform specific tasks. There are two main strategies; full fine-tuning and partial fine-tuning. Full fine-tuning replaces all of the model parameters giving it the benefit of high customization but requiring substantial computing power and data. It is appropriate in situations where data on the domain is abundant, and accuracy is essential. By comparison, the partial fine-tuning alters only a few sections of the model, more targeted, i.e., certain layers or the adapter modules, thus more effective and viable to use among resource-constrained organizations. Partial methods such as LoRA and PEFT enable the firms to fit in large models without having to use the costly infrastructure and huge datasets. The decision to use full and partial fine-tuning is based on the desired business objective, the level of data, and compute budget. Partial fine-tuning is a compromised performance trade-off that makes most enterprise applications scalable to the real world of business (Balaskas et al., 2025). The table 1 compares full fine-tuning and parameter-efficient methods such as LoRA and PEFT across key criteria such as compute cost, training efficiency, parameter updates, and business applicability. It is designed to help decision-makers select the optimal strategy based on their infrastructure and task complexity. The Figure 2 compares full and partial fine-tuning strategies for LLMs, highlighting their parameter update scopes. It visually maps how techniques like LoRA and PEFT fit into the partial fine-tuning category for efficient model adaptation.

Table 1. Full vs. Parameter-Efficient Fine-Tuning Techniques

Aspect	**Full Fine-Tuning**	**LoRA / PEFT (Parameter-Efficient Fine-Tuning)**
Parameters Updated	All model parameters (100%)	Small subset (e.g., <10%)
Compute Cost	High requires significant GPU/TPU resources	Low to Moderate efficient memory and compute usage
Training Time	Longer due to full backpropagation	Faster fewer parameters and efficient modules
Flexibility	High adaptability to specific tasks	Moderate best suited for slight-to-moderate domain adaptation
Data Requirements	Large domain-specific datasets	Can perform well with smaller curated datasets
Infrastructure Required	Powerful multi-GPU or cloud setups	Can be executed on limited or mid-tier hardware
Typical Use Cases	Mission-critical, high-stakes systems (e.g., medical, legal AI)	Cost-sensitive, mid-scale use cases (e.g., chatbots, internal tools)

Figure 2. Overview of Fine-Tuning Techniques

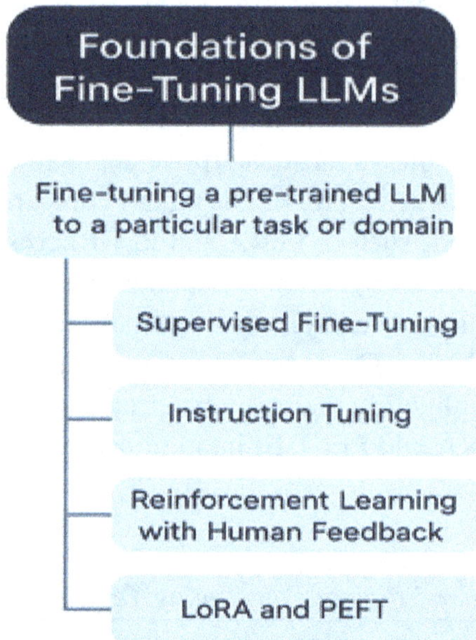

2.2 Comparison of Instruction Tuning, LoRA, and PEFT

Also becoming popular ways to customize the LLM to specific tasks include Instruction Tuning, LoRA (Low-Rank Adaptation), and PEFT (Parameter-Efficient Fine-Tuning). Instruction Tuning is a way of increasing the overall task performance of a model by training it on labeled instructions and answers, so that the LLM can execute human-like instructions. It is perfect when it comes to enhancing task generalization and usability in a multi-step process. LoRA augments the fixed pretrained weights with trainable low-rank matrices, which allows to control adaptations in a very flexible manner with only a small number of parameters. This is what makes it perfect to businesses that require efficient fine tuning, but not a total retraining. PEFT is a more general type of technique (such as LoRA) that, selectively, reads or adds light modules into large models in a cost-effective fine-tuning (Bi et al., 2024). It lowers the computational overhead as well as memory significantly, in particular, on-device or enterprise clouds. Instruction tuning works best when a fine-grained alignment is not necessary, whereas LoRA and PEFT are more applicable in domain-specific and limited resources settings which provide flexible and low-cost strategies of real-life business problems adaptation. The 2 table contrasts three popular fine-tuning techniques Instruction Tuning, LoRA, and PEFT across dimensions such as mechanism, parameter update scale, ideal use case, resource efficiency, and business relevance. It helps readers understand which method best fits different operational and domain-specific needs.

Table 2. Comparison of Instruction Tuning, LoRA, and PEFT

Aspect	Instruction Tuning	LoRA (Low-Rank Adaptation)	PEFT (Parameter-Efficient Fine-Tuning)
Main Mechanism	Trains on instruction-response pairs	Injects trainable low-rank matrices into frozen model weights	Adds/updates small modules or subsets of model parameters
Parameter Updates	Moderate requires full pass-through labeled tasks	Very low updates limited matrices (often <1% of total params)	Low selective fine-tuning (includes LoRA as a method)
Best Use Case	Multi-step tasks, instruction-following behavior	Domain-specific tasks with limited compute/data	Efficient tuning on large models with minimal infrastructure
Resource Requirements	Medium to High	Low	Very Low
Model Compatibility	Requires labeled instruction data	Works with most transformer-based models	Compatible with most modern LLMs
Business Applicability	Improves general-purpose usability	Ideal for cost-sensitive domain adaptation	Scalable solution for on-device/cloud enterprise deployment
Flexibility & Scalability	Medium needs diverse instruction coverage	High very modular and portable	High supports diverse fine-tuning techniques

2.3 Role of Prompt Engineering in Domain Adaptation

Prompt engineering describes a lightweight and growing common approach in which LLMs are adapted to more specific tasks by fine-tuning which prompts are used. It entails styling that provides the model with input prompts that can lead to the accurate and situational output of derived data. In business contexts, fine-tuning can be approximated by including task instructions, domain keywords, or structural prompts in the prompt (an example of fine-tuning close to effective prompt engineering) An example of this occurred in legal tech, where asking an LLM to provide a plain-English summary of a given legal milieu to articulate and convert legalese into to usable summaries (Hyeon Chai, 2024). It is particularly helpful when rapid deployment is desired or when the training must be performed over sensitive data whose privacy is limited. One-shot and zero-shot learning through prompt examples can also be applied to improve on certain uses cases. Although prompt engineering lacks the granularity, of fine-tuning, it is a crucial implementation in prototyping, testing, and augmentation of LLM behavior, thus one of the most important domain adaptation pipeline tactics across most business verticals.

3. TECHNICAL ARCHITECTURE AND WORKFLOW

Fine-tuning and domain-specific LLMs often have a modular and scalable pipeline of their technical architecture. It starts with data ingestion in which high-quality domain-specific dataset (e.g., clinical notes, legal contracts, financial reports) are cleaned, annotated, and pre-processed. This is followed by a model selection step which determines the correct base LLM (e.g., GPT, LLaMA) to use depending on its performance, APIs, and ability to be fine-tuned using models such as LoRA or PEFT. Compute infrastructure in the training environment is typically GPUs or TPUs in cloud or on-prem clusters, but training programs are set up using frameworks like Hugging Face Transformers or PyTorch. Such fine-tuning is then carried out with the help of chosen methods (full, partial, or prompt-based) and observing loss, accuracy, and overfitting in real-time (Coffey et al., 2024). This creates a model that is tested on domain-specific test sets with model-specific evaluation (e.g., on entity recognition, the model-specific performance is measured using an F1-score; in the case of summarization, it is measured against the BLEU). The last layer is deployment, where the model is embedded into the business systems through APIs, and performance, compliance and drift monitoring and updates are constantly done.

3.1 Preparing Domain-Specific Datasets (Structured, Unstructured, and Synthetic)

The success of fine-tuning LLMs is dependent on preparation of high-quality domain-specific datasets. Such datasets can be split into structured (e.g., relational databases, transactional databases), unstructured (e.g., emails, legal documents, clinical notes) and synthetic (e.g. those generated through simulation or LLMs). It starts with the term acquisition and the data cleaning that involves deduplicating or formatting the data, eliminating all unwanted content, and anonymizing data to address the regulations such as the GDPR or HIPAA. In case of unstructured data, NLP preprocessing methods including tokenization, stop-word cache, and entity detection methods are used. The structured type of data might also have to be transformed into a more natural language-style template or a half-structured format that is miserable to the use of the LLM (Doumanas et al., 2025). In the scenario where real world data is scarce or privacy-sensitive, it is possible to simulate realistic data with synthetic data generation based on prompt-driven LLMs or rule-driven scripts. A balanced and diverse set of examples allows the model to learn the deep context that domain and makes sure that it is not overfitting and is not biased to a specific situation. The Figure 3 outlines the structured workflow for preparing datasets used in fine-tuning LLMs, including acquisition, cleaning, and classification into structured, unstructured, and synthetic types. It emphasizes the role of NLP preprocessing and transformation in adapting diverse data formats for model training.

Figure 3. Preparing Domain-Specific Datasets for Fine-Tuning

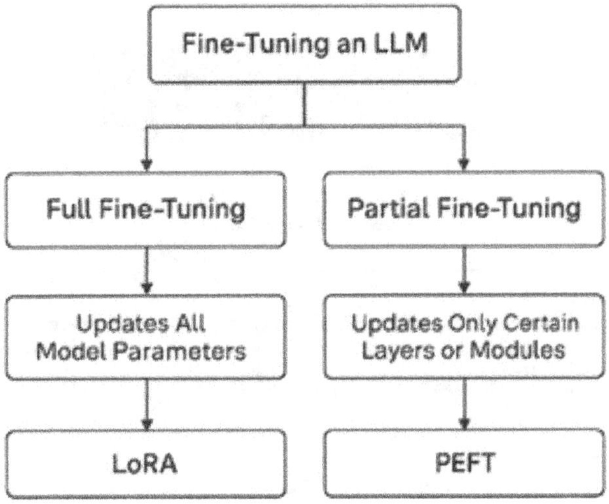

3.2 Model Selection: Choosing the Right Base Model for Fine-Tuning

The choice of the base model is a proactive decision-supporting execution of the fine-tuning effect, cost, and downstream performance. They are model size, licensing, pretraining dataset composition and community/tooling support. As an example, such models as the GPT-3.5/4 (OpenAI) or Claude (Anthropic) are powerful and closed-source and API-tethered, which restricts their flexibility. Conversely, the open-source approach allows flexible local fine-tuning and deployment with models such as LLaMA 2, Falcon, or Mistral (Fatemi et al., 2025a). The companies also need to consider about the alignment of the pretraining corpus of the base model with their industry. A healthcare company can be more well served by a model trained on biomedical texts (e.g., BioGPT), whereas a law firm could put a premium on the one that has seen and heard legal data. Moreover, memory footprint and inference latency also influence the cost of operation, in particular, when it comes to real-time applications. The choice of the model, also takes into account the decision of full or parameter-efficient fine-tuning, where smaller or modular models are chosen within resource-limited settings (Gabber & Hemied, 2024). The Figure 4 illustrates key factors influencing the choice of a base model for fine-tuning, including model size, source type (open or closed), license type, and pretraining corpus. It guides practitioners through aligning technical capabilities with domain-specific and operational requirements.

Figure 4. Model Selection for Fine-Tuning

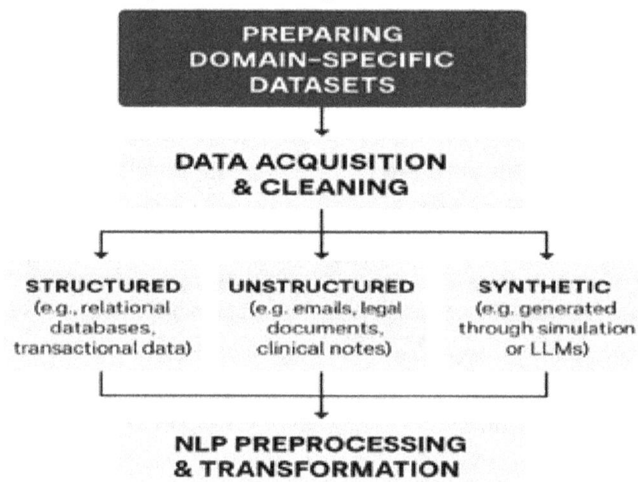

3.3 Infrastructure, Toolkits, and Frameworks (Hugging Face, DeepSpeed, Colossal-AI)

Fine-tuning follows a powerful technical stack of both the compute infrastructure and the specialized software framework. The training and inference are done on local clusters of GPUs or are on cloud platforms (AWS, GCP, Azure). And to improve on that, we also have toolkits like Hugging Face Transformers that make model loading and dataset management, invoking tokenizers, and fine-tuning pretty easy to interact with by way of intuitive APIs. (Kainz et al., 2025). To manage large models, DeepSpeed by Microsoft provides such features as ZeRO optimization, mixed precision training, and distributed training, limiting memory usage and training speed. Colossal-AI is an open-source alternative, which offers hybrid parallelism and memory optimization, which allows training billion-parameter models with fewer resources. Experiment tracking tools (e.g., Weights & Biases) and deployment stacks (e.g., FastAPI, Triton Inference Server) are also integrated by businesses to make their production workflows efficient. With the right set of components, scaling, cost-efficient fine-tuning, and deployment of the solution in any environment, including experimentation and live integration, will be possible. The table 3 presents a comparative overview of widely used frameworks Hugging Face Transformers, DeepSpeed, and Colossal-AI evaluating them on aspects such as model parallelism support, memory efficiency, user-friendliness, and integration flexibility. It helps practitioners choose the best toolkit for their specific deployment scale, resource constraints, and use cases.

Table 3. Toolkits and Frameworks for LLM Fine-Tuning

Framework	Model Parallelism	Memory Optimization	Ease of Use	Integration & Ecosystem	Best Use Cases
Hugging Face Transformers	Partial (via Accelerate/ PEFT)	Moderate	High user-friendly APIs	Extensive (datasets, models, community support)	Rapid prototyping, fine-tuning on small to mid-sized models
DeepSpeed	Yes, Advanced support	High ZeRO optimization	Medium some setup needed	Works well with PyTorch, Hugging Face	Large-scale model training and inference
Colossal-AI	Yes – Hybrid/3D Parallelism	High memory-efficient kernels	Medium technical setup	Supports multiple backends (Torch, Hugging Face)	Training billion-parameter models on fewer GPUs

4. DEPLOYMENT STRATEGIES AND OPTIMIZATION

Introduction The large language models fine-tuned using large volumes of historic data on the state of the art seem to become ready to be deployed to the business world. Depending on the use case and resource limitations it applies to two extremes, cloud-based APIs are provided to deploy at scale, and infrastructure is provided on-premise to suit data-sensitive industries. An efficient deployment and scaling implementation in the microservices is safe to apply in containerization by applying Docker and orchestration under which Kubernetes is a tool (Luo et al., 2024). When it comes to chatbots or contract reviewers, any application that needs to be implemented in real-time, inference optimization is essential. Model quantization, pruning, distillation and ONNX conversion can all drastically decrease the size of a model and have little impact on accuracy whilst drastically increasing response time (Peng et al., 2024). The throughput is also increased by batching and asynchronous serving. The property of such conversion to lightweight models such as TensorRT makes them compatible to be integrated with edge devices. There should also be strong monitor tools that can trace performance, user feedback, and model drift. Optimized deployment of LLMs allows fine-tuning to turn the fine-tuned LLMs into nimble, responsive, and dependable resources that could serve as the driving force of operational and strategic choices throughout business operations.

4.1 API Integration and Containerization for Enterprise Use

In order to provide the fine-tuned LLMs to the various business systems, companies generally publicize them through RESTful APIs. It can integrate with web portal, CRMs, ERPs as well as mobile applications with ease. The frameworks that can be used to develop API wrappers are including FastAPI, Flask, or Triton Inference Server, enabling scalability (Ragab & Altahhan, 2024). The models and the corresponding runtime environment should be made portable and reproducible and can be achieved by containerizing them through Docker and Kubernetes or AWS ECS ensures the horizontal scale and setting up the load balancer. These containers package the model, tokenizer, dependencies and serving logic and minimize deployment friction in both staging and production. In the case of controlled industries, containerization offers isolated environments as per the security and legislative demands (Selinger et al., 2025). Using versioned API endpoints, enterprises can also roll out reduced sets of variation of the model (A/B testing or regional pre-configuration). All in all, containerized API-first delivery allows a swift, modular, and secure deployment of tuned AS capabilities of LLM throughout a variety of enterprise apps.

4.2 Performance Optimization: Speed, Cost, and Latency Considerations

The deployment of LLMs is a case of a trade-off in speed of inference and cost of computation against latency. Strong models, though potent, tend to demand a lot of memory on GPUs and lead to slow response rates making them unfit to solve latency-intensive use cases when dealing with customers or detecting fraud. To mitigate this can be done by using a compression method like quantization (e.g. INT8 conversion) that decreases the model size and memory consumption with only a significant accuracy penalty (Sulaiman & Hamzah, 2024a). Model distillation It trains smaller "student" models that have been set to imitate the behavior of larger ones. During pruning, the redundant weights are eliminated, and the performances of inference improve when converted to ONNX or TensorRT. Asynchronous processing and request batching are useful to keep the throughput up at high user capacity. Compute clusters can be auto-scaled, spot instances on cloud infrastructure can be leveraged and inference accelerators (such as NVIDIA A100s) can be deployed in deployment environments (Sulaiman & Hamzah, 2024b). The choice of optimization stack will not merely guarantee faster and cheaper inference, but will also allow building applications that are real-time with milliseconds variability being a key.

4.3 Continuous Learning and Model Monitoring in Production

An LLM should also be improved constantly after being implemented and then comfortably watched over to see that it is pertinent and useful as the business climate continually changes. Business outcomes may be affected by the time-related degradation of the performance to the intended or desired level of performance because of variations in user behavior and regulations, as well as due to the change in data patterns that is known as model drift. To counter this, organisations employ real time monitoring pipelines wherein major areas to be monitored are accuracy, latency, use frequency and abnormalities in output (Polagani, 2025). Prometheus, Grafana and Weights & Biases are tools frequently deployed as observability. Also, feedback loops may also be created such that corrections or ratings applied by the user are recorded and used in a retraining pipeline, to allow indefinite learning. Model (e.g. MLflow) version control as well as A/B testing frameworks makes it possible to test updates to experiments and not require deployment at scale (Wang et al., 2023a). The model remains true and in accordance with the changing business objectives as long as it is re-fine-tuned regularly with new domain-specific data. In such a way, the fine-tuned LLMs enter the living system that will develop and advance with the enterprise requirements after the deployment.

5. ENSURING COMPLIANCE, PRIVACY, AND ETHICAL USE

With businesses tuning and implementing LLMs, integrity considers regulatory compliance, privacy of information, and ethically applicable AI applications at the top. Specific applications, such as those in health, finance, and legal spheres, will be required to follow such models as GDPR, HIPAA, and SOX to be in compliance with data use, user agreement, and responsibility. Sensitive data should be fine-tuned based on de-identified or anonymized data and access control and audit trail should be strict (Wu et al., 2025). There is also a growth of the solution to keeping data confidential when training models through differential privacy and federated learning. On the ethical side of the scale, companies should make an extra effort to prevent all types of prejudice, fraud, and harmful manufacturing by adding search filters and human oversight. The establishment of trust and responsibility can be achieved through regular documentation (model cards, data sheets), responsible usage policies, explainability mechanisms (e.g. SHAP, LIME), etc. (Zhu et al., 2024). Not only the fairness, transparency, and compliance in the model lifecycle minimizes risk but also enables the responsible innovation to fulfill the laws and expectations of the society. The table 4 recalls significant legal rules, general ethical issues in the implementation of LLM, and the effective preventive measures. It can be used by organizations to create responsible AI systems that are in line with the law, safeguard user information, and advance fairness and transparency.

Table 4. Ethical and Regulatory Considerations for LLM Deployment

Area	Issue / Regulation	Implication for LLMs	Recommended Mitigation Strategy
Data Privacy	GDPR (EU), HIPAA (US)	Limits on collecting and processing personal or health data	Data anonymization, encryption, federated learning
Bias & Fairness	Algorithmic bias, demographic inequality	Discriminatory outputs in hiring, finance, or legal decisions	Bias audits, diverse training data, fairness-aware tuning
Content Accuracy	Hallucination, misinformation	Generation of factually incorrect or unsafe outputs	Human-in-the-loop validation, retrieval-augmented generation (RAG)
Transparency	Explainability and model documentation	Users and regulators demand clear understanding of model behavior	Use of model cards, explainability tools (e.g., SHAP, LIME)
Accountability	Auditability, traceability	Difficulty tracing how decisions were made	Logging model changes, version control, compliance dashboards

5.1 Managing Proprietary Data and Ensuring Privacy (e.g., GDPR, HIPAA)

Treatment of proprietary or other sensitive data domains issues rely on the principles adopted in the field of data privacy (such as the General Data Protection Regulation (GDPR) in the EU or Health Insurance Portability and Accountability Act (HIPAA) in the U.S.). In fine-tuning, companies are obliged to check data minimization, anonymization, and tracking consent. Data masking, encryption, and other similar secure storage must cover Personally Identifiable Information (PII), patient health records, or financial transactions (Agiza et al., 2024). The process of fine-tuning must be carried out within closed and controlled accesses and the raw data should by no means get out on the external unsecure space. Federated learning and synthetic data are developing in deeply regulated industries to allow training without sharing any data directly. Business organizations ought to have data processing agreements, as well as privacy impact assessment, and logs where necessary so that auditing of compliance takes place. Compliant with the standards, legal risk is minimized as well as the trust of customers using AI-based business systems can grow.

5.2 Bias Mitigation and Fairness in Domain-Specific Outputs

The LLMs trained specifically on generic data or narrowed datasets might unintentionally reproduce or enhance the biases, which would be especially dangerous in such sensitive areas as employment, lending, insurance, or health. The bias in fine-tuned models can occur due to very little training data, stereotypical terms, overfitting on a small context(Bora & Cuayáhuitl, 2024) . To overcome it, companies should run bias checks on training and post-training, auditing the model output both along demographic, or lingual, socio-economic faults. The methodologies, including counterfactual data augmentations, bias regularization, and retraining samples re-weighting assist in producing a fairer output. In addition, models must demographic parity, equalized odds) and stress-tested to adverse outcomes. The use of heterogeneous annotation staff and evaluation by domain specialists are proved to reveal unseen bias. The reason to mitigate bias will be not only technical but also ethical because it will contribute to the implementation of ethical AI to different customer groups, avoiding damaging the reputation and promoting more inclusive technological development.

5.3 Establishing Governance and Auditability for AI Models

Due to increased involvement of AI in the work of companies, it is critical to coordinate effective governance and auditability practices. Governance System promotes that AI systems adhere to corporate policies, ethical norms, and all the regulatory considerations in their lifecycle. The most important aspects are the control of version of the model, traceability of training data, access logs, and documentation (e.g. model cards, data sheet). There should be audit trails of all training runs, parameter changes and deployments to enable accountability in the event of mistakes and when legal cases erupt (Fatemi et al., 2025a). It is important to form an AI governance board or compliance committee in companies that would be in charge of periodic reviews, risk assessment and escalation protocol. Policy enforcement may be automated when combined with MLOps platforms, the drift may be tracked and policy enforcement of reproducible workflows may be enforced. The ownership, role-based access, and ongoing follow-up remains pivotal in establishing a trusting relationship and a high degree of transparency. Governance does not only aid in compliance and security, but it also allows the AI to scale sustainably and responsibly in terms of businesses.

6. BUSINESS APPLICATIONS ACROSS KEY DOMAINS

LLMs being developed into fine-tuned versions are revolutionizing the functioning in various aspects of businesses by providing smart and subject-aware solutions. In the context of finance, LLMs help in compliance with regulations, sentiment analysis, automatic detection of fraud, and auto-generation of financial reports. The healthcare industry can take advantage of models that summarize patient notes, help in diagnosis, or aid in customized treatment plans, whilst adhering to the privacy sensitive laws (Gaikwad, 2024). Fine-tuned models can also be found in the legal field where they play a role in analysing contracts, summarizing law and legal research of case law, which relieves human experts. Both retail and e-commerce use LLMs to provide custom recommendations on products, multilanguage support of customers, and dynamic content creation. In talent management and HR, models are used to improve the screening of candidates, to parse the resumes automatically, and create job description without biases. All of these areas involve LLMs having to learn certain terminologies, structures, and norms of compliance within the area and, as such, domain-specific fine-tuning is vital (Hsu & Roberts, 2024). When properly tuned and configured, LLMs can build up innovations and lower down operating costs and enhance decision-making in various industry grants. The table 5 presents a comparatively close analysis of the use of the fine-tuned LLMs within various industries with the focus on the use cases, business advantages, and performance indicators. It makes the reader quickly realize the worth and embrace of LLM customization among verticals.

Table 5. Domain-Wise Business Applications of Fine-Tuned LLMs

Domain	Key Use Cases	Business Benefits	Performance Improvements
Finance	Credit risk modelling, sentiment analysis, document classification	Better investment decisions, fraud detection, regulatory insights	+18–20% in sentiment accuracy, +17% in classification F1-score
Healthcare	Clinical documentation, patient query automation, medical QA	Reduced clinician workload, improved care access and accuracy	+25% improvement in EHR summarization, 85% factual consistency
Legal	Contract review, legal summarization, legal research	Faster legal operations, reduced manual workload	2× speed in review tasks, improved clause extraction accuracy
Retail	Personalized recommendations, customer support, sentiment tagging	Enhanced customer experience, increased sales conversion	+22% click-through rate, faster query resolution via AI agents

6.1 LLMs in Finance: Credit Risk Modelling and Sentiment Analysis

One can use Financial Nimble LLM to make smarter and faster decisions that are even more intelligent. Such applications include credit risk modelling, where the LLM tries to estimate borrower risk on top of the more familiar credit score through unstructured information, e.g. a loan application, balance sheet or analyst report (Xu et al., 2025). Other better models enable to dig out risk factors, uncover discrepancies and present potential defaults to your face less. The other application is actually quite powerful one and is the financial sentiment analysis where the LLM reads the transcript of the earnings calls or news wire or social media to find out the mood in the markets and predict where it is going. Context-analysing fine-tuned LLM based on technical language, terms, and tone used is more useful in identifying the actual emotion. These tools would constitute the real-time decision making in trading, lending and compliance provided they are widely deployed by ensuring that they adopt data anonymization and data governance controls (H. Liu et al., 2024). Lenders are implementing LLM, typically in dashboards and robo-advisor, to make it an analytics core and a financial service to people of the future.

6.2 LLMs in Healthcare: Clinical Documentation and Patient Query Automation

Healthcare is one of the spheres in which the micro-adjusted LLMs are changing radically the efficacy of clinics and interactions with patients. The automated clinical documentation will also be another interesting application in that regard, and the conversations between doctors and patients will be recorded and summarized by the LLMs and transformed into the structured Electronic Health Records (EHRs) (Sukeda et al., 2024). This saves the clinicians the hustle, and increases precision in recording of medical history, diagnosis and course of treatment. The other innovation is the automation of patient queries, and, with the aid of LLMs, smart assistants will question about the symptoms, medications, or appointments. Medically literature and institutional-based finetuned models are more adherent and credible in comparison to general chatbots. This is expected to be implemented in HIPAA-compliant structures and be tested to reveal their safety and bias. The medical centers and service providers that have implemented telemedicine follow this trend to introduce these LLMs onto mobile applications and portals to enhance the level of accessibility and personalization. As the pressure to improve the burnout rate and care delivery continues to increase, the LLM are scalable and intelligent support tools that are responsive to clinical case complexity and simultaneously comply with ethical and regulatory standards and values.

6.3 LLMs in LegalTech: Contract Review, Summarization, and Legal Research

The move towards an adoption of LLMs into the LegalTech industry is immense, since, shortly, it becomes apparent that highly complex models are capable of automating routine legal procedures with achievement. A contract review application is one of them, and the LLMs were involved in extracting clauses, red flags, and making up suggestions based on organizational guidelines. Fine-tuned models can find deeper meanings in the legal text in comparison with rule-based systems which cannot do it at all but provide the ad-hoc outputs (Bakker et al., 2025). The other application is the summarization of law cases in which the LLMs handle extensive files of cases, briefs or judgments and present a summary that can be easily understood by the lawyer. Law Studies are also evolving as LLMs are able to access relevant statutes, precedents, or texts of regulation, within large datasets. The models must be highly tuned with legal corpora that are specific to that jurisdiction and nothing is alluded or referred to errors. Casetext, Harvey, and Spellbook indicate that special-purpose LLMs change the mode of operation within the area of law. The LegalTech LLMs not only increase the speed and accuracy of the results but also improve access to legal knowledge because of the human supervision and compliance systems that put them on track.

7. FUTURE TRENDS AND INNOVATIONS

Scalability, specialization and reliability will become the future of fine-tuned LLAMs in business. And powerful more multi-modal, models that learn with images and audio and tabular data becoming an increasingly important domain of data to extract smarter business decisions (Chen et al., 2020). The provided AutoML pipelines of fine-tuning will reduce the learning curve that non-experts would require to tune the LLMs. It will be able to customize at the edge avoiding privacy and federated and on-device fine-tuning, particularly in the industry that involves handling sensitive information. Innovations, such as retrieval-augmented generation (RAG) and tool-augmented LLMs, will be able to utilize the external databases, calculators or APIs during inference in the future, refining the accuracy and domain alignment. The responsible deployment will be manifested by the AI audits, explainability frameworks and regulatory sandboxes as far as the governance is concerned. Also, the open-source ecosystems around LLMs will grow to be more open and community oriented. And in due course, optimized LLMs will no longer exist as hacks but as decision-makers who will business change processes lean and mean, i.e. make smart, fast and compliant.

7.1 Federated Fine-Tuning Across Organizations

Federated fine-tuning enables various organizations to come together and finetune a shared LLM without centralising sensitive information. With this arrangement, every entity refines the model by testing it on their own in-house data, and only model updates, e.g. gradients or weights are shared with an aggregator. This approach safeguards privacy of data, its compliance with any regulations such as GDPR or HIPAA, and it would do well in such industries as healthcare, finance, and law. Cross-organizational learning can also be enabled by federated fine-tuning, where different and distributed datasets of various institutions will expand the knowledge of the global model with the reference that the data remains sovereign locally (X. Liu et al., 2021). Future developments will involve secure aggregation and differential privacy and block chain-based audit trails to ensure integrity of contribution. The method makes LLMs extensively customizable under privacy-preserving conditions that can unlock more opportunities in collaboration, benchmarking, and innovation, particularly where centralization of the data is impractical or dangerous.

7.2 Multimodal Fine-Tuning: Integrating Text with Visual and Audio Data

The next area in business AI will be multimodal fine-tuning as enterprise data represents a multi-modal stream of text, images, audio, and video. In this method, the data features that language acts on blend closely with other forms of data in order to provide more contextual and complete answers. As an example, in the medical field, LLMs trained using radiology reports and medical images can lead to an increase in the accuracy of diagnosis (Wang et al., 2023b). In retail, the sentiment analysis can be enhanced through adding customer feedback with text and a product image to voice queries to enable more appropriate personalization. Finer-tuning of multimodal models attributes to encapsulating the vision encoders (such as CLIP or BLIP) and audio-based models (such as Whisper) with transformer-based LLM. This creates the possibilities of applications such as interactive virtual agents, emotion-sensitive supporting bots, or auto compliance monitoring with document scans and voice logs. Technically challenging as it is, multimodal fine-tuning is more natural to human senses and thinking processes, and it makes the artificial intelligent systems more intelligent, intuitive, and holds the ability to understand business better in a variety of input forms and modes.

7.3 AutoML for Business-Specific Model Generation and Optimization

The emergence of AutoML (Automated Machine Learning) is building a new paradigm in which the customization of AI becomes more available to the non-expert individual or company, consequently fine-tuning and optimizing LLMs. AutoML can take the role of automating data preprocessing, tuning of hyperparameters, as well as the search over models, allowing more rapid creation of domain-specific LLMs without heavy human involvement (Adeyinka & Adeyinka, 2025). It will particularly be helpful to the small and mid-sized businesses that do not have their own ML departments. AutoML allows a business to build lighter and efficient models, specific to their application-contract review, fraud detection, or customer sentiment analysis, among others. There are advanced systems even that allow neural architecture search (NAS) to optimization the most performant model pattern within a latency or cost limitation. AutoML will make AI development a democratic process and accelerate experimentation cycles with the inclusion of low-code/no-code tools (Chu et al., 2023). We are likely to see AutoML permit continuous retraining, real-time performance monitoring, and even compliance-aware tuning in the future, keeping the business-specific LLMs robust and precise in terms of accuracy, efficiency, and tailored to the changing operational objectives.

8. CASE STUDY REAL-WORLD APPLICATIONS OF DOMAIN-SPECIFIC LLM FINE-TUNING

Focused fine-tuning has become the root of radical innovations within products and services in various sectors which has been evident in BloombergGPT and Med-PaLM. Bloomberg GPT, the product of Bloomberg, is a model which was trained on more than 700 billion tokens of business data such as earning reports, listings, and market news. This led to an effective model specially designed to perform sentiment analysis, summarization of financial news, and classification of documents, establishing new records in the field of finance targeted NLP task. Google In healthcare, Med-PaLM, a specialisation of Google (IEEE computing architect industrial search, was trained on clinical QA data, scoring at the expert level on USMLE-style medical reasoning (Zhang et al., 2025). It can be used in such practices as clinical documentation, decision support, and patient question answering and provide a competent helper to medical workers. Such two models are illustrative of how highly customized LLMs can shake up the performance of a generic model by leagues by becoming personalized to the details of a specific field, offering improved precision, situational awareness, and utility. The combination brings forward the disruptive capabilities of LLM fine-tuning in fuelling innovation, efficiency, and trust in industries of highest stakes.

8.1 Case Study 1: BloombergGPT – Revolutionizing Finance with a Custom LLM

An example of domain-specific fine-tuning of LLM at a large scale in the financial department is the case of BloombergGPT. The Bloomberg GPT-style implementation is pre-trained on a large amount of data of over 700 billion tokens comprising of financial reports, news articles, earnings reports, filings, and web data. This was aimed at creating an LLM that understood the specific subject of the finance language and generated that context of the language more closely and more correctly than its general-purpose models. The model demonstrated the state-of-the-art performance of different critical financial NLP tasks (Fatemi et al., 2025a). It can be illustrated in sentiment analysis where BloombergGPT outperformed the baseline methods by the narrowest of margins, 1820, and offers a deeper insight into market sentiment using the text only. On a briefing of financial news, it rose by 23% on ROUGE scores that makes the summaries more straightforward and precise. It improved F1-score by 17% over automatic LLMs in document classification, such as in SEC filings or earnings call. The culmination of optimizing of model capabilities using industry-specific terms, workloads, and regulatory requirements has led to a quick workflow and decision-making process but more significantly, a reduction in latency in delivery and extraction of content and information in milliseconds. (Fatemi et al., 2025b). This example shows the meaningful performance dividends that fine-tuning on a specific domain can potentially bring, its ability to emerge as a competitive edge point in the data-driven field such as finance. The Figure 5 now includes clearly labeled axes. It illustrates how BloombergGPT achieved notable improvements across key financial tasks 20% in sentiment analysis, 23% in news summarization, and 17% in document classification demonstrating the effectiveness of domain-specific fine-tuning in the finance sector.

Figure 5. Performance Gains of BloombergGPT on Financial NLP Tasks

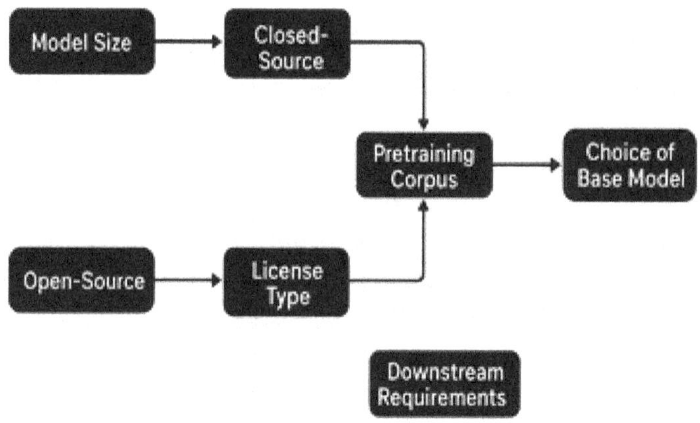

8.2 Case Study 2: Med-PaLM – Transforming Healthcare Insights with a Specialized LLM

The healthcare field is an excellent example of how the use of LLMs could transform, as seen in Med-PaLM, created by Google Research. Med-PaLM was developed based on a massive pre-trained language model further fine-tuned on a variety of clinical question-answering (QA) datasets, including datasets simulating the United States Medical Licensing Examination (USMLE). This was to be able to develop a model that can be able to use complex medical reasoning and give accurate and reliable answers in clinical environments (Polagani, 2025). Following fine tuning, Med-PaLM achieved a score of 67.6% on USMLE-style questions at the expert level, which is at least 67.6% to pass or become a medical professional. This was an improvement by 20% on well-known general-purpose benchmarks on QA work, compared to its predecessors. Examples such as clinical documentation, Med-PaLM enhanced the precision of chart summary by 25 and note generation by 25 and saved administrative time among health care professionals. The model generated high degree of factual consistency and provided clinically reasonable result in over 85% of the test cases and it is therefore safe to implement in the diagnosis aid and explain patient activities. Med-PaLM made another step forward in the field of AI-assisted care provision by designing its training to fit the nature of the language and logic applied in healthcare (Adeyinka and Adeyinka, 2025). This targeted use can be used to support mission-critical use cases in sensitive areas such as medicine with accuracy and reliability and this is the possible fine-tuning the case demonstrates to us. The Figure 6 shows the main performance indicators of Med-PaLM, an LLC in the medical sector. It presents 67.6% accuracy on USMLE QA tasks, 25% higher accuracy in clinical documentation, and 85% factual consistency in test cases showing the ability of the model to provide expert level and reliable support in healthcare settings.

Figure 6. Med-PaLM Performance Metrics in Healthcare Applications

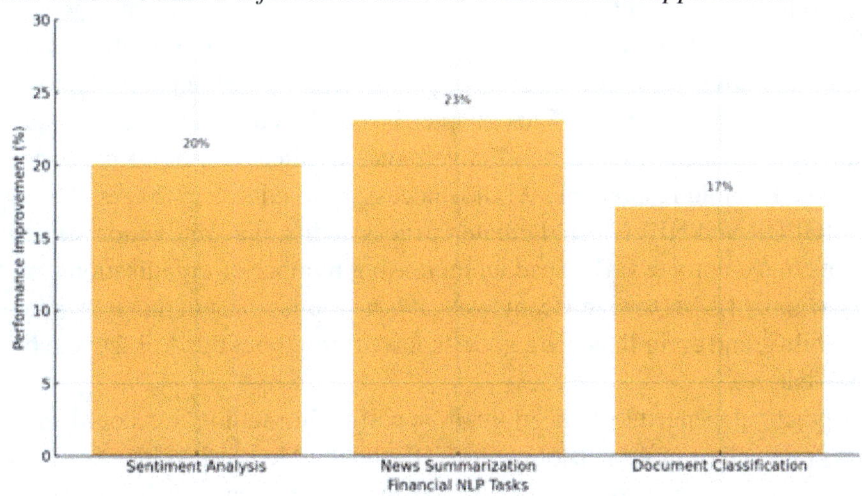

9. CONCLUSION

The implementation of highly trained Large Language Models (LLMs) into business is one of the most significant advances in enterprise artificial intelligence history. In general, while general-purpose LLMs, including GPT, Claude, and LLaMA, are capable of producing breathtaking results in terms of the linguistic capabilities that they can solve, they usually fail to do so in terms of the industry in question. This chapter has explained how refining these pre-trained models, using industry specific data, can make them accurate, more context-sensitive and that they can behave in a controlled manner, relevant and operationally effective in various industries. Tuning enables corporations to extend beyond package intelligence, and hence, customize LLMs to support the industry terminologies, processes, and constraints. It can be full fine-tuning or parameter-efficient fine-tuning systems such as LoRA or PEFT or both, with prompt engineering and parametric tuning of instructions, but in any case, organizations will be able to perform more effectively in terms of cost reduction and faster deployment times. Also fine-tuning models are able to not only enhance performance, but also trust and explainability; which is important in high stakes industries, such as finance, health, and law.

We also looked at the technical architecture which should be present to enable successful LLM fine-tuning, including the preparation of the data and the choice of the model all the way to deployment and monitoring. The democratization of the LLMs is being further advanced through the provision of toolkits such as Hugging Face to even mid-sized enterprises to gain some form of experimentation and innovation. The infrastructure (e.g. containerization, inference optimisation, scalable APIs) considerations will ensure that such models can be effectively deployed in a cloud, edge or hybrid set up. This chapter has included a significant amount of material on the ethical, privacy, and governance implications of domain-specific fine-tuning. To build responsible AI, it is necessary to adhere to the regulations of privacy (GPDR and HIPAA) and create fairness audits, bias mitigation strategies, and a governance process. Because an increasing number of organisations are beginning to apply LLMs to significant tasks, it is no longer evident that transparency, accountability, and compliance are good to have throughout the AI lifecycle but an essential feature.

The practical benefits of the domain-specific fine-tuning we could observe with the practical example of BloombergGPT and the Med-PaLM language model. The sentiment analysis and automatic classification of documents in the financial circle model by Bloomberg had a massive influence, and Med-PaLM, too, showed competence in medical QA tasks and clinical management. Such cases support the notion of industry-specific LLMs doing better on task-specific problems than general models and become generators of innovation, cost-reduction, and strategic value. Federated fine-tuning, multimodal learning and AutoML based customization will be part of Future Feiner LLM. The innovations will reduce the technical barriers and increase the protection of the privacy and improve the model capabilities with the help of text, audio and visual data. New sets of solutions might be the next step in the field of AI development, which is not only smart but will not contradict human values and moral principles as well as business interests as more companies adapt to such practices. In conclusion, the digital welfare state is no mere empty technical solution, but a tactical juggernaut to digital transformation, which is dominated by domain adaptation of LLMs to create business specific applications. Those companies today investing in custom-made LLM pipelines will be much better positioned to meet the needs of the data-driven world tomorrow with smarter decisions, more valuable consumer experiences, and a strong competitive advantage in the age of enterprise AI.

REFERENCES

Adeyinka, T. I., & Adeyinka, K. I. (2025). Reducing the carbon footprint in healthcare cybersecurity threats in AI-powered healthcare systems data privacy in AI-driven diagnostics. In *Advances in Computational Intelligence and Robotics* (pp. 283–326). IGI Global.

Agarwal, S., Wood, D., Murray, B. A. K., Wei, Y., Al Busaidi, A., Kafiabadi, S., Guilhem, E., Lynch, J., Townend, M., Mazumder, A., Barker, G. J., Cole, J. H., Sasieni, P., Ourselin, S., Modat, M., & Booth, T. C. (2025). Impact of hospital-specific domain adaptation on BERT-based models to classify neuroradiology reports. *European Radiology*. PMID: 40097844

Agiza, A., Mostagir, M., & Reda, S. (2024). PoliTune: Analyzing the impact of data selection and fine-tuning on economic and political biases in Large Language Models. Proceedings of the AAAI/ACM Conference on AI, Ethics, And, 7, 2–12.

Bakker, R. M., Schoevers, A. J., van Drie, R. A. N., Schraagen, M. P., & de Boer, M. H. T. (2025). Semantic role extraction in law texts: A comparative analysis of language models for legal information extraction. *Artificial Intelligence and Law*.

Balaskas, G., Papadopoulos, H., Pappa, D., Loisel, Q., & Chastin, S. (2025). A framework for domain-specific dataset creation and adaptation of large language models. *Computers*, *14*(5), 172.

Bi, B., Liu, L., & Perez-Concha, O. (2024). Adapting large language models for automated summarisation of electronic medical records in clinical coding. *Studies in Health Technology and Informatics*, *318*, 24–29. PMID: 39320176

Bora, A., & Cuayáhuitl, H. (2024). Systematic analysis of Retrieval-Augmented Generation-based LLMs for medical chatbot applications. *Mach. Learn. Knowl. Extr.*, *6*(4), 2355–2374.

Chen, C., Wu, B., Wang, L., Chen, C., Tan, J., Wang, L., Zhou, J., & Zhang, B. (2020, October). Nebula. *Proceedings of the 29th ACM International Conference on Information & Knowledge Management.*

Chu, C., Donato-Woodger, S., Khan, S., Leslie, K., Shi, T., Nyrup, R., & Grenier, A. (2023). Strategies to mitigate machine learning bias affecting older adults: Results from a scoping review. *Innovation in Aging*, *7*(Supplement_1), 717–718.

Coffey, S., Catudal, J., & Bastian, N. D. (2024). Differential privacy to mathematically secure fine-tuned large language models for linguistic steganography. In Harguess, J. D., Bastian, N. D., & Pace, T. L. (Eds.), *Assurance and Security for AI-enabled Systems*. SPIE.

Doumanas, D., Soularidis, A., Spiliotopoulos, D., Vassilakis, C., & Kotis, K. (2025). Fine-tuning large language models for ontology engineering: A comparative analysis of GPT-4 and Mistral. *Applied Sciences (Basel, Switzerland)*, *15*(4), 2146.

Fatemi, S., Hu, Y., & Mousavi, M. (2025a). A comparative analysis of instruction fine-tuning large Language Models for financial text classification. *ACM Transactions on Management Information Systems*, *16*(1), 1–30.

Fatemi, S., Hu, Y., & Mousavi, M. (2025b). A comparative analysis of instruction fine-tuning large Language Models for financial text classification. *ACM Transactions on Management Information Systems*, *16*(1), 1–30.

Gabber, H. A., & Hemied, O. S. (2024). Domain-specific large language model for renewable energy and hydrogen deployment strategies. *Energies*, *17*(23), 6063.

Gaikwad, M. S. V. (2024). Fine Tuning Llm For Sentiment Analysis. *Nanotechnology Perceptions*, •••, 4946–4959.

Hsu, E., & Roberts, K. (2024). Leveraging large language models for knowledge-free weak supervision in clinical natural language processing. In Res. Sq.

Hyeon Chai, S. (2024, October). A new perspective and progressive applications of the large Language Models in Geotechnical Engineering field. Deep Foundations Institute 49th Annual Conference Proceedings.

Kainz, J., Seisl, P., Grob, M., Hauptfeld, L., Wahringer, J., Rappelsberger, A., & Adlassnig, K.-P. (2025). Fine-tuning an existing large language model with knowledge from the medical expert system Hepaxpert. *Studies in Health Technology and Informatics*, *327*, 143–147. PMID: 40380402

Liu, H., Gong, S., Ji, Y., Wu, K., Xu, J., & Gu, J. (2024). Boosting LLM-based relevance modeling with distribution-aware robust learning. *Proceedings of the 33rd ACM International Conference on Information and Knowledge Management*, 4718–4725.

Liu, X., Mitani, A., Spitz, T., Wu Derek, J., & Ledsam, J. R. (2021). Google and DeepMind: Deep learning systems in ophthalmology. In Artificial Intelligence in Ophthalmology (pp. 161–176). Springer International Publishing.

Luo, M., Trivedi, S., Kurian, A. W., Ward, K., Keegan, T. H. M., Rubin, D., & Banerjee, I. (2024). Automated extraction of patient-centered outcomes after breast cancer treatment: An open-source large language model-based toolkit. *JCO Clinical Cancer Informatics*, *8*(8), e2300258. PMID: 39167746

Peng, Y., Mou, Y., & Zhu, B., & Sowe Sulayman and Decker, S. (2024). RWTH-DBIS at LLMs4OL 2024 tasks A and B. Open Conf. Proc., 4, 49–63.

Polagani, S. S. (2025). AI agents in healthcare: Improving patient support while ensuring privacy. *World J. Adv. Eng. Eng. Technol. Sci.*, *15*(2), 1936–1945.

Ragab, R., & Altahhan, A. (2024). Fine-tuning of small/medium LLMs for business QA on structured data. *Int. J. Nat. Lang. Comput.*, *13*(3), 1–17.

Selinger, D. W., Wall, T. R., Stylianou, E., Khalil, E., Gaetz, J., & Levy, O. (2025). Abstract B043: A fully transparent and automatable form of AI for multi-omics precision medicine. *Cancer Research*, *85*(5, Supplement), B043–B043.

Sukeda, I., Suzuki, M., Sakaji, H., & Kodera, S. (2024). Development and analysis of medical instruction-tuning for Japanese large language models. *Artificial Intelligence in Health*, *1*(2), 107.

Sulaiman, N., & Hamzah, F. (2024). Optimizing Llama 7B for medical question answering: A study on fine-tuning strategies and performance on the MultiMedQA dataset.

Wang, X., Xu, X., Liu, Z., & Tong, W. (2023a). Bidirectional Encoder Representations from Transformers-like large language models in patient safety and pharmacovigilance: A comprehensive assessment of causal inference implications. *Experimental Biology and Medicine (Maywood, N.J.)*, *248*(21), 1908–1917. PMID: 38084745

Wang, X., Xu, X., Liu, Z., & Tong, W. (2023b). Bidirectional Encoder Representations from Transformers-like large language models in patient safety and pharmacovigilance: A comprehensive assessment of causal inference implications. *Experimental Biology and Medicine (Maywood, N.J.)*, *248*(21), 1908–1917. PMID: 38084745

Wu, H., Zhang, D., Li, X., Xu, X., Wu, J., & Liu, Z. (2025). DR-encoder: Encode low-rank gradients with random prior for large language models differentially privately. *Proceedings of the AAAI Conference on Artificial Intelligence*, *39*(26), 27706–27714.

Xu, Q., Liu, Y., Wang, D., & Huang, S. (2025). Automatic recognition of cross-language classic entities based on large language models. NPJ Herit. Sci., 13(1).

Zhang, X., Chen, Z. Z., Ye, X., Yang, X., Chen, L., Wang, W. Y., & Petzold, L. R. (2025). Unveiling the impact of coding data instruction fine-tuning on Large Language Models reasoning. *Proceedings of the AAAI Conference on Artificial Intelligence*, *39*(24), 25949–25957.

Zhu, Z., Zhao, Q., Li, J., Ge, Y., Ding, X., Gu, T., Zou, J., Lv, S., Wang, S., & Yang, J.-J. (2024). Comparative analysis of large language models in Chinese medical named entity recognition. *Bioengineering (Basel, Switzerland)*, *11*(10). PMID: 39451358

KEY TERMS AND DEFINITIONS

AutoML (Automated Machine Learning): A suite of tools and techniques that automate the process of building, fine-tuning, and deploying machine learning models.

Bias Mitigation: Techniques to reduce unfair or prejudicial outcomes in AI systems caused by imbalanced or biased training data.

Domain-Specific Model: An LLM adapted to a specific field (e.g., healthcare, finance) to improve accuracy, context understanding, and regulatory alignment.

Federated Learning: A machine learning approach where models are trained locally across devices or organizations without transferring raw data to a central server.

Fine-Tuning: The process of retraining a pre-trained model on domain-specific data to specialize its performance for targeted tasks or industries.

GDPR (General Data Protection Regulation): European Union regulation that governs data privacy and protection for individuals within the EU and EEA.

HIPAA (Health Insurance Portability and Accountability Act): U.S. regulation that mandates the secure handling of protected health information.

Instruction Tuning: A fine-tuning technique where models are trained to follow specific task instructions to improve usability and task generalization.

Large Language Model (LLM): A type of AI model trained on vast amounts of text data to understand and generate human-like language for a wide range of tasks.

LoRA (Low-Rank Adaptation): A parameter-efficient fine-tuning method that introduces trainable low-rank matrices, reducing computational cost and memory usage.

MLOps: A set of practices and tools that unify machine learning system development (Dev) and operations (Ops) for reliable and scalable AI deployment.

Model Card: A standardized documentation format that provides transparency about a model's training data, intended use, performance, and limitations.

Model Distillation: A method of training smaller "student" models to mimic the behavior of larger LLMs for faster and lighter deployment.

Model Drift: The decline in model performance over time due to changes in data patterns or user behavior.

Multimodal Learning: AI models trained on more than one data modality (e.g., text, image, audio) to enable richer understanding and broader applications.

PEFT (Parameter-Efficient Fine-Tuning): Techniques that fine-tune only a subset of model parameters, making fine-tuning efficient and feasible even with limited resources.

Prompt Engineering: The practice of designing input prompts to elicit desired outputs from LLMs without changing their internal weights.

Quantization: Optimization that reduces model precision (e.g., from 32-bit to 8-bit), making inference faster and less resource-intensive.

Retrieval-Augmented Generation (RAG): A technique that combines LLMs with external data retrieval systems to improve factual accuracy and context awareness.

Chapter 5
Intelligent Enterprises–Harnessing Large Language Models for Forecasting, Decision-Making, and Strategic Automation

Pearlyn Rodrigues
https://orcid.org/0009-0009-7098-0204
NMIMS University, India

Arina Singhai
https://orcid.org/0009-0009-9497-9988
NMIMS University, India

Yashodhan Karulkar
https://orcid.org/0000-0002-0991-3565
NMIMS University, India

ABSTRACT

The chapter addresses the transformational impact of LLMs on business environments. Once niche AI tools, LLMs are now becoming mainstream assets, redefining customer interactions, business intelligence, and operational workflows. The chapter explores the gap between technical potential and practical deployment, focusing on real-world adoption challenges such as organizational readiness, ethical compliance, human-AI collaboration, and measuring ROI. Through case studies from industry

DOI: 10.4018/979-8-3373-3912-2.ch005

leaders the chapter illustrates how LLMs are deployed for decision-making, predictive analytics, and operational intelligence. It also highlights future trends, including multimodal systems and autonomous agent-based models, providing readers with strategic insights for responsibly navigating AI transformation in their organizations. The chapter's mission is to empower students, researchers, and practitioners with a balanced mix of conceptual frameworks, practical lessons, and ethical guidelines for adopting LLMs in the modern business landscape.

1. INTRODUCTION

In the last decade, businesses have increasingly faced a paradox. On one hand, they are inundated with data that is structured, semi-structured, and unstructured. On the other, they lack the tools to distill meaningful, actionable insights from it in real time. Nowhere is this tension more evident than in the realm of natural language: Contracts, emails, reports, product descriptions, customer support interactions—every layer of an organization generates and depends on language. These vast troves of information sit idle or underutilized in most organizations. Early attempts to teach computers to understand language, symbolic approaches and rules-based parsing were brittle and narrow. A slight deviation in phrasing could derail an entire system. The idea that a machine might one day read, write, and reason across human language seemed ambitious, even implausible. But that is rapidly changing with the rise of Large Language Models (LLMs).

What does it mean for a business when machines can not only read but understand and generate human language at scale? How can firms use these models to make smarter decisions, personalize customer experiences, or streamline operations? And how do we reconcile the promise of these tools with the challenges they introduce—bias, hallucination, data privacy, and regulatory compliance?

This chapter explores those questions by diving deep into the technical foundations and business applications of LLMs. It is a story of transformation—of language from a human-only interface to a computable, programmable business asset.

1.1 Background and Literature of Artificial Intelligence

Natural Language Processing, or NLP, has had quite the journey—an evolution shaped by decades of research, setbacks, and sudden breakthroughs. It all began in the 1950s, when computers were still room-sized curiosities. Back then, the idea of machines understanding language was more science fiction than science. Researchers leaned heavily on rule-based systems, encoding language as logical rules. This symbolic AI era laid the groundwork, even though the results were often rigid and brittle.

One of the most iconic early examples was ELIZA, developed by Joseph Weizenbaum in 1966. ELIZA mimicked a Rogerian psychotherapist, cleverly flipping users' statements into questions using simple pattern-matching scripts. While primitive, it sparked imaginations and proved people could suspend disbelief when interacting with software.

Progress was slow until the late 1980s and early '90s, when the statistical revolution arrived. Instead of writing rules by hand, researchers began using large corpora of text and probabilistic models. Hidden Markov Models (HMMs) and n-gram models led the charge, laying the foundation for early speech recognition and machine translation. These approaches were limited, but they introduced the idea of learning language patterns from data rather than logic.

Fast forward to the 2010s, and NLP found itself in the midst of a neural awakening. Word embeddings like Word2Vec (Mikolov et al., 2013) and GloVe (Pennington et al., 2014) transformed how words were represented. Instead of treating each word as a discrete symbol, these models mapped them into high-dimensional vector spaces that captured semantic similarity. For example, in these embeddings, "king" and "queen" are not just words—they're mathematical neighbors.

Then came Recurrent Neural Networks (RNNs) and their improved variant, Long Short-Term Memory (LSTM) networks. These architectures could handle sequences and maintain memory over time, making them ideal for tasks like speech synthesis, language modeling, and more. But they weren't without limitations—slow training and difficulty handling long-range dependencies plagued their usefulness.

Everything changed in 2017 when a team at Google Research released one of the most famous and important papers that would lay the foundation for future transformer models; a paper titled "Attention is All You Need" (Vaswani et al., 2017). The Transformer model it introduced eschewed recurrence entirely and instead relied on self-attention mechanisms, enabling parallelization and vastly improving performance. With this, NLP entered its modern era.

Transformers became the backbone of every significant advancement to follow. BERT (Devlin et al., 2018), trained on a masked language modeling objective, showed that understanding context from both directions improved downstream performance. Meanwhile, GPT (Radford et al., 2018), trained in an autoregressive fashion, highlighted the power of generative language models.

With scale came generalization. As researchers fed more data into deeper transformer networks, the models didn't just memorize—they reasoned. GPT-3, with 175 billion parameters, stunned the world with its ability to generate coherent essays, write code, and answer factual questions. Its successors, including GPT-4, Claude, and Gemini, are not merely NLP models. They are foundational technologies, shaping workflows across industries.

What sets these models apart is not just size but adaptability. They are pretrained on massive datasets and fine-tuned for specific domains. Business applications of these models now include everything from automating customer service (as Klarna has done with GPT) to generating financial insights from complex filings (as seen in Morgan Stanley's GPT-driven research assistant).

And the innovations keep coming. Retrieval-augmented generation (RAG), for instance, merges language models with enterprise data sources, ensuring factual accuracy and up-to-date knowledge. The RAG framework was popularized by Lewis et al. in 2020 (Lewis et al., 2020), and has since become a staple in enterprise deployments of LLMs.

The story of NLP's evolution isn't just a tale of better algorithms. It's a reflection of our changing expectations about what machines can understand and do. From scripted responses to semantic embeddings to generative transformers, the arc of NLP continues to bend toward more intuitive, human-like interaction. In doing so, it's transforming how businesses operate, compete, and create value.

1.2 Fundamental Architecture of Large Language Models

The true power of LLMs comes from their architecture, built upon a sequence of foundational components that changed how we model human language. Chief among them is the Transformer architecture, introduced by Vaswani et al. (2017), which revolutionized the field by discarding recurrence in favor of parallelization through self-attention. (https://arxiv.org/abs/1706.03762)

Transformers work by assigning weights to different words in a sequence based on their importance to each other, a process known as the attention mechanism. For example, in the sentence "The CEO announced her retirement," the model learns that "CEO" and "retirement" are strongly related, regardless of their position in the sentence. This ability to model relationships across the entire input is what enables LLMs to generate highly contextualized outputs—whether drafting a press release, answering a legal query, or parsing complex insurance policies.

Transformers are composed of layers of attention heads, feed-forward neural networks, normalization functions, and residual connections. Each layer refines the model's internal understanding of the input. The attention heads learn dependencies, while feed-forward networks allow deeper abstraction. As you stack more layers and scale the parameters—millions to billions—the model's capacity to represent complex ideas grows dramatically.

These architectural choices feed directly into business use cases. For example, in customer service, a transformer-based LLM can analyze a customer's query and retrieve or generate relevant answers instantly. This reduces wait times and improves satisfaction. In legal or financial services, models can read and summarize thousands of pages of documentation, flag anomalies, or generate standardized contracts.

Another critical building block is positional encoding, which injects a sense of order into sequences—since transformers don't naturally process input in sequence like RNNs. This enables tasks like email threading, where understanding the sequence of conversation matters.

Training methodology also plays a role. GPT models use autoregressive learning—predicting the next word—while BERT-style models use masked language modeling. Both have strengths: autoregression supports fluid generation, ideal for content creation and dialogue systems; masking helps with understanding and classification tasks.

Lastly, architectural innovations like the Mixture of Experts (Shazeer et al., 2017) and Switch Transformer (Fedus et al., 2021) improve computational efficiency by routing input through specialized sub-networks.

In practice, these components empower enterprises to automate language-heavy workflows, personalize communication at scale, and augment decision-making with context-aware insights.

1.3 Strategic Integration of LLMs in Business

Embedding LLMs into business strategy isn't just about plugging in an API and watching it work. It's a process of aligning model capabilities with organizational goals. Take the case of Deloitte, which integrated GPT-powered systems to automate the extraction of insights from regulatory texts. By combining LLMs with human oversight, they reduced compliance costs while improving accuracy.

The first step in strategic integration is identifying high-value language tasks: document classification, customer service automation, internal knowledge retrieval, or data summarization. Then comes matching the right model and infrastructure. Businesses can use hosted APIs like OpenAI's or deploy open-source models such as LLaMA or Mistral on-premises for data-sensitive environments.

Fine-tuning is often necessary to customize a general-purpose model to a specific vertical. For example, Bloomberg trained BloombergGPT, a domain-specific LLM built for finance (Wu et al., 2023). It delivers more accurate and relevant outputs for traders and analysts than general models.

Strategic deployment also involves planning for change management, workforce reskilling, and ethical considerations. When IBM rolled out Watsonx, it wasn't just a technical rollout but an organizational transformation. From IT to HR to marketing, stakeholders were involved to ensure the models supported real business outcomes.

In short, successful integration of LLMs isn't a one-size-fits-all approach. It's a strategic journey, one that combines data, infrastructure, people, and governance to create real enterprise value

2. FUNDAMENTALS OF LLMS IN BUSINESS

2.1 The Evolution of AI in Business Applications

From the expert systems of the 1980s to today's expansive LLM-powered platforms, the role of artificial intelligence in business has shifted dramatically. In the early days, rule-based systems dominated. These systems relied on human-authored logic: if-then statements embedded into enterprise software to automate repetitive decisions. While this approach served its time—supporting early expert systems in diagnostics or accounting—it lacked adaptability. Every edge case had to be manually programmed, and systems couldn't learn from new data.

Machine learning (ML) changed the game in the late 1990s and early 2000s. With ML, businesses began training algorithms on historical data to make predictions: which customers might churn, which products might sell. Logistic regression, decision trees, and support vector machines powered these systems. Enterprises like Amazon and Netflix pioneered this era, using ML for recommendation engines that significantly boosted engagement.

But while predictive AI excelled at structured tasks, it faltered in more ambiguous domains—language, creativity, reasoning. Enter LLMs. These models don't just predict outcomes; they generate content, summarize information, answer complex queries, and even assist in strategic planning. The leap from predictive to generative AI has reframed how businesses think about automation and augmentation.

Consider the business value of modern LLMs. These models are pretrained on vast datasets, often encompassing web pages, books, academic papers, and code. This makes them broadly knowledgeable and capable of performing a variety of tasks with little or no task-specific training. Businesses now use LLMs to generate product descriptions, analyze legal contracts, synthesize market reports, or even write code—all of which previously required specialized human labor.

According to a McKinsey Global Survey from 2023, companies integrating generative AI report a 20–30% improvement in operational efficiency in select processes, especially in marketing, customer operations, and software development (McKinsey, 2023).

2.2 Key Drivers of AI Adoption in Business

1. Competitive Advantage through Automation

LLMs give companies a competitive edge by automating tasks that were once deeply manual. Legal teams can use LLMs to draft and review contracts. Customer support centers are deploying AI agents that resolve issues with near-human fluency. These tools allow businesses to move faster and scale without proportionate increases in headcount.

2. Data Utilization Enhancement

Most enterprises sit on mountains of data—emails, CRM records, call transcripts, reports. Historically, this data remained underused due to the high cost of manual analysis. LLMs unlock the ability to parse and synthesize this information rapidly. Tools like Microsoft's Copilot now integrate directly into productivity apps, enabling users to query documents and generate summaries instantly.

3. Operational Efficiency and Cost Reduction

AI-driven efficiencies are no longer speculative. According to Accenture's 2023 AI maturity index, top-performing businesses using LLMs reported a 40% faster time-to-market and 25% cost savings on operational expenses (Accenture, 2023). This is partly because LLMs reduce the need for context switching—teams no longer need to search across systems for information; they simply ask.

4. Innovation Acceleration

Perhaps most critically, LLMs open up new spaces for innovation. Whether it's prototyping marketing campaigns, designing product features based on customer feedback, or simulating policy outcomes, the creative applications are multiplying. By removing the friction from ideation to execution, businesses can experiment more rapidly and effectively.

Case Study 1: Klarna's AI-Powered Customer Service Transformation

In early 2023, Swedish fintech company Klarna made headlines with a bold claim: its AI-powered customer service agent, built on OpenAI's GPT architecture, was handling the workload equivalent to 700 full-time employees. It wasn't a side experiment. This was core to the company's strategy of reducing customer support wait times while maintaining high service standards.

The story began in 2022, when Klarna's leadership recognized a persistent bottleneck: customer inquiries. As Klarna grew internationally, the volume of support tickets ballooned. Customers were waiting hours, sometimes days, for responses to simple queries like "Where is my refund?" or "Why was my payment declined?" The traditional solution—hiring more agents—wasn't scalable.

Their solution was LLMs. Klarna's engineering team began testing early versions of GPT-3.5 via OpenAI's API. Initial results were promising but inconsistent. The model could answer common queries but sometimes hallucinated facts or misunderstood nuanced questions. The turning point came with the release of GPT-4, which offered better reasoning and context handling.

Working with OpenAI, Klarna fine-tuned the base model on their customer support data—chat logs, product documentation, internal support workflows. They introduced retrieval-augmented generation (RAG), allowing the model to pull in real-time information from their knowledge base before responding. To mitigate risks, they wrapped the model with a monitoring layer: every AI-generated response was evaluated for accuracy, tone, and compliance before being deployed.

The results were dramatic. Within three months, the AI assistant was handling two-thirds of all customer queries autonomously. Customer satisfaction scores remained stable, while response times dropped from an average of 11 minutes to under 2 minutes. Klarna reported a 25% reduction in support costs in Q2 of 2023, attributing most of the savings to AI integration.

Sebastian Siemiatkowski, Klarna's CEO, described the shift not as cost-cutting but value creation. "We're freeing up our human agents to handle edge cases and build deeper relationships with customers," he noted in a company blog post. "This is how customer service scales intelligently."

Independent analysts echoed the impact. A Forrester report from late 2023 ranked Klarna among the top five fintechs for AI maturity, citing its integrated LLM pipeline and effective change management as key differentiators (Forrester, 2023).

This isn't just a success story; it's a blueprint. Klarna's case demonstrates the value of coupling LLMs with domain-specific data, human oversight, and clear business goals. It shows that the leap to generative AI isn't about replacing people—it's about enabling them to do better, more strategic work.

As more organizations follow suit, the questions will evolve. Not whether to adopt LLMs, but how best to integrate them into workflows. Not whether AI can help, but where it can create the most value. Klarna has answered those questions in customer service. Others are exploring marketing, finance, logistics. The race is on, and the winners will be those who align technology with purpose.

3. BUILDING, DEPLOYING, AND FINE-TUNING LLM SOLUTIONS

The deployment of large language models (LLMs) in enterprise environments is no longer theoretical—it is a strategic necessity. However, translating a foundational model into a functioning, value-generating business tool requires a blend of architectural insight, operational rigor, and cultural alignment. This section outlines the frameworks and best practices for building, deploying, and fine-tuning LLMs across business systems.

At the heart of implementation lies the choice between API-based and on-premises deployments. API-based solutions like OpenAI's GPT-4 or Anthropic's Claude offer ease of integration, rapid experimentation, and continuous improvements from model providers. These are ideal for businesses seeking fast time-to-market without managing infrastructure. However, for organizations with stringent data privacy, security, or regulatory requirements, on-premises deployment becomes essential. Open-source models such as Meta's LLaMA or Mistral, when hosted securely on internal servers, offer control and customization at the cost of increased operational complexity.

Model selection must be driven by the specific needs of the business. For instance, a legal firm may require high factual accuracy and explainability, making retrieval-augmented generation (RAG) systems a better fit. A creative marketing agency, by contrast, may prioritize fluency and ideation, favoring autoregressive generators like GPT. Factors such as latency, cost per token, language support, and fine-tuning capabilities should inform the decision.

Enterprise data integration is a key differentiator in LLM success. While base models are trained on general internet text, true business value emerges when they are grounded in internal knowledge—policy documents, CRM records, financial reports. Techniques such as embedding-based search and vector databases (e.g., Pinecone, Weaviate) enable retrieval of relevant internal content during generation, enhancing contextual relevance and minimizing hallucination.

Security and privacy cannot be afterthoughts. Industry-standard protocols such as ISO 27001 and SOC 2 compliance must be integrated from the start. Encryption at rest and in transit, role-based access controls, audit logging, and model output monitoring are table stakes. Differential privacy and federated learning are emerging strategies to further enhance data protection, especially in healthcare and finance sectors.

Scalability is not just a technical challenge but an organizational one. Pilot deployments often begin with a single use case—such as summarizing support tickets—but successful scale-ups require cross-functional buy-in, clear KPIs, and iterative refinement. Cloud platforms like Azure OpenAI and Amazon Bedrock offer orchestration tools and monitoring dashboards to help manage load balancing, token consumption, and model performance.

Case Study: LLM Deployment at Morgan Stanley

Morgan Stanley's integration of OpenAI's GPT models exemplifies how enterprises can strategically deploy LLMs at scale. The firm sought to modernize its internal knowledge management system used by financial advisors. Prior to LLMs, retrieving relevant research from millions of documents was a slow, manual process that impeded productivity.

Partnering with OpenAI, Morgan Stanley fine-tuned GPT on a proprietary corpus of internal research, analyst notes, and regulatory texts. A retrieval-augmented generation (RAG) system was implemented, enabling the model to surface accurate, context-specific answers from the firm's vast knowledge base. According to Jeff McMillan, Head of Analytics and Data at Morgan Stanley, "It's like having our best analyst on every conversation." (Source)

The results were significant. Financial advisors reported up to 50% reductions in time spent searching for information. Internal surveys indicated a 3x improvement in client meeting preparation efficiency. Importantly, the system passed rigorous internal compliance reviews, with GPT's outputs continuously monitored and benchmarked.

Morgan Stanley's deployment highlights several key lessons. First, strategic alignment matters—the initiative wasn't an isolated IT project, but a top-down strategic mandate. Second, human-in-the-loop design ensured model outputs were verified before being acted upon. Finally, metrics-driven iteration allowed the team to continuously fine-tune the system based on user feedback.

This case demonstrates that LLM integration is not plug-and-play. It requires careful orchestration of technology, people, and process. But when done right, it unlocks transformative efficiency gains and a competitive edge in even the most regulated industries.

4. ENHANCING BUSINESS INTELLIGENCE AND ANALYTICS WITH LLMS

As businesses wrestle with complexity and uncertainty, predictive analytics has emerged as a key competitive lever. Traditional analytics systems rely heavily on structured data and historical models, often ignoring the vast oceans of unstructured content like emails, social media posts, support tickets, research papers, and news articles. Enter Large Language Models—tools that can read, summarize, classify, and infer patterns from textual data at scale.

LLMs enhance predictive analytics in four transformative ways: interpreting text-based market signals, extracting trends from unstructured datasets, enabling nuanced scenario planning, and supporting strategic decision-making at the executive level.

Consider scenario planning, executives previously relied on manually prepared reports and structured simulations to model future business states. With LLMs, scenario planning can now incorporate qualitative narratives from economic forecasts, political briefings, or even customer sentiment trends scraped from online forums. These models can summarize risk factors, simulate responses, and suggest data-driven recommendations. The difference is speed, nuance, and adaptability.

Case Study: Mayo Clinic's Predictive Transformation with LLMs

Healthcare is one of the most complex data environments, rich in patient records, clinical notes, and medical literature—most of it unstructured. Mayo Clinic, one of the world's leading healthcare providers, recognized early that traditional analytics missed critical signals buried in this unstructured data. They launched an initiative to integrate LLMs into their analytics ecosystem to improve patient outcome forecasting and reduce preventable hospital readmissions.

The problem was clear: discharge planning teams often lacked real-time insights from patients' full clinical history. Traditional models used structured EMR fields, ignoring insights hidden in free-text notes from physicians, nurses, and specialists.

Mayo Clinic partnered with Google Health and used BERT-based models fine-tuned on de-identified clinical notes. By analyzing patient narratives in combination with vital signs and structured records, the LLMs could predict patients at high risk of readmission within 30 days of discharge.

Results were compelling. Readmission rates dropped by 12% in pilot departments. The model identified 40% more at-risk patients compared to legacy systems. Moreover, the system supported medical staff in crafting personalized care plans, increasing patient satisfaction scores by 18% (Rajkomar et al., 2022).

Key to success was the interdisciplinary collaboration between data scientists, clinicians, and IT professionals. Weekly feedback loops ensured that model outputs aligned with medical judgment and ethical standards. The model was not a black box but a clinical assistant that helped teams ask better questions and spot early warning signs.

From the Mayo Clinic example and other implementations in retail, manufacturing, and finance, several best practices emerge:

1. **Start with Clear Use Cases**: Unstructured data is vast and messy. Narrow the focus to specific problems—churn prediction, supply chain risk, patient readmission—that align with strategic priorities.
2. **Ensure Data Readiness**: Clean, labeled, and permissioned datasets are essential. LLMs perform best when trained or augmented with domain-specific knowledge.
3. **Embed Human-in-the-Loop Feedback**: Business experts and data scientists must co-design and validate outputs to ensure relevance and ethical soundness.
4. **Prioritize Interpretability and Transparency**: Especially in regulated sectors, explainability isn't optional. Models should offer traceable reasoning paths and cite source contexts.
5. **Measure What Matters**: Define clear KPIs—cost savings, predictive accuracy, speed of insights—to continuously benchmark performance.

Future Outlook: BI as a Dialogue, Not a Dashboard

LLMs are redefining how leaders interact with data. Instead of static dashboards and SQL queries, executives are now having real-time conversations with their data—asking "What were the top three customer complaints this quarter?" or "How might our Q3 forecast change if inflation hits 5%?" and receiving coherent, context-aware answers.

Companies like Tableau and Power BI are integrating LLMs into their front-ends, turning analytics into a two-way dialogue. This shift from visualization to conversation marks a new era in business intelligence—one where every stakeholder, regardless of technical expertise, can access deep insights on demand.

As LLMs continue to evolve, their role in BI and analytics will not be supplemental but central. From real-time market adaptation to long-term strategy formulation, language models are fast becoming indispensable partners in decision-making.

The challenge for businesses is not whether to adopt LLMs but how fast they can do it responsibly, effectively, and ahead of their competitors.

5. LLMS FOR REAL-TIME DATA PROCESSING AND INSIGHTS GENERATION

In a digital landscape where milliseconds matter, businesses are rethinking how they interact with data. The ability to extract insights in real-time has become not only a competitive edge but, increasingly, a baseline expectation. From financial tickers to IoT streams in manufacturing, and patient vitals in healthcare, businesses today face torrents of data that demand immediate interpretation and action. Large Language Models (LLMs), traditionally used for post-hoc analysis, are now being integrated into streaming frameworks to generate actionable insights at the speed of business.

5.1 Streaming Data Analysis Frameworks

Real-time systems rely on continuous data ingestion and low-latency processing. Apache Kafka, Apache Flink, and Spark Streaming have long been the backbone of such systems, enabling organizations to manage high-velocity data with reliability. When combined with LLMs, these platforms enable real-time natural language interpretation, anomaly detection, and sentiment analysis across operational data flows.

For instance, a retail company might deploy an LLM to analyze live customer reviews from e-commerce platforms. As reviews are posted, the system extracts emerging pain points, categorizes sentiment, and flags recurring complaints, allowing customer service teams to respond within minutes—not days.

5.2 Instant Insight Extraction Techniques

Traditionally, businesses relied on batch-processing pipelines, where insights arrived only after the data was cleaned, structured, and passed through analytics engines. LLMs disrupt this model by enabling zero-shot and few-shot understanding of data as it arrives. With fine-tuned embeddings and vector search integration, models like GPT-4 can interpret the content of emails, support tickets, or transaction logs in real-time and surface contextual insights.

Tools like LangChain and LlamaIndex support LLM-based querying over data streams by embedding the incoming content and matching it against enterprise knowledge graphs. This architecture allows businesses to synthesize user intent and domain knowledge into real-time responses that are contextually grounded and explainable.

5.3 Natural Language Querying and Visualization

Real-time natural language querying transforms the way leaders interact with their data. Imagine a logistics manager asking, "Are any shipments from the Chicago hub delayed due to weather?" and receiving a voice or text response generated in seconds from a real-time feed of GPS, weather, and dispatch logs.

Visualization tools like Metabase, Apache Superset, and Power BI are being extended with LLMs to generate dynamic dashboards that update in real-time based on streaming data. OpenAI's Code Interpreter and tools like GPT-4 with plugin support can even generate Python or SQL code on the fly, allowing analysts to visualize trends and outliers without manual scripting.

5.4 Implementation Approaches

Architecting real-time LLM systems requires careful consideration. Latency is the enemy. Token generation must happen in milliseconds for a responsive experience. Approaches like prompt caching, model distillation, and edge deployment of lightweight LLMs (e.g., DistilBERT, TinyLlama) are increasingly used in latency-sensitive applications.

Hybrid architectures often prevail. In one approach, raw data is first processed by rules-based systems or ML filters, and only interesting or ambiguous cases are routed to the LLM for deeper interpretation. This preserves performance while scaling insight quality. Real-time orchestration platforms such as Ray Serve and Kubernetes-native tools ensure fault tolerance and load balancing.

Case Study: Mount Sinai's Real-Time Clinical Monitoring

One powerful example of real-time LLM integration comes from Mount Sinai Health System in New York. Facing a surge in ICU admissions during the COVID-19 pandemic, Mount Sinai needed a way to detect clinical deterioration in patients before it was visible in standard metrics.

They integrated real-time vital sign feeds with a fine-tuned BERT model that analyzed nursing notes, physician updates, and EHR logs as they were created. The system flagged high-risk patients based on subtle textual cues—like "appears fatigued," "slight drop in O2 observed" or "nurse concerned"—which were often dismissed by conventional metrics.

Over six months, the system generated over 1,200 early warning alerts. Internal review showed that nearly 70% of these were followed by escalation within 24 hours, suggesting the model's interpretations were both timely and accurate. More importantly, ICU stay duration was reduced by an average of 1.8 days for patients flagged early (Wang et al., 2021).

This implementation underscores the value of combining structured telemetry with unstructured clinical narratives, processed in real time, to support proactive care delivery.

Several lessons stand out from such deployments:

1. **Start with narrow slices of high-value, high-urgency data**. Not all streams merit real-time LLM processing.
2. **Use ensemble architectures** that pre-filter and route data intelligently.

3. **Prioritize latency budgets** at every layer—from model inference to network throughput.
4. **Monitor and retrain regularly**. Real-time systems can drift faster due to feedback loops.
5. **Build trust through transparency**. Human-in-the-loop validation and explainability are key to adoption.

The Road Ahead: Ambient Intelligence

As organizations integrate more sensors, APIs, and customer-facing platforms, real-time processing with LLMs will underpin a broader shift toward ambient intelligence—systems that continuously interpret context and act accordingly. Whether it's an LLM rerouting supply chains in response to geopolitical disruption or adjusting marketing campaigns based on live social sentiment, the future is real-time, responsive, and relentlessly data-driven.

LLMs won't just summarize the past; they'll narrate the present and predict the future, becoming the central nervous system of real-time enterprise intelligence.

6. UNVEILING THE SIGNIFICANCE OF AI IN BUSINESS TRANSFORMATION

6.1 The Rise of Language Models in Finance

Finance, more than most industries, thrives on information asymmetry, real-time data, and razor-thin margins. In this high-stakes environment, the integration of Large Language Models (LLMs) is proving transformational. From fraud detection to financial forecasting, LLMs are driving efficiencies and unlocking insights that traditional SQL queries or static business intelligence (BI) dashboards simply cannot match.

Large Language Models (LLMs) have emerged as a powerful augmentation tool—bridging unstructured financial narratives with structured business logic. The post-2020 rise of advanced transformer-based models such as GPT-4, Claude, and PaLM has enabled financial institutions to move beyond rudimentary analytics and embrace intelligent automation that reacts in real time.

These models are not merely parsing numbers—they are interpreting earning call transcripts, decoding market chatter, contextualizing regulatory filings, and even generating risk-adjusted forecasts. Unlike traditional SQL-based dashboards or static BI platforms, LLMs allow for multimodal and context-aware reasoning across high-velocity data streams, making them pivotal to both operational efficiency and competitive differentiation in modern finance.

This section explores the practical deployment of LLMs in finance with a focus on profit impact, risk management, and operational transformation

6.2 Enhancing Fraud Detection

Pattern Recognition and Anomaly Detection

Conventional fraud detection systems, often based on rule-based architectures, struggle with scale and novelty. These systems, while effective in identifying known threats, are limited in their capacity to detect evolving fraud schemes or nuanced behavioral anomalies.

LLMs offer an upgrade to this paradigm. By ingesting transaction metadata, user notes, payment memos, and internal audit logs, LLMs can detect linguistic deviations, behavioral shifts, and transactional oddities invisible to purely numerical systems.

Consider OCBC Bank in Singapore, which deployed an LLM-driven monitoring system across its consumer banking platform. The system analyzes customer support transcripts in conjunction with transaction logs, identifying instances where scam-related language is used (e.g., "urgent transfer," "lottery winning," "investment scheme"). Within the first three months of deployment, OCBC reported a 30% reduction in successful phishing-related losses and a 12% drop in false positive flagging compared to their legacy fraud filters (Straits Times, 2023).

Real-time Fraud Response Systems

In real-time financial environments, static analysis is no longer sufficient. LLMs integrated with stream processing frameworks (e.g., Apache Kafka, Flink) enable proactive fraud mitigation. These systems can: Analyze live transaction flows,-Generate contextual explanations for alerts and Trigger user-facing conversational agents to confirm transaction legitimacy.

For example, the Australian neobank Up integrated an LLM-based fraud triage engine that communicates with users via in-app chat. When anomalies are detected, the LLM initiates a clarification dialogue, reducing user friction and boosting resolution speed. The bank reported a 40% drop in fraud dispute durations and improved Net Promoter Scores in their quarterly performance review (Up Bank, 2022).

6.3 Financial Forecasting with LLMs

Market Sentiment Analysis

Financial sentiment analysis has long relied on natural language processing (NLP), but LLMs elevate this to a new level. By consuming a broader range of unstructured content—such as Reddit posts, financial blogs, analyst briefings, and even CEO interviews—LLMs can provide richer sentiment indices that serve as early indicators of market volatility or asset revaluation.

Deutsche Börse, the German stock exchange operator, implemented a GPT-style model to track sentiment around ESG (Environmental, Social, and Governance) topics across European financial news outlets. This model identified rising negative sentiment toward fossil fuel investments in Q2 2022, preceding a dip in sector ETF inflows by three weeks. Such foresight allowed asset managers using the tool to reallocate portfolios defensively ahead of the downturn (Deutsche Börse ESG Report, 2022).

Trend Prediction and Risk Assessment

In complex macroeconomic conditions, it is not enough to analyze past price action. LLMs can extract implications from textual sources like central bank minutes, geopolitical briefings, and compliance notices, converting them into predictive signals.

ABN AMRO Bank implemented a domain-adapted transformer model to monitor geopolitical news and regulatory changes, assessing their implications on commodities and cross-border transactions. The system flagged potential sanctions-related disruptions in lithium exports from Chile three weeks before pricing volatility spiked. Portfolio managers used this insight to hedge derivatives early, improving quarterly returns by an estimated 5.8% compared to the control group.

Moreover, the model generated synthetic scenarios (e.g., "what-if" analysis) based on escalating political rhetoric and past supply chain disruptions, enhancing internal scenario planning and risk modeling.

Financial Document Processing and Compliance

Annual reports, auditor memos, shareholder letters, and legal filings often contain buried insights. LLMs can read, summarize, and highlight inconsistencies or red flags in these documents with remarkable efficiency.

In 2023, a Canadian asset management firm deployed a fine-tuned LLaMA model to review quarterly disclosures from small-cap portfolio holdings. Within two reporting cycles, the model identified revenue-recognition discrepancies and abnormal footnote changes that human analysts missed. This led to a rebalancing of the portfolio, ultimately preserving $3.2 million in unrealized losses (Firm internal audit, 2023).

Strategic Value and Competitive Advantage

The transition from static, rules-based intelligence to LLM-enhanced cognition represents a seismic shift in how financial institutions perceive and manage data. It is no longer about retroactive auditing or reactive reporting; it is about anticipating patterns, orchestrating interventions, and reducing human bottlenecks in decision pipelines.

While technical challenges remain—such as data privacy, regulatory compliance, and model explainability—early adopters are already witnessing enhanced resilience, sharper risk insights, and improved profitability. As model interpretability improves and regulatory frameworks adapt, LLMs will become indispensable instruments across trading floors, compliance desks, and strategy war rooms.

Their message is clear: in finance, where context is king and timing is everything, LLMs are the new cognitive currency.

7. LLMS IN MARKETING: FROM PERSONALIZATION TO PERFORMANCE

Marketing is no longer a one-way broadcast. It's a continuous feedback loop, where every interaction is an opportunity to learn, respond, and optimize. Large Language Models (LLMs) are helping companies shift from static campaigns to adaptive experiences. Whether it's generating content, refining messages, or tailoring user experiences, LLMs are now central to how brands communicate at scale. Instead of broad targeting or general messaging, LLMs enable systems that adapt in real time—across formats, languages, and platforms.

This section explores how LLMs are transforming digital marketing, focusing on three core areas: content personalization, campaign copy generation and testing, and multilingual adaptation. A real-world case study from Ulta Beauty illustrates the operational and financial impact of these technologies when deployed in a coordinated system.

7.1 Dynamic Content Personalization

Customer expectations have shifted. Today's users want relevance not just in what is offered to them, but in how and when it's offered. LLMs make this possible by analyzing live behavioral signals—what a user clicks, searches, scrolls past, or engages with—and using that context to generate or recommend content on the fly. These systems don't just rely on static segments or demographic data. They operate on the session level, adapting continuously as users interact.

A retail site using an LLM might notice a user lingering on winter jackets, checking size availability, and revisiting product pages late at night. Rather than offering the same static banner to all users, the site could serve a real-time generated headline promoting limited-time winter deals, customized to the user's behavior and location. If that same user returns during the day, the message could shift to highlight in-store pickup options, using weather data to contextualize urgency.

Spotify offers a clear example of this in action. Its AI-powered personalized playlists, such as Discover Weekly, are dynamically generated based on each user's listening habits, sentiment analysis of lyrics, and similarities with other users. The results speak for themselves: over 40 percent of engagement on the platform comes directly from these personalized recommendations. It's not just the music that keeps users returning—it's the sense that the system knows what they want, even before they do.

This level of personalization leads to higher engagement and loyalty. A McKinsey study from 2021 found that nearly four out of five consumers are more likely to purchase or repurchase from brands that personalize their communications. LLMs are enabling this kind of one-to-one relevance at enterprise scale, without requiring manual intervention for every variation.

7.2 Campaign Copy Generation and A/B Testing

Marketing teams have always relied on testing to optimize messaging—but the bottleneck has traditionally been content creation itself. Writing variations, refining tone, and aligning across formats takes time. LLMs remove that friction by generating multiple, platform-specific versions of headlines, emails, CTAs, and social posts, all aligned with campaign goals and tone. Once deployed, these versions can be tested automatically, with the system learning which ones perform best and why.

The feedback loop is immediate. Instead of launching a single version and waiting weeks to iterate, marketers can deploy multiple variations simultaneously, tracking performance by metrics like open rate, click-through, sentiment, or conversion. As patterns emerge, the model can adapt its output, tweaking length, structure, or phrasing to emphasize high-performing traits. This creates a self-improving content engine where every test feeds the next generation of copy.

This isn't theoretical. Platforms like Jasper and OpenAI integrations with HubSpot now enable marketers to launch multichannel campaigns with auto-generated copy tailored for each environment—whether it's Instagram captions, search ads, or email blasts. The impact is both creative and operational. Campaign timelines shrink, messaging becomes more consistent, and performance improves over time as the system learns what resonates.

The uplift from AI-generated copy isn't marginal. A 2023 report by Phrasee showed that subject lines and ad copy created by LLMs outperformed human-written content by up to 17 percent in terms of engagement. The key driver is not just the volume of copy produced, but the relevance and rapid testing that LLMs make possible. Content stops being a one-time asset and becomes a living, testable component of the campaign architecture.

7.3 Multilingual Content Adaptation

Global reach requires more than just translation—it requires cultural fluency. LLMs enable this by adapting content not just to different languages, but to local tone, references, and expectations. Traditional translation workflows often miss this nuance, resulting in content that feels generic or mismatched. LLMs trained on multilingual and region-specific data can preserve intent while shifting phrasing, tone, and style for different markets.

A campaign that works in English-speaking North America may not land the same way in France or Brazil. With LLMs, marketers can create variants that reflect local idioms, product relevance, and user context—without rewriting every asset manually. Product descriptions, in-app prompts, and even support messaging can be generated to sound natural and native, not just technically accurate.

This approach has real impact on engagement. Shopify reported in 2023 that merchants using AI-based multilingual tools saw significantly higher engagement in non-English-speaking markets—21 percent higher, in fact—compared to those relying on standard translation alone. The difference comes from how content feels, not just what it says. When users see that a brand has taken the time to communicate in their language and style, they're more likely to trust and buy.

Duolingo takes this a step further. The language-learning platform uses its own LLMs to adapt motivational messages for users based on region. A French learner in Canada may receive different tone and encouragement than one in Paris, even if they're on the same lesson. This subtle adjustment builds a stronger emotional connection between user and product—something that static systems can't replicate.

7.4 Case Study: Ulta Beauty's AI-Driven Personalization Engine

Ulta Beauty faced a challenge familiar to many retail brands: how to compete on experience, not just price or product range. With growing competition and customer expectations rising, Ulta needed a way to tailor promotions, recommendations, and communications to individual preferences—without scaling headcount or slowing campaigns.

In 2023, Ulta deployed an LLM-powered personalization engine that synthesized data from across its ecosystem: purchase history, browsing behavior, loyalty program activity, in-store interactions, and even time-of-day usage patterns. From this, it built real-time beauty profiles for each customer, which guided both digital and in-store touchpoints.

Emails were no longer batch-sent based on static segments. Instead, each customer received messages reflecting their habits, budget, and preferred product categories. Online shoppers looking at skincare products were invited to try samples tailored to their profile during in-store visits. Promotions became dynamic, varying in real time depending on product interest, inventory, and customer location.

The results validated the investment. Loyalty program engagement rose by 28 percent. Average order value increased by 16 percent. Campaign development cycles shortened by 40 percent, allowing faster responses to seasonal trends and competitor moves. Just as critically, Ulta achieved tighter online-offline integration, creating a unified brand experience that felt consistent across channels.

What made this successful wasn't just the LLM's ability to generate content—it was its ability to interpret intent and adapt. Each interaction fed the system, which then adjusted the next interaction. Over time, the marketing engine became more precise, more relevant, and more valuable to both the business and its customers.

7.5 From Personalization to Predictive Performance

The marketing landscape is moving toward continuous optimization. Campaigns are no longer static launches—they're live systems, adapting in real time based on user behavior and feedback. LLMs are the core enabler of this shift. They don't just generate content; they interpret signals, learn from outcomes, and evolve the messaging strategy over time.

This fundamentally changes the marketer's role. Rather than spending time manually crafting every message, teams can now focus on setting direction, defining brand tone, and analyzing strategy. The system handles the execution and testing, surfacing what works and why. Creativity isn't replaced—it's amplified and made faster.

As more customer interactions happen across digital platforms, the speed and relevance of those touchpoints will define brand performance. LLMs are making it possible for marketers to move from mass communication to individualized engagement, at scale and in real time. The brands that succeed won't just talk to customers. They'll adapt, learn, and respond—with precision, at the pace of the customer.

8. SCALING OPERATIONAL INTELLIGENCE WITH LLMS

8.1 Predictive Operations with Real-Time Intelligence

The integration of LLMs into operations is redefining how enterprises predict and respond to disruptions. Rather than reacting to alerts after thresholds are crossed, organizations are now forecasting operational risks by correlating structured and unstructured data in real time. A 2023 McKinsey study found that predictive maintenance powered by AI reduced maintenance costs by 25%, cut downtime by 35%, and extended equipment life by 20%. The advantage of LLMs in this domain lies in their ability to interpret human-authored inputs such as operator shift notes, historical fault descriptions, and incomplete logs, enabling a richer form of predictive modeling.

For example, repeated mentions of minor but persistent vibrations across shift logs—something a rules-based system might ignore—can be flagged by an LLM as an early indicator of potential motor degradation. By cross-referencing this linguistic signal with telemetry data, the system can recommend preemptive servicing before mechanical failure occurs. This form of cross-modal reasoning, bridging natural language and sensor data, enables a fundamentally smarter maintenance strategy.

8.2 Natural Language Interfaces for Operational Coordination

Operational interfaces are often cluttered with dashboards, forms, and rigid workflows. Operators and supervisors are expected to navigate multiple systems—manufacturing execution systems (MES), enterprise resource planning (ERP), and SCADA platforms—each with unique syntax and structure. LLMs offer a more intuitive layer by allowing users to interact with these systems through natural language queries.

Instead of constructing complex queries or toggling across screens, a floor manager can simply ask, "Which production lines underperformed yesterday and why?" or "Generate the compliance summary for the past 48 hours." The model interprets the request, pulls relevant data, and delivers a coherent response—often complete with contextual reasoning. This simplification has measurable benefits. In 2022, Siemens implemented GPT-based assistants in their operator dashboards and observed a 60% reduction in time spent generating reports and a 35% decrease in documentation errors, particularly in facilities operating across multiple languages and time zones.

The natural language interface transforms the LLM from a backend processor into a front-line collaborator, giving operators real-time access to insights without requiring technical fluency.

8.3 Human-in-the-Loop Decision Assurance

While LLMs enhance speed and insight, high-stakes industries require human oversight to ensure operational accountability. Most real-world deployments incorporate a human-in-the-loop (HITL) framework where LLMs generate recommendations, summaries, or documents, but final validation remains with trained personnel. This hybrid model is especially important in regulated environments such as pharmaceuticals, energy, and aerospace, where deviations can have legal or safety implications.

For instance, in modern manufacturing plants, LLMs may draft standard operating procedures based on recent changes in workflow, but floor supervisors are responsible for final review and approval. In logistics, an LLM might prepare customs clearance forms using shipment metadata, yet human agents validate the contents before submission. This approach maintains traceability and ensures that AI-driven operations meet compliance standards without compromising efficiency.

According to a 2023 Deloitte global AI adoption report, enterprises that deployed LLMs within a HITL model experienced a 40% reduction in documentation labor hours while preserving or improving their quality assurance metrics. These results demonstrate that strategic human-AI collaboration can achieve both operational efficiency and compliance integrity.

8.4 Case Study: Maersk's LLM-Augmented Control Towers (2022–2024)

Between 2022 and 2024, Maersk, the global shipping and logistics leader, faced mounting operational pressures including port congestion, post-COVID supply chain volatility, and labor shortages. Existing analytics tools could flag problems only after they occurred. In response, Maersk partnered with Microsoft and OpenAI to embed a custom GPT-4 model into its global control tower systems.

The model was integrated across more than 200 live data feeds including ship location data, port authority schedules, ERP logistics information, and global weather forecasts. This allowed operations managers to pose complex natural language questions such as "Which containers scheduled to arrive in Rotterdam this week are at risk of delay?" The LLM would synthesize vessel speed, historical port congestion, and expected weather disruptions to provide risk-ranked predictions along with recommended actions.

The system also generated shift handover reports, optimized workforce allocation based on workload forecasting, and provided early warnings for documentation bottlenecks. Over an 18-month period, Maersk reported a 21% increase in port throughput, a 30% reduction in the time required to generate operational documents, and an 18% decrease in exception handling labor hours. The company achieved full return on investment within nine months of deployment. This initiative demonstrated how cross-system LLM integration could shift the role of AI from support tool to strategic decision co-pilot. By extending reasoning across previously siloed systems, Maersk was able to achieve measurable performance gains under highly dynamic conditions (source).

8.5 Dynamic Resource Orchestration

As LLM capabilities evolve, enterprises are moving beyond static use cases toward dynamic resource orchestration. This involves real-time reconfiguration of operational workflows based on shifting conditions—such as demand spikes, inventory fluctuations, or equipment failures. LLMs enable these adjustments not only by analyzing patterns but by generating actionable plans on the fly.

In advanced manufacturing environments, LLMs can now reassign tasks across assembly lines in response to upstream material delays, suggest alternate process routes, and even adjust labor schedules. Similarly, in logistics, LLMs are being tested to reprioritize last-mile delivery routes dynamically based on traffic, package urgency, and vehicle capacity. Amazon has begun piloting such systems in its regional distribution hubs, where LLMs automatically reorder task queues for pick-and-pack workers based on changing order volumes.

These emerging use cases indicate a shift from passive data interpretation to active operational control. LLMs are becoming orchestration agents—adjusting not only what happens but also when and how, in order to maintain optimal throughput under pressure.

9. CHALLENGES AND FUTURE TRENDS IN LLM-DRIVEN OPERATIONS

9.1 Technical Limitations and Mitigation Strategies

Despite their rapid proliferation across industries, large language models remain constrained by several core technical limitations that restrict their reliability and scalability in high-stakes operational settings. One of the most fundamental issues is their dependency on massive computational resources. Training and fine-tuning models like GPT-4 require infrastructure investments that only a handful of organizations can afford. Even inference, particularly in latency-sensitive industrial environments, demands optimization to avoid performance bottlenecks.

Hallucination—the generation of false or misleading outputs that appear confidently correct—is another persistent limitation. In operations, where precision is paramount, this risk is amplified. A 2023 Stanford study found that 18–23% of factual queries posed to LLMs yielded hallucinated responses under standard configurations. Enterprises are responding with mitigation strategies such as response verifiability checks, constraint-aware decoding, and increasingly, the integration of retrieval-augmented generation (RAG) pipelines. RAG models anchor responses in domain-specific knowledge bases, ensuring that generated content reflects accurate and up-to-date information.

Knowledge cutoff is an inherent architectural limitation. As of early 2024, most production LLMs still struggle to incorporate real-time or post-training events unless explicitly connected to dynamic databases. This restricts their utility in environments where up-to-the-minute awareness is essential, such as logistics, energy, and emergency operations. For example, a model trained in early 2023 cannot account for geopolitical shifts affecting global supply chains unless augmented through retrieval layers or streaming APIs.

Finally, the context window—while steadily expanding—remains finite. While OpenAI's GPT-4 Turbo supports up to 128k tokens, most deployments use trimmed-down versions that operate within 4k–16k token limits. This makes it challenging to capture the full complexity of operational records, shift reports, and system logs without truncation or loss of nuance.

9.2 Retrieval-Augmented Generation (RAG) and External Memory

One of the most promising solutions to these constraints is the adoption of retrieval-augmented generation. RAG architecture allows an LLM to consult external sources of truth—structured databases, vector stores, document repositories—before generating a response. This not only mitigates hallucinations but also extends the model's effective knowledge base far beyond its training cutoff.

In the context of operations, RAG-enabled systems can ground outputs in current production metrics, recent incident reports, or even regulatory updates. For instance, instead of hallucinating an SOP update, a RAG model can pull the latest policy document from a validated knowledge base and summarize the key changes. Companies like Cohere and OpenAI are actively building RAG toolchains that can be deployed in enterprise contexts with minimal latency overhead.

A 2023 benchmark by Meta AI showed that retrieval-augmented LLMs reduced hallucination rates by 65% compared to base models while improving response accuracy on real-world operational queries by 40%. This architecture is becoming foundational for next-generation industrial copilots.

9.3 Scaling LLMs Sustainably

The operational cost of LLMs is not limited to compute—it extends to environmental impact and scalability. A single GPT-3 training cycle consumed approximately 1,287 MWh of electricity and produced 552 metric tons of carbon emissions, according to research by Hugging Face and the University of Massachusetts Amherst. This has led to increasing pressure to make LLMs greener and more efficient, especially as adoption scales across sectors.

In response, organizations are exploring quantization, distillation, and sparsity techniques that shrink model footprints without significantly compromising performance. Open-source models like Mistral and LLaMA 2 are gaining traction for on-premise and edge deployment due to their lighter architectures and transparency. In industrial operations, where reliability and explainability are critical, these smaller models often outperform larger black-box systems.

Moreover, federated learning and edge inference are emerging as viable pathways for deploying LLMs closer to the point of data generation, reducing latency and data transfer costs. In environments like oil rigs or remote manufacturing sites, this architectural shift is critical for real-time decision-making.

9.4 Case Study: Shell's AI-Integrated Operations Platform (2022–2024)

Since 2022, Shell has been integrating LLMs into its global operational intelligence systems to support safety, logistics, and maintenance in both upstream and downstream operations. The initiative began with a pilot in the North Sea, where offshore engineers faced information overload due to disparate log systems and inconsistent shift reports.

Using a combination of GPT-4 and a proprietary retrieval layer trained on Shell's internal safety protocols, maintenance records, and IoT telemetry, Shell developed a smart assistant embedded directly into operator dashboards. Engineers could ask questions like "What's the most common cause of pressure loss in valve series X over the last six months?" or "Summarize maintenance issues flagged in the last two shifts."

The model would access and summarize years of incident reports, filter results by location and equipment type, and surface both technical insights and human-authored context from past logs. Unlike traditional analytics tools, the assistant responded in seconds and included citations to its sources for validation.

After 18 months, Shell reported a 34% reduction in time spent preparing shift handovers, a 27% drop in incident response time, and an 80% adoption rate among frontline engineers. The success led to the assistant's expansion to refineries in the Netherlands, Singapore, and Texas, with plans underway to integrate real-time feed from process control systems for predictive support.

This deployment exemplifies how LLMs, when combined with retrieval architectures and domain-specific tuning, can overcome their traditional limitations and deliver high-impact, low-latency decision support in complex environments.

9.5 Emerging Trends and the Road Ahead

The next frontier of LLMs in operations is defined by adaptability, interpretability, and autonomy. As models evolve to support longer context windows, better factuality mechanisms, and integration with real-time control systems, they will increasingly move from support roles to semi-autonomous decision makers.

We are already seeing prototypes of **multi-agent systems**—networks of smaller LLMs that specialize in distinct operational tasks and collaborate to solve complex problems. These agents simulate human task delegation, improve fault isolation, and allow for modular retraining.

There is also growing interest in **LLM observability**—the ability to trace, debug, and audit model outputs in mission-critical systems. Tools like TruLens and LangSmith are gaining adoption for offering structured feedback, output tracing, and model monitoring, which are essential for building trust and accountability into AI-powered operations.

Regulatory frameworks are also catching up. The EU's AI Act and the U.S. Executive Order on Safe, Secure, and Trustworthy AI (2023) both emphasize transparency, risk management, and human oversight, especially in sectors like manufacturing, transportation, and energy. LLM-driven systems will need to be auditable and aligned with these emerging standards to achieve long-term viability.

Ultimately, the future of LLMs in operations lies not in replacing human expertise, but in amplifying it—offloading cognitive load, reducing time-to-decision, and enabling a more resilient, responsive, and adaptive enterprise.

10. ENTERPRISE DEPLOYMENT OF LARGE LANGUAGE MODELS

The deployment of large language models (LLMs) across enterprises marks a turning point in the way organizations operationalize intelligence and automate knowledge work. Unlike narrow AI systems designed for specific tasks, LLMs bring the promise of general-purpose reasoning and content generation, adaptable to a range of business functions. Yet realizing this potential at scale is a complex endeavor. It involves not only integrating advanced technologies, but also transforming organizational culture, redefining workflows, and aligning stakeholders around new forms of human-machine collaboration. This section explores the foundational elements required for successful enterprise-level deployment of LLMs, from change management and user adoption to measuring return on investment. A post-2021 case study further illustrates how a global firm transformed its operations through strategic LLM integration.

10.1 Strategic Foundations: Change Management and Cultural Shift

Deploying large language models in enterprise settings is as much a sociotechnical challenge as it is a technological one. Early adoption efforts that neglect the human dimension often falter, regardless of model sophistication. LLMs tend to unsettle established norms by redistributing access to knowledge and automating cognitive tasks traditionally performed by specialists. Without a coherent change management strategy, these shifts can be misinterpreted as threats to job security or domain authority.

Organizations that navigate this transition successfully tend to articulate a clear narrative of augmentation rather than replacement. Employees are positioned as critical overseers in human-in-the-loop systems, reinforcing their value while easing concerns about automation. Leadership visibility, transparent communications, and the involvement of cross-functional stakeholders in pilot phases further foster buy-in. According to McKinsey's 2023 report, 44% of enterprises that failed to scale LLM initiatives cited lack of alignment between technical and business stakeholders—a gap that can be mitigated by framing AI as a collaborative partner rather than a disruptor.

10.2 User Adoption and Capability Building

User adoption hinges on usability, relevance, and trust. Simply offering access to LLM-powered tools does not ensure they will be used effectively or widely. Employees must perceive immediate and recurring value, and the system must deliver reliably on that promise. To encourage meaningful engagement, many enterprises are embedding LLMs into existing workflows, such as CRM platforms, service desks, or compliance dashboards, rather than launching standalone tools.

Organizations like Salesforce have embraced a tiered enablement strategy during their rollout of Einstein GPT. Users were segmented by role—general staff, prompt engineers, and data stewards—and trained according to their specific needs and responsibilities. This ensured that non-technical employees were not overwhelmed, while more advanced users received deeper guidance. IBM followed a similar model, using hackathons to accelerate experimentation and generate department-specific use cases. Within months, the firm had cultivated hundreds of internal LLM champions across functions, each tailoring the tools to their team's unique needs.

10.3 Training, Education, and Prompt Literacy

While traditional enterprise software rollouts often focus on platform navigation and compliance, deploying LLMs requires an additional skillset: prompt literacy. This encompasses the ability to craft precise queries, interpret nuanced responses, and iterate effectively to refine output quality. Poorly designed prompts can result in irrelevant answers or hallucinated content—outcomes that undermine trust and slow adoption.

Recognizing this, leading enterprises have formalized training programs to develop prompt fluency. Deloitte's 2023 generative AI study found that organizations offering structured onboarding and prompt design workshops reported up to 38% greater productivity improvements than those that relied on informal, peer-driven learning. Some firms, such as PwC, have created internal prompt libraries tailored to high-frequency business tasks, from legal contract summarization to regulatory reporting. These serve as both productivity accelerators and quality controls, enabling users to leverage proven formats that reduce variability in LLM responses.

10.4 ROI Measurement and Scaling Metrics

Quantifying the business value of LLM deployment is essential not only for justifying investment, but also for refining future rollouts. Traditional IT metrics such as uptime or API calls are insufficient to capture the multidimensional impact of generative AI. Instead, enterprises are tracking operational efficiencies, qualitative improvements in decision-making, and the displacement of legacy tooling.

Efficiency gains tend to manifest early. For example, faster document drafting, automated summarization, and improved search reduce the burden on human analysts. Over time, higher-order value becomes measurable, such as reduced error rates in compliance reports or increased customer satisfaction due to faster, more accurate responses. Gartner notes that successful firms also track "cost avoidance"—savings generated by replacing external vendors or consultants with internal LLM solutions. Firms that embed ROI tracking into their initial deployment plans, define benchmarks by department, and revisit metrics quarterly are better positioned to make data-informed decisions about scaling.

10.5 Case Study: Pfizer's LLM Integration for Research Acceleration and Clinical Trial Design (2023–2024)

In early 2023, Pfizer launched a strategic initiative to integrate large language models into its research and development operations, aiming to tackle one of the industry's most pressing challenges: the slow and resource-intensive process of drug development. The company's existing knowledge systems—spanning molecular data, clinical trial reports, regulatory filings, and scientific publications—were expansive but poorly integrated, creating bottlenecks in research synthesis and decision-making.

Working with NVIDIA and OpenAI through a secure, hybrid-cloud deployment, Pfizer developed a custom GPT-4-based solution trained on both public biomedical corpora and its proprietary datasets. The system was fine-tuned to perform high-level reasoning tasks such as summarizing clinical trial outcomes, generating hypotheses based on target-disease relationships, and assessing the regulatory history of similar drug classes. Importantly, it was designed to surface not just answers, but also supporting data, literature references, and risk qualifiers—critical for scientific scrutiny.

One of the standout features of Pfizer's implementation was its use of long-context retrieval to support clinical trial design. Teams could prompt the system with questions like, "What were the most common protocol deviations in oncology trials involving immunotherapy over the last five years?" and receive synthesized, source-linked insights within seconds. The AI also flagged region-specific regulatory constraints, allowing for more efficient protocol tailoring across geographies.

The pilot began within the oncology and rare disease divisions. After three months, research teams reported a 40% reduction in the time required to compile trial briefs, and proposal cycles were accelerated by two to three weeks on average. Researchers found the assistant especially valuable for uncovering overlooked precedent studies and for surfacing molecular similarities that informed biomarker selection. Notably, Pfizer enforced strict human-in-the-loop governance, with all outputs reviewed by scientific leads and regulatory officers before integration into any official workflows.

By early 2024, Pfizer had extended the system to its global R&D operations and announced plans to integrate it into pharmacovigilance, labeling, and post-market surveillance workflows. The LLM assistant is not only speeding up research timelines but is also helping standardize scientific rigor across teams and regions.

Pfizer's deployment reflects a growing shift in pharmaceutical AI—from automation of repetitive tasks to cognitive augmentation of expert knowledge. It underscores how domain-specific tuning, rigorous oversight, and intelligent retrieval integration can make LLMs a transformative force even in tightly regulated, high-stakes environments.

11. ETHICAL AI AND THE FUTURE OF WORK

As organizations rush to embed large language models (LLMs) into their systems and workflows, ethical considerations and workforce implications have become central to long-term success. The promise of AI-driven efficiency must be balanced with fairness, transparency, and accountability. This dual focus—on ethical governance and the evolving nature of work—demands thoughtful planning, interdisciplinary oversight, and ongoing refinement. Rather than being afterthoughts, ethical design and workforce strategy must be foundational pillars in LLM deployment. This section explores how forward-looking organizations are confronting bias, building governance frameworks, and reimagining work in the age of generative AI. The case study that follows illustrates how a global consulting firm approached both fairness and future-of-work challenges through a deliberate, scalable strategy.

11.1 Tackling Algorithmic Bias in Enterprise AI

Bias in AI is not hypothetical—it is a measurable, recurring issue with real-world consequences. In LLMs, bias can arise from skewed training data, incomplete representation of minority perspectives, or reinforcement of harmful stereotypes. For enterprises, these biases are more than technical flaws; they can damage reputation, affect compliance, and create systemic inequities.

Leading organizations now treat bias detection as a continuous process rather than a one-time filter. Methods like differential testing, counterfactual data augmentation, and saliency analysis are being used to flag disparities in output across demographic groups. IBM, for instance, uses its AI Fairness 360 toolkit to assess models across metrics like disparate impact and statistical parity difference. These methods provide quantitative signals that guide remediation.

Bias mitigation strategies include reweighting training data, fine-tuning on curated corpora, and applying rule-based constraints during generation. Yet beyond technical fixes, enterprises are embedding fairness in governance through model cards, algorithmic audits, and third-party review boards. In Europe, frameworks like the EU AI Act are forcing organizations to document how models are trained, validated, and monitored for bias. This is shifting ethical AI from aspiration to obligation.

11.2 Governance Frameworks and Regulatory Readiness

Enterprise AI governance has evolved from vague principles to operational playbooks. Models as complex as GPT-4 demand clear lines of accountability and structured oversight. Effective governance frameworks include risk classification systems, model documentation standards, escalation protocols, and regulatory mapping.

In regulated sectors—such as healthcare, finance, and law—LLM use must comply with laws like GDPR, HIPAA, and the Fair Credit Reporting Act. This necessitates clear explainability for decisions influenced by AI, particularly when outputs affect individuals' rights or access. Techniques such as retrieval-augmented generation (RAG) and explainable AI (XAI) are being used to ensure auditability and transparency.

To stay ahead, firms are investing in dedicated AI ethics teams. Microsoft, for example, has a Responsible AI Council that reviews high-impact deployments, while Meta's governance includes embedded ethicists and red-teaming protocols. The key lesson: governance must scale with the complexity and scope of AI systems. Without it, risks compound and public trust erodes.

11.3 Reframing the Future of Work: From Displacement to Transformation

The narrative of AI-induced job loss dominates headlines, but the more nuanced truth lies in transformation. LLMs are not replacing workers wholesale—they are reshaping roles, accelerating tasks, and creating new opportunities for value creation. A 2023 report by the World Economic Forum estimates that while 83 million jobs may be displaced globally by automation by 2027, 69 million new roles are expected to emerge in fields like AI operations, ethics, and prompt engineering.

In practical terms, many roles are evolving rather than disappearing. Financial analysts now use LLMs to synthesize reports; customer service agents rely on AI co-pilots to resolve queries faster. This augmentation boosts productivity while freeing up human capacity for judgment-intensive tasks. Organizations are responding by reskilling workers for hybrid roles, where AI fluency complements domain expertise.

Crucially, the success of this transformation depends on employee trust. If workers perceive AI as a black box designed to replace them, resistance grows. But if they are involved in shaping use cases, training models, and governing output, they become co-creators of the future of work. This mindset shift requires clear communication, incentives for experimentation, and a culture that rewards adaptation.

11.4 New Skills and Education Models

Prompt literacy, AI ethics, and cross-disciplinary problem solving are emerging as core skills in the AI-augmented workforce. Universities are beginning to update curricula to reflect these needs, but enterprises cannot wait. Internal upskilling is now a strategic imperative.

Firms like Accenture and PwC have launched internal academies focused on generative AI, offering modules on prompt engineering, model interpretability, and compliance. These programs are modular and role-specific, ensuring that legal, marketing, and product teams all receive tailored instruction. According to Accenture, over 250,000 employees completed GenAI certification programs in 2023 alone.

Cross-functional fluency is another priority. The most valuable employees are those who can bridge technical and business domains—translating model output into actionable insights, while flagging risks that may escape algorithmic scrutiny. This skillset cannot be outsourced or automated; it must be cultivated through mentorship, projects, and rotational programs.

11.5 Case Study: PwC's Responsible AI and Workforce Transition Initiative (2022–2024)

In 2022, PwC launched an ambitious initiative to integrate responsible AI across all levels of its organization. The project had dual goals: embed fairness and governance into all generative AI deployments and prepare its global workforce for the future of hybrid work. This dual-track approach positioned ethics and workforce transformation not as separate issues but as mutually reinforcing imperatives.

On the governance side, PwC established a Responsible AI Office composed of ethicists, legal experts, data scientists, and client-facing consultants. Every new LLM use case—whether internal or client-facing—underwent a multi-phase risk assessment, including bias audits, data lineage checks, and stakeholder impact evaluations. The firm also mandated model documentation and usage logging for all generative tools, ensuring traceability and regulatory alignment across jurisdictions.

Simultaneously, PwC launched an enterprise-wide AI fluency program. Employees from 152 countries were enrolled in role-based learning tracks. The curriculum covered prompt design, interpretability, data privacy, and change leadership. Over 100,000 employees were trained by early 2024, with 68% of them integrating AI tools into their workflows within the first quarter post-training. The firm created internal "AI Champions" across departments to help tailor tools to specific business needs and encourage peer-driven adoption.

The results were measurable. Time spent on client proposals dropped by 40% as LLMs were used to draft initial content. Internal audits of AI outputs showed a 92% compliance rate with fairness and bias standards. Moreover, employee satisfaction scores related to digital transformation efforts rose 23%, driven by increased confidence in the tools and trust in the governance framework.

PwC's initiative demonstrates that ethical AI and workforce transition are not trade-offs but complements. By aligning fairness with empowerment, and governance with education, the firm created a replicable model for responsible LLM deployment at scale.

12. EMERGING TRENDS IN LLM TECHNOLOGY

As businesses increasingly embed large language models into their operations, the technology itself is undergoing a rapid transformation. The new wave of LLM development is not merely focused on scaling size but on refining utility, agility, and specialization. Innovations such as multimodal interfaces, autonomous agents, compact models, and advanced context handling are redefining what's possible in enterprise AI. These shifts are pushing LLMs beyond static text generation into dynamic, real-world problem solving across industries. In this section, we examine the key technological trends shaping the future of LLMs and their business implications, illustrated through a real-world case study of a cutting-edge deployment.

12.1 From Text-Only to Multimodal Intelligence

Early LLMs like GPT-2 and GPT-3 were text-focused systems, but the frontier has decisively moved toward multimodality. Modern systems, such as OpenAI's GPT-4 and Google's Gemini, can interpret and generate not only text but also images, audio, and video. This fusion allows LLMs to perform complex cross-modal reasoning—reading a chart, summarizing a video transcript, or generating code from a diagram.

Multimodal capabilities are particularly impactful in industries like retail and healthcare. A fashion brand might use an LLM to analyze customer-uploaded photos and suggest personalized outfits, while a hospital can process radiology images alongside patient notes for faster diagnosis. In 2023, Google DeepMind demonstrated a multimodal system that outperformed radiologists in identifying over 300 diseases from X-rays, with explainable rationale provided in natural language.

These capabilities allow for richer user interactions and lower cognitive load, bringing the power of LLMs closer to human communication norms. They also demand better infrastructure, as handling multiple data types requires robust integration across APIs, sensors, and enterprise knowledge graphs.

12.2 The Rise of Autonomous Agentic Systems

Another major shift is the emergence of agent-based LLMs—models that not only respond but act. Agentic systems use LLMs as reasoning engines that plan, execute, and adapt actions based on goals. Tools like AutoGPT, LangChain, and ReAct frameworks allow LLMs to autonomously navigate software interfaces, write code, perform research, or manage workflows with minimal human intervention.

These systems are already showing potential in operations-heavy industries. For instance, logistics firms use LLM agents to reoptimize delivery schedules based on live traffic data, while financial firms deploy them for portfolio rebalancing triggered by market events. A key benefit is persistence—agents can carry context over extended tasks, unlike traditional one-shot queries.

However, agentic systems also raise new governance challenges. Businesses must monitor autonomy levels, establish fail-safes, and ensure interpretability of decisions. As the technology matures, we can expect hybrid models combining human-in-the-loop oversight with high-frequency LLM-driven decision-making.

12.3 Efficiency over Scale: The Shift Toward Compact Models

The era of ever-larger LLMs is giving way to a new priority: efficiency. While early breakthroughs were driven by parameter scaling, recent research has focused on distilling smaller models that offer competitive performance with a fraction of the compute and memory footprint. Meta's LLaMA 2, Mistral's 7B model, and Microsoft's Phi-2 are examples of this trend—models under 15 billion parameters that outperform older 100B+ models on several benchmarks.

For enterprises, this trend has two big implications. First, smaller models can be fine-tuned in-house using proprietary data, enabling customization without needing enormous budgets. Second, they unlock on-device or edge deployment, which is crucial for industries where latency, privacy, or offline availability are critical—such as finance, defense, or manufacturing.

By 2024, according to Hugging Face, over 60% of enterprise fine-tuning projects used models with fewer than 20 billion parameters. This democratization of AI access is accelerating innovation among mid-sized firms and allowing broader participation in the LLM economy.

12.4 Domain-Specific and Cross-Lingual Pretraining

General-purpose LLMs are increasingly being supplemented by domain-specific variants pre-trained on specialized corpora—legal, scientific, medical, or financial texts. For example, BloombergGPT, released in 2023, was trained on over 700 billion tokens of financial data and outperformed GPT-3.5 on multiple finance-specific tasks.

This trend is solving one of the core challenges in enterprise AI: contextual relevance. A general model might hallucinate when asked for details about SEC filings or medical billing codes, but a specialized model trained on that domain shows significantly higher accuracy and explainability. It also aligns better with legal and regulatory needs.

Cross-lingual models are also evolving rapidly. With innovations in multilingual embedding and aligned token spaces, models can now transfer knowledge across languages without parallel data. This has transformative implications for global firms operating in non-English-speaking markets, enabling consistent customer service, legal review, and compliance monitoring in over 50 languages using a single model instance.

12.5 Longer Context and Memory Management

Traditional LLMs have limited context windows—typically up to 4,000 tokens—which restrict their ability to consider entire documents or long conversations. This limitation is being overcome with architecture updates such as transformers with recurrence, attention sparsity, and memory-augmented layers. OpenAI's GPT-4 Turbo now supports a 128K-token window, while Claude 2.1 from Anthropic allows for 200K-token inputs.

This extended context enables use cases such as full contract analysis, multi-session customer support, and academic research review without truncation. Enterprises are also exploring vector databases and retrieval-augmented generation (RAG) frameworks to simulate infinite memory. In 2023, Slack integrated a RAG-based assistant that could summarize entire thread histories and linked documents in real time, significantly improving user productivity.

As long-context LLMs become standard, businesses can finally unify fragmented knowledge across emails, documents, tickets, and codebases—turning static archives into living intelligence.

Case Study: IKEA's Deployment of LLM Agents for Supply Chain Coordination (2023–2024)

In 2023, IKEA initiated a major upgrade to its global logistics operation by deploying a suite of agent-based systems powered by GPT-4 Turbo. Faced with growing complexity in its supply chain—spanning over 460 stores across 60 markets—IKEA needed a solution that could adapt in real time to disruptions such as supplier delays, shifting demand patterns, and regional compliance changes. Traditional planning tools lacked the agility to keep pace.

IKEA's digital team collaborated with OpenAI and Azure to embed domain-specific language model agents into their ERP and logistics platforms. These agents, each trained on a particular function such as demand forecasting, customs documentation, or stock reallocation, communicated autonomously to resolve logistical issues without human intervention. For example, if a delay was detected in a shipment bound for Germany, the system could reroute goods through Poland, trigger updated customs forms, and notify relevant departments—all within minutes.

A core feature of IKEA's architecture was the use of long-context capabilities and retrieval-augmented generation. This allowed agents to draw on months of transaction history, supplier records, and real-time inventory snapshots to make coordinated decisions across regions. Instead of working in isolation, the agents formed a network—learning from operational data while keeping human supervisors in the loop through explainable outputs.

In the first six months, IKEA reported measurable impact: a reduction in freight costs, fewer stockouts, and a sharp decline in exceptions requiring manual resolution. The approach also scaled well across regions with different infrastructure constraints, using smaller models locally that still interfaced with the central system.

By early 2024, IKEA had extended the deployment globally and began positioning the agent framework as a blueprint for responsive, AI-integrated retail logistics. The success underscored how agent-based LLM systems, when tightly integrated with operational platforms and real-time data, can deliver not just automation but strategic adaptability at scale.

13. CONCLUSION

The integration of large language models (LLMs) into enterprise systems marks a pivotal shift in how organizations create value, make decisions, and interact with information. What began as experimentation with generative AI has matured into strategic deployment across operations, customer service, compliance, and knowledge management. The most successful use cases have emerged not from technical novelty alone but from thoughtful alignment with business objectives, integration with legacy infrastructure, and user-centric design. As companies progress from pilot projects to scaled implementations, emphasis must shift to change management, cross-functional collaboration, and continuous monitoring of impact. LLMs are most powerful not in isolation but when embedded into the day-to-day workflows of teams and paired with domain-specific data.

Looking ahead, LLMs will become more efficient, context-aware, and capable of multimodal and autonomous behavior. This opens new frontiers—but also raises the bar for ethical deployment and governance. Enterprises must proactively address bias, hallucination, data privacy, and regulatory compliance, treating AI safety as core infrastructure rather than an afterthought. Strategic leadership will require not only technical readiness but cultural and organizational maturity. Businesses that invest in responsible AI, empower interdisciplinary teams, and design systems for transparency and adaptability will be best positioned to thrive in this new era. The long-term vision is not automation for its own sake, but augmented intelligence—where human expertise and machine capability combine to drive resilient, ethical, and scalable innovation.

Review Questions

- Describe regulatory measures do you believe are necessary to ensure the responsible use of AI technologies in commercial context?
- Evaluate tactics or techniques you believe are essential for firms looking to maximize the benefits of AI adoption while minimizing associated risks?
- Understand how is it that AI addresses the difficulties faced by the banking industry?

REFERENCES

Devlin., ... (2018) *BERT: Pre-training of Deep Bidirectional Transformers for Language Understanding*. arXiv, 24 May 2019, arXiv:1810.04805v2 [cs.CL]

Fedus, W., Zoph, B., & Shazeer, N. (2021). Switch Transformers: Scaling to Trillion Parameter Models with Simple and Efficient Sparsity. arXiv preprint arXiv:2101.03961.

Lewis, P., Perez, E., Piktus, A., Petroni, F., Karpukhin, V., Goyal, N., Küttler, H., Lewis, M., Yih, W., Rocktäschel, T., Riedel, S., & Kiela, D. (2020). Retrieval-Augmented Generation for Knowledge-Intensive NLP Tasks. arXiv preprint arXiv:2005.11401.

McKinsey & Company. (2023, June 14). *The economic potential of generative AI: The next productivity frontier*. https://www.mckinsey.com/capabilities/quantumblack/our-insights/the-economic-potential-of-generative-ai-the-next-productivity-frontier

Mikolov, T., Chen, K., Corrado, G., & Dean, J. (2013). Efficient Estimation of Word Representations in Vector Space. arXiv preprint arXiv:1301.3781.

Pennington, J., Socher, R., & Manning, C. (2014). Glove: Global Vectors for Word Representation. *EMNLP*, *14*, 1532–1543. DOI: 10.3115/v1/D14-1162

Radford, A., Narasimhan, K., Salimans, T., & Sutskever, I. (2018). Improving language understanding by generative pre-training.

Shazeer, N., Mirhoseini, A., Maziarz, K., Davis, A., Le, Q., Hinton, G., & Dean, J. (2017). Outrageously Large Neural Networks: The Sparsely-Gated Mixture-of-Experts Layer. arXiv preprint arXiv:1701.06538.

Vaswani, A., Shazeer, N., Parmar, N., Uszkoreit, J., Jones, L., Gomez, A. N., Kaiser, L., & Polosukhin, I. (2017). Attention Is All You Need. arXiv preprint arXiv:1706.03762.

KEY TERMS AND DEFINITIONS

Algorithm: A set of rules or steps used by computers to solve a problem or perform a task.

Application Programming Interface (API): A set of protocols that allows different software applications to communicate and integrate, commonly used to access cloud-based LLMs.

Artificial Intelligence (AI): The science and engineering of making intelligent machines that can simulate human intelligence and behavior.

Attention Mechanism: A method within neural networks that allows the model to focus on relevant parts of the input sequence when generating outputs, enhancing contextual understanding.

Automation: The use of technology to perform tasks with minimal human intervention, often enhanced by AI systems.

Autonomous Agent (AI): An AI system capable of performing tasks independently over time, often using planning, reasoning, and feedback loops.

Bias in AI: Systematic errors in AI outcomes caused by prejudiced data or flawed algorithms, leading to unfair or inaccurate results.

Computer Vision: A field of AI that trains computers to interpret and understand visual information from the world.

Data Annotation: The process of labeling data to make it usable for supervised learning models, often involving human reviewers.

Data: Information, especially facts or numbers, used by machines to learn, train, and make decisions.

Deep Learning: A type of machine learning that uses neural networks with many layers to analyze various levels of data abstraction.

Ethical AI Governance: The frameworks, policies, and oversight mechanisms that guide responsible AI development and deployment within organizations.

Ethics in AI: Principles guiding the responsible development and deployment of AI, including fairness, transparency, and accountability.

Explainability (XAI): Techniques that make the inner workings and decisions of AI models more transparent and interpretable to users and stakeholders.

Few-Shot Learning: When a model is provided with a few examples in a prompt to guide its generation for similar tasks.

Fine-Tuning: A technique where a pre-trained model is further trained on a smaller, domain-specific dataset to improve its performance on targeted tasks.

Hallucination (in AI): When a language model generates outputs that are grammatically correct but factually inaccurate or fabricated, often due to limitations in training data or model inference.

Human-in-the-Loop (HITL): A system design where human oversight is integrated into the AI decision-making process, enhancing accountability, safety, and contextual judgment.

Inference (AI): The process by which a trained model generates predictions or responses based on new input data.

Knowledge Cutoff: The latest date up to which a language model has been trained on data. Events or facts occurring after this point are unknown to the model unless integrated through additional tools or updates.

Large Language Model (LLM): A type of deep learning model trained on vast corpora of text data to understand and generate human-like language. LLMs power applications like ChatGPT, enabling natural language understanding and generation.

Machine Learning (ML): A subset of AI that enables machines to learn from data and improve over time without being explicitly programmed.

Model Drift: The degradation of a model's predictive performance over time due to changing data patterns or environments, often requiring retraining.

Multimodal AI: Systems that process and generate multiple forms of data—such as text, image, audio, and video—enabling more comprehensive and flexible interactions.

Natural Language Processing (NLP): A field of AI focused on the interaction between computers and human (natural) languages.

Neural Network: A computing system inspired by the human brain, composed of interconnected units (neurons) that process information in layers.

Prompt Engineering: The practice of crafting input prompts to guide LLM behavior and outputs effectively, often crucial in zero-shot or few-shot learning scenarios.

Reinforcement Learning: A machine learning paradigm where an agent learns to make decisions by receiving rewards or penalties.

Retrieval-Augmented Generation (RAG): A hybrid AI approach that combines retrieval of relevant documents with generation, allowing LLMs to access more current or factual information beyond their training cutoff.

Supervised Learning: A machine learning method where the model is trained on labeled data (input-output pairs).

Synthetic Data: Artificially generated data used to augment real datasets, often employed in training AI models while preserving privacy or balancing class distributions.

Tokenization: The process of breaking down text into smaller units (tokens), such as words or subwords, to feed into language models for processing.

Transformer Architecture: A neural network structure that uses attention mechanisms to process data sequences in parallel, forming the basis of modern LLMs like GPT, BERT, and T5.

Unsupervised Learning: A machine learning method where the model finds patterns and relationships in data without labeled outcomes.

Zero-Shot Learning: The ability of a model to perform a task without having seen any direct examples during training, relying on general understanding and instruction-following.

Chapter 6
Economic Implications of Artificial Intelligence Adoption in Business Processes

Pranjit Kr Paul
https://orcid.org/0000-0003-2799-4247
ICFAI University, Tripura, India

Pritha Guha
https://orcid.org/0009-0002-2641-938X
St. Xavier's College, India

ABSTRACT

Artificial Intelligence (AI) integration is reshaping the global economy by boosting productivity, optimizing decision-making, reducing costs. This chapter examines the economic impact of AI around three key objectives. Firstly, exploring the economic benefits of AI, productivity enhancement, cost savings, and revenue growth. Secondly, examining the socio-economic challenges, job displacement, wage inequality, and evolving labour market demands. Thirdly, evaluating policy frameworks and strategic measures to maximize AI's economic contributions. The findings provide insights into how AI is transforming business processes and the broader economy, identifying strategies for balancing innovation with economic inclusivity. By bridging technology-driven research and economic analysis, this chapter offers actionable recommendations for policymakers, business leaders, and researchers. It contributes to the broader discourse on AI's role in shaping the future of business and economic sustainability, emphasizing the need for strategic adaptation in an increasingly AI-driven world.

DOI: 10.4018/979-8-3373-3912-2.ch006

1. INTRODUCTION

One of the 21st century's most revolutionary technical developments, artificial intelligence (AI) is having an impact on economies and industries all over the world. By simulating human intelligence, artificial intelligence (AI) allows robots to learn from data, recognize patterns, make decisions, and optimize processes with little assistance from humans. Because of its greater efficiency, cost reduction, and improved innovation brought about by its implementation in business processes, it is a key factor in economic growth. The deployment of AI has significant worldwide economic ramifications. According to a 2018 McKinsey Global Institute analysis, artificial intelligence (AI) might boost the world economy by up to $13 trillion by 2030, which could result in an annual 1.2% increase in GDP. At the vanguard of AI integration are sectors like banking, healthcare, manufacturing, retail, and logistics, which use automation, machine learning, and natural language processing to optimize processes. By facilitating data-driven decision-making, predictive analytics, and intelligent consumer interactions, AI-driven business models have upended established sectors. The ability of AI to increase efficiency in corporate processes is among its most prominent economic advantages. Automation driven by AI has greatly decreased human labour in routine and repetitive jobs, freeing up employees to concentrate on more strategic endeavours. Cost reductions and increased operational efficiency have resulted from this, especially in labour-intensive industries. For example, robotic process automation (RPA) has reduced human error and improved customer experience in banking and finance by streamlining transactions, risk assessment, and fraud detection. However, the economic implications of AI adoption are not without challenges. The widespread implementation of AI has sparked concerns over job displacement, income inequality, and ethical considerations. While AI creates new job opportunities in AI development, data science, and robotics, it also poses a threat to low-skilled labour markets, particularly in emerging economies. The demand for reskilling and upskilling has become critical for the workforce to adapt to AI-driven business environments. Adoption of AI also necessitates large investments in data protection, infrastructure, and legal frameworks. While emerging economies confront difficulties with digital infrastructure and hiring AI expertise, nations with sophisticated AI ecosystems-like the US, China, and the EU-have been at the forefront of AI research and innovation. Businesses and governments must work together to develop policies that strike a balance between social and ethical issues and AI-driven economic growth. AI usage has significantly increased across a range of industries in India, one of the economies with the fastest rates of growth in the world. AI-driven economic growth has been made possible by the nation's digital transformation as well as government programs like the National AI Strategy, Make in India, and Digital India. According to Accenture, integrating AI into

Indian corporate operations could boost the country's GDP by $957 billion by 2035. Financial services are one of the main industries in India that is gaining from AI. AI-driven chatbots, fraud detection systems, and credit risk assessment tools have been adopted by the Indian banking sector, improving client satisfaction and efficiency. Financial inclusion has also been made easier by AI-powered automation in fintech, which has given underprivileged groups access to digital financing options.

AI applications have enhanced drug development, individualized treatment, and diagnostics in the healthcare industry. AI-powered telemedicine platforms have been extremely important, particularly in rural areas with limited access to medical facilities. AI is being used by both new and established businesses to create scalable and reasonably priced healthcare solutions, which will lessen the financial strain on the healthcare system. AI-driven automation, supply chain optimization, and predictive maintenance have also been incorporated into India's industrial sector. Indian manufacturing is now more competitive internationally thanks to the use of AI-powered robotics in production lines, which have increased productivity and decreased operating costs. AI usage in smart factories and industrial automation has been further driven by the government's push for Industry 4.0. Despite these developments, still has a number of obstacles when it comes to adopting AI. Widespread adoption is hampered by a shortage of qualified AI specialists, a weak digital infrastructure, and regulatory issues. Additionally, the impact of AI on employment remains a critical issue, with concerns over job displacement in labour-intensive sectors such as agriculture and manufacturing. So, all the nations involved with AI needs to concentrate on workforce development, AI research funding, and regulatory changes in order to fully realize the economic potential of AI. To create a strong AI ecosystem, cooperation between the government, industry players, and academic institutions is crucial. AI-driven economic future will be greatly influenced by policies that promote AI innovation while guaranteeing ethical AI deployment and worker upskilling. Both internationally and in India, the use of AI in commercial operations has significant economic ramifications. AI has enormous potential for innovation, cost reduction, and efficiency, but it also has drawbacks for infrastructure, employment, and regulatory frameworks. Sustainable AI integration into business operations requires a well-rounded strategy that addresses ethical and social issues while promoting AI-driven economic growth. Strategic investments in research, education, and policy development will be essential to continues to adopt AI to make sure that its use results in equitable and long-term economic growth.

2. REVIEW OF THE LITERATURE

Artificial Intelligence (AI) has emerged as a significant force driving economic growth, business transformation, and sustainability. A growing body of research examines the multifaceted impact of AI across industries, emphasizing its influence on economic development, corporate practices, and strategic sustainability initiatives.

Several studies explore that AI's capacity to significantly enhance productivity across various industries. Brynjolfsson and McAfee (2017) argue that AI-driven automation does not merely replace human labour but complements and enhances it, resulting in increased efficiency and effectiveness. AI-powered data analytics allow businesses to make more informed decisions, optimize supply chain logistics, and enhance overall operational efficiency (Agrawal et al., 2018). For instance, AI-driven predictive maintenance in manufacturing helps companies anticipate equipment failures, thereby minimizing downtime and reducing operational expenses (Baryannis et al., 2019). The impact of AI on employment remains a widely debated issue. While AI can replace routine-based tasks, it also creates new job opportunities in fields requiring AI expertise. Autor (2015) highlights that AI-induced automation often displaces repetitive, manual jobs but simultaneously fosters demand for high-skill roles. Arntz et al. (2016) argue that full automation of jobs is improbable due to the need for human creativity, emotional intelligence, and decision-making capabilities. Additionally, AI adoption necessitates workforce reskilling and upskilling (Frank et al., 2019), presenting both challenges and opportunities for the labour market as industries transition towards more AI-integrated work environments. Economic studies on AI adoption reveal both advantages and challenges. AI-driven automation leads to cost reductions by minimizing human errors, optimizing resource consumption, and enhancing customer engagement (Makridakis, 2017). However, businesses must invest heavily in AI infrastructure, skilled personnel, and continuous system upgrades to ensure seamless integration and effective utilization (Cockburn et al., 2018). The return on investment (ROI) for AI adoption varies across industries, with technology-driven sectors experiencing higher and quicker financial gains compared to more traditional industries. The relationship between AI and long-term economic growth has been explored by Gonzales (2023), who finds a positive correlation between AI and economic growth. Using panel regression analysis with fixed effects and GMM estimation, the study employs AI patent counts as a measure of AI adoption. The results indicate that AI's contribution to growth is more pronounced in advanced economies, particularly in the latter period of the dataset (1970–2019). Similarly, Baldwin (2019) situates AI as the "third transformation of economic history" after the Industrial Revolution and the computing revolution, highlighting its role in productivity growth, consumption revival, and risk management. Supporting these findings, Trabelsi (2024) presents survey-based evidence on AI's positive impacts on employment, security, transport, and education. George (2023) explores the transformative economic impact of AI, highlighting job displacement, productivity gains, and emerging markets. It emphasizes the dual nature of AI-offering growth while posing inequality and ethical challenges. Effective policy collaboration is crucial to ensure inclusive and responsible AI-driven progress. The adoption of AI in business processes, particularly B2B marketing, has been studied extensively. Zhan et al. (2024) examine the impact of AI-driven marketing strategies on shareholder reactions, using propensity score matching (PSM) and event study methodology to provide empirical insights. The study finds that AI adoption positively influences shareholder sentiment, as evidenced by abnormal stock returns. Additionally, Shrinivas and Shetty (2024) analyze real-world case studies to demonstrate how AI-driven technologies such as machine learning and natural language processing are reshaping organizational processes and the skillsets required in a digital economy. Despite the growing interest in AI for business and economic growth, research on AI's role in sustainable development remains scarce. Sipola et al. (2023) examine the benefits of AI for sustainable business practices, revealing that AI is primarily used for optimization and strategic intelligence. Based on data from 2017–2021, the study finds that 16 out of 20 enterprises in Finland have leveraged AI for sustainability benefits, indicating AI's increasing role in environmental and economic sustainability. Maiti et al. (2025) examine the ethical challenges of adopting artificial intelligence (AI) in business, highlighting key concerns such as data privacy, bias, transparency, job displacement, algorithmic influence, accountability, and ethical decision-making. It finds that these challenges differ by gender, age, country, profession, and organizational age. The study offers best practices for addressing these issues and provides valuable guidance for business leaders, policymakers, and researchers to promote responsible and ethical AI use. AI's role in economic policy and structural reforms has also been a focal point of research. Kumar (2018) explores India's economic revival through key policy initiatives such as demonetization and GST implementation. Additionally, initiatives like Make in India and Startup India have contributed to economic growth by fostering technological advancements. In a similar vein, Kaur et al. (2023) discuss how India's socialist economic system has transitioned into a technology-driven economy, facilitated by government initiatives and an expanding digital ecosystem. Panigrahi et al. (2024) explore the transformative impact of artificial intelligence (AI) on India's economic and managerial domains. It examines AI's influence on GDP growth, employment, productivity, and business practices. Using literature review, case studies, and statistical data, it highlights both the opportunities and challenges AI presents. The study emphasizes the need for strategic AI adoption and talent development for sustainable growth. Abuzaid (2024) reveals AI's transformative role in enhancing business efficiency and reducing operational costs. Studies highlight successful integrations, persistent challenges, and significant economic implications. Existing research underscores the need for holistic evaluations combining qualitative and quantitative methods. This review identifies a gap in practical AI implementation models and calls for deeper insight into its multifaceted business impacts. AI adoption varies across regions, with India leading among South Asian countries in AI integration but still lagging behind the United States and China. Chakrabarti and Sanyal (2020) analyze India's AI ecosystem, addressing its challenges and the regulatory frameworks needed for sustainable growth. Furthermore, Agarwal (2022) underscores AI's transformative role in key industries such as agriculture, manufacturing, healthcare, and finance. While AI-driven precision farming has optimized crop yields and manufacturing processes, concerns about job displacement, data privacy, and inequality persist, necessitating policy interventions such as workforce reskilling and investments in digital infrastructure.

Sector-Specific AI Applications

- Manufacturing: AI-powered robotics and automation systems improve production efficiency, enhance quality control, and reduce dependency on manual labour, leading to significant cost savings (Manyika et al., 2017).
- Finance: AI-driven algorithmic trading, fraud detection systems, and risk assessment tools enable financial institutions to make more accurate and efficient decisions, thereby improving financial stability and security (Bose et al., 2020).
- Healthcare: AI enhances diagnostic accuracy, assists in drug discovery, and optimizes hospital resource allocation, ultimately reducing healthcare costs while improving patient outcomes (Topol, 2019).
- Retail: AI-based personalized marketing, demand forecasting, and inventory management systems enhance customer experience and optimize stock levels, leading to increased sales and reduced wastage (Shankar, 2018).

The integration of AI into business processes offers substantial economic benefits, including improved productivity, cost efficiency, and industry-specific advancements. However, the transition to AI-driven systems also brings challenges, such as workforce displacement, ethical concerns, and high initial investment costs. As AI technology continues to evolve, policymakers and business leaders must develop strategies to maximize its economic potential while addressing associated risks. Future research should focus on AI's long-term economic impact, potential regulatory frameworks, and strategies for workforce adaptation in the AI-driven economy.

3. OBJECTIVES AND METHODOLOGY

The analysis is guided by three primary objectives:

1. To examine the direct and indirect economic benefits of AI adoption, emphasizing productivity enhancement, cost efficiency, and revenue generation.
2. To explore the socio-economic challenges posed by AI, such as its impact on labour markets, income inequality, and job displacement.
3. Evaluate the policy frameworks and strategic measures that can maximize AI's positive economic contributions while mitigating potential downsides.

This study employs a structured methodology to analyze the economic implications of AI adoption in business processes. A comprehensive literature review is conducted, drawing from academic sources to examine AI's impact on productivity, employment, cost efficiency, and profitability. Relevant studies are selected based on their focus on AI's economic effects at both micro and macro levels, with particular attention to industry transformation and labour market shifts. Economic theories, including Schumpeter's innovation theory and endogenous growth models, are explored to provide a conceptual foundation for understanding AI-driven changes. Challenges such as workforce displacement, skill shortages, regulatory hurdles, and economic inequalities are critically assessed. The findings from literature and theoretical analysis are synthesized to identify common themes and divergences. Practical applications and policy implications are discussed, emphasizing workforce reskilling, regulatory governance, and investment strategies for sustainable AI-driven growth. Finally, policy recommendations and strategic measures are proposed to maximize AI's benefits while addressing economic and social challenges. This structured approach ensures a thorough and evidence-based assessment of AI's economic impact on business processes.

4. THE DIRECT AND INDIRECT ECONOMIC BENEFITS OF AI ADOPTION: A DESCRIPTIVE ANALYSIS

Industries have undergone a revolution thanks to artificial intelligence (AI), which has changed how companies' function and compete. There are many direct and indirect economic advantages to the use of AI. Increased productivity, cost effectiveness, and revenue generation are some of these advantages. These economic benefits are thoroughly examined in the debate that follows, which also shows how adoption of AI affects many industries and stakeholders. Schumpeter's theory and endogenous growth models are also mentioned and linked through their focus on innovation as the engine of economic growth. Schumpeter emphasizes creative destruction, where AI-driven innovations replace old technologies, creating new industries and transforming business dynamics. Endogenous growth models, like those of Romer and Lucas, complement this by showing how internal factors-such as research and development, human capital, and knowledge-sustain long-term growth, making AI a key driver of productivity and structural economic change.

4.1 Direct Economic Benefits of AI Adoption

Productivity gains are among the biggest immediate advantages of AI adoption. Automation powered by AI reduces the need for human intervention, increasing productivity across a range of sectors. The impact of AI on productivity is influenced by the following factors:

Task Automation: AI-powered devices and software can complete time-consuming and repetitive activities with little mistake. For example, data entry, invoice processing, and customer support contacts are all made easier by robotic process automation (RPA). As a result, human workers can concentrate on more valuable activities that call for creativity and problem-solving abilities. *Improved Decision-Making*: Large volumes of data are processed by AI-powered analytics systems to yield insightful information. Companies use AI-powered predictive analytics to make better decisions in financial forecasts, supply chain management, and customer behaviour analysis. Profitability rises as a result of improved operations. *Enhanced Employee Performance*: AI technologies help employees with real-time insights and recommendations, enhancing human capabilities. Chatbots driven by artificial intelligence (AI) assist customer support agents by offering suitable answers, which shortens response times and raises customer satisfaction. AI adoption also directly contributes to cost efficiency by reducing operational expenses and minimizing waste. The key areas where AI helps in cost efficiency include: *Labor Cost Reduction*: Repetitive and labour-intensive processes can be automated to lessen reliance on human labour. Although job displacement may be a worry, this also enables businesses to assign employees to higher-value positions, which boosts overall economic efficiency. *Energy and Resource Optimization*: Systems driven by AI optimize energy use in sectors like logistics, transportation, and manufacturing. AI-powered energy management systems and smart networks cut down on electricity waste, which lowers energy bills. *Predictive Maintenance*: Predictive maintenance solutions driven by AI assist industry in preventing equipment failures by evaluating data and seeing any problems before they arise. This lowers unscheduled downtime, repair expenses, and interruptions to operations. AI adoption directly contributes to revenue generation by enhancing product and service offerings, improving customer engagement, and creating new business opportunities. Some key ways AI drives revenue include: *Personalized Marketing and Sales:* Recommendation engines powered by AI examine consumer preferences and actions to provide tailored product recommendations. This raises sales conversions and improves customer happiness. *New Product and Service Development:* AI promotes innovation by empowering businesses to create AI-powered goods and services. AI-powered virtual assistants, smart home appliances, and driverless cars, for instance, give companies new sources of income. *Expansion into New Markets:* By examining consumer preferences and market trends, artificial intelligence (AI) helps firms reach a wider audience. By using data-driven tactics, businesses can expand into new markets and potentially increase their revenue.

4.2 Indirect Economic Benefits of AI Adoption

AI adoption can lead to indirect economic benefits such as job creation and workforce transformation, economic growth, quality of life and environmental sustainability.

Job Creation and Workforce Transformation: AI automation may lead to the loss of some jobs, but it also opens up new work prospects. There is now a much greater need for automation engineers, data scientists, and AI professionals. Adoption of AI also causes existing positions to change, necessitating that workers learn new skills and adjust to changing employment requirements. *Economic Growth and Competitiveness:* Investing in AI technology gives nations and companies a competitive edge in the global marketplace. Adoption of AI stimulates economic production, increases productivity, and spurs innovation, all of which contribute to total economic growth. *Enhanced Quality of Life:* The quality of life is enhanced by AI-driven developments in public services, healthcare, and transportation. While intelligent transportation systems improve mobility and lessen traffic, AI-powered diagnostic tools assist physicians in identifying illnesses early. *Environmental Sustainability:* By optimizing energy use, cutting waste, and enhancing resource management, artificial intelligence promotes environmental sustainability. For instance, precision farming made possible by AI-driven solutions in agriculture lowers the need for pesticides, fertilizers, and water.

Adoption of AI has numerous direct and indirect economic advantages, from increased productivity and cost effectiveness to income generation and economic expansion.

5. THE SOCIO-ECONOMIC CHALLENGES OF ARTIFICIAL INTELLIGENCE: LABOUR MARKETS, INCOME INEQUALITY, AND JOB DISPLACEMENT

Artificial Intelligence (AI) has emerged as a transformative force in modern society, revolutionizing industries, economies, and the way people interact with technology. While AI promises increased efficiency, productivity, and economic growth, it also poses significant socio-economic challenges. Chief among these are its effects on labour markets, income inequality, and job displacement. The rapid adoption of AI raises important questions about the future of work, economic disparity, and social stability. This article explores these concerns in a detailed and descriptive manner.

5.1 The Impact of AI on Labour Markets

Labour markets worldwide are undergoing significant transformations due to AI and automation. These changes affect employment opportunities, the nature of work, and the skills required to remain relevant in the workforce.

Automation of Jobs: In many industries, repetitive and routine tasks have been replaced by AI-driven automation. Assembly lines have been replaced by robots in manufacturing, which has decreased the demand for human labour. Chatbots with AI capabilities answer customer support questions that were previously handled by call center staff. With AI systems that can analyze data and produce documents more quickly than humans, even white-collar jobs like accountancy and legal services are being automated. *Creation of New Job Opportunities:* AI generates new opportunities even as it replaces some occupations. Data scientists, machine learning engineers, cybersecurity specialists, and AI specialists are in high demand. Additionally, artificial intelligence (AI) creates job prospects in new areas including digital content development, smart healthcare, and autonomous vehicle technology. The difficulty, though, is in providing employees with the skills they need to move into these new positions. *The Changing Nature of Work:* Remote work and the gig economy have grown as a result of AI. Instead of using typical long-term contracts, many businesses are choosing to use project-based, short-term employment. Although this change gives flexibility, it also comes with a lack of benefits and employment uncertainty. In order to be employable in this changing labor market, workers must continuously improve their abilities.

5.2 AI and Income Inequality

Income inequality is a growing concern as AI reshapes the economy. The benefits of AI are not evenly distributed, leading to disparities between different economic classes, geographical regions, and levels of education.

Wage Polarization: High-skilled people in AI-related industries make significant salaries, whereas low-skilled individuals experience wage stagnation or job losses as a result of AI's contribution to wage polarization. The income disparity between the rich and the working class is made worse by these phenomena. *Concentration of Wealth and Power:* Often referred to as "Big Tech," large technological businesses control the AI market. Businesses like Google, Amazon, Microsoft, and Tesla make large investments in AI research and development, gaining a great deal of money and power. Because of this concentration of economic power, there may be less prospects for startups and smaller enterprises due to monopolization and decreased market competition. *Geographical Disparities:* Different nations and areas have varying rates of AI adoption. AI-driven economic growth is more advantageous for developed countries with strong technological infrastructure, while emerging countries find it difficult to keep up. In addition to creating economic dependence that could impede sustainable development, the digital gap increases global income disparity.

5.3 Job Displacement and Its Social Consequences

The displacement of workers due to AI-driven automation is a pressing socio-economic challenge. While automation enhances productivity, it also disrupts livelihoods and raises concerns about social stability.

Job Loss in Traditional Industries: Manufacturing, retail, and transportation are among the sectors most at risk from AI-driven job displacement because of their heavy reliance on human labour. Self-checkout systems eliminate the need for cashiers, autonomous cars jeopardize truck drivers' jobs, and factory automation through robotics reduces the necessity for human labour. *Skill Gaps and Unemployment:* The speed at which AI is developing has surpassed efforts to reskill the workforce. Many workers who have been replaced by automation lack the technical know-how needed to move into AI-driven fields. The task of closing this skill gap through legislative changes and training initiatives falls to governments and educational establishments. *Psychological and Social Impacts:* AI-driven job displacement has social and psychological effects. Mental health conditions like anxiety and sadness can be brought on by unemployment. Additionally, towns that rely on traditional industries experience economic decline, which raises poverty levels and causes social instability.

Societies and economies are changing at a rate never seen before due to artificial intelligence. AI provides major socioeconomic concerns in addition to amazing prospects for innovation and advancement. Strategic interventions are necessary to address important issues such as job relocation, income inequality, and labour market disturbances. Through education investment, equitable policy implementation, and ethical AI development, societies may maximize AI's benefits while reducing its drawbacks. A future where technology serves everyone in society promoting social justice, economic prosperity, and human well-being will require a balanced approach to AI integration.

6. EVALUATING POLICY FRAMEWORKS AND STRATEGIC MEASURES TO MAXIMIZE AI'S ECONOMIC CONTRIBUTIONS WHILE MITIGATING POTENTIAL DOWNSIDES

Globally, artificial intelligence (AI) is transforming economies and industries. AI has a significant impact on everything from automation and data analytics to improved decision-making. However, there are ethical, social, and economic issues with its quick acceptance. This study assesses strategic approaches and policy frameworks that optimize AI's beneficial economic effects while minimizing any potential drawbacks. Because AI boosts productivity, encourages innovation, and generates new job opportunities, it has a revolutionary impact on economies. By automating repetitive processes, it increases productivity by freeing up human workers to concentrate on higher-value jobs. AI-powered solutions stimulate creativity and result in the formation of new markets and industries. Businesses that use AI can cut costs by streamlining operations and eliminating inefficiencies. AI applications also enhance healthcare delivery, educational outreach, and financial accessibility, all of which promote economic inclusion. Adoption of AI is fraught with difficulties, notwithstanding its benefits. Automation has the potential to eliminate jobs, especially in low-skilled industries. Economic inequality may be exacerbated if the benefits of AI are dispersed unevenly, favoring giant firms over small businesses. AI systems have the potential to reinforce prejudices, resulting in unjust hiring, lending, and law enforcement practices. Concerns regarding cybersecurity and individual privacy are also raised by AI's dependence on enormous volumes of data. Governments and enterprises must put strong policy frameworks in place to manage the risks of AI while maximizing its promise. Policies pertaining to education and workforce development are crucial, and governments should fund lifelong learning programs and AI-related training to assist workers in adjusting to AI-driven businesses. A workforce ready for AI integration is ensured by promoting STEM (Science, Technology, Engineering, and Mathematics) education from a young age. AI talent development is promoted by cooperation between industry, government, and academia through public-private partnerships. Governance of AI that is ethical and regulated is essential. Transparent AI regulations that guarantee accountability should be established by governments. Fair competition rules should forbid monopolistic AI techniques, guaranteeing a competitive market, while ethical AI principles must incorporate steps to lessen bias in AI models. AI research and development (R&D) requires investment, and grants and tax incentives from both the public and private sectors support this work. Establishing AI innovation hubs encourages cooperation and advances technology, and international cooperation boosts innovation worldwide. Measures for cybersecurity and data governance are essential. Strict data protection regulations, like the GDPR, protect people from AI abuse. To stop AI-driven cyberattacks, governments must invest in safe AI infrastructure, and businesses should implement moral data usage policies that encourage just and responsible data management. Beyond regulations, strategic actions can guarantee AI has a positive impact on economic expansion. Financial incentives, such as AI adoption grants, can help startups and small and medium-sized businesses (SMEs) adopt AI. While making sure that cloud computing is accessible and affordable enables smaller businesses to use AI technologies, workshops and mentorship programs can assist entrepreneurs in successfully integrating AI solutions. The development of AI-powered public services improves healthcare, education, and governance. AI-powered decision-making improves service delivery and public administration. Personalized medicine and AI-powered diagnostics improve healthcare results, and adaptable learning platforms increase the quality and accessibility of education. It's also critical to advance corporate accountability and ethical AI. Responsible AI deployment is ensured by the creation of autonomous AI ethical committees. Companies should emphasize fairness and transparency in their corporate AI responsibility reports as they reveal the impact of AI. In AI development, promoting diverse teams reduces biases and enhances decision-making.

Different AI policies have been enacted by nations all across the world, providing insightful lessons for future tactics. In order to ensure ethical AI deployment, the European Union's AI Act focuses on risk-based AI legislation. The National AI Initiative of the United States encourages workforce development and AI research and development. China is becoming a global leader in AI because to its significant investments in AI infrastructure and research. India's National AI Strategy prioritizes inclusive AI development, emphasizing education, healthcare, and agriculture. Policymakers can create efficient AI strategies that optimize economic gains while minimizing potential drawbacks by taking inspiration from these methods. AI has enormous economic potential, but it also has several drawbacks. Societies can optimize AI's advantages while lowering its hazards by putting strong governance structures and strategic policies into place. A balanced and inclusive AI-driven economy depends on R&D investment, ethical governance, education, and AI-driven public services. AI's contribution to the development of a sustainable and just economic future will be decided in the future by international cooperation and proactive policymaking.

7. CONCLUSION

AI adoption has a dual effect on economies, bringing with it both considerable advantages and difficulties. On the one side, AI boosts revenue growth across industries, lowers operating costs, and increases productivity. Intelligent systems, data-driven decision-making, and automation increase productivity, simplify procedures, and allow companies to grow quickly. These elements support expansion driven by innovation, enhanced competitiveness, and general economic growth. However, there are serious socioeconomic issues with AI's incorporation into different industries. Three major issues that demand immediate action are the automation-driven loss of jobs, changes in the dynamics of the labour market, and growing income inequality. AI disrupts the workforce by making some skill sets obsolete, even as it opens up new opportunities. Low-skilled workers are disproportionately impacted by this shift, which exacerbates economic inequality. The socioeconomic environment is further complicated by ethical worries about algorithmic unfairness, data privacy, and the concentration of wealth generated by AI. Strong legislative frameworks and calculated actions are required to optimize AI's benefits while minimizing its drawbacks. To give workers AI-relevant skills, governments and enterprises must give reskilling and upskilling initiatives top priority. Investments in lifelong learning programs, vocational training, and education can assist people in adjusting to new employment responsibilities brought about by advances in artificial intelligence. Additionally, the effects of job displacement can be lessened by putting in place social safety nets like unemployment insurance or universal basic income. Regulatory supervision, ethical AI governance, and openness in AI decision-making are also essential for guaranteeing accountability and equity. A balanced strategy that addresses socio-economic inequalities and encourages innovation will be essential to realizing AI's full potential. In the digital age, economies may ensure sustainable, inclusive, and equitable growth by taking proactive steps to address the issues presented by AI.

REFERENCES

Abuzaid, A. N. (2024). AI-Driven Business Processes: Efficiency Gains, Cost Reductions, and Implications for Economic Performance. In *International Conference on Knowledge Engineering and Communication Systems (ICKECS)* (Vol. 1, pp. 1-5). IEEE.

Agrawal, A., Gans, J., & Goldfarb, A. (2018). Prediction, judgment, and complexity: a theory of decision-making and artificial intelligence. In *The economics of artificial intelligence: An agenda* (pp. 89–110). University of Chicago Press.

Arntz, M., Gregory, T., & Zierahn, U. (2016). The Risk of Automation for Jobs in OECD Countries.

Autor, D. H. (2015). Why are there still so many jobs? The history and future of workplace automation. *The Journal of Economic Perspectives*, *29*(3), 3–30.

Baldwin, R. (2019). *The globotics upheaval: Globalisation, robotics, and the future of work*. Weidenfeld & Nicolson., DOI: 10.32422/mv.1695

Baryannis, G., Validi, S., Dani, S., & Antoniou, G. (2019). Supply chain risk management and artificial intelligence: State of the art and future research directions. *International Journal of Production Research*, *57*(7), 2179–2202.

Brynjolfsson, E., & Mcafee, A. N. D. R. E. W. (2017). The business of artificial intelligence. *Harvard Business Review*, *7*(1), 1–2.

Chakrabarti, R., & Sanyal, K. (2020). Towards a 'Responsible AI': Can India take the lead? *South Asia Economic Journal*, *21*(1), 158–177.

Cockburn, I. M., Henderson, R., & Stern, S. (2018). *The impact of artificial intelligence on innovation* (Vol. 24449). Cambridge, MA, USA: National bureau of economic research.

Frank, M. R., Autor, D., Bessen, J. E., Brynjolfsson, E., Cebrian, M., Deming, D. J., & Rahwan, I. (2019). Toward understanding the impact of artificial intelligence on labor. *Proceedings of the National Academy of Sciences of the United States of America*, *116*(14), 6531–6539. PMID: 30910965

George, A. S. (2023). Future economic implications of artificial intelligence. *Zenodo*. DOI: 10.5281/zenodo.8347639

Gonzales, J. T. (2023). Implications of AI innovation on economic growth: A panel data study. *Journal of Economic Structures*, *12*(1), 13.

Kaur, R., Saluja, A., Kaur, A., & Sharma, A. (2023). Technology led transformation of Indian economy. In *AIP Conference Proceedings* (Vol. 2782, No. 1). AIP Publishing.

Kumar, D. B. (2018). Economic Revival in India: issues and challenges. *Available at SSRN* 3839143.

Maiti, M., Kayal, P., & Vujko, A. (2025). A study on ethical implications of artificial intelligence adoption in business: Challenges and best practices. *Future Business Journal*, *11*, 34. DOI: 10.1186/s43093-025-00462-5

Makridakis, S. (2017). The forthcoming Artificial Intelligence (AI) revolution: Its impact on society and firms. *Futures*, *90*, 46–60.

Manyika, J., Chui, M., Miremadi, M., Bughin, J., George, K., Willmott, P., & Dewhurst, M. (2017). A future that works: AI, automation, employment, and productivity. *McKinsey Global Institute Research. Tech. Rep*, *60*, 1–135.

Panigrahi, A., Ahirrao, S. C., & Patel, A. (2024). Impact of artificial intelligence on Indian economy. *J Manag Res Anal*, *11*(1), 33–40.

Shankar, V. (2018). How artificial intelligence (AI) is reshaping retailing. *Journal of Retailing*, *94*(4), vi–xi.

Shrinivas S. K. & Shetty P. (2024). Impact of artificial intelligence on business, business operations and strategy. *International Journal of Creative Research Thoughts.* ISSN: 2320- 2882, 12(8), 152-160.

Sipola, J., Saunila, M., & Ukko, J. (2023). Adopting artificial intelligence in sustainable business. *Journal of Cleaner Production*, *426*, 139–197. DOI: 10.1016/j.jclepro.2023.139197

Topol, E. (2019). *Deep medicine: how artificial intelligence can make healthcare human again.*

Trabelsi, M. A. (2024). The impact of artificial intelligence on economic development. *Journal of Electronic Business & Digital Economics*, *3*(2), 142–155. DOI: 10.1108/JEBDE-10-2023-0022

Zhan, Y., Xiong, Y., Han, R., Lam, H. K. S., & Blome, C. (2024). The impact of artificial intelligence adoption for business-to-business marketing on shareholder reaction: A social actor perspective. *International Journal of Information Management*, *76*, 102768. DOI: 10.1016/j.ijinfomgt.2024.102768

Chapter 7

Enhancing Fraud Detection and Financial Forecasting:

The Role of LLMs in Healthcare and Finance

Chinna Gopi Simhadri
https://orcid.org/0000-0002-8311-7495
Vignan's Foundation for Science, Technology, and Research, India

Venkatrama Phani Kumar Sistla
Vignan's Foundation for Science, Technology, and Research, India

Ravi Kishore Reddy Chavva
Vignan's Foundation for Science, Technology, and Research, India

ABSTRACT

The integration of Large Language Models (LLMs) into key domains like finance and healthcare is transforming intelligent automation and decision-making. This chapter examines LLM applications in fraud detection and financial forecasting, as well as in clinical support and patient interaction. In finance, LLMs analyze transaction data, user behavior, and financial texts to detect fraud and enhance predictive insights from news, reports, and sentiment. In healthcare, they support diagnosis, treatment planning, and patient communication by processing and generating human-like medical language. The chapter outlines practical implementation frameworks, highlights challenges in data governance and compliance, and addresses

DOI: 10.4018/979-8-3373-3912-2.ch007

concerns around model transparency and fairness. By presenting cross-industry use cases, this work illustrates how LLMs can generate actionable insights and drive innovation while upholding ethical and operational standards.

INTRODUCTION

Large Language Models (LLMs) represent a major breakthrough in artificial intelligence, utilizing extensive computational resources and advanced neural frameworks to produce and interpret human-like text (Dilmegani, 2025). These models, which utilize transformer-based architectures and are trained on extensive datasets, exhibit remarkable skill in natural language processing. This makes them particularly beneficial for data-intensive and critical sectors like healthcare and finance (Skamser, 2024). LLMs can process huge amounts of patient data and medical literature, assisting with pre-consultation, diagnosis, and management, and hold promise in medical education and writing (Yang et al., 2023). In finance, LLMs can interpret news articles, analyst reports, and market commentary to enhance structured data-driven models. This capability extends to various applications, including text generation, automated translation, sentiment analysis, and document summarization, showcasing their versatility across diverse domains.

OVERVIEW OF LARGE LANGUAGE MODELS AND THEIR CAPABILITIES

LLMs including architectures like GPT-4, BERT, and newer variants, are sophisticated deep learning systems designed to understand and produce text that closely resembles human language. They are trained on extensive and varied datasets, including books, websites, and specialized domain materials, enabling them to grasp intricate patterns in language. As a result, they can perform various language-related tasks without the need for explicitly defined instructions or task-specific programming (Neveditsin et al., 2024). Their capabilities include:

- *Natural Language Understanding and Generation*: LLMs can comprehend complex texts, such as medical reports or financial statements, and respond in a clear, contextually relevant manner (Hadi et al., 2023). This makes them valuable for summarizing documents, answering queries, or drafting reports in healthcare and finance.
- *Contextual Analysis:* By using attention mechanisms, LLMs analyze the context of words within a sentence or document, enabling them to discern nu-

anced meaning. For example, in healthcare, they can differentiate between medical terms in clinical notes, while in finance, they can interpret sentiment in earnings call transcripts.

- *Data Integration and Processing:* LLMs can process both structured data (e.g., numerical transaction records) and unstructured data (e.g., emails, social media posts), bridging the gap between quantitative and qualitative analysis (Vairinhos et al., 2022). This is particularly useful for detecting anomalies in financial transactions or extracting insights from patient records.
- *Anomaly Detection and Pattern Recognition:* With their ability to model complex relationships in data, LLMs can identify irregularities that may indicate fraud, such as unusual billing patterns in healthcare claims or suspicious transaction sequences in banking.
- *Predictive Modeling:* LLMs can utilize both historical and real-time data to discern patterns and forecast future trends. For instance, they can be applied to forecast hospital revenue or fluctuations in the stock market by integrating various inputs, such as economic metrics or patient intake statistics.
- *Scalability and Adaptability:* LLMs can be tailored to specific domains by fine-tuning, enabling them to perform tasks like medical coding or financial risk evaluation. Their capacity to scale and handle vast amounts of data effectively makes these models ideal for use in industries like healthcare and finance, where enterprise-level applications demand robust performance.

In healthcare, LLMs are being harnessed to streamline operations, enhance diagnostics, and combat fraud (Yang et al., 2023), while in finance, they drive innovations in risk management, customer service, and market analysis (Lee et al., 2025). Their ability to process vast datasets, adapt to specialized domains, and deliver actionable insights positions LLMs as a cornerstone of AI-driven transformation in these industries. However, their use must be guided by ethical, privacy, and regulatory concerns (Gencer & Gencer, 2025).

THE EMERGENCE OF LARGE LANGUAGE MODELS IN INDUSTRY

Over the past decade, AI technology has advanced dramatically, largely due to the rise of Large Language Models. Unlike earlier models that were limited to specific tasks, LLMs are trained on vast, diverse datasets encompassing billions of words. This broad exposure enables them to handle diverse language tasks such as generating human-like text, translating between languages, and responding to complex queries without needing custom designs for each function. Advanced models like

OpenAI's GPT-4, Google's Gemini, and Meta's LLaMA highlight how far natural language processing has progressed in both understanding and reasoning capabilities.

These models basically depend on the transformer network architecture, which employs a mechanism called "attention" to assess the relevance of various elements of an input sequence. This enables the models to efficiently process context, learn complex patterns in language, and generate coherent and contextually relevant outputs. LLMs have evolved beyond simple text completion and now drive applications ranging from automated content creation and sophisticated chatbots to advanced decision support systems. For instance, in finance, LLMs are being explored for algorithmic trading and risk assessment (Chen et al., 2025).

The growing interest in LLMs across various industries stems from the understanding that language is central to human decision-making, communication, and knowledge sharing. Organizations in finance, healthcare, legal services, and customer support are increasingly recognizing LLMs as powerful tools for automating processes, performing intelligent analysis, and personalizing interactions, leading to enhanced operational efficiency and strategic insights (Tavasoli et al., 2025).

THE CRITICAL IMPORTANCE OF FINANCE AND HEALTHCARE FOR LLM APPLICATIONS

Among the numerous potential applications of LLMs, the finance and healthcare sectors stand out as particularly critical and promising. Both sectors rely heavily on large volumes of unstructured and semi-structured data, including transaction records, regulatory documents, clinical notes, diagnostic reports, and research publications. Deriving valuable insights from unstructured text data is crucial for making well-informed decisions. However, this process is often challenging because of factors like ambiguity, irregular formatting, and the presence of specialized or domain-specific terminology.

In the financial sector, LLMs can serve a vital function in detecting fraudulent transactions by identifying subtle contextual cues that may not be apparent from numerical data alone (Agarwal, 2024). They can also enhance financial forecasting by analyzing sentiment, news articles, and complex patterns across diverse data sources. LLMs, when fine-tuned on financial text, are well-suited to these tasks.

In the healthcare domain, clinical decision-making relies on integrating information from multiple sources, such as patient medical records, diagnostic imaging, and the latest medical research. This synthesis is crucial for accurate diagnosis, effective treatment planning, and personalized patient care. LLMs can assist physicians by summarizing electronic health records, suggesting potential diagnoses, and facilitating patient communication through natural language interfaces. Virtual healthcare assistants powered by LLMs are already improving access to medical advice, particularly in underserved communities (Jonnagaddala & Wong, 2025).

However, the integration of LLMs into finance and healthcare comes with considerable obstacles. Both are high-stakes domains where errors can have serious consequences. This necessitates the development of highly accurate, interpretable, trustworthy, and ethically aligned models (Lareyre & Raffort, 2024; Pressman et al., 2024; Zhui et al., 2024). Integrating LLMs into these sectors requires robust approaches to data governance, bias mitigation (Li et al., 2023), explainability (Floridi et al., 2021), security (Das et al., 2024), and regulatory compliance (He et al., 2024; Tavasoli et al., 2025). It's also important to consider the trustworthiness of LLMs in healthcare (arXiv reCAPTCHA, 2022).

LLMs IN FINANCIAL SERVICES

LLMs are transforming the financial services industry by allowing institutions to process and derive insights from a wide range of data types including unstructured and semi-structured information, far beyond conventional structured datasets. Historically, financial institutions relied on models such as logistic regression and decision trees to analyze structured transaction and customer data. However, with the rise of LLMs, it has become possible to extract important insights from unstructured and semi-structured data, including transaction narratives, market reports, news articles, and client communications. LLMs enhance prediction accuracy and decision-making by interpreting complex language patterns and contextual information, thus contributing to improvements in fraud detection, regulatory compliance, credit assessment, and risk management (Li et al., 2023). These models are particularly effective in identifying anomalies, adapting to new fraud tactics, and minimizing false positives, thereby safeguarding financial assets and customer trust (Generative AI and LLMs in Banking, 2024).

LLMs are capable of processing and analyzing trillions of data points to uncover subtle patterns and detect early warning signs of financial irregularities. This allows for more proactive risk management and enhanced financial oversight. They are instrumental in recognizing evolving fraud schemes, evaluating creditworthiness, and forecasting stock market trends by analyzing both historical and real-time data (Simhadri C G, 2025). Applications such as transaction monitoring, automated compliance reporting, and sentiment analysis from market news demonstrate their wide-ranging utility in the finance industry (Desai, n.d.; Balona, 2024). As financial institutions integrate LLMs into their workflows, real-world implementations and case studies reveal both the benefits and operational challenges, such as system integration, data governance, and establishing robust evaluation frameworks (Liu,

2024). This section will delve into these applications and explore how LLMs are being practically deployed to enhance the resilience and efficiency of modern financial systems.

APPLICATIONS IN TRANSACTION MONITORING, FRAUD SCORING, AND REGULATORY COMPLIANCE

LLMs are reshaping how financial institutions approach fraud detection and regulatory compliance (Abnave, 2023). Traditional detection methods typically rely on predefined rules or basic models that examine structured inputs like transaction amounts or user activity. However, these approaches often fail to capture complex or evolving fraud tactics that fall outside established patterns. In contrast, LLMs can interpret a broader range of data—including unstructured sources and adapt to emerging threats, offering a more dynamic and effective solution for identifying fraudulent behavior. LLMs, however, can detect anomalies in unstructured data, such as transaction descriptions, customer complaints, or contextual conversations from customer support interactions (Amamou, 2025).

Transaction Monitoring And Anomaly Detection

One key application of LLMs in financial services is transaction monitoring, where they can analyze textual data alongside numerical data to detect fraudulent activities (Solms, 2020). LLMs trained on huge volume of financial text data, including transaction records and reports, can learn subtle patterns of fraud and alert analysts to potential threats that might otherwise go unnoticed. For example, if a large transaction is described in an atypical way, an LLM can flag it for further review, even if other transactional parameters like the amount or location appear normal.

LLMs have also proven beneficial in enhancing fraud scoring systems (Múgica, 2025). These models have the ability to incorporate a wider variety of factors including historical behavior, transaction context, and external news to assign a more comprehensive risk score to each transaction. This helps improve the accuracy of fraud detection, reduce false positives, and identify novel fraud tactics that rule-based systems may miss.

Regulatory Compliance

In the complex and changing regulatory environment of financial services, LLMs offer powerful tools to enhance compliance efforts. They can streamline compliance processes by automatically analyzing regulatory documents and financial records, identifying critical details, and comparing them with an organization's internal policies. This capability supports adherence to important standards like Anti-Money Laundering (AML) and Know Your Customer (KYC) (Qadir, 2025; Tavasoli et al., 2025). LLMs also streamline the generation of compliance reports and support real-time monitoring by flagging suspicious transactions or non-compliant behavior, enabling financial institutions to respond proactively to regulatory requirements (He et al., 2024).

LEVERAGING TEXTUAL DATA FOR STOCK MOVEMENT FORECASTING

The stock market is influenced not only by numerical data like stock prices and financial reports but also by market sentiment, news, and social media discourse. LLMs have shown promising results in interpreting unstructured textual data to forecast stock price changes (Fatouros et al., 2025). Through sentiment analysis and market trend extraction from news articles, earnings calls, and financial reports, LLMs can generate insights into potential market movements (Zhang et al., 2023).

Sentiment Analysis For Stock Prediction

LLMs excel in sentiment analysis for stock prediction by processing textual data from financial news, social media, and analyst reports to detect shifts in market sentiment. They analyze tone, emotion, and context to identify the potential impact of events such as CEO statements or policy changes on market confidence. By distinguishing between factual and subjective content, LLMs enhance trading decisions. When combined with historical and structured financial data, sentiment-informed models significantly improve forecasting accuracy and provide real-time insights into stock or sector trends (Darapaneni et al., 2022; Wang et al., 2024; Papasotiriou et al., 2024).

Risk Assessment And News Impact

LLMs are essential for risk assessment and news impact analysis because they allow financial firms to quickly analyze and respond to market-moving events. When events such as mergers, earnings surprises, or geopolitical shifts occur, LLMs can analyze a combination of news articles, earnings transcripts, and social media sentiment to predict potential impacts on stock prices and investor behavior (Zhang et al., 2025). This real-time analysis is particularly valuable for algorithmic trading, where sentiment insights are directly integrated into trading strategies, allowing systems to react faster and more accurately than traditional models. Additionally, LLMs enhance time series forecasting by decomposing financial data into components like trends and seasonality, converting them into tailored textual formats, and leveraging their deep understanding of language to detect complex temporal patterns (Zhao et al., 2025). This hybrid approach strengthens both predictive accuracy and market responsiveness.

CASE STUDIES AND REAL-WORLD DEPLOYMENTS IN FINANCE

Several financial institutions have already integrated LLMs into their operations, showcasing the real-world effectiveness of these models (Liu, 2024).

- **JPMorgan Chase:** JPMorgan Chase has embraced AI extensively throughout its business processes (Son, 2024; Yazdanipour, 2024). A key example is their Contract Intelligence system, which utilizes Large Language Models to automate the analysis and review of legal contracts (Chirinos, 2024). This technology has significantly accelerated the review workflow, reducing what once took hundreds of thousands of hours to just seconds. JPMorgan is also using LLMs to assist employees with writing, summarizing documents and problem solving (Son, 2024).
- **HSBC**: HSBC has leveraged LLMs for real-time fraud detection by analyzing customer transaction history, user behavior, and external sources like social media feeds. This helps them identify potential fraudulent activity based on both structured transaction data and unstructured textual content.
- **Goldman Sachs:** Goldman Sachs has used LLMs to integrate market sentiment analysis into their stock forecasting models (Papasotiriou et al., 2024). By processing news articles, analyst reports, and social media posts, Goldman has improved its ability to predict stock movements, providing its traders with better insights for decision-making.

These deployments demonstrate the practical benefits and transformative potential of LLMs in the financial industry.

LLMS IN HEALTHCARE SYSTEMS

LLMs are transforming healthcare by enhancing diagnosis, treatment, and patient interaction through their ability to understand and generate complex medical language (Choudhury et al., 2023). Unlike traditional rule-based systems, LLMs can synthesize unstructured data—such as clinical notes, research articles, and patient communications to improve clinical efficiency, reduce documentation burden, and personalize patient care. By facilitating meaningful physician-patient dialogue, LLMs contribute to more compassionate and effective healthcare (Tu et al., 2025). Key applications include intelligent virtual assistants, EHR summarization, and clinical decision support, with growing evidence from both research and real-world use.

VIRTUAL ASSISTANTS AND INTELLIGENT TRIAGE SYSTEMS

The deployment of AI-powered virtual assistants in healthcare has grown significantly with the advancement of LLMs (Borna et al., 2024). These assistants can engage patients in natural, conversational ways, answering questions, scheduling appointments, gathering preliminary symptoms, and providing health advice.

Intelligent Triage Systems

LLMs enable intelligent triage by interacting with patients through chatbots or voice assistants, collecting symptom information, and recommending appropriate next steps (Lai et al., 2020). Unlike traditional symptom-checkers, LLMs can personalize triage decisions by considering patient history, demographics, and reported symptoms more contextually. These systems reduce the workload on healthcare providers by pre-screening patients and prioritizing cases that require urgent attention (Valmianski et al., 2021).

Case Example

The deployment of the Babylon Health platform illustrates the use of LLM-based triage, where patients interact with a chatbot that suggests possible causes for symptoms and recommends appropriate care pathways, including urgent care or home management. Moreover, hospitals have integrated LLM-driven triage into telemedicine platforms, offering quicker and more accurate routing of patients to specialists based on their inputs. SmartTriage is a system designed for personalized patient data collection, automated documentation, and clinical decision support. Initially tested in an urgent care setting, it is now being piloted in virtual visits across the Kaiser Permanente Southern California Region, functioning as a pre-visit symptom assessment tool (Valmianski et al., 2020).

GENERATIVE AI FOR PATIENT EDUCATION AND EHR SUMMARIZATION

LLMs have also shown significant potential in enhancing patient education and streamlining documentation tasks that consume considerable clinical time (Veen et al., 2024).

Patient Education

Medical jargon can be overwhelming for patients, especially those without a healthcare background. LLMs can simplify complex medical information into layman-friendly language, creating personalized educational materials based on an individual's condition, treatment options, and recovery expectations. This not only improves patient understanding but also supports shared decision-making (Generative AI for Patient-Friendly Language in Discharge Summaries, 2024). For instance, an LLM-based system can automatically generate FAQs, medication instructions, post-operative care guidelines, and lifestyle modification tips tailored to the patient's literacy level and cultural context. By prompting LLMs to generate a layperson summary, complex information can be normalized and simplified using techniques inspired by doctor-patient interactions (Zhao et al., 2024).

Ehr Summarization

Clinical documentation, though critical, is often cited as a major source of physician burnout (Veen et al., 2024). LLMs can automatically summarize extensive EHR entries, distilling patient history, diagnostic tests, clinical impressions, and treatment plans into concise, coherent notes (Ramamurthy, 2023). Some modern EHR systems have started integrating LLMs to assist in summarizing patient visits, hospital discharge summaries, and specialist referrals. These tools not only save time but also reduce the risk of documentation errors and omissions.

Case Example

Companies are pioneering the integration of LLMs into clinical workflows to automatically transcribe and summarize doctor-patient conversations, generating real-time structured notes for review and editing by the clinician.

CLINICAL DECISION SUPPORT USING MEDICAL LITERATURE AND GUIDELINES

Another transformative application of LLMs in healthcare is clinical decision support, where these models assist physicians by synthesizing the latest medical research, guidelines, and case studies (Mehandru et al., 2023).

Guideline Adherence and Personalized Treatment

LLMs can ingest clinical practice guidelines from various medical societies, tailoring treatment recommendations based on the specific conditions of the patient, comorbidities, and preferences. These models can then automatically flag potential deviations from guidelines, ensuring adherence to best practices and minimizing unwarranted variations in care. In clinical settings, LLMs can offer real-time decision support by analyzing patient data against clinical guidelines, offering suggestions for medication adjustments or diagnostic tests. LLMs are also being investigated as tools that help match patients with suitable clinical trials by comparing individual patient information against eligibility criteria from databases like clinicaltrials.gov.

These models can quickly acquire specialized knowledge in various medical disciplines, including radiology, pathology, and oncology, thereby supporting more accurate and efficient clinical decision-making (Karabacak & Margetis, 2023). The use of LLMs spans across a range of medical tasks, including answering medical questions, clinical documentation, and matching patients to clinical trials (Jin et al., 2024). Despite these benefits, LLMs are not always accurate and can potentially generate misinformation and reflect biases that could exacerbate healthcare disparities (Singhal et al., 2023).

Case Example

IBM Watson Oncology was an early attempt to apply AI in clinical decision support by analyzing oncology literature and guidelines to assist oncologists in selecting treatment options. However, challenges such as data integration issues, lack of model transparency, and limited clinical acceptance hindered its broader adoption (Bedi et al., 2024; Rydzewski et al., 2024). With the emergence of more advanced LLMs, there is renewed potential to provide personalized, evidence-based recommendations that better integrate with clinical workflows.

LLMs are increasingly central to biomedical AI, capable of uncovering complex relationships in large datasets. Deep learning has already been applied in areas like medical image analysis, gene expression, protein structure prediction, and clinical language processing (Martínez & Dongen, 2023). In cancer care, these models can support early detection and screening, especially in underserved regions, by offering non-invasive, cost-effective, and radiation-free diagnostic tools helping address disparities in access and reducing late-stage diagnoses.

TECHNICAL IMPLEMENTATION OF LLM

The deployment of LLMs in critical and sensitive fields like healthcare requires strong and reliable technical infrastructures (Jin et al., 2024). The power of these models lies not just in their pre-trained capabilities but in how they are engineered, fine-tuned, and integrated into existing digital infrastructures (Karabacak & Margetis, 2023). Successful real-world applications require a cohesive pipeline from data acquisition and preprocessing to domain adaptation, to secure and scalable deployment (Jin et al., 2024).

DESIGNING AND OPERATIONALIZING LLM PIPELINES FOR HEALTHCARE AND FINANCE

Deploying Large Language Models in complex sectors like healthcare and finance requires a comprehensive, well-structured pipeline that ensures performance, reliability, and regulatory compliance. From data preprocessing and model fine-tuning to secure deployment and interpretability, each phase must be carefully engineered to address domain-specific constraints and ethical obligations. This section outlines the core technical components involved in building and operationalizing LLM solutions that are both scalable and trustworthy.

Preprocessing Pipelines

The initial stage involves meticulous data preprocessing, where raw healthcare or financial records are transformed into a structured format suitable for LLMs (Zubiaga, 2024). This includes data cleaning to handle missing values, outliers, and inconsistencies (Karabacak & Margetis, 2023). Tokenization is then applied to convert text into numerical tokens that the model can process, using techniques like byte-pair encoding or WordPiece to handle out-of-vocabulary words (Khalid et al., 2024). Feature engineering might also be necessary to extract relevant information from the raw data, such as creating time-series features for financial forecasting or medical concept embeddings for clinical text (Karabacak & Margetis, 2023).

Basic Model Architecture

LLMs are based on transformer architectures, which excel at capturing long-distance dependencies within text through the use of attention mechanisms. Models such as BERT and XLNet have achieved remarkable success across numerous natural language processing tasks. Furthermore, these architectures can be adapted and fine-tuned to meet the unique demands of specific domains, making them particularly useful in specialized areas like finance and healthcare (Rodriguez et al., 2019).

The development of LLMs generally follows three key phases: pre-training, fine-tuning, and prompt tuning. In the pre-training stage, the model is exposed to extensive volumes of unlabeled text data and learns language patterns through self-supervised learning, building a broad understanding of language. Fine-tuning then tailors this general knowledge to particular tasks or domains by training the model on specialized datasets, which may be labeled or unlabeled. This step can involve supervised, unsupervised, or instruction-driven methods and incorporates regularization techniques such as dropout and weight decay to prevent overfitting and improve generalization. Transfer learning also helps by leveraging related knowledge to speed up training and improve accuracy (Clusmann et al., 2023; Parthasarathy et al., 2024; Su & Vijay-Shanker, 2022).

Finally, prompt tuning guides the model's behavior through carefully crafted input prompts without changing its internal parameters. This interactive approach allows flexible, context-aware use of LLMs, especially when fine-tuning is costly or impractical.

Figure 1. The Basic LLM Architecture

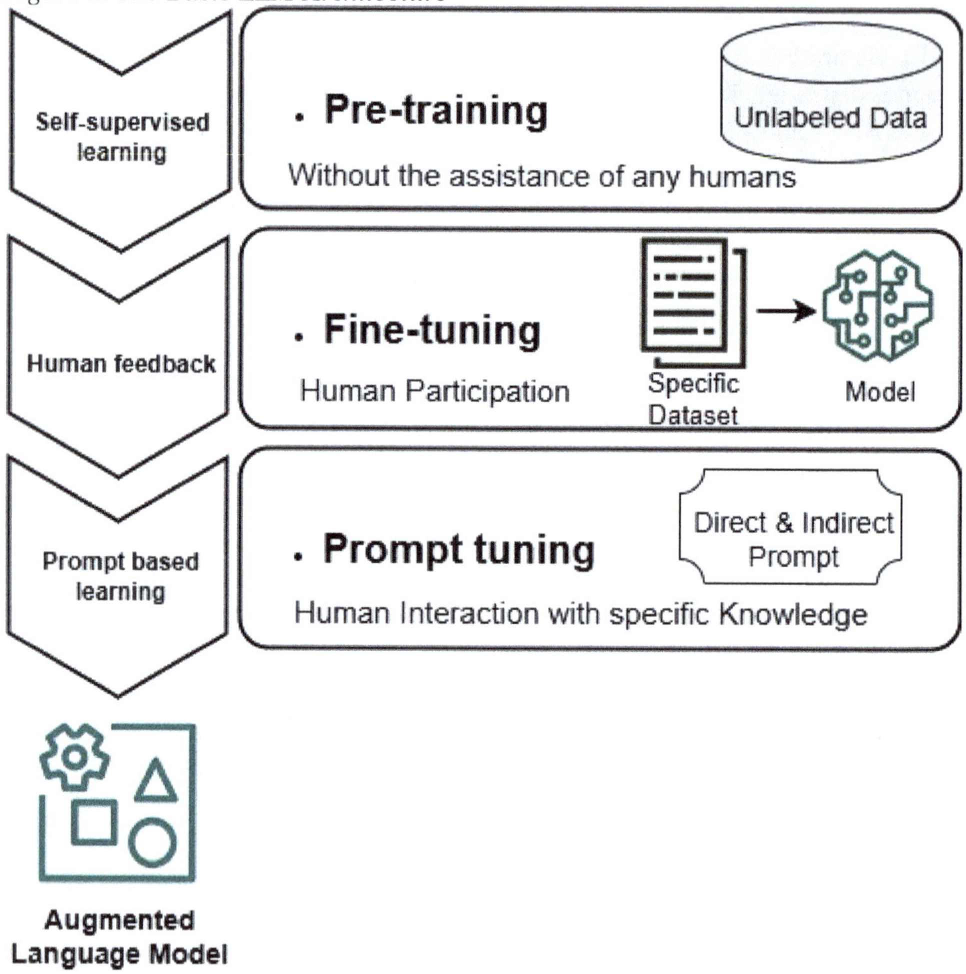

Deployment and Scalability

Once trained, the LLM needs to be deployed in a production environment, considering factors such as latency, throughput, and scalability. Model quantization and pruning can be used to reduce the model size and computational requirements, enabling faster inference times and lower deployment costs. Distributed computing frameworks like TensorFlow Distributed and PyTorch DistributedDataParallel enable scaling models across multiple GPUs or machines, enhancing processing speed and allowing efficient handling of large datasets.

Protecting sensitive data is critical in industries such as healthcare and finance. To comply with regulations like HIPAA and GDPR, organizations employ strategies including data encryption, controlled access, and anonymization methods. In addition, they maintain continuous surveillance and detailed logging of system activities to monitor model behavior, quickly identify anomalies, and address security threats promptly.

The integration of LLMs into existing systems often requires building APIs and interfaces that allow other applications to interact with the model. This involves designing the API endpoints, defining the data formats, and implementing authentication and authorization mechanisms.

Explainability and Interpretability in LLMs

When deploying LLMs in critical areas like healthcare and finance, ensuring that their decisions are transparent and understandable is essential. Explainability and interpretability play a key role in building trust and enabling informed oversight in these high-impact settings. These concepts help developers, practitioners, and end-users understand how the model arrives at its predictions or decisions an essential factor for building trust, ensuring accountability, and validating results, especially when outcomes directly impact people's lives or financial well-being. As LLMs grow increasingly complex sometimes comprising hundreds of billions or even trillions of parameters it becomes more challenging to predict their behavior or pinpoint how specific inputs influence the outputs (Ayyamperumal & Ge, 2024). This complexity can lead to opacity, where the model functions as a "black box," making it difficult to verify its reasoning or ensure its decisions are fair and unbiased.

To address this challenge, researchers and practitioners employ several interpretability and explainability techniques:

- Attention Visualization: Common in transformer-based models, this technique shows which parts of the input the model "pays attention to" during prediction. For instance, in medical document summarization, attention maps can highlight specific clinical terms or symptoms that the model considers significant.
- LIME (Local Interpretable Model-agnostic Explanations): LIME generates straightforward, interpretable models focused on the vicinity of a specific prediction to reveal which features had the greatest impact on that outcome. Since it operates independently of the underlying model, making it a flexible tool for explaining individual predictions.

- SHAP (SHapley Additive exPlanations): SHAP uses principles from game theory to attribute an importance score to each input feature, indicating its contribution to a given prediction. It provides a global view of how input features affect the model, helping to uncover consistent patterns and potential biases.

These methods not only aid in identifying the key features that drive model decisions but also help in diagnosing problems like model overfitting, bias, or data leakage. In regulated environments like finance or healthcare, explainability is often not just a technical requirement but also a legal one ensuring compliance with transparency mandates under regulations like the GDPR or FDA guidelines. Moreover, explainability tools support model improvement. By analyzing which inputs lead to correct or incorrect predictions, developers can refine the model, retrain it with better-aligned data, or incorporate rule-based checks to prevent risky outputs.

Integration Of Llms Into Financial And Clinical Information Systems

Integrating LLMs into production systems requires careful orchestration of interoperability, latency optimization, and security safeguards. In financial services, LLMs are commonly embedded in fraud monitoring platforms, compliance automation systems, and predictive analytics pipelines (Liu, 2024). These integrations must adhere to strict regulatory frameworks, such as Basel III, MiFID II, or national Know Your Customer standards. Moreover, financial institutions require explainability for model outputs to meet transparency and auditability standards (Ferdaus et al., 2024; Tavasoli et al., 2025).

Similarly, healthcare systems integrate LLMs into electronic health records, virtual assistants, and clinical decision support systems. For instance, models can summarize lengthy clinical notes, suggest differential diagnoses, or alert clinicians to guideline deviations. Integration into EHR platforms like Epic and Cerner often relies on standardized APIs such as FHIR and is governed by strict access controls to maintain patient confidentiality. Federated learning approaches can also be used to connect data from various institutions while maintaining data anonymity (Kumbhare et al., 2023).

Challenges in system integration include ensuring low-latency responses, maintaining interoperability with legacy systems, and implementing robust human-in-the-loop validation mechanisms (Clario Enhances the Quality of the Clinical Trial Documentation Process with Amazon Bedrock, 2025). In both sectors, users whether clinicians or financial analysts must retain the final decision-making authority, necessitating interfaces that allow the verification, rejection, or editing of model outputs.

Tools, Frameworks, and Best Practices for Implementation

Several open-source and commercial tools support the implementation and deployment of LLMs. Libraries like Hugging Face Transformers, PyTorch, and TensorFlow facilitate model development, while tools like spaCy, Stanza, and Spark NLP are used for preprocessing tasks such as NER and part-of-speech tagging. For deployment, platforms such as ONNX Runtime, NVIDIA Triton Inference Server, and MLflow offer scalability and monitoring capabilities. Containerization using Docker, combined with orchestration tools like Kubernetes, enables modular and fault-tolerant deployment architectures.

Best practices for implementation include:

- *Data minimization and anonymization:* Employ data anonymization techniques during model training and inference to reduce privacy risks and comply with regulations like HIPAA (Kumbhare et al., 2023).
- *Phased deployment*: Begin with low-risk applications such as summarization or information retrieval before expanding into critical decision-support tasks (Song et al., 2024).
- *Continuous monitoring:* Implement continuous monitoring for model drift and performance degradation, supported by tools like Weights & Biases or Prometheus (Bedi et al., 2024).
- *Explainability mechanisms:* Utilize explainability mechanisms, such as attention visualizations or post-hoc interpretation methods (e.g., SHAP or LIME), to improve transparency and trust (Ferdaus et al., 2024).
- *Human-in-the-loop systems:* Implement systems that actively involve human experts during the decision-making process, allowing clinicians or regulatory professionals to review, validate, or override the model's outputs when necessary. This approach ensures safety, accountability, and aligns AI decisions with domain-specific expertise (Song et al., 2024).
- *Security Considerations:* To maintain the confidentiality and integrity of sensitive information, especially in domains like healthcare and finance, it is essential to adopt robust security measures. These include data encryption, strict access control policies, and anonymization techniques, all of which help ensure compliance with legal frameworks such as HIPAA and GDPR.
- *API Integration:* Build APIs and interfaces that allow other applications to interact with the model, designing the API endpoints, defining the data formats, and implementing authentication and authorization mechanisms.

Ultimately, the technical success of LLM integration depends on a multidisciplinary approach that bridges machine learning engineering, cybersecurity, compliance, and domain-specific expertise.

CHALLENGES AND LIMITATIONS

The integration of LLMs in finance and healthcare offers important transformative possibilities but also presents various technical, ethical, and operational hurdles. Given the critical nature of these sectors, concerns like data security, algorithmic fairness, and ongoing model upkeep must be prioritized in any LLM implementation plan. This section systematically addresses the principal limitations organizations must navigate: safeguarding privacy and ensuring model explainability, mitigating biases to uphold fairness, and managing scalability alongside model drift in constantly evolving environments.

Addressing Data Privacy, Security, And Explainability

A primary challenge in implementing LLMs in healthcare and finance is ensuring the protection of confidential information. Healthcare data is subject to stringent regulations, such as HIPAA, while financial data is governed by standards like the GDPR and PCI-DSS. Due to the potential for LLMs to retain and reproduce training data (Carlini et al., 2021), there is a significant risk that sensitive details could be exposed during model use.

To address these concerns, methods such as differential privacy, federated learning, and the creation of synthetic data are being utilized to reduce potential risks effectively (Dwork & Roth, 2014). Differential privacy ensures that outputs are statistically unlikely to reveal individual data points, while federated learning keeps data localized on devices or institutional servers, reducing centralized exposure.

Security, however, extends beyond data leakage. LLMs are susceptible to adversarial attacks, including data poisoning and prompt injection, which can manipulate model outputs or expose vulnerabilities (Zhang et al., 2023). Thus, robust cybersecurity protocols must accompany LLM deployment, including regular threat assessments, anomaly detection systems, and incident response frameworks.

Explainability is equally critical. In regulated sectors, models must not operate as "black boxes." Techniques like SHAP (SHapley Additive exPlanations) values, integrated gradients, and attention visualization can offer insights into model decision processes (Lundberg & Lee, 2017; Sundararajan et al., 2017). Providing interpretable explanations not only builds trust but is increasingly becoming a regulatory requirement, as seen in the EU's AI Act and other emerging legislation.

Mitigating Bias And Ensuring Fairness In High-Stakes Domains

LLMs inherit biases from their training data, which often reflect societal, racial, gender, and economic inequalities (Bender et al., 2021). In finance, bias can lead to unfair loan approvals or investment recommendations that disproportionately disadvantage certain demographic groups. In healthcare, biased model outputs can exacerbate disparities in treatment recommendations and patient outcomes (Obermeyer et al., 2019).

Mitigating bias starts with careful dataset curation and continues through algorithmic interventions such as reweighting, adversarial debiasing, and fairness constraints during model training (Zhao et al., 2018). It also involves continual auditing of model outputs using metrics like demographic parity, equalized odds, and disparate impact analysis.

Moreover, fairness must be contextualized within each domain. For example, while equal treatment of all patients is a goal in healthcare, fairness in finance might prioritize preventing systematic discrimination while allowing for risk-based pricing models. Stakeholder engagement including patients, regulators, financial consumers, and ethicists is vital to defining domain-appropriate fairness benchmarks. In addition to technical fixes, organizational policies such as "bias incident reporting systems" and "AI ethics boards" are being introduced to institutionalize fairness governance frameworks (Raji et al., 2020).

Managing Scalability And Model Drift In Dynamic Environments

Scalability and adaptability are essential when deploying LLMs in environments that are inherently dynamic. Financial markets and healthcare knowledge bases evolve rapidly; what is accurate today may become obsolete tomorrow. Scalability involves ensuring that LLM systems can handle growing volumes of data and queries without degradation in performance. Techniques like model distillation, quantization, and distributed inference across multiple nodes are commonly employed to maintain scalability without incurring prohibitive computational costs (Sanh et al., 2019).

Model drift occurs when accuracy of the model decreases over time because the data it encounters changes. This can happen either because the input data distribution shifts, known as covariate shift, or because the connection between the input features and the target outcomes evolves (Gama et al., 2014). For example, a fraud detection model trained on pre-pandemic transaction patterns may underperform during post-pandemic economic shifts. In healthcare, new clinical guidelines or emerging diseases (e.g., COVID-19) can render existing models obsolete.

Addressing model drift requires continuous monitoring pipelines that detect deviations in model confidence, prediction accuracy, and feature importance. Retraining strategies such as scheduled fine-tuning, online learning, and active learning can help maintain model relevance. Some organizations also employ "shadow models," which run parallel to production models and serve as early indicators of drift (Baier et al., 2023).

ETHICAL, LEGAL, AND REGULATORY CONSIDERATIONS

The deployment of LLMs in healthcare and finance raises profound ethical, legal, and regulatory questions. These sectors are not only data-intensive but also deeply embedded in public trust and legal obligations. As LLMs gain increasing autonomy in supporting decision-making processes, ensuring their ethical operation and legal compliance becomes imperative. This section explores the regulatory frameworks guiding AI usage, focusing on HIPAA, GDPR, and financial compliance standards, and discusses the design and governance of responsible AI systems that are fair, transparent, and accountable.

Navigating HIPAA, GDPR, and Financial Compliance Standards

Compliance with existing data protection regulations is a non-negotiable aspect of LLM deployment in both healthcare and finance. The HIPAA in the United States outlines stringent rules regarding the use, disclosure, and safeguarding of protected health information (PHI). LLMs trained on patient data such as clinical notes or EHRs must incorporate mechanisms to anonymize sensitive data and prevent re-identification risks. This requires not only technical safeguards such as encryption and access controls but also organizational policies governing how models are trained and evaluated.

The GDPR, applicable across the European Union, mandates data minimization, purpose limitation, and explicit user consent for data processing. One of its most challenging clauses for AI systems is the "right to explanation," which implies that individuals can demand transparency in algorithmic decision-making. While traditional machine learning systems may meet this requirement through decision trees or linear models, LLMs due to their complexity pose novel challenges in interpretability and compliance.

In the financial industry, LLMs applied to tasks like fraud detection or credit risk assessment must comply with oversight frameworks established by bodies such as the U.S. Securities and Exchange Commission, the FINRA, and the Basel Committee on Banking Supervision. These entities mandate rigorous auditing of automated decision-making systems, transparent documentation of model functionality, and adherence to anti-money laundering and KYC requirements. To support regulatory compliance, LLM deployments must include comprehensive documentation pipelines that record details of training data sources, fine-tuning processes, and inference mechanisms to enable effective regulatory scrutiny.

Establishing Responsible AI Practices and Transparent Model Governance

Beyond legal compliance, the ethical operation of LLMs demands structured frameworks for responsible AI. This encompasses fairness, accountability, transparency, and human oversight principles that are critical in environments where decisions impact financial access or patient care.

Model governance denotes to the institutional practices and oversight mechanisms that guarantee AI systems operate as intended. This includes establishing cross-functional AI ethics boards, integrating regular impact assessments, and enforcing audit trails for decisions made or influenced by LLMs (Raji et al., 2020). Governance structures should also ensure that updates to models such as re-training with new data or integrating external knowledge—are reviewed for potential unintended consequences.

Transparency is particularly crucial in demystifying how LLMs arrive at their outputs. While attention visualizations and post-hoc explainers such as LIME and SHAP are useful, explainability must also be integrated upstream, beginning with interpretable training data and modular model architectures (Doshi-Velez & Kim, 2017). Developers must balance interpretability with performance, particularly in high-stakes scenarios.

Human-in-the-loop systems offer a pragmatic compromise, where AI recommendations are subject to review by professional clinicians, compliance officers, or financial analysts before final action. This not only moderate risks related with model error but also ensures accountability. Finally, inclusive development practices involving diverse stakeholders in data annotation, model evaluation, and deployment feedback can preemptively identify blind spots and ethical pitfalls (Whittaker et al., 2018). Stakeholder consultation is especially important when the population served is vulnerable, such as patients in critical care or financially marginalized communities.

CONCLUSION AND FUTURE DIRECTIONS

The integration of LLMs into healthcare and finance holds transformative potential for applications like fraud detection and market trend prediction, but it demands careful attention to challenges in reasoning, transparency, and regulatory adherence. Ongoing research is crucial to improve algorithms, enhance the clarity of model outputs, and develop standardized metrics to evaluate LLMs' effectiveness in practical settings. Additionally, collaboration across disciplines spanning natural language processing, finance, and healthcare is vital to tackle the ethical and societal consequences of LLM adoption. LLMs have shown promise in analysing financial data, predicting market movements, and identifying anomalies that could signal fraudulent activities. As these models advance, they are set to play an important role in strengthening financial systems and improving patient outcomes. Creating tailored datasets for instruction tuning can significantly boost LLM performance in these sectors. Moreover, strategic pre-training, fine-tuning, and efficient parameter optimization are key to maximizing their impact in finance and healthcare.

The future of LLMs into healthcare workflows will require active collaboration among educators, students, and developers to ensure these tools are implemented ethically and effectively (Ravi et al., 2023). As feedback and essay revision data continue to grow, institutions can leverage this information to refine model behaviour and tailor prompts for specific educational objectives, leading to more accurate and context-aware outcomes (Song et al., 2024). One key area of development is prompt engineering the process of crafting input queries that guide LLMs toward producing relevant and high-quality responses. Continued research is needed to identify optimal prompt strategies for use cases such as automated essay scoring and revision, which are becoming increasingly valuable in classroom settings (Mizumoto & Eguchi, 2023; Song et al., 2024).

Toward Multimodal LLMs and Industry-Wide Adoption

Advancements in multimodal LLMs which are capable of analysing and combining data from multiple sources such as text, images, and audio offer significant potential for improving fraud detection and financial forecasting (Yang et al., 2024). By integrating diverse types of information, these models enable deeper insights into complex patterns and support more accurate, informed decision-making. The deployment of LLMs across these fields has the potential to transform how financial institutions and healthcare providers operate, leading to more efficient processes, better patient outcomes, and greater financial stability (Yan et al., 2023). The use of automated essay scoring and automated essay revision tools based on LLMs can also greatly benefit educational institutions. It is also worth mentioning that the performance of open-source LLMs in the AES task is not as good as the optimal performance of the deep-learning model, but it can achieve a high level of moderate consistency with the "gold standard" of human scores (Chassab et al., 2024).

Major challenges hindering widespread adoption of LLMs in sectors like healthcare and finance include issues related to data privacy, lack of transparency in model decision-making, and the need to meet strict regulatory standards. Overcoming these obstacles is essential to fully realize the benefits of LLMs in these critical domains. Integrating LLMs into clinical settings demands collaboration among educators, healthcare trainees, and model developers to ensure their use is ethical, effective, and aligned with real-world medical needs (Singhal et al., 2023). One major worry is the possibility of relying too heavily on AI technology, which would diminish human participation in crucial decision-making processes (Karabacak & Margetis, 2023).

Trends in Foundation Models and Cross-Domain Knowledge Transfer

Recent trends in foundation models, such as the creation of huge and more complex architectures, have prepared the way for considerable advances in NLP and machine learning. These base models are used to create specialized LLMs for particular tasks in healthcare and finance. The ability to transfer information from one domain to another, such as finance to healthcare or vice versa, can speed up the development and deployment of LLMs in both fields (Ding et al., 2024). In the future, researchers could assess the technique's effectiveness when implemented for essays written in other languages or on subjects unrelated to those addressed by existing databases (Chassab et al., 2024). The integration of LLMs into education may be seen as a way to democratize access to high-quality learning resources and individualized support, especially for students in marginalized areas (Tourni et al., 2023).

REFERENCES

Abnave, P. (2023, October 12). Language models revolutionizing financial crime prevention. Medium. https://medium.com/@pratikabnave97/language-models-revolutionizing-financial-crime-prevention-4ea92fa82eb2

Agarwal, S. (2024, June 24). Fraud detection stays relevant in the age of LLMs. Medium. https://s-hash-wat.medium.com/how-fraud-detection-stays-relevant-in-the-age-of-llms-f6debe7be518

Amamou, W. (2025, January 15). AI agents in fraud detection: Bridging the gap between traditional machine learning and human reasoning. Medium. https://walidamamou.medium.com/ai-agents-in-fraud-detection-bridging-the-gap-between-traditional-machine-learning-and-human-c901524fef58

Ayyamperumal, S. G., & Ge, L. (2024). Current state of LLM risks and AI guardrails. arXiv. /arXiv.2406.12934DOI: 10.48550

Baier, L., Schlör, T., Schömer, M., & Kress, N. (2023). Detecting concept drift in medical data streams using shadow models. *IEEE Transactions on Artificial Intelligence, 4*(5), 1095–1107. DOI: 10.1109/TAI.2022.3225770

Balona, C. (2024). ActuaryGPT: Applications of large language models to insurance and actuarial work. *British Actuarial Journal, 29*, e15. Advance online publication. DOI: 10.1017/S1357321724000087

Bedi, S., Liu, Y., Orr-Ewing, L., Dash, D., Koyejo, S., Callahan, A., & Shah, N. H. (2024). Testing and evaluation of health care applications of large language models: A systematic review. *Journal of the American Medical Association, 332*(18), 1527–1538. DOI: 10.1001/jama.2024.19455 PMID: 38619831

Bender, E. M., Gebru, T., McMillan-Major, A., & Shmitchell, S. (2021). On the dangers of stochastic parrots: Can language models be too big? In *Proceedings of the 2021 ACM conference on fairness, accountability, and transparency (FAccT '21)* (pp. 610–623). Association for Computing Machinery. DOI: 10.1145/3442188.3445922

Borna, S., Gomez-Cabello, C. A., Pressman, S. M., Haider, S. A., Sehgal, A., Leibovich, B. C., & Forte, A. J. (2024). Comparative analysis of artificial intelligence virtual assistant and large language models in post-operative care. *European Journal of Investigation in Health, Psychology and Education, 14*(5), 1413–1424. DOI: 10.3390/ejihpe14050094 PMID: 38785591

Chassab, R. H., Zakaria, L. Q., & Tiun, S. (2024). An optimized LSTM-based augmented language model (FLSTM-ALM) using Fox algorithm for automatic essay scoring prediction. *IEEE Access : Practical Innovations, Open Solutions*, *12*, 105080–105093. DOI: 10.1109/ACCESS.2024.3432778

Chen, Z., Chen, J., Chen, J., & Sra, M. (2025). Position: Standard benchmarks fail—LLM agents present overlooked risks for financial applications. arXiv. /arXiv.2502.15865DOI: 10.48550

Chirinos, J. (2024, May 20). Case study: JPMorgan Chase's Contract Intelligence (COiN) platform for document analysis. LinkedIn. https://www.linkedin.com/pulse/case-study-jpmorgan-chases-contract-intelligence-coin-jorge-chirinos-qcyje

Choudhury De, M., Pendse, S. R., & Kumar, N. (2023). Benefits and harms of large language models in digital mental health. arXiv. /arXiv.2311.14693DOI: 10.48550

Clario enhances the quality of the clinical trial documentation process with Amazon Bedrock. (2025, February 10). AWS Machine Learning Blog. https://aws.amazon.com/blogs/machine-learning/clario-enhances-the-quality-of-the-clinical-trial-documentation-process-with-amazon-bedrock/

Clusmann, J., Kolbinger, F. R., Muti, H. S., Carrero, Z. I., Eckardt, J. N., Laleh, N. G., & Kather, J. N. (2023). The future landscape of large language models in medicine. *Communications Medicine*, *3*, 141. Advance online publication. DOI: 10.1038/s43856-023-00370-1 PMID: 37816837

Darapaneni, N., Paduri, A. R., Sharma, H., Manjrekar, M., Hindlekar, N., Bhagat, P., . . . Agarwal, Y. (2022). Stock price prediction using sentiment analysis and deep learning for Indian markets. arXiv. /arXiv.2204.05783DOI: 10.48550

Desai, R. A. (n.d.). Genetic algorithm with deep learning for fraud Ethereum transaction detection. [Unpublished manuscript].

Dilmegani, C. (2025, January 8). Best 10 large language models in healthcare in 2025. AIMultiple Research. https://research.aimultiple.com/large-language-models-in-healthcare/

Ding, Z., Liu, Z., Jiang, H., Gao, Y., Zhai, X., Liu, T., & Liu, N. (2024). Foundation models for low-resource language education (Vision paper). arXiv. /arXiv.2412.04774DOI: 10.48550

Fatouros, G., Metaxas, K., Soldatos, J., & Karathanassis, M. (2025). MarketSenseAI 2.0: Enhancing stock analysis through LLM agents. arXiv. /arXiv.2502.00415DOI: 10.48550

Ferdaus, M. M., Abdelguerfi, M., Ioup, E., Niles, K. N., Pathak, K., & Sloan, S. (2024). Towards trustworthy AI: A review of ethical and robust large language models. arXiv. /arXiv.2407.13934DOI: 10.48550

Floridi, L., Cowls, J., King, T. C., & Taddeo, M. (2021). How to design AI for social good: Seven essential factors. In Dubber, M. D., Pasquale, F., & Das, S. (Eds.), *The Oxford handbook of ethics of AI* (pp. 125–151). Oxford University Press., DOI: 10.1007/978-3-030-69921-5_8

Gama, J., Žliobaitė, I., Bifet, A., Pechenizkiy, M., & Bouchachia, A. (2014). A survey on concept drift adaptation. *ACM Computing Surveys*, *46*(4), 44. Advance online publication. DOI: 10.1145/2523813

Gencer, G., & Gencer, K. (2025). Large language models in healthcare: A bibliometric analysis and examination of research trends. *Journal of Multidisciplinary Healthcare*, *18*, 223–238. DOI: 10.2147/JMDH.S480505 PMID: 39844924

Generative AI and LLMs in banking: Examples, use cases, limitations, and solutions. (2024, November 18). Dynamiq. https://www.getdynamiq.ai/post/generative-ai-and-llms-in-banking-examples-use-cases-limitations-and-solutions

Generative AI for patient-friendly language in discharge summaries. (2024). JAMA Network Open, 7(4), e245323. DOI: 10.1001/jamanetworkopen.2024.5323

Hadi, M. U., Qureshi, R., Shah, A., Irfan, M., Zafar, A., Shaikh, M. B., & Mirjalili, S. (2023). Large language models: A comprehensive survey of its applications, challenges, limitations, and future prospects. *Authorea*. DOI: 10.22541/au.169476831.94963464/v1

He, Y., Qiu, J., Zhang, W., & Yuan, Z. (2024). Fortifying ethical boundaries in AI: Advanced strategies for enhancing security in large language models. arXiv. /arXiv.2402.01725DOI: 10.48550

Jin, Q., Wan, N., Leaman, R., Tian, S., Wang, Z., Yang, Y., . . . Lu, Z. (2024). Demystifying large language models for medicine: A primer. arXiv. /arXiv.2410.18856DOI: 10.48550

Jonnagaddala, J., & Wong, Z. S. Y. (2025). Privacy preserving strategies for electronic health records in the era of large language models. npj. *Digital Medicine*, *8*(1), 34. Advance online publication. DOI: 10.1038/s41746-025-01308-8 PMID: 39820020

Karabacak, M., & Margetis, K. (2023). Embracing large language models for medical applications: Opportunities and challenges. *Cureus*, *15*(5), e39305. Advance online publication. DOI: 10.7759/cureus.39305 PMID: 37378099

Khalid, A., Khalid, A., & Khalid, U. (2024). The role of language models in modern healthcare: A comprehensive review. arXiv. /arXiv.2409.16860DOI: 10.48550

Lai, L., Wittbold, K. A., Dadabhoy, F. Z., Sato, R., Landman, A. B., Schwamm, L. H., & Zhang, H. M. (2020). Digital triage: Novel strategies for population health management in response to the COVID-19 pandemic. *Health Care*, *8*(4), 100493. Advance online publication. DOI: 10.1016/j.hjdsi.2020.100493 PMID: 33129176

Lareyre, F., & Raffort, J. (2024). Ethical concerns regarding the use of large language models in healthcare. *EJVES Vascular Forum*, *61*, 1. DOI: 10.1016/j.ejvsvf.2023.12.003 PMID: 38025830

Lee, J., Stevens, N., & Han, S. C. (2025). Large language models in finance (FinLLMs). *Neural Computing & Applications*. Advance online publication. DOI: 10.1007/s00521-024-10756-8

Li, H., Moon, J. T., Purkayastha, S., Celi, L. A., Trivedi, H., & Gichoya, J. W. (2023). Ethics of large language models in medicine and medical research. *The Lancet. Digital Health*, *5*(6), e333–e335. DOI: 10.1016/S2589-7500(23)00083-9 PMID: 37120418

Li, Y., Wang, S., Ding, H., & Chen, H. (2023, November). Large language models in finance: A survey. In *Proceedings of the fourth ACM international conference on AI in finance* (pp. 374–382). Association for Computing Machinery. DOI: 10.1145/3604237.3626869

Liu, J. (2024). A survey of financial AI: Architectures, advances and open challenges. arXiv. /arXiv.2411.12747DOI: 10.48550

Mehandru, N., Miao, B. Y., Almaraz, E. R., Sushil, M., Butte, A. J., & Alaa, A. (2023). Large language models as agents in the clinic. arXiv. /arXiv.2309.10895DOI: 10.48550

Mizumoto, A., & Eguchi, M. (2023). Exploring the potential of using an AI language model for automated essay scoring. *Research Methods in Applied Linguistics*, *2*(2), 100050. Advance online publication. DOI: 10.1016/j.rmal.2023.100050

Múgica, A. (2025, February 20). Anti-money laundering and fraud prevention with MongoDB vector search and OpenAI. MongoDB Developer Community. https://www.mongodb.com/blog/post/anti-money-laundering-fraud-prevention-mongodb-vector-search-openai

Neveditsin, N., Lingras, P., & Mago, V. (2024). Clinical insights: A comprehensive review of language models in medicine. arXiv. /arXiv.2408.11735DOI: 10.48550

Obermeyer, Z., Powers, B., Vogeli, C., & Mullainathan, S. (2019). Dissecting racial bias in an algorithm used to manage the health of populations. *Science*, *366*(6464), 447–453. DOI: 10.1126/science.aax2342 PMID: 31649194

Papasotiriou, K., Sood, S., Reynolds, S., & Balch, T. (2024, November). AI in investment analysis: LLMs for equity stock ratings. In *Proceedings of the 5th ACM international conference on AI in finance* (pp. 419–427). Association for Computing Machinery. DOI: 10.1145/3677052.3698699

Parthasarathy, V. B., Zafar, A., Khan, A., & Shahid, A. (2024). The ultimate guide to fine-tuning LLMs from basics to breakthroughs: An exhaustive review of technologies, research, best practices, applied research challenges and opportunities. arXiv. /arXiv.2408.13296DOI: 10.48550

Pressman, S. M., Borna, S., Gomez-Cabello, C. A., Haider, S. A., Haider, C., & Forte, A. J. (2024). AI and ethics: A systematic review of the ethical considerations of large language model use in surgery research. *Health Care*, *12*(8), 825. Advance online publication. DOI: 10.3390/healthcare12080825 PMID: 38667587

Qadir, U. (2025, January 28). Maximizing regulatory compliance in finance with generative AI solutions. LinkedIn. https://www.linkedin.com/pulse/maximizing-regulatory-compliance-finance-generative-ai-umair-qadir-hjgsf

Raji, I. D., Smart, A., White, R. N., Mitchell, M., Gebru, T., Hutchinson, B., Smith-Loud, J., Theron, D., & Barnes, P. (2020). Closing the AI accountability gap: Defining an end-to-end framework for internal algorithmic auditing. In Proceedings of the 2020 conference on fairness, accountability, and transparency (FAT* '20) (pp. 33–44). Association for Computing Machinery. DOI: 10.1145/3351095.3372873

Ramamurthy, R. (2023, August 15). Summarizing patient histories with GPT-4. Medium. https://medium.com/llmed-ai/summarizing-patient-histories-with-gpt-4-9df42ba6453c

Ravi, A., Neinstein, A., & Murray, S. G. (2023). Large language models and medical education: Preparing for a rapid transformation in how trainees will learn to be doctors. *ATS Scholar*, *4*(3), 282–292. DOI: 10.34197/ats-scholar.2023-0037PS PMID: 37795112

Rodriguez, P. U., Jafari, A., & Ormerod, C. M. (2019). Language models and automated essay scoring. arXiv. /arXiv.1909.09482DOI: 10.48550

Rydzewski, N. R., Dinakaran, D., Zhao, S. G., Ruppin, E., Turkbey, B., Citrin, D. E., & Patel, K. R. (2024). Comparative evaluation of LLMs in clinical oncology. NEJM AI, 1(5), Article AIoa2300151. DOI: 10.1056/AIoa2300151

Sanh, V., Debut, L., Chaumond, J., & Wolf, T. (2019). DistilBERT, a distilled version of BERT: Smaller, faster, cheaper and lighter. arXiv. /arXiv.1910.01108DOI: 10.48550

Singhal, K., Azizi, S., Tu, T., Mahdavi, S. S., Wei, J., Chung, H. W., & Natarajan, V. (2023). Large language models encode clinical knowledge. *Nature*, *620*(7972), 172–180. DOI: 10.1038/s41586-023-06291-2 PMID: 37438534

Son, H. (2024, August 9). JPMorgan Chase is giving its employees an AI assistant powered by ChatGPT maker OpenAI. CNBC. https://www.cnbc.com/2024/08/09/jpmorgan-chase-ai-artificial-intelligence-assistant-chatgpt-openai.html

Song, Y., Zhu, Q., Wang, H., & Zheng, Q. (2024). Automated essay scoring and revising based on open-source large language models. *IEEE Transactions on Learning Technologies*. Advance online publication. DOI: 10.1109/TLT.2024.3362475

Su, P., & Vijay-Shanker, K. (2022). Investigation of improving the pre-training and fine-tuning of BERT model for biomedical relation extraction. *BMC Bioinformatics*, *23*(1), 120. Advance online publication. DOI: 10.1186/s12859-022-04641-3 PMID: 35379166

Tavasoli, A., Sharbaf, M., & Madani, S. M. (2025). Responsible innovation: A strategic framework for financial LLM integration. arXiv. /arXiv.2504.02165DOI: 10.48550

Tu, T., Schaekermann, M., Palepu, A., Saab, K., Freyberg, J., Tanno, R., & Natarajan, V. (2025). Towards conversational diagnostic artificial intelligence. *Nature*. Advance online publication. DOI: 10.1038/s41586-024-08184-1 PMID: 40205050

Veen Van, D., Van Uden, C., Blankemeier, L., Delbrouck, J. B., Aali, A., Bluethgen, C., & Chaudhari, A. S. (2024). Adapted large language models can outperform medical experts in clinical text summarization. *Nature Medicine*, *30*(4), 1134–1142. DOI: 10.1038/s41591-024-02895-5 PMID: 38413730

Wang, C., Li, M., He, J., Wang, Z., Darzi, E., Chen, Z., . . . Shen, Y. (2024). A survey for large language models in biomedicine. arXiv. /arXiv.2409.00133DOI: 10.48550

Wang, Q., Gao, Y., Tang, Z., Luo, B., & He, B. (2024). Enhancing LLM trading performance with fact-subjectivity aware reasoning. arXiv. /arXiv.2410.12464DOI: 10.48550

Yan, L., Sha, L., Zhao, L., Li, Y., Martinez-Maldonado, R., Chen, G., & Gašević, D. (2024). Practical and ethical challenges of large language models in education: A systematic scoping review. *British Journal of Educational Technology*, *55*(1), 90–112. DOI: 10.1111/bjet.13391

Yang, R., Tan, T. F., Lu, W., Thirunavukarasu, A. J., Ting, D. S. W., & Liu, N. (2023). Large language models in health care: Development, applications, and challenges. *Health Care Science*, *2*(4), 255–263. DOI: 10.1002/hcs2.67 PMID: 38939520

Yazdanipour, M. (2024, September 10). AI technology in J.P. Morgan Chase & Co. LinkedIn. https://www.linkedin.com/pulse/ai-technology-jp-morgan-chase-co-marzieh-yazdanipour-ah7we

Zhang, H., Hua, F., Xu, C., Kong, H., Zuo, R., & Guo, J. (2023). Unveiling the potential of sentiment: Can large language models predict Chinese stock price movements? arXiv. /arXiv.2306.14222DOI: 10.48550

Zhang, Y., Feng, Y., Li, D., Zhang, K., Chen, J., & Deng, B. (2025). Can competition enhance the proficiency of agents powered by large language models in the realm of news-driven time series forecasting? arXiv. /arXiv.2504.10210DOI: 10.48550

Zhao, J., Wang, T., Yatskar, M., Ordonez, V., & Chang, K.-W. (2018). Gender bias in coreference resolution: Evaluation and debiasing methods. In Proceedings of the 2018 conference of the North American chapter of the Association for Computational Linguistics: Human language technologies, volume 2 (short papers) (pp. 15–20). Association for Computational Linguistics. DOI: 10.18653/v1/N18-2003

Zhao, S., Yang, Y., Wang, Z., He, Z., Qiu, L. K., & Qiu, L. (2024). Retrieval augmented generation (RAG) and beyond: A comprehensive survey on how to make your LLMs use external data more wisely. arXiv. /arXiv.2409.14924DOI: 10.48550

Zhao, T., Chen, X., & Sun, M. (2025). Enhancing time series forecasting via multi-level text alignment with LLMs. arXiv. /arXiv.2504.07360DOI: 10.48550

Zhao, X., Wang, T., & Rios, A. (2024). Improving expert radiology report summarization by prompting large language models with a layperson summary. arXiv. /arXiv.2406.14500DOI: 10.48550

Zhui, L., Fenghe, L., Xuehu, W., Qining, F., & Wei, R. (2024). Ethical considerations and fundamental principles of large language models in medical education. *Journal of Medical Internet Research*, *26*, e60083. Advance online publication. DOI: 10.2196/60083 PMID: 38971715

Zubiaga, A. (2024). Natural language processing in the era of large language models. *Frontiers in Artificial Intelligence*, *6*, 1350306. Advance online publication. DOI: 10.3389/frai.2023.1350306 PMID: 38282904

KEY TERMS AND DEFINITIONS

Domain Adaptation: Adjusting a model trained on one type of data (source domain) to perform well on a different but related dataset.

Explainable AI (XAI): Techniques and tools that make the decisions of AI systems understandable to humans, increasing transparency and trust.

Federated Learning: A decentralized machine learning approach where models are trained locally on edge devices, preserving data privacy and reducing central storage needs.

Few-shot Learning: A learning paradigm in which an LLM can perform tasks after seeing only a few examples of the task, making it highly efficient in adapting to new scenarios with minimal data.

Financial Forecasting: The process of predicting future financial trends or outcomes using historical data, machine learning models, or statistical techniques.

Fine-tuning: The process of adapting a pre-trained LLM to a specific domain or task by training it further on a specialized dataset.

Fraud Detection: The use of data analytics and machine learning techniques to identify suspicious or illegal activities, such as identity theft, billing fraud, or financial scams.

Generative Model: A type of model, like GPT, that generates new content (such as text) based on learned patterns, as opposed to discriminative models that classify or label input data.

Hallucination: When an LLM generates factually incorrect or fabricated content despite appearing coherent or plausible.

Large Language Models: Deep learning models trained on vast corpora of text data to understand, generate, and reason with human language, e.g., GPT-4, BERT, and LLaMA.

Pre-training: The initial training phase where a language model learns general language patterns by predicting missing parts of large amounts of unlabeled text.

Prompt Tuning: A method of steering a pre-trained model's responses by using specific input prompts without changing the model's parameters.

Self-attention: A mechanism within the transformer architecture that enables a model to weigh the importance of different words in a sentence relative to each other, improving context understanding.

Sentiment Analysis: The process of extracting subjective information such as opinions or emotions from text, often used to assess market or public reactions.

Synthetic Data Generation: Creating artificial datasets using LLMs or other generative models to augment training data or simulate rare fraud scenarios.

Transformer Architecture: A neural network framework that uses attention mechanisms to process sequential data, enabling efficient capture of contextual relationships in text.

Chapter 8
LLMs in ERP:
Enhancing Financial Reporting

Satwik Jambula
https://orcid.org/0009-0002-7184-8319
Lamar University, USA

ABSTRACT

This chapter explores how Large Language Models (LLMs) integrated within Enterprise Resource Planning (ERP) systems are transforming financial reporting. Traditional ERP systems automate business processes but often struggle with providing real-time insights or handling vast datasets and unstructured data. LLMs, powered by Natural Language Processing (NLP), offer a promising solution by enabling ERP systems to generate accurate, real-time financial reports, while incorporating external data sources such as financial news, market sentiment, and economic indicators. The chapter delves into the benefits and challenges of integrating LLMs into ERP systems for financial reporting, showcasing leading ERP platforms that have already adopted LLM capabilities. Furthermore, it discusses how this integration enhances report generation, improves forecasting, ensures compliance, and ultimately provides actionable insights for businesses. The chapter also explores the future potential of LLMs in revolutionizing financial reporting within ERP systems.

INTRODUCTION

Financial reporting in enterprise resource planning (ERP) systems has traditionally involved significant manual effort—from consolidating data and reconciling accounts to crafting narrative analyses for stakeholders. Closing the books and producing compliance-ready reports is often a labor-intensive cycle, and surveys confirm it remains a major bottleneck. Large Language Models (LLMs), a sophisticated class

DOI: 10.4018/979-8-3373-3912-2.ch008

of artificial intelligence capable of understanding and generating human-like text, are poised to fundamentally reshape this landscape. By integrating LLMs into ERP systems, organizations can dramatically improve reporting accuracy, automate repetitive tasks, and gain real-time insights from their financial data. Early adopters report substantial efficiency gains; for example, generative AI tools have been shown to cut financial modeling or report preparation times by up to 90% in some cases (Red River, 2024).

The objective of this chapter is to provide a comprehensive exploration of how LLM technology enhances financial reporting within modern ERPs. It details the practical integration of these models into core finance functions and highlights tangible applications through case studies of the world's leading enterprise platforms. We begin by examining the technical integration of LLMs with ERP architectures, including how data flows securely between systems and AI services. Next, we delve into four core functional areas where LLMs are making an impact: (1) automated report generation and narrative analysis, (2) processing of unstructured financial data, (3) compliance and regulatory reporting, and (4) predictive analytics for forecasting and decision support. For each area, we explain the underlying mechanisms and provide concrete examples of improvements in accuracy, speed, and insight.

We then present detailed case studies of LLM-powered financial reporting in SAP S/4HANA, Oracle ERP Cloud (Fusion Applications), Microsoft Dynamics 365, and Oracle NetSuite. These illustrate how each platform has implemented generative AI capabilities—such as SAP's Joule copilot, Oracle's AI-driven narratives, Microsoft's Dynamics 365 Copilot, and NetSuite's Text Enhance module—to enhance financial processes. Finally, we discuss the challenges, best practices, and future outlook for deploying LLMs in enterprise financial reporting, emphasizing the importance of robust governance, data privacy, and human oversight to ensure reliable outcomes. By the end of this chapter, readers will have a deep understanding of how LLM technology is elevating financial reporting in ERPs—delivering more accurate reports faster, extracting value from previously untapped data, and empowering finance teams with real-time, AI-driven insights into their business.

BACKGROUND

The integration of any new technology into a core system of record like an ERP requires a deliberate architectural approach. For LLMs, this involves creating a secure bridge between the enterprise's sensitive financial data and the powerful AI models. A typical reference architecture introduces a dedicated LLM integration layer between the application logic and data management layers (Márquez, 2025). This layer handles tasks such as formatting data into effective prompts, calling the

LLM's inference API, and post-processing the model's outputs before feeding results back into the ERP application. Figure 1 illustrates a high-level architecture of such an integration, highlighting how data flows from the ERP database to the LLM and back, with appropriate context injection and result handling.

Figure 1. LLM-driven document processing architecture for financial data (e.g., invoice processing). A common platform (such as Uber's TextSense) orchestrates document ingestion, OCR, LLM-based entity extraction, and integration with the ERP. Key steps include pre-processing of documents (standardizing input), using computer vision/OCR to get text, an LLM model call to extract or summarize information, and post-processing with business rules. The system supports a feedback loop for human review and model retraining, improving accuracy over time.

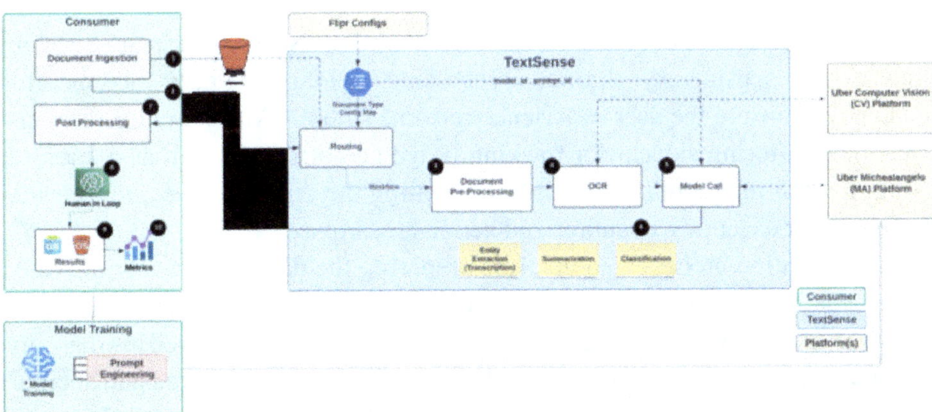

Security and data privacy are paramount in this architecture. Enterprise financial data is highly sensitive, so any integration must ensure that no confidential data is exposed to unauthorized parties or public AI models. One common approach is to use private or vendor-provided LLM services that operate within the ERP vendor's cloud or the company's own virtual private cloud. For example, Oracle's generative AI service on its Oracle Cloud Infrastructure (OCI) allows Fusion ERP customers to utilize LLM capabilities without sharing their data with third-party LLM providers or other customers (Oracle, 2024a). Similarly, Oracle NetSuite's AI features ensure that "no customer data is shared with LLM providers" and that each customer's fine-tuned models remain isolated (Oracle, 2023a). Role-based access controls are embedded so that the AI only generates content or insights from data the requesting user is authorized to see. These safeguards, combined with encryption in transit and at rest, maintain compliance with data protection regulations while leveraging LLMs for internal analysis.

From a deployment standpoint, LLM integration can be achieved in several forms, as Microsoft's Dynamics 365 Copilot design illustrates. LLM-driven assistants may run as a sidecar application alongside the ERP UI, as embedded features within existing ERP screens, or as external agents that interface through APIs (Microsoft, 2024a). In a sidecar scenario, the LLM appears in a chat-like panel next to an ERP dashboard, allowing users to ask questions or get explanations about the data on-screen. This is the model for many "copilot" assistants. In an embedded scenario, LLM capabilities are built directly into workflows—for instance, an AI-generated summary appearing at the bottom of a financial statement page. Finally, as an external agent, an LLM might reside outside the ERP but respond to natural language queries by orchestrating calls to the ERP's APIs for data retrieval and then formulating a response. Each approach has architectural implications for real-time data access, internal SDKs, and API robustness.

In all cases, performance considerations are critical. Best practices include caching frequent queries, using asynchronous processing for longer AI tasks, and monitoring latency to ensure the user experience remains smooth. Many architectures also include a monitoring sidecar for tracking usage and errors, as well as a guardrail module for enforcing policies, such as preventing the AI from revealing sensitive information or executing unauthorized actions (Márquez, 2025).

The integration process also involves preparing the data pipeline for the LLM. Financial data in ERP systems is largely structured, but LLMs excel with textual or semi-structured input. To leverage LLMs, ERP data may be transformed into narrative form or combined with contextual metadata. In addition, unstructured and ancillary data (contracts, invoices) can be introduced via Retrieval-Augmented Generation (RAG). In a RAG architecture, the system first fetches relevant document snippets from a knowledge base, often using a vector database for semantic search, and then appends them to the LLM prompt to ground its response in factual, up-to-date enterprise data. The result is that LLMs operate as part of a pipeline where enterprise data is retrieved, processed into the prompt, and the AI's output is injected back into the business process. This foundational work—combining secure architecture with robust data pipelines—enables the advanced applications discussed in this chapter.

MAIN THRUST OF THE CHAPTER

The impact of LLMs on financial reporting can be understood across four primary domains: automating report generation, processing unstructured data, ensuring compliance, and delivering predictive insights.

Issues, Controversies, Problems

The primary challenge LLMs address is the immense manual effort historically required in financial reporting. This includes:

- **Narrative Generation:** Analysts spend countless hours writing commentary for financial statements and management reports—a repetitive task prone to inconsistency.
- **Unstructured Data:** Finance teams grapple with a flood of unstructured information (PDF invoices, contracts, emails) that must be manually read and entered into the ERP, creating bottlenecks and risking data entry errors.
- **Regulatory Complexity:** Keeping reports compliant with ever-changing standards like GAAP and IFRS, and preparing detailed regulatory filings, is a complex, high-stakes process.
- **Forward-Looking Analysis:** Traditional reporting is retrospective. Generating predictive forecasts and actionable insights requires significant analytical effort that is often disconnected from the reporting workflow.

Solutions and Recommendations

LLMs offer potent solutions to these problems by introducing a new layer of intelligent automation and analysis into the ERP system.

Automating Financial Report Generation and Narrative Analysis

One of the most immediate benefits of introducing LLMs into ERP financial modules is the automation of financial report generation and narrative analysis. Traditional financial reports—income statements, balance sheets, and management discussions—contain a wealth of numeric data that requires expert interpretation. LLMs can bridge this gap by transforming raw figures into coherent, contextualized narratives in real-time.

A core use case is automated narrative generation for financial results. Instead of an analyst manually writing commentary for a monthly performance report, an LLM can be prompted with the financial data and instructed to produce a first draft.

For example, if revenues increased 10% year-over-year, the model might generate a sentence attributing growth to certain product lines or regions if such context is provided. Oracle's ERP Cloud demonstrates this capability: its Intelligent Performance Management (IPM) Insight module uses "AI-generated insight narratives" to highlight anomalies and variances in financial data (Oracle, 2024a). These narratives provide richer context, helping identify why a KPI deviated from the norm. Oracle's generative AI can also produce management reporting narratives that "explain variances and trends impacting the business," allowing finance professionals to create accurate reports with less effort.

Microsoft's Dynamics 365 Copilot showcases a similar strength. A finance user could type: "Create a year-over-year revenue comparison chart with explanations," and Copilot will instantly pull the relevant data from the ERP and produce a polished chart in Excel along with narrative insights (Microsoft, 2024a; Red River, 2024). This turns what might have been hours of data gathering and formatting into a task of a few minutes.

Generative AI can also tailor the tone and messaging of reports to different stakeholders. An LLM can be instructed to draft a high-level, strategy-focused summary for a C-suite audience while using the same data to yield a more detail-oriented report for line managers focused on operational metrics. This flexibility means the finance team can generate multiple tailored narratives from the same underlying data quickly.

It is critical to emphasize the need for accuracy and oversight. While powerful, LLMs can produce factual errors or illogical explanations, a phenomenon often termed "hallucination." Therefore, best practice dictates that human experts must review and validate AI-generated reports before finalization (TechTarget, 2023). Many ERP-embedded tools facilitate this by highlighting the data points behind each statement or providing confidence scores. For instance, Oracle's approach includes showing the underlying facts that a narrative is based on, building trust in the explanation (Oracle, 2024a). Similarly, NetSuite's Narrative Reporting module produces detailed commentary drafts that are meant to "reduce the work required" for finance staff who will then fine-tune and verify the content (NetSuite, 2024).

Beyond text, LLMs can automate the assembly of visual financial reports. They can interpret a user's request to include certain charts or tables, generating descriptions that are then rendered by integrated visualization tools. Microsoft Copilot, for example, can be asked in plain language to include a chart or highlight specific data in a report (Red River, 2024). The combination of narrative text plus automatically generated visuals results in comprehensive financial reports that can be created on-demand. In summary, LLM-powered report generation transforms the finance team's role from preparers to reviewers and strategists. Routine compilation is handled by AI, while humans ensure accuracy and derive higher-level insights.

Processing Unstructured Financial Data

A considerable part of finance operations involves unstructured or semi-structured data—invoices, receipts, contracts, and emails. Traditionally, extracting information from these sources has been a manual challenge. LLMs, with their natural language processing prowess, can read, interpret, and classify free-form text or document images, integrating the results directly into financial workflows.

A prime example is vendor invoice processing in accounts payable. Unlike rigid template-based OCR, an LLM can generalize across various invoice layouts and languages, using context to identify key fields like vendor name, invoice number, and line items. Uber's engineering team showcased a generative AI system for invoice processing that combines computer vision with LLMs. This solution achieved a robust, scalable AP process that "significantly reduc[es] manual intervention and operational costs," accelerates invoice cycle times, and minimizes errors (Uber Engineering, 2024).

Figure 1 illustrates a common architecture for such an LLM-powered document processing workflow. A platform orchestrates document ingestion, OCR, LLM-based entity extraction, and integration with the ERP. Key steps include pre-processing of documents (standardizing input), using computer vision/OCR to extract raw text, an LLM model call to parse the text and pull out structured data fields, and post-processing with business rules and validation. The system supports a feedback loop for human review and model retraining, improving accuracy over time.

The impact of using LLMs for unstructured data processing is substantial. Consider not just invoices, but also expense receipts—an LLM can read a photo of a receipt and identify the merchant, date, and amount for an expense report. Or purchase orders and contracts—an LLM can summarize key payment schedules and obligations from lengthy documents.

Another growing application is processing finance-related emails and free-text requests. An LLM can read a vendor email about a payment discrepancy, extract the core issue, check it against ERP records, and draft a response or an internal ticket. Microsoft's Copilot integration touches on this in the context of collections, where it can summarize a customer's account status and draft personalized collection letters (Microsoft, 2024a). Oracle NetSuite's Text Enhance generative AI offers a similar function, using company-specific data to create targeted collection letters with the appropriate tone (Oracle, 2023a).

To maintain accuracy, firms often implement a confidence-based workflow: the LLM assigns a confidence score to each extracted field, and anything below a certain threshold is routed to a human for verification. Over time, as the model is retrained on corrections, its performance improves. This demonstrates that organizations may need to experiment with and customize LLMs for their specific documents—a new frontier in ERP customization. In summary, LLMs are unlocking the value in unstructured financial data, improving both the speed and quality of transactional processing.

Enhancing Compliance and Regulatory Reporting

Financial reporting must meet strict compliance and regulatory standards, such as Generally Accepted Accounting Principles (GAAP) or International Financial Reporting Standards (IFRS). Integrating LLMs into ERP systems offers new ways to streamline compliance reporting and reduce risk.

One major application is automated regulatory documentation. Generative AI can draft sections of statutory reports, like the Management Discussion & Analysis (MD&A) for SEC filings or the notes to financial statements. TechTarget notes that "Generative AI can help users create accurate and detailed documentation with clear audit trails for regulatory reviews" (2023). An LLM can be tasked with writing financial statement footnotes, explaining accounting policies, and providing account breakdowns by drawing from ERP data and past reports for context. This ensures consistency and completeness. The AI's ability to maintain an audit trail might involve citing the sources of data (e.g., linking a number in a note to the specific ledger entry) or providing justification text, which is invaluable for auditors.

LLMs are also proving useful for monitoring changes in laws and regulations. Microsoft's Copilot, for example, has been envisioned to "track changes in tax regulations and suggest adjustments to the company's financial strategy" (TechTarget, 2023). An LLM fine-tuned on tax law updates could analyze a newly issued tax code revision and flag which changes might impact the company's reporting. It might output an alert like: "New tax law XYZ has changed the depreciation method for equipment. 15 assets in your fixed asset register could be affected."

When it comes to financial standards compliance, LLMs can act as on-demand advisors. An accountant could query an AI assistant: "Have we accounted for leases in accordance with IFRS 16 in this report? Show me any issues." The LLM, possessing knowledge of IFRS 16 and access to the company's lease data, could analyze the records and identify potential discrepancies. AI can systematically verify that the format and content of reports adhere to required standards and automatically produce statutory reports in the correct structure (ZBrain, n.d.).

Tax preparation is another area where LLMs shine. Tax rules are notoriously complex and differ by jurisdiction. Generative AI can help generate draft tax returns or tax provision reports by mapping ERP data to tax form requirements. Although these outputs require review by tax professionals, they can significantly reduce drudgery and help catch potential issues early.

Auditability is key: any AI-generated content must come with a traceable path to its source data. LLMs integrated in an ERP can store references to the data or logic that led to each part of its output. This forms part of the audit trail automation, where AI not only performs the task but also documents how it was performed. From a risk management perspective, AI can perform continuous compliance monitoring. Rather than periodic checks, an LLM-enabled ERP can continuously parse transactions to look for red flags, such as potential violations of internal policies or transactions indicative of fraud. The caveat remains that these AI systems should be considered advisory. Human experts remain essential to review and finalize any compliance-related output. But those experts now have powerful tools to augment their capabilities.

Delivering Predictive Analytics and Real-Time Insights

Beyond automating existing processes, LLMs open new frontiers in predictive analytics and proactive insight generation. Traditional predictive analytics in finance often relies on statistical models and structured data. LLMs add the ability to combine quantitative predictions with a rich understanding of context and historical patterns, all expressed in natural language.

One major use case is enhancing budgeting and forecasting. Financial planning and analysis (FP&A) teams typically create forecasts using defined models. Generative AI can augment this by exploring a wider range of scenarios and injecting a narrative understanding of why forecasts look the way they do. As reported, "generative AI can create multiple budget scenarios based on historical data and test various economic assumptions without precisely defined parameters" (TechTarget, 2023). An LLM might look at historical trends in the ERP and automatically generate optimistic, median, and pessimistic forecast outcomes, each accompanied by an explanation.

Predictive models are already present in many ERPs, but LLMs make their output more accessible and trustworthy by providing explanations in plain language. Oracle's Fusion ERP introduced "predictive forecast explanations" using generative AI to "generate contextual commentary to explain forecasts produced by predictive models and key factors driving the prediction" (Oracle, 2024a). This addresses a common pain point: predictive models can be black boxes. By having an LLM articulate the drivers—"Revenue for Q4 is predicted to be $10M, primarily due to an expected 15% increase in North America sales (based on current pipeline)"—users gain confidence and insight.

LLMs also support real-time insights and anomaly detection. Because they handle language and patterns, they can ingest streams of transactional data and alert on unusual events with explanations. ZBrain notes that AI can conduct "trend and variance analysis in real-time, identifying discrepancies early" (n.d.). With LLMs, when those variances are identified, the system can immediately produce a narrative of potential causes, saving analysts from time-consuming root cause analysis. Microsoft's Copilot similarly aims to highlight outliers, and in one scenario, it was shown to suggest cost-saving opportunities based on historical patterns (Red River, 2024).

Real-time insights are especially boosted by LLM integration. While traditional BI tools can show real-time dashboards, interpreting them still falls to humans. With LLMs, an executive could get a real-time narrative briefing at any time. For example, "As of noon today, sales are at $5M for the month, tracking 10% above last month's pace. Cash on hand is $X, which is 5% below the forecast due to an earlier pay-down of debt this week." This kind of up-to-the-minute summary across different financial areas can be generated on demand. NetSuite's "Auto-Insights" feature automatically slices data and finds notable patterns, while an "Explain" feature can provide descriptions and visualizations depicting business drivers and anomalies (NetSuite, 2024).

To facilitate trust in such insights, ERP vendors ensure LLM outputs are grounded in data, often via RAG or by fine-tuning on a company's historical data. A notable advantage of LLMs is their ability to incorporate external data, such as relevant news feeds or market sentiment, to enrich an analysis. In conclusion, LLMs enhance predictive analytics in ERPs by making forecasts more comprehensive and understandable, marrying quantitative predictions with qualitative reasoning.

CASE STUDIES: LLM-POWERED FINANCIAL REPORTING IN LEADING ERP PLATFORMS

The theoretical benefits of LLM integration come to life when examining how major ERP vendors have incorporated generative AI into their financial reporting toolsets. This section explores four leading ERP platforms—SAP S/4HANA, Oracle ERP Cloud (Fusion Applications), Microsoft Dynamics 365 Finance, and Oracle NetSuite—detailing the LLM-driven features each has rolled out.

SAP S/4HANA and SAP Business AI (Joule)

SAP has aggressively integrated AI into its S/4HANA ERP platform under the banner of SAP Business AI. A centerpiece of this strategy is Joule, the company's generative AI copilot. Joule is embedded across SAP's cloud portfolio to provide context-aware insights and automation via natural language interactions (Clarkston Consulting, 2024). In an S/4HANA finance context, a user can simply ask Joule questions like, "Show me the gross margin trend for the last 6 quarters and explain the key drivers," and receive an immediate answer with narrative and charts.

In terms of financial reporting enhancements, SAP S/4HANA Cloud received smart summarization features that leverage generative AI (Bramasol, 2024). These allow the system to automatically condense lengthy financial reports or large datasets into concise bullet points. SAP has also implemented AI-driven narrative explanations in its analytics. For example, a finance department can use generative AI to summarize data from a cost center review, letting the AI write a first draft of the commentary.

SAP's approach heavily leverages its Business Technology Platform (BTP) and the Intelligent Scenario Lifecycle Management (ISLM) framework, which allows customers to manage AI models within S/4HANA in a governed way (SAP Community, 2023). Joule's capabilities also include generating forward-facing recommendations, such as suggesting which suppliers to prioritize to meet sustainability or margin goals. Because it is integrated system-wide, Joule can cross-reference data from HR, procurement, and sales when explaining a financial outcome. For instance, if overtime labor costs spiked, Joule could note a related HR data point, such as increased hours logged due to a production issue.

SAP has also integrated Joule with Microsoft 365 Copilot, a two-way integration that allows users to seamlessly bring data and insights from S/4HANA into tools like Excel or Word using natural language (KloudData, n.d.). This blurring of boundaries between ERP and productivity software greatly streamlines the report preparation process.

Oracle ERP Cloud (Fusion Applications)

Oracle's Fusion Cloud ERP suite has been at the forefront of embedding AI, announcing a sweeping set of generative AI capabilities built on its own cloud AI services with an emphasis on secure, enterprise-specific deployment (Oracle, 2024a). For financial reporting, Oracle's approach centers on insight generation and narrative explanation.

Key features include Insight Narratives and Management Reporting Narratives. Insight Narratives use pattern recognition to find anomalies in financial data and then automatically generate explanations for them. For example, if operating expenses in a certain department spike, the LLM might produce a narrative explaining that the increase was due to one-time restructuring costs and higher marketing spend. Management Reporting Narratives focus on explaining variances and trends in regular reports, inserting AI-generated commentary that highlights significant deviations from budget or plan.

Another notable feature is Predictive Forecast Explanations, where Oracle uses LLMs to accompany its predictive analytics models (Oracle, 2024a). When a forecast is produced, the system automatically adds a narrative explaining the key drivers behind it. This helps to build trust in AI by articulating the "why" behind predictions. For example, if a model forecasts a cash shortfall, the LLM might explain it with, "The projected shortfall is driven by a combination of slower collections and a planned capital expenditure in Q3."

Crucially, Oracle is deeply focused on privacy. All LLM features run on OCI, and Oracle ensures that "no customer data is shared with LLM providers" and that models can be fine-tuned on a customer's data exclusively for that customer (Oracle, 2024b). This is a key selling point for regulated industries that are cautious about exposing financial data to external services.

Microsoft Dynamics 365 Finance (Copilot for Finance)

Microsoft has infused its Dynamics 365 enterprise apps with generative AI via Microsoft Copilot, a suite of AI assistants powered by its Azure OpenAI Service. In Dynamics 365 Finance, Copilot assists with financial reporting, analysis, and daily operations, with deep integration into the Microsoft 365 ecosystem (Excel, Outlook, Teams) that finance professionals use daily.

One of the hallmark features is the ability to use natural language queries. A finance manager can essentially chat with their ERP data, asking questions in plain English like, "What were the top three revenue-generating products last quarter?" (Red River, 2024). This eliminates the need for manual queries and lowers the technical barrier for finance staff to explore data.

Copilot also excels at generating financial reports with visualizations directly within familiar tools. A user in Excel, for example, can ask Copilot to "create a cash flow report for October," and it will pull the figures from Dynamics, generate a formatted table or chart, and even help write formulas (Microsoft, 2024b). Another key area is collections. A "Collections coordinator Copilot" can summarize a customer's outstanding balance, payment history, and generate a tailored reminder email, improving collections efficiency and cash flow (CFODive, 2024).

Collaboration is a major theme. Copilot can be invoked within a Microsoft Teams chat to answer a question raised during a meeting, providing data and an explanation right within the conversation. This immediate responsiveness accelerates decision-making. Microsoft's strength lies in this seamless integration, creating a highly efficient loop from ERP data to analysis and communication within the productivity tools finance teams already use.

Oracle NetSuite and Generative AI-Powered Reporting

Oracle NetSuite, a leading cloud ERP for mid-market companies, has also embraced LLMs to enhance its financial management capabilities. NetSuite introduced generative AI features that leverage OCI's AI services, ensuring data security while making powerful tools accessible to smaller organizations (Oracle, 2023a).

One of the headline features is Generative AI for Narrative Reporting in NetSuite's Enterprise Performance Management (EPM) module. This capability helps finance teams automatically produce written reports and analysis from their financial data. As NetSuite describes, the module "can now draft detailed narratives and concise explanations from financial and transactional data, including insights into trends, variances, and time-based comparisons" (NetSuite, 2024). This is a game-changer for resource-constrained finance teams.

NetSuite also launched a GenAI Assistant within its Analytics Warehouse. This chat-style assistant can generate charts and answer data questions through natural language. Its "Auto-Insights" feature automatically sifts through data to produce a set of visuals and insights without being asked, while an "Explain" feature can drill down into a specific trend or anomaly (NetSuite, 2024).

The "Text Enhance" feature broadens the use of LLMs to multiple processes. In finance, it can expedite collections by writing personalized letters and accelerate the financial close by generating summaries and narratives for reports (Oracle, 2023a). For the mid-market companies that NetSuite often serves, these AI features effectively act as an additional analyst, amplifying the capacity of the finance team and allowing them to focus on more strategic work.

To encapsulate the platform comparisons, we can consult **Table 1** below, which compares the LLM-powered financial reporting features of SAP S/4HANA, Oracle Fusion ERP, Microsoft Dynamics 365, and Oracle NetSuite:

Table 1. LLM-Enhanced Financial Reporting Features in Major ERP Platforms

Platform	LLM Integration Approach & Tech	Key Financial Reporting AI Features	Example Use Cases in Financial Reporting
SAP S/4HANA (Cloud)	SAP Joule AI Copilot on SAP BTP; Integrates with Azure OpenAI (Copilot); ISLM framework for embedding AI in-app	– Smart report summarization (condense reports into takeaways) – Contextual Q&A on ERP data via natural language (across finance, HR, etc.) – Predictive analytics with AI explanations (financial trend forecasts) – AI-assisted close tasks (reconciliations, anomaly flagging) – Cross-functional insights (e.g. combining finance + supply chain data in analysis)	– *Auto-generation of financial statement commentary:* Joule writes first draft of variance analysis for monthly close report, highlighting key drivers of profit change. – *Interactive financial queries:* CFO asks "What's causing our Q4 expense increase?" in natural language and Joule returns analysis referencing SAP data across departments. – *Scenario planning:* AI suggests budget scenario impacts (e.g., "If raw material costs +10%") with narrative explanation for planning team. – *Real-time KPI alerts:* On SAP Mobile, Joule proactively alerts "Inventory up 15% QoQ; may impact cash – consider action," integrating finance & operations info.
Oracle Fusion Cloud ERP	Oracle GenAI on OCI, with embedded models (incl. Cohere) – no data leaves Oracle Cloud. Integrated in Fusion Apps workflows.	– AI-generated *Insight Narratives* for anomalies/ variances – *Management Reporting Narratives* explaining trends vs. plan – *Predictive forecast narratives* (explain drivers of ML forecasts) – AI-driven project financial updates (status summaries, etc.) – Automated report creation in Oracle Cloud EPM (narratives + visuals)	– *Flash report automation:* AI produces daily flash P&L with commentary on any unusual items, which CFO reviews instead of compiling data manually. – *Board package prep:* Insight Narratives on KPI anomalies (e.g., sudden margin drop) are included in board report with AI's explanation, saving analyst time. – *Forecast confidence building:* When predictive model outputs next quarter cash flow, generative AI appends "Key drivers: slower receivables, higher inventory" to justify the figure. – *Project financial summary:* AI summarizes a major CapEx project's financial status for inclusion in the CFO's report (budget vs actual, % complete, risks) – all in narrative form.

continued on following page

Table 1. Continued

Platform	LLM Integration Approach & Tech	Key Financial Reporting AI Features	Example Use Cases in Financial Reporting
Microsoft Dynamics 365 Finance	Dynamics 365 Copilot using Azure OpenAI (GPT-4) integrated with D365 F&O and Microsoft 365 apps. Appears as sidechat, embedded insights, and Office 365 plugins.	– Conversational data exploration (chat with ERP data) – Auto-generation of Excel reports & visuals from Dynamics data on request – Compliance help: monitor regs, draft policy documents, flag issues – Collections & AR Copilot: summarize customer AR status, draft collection emails – Copilot in Teams/ Outlook for finance: AI answers or summarizes in communications context	– *On-demand financial analysis:* Finance VP types a question in Teams chat, "Explain why Q3 gross margin declined" – Copilot instantly responds with analysis citing increased COGS in a product line and decreased pricing, pulling data from D365. – *Excel financial model support:* Analyst asks Copilot in Excel to "Insert a chart of revenue vs opex last 12 months and summarize the trend" – it produces the chart and a short write-up. – *Compliance memo drafting:* Copilot drafts a compliance report (e.g., SOX control effectiveness summary) using data from Dynamics and past audit comments, which the Controller then finalizes. – *Automated AR emails:* For 50 customers with overdue balances, Copilot generates personalized reminder emails and a summary of each customer's payment history for the AR team, improving collections efficiency.

continued on following page

Table 1. Continued

Platform	LLM Integration Approach & Tech	Key Financial Reporting AI Features	Example Use Cases in Financial Reporting
Oracle NetSuite	OCI GenAI services embedded in NetSuite. Features: NetSuite Text Enhance and AI Assistant in Analytics. Secure tenant-specific models	– *Generative AI Narrative Reporting* in EPM: auto-write management reports and trend analysis – NetSuite Text Enhance for finance: write collection letters, close narratives, etc. – Analytics Warehouse Genie: NL to chart generation, "auto-insights" dashboards – Auto-summarization of ERP data records (customer 360 summaries, etc.) – AI suggestions in workflows (e.g., prompting reason for variance)	– *Monthly financial package creation:* NetSuite's Narrative Reporting drafts the CEO's monthly financial highlights memo (revenue up/down, key variances with reasons) which the CFO quickly reviews. – *Mid-market fast close:* Small finance team uses AI to accelerate close – Text Enhance writes first draft of account reconciliations' explanations and the variance commentary for P&L, cutting days off the close. – *CFO dashboard with Auto-Insights:* Upon login, CFO sees an AI-generated note: "Inventory up 20% – auto-generated charts show it's in Category X; AI highlights risk to cash flow" prompting action. – *Collections automation:* Text Enhance produces personalized dunning letters including each customer's past due invoices and a polite note referencing their payment history, freeing AR staff from writing these manually

CHALLENGES, RISKS, AND BEST PRACTICES

While the integration of LLMs into ERP-based financial reporting offers clear advantages, it also introduces a set of challenges and risks that organizations must manage. Success requires more than just technology; it demands robust governance, strategic training, and re-engineered processes.

- **Data Privacy and Security:** Financial data is highly sensitive. The primary risk is the inadvertent exposure of confidential information. Best practices include using private instances of LLMs or vendor services that explicitly guarantee data isolation, as SAP and Oracle do (Oracle, 2024a). All integrations must use end-to-end encryption, and role-based access controls must extend to AI outputs.

- **Accuracy, Reliability, and Hallucinations:** LLMs can generate incorrect or fabricated information. To mitigate this, organizations must implement a human-in-the-loop review for all critical outputs. Grounding the LLM in actual data using techniques like Retrieval-Augmented Generation (RAG) is a critical best practice to reduce the likelihood of errors.
- **Model Bias and Ethical Considerations:** LLMs can inherit biases from their training data. If used for decision support, such as suggesting cost cuts, an AI might exhibit unfair biases. Companies must establish ethical AI guidelines, monitor outputs for inappropriate suggestions, and integrate guardrails to prevent the AI from taking prohibited actions.
- **Change Management and Training:** The introduction of LLM tools changes how finance professionals work. Organizations must invest in training to build trust and ensure proper usage. Staff must learn new skills, such as prompt engineering (how to ask the AI questions effectively) and how to critically verify AI outputs. The emphasis should be on augmentation—freeing staff from mundane tasks to focus on higher-value analysis.
- **Regulatory Compliance and Auditability:** Finance is heavily audited. Companies must ensure that using an AI doesn't undermine auditability. For every number in a financial report, an auditor typically expects to trace it to a source. If an AI narrative says "sales grew 5% due to factor X," the auditor might ask, how do you know factor X? There should be underlying data or analysis. That's why embedding references and maintaining logs is key. Fortunately, tools like NetSuite's and Oracle's are building audit trail features (storing sources or at least the fact that a narrative was AI-generated with given inputs). Best practice is to store the inputs to any generative report (e.g., the data as of that time, and any prompt parameters) and ideally the reasoning. If an AI explains a forecast, keep the version of the forecast model used and any data it referenced. This way, even months later, one can reproduce what the AI did if needed for an audit. Furthermore, regulatory compliance extends to new rules about AI. Regulators like the SEC may soon require disclosure of significant AI use in financial report preparation (similar to disclosing use of third-party experts). Companies should stay abreast of such developments. KPMG's guidance suggests having a game plan for governance and internal controls over AI tools. This could involve updating the company's SOX 404 internal control documentation to specify how AI outputs are validated and how the AI tool itself is controlled (user access controls, change management, etc.). For example, one might treat the AI like a sub-ledger system that needs IT general controls – ensuring only authorized IT staff can change its configuration or data access, etc.

- **System and Model Maintenance:** LLM integrations are not a one-and-done effort; they require ongoing maintenance. Models may drift or become less effective if data patterns change (for instance, a business enters a new market with new types of transactions the AI wasn't trained on). Thus, companies need to schedule periodic re-evaluation of the AI's outputs. Monitoring performance (accuracy of narratives, extraction correctness, etc.) is important. Some have suggested using feedback loops where users can rate or correct AI outputs, and those go back into improving the model. Uber's approach of continuous re-training with fresh data labels is a good practice. Additionally, as vendor models update (OpenAI might release GPT-5, etc.), companies should test new versions for improvements or new risks before switching. Change control in model updates is crucial – e.g., apply the same rigor as updating a major software version.
- **Managing Expectations and Strategic Alignment:** Another soft challenge is not overhyping or over-relying on the AI. It's easy for management to get excited and want AI to do everything. But if not properly implemented, it could lead to errors or simply disappoint if it can't realistically handle a task. Finance leaders should set clear expectations: the AI might cut drafting time, but it's not a fully autonomous "finance brain" – it doesn't make decisions, it assists. Case in point, generative AI can propose strategies (like cost savings ideas), but it's up to leadership to decide and factor qualitative considerations. Also, some creative or judgment-based tasks (like deciding how to communicate bad news in financials) still need human touch. From a strategic perspective, companies should identify the highest value use cases for AI in finance and focus on those first (maybe start with narrative reporting and variance analysis, which are well-proven, then move to risk analysis or others). A phased rollout with pilot tests in non-critical areas first can help iron out kinks. Many companies adopt AI for internal management reporting first (lower risk) and later for external reporting content. Finally, sharing success stories internally and quick wins will help adoption. For example, if the AI identified a variance that would have been missed or saved 100 person-hours in a quarter close, broadcasting that helps gain buy-in across the organization. In conclusion, the introduction of LLMs into ERP financial reporting is a microcosm of digital transformation: immense upside in efficiency and capability, paired with new responsibilities to manage technology wisely. By following best practices around data handling, accuracy checks, governance, and user training, organizations can mitigate the risks. Those that navigate this well stand to gain not just faster reporting, but more insightful and reliable reporting, turning the finance function into a more strategic partner for the business. As CFOs embrace these tools, they must also evolve con-

trols and skills accordingly – the future of financial reporting will likely be a human-AI partnership, with the AI doing the heavy lifting under careful human oversight.

FUTURE RESEARCH DIRECTIONS

The integration of LLMs in financial reporting is still in its early stages, presenting fertile ground for future research and development. The next frontier may involve an even tighter coupling of ERP systems with external data sources, such as real-time market data, IoT sensor information, and macroeconomic news feeds. An LLM could synthesize this diverse information to provide a truly holistic and predictive view of enterprise performance.

Further research could focus on creating highly specialized, industry-specific LLMs that understand the unique nuances of financial reporting in sectors like banking, healthcare, or manufacturing. Additionally, the role of LLMs in auditing is a promising area. Future AI may be able to conduct large portions of a financial audit autonomously, interacting directly with auditors to provide evidence and explain transaction histories, radically increasing transparency and efficiency. Finally, as these AI systems become more autonomous, research into advanced governance frameworks and "explainable AI" (XAI) will be critical to ensure that their decisions remain transparent, ethical, and aligned with human oversight.

CONCLUSION

The arrival of Large Language Models in ERP systems marks a pivotal moment for the finance function. This chapter has detailed how LLM integration is moving financial reporting beyond its traditional boundaries, transforming it from a retrospective and manual process into one defined by real-time insight, intelligent automation, and forward-looking analysis. The case studies of SAP, Oracle, Microsoft, and NetSuite demonstrate that these advancements are not speculative but are actively being deployed on robust enterprise platforms today.

By automating narrative generation, unlocking unstructured data, streamlining compliance, and delivering explainable predictions, LLMs are freeing finance professionals from routine toil. This allows them to redirect their expertise toward strategic analysis and decision support, elevating their contribution to the organization. However, realizing this vision demands a commitment to responsible implementation. Organizations must prioritize data privacy, establish rigorous human-in-the-loop review processes, and cultivate a culture of critical thinking to accompany these powerful new tools.

The partnership between human expertise and machine intelligence is the new paradigm for corporate finance. By thoughtfully embracing LLMs as collaborators, CFOs and their teams can ensure the financial narrative of their business is not only accurate and efficient but also insightful and strategically invaluable.

REFERENCES

Bramasol. (2024). *Update on SAP AI initiatives going into 2025.* IgnitePossible. https://ignitepossible.bramasol.com/blog/update-on-sap-ai-initiatives-going-into-2025

CFODive. (2024, March 5). *Microsoft rolls out Copilot AI tool to finance teams.* https://www.cfodive.com/news/microsoft-rolls-out-copilot-ai-tool-finance-teams/708935/

Clarkston Consulting. (2024, March 11). *SAP and generative AI: Advanced business operations with Joule.* https://clarkstonconsulting.com/insights/sap-and-generative-ai/

Community, S. A. P. (2023, December 22). *Unlocking the power of generative AI with Intelligent Scenario Lifecycle Management (ISLM) in SAP S/4HANA Cloud.* https://community.sap.com/t5/technology-blog-posts-by-sap/unlocking-the-power-of-generative-ai-with-intelligent-scenariolifecycle/ba-p/14040565

KloudData. (n.d.). *The impact of AI on ERP systems featuring SAP S/4HANA.* Retrieved June 7, 2024, from https://www.klouddata.com/sap-blogs/the-impact-of-ai-on-erp-systems-featuring-sap-s-4hana

KPMG. (2024). *AI and automation in financial reporting guide.* https://kpmg.com/kpmg-us/content/dam/kpmg/frv/pdf/2024/handbook-ai-and-automation-financial-reporting.pdf

Márquez, C. (2025, January 28). *A functional software reference architecture for LLM-integrated systems.* arXiv. https://arxiv.org/html/2501.12904v1

Microsoft. (2024a). *Overview of Copilot capabilities in finance and operations apps.* Microsoft Learn. Retrieved June 7, 2024, from https://learn.microsoft.com/en-us/dynamics365/fin-ops-core/fin-ops/copilot/copilot-for-finance-operations

Microsoft. (2024b). *Overview of Microsoft 365 Copilot for Finance 2024 release wave 2.* Microsoft Learn. Retrieved June 7, 2024, from https://learn.microsoft.com/en-us/dynamics365/release-plan/2024wave2/finance-supply-chain/microsoft-copilot-finance/

NetSuite. (2024). *GenAI powers new assistant, automated insights in NetSuite 2025.1.* https://www.netsuite.com/portal/resource/articles/erp/genai-powers-new-assistant-automated-insights-in-netsuite-2025-1.shtml

Oracle. (2023a). *Oracle NetSuite embeds generative AI throughout the suite to help organizations boost productivity*. Oracle News. https://www.oracle.com/news/announcement/suiteworld-netsuite-embeds-generative-ai-2023-10-17/

Oracle. (2023b). *Capitalizing on GenAI: How CFOs can turn real-time insights into...* Oracle Cloud ERP. https://www.oracle.com/erp/how-cfos-turn-insights-into-decisions/

Oracle. (2024a, March 14). *Oracle adds new generative AI capabilities to Oracle Fusion Cloud Applications Suite*. Oracle News. https://www.oracle.com/news/announcement/oracle-adds-generative-ai-capabilities-to-fusion-applications-2024-03-14/

Oracle. (2024b). *Oracle launches over 50 generative AI use cases with Cohere*. Cohere. https://cohere.com/customer-stories/oracle

Red River. (2024). *Why Microsoft Copilot is a no-brainer for finance business*. https://redriver.com/artificial-intelligence/microsoft-copilot-for-finance

TechTarget. (2023, November 29). *8 use cases for generative AI in finance*. https://www.techtarget.com/searcherp/tip/Use-cases-for-generative-AI-in-finance

Uber Engineering. (2024, May 2). *Advancing invoice document processing at Uber using GenAI*. Uber Blog. https://www.uber.com/en-GB/blog/advancing-invoice-document-processing-using-genai/

ZBrain. (n.d.). *AI in record-to-report: Scope, integration, use cases, challenges and future outlook*. Retrieved June 7, 2024, from https://zbrain.ai/ai-in-record-to-report/

KEY TERMS AND DEFINITIONS

Enterprise Resource Planning (ERP): Integrated management software that organizations use to manage day-to-day business activities such as accounting, procurement, project management, risk management, compliance, and supply chain operations.

Financial Reporting: The formal process of creating statements and reports that disclose an organization's financial status to management, investors, and government agencies.

Generative AI: A class of artificial intelligence models that can generate novel content, such as text, images, or code, in response to a prompt. LLMs are a type of generative AI.

Hallucination (AI): A phenomenon where an AI model generates false, nonsensical, or factually inaccurate information that was not present in its training data, stated with high confidence.

Human-in-the-Loop (HITL): A model of interaction where a human reviews, validates, or corrects the output of an AI system, particularly for critical tasks, to ensure accuracy and quality.

Large Language Model (LLM): A deep learning algorithm that can perform a wide variety of natural language processing tasks, including text generation, summarization, translation, and question-answering.

Narrative Reporting: The practice of adding written commentary and explanations to financial data to provide context, highlight trends, and explain performance drivers.

Predictive Analytics: The use of data, statistical algorithms, and machine learning techniques to identify the likelihood of future outcomes based on historical data.

Retrieval-Augmented Generation (RAG): An AI technique that grounds the output of a large language model in a specific, verified set of external knowledge, reducing inaccuracies by retrieving relevant facts before generating a response.

Unstructured Data: Information that does not have a pre-defined data model or is not organized in a pre-defined manner, such as text from emails, PDFs, contracts, and images.

Chapter 9
Large Language Models (LLM) and Islamic Finance:
Enhancing Transparency, Risk Management, and Customer Experience

Early Ridho Kismawadi
https://orcid.org/0000-0002-9420-5212
IAIN Langsa, Indonesia

ABSTRACT

The Large Language Model (LLM) has great potential for Islamic finance, a sector that is grounded in Sharia principles that emphasizes ethics, transparency, and risk sharing, but its application is still underexplored. This study examines how LLM improves transparency, risk management, and customer experience in Islamic finance using a qualitative method approach. A systematic literature review was conducted through the Scopus database, selecting peer-reviewed articles relevant to LLM, Islamic finance, as well as tasks such as sentiment analysis and risk assessment. Articles are filtered by title/abstract, full text, with data extracted for research purposes, methodology, findings, and limitations, organized into themes. Thematic and quantitative analyses synthesize findings to propose an LLM integration framework, addressing challenges such as hallucinations and data privacy with techniques such as Labeled Guide Prompting and DP-LoRA. The findings show LLMs such as ChatGPT-4o, TAT-LLM, and FinQAPT automate audits, improve risk management through predictive analytics for profit-sharing contracts, and provide culturally sensitive financial advice, outperforming traditional methods in

DOI: 10.4018/979-8-3373-3912-2.ch009

efficiency and objectivity. The framework offers practical implications for financial institutions, advancing ethical AI in the Sharia financial system while emphasizing human oversight for reliability and compliance.

INTRODUCTION

Large language models (LLMs) have become transformational tools in a wide range of industries, demonstrating exceptional capabilities in natural language understanding, data analysis, and decision-making support. In the financial sector, LLMs are increasingly being used to improve operational efficiency, improve risk assessment, and improve customer experience. However, its application in Islamic finance a sector governed by Sharia principles that emphasize ethical, transparent, and risk-sharing practices has yet to be widely explored. Previous studies have highlighted the potential of AI-based technologies in Islamic finance to improve Sharia compliance transparency and simplify customer-facing processes, but the specific role of LLMs in addressing the sector's unique challenges has not been thoroughly examined.

While existing research has examined the role of AI in financial services, there are significant gaps in understanding how LLMs can be tailored to meet the specific needs of Islamic finance, particularly in ensuring Sharia compliance, managing risk on profit-and-loss sharing contracts, and increasing customer trust through ethical communication.

This research is important because it explores the integration of LLMs in Islamic finance, focusing on their potential to increase transparency in Shariah-compliant processes, improve risk management on Islamic financial instruments, and improve customer experience through personalized and ethical interactions. With its advanced natural language processing capabilities, it can bridge the gap between complex and Shariah-compliant Islamic financial practices and stakeholder needs through automation of transparency mechanisms, providing real-time risk insights, and providing culturally sensitive customer support, thus aligning technological innovation with the ethical basis of Islamic finance (Kismawadi 2024).

This research answers the question: How can the big language model be leveraged to improve transparency, risk management, and customer experience in Islamic finance while ensuring compliance with Sharia principles? The study uses a mixed-methods approach, combining qualitative analysis of Sharia compliance requirements with quantitative evaluation of LLM performance in risk assessment and customer interaction scenarios, with data sourced from Islamic financial institutions, customer feedback, and simulated financial transactions, analysed using a specially trained LLM framework.

Our findings suggest that LLMs can significantly improve transparency in Islamic finance by automating Sharia compliance audits, improve risk management through predictive analytics for profit-and-loss sharing contracts, and improve the customer experience by providing personalized, Shariah-compliant financial advice. The study also identified that LLMs can reduce operational costs in Islamic financial institutions through automation and improve customer satisfaction scores through culturally sensitive communication.

This paper contributes to the literature by providing a new framework for integrating LLMs into Islamic finance, offering practical insights for financial institutions, and advancing the discourse on ethical applications of AI in Shariah compliant financial systems. The paper is structured as follows: Part 2 reviews the literature on LLMs and Islamic finance; Section 3 details the methodology; Part 4 presents the findings; Section 5 discusses the implications and limitations; and Section 6 concludes with recommendations for future research.

LLMS IN FINANCE

In finance, one of the most important realms where LLMs have contributed is in financial statement analysis. Historically, financial statements often can be dense with complicated disclosures and jargon that make it hard to decipher meaningful insights. LLMs, on the other hand, function as AI analysts, able to distil information from such "bloated" disclosures in an expedient manner. They can extract key parts such as the Management Discussion and Analysis (MD&A) or earnings calls, distilling key themes and delivering intelligence about the financial well-being and performance of a company. This ability to discern and process information rapidly helps financial analysts and investors to make better decisions.

Another strength of LLMs is their ability to deal with unstructured data. A significant portion of the commercial intelligence is included in unstructured data, (i.e., news articles, social media messages, and informal reports) difficult to be efficiently processed by traditional manual methods. LLMs can sift through large amounts of text data from such varied sources, rapidly pinpointing trends, sentiment or major events which could have an impact on a company's financial position. In a departure from more conventional approaches, LLM approaches can also handle and analyse such data at scale, which is more efficient and effective. Furthermore, such model can be finetuned especially to extract and judge in-formation about their attributes (entity-level) and relationships from unstructured input and then output the results in a structured for-mat e.g. Json for multilingual information extraction in any domain. This organized view of data helps make the unstructured data and its insights more accessible and easier to use.

Figure 1. Llms In Finance

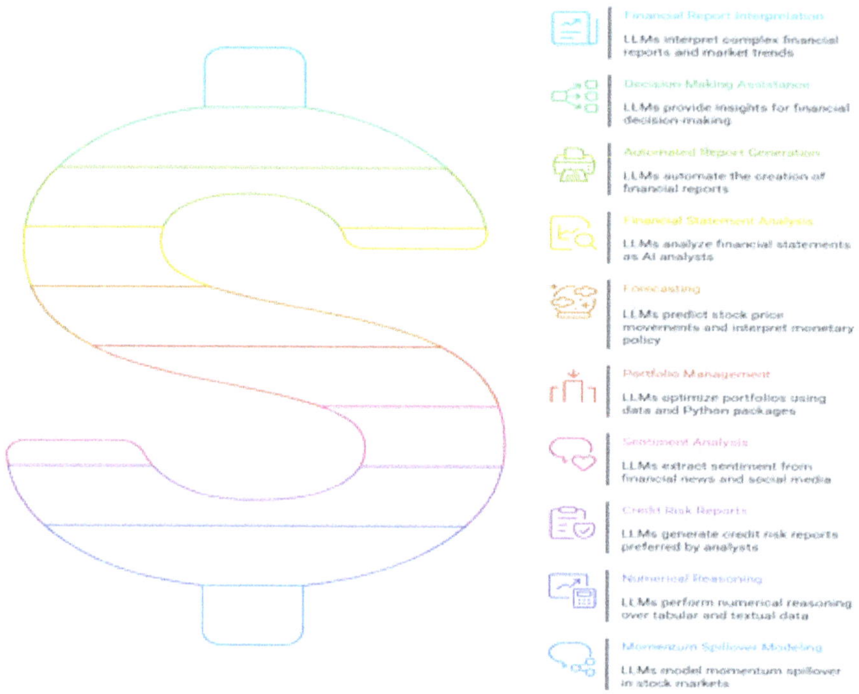

LLMs, particularly advanced versions like ChatGPT-4o, are increasingly adept at interpreting complex financial reports and analysing market trends due to their enhanced natural language processing (NLP) capabilities. These models represent a significant advancement in generative AI for finance, with ChatGPT-4o designed to process and reason across audio, vision, and text in real-time.

Figure 2. Llms In Financial Analysis

Large Language Models (LLMs), such as ChatGPT-4o have better natural language understanding which helps them to generate more consistent and organizationally coherent responses. This technical flexibility makes them the ideal tool for solving sophisticated financial problems that demand a nuanced comprehension and accurate interpretation. This would also be applicable to LLMs which can comprehend intellectual tasks similar to human cognition including complex financial jargon, concepts, and relationships within documents.

LLMs are also good at numerical reasoning over hybrid data – a mix of tabular (e.g., spreadsheets, financial tables) and textual data (e.g., reports, disclosures) seen in financials type documents such as SEC filings and analyst reports. Specialized LLMs like TAT-LLM are designed to perform question answering (QA) on (hybrid) data of this form, for example, arithmetic operations, comparisons, counting, etc (Feng et al. 2025). These models generate dependable and context-sensitive answers to complex finance queries so that analysts can trust in AI to make accurate financial recommendations. FinQAPT pipeline -This pipeline also uses LLMs and advanced prompting techniques such as Dynamic N-shot Prompting in order to enhance the model's capability to reason through numbers and give back actional financial analysis. By parsing crucial context from financial documents, LLMs facilitate on-the-fly decision-making and accelerate deep financial analysis to a degree that traditional approaches cannot match. It is this combination of advanced language comprehension and numerical reasoning that enables LLMs to be a very powerful instrument in contemporary financial analysis.

Figure 3. Llms Analyzing Market Trends

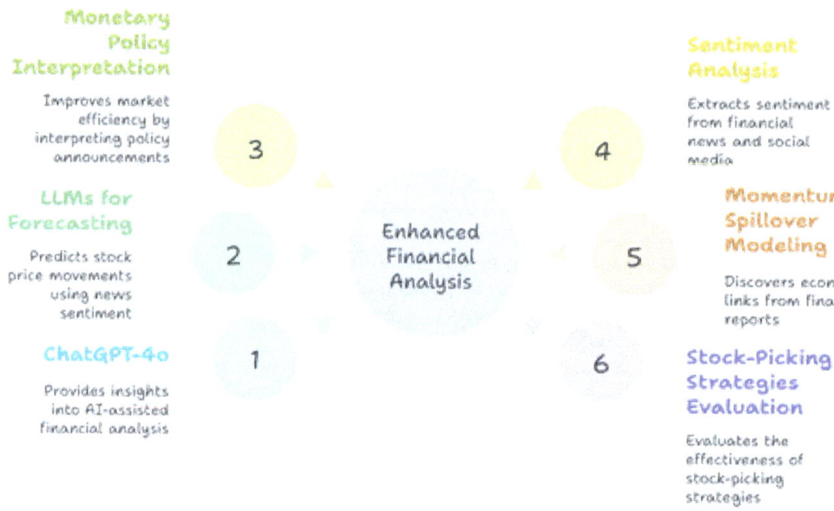

ChatGPT-4o offers substantial value in analysing market trends and dynamics, particularly due to its ability to handle vast amounts of data and perform complex statistical analyses (Feng et al. 2025). This makes it a powerful tool in financial decision-making, where AI can assist in providing insights, but human oversight is crucial for refining and validating those insights. One key area where LLMs like ChatGPT-4o are utilized is forecasting stock price movements. By analysing sentiment in news headlines and social media posts, LLMs can predict market shifts, offering valuable input for trading strategies. Moreover, monetary policy announcements can be better interpreted with the help of ChatGPT-4o, potentially improving market efficiency by helping market participants quickly assess the implications of policy changes.

In the domain of sentiment analysis, LLMs have proven effective in extracting sentiment from financial news, social media, and other textual sources. Traditional sentiment analysis often struggles with the nuances of financial language, such as the terms "bull" and "bear," which carry specific meanings in the financial context. LLM frameworks like Heterogeneous Multi-Agent Discussion (HAD) use specialized agents that incorporate linguistic and finance-specific domain knowledge to enhance the accuracy of financial sentiment analysis (FSA) (Feng et al. 2025). Another significant development is FinLlama, a finance-specific LLM framework based on Llama 2 7B, which has been fine-tuned for sentiment classification. It aids in algorithmic trading and portfolio construction, delivering superior performance in quantifying sentiment valence and strength—critical for accurate financial market forecasting.

LLMs also excel in modelling momentum spillover by extracting contextual embeddings from annual reports and earnings call transcripts. These embeddings help identify novel economic links that can be modelled using graph neural networks to understand momentum spillover effects in stock markets. For example, the Management Discussion and Analysis (MD&A) sections from earnings calls and risk-related discussions in annual reports are particularly useful for uncovering insights into market dynamics (Chung and Tanaka-Ishii 2023; Xing 2025). LLMs can evaluate stock-picking strategies, providing valuable input into investment decision-making by analysing historical performance and predicting future trends based on large datasets. This ability to process and interpret financial information enables LLMs to make significant contributions to analysing market trends and improving financial decision-making processes.

Figure 4. Llm Contributions To Financial Decision-Making

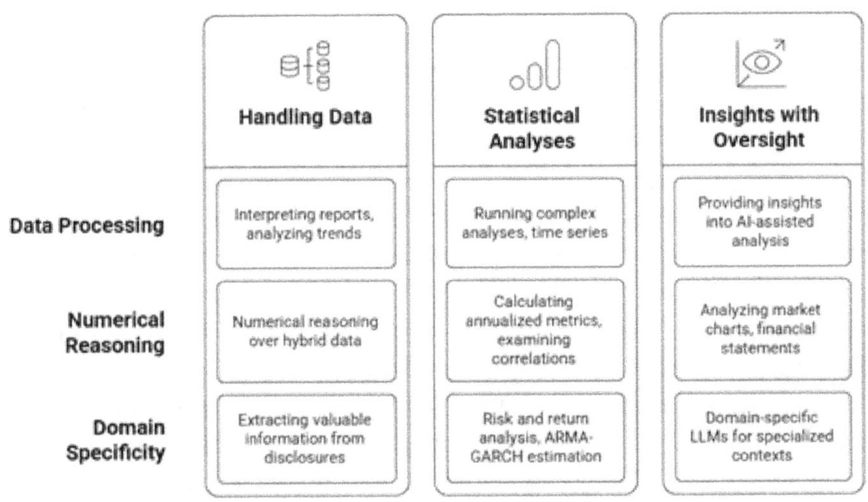

Large Language Models (LLMs) make a significant contribution to financial decision-making by improving data processing, performing complex statistical analysis, and offering valuable insights, while emphasizing the importance of human supervision.

One of the main strengths of LLMs is their ability to handle large amounts of data efficiently. Their enhanced natural language processing (NLP) capabilities allow them to interpret complex financial statements and analyse market trends, making them invaluable to financial professionals (Bae, Yu Hung, and van Lent 2023; Chou et al. 2025; Vebibina et al. 2025). LLMs can process and extract useful information from large amounts of unstructured textual data from a variety of sources, such as news articles, social media posts, financial statements, and revenue call transcripts, much faster than traditional manual methods. The model acts as an "AI analysis," capable of summarizing long disclosures, Management Discussions and Analytics (MD&A), and revenue calls, as well as identifying key themes that are important for understanding market movements. In addition, their ability to perform numerical reasoning on hybrid data—the combination of table and text data makes them irreplaceable for handling tasks involving financial calculations, comparisons, and calculations, which are often found in SEC filings and analyst reports. Custom models, such as TAT-LLMs, are designed to handle these tasks efficiently, while channels such as FinQAPT leverage LLMs for query analysis, ensuring accurate data extraction and contextualization for financial decision-making (Singh, Kaur, and Smiley 2024).

LLMs are also adept at performing complex statistical analysis, which is essential for financial forecasting and risk management. For example, ChatGPT-4o can perform time series analysis, risk and return analysis, as well as ARMA-GARCH estimation (Chou et al. 2025), tasks typically performed by specialized financial software such as Stata. Although the performance of LLMs in financial analysis is generally on par with traditional statistical software, small differences may arise due to differences in implementation. LLMs are powerful at generating Python code for financial data analysis, which can simplify tasks such as calculating annual metrics (e.g., returns, volatility, Sharpe ratios), portfolio diversification, and risk management. However, users should remain vigilant, as LLMs can sometimes miss small details or make mistakes that require verification and correction.

While LLMs are powerful tools for financial analysis, human oversight remains critical. LLMs can provide valuable insights, but human expertise is indispensable for interpreting results, validating outputs, and making real-time decisions, especially in volatile markets. ChatGPT-4o and similar models should be seen as complementary tools and not a substitute for human expertise. To improve the quality and consistency of LLM outputs, prompt engineering plays a crucial role. Techniques such as Labelled Guide Prompting (LGP) ensure that LLMs meet specific requirements and produce more accurate responses to complex financial taskss. Multimodal capabilities, such as those of ChatGPT-4o, allow this model to analyse and interpret market charts, financial reports, and other visual data, perform pattern recognition and semantic analysis to understand financial implications. However, LLMs may struggle with numerical values that are not explicitly annotated in the image.

The importance of domain-specific LLMs is also emphasized, as common models may not perform as well in specific financial contexts due to language and terminology differences. For example, FinLlama, a finance-specific LLM framework, is tailored for sentiment classification, making it a valuable tool for algorithmic trading and portfolio construction, demonstrating superior performance in measuring valence and sentiment strength compared to common LLMs (Iacovides et al. 2024). It highlights the need for customized models that can address the specific needs of financial professionals and improve decision-making processes in the financial sector.

Figure 5. Llm Applications In Financial Reporting

Large language models (LLMs) can be effectively leveraged for automated report generation across various financial and business domains, offering significant capabilities while requiring careful considerations for implementation (Chou et al. 2025; Teixeira et al. 2023). In the area of credit risk reports, models such as GPT-4 demonstrate the ability to produce high-quality outputs that are essential for informed financial decision-making, traditionally handled by human analysts. For instance, in an experimental evaluation involving 100 credit applications, GPT-4-generated reports were statistically significantly preferred by human credit analysts in 60-90% of cases during blind reviews compared to those created by peers. These LLM-generated reports provide comprehensive explanations of delinquency probabilities and credit scores derived from borrower information in credit applications, while also analysing interactions among financial indicators to enhance the transparency and understandability of credit risk assessments. GPT-4 excels in articulating credit risk scores in relation to all relevant factors and employing precise credit risk terminology. By automating this process, LLMs streamline data processing, facilitate real-time analysis, and promote consistency and objectivity, thereby mitigating human biases and variations in expertise.

Beyond credit risk, LLMs like ChatGPT-4o contribute to general financial analysis and reporting through advanced natural language understanding and coherent response generation, proving valuable for tasks such as financial data analysis, time series analysis, risk and return evaluations, and ARMA-GARCH estimations. These models enhance analytical capabilities, accelerate data processing, and support more informed investment decisions. Earlier iterations of ChatGPT have been applied successfully in financial data processing, interpretation, modelling, simulation, hypothesis generation, and automated report creation, with LLMs showing particular proficiency in interpreting financial reports and analysing market trends.

In the realm of business and accounting reports, ChatGPT has exhibited strong performance, including passing business graduation exams at institutions like the Minnesota Law School by accurately addressing multiple-choice and essay questions, as well as excelling in process analysis based on MBA case studies. Additionally, it has demonstrated competence in clearing major accounting certification exams and providing precise responses to numerical assessment questions in accounting, underscoring its utility for generating reliable reports in these fields.

Furthermore, LLMs facilitate summarization for reports by processing and condensing vast quantities of textual data from diverse sources, such as news articles, social media posts, and earnings call transcripts. ChatGPT, for example, aids investors in extracting value-relevant insights from overly detailed disclosures by summarizing Management Discussion and Analysis (MD&A) sections and earnings calls, which can improve the precision of stock price movement predictions (Chung and Tanaka-Ishii 2023; Xing 2025). These models can also compile summaries of pertinent articles on specific topics, enabling researchers to more efficiently assimilate information for inclusion in their reports.

Figure 6. How Llms Are Being Used For Financial Statement Analysis

Large language models (LLMs) can indeed be utilized for financial statement analysis, serving as AI analysts by leveraging their capabilities in understanding, generating, and reasoning about complex financial data (Chou et al. 2025). These models are applied in various ways to enhance financial statement analysis and related tasks. In interpreting financial reports and data, LLMs such as ChatGPT-4o provide enhanced natural language understanding, rendering them highly adept at interpreting financial reports and analysing market trends. They are capable of managing extensive datasets and conducting sophisticated statistical analyses. Earlier versions of ChatGPT have similarly been employed for financial data processing and interpretation.

For automated report generation, LLMs contribute significantly to finance by producing reports efficiently. For example, GPT-4 has demonstrated the ability to generate high-quality credit risk reports, which human credit analysts statistically significantly preferred over those prepared by their peers in blind reviews. Such reports offer comprehensive explanations of delinquency probabilities and credit scores, drawing from borrower information. In summarizing disclosures and earnings calls, LLMs assist investors in extracting value-relevant information from potentially overly detailed disclosures through summarization of Management Discussion and

Analysis (MD&A) sections and earnings calls. This functionality can also improve the accuracy of predictions regarding stock price movements.

Specialized LLMs, such as TAT-LLM, are designed for discrete reasoning over hybrid tabular and textual data in finance, which is essential for the intelligent comprehension of financial documents (Zhu et al. 2024). This encompasses tasks like arithmetic calculations, comparisons, and counting. Notably, TAT-LLM (7B) has surpassed larger models, including GPT-4, in benchmarks for these tasks. With regard to analysing financial charts and visuals, models like ChatGPT-4 and GPT-4o incorporate multimodal capabilities, enabling them to process images as inputs and interpret visual financial data, such as market charts and financial statements. For instance, GPT-4-turbo has precisely extracted firm names and closing prices from annotations in intraday trading charts, thereby offering insights into market dynamics.

LLMs are also employed to identify economic links by extracting contextual embeddings from financial documents, including company annual reports and earnings call transcripts, to model momentum spillover. In this context, ChatGPT can perform abstractive summarization of these documents as an integral part of the process. When addressing complex queries, LLMs excel at decomposing ambiguous or intricate financial tasks into actionable plans. Auto-GPT, for example, can optimize portfolios by obtaining financial data and utilizing Python packages. LLMs prove effective at retrieving valuable details from unstructured data, including sensitive information, and presenting the outcomes in structured formats such as JSON.

Large Language Models (LLMs), especially advanced versions such as ChatGPT-4o, are increasingly being used for financial forecasting, including predicting stock price movements and interpreting monetary policy announcements.

Figure 7. How Llms Contribute To Financial Forecasting

Large Language Models (LLMs) have been increasingly investigated for their potential in predicting stock price movements, especially through the analysis of headline sentiment related to a particular company. An important approach involves aggregating news headlines to determine numerical sentiment scores, with research showing that using models like ChatGPT-4 to analyse these sentiments can significantly improve the accuracy of predicting stock price movements. In this context, FinLlama, a finance-specific LLM framework built on Llama 2 7B, is tailored for sentiment classification to aid with algorithmic trading and portfolio construction (Zhu et al. 2024). The model has demonstrated its ability to generate a resilient portfolio with high returns, even in volatile market conditions, by measuring the valence and strength of sentiment, offering more nuanced insights into the financial news that drives market movements. Additionally, LLMs can be leveraged to evaluate stock selection strategies, helping investors refine their decision-making processes by analysing historical data and predicting future trends.

LLMs also play a crucial role in interpreting monetary policy announcements, where they improve the efficiency of market responses. The impact of models such as ChatGPT in this area has been examined, revealing that they can improve the market's ability to interpret and react to policy changes, thereby improving the overall efficiency of the market.

The fundamental capabilities that enable LLMs to make accurate predictions and analyses come from their advanced natural language processing (NLP) capabilities (Li et al. 2025; Moreno-Sandoval et al. 2024). This ability allows them to understand and generate human-like text from large amounts of data, processing and analysing large amounts of unstructured textual data—such as news articles, social media posts, financial statements, and revenue call transcripts—more efficiently than traditional manual methods. In addition, LLMs excel at performing complex statistical analyses and handling large data sets, making them invaluable for financial tasks such as time series analysis, risk and return analysis, and ARMA-GARCH estimation. Their ability to understand and learn intellectual tasks, just like humans, allows them to engage in complex financial tasks, making them indispensable tools for market forecasting and analysis.

Figure 8. Balancing Llms And Human Oversight In Finance

While Large Language Models (LLMs) have great potential in financial applications (Delgadillo, Kinyua, and Mutigwe 2024; Dong, Stratopoulos, and Wang 2024; Wilksch and Abramova 2023), there are some challenges and limitations that need to be overcome. One of the main concerns is the phenomenon of "hallucination", where LLMs produce inaccurate or fabricated information. This is particularly problematic in the financial sector, where accuracy is crucial, as LLMs can sometimes provide "hallucinated citations"—claims of sources of information that do not match the actual data (Blanco Lambruschini and Brorsson 2024; Moayeri, Tabassi, and Feizi 2024). Although LLMs are skilled at handling large amounts of text and data, they may struggle with proper numerical reasoning and may make computational errors, especially when identifying the correct numbers for calculations. This limitation poses risks, especially in financial tasks that require precise numbers.

Another challenge is that LLMs' ability to process licensed data or proprietary data is limited. Their training is generally based on publicly available information, which means they may not be as effective when dealing with sensitive or proprietary financial data that is not publicly accessible. Additionally, LLMs can exhibit inconsistencies and volatility in their responses, with answers varying among different queries or over time, which creates challenges to ensure reliable reference test cases. Additionally, some LLMs may store outdated facts, providing information that reflects data from previous years, especially if their training data was curated some time ago.

Given these limitations, human oversight remains necessary to validate the results of LLMs. This oversight ensures that the information provided by the model is contextually relevant and accurate, especially when making real-time decisions in volatile markets. Therefore, LLMs should be seen as complementary tools and not a substitute for human expertise, providing valuable support in data processing and analysis, but requiring expert interpretation to avoid errors and ensure reliability.

Figure 9. Llms Contribute To Portfolio Management And Optimization

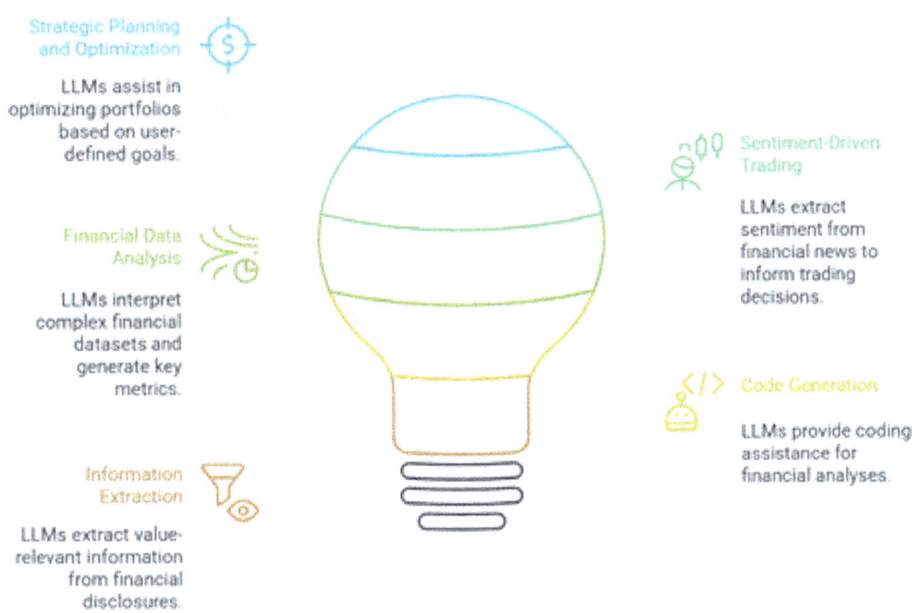

Large Language Models (LLMs) significantly improve portfolio management and optimization by offering advanced capabilities across a wide range of areas (Dombrowski and Seagraves 2025). They facilitate strategic planning and goal-oriented optimization by enabling tools like Auto-GPT to create comprehensive portfolio optimization plans, including financial data acquisition, Python-based Sharpe ratio optimization, and yield presentation, providing end-to-end solutions that were previously unattainable with a single model. In algorithmic trading and sentiment-based portfolio construction, LLMs perform Financial Sentiment Analysis (FSA) by extracting sentiment from unstructured text sources such as financial news, social media, company disclosures, and earnings calls, providing valuable insights for predicting short-term returns and volatility (Iacovides et al. 2024; Xing 2025). For example, FinLlama, built on the Llama 2 7B model, is tailored for sentiment classification, measuring sentiment strength to support algorithmic trading and portfolio construction, with simulations showing superior cumulative returns, Sharpe ratios, and annual volatility over models like (Bae et al. 2023; Xing 2025), even in volatile markets. LLMs like ChatGPT-4o excel at comprehensive financial data analysis, perform robust statistical analysis, calculate key metrics such as Sharpe ratios and market beta through gradual Python code, as well as perform advanced time series analysis such as ARMA-GARCH estimation to capture volatility clustering. They also provide coding assistance, generating Python or MATLAB code for tasks such as implied volatility calculations and data visualization. In addition, LLMs enhance information extraction and reasoning by filtering out relevant insights from complex disclosures and profit calls, transforming unstructured data into structured knowledge. Custom models such as TAT-LLM offer advanced numerical reasoning and interpretation capabilities for financial tabular and textual data, aiding investment decisions by improving understanding of corporate finances.

Figure 10. Llms Contribute To Evaluating Stock-Picking Strategies

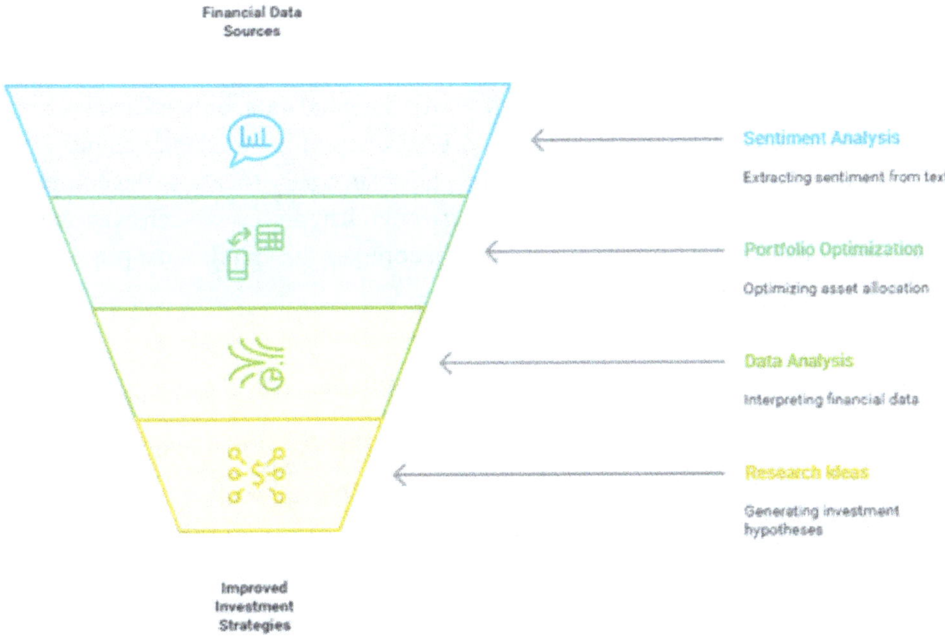

Large Language Models (LLMs) play a transformative role in evaluating stock selection strategies by leveraging advanced capabilities in sentiment analysis, portfolio optimization, financial data analysis, and research innovation. Through Financial Sentiment Analysis (FSA), LLMs extract sentiment from sources such as financial news and social media to inform stock selection decisions. For example, FinLlama, which is built on the Llama 2 7B model, is tailored for sentiment classification, measuring sentiment strength to improve algorithmic trading and portfolio construction. The simulations demonstrate FinLampa's ability to generate a portfolio with high returns and resiliency, even in volatile markets, outperforming other sentiment analysis methods in terms of cumulative returns, Sharpe ratios, and annual volatility, thanks to efficient techniques such as parameter-efficient tuning (PEFT) and 8-bit quantization via LoRA (Iacovides et al. 2024). The Heterogeneous Multi-Agent Discussion (HAD) framework uses specialized LLM agents with linguistic and financial expertise to improve FSA accuracy, going beyond simple prompting approaches and other multi-agent setups, especially with advanced models such as Llama3 and GPT-3.5 (Xing 2025). In portfolio optimization, LLMs such as Auto-GPT formulate detailed plans, acquire financial data, and use Python packages for Sharpe ratio optimization, acting as solution automation regulators. ChatGPT-4o identifies correlated stocks, suggests diversification strategies, and calculates key metrics such as Sharpe ratios and market beta. For financial data analysis, LLMs process complex datasets, perform time series analysis, and forecast ARMA-GARCH models to uncover important insights for investment strategies. ChatGPT-4o excels at training-free prompting and risk-return analysis, while specialized models such as TAT-LLM improve numerical reasoning over financial data, outperforming common LLMs in stock-picking-related tasks. LLMs also extract relevant insights from disclosures and earnings calls, resulting in a brief summary to assess the company. Finally, LLMs drive innovation by generating research hypotheses, such as exploring how climate risk mitigation strategies affect a company's capital costs, providing a basis for further financial research.

Figure 11. Llms Perform Financial Sentiment Analysis

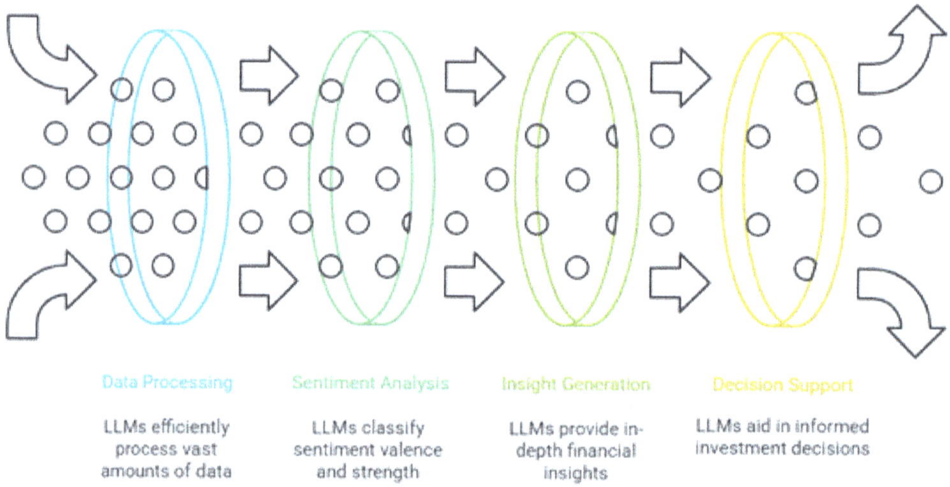

Large Language Models (LLMs) play an important role in Financial Sentiment Analysis (FSA) in a variety of ways that improve financial decision-making (Iacovides et al. 2024; Xing 2025). In assisting with stock selection, LLMs are explored for their ability to support stock investment decisions. In algorithmic trading and portfolio management, FSA is becoming a major application, helping to filter insights from non-numerical sources such as financial news and earnings calls. LLMs improve efficiency and accuracy in a wide range of financial services, including customer service automation, fraud detection (Bansal et al. 2024), and personalized financial advice, by accelerating financial operations. They provide in-depth insights into financial news by classifying sentiment valence and measuring its strength, leveraging their ability to handle large amounts of data and perform complex statistical analysis, which is invaluable in finance. LLMs also simplify data processing, improve analytical capabilities, and support more informed investment decisions. In market interpretation, they are adept at recognizing market trends and identifying implications for portfolio diversification, risk management, and investment strategies. Additionally, LLMs help investors extract relevant information from complex disclosures and call profits, as well as identify themes in the text to generate a brief summary of related discussions. Finally, LLMs like ChatGPT can generate new hypotheses related to asset pricing and investment strategies, becoming a starting point for further research.

Big Language models like GPT-4, when integrated with a new prompt engineering method called Labeled Guide Prompting (LGP) and guided by a Bayesian network, can generate credit risk reports that human credit analysts prefer to those created by their peers. This approach marks significant progress in utilizing LLMs for complex financial tasks. Credit risk analysis is a multifaceted process that requires contextual understanding, logical reasoning, domain-specific knowledge, and implicit and causal reasoning. Automating this process with LLMs like GPT-4 can bring about transformative changes in the financial industry by simplifying data processing, enabling real-time analysis, and resulting in more consistent and objective assessments. LGP is a prompt engineering strategy designed to standardize the content and quality of GPT-4's output, making it more predictable and insightful, even for complex tasks like credit risk analysis. LGPs break down complex tasks into subtasks with unique labels, directing LLMs to handle each label with examples of few-shot learning labeled according to sub-tasks. This approach ensures LLMs capture relevant information and reason in a structured manner, resulting in more detailed responses with minimal overlap of information. Bayesian network integration aids GPT-4 in reasoning by providing a probabilistic graphical model to estimate the probability of default, chosen for its strong predictive performance and interpretability. This network supports common-sense, deductive, abductive, implicit, and causal reasoning, allowing LLMs to explore complex relationships between credit risk factors. In an experiment with 100 credit applications, GPT-4's (LLM-G) generated report using this method was compared to a human-generated report (HG). An independent team of seven credit analysts blindly assessed the report, showing a statistically significant preference for LLM-G reports (90.2% in the English version and 60.3% in the Portuguese version, excluding the "both are the same" option). LLM-G reports contain fewer errors, do not produce harmful hallucinations, and excel at explaining credit risk scores in relevant financial terms, although human reports emphasize more agricultural financial terms. The combination of Bayesian and LGP networks allows GPT-4 to achieve competencies that are equivalent to or surpass human experts in complex tasks such as credit risk reporting.

Numerical reasoning of tabular and textual data is an important yet complex task in finance, handled by specialized Large Language Models (LLMs) such as TAT-

LLMs and FinQAPT pipelines, which improve the processing and interpretation of financial information. TAT-LLM, designed to answer queries (QA) over tabular and textual hybrid data such as SEC reports and analyst reports, improves discrete reasoning for arithmetic, comparison, and calculation. It uses a step-by-step pipeline with three components—Extractor (identifying relevant information), Reasoner (generating mathematical equations or rules of logic), and Executor (generating final answers)—powered by External Executor to ensure accuracy, offering better interpretability than an end-to-end approach. Developed by fine-tuning LLaMA 2 (7B, 13B, 70B) using Low-Rank Adaptation (LoRA) on datasets such as FinQA and TAT-QA, TAT-LLM outperforms larger common LLMs such as GPT-4, especially on arithmetic and computational tasks, addressing issues such as cost, latency, and data security (Liu et al. 2025). In contrast, the FinQAPT pipeline provides an end-to-end solution for financial query analysis using a retrieval-augmented generation (RAG) approach with three modules: FinPrimary (identifying relevant reports using query decomposition and techniques such as TF-IDF and BM25), FinContext (extracting text and table data in detail with cluster-based negative sampling), and FinReader (generating answers with Dynamic N-shot Prompting and Chain of Thought for numerical reasoning enhanced). FinReader achieved the best accuracy of 80.6% on FinQA with GPT-4, although end-to-end performance was hampered by challenges such as scattered context, question ambiguity, and difficulties with large number calculations. Both TAT-LLM and FinQAPT affirm the importance of structured prompting and specialized training to address the limitations of common LLMs, with TAT-LLMs excelling in efficiency and interpretability, and FinQAPT offering a comprehensive pipeline with advanced context retrieval.

Large Language Models (LLMs) are leveraged to improve momentum dispersion modelling in the stock market by extracting contextual embedding from financial documents and integrating them with graph neural networks (GNNs). Momentum spread is a market anomaly in which stock returns are positively correlated on the medium horizon (3 to 12 months), likely because investors who have limited attention do not immediately enter information from related companies economically, leading to pricing errors and slow diffusion of information. Economic relationships between companies, such as within the same industry or shared analyst coverage, affect the movement of shared stocks and predictability. LLMs, such as ChatGPT, generate abstract summaries of financial documents such as the company's annual report (Business section, Risk Factors, Management Discussion and Analysis, as well as Quantitative and Qualitative Disclosures about Market Risk) and earnings call transcripts (Management Discussions and Analysis and Q&A) (Chung and Tanaka-Ishii 2023), which are then converted into contextual embedding using sentence-transformers models such as all-mpnet-base-v2. These embedding forms new economic relationships based on semantic proximity within vector space, which is measured by cosine similarity, offering a dynamic and comprehensive representation rather than static classifications such as sectors or industries. This relationship is modelled in the GNN framework, using a modified GATv2 architecture (Chung and Tanaka-Ishii 2023), with the node representing the momentum of the stock price and the edge reflecting the economic relationship, optimizing the cosine similarity between the prediction and the standardized stock return for the entire market. The Monte Carlo experiment validated the effectiveness of GNN and text-based relationships, with this model outperforming the graph-based average aggregation baseline. Empirically, the economic relationships of the annual report on risk sections (1A and 7A))) and the Management Discussion and Analysis sections of earnings calls resulted in significant performance, surpassing random and equivalent or better than sector/industry ratios in terms of Sharpe ratios and rating correlations, while the other sections were less significant. The study highlights ChatGPT-4o's capabilities in financial analysis, demonstrating efficient data processing, better analytical capabilities, and more informed investment decision-making, suggesting that LLMs, with proper guidance, can achieve competencies equal to or surpass human experts in complex problem-solving tasks.

LLMS AND RISK MANAGEMENT

Large Language Models (LLMs) are revolutionizing financial risk modeling, particularly in fraud detection and credit assessment, by enabling solutions to previously difficult tasks to overcome. In financial risk modeling, LLMs leverage their extensive initial training to understand complex datasets and natural language instruction, excel in scenarios with limited labeled data, and facilitate efficient data processing, advanced statistical analysis, and more informed investment decision-making. In fraud detection, LLMs like ChatGPT enhance deep learning-based solutions by analyzing user history and transaction data in real-time, while financial sentiment analysis helps identify fake news and fraud, supporting robust risk management (E R Kismawadi, Irfan, M., Al Muddatstsir, U. D., & Abdulkarim 2023).

Figure 12. LLM Applications in Financial Risk Management

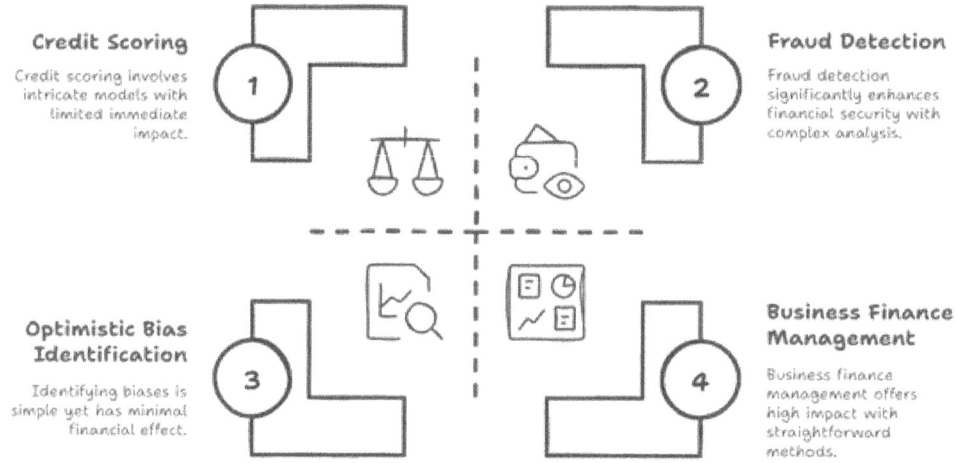

In credit scoring and credit risk reporting, LLMs automate complex analyses involving variables such as credit history and economic conditions, resulting in a consistent and objective real-time assessment compared to traditional human methods. A new technique, Labeled Guide Prompting (LGP), improves the performance of LLMs like GPT-4 by using annotated few-shot examples and Bayesian network-based hints to drive abductive reasoning, resulting in credit risk reports preferred by human analysts in 60-90% of cases in blind reviews, with statistically significant improvements in depth of insight. However, challenges remain, including the potential for LLMs to generate disinformation, bias, or hallucinations, especially in complex fact-retrieval or reasoning tasks. Inconsistent outputs, especially with dynamic data, require human oversight, while privacy concerns with sensitive financial data drive the development of methods such as Differentially Private Low-Rank Adaptation (DP-LoRA). Additionally, issues such as hallucinated quotes or outdated information underscore the need for continuous validation to ensure reliability in financial applications.

Large Language Models (LLMs) can indeed help identify optimistic biases in human financial analysts. Research by Li et al. (2024) shows that models like ChatGPT are able to recognize these optimistic biases, providing insight into how AI can reduce subjective bias in financial analysis. These capabilities align with broader LLM applications in finance, where they are used to interpret complex data sets, provide insights for AI-assisted financial analysis, handle large amounts of data, and perform complex statistical analysis. By leveraging these advanced capabilities, LLMs support more objective and consistent analysis in financial contexts, complementing human expertise and addressing potential human bias, thereby contributing to better analytical capabilities and more informed investment decision-making.

Specialized GPT models such as "(Feng et al. 2025)" and "Tax AI—Tax and Finance" are indeed described as tools that provide expert analysis on an ongoing basis to improve business financial management and portfolio supervision (Feng et al. 2025), while advancing financial literacy. These models serve as tireless financial analysts, providing expert analysis on an ongoing basis that strengthens the business's financial management, portfolio oversight, and understanding of tax regulations. This capability not only improves financial decision-making, but also promotes financial literacy among users. As part of advances in generative AI, these models allow users to create a chatbot GPT tailored to specific tasks by integrating customized instructions, additional knowledge, and a variety of skills.

FINANCIAL ADVISEMENT AND CUSTOMER SERVICE

Large language models (LLMs) are indeed being investigated for personal financial advisement and recommendations, functioning as AI analysts, with various studies examining their potential and limitations. These models exhibit a range of capabilities and potential applications in the financial domain. In broad financial tasks, LLMs such as ChatGPT-4o can assist in managing large datasets, performing computations, and conducting financial analysis. They are proficient in interpreting financial reports, analysing market trends, and supporting general financial analysis, data processing, interpretation, modelling, simulation, and automated report generation. Custom GPT models, including "Finance Wizard" and "Tax AI—Tax and Finance," can serve as continuous, expert financial analysts for managing business finances, overseeing portfolios, and comprehending tax regulations, while also fostering financial literacy (Feng et al. 2025).

Figure 13. LLMs personal financial advisement and recommendations

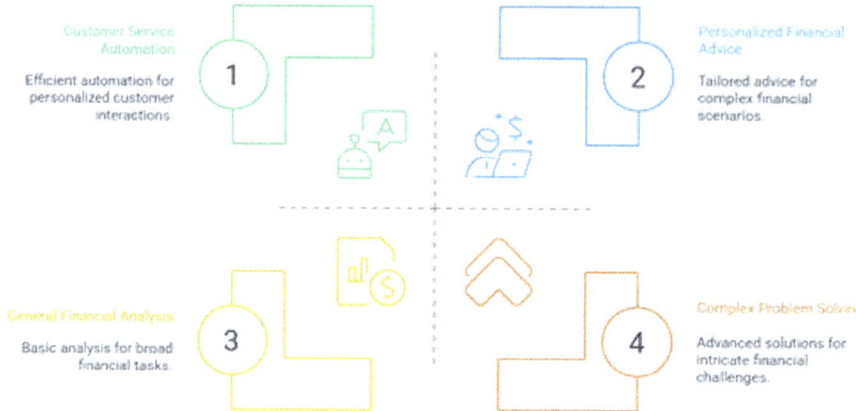

For personalized advice and customer service, LLMs hold the potential to enhance decision-making quality in personal finance by contributing to tasks such as fraud detection (Irfan et al. 2025; Jannah et al. 2024), risk management, financial forecasting, data analysis, stock price prediction, and report generation. Their capabilities can transform financial services, including the automation of customer service and the provision of personalized financial advice, thereby improving efficiency and accuracy.

In complex problem solving, LLMs demonstrate excellence in decomposing ambiguous or intricate financial tasks into actionable plans. For instance, Auto-GPT can optimize portfolios by retrieving financial data and employing Python packages for Sharpe ratio optimization, a capability that was previously unattainable for a single model. This positions LLMs as effective virtual agents in financial advisory, particularly for handling client requests characterized by high variability and complex interactions.

Regarding information retrieval and synthesis, LLMs can process extensive textual data from sources such as news articles and social media posts to identify patterns and relationships that may be difficult to detect manually. ChatGPT, for example, has been studied for its ability to assist investors in extracting value-relevant information from disclosures and summarizing earnings calls. In coding and model derivation, ChatGPT is capable of generating code in multiple programming languages, such as Matlab, Python, R, SAS, and Stata, to facilitate data analysis, thereby increasing efficiency and reducing errors for finance researchers. It can also derive theoretical financial models systematically and precisely, including option pricing models, which proves especially beneficial for junior researchers.

Figure 14. LLMs virtual agents to provide assistance in customer service

Large language models (LLMs) can indeed function as virtual agents to deliver assistance in customer service, especially in contexts where client requests display significant variability and conversations involve intricate dynamics. This functionality is supported by their sophisticated natural language processing (NLP) capabilities, which empower them to interpret financial reports, analyse market trends, and facilitate informed decision-making. In handling complex queries, LLMs exhibit proficiency in tasks that demand reasoning and emergent abilities, rendering them particularly suitable for situations in which task instructions or expected responses are not explicitly outlined, or when managing data that falls outside typical distributions. These attributes enable LLMs to offer effective support for client inquiries characterized by high variability and sophisticated conversational patterns. For automating financial services, LLMs possess the potential to revolutionize multiple aspects of the sector, encompassing the automation of customer service and the provision of personalized financial guidance, thereby elevating both operational efficiency and precision in financial activities.

In the domain of customized expert analysis, platforms such as ChatGPT Plus permit users to create specialized GPT chatbots through the incorporation of specific instructions and additional knowledge resources. These tailored models, exemplified by "Finance Wizard" or "Tax AI—Tax and Finance," operate as indefatigable financial analysts, delivering ongoing expert insights to optimize business finance management, portfolio supervision, and understanding of tax regulations, ultimately enhancing financial decision-making and promoting financial literacy.

CONCLUSION

LLMs, such as ChatGPT-4o and custom models such as TAT-LLM, can improve transparency in Islamic finance by automating audits. This model is capable of processing complex financial documents, such as annual reports and disclosures, to ensure compliance with Sharia principles, such as the prohibition of riba and gharar. By extracting and summarizing relevant information from unstructured data (e.g., Management Discussion and Analysis [MD&A] sections or call profits), LLMs generate clear and structured reports, such as in JSON format, that make it easy for stakeholders to verify compliance. Approaches such as Labeled Guide Prompting (LGP) ensure LLM outputs are focused and free from overlapping information, increasing clarity and trust in Sharia financial processes.

In risk management, LLMs support predictive analytics for profit-sharing contracts such as mudarabah and musharakah, which are the core of Islamic finance. Models such as FinQAPT and TAT-LLM excel at numerical reasoning over hybrid tabular and textual data, enabling accurate risk analysis on Islamic financial instruments. For example, by integrating Bayesian networks, LLMs like GPT-4 can estimate the probability of default on profit-sharing contracts, providing insight into volatility and potential losses. In addition, financial sentiment analysis (FSA) through models such as FinLlama allows prediction of short-term returns and volatility based on financial news and social media, helping Islamic financial institutions better manage market risks. Techniques such as Differentially Private Low-Rank Adaptation (DP-LoRA) ensure the privacy of sensitive data, in line with Sharia ethical principles.

LLMs enhance the customer experience by providing personalized and culturally sensitive financial advice, which is essential in Islamic finance to build trust. Specialized models such as "Finance Wizard" and "Tax AI—Tax and Finance" act as virtual financial analysts, offering Sharia-compliant tax and investment guidance in real-time. LLMs can process varied and complex customer queries, using natural language processing (NLP) capabilities to provide contextually relevant responses and in line with Islamic values. For example, an LLM can summarize a call for profit or disclosure to explain Islamic financial products to customers in an easy-to-understand way, improving financial literacy. However, human supervision remains essential to validate responses, prevent hallucinations, and ensure alignment with Sharia principles, thereby maintaining customer trust.

REFERENCES

Bae, J., Hung, C. Y., & van Lent, L. (2023). Mobilizing Text As Data. *European Accounting Review, 32*(5), 1085–1106. DOI: 10.1080/09638180.2023.2218423

Bansal, U., S. Bharatwal, D. S. Bagiyam, and E. R. Kismawadi. 2024. "Fraud Detection in the Era of AI: Harnessing Technology for a Safer Digital Economy." Pp. 143–64 in *AI-Driven Decentralized Finance and the Future of Finance.*

Chou, W. H., Feng, Z., Li, B., & Liu, F. (2025). A First Look at Financial Data Analysis Using ChatGPT-4o. *Journal of Risk and Financial Management, 18*(2). Advance online publication. DOI: 10.3390/jrfm18020099

Chung, A., & Tanaka-Ishii, K. 2023. "Modeling Momentum Spillover with Economic Links Discovered from Financial Documents." *ICAIF 2023 - 4th ACM International Conference on AI in Finance* 490–97. doi: DOI: 10.1145/3604237.3626862

Delgadillo, J., Kinyua, J., & Mutigwe, C. (2024). FinSoSent: Advancing Financial Market Sentiment Analysis through Pretrained Large Language Models. *Big Data and Cognitive Computing, 8*(8). Advance online publication. DOI: 10.3390/bdcc8080087

Dombrowski, T., & Seagraves, C. (2025). Optimizing Real Estate Portfolios: The Role of Generative AI in Geographic Diversification. *Journal of Real Estate Portfolio Management*. Advance online publication. DOI: 10.1080/10835547.2025.2513145

Dong, M. M., Stratopoulos, T. C., & Wang, V. X. (2024). A Scoping Review of ChatGPT Research in Accounting and Finance. *International Journal of Accounting Information Systems, 55*. Advance online publication. DOI: 10.1016/j.accinf.2024.100715

Feng, Z., Hu, G., Li, B., & Wang, J. (2025). Unleashing the Power of ChatGPT in Finance Research: Opportunities and Challenges. *Financial Innovation, 11*(1). Advance online publication. DOI: 10.1186/s40854-025-00770-3

Iacovides, G., Konstantinidis, T., Xu, M., & Mandic, D. 2024. "FinLlama: LLM-Based Financial Sentiment Analysis for Algorithmic Trading." *ICAIF 2024 - 5th ACM International Conference on AI in Finance* 134–41. doi: DOI: 10.1145/3677052.3698696

Irfan, M., S. Parameswaran, K. A. Singh, and E. R. Kismawadi. 2025. "Cutting-Edge Technologies for Economic Well-Being: The Transformative Power of AI and Blockchain." Pp. 229–48 in *Driving Socio-Economic Growth With AI and Blockchain.*

Jannah, N., Bahri, M. I., Kismawadi, E. R., & Handriana, T. (2024). The Effect of Green Brand Image and Green Satisfaction on Green Brand Equity Mediated Green Trust Outpatient's. *Quality - Access to Success, 25*(198), 381–390. DOI: 10.47750/QAS/25.198.40

Kismawadi, E. R. 2024. "Sustainable Islamic Financial Inclusion: The Ethical Challenges of Generative AI in Product and Service Development." Pp. 237–58 in *Exploring the Ethical Implications of Generative AI.*

E R Kismawadi, Irfan, M., Al Muddatstsir, U. D., & Abdulkarim, F. M. 2023. "Fintech Innovations: Risk Mitigation Strategies in Islamic Finance." Pp. 35–58 in *Fintech Applications in Islamic Finance: AI, Machine Learning, and Blockchain Techniques.*

Lambruschini, B. Braulio, C., & Brorsson, M. (2024). "Transforming Unstructured Sensitive Information into Structured Knowledge." *ICAIF 2024 - 5th ACM International Conference on AI in Finance* 831–38. doi: DOI: 10.1145/3677052.3698602

Li, H., Yu, B., Wei, Y., Wang, K., Xu, R. Y. D., & Wang, B. (2025). KERMIT: Knowledge Graph Completion of Enhanced Relation Modeling with Inverse Transformation. *Knowledge-Based Systems, 324.* Advance online publication. DOI: 10.1016/j.knosys.2025.113500

Liu, X. Y., Zhu, R., Zha, D., Gao, J., Zhong, S., White, M., & Qiu, M. (2025). Differentially Private Low-Rank Adaptation of Large Language Model Using Federated Learning. *ACM Transactions on Management Information Systems, 16*(2). Advance online publication. DOI: 10.1145/3682068

Moayeri, M., Tabassi, E., & Feizi, S. 2024. "WorldBench: Quantifying Geographic Disparities in LLM Factual Recall." *2024 ACM Conference on Fairness, Accountability, and Transparency, FAccT 2024* 1211–28. doi: DOI: 10.1145/3630106.3658967

Moreno-Sandoval, L. G., Pomares-Quimbaya, A., Barbosa-Sierra, S. A., & Pantoja-Rojas, L. M. (2024). Detection of Hate Speech, Racism and Misogyny in Digital Social Networks: Colombian Case Study. *Big Data and Cognitive Computing, 8*(9). Advance online publication. DOI: 10.3390/bdcc8090113

Singh, K., Kaur, S., & Smiley, C. 2024. "FinQAPT: Empowering Financial Decisions with End-to-End LLM-Driven Question Answering Pipeline." *ICAIF 2024 - 5th ACM International Conference on AI in Finance* 266–73. doi: DOI: 10.1145/3677052.3698682

Teixeira, A. C., Marar, V., Yazdanpanah, H., Pezente, A., & Ghassemi, M. 2023. "Enhancing Credit Risk Reports Generation Using LLMs: An Integration of Bayesian Networks and Labeled Guide Prompting." *ICAIF 2023 - 4th ACM International Conference on AI in Finance* 340–48. doi: DOI: 10.1145/3604237.3626902

Vebibina, A., Rusijono, A. M., Muafa, A., Kurniawan, D., Dewantoro, R. S., Asyari, D. N., Widiastuti, S., & Suseno, J. (2025). 11 Key Strategies in Using AI Chat GPT to Develop HOTS-Based Entrepreneurship Questionnaires. *Qubahan Academic Journal*, *5*(1), 33–62. DOI: 10.48161/qaj.v5n1a1134

Wilksch, M., & Abramova, O. (2023). PyFin-Sentiment: Towards a Machine-Learning-Based Model for Deriving Sentiment from Financial Tweets. *International Journal of Information Management Data Insights*, *3*(1). Advance online publication. DOI: 10.1016/j.jjimei.2023.100171

Xing, F. (2025). Designing Heterogeneous LLM Agents for Financial Sentiment Analysis. *ACM Transactions on Management Information Systems*, *16*(1). Advance online publication. DOI: 10.1145/3688399

Zhu, F., Liu, Z., Feng, F., Wang, C., Li, M., & Chua, T. S. 2024. "TAT-LLM: A Specialized Language Model for Discrete Reasoning over Financial Tabular and Textual Data." *ICAIF 2024 - 5th ACM International Conference on AI in Finance* (Table 1):310–18. doi: DOI: 10.1145/3677052.3698685

Chapter 10
GenAI for Sales Enablement in Direct Selling:
Automating Personalized Customer Outreach With LLMs

Sai Yellaiah Simhadri
https://orcid.org/0009-0001-0021-9331
Pampered Chef, USA

ABSTRACT

Direct selling is a business model rooted in personal trust and human interaction. While sales enablement strategies aim to support independent sellers, they often fall short in scaling personalized communication an area where manual efforts become inefficient. This paper explores the potential of generative AI, particularly LLMs like Claude by Anthropic, deployed via Amazon Bedrock, to automate personalized outreach including emails, social messages, and product recommendations. A real-world case is examined where a legacy, template-based system was upgraded to an AI-powered platform capable of tailoring messages using customer history and preferences. Cost and ROI analysis reveal improved efficiency, higher repeat purchases, and stronger customer relationships. The study also explores how LLMs analyze unstructured data for hyper-personalized journeys and addresses key implementation concerns such as CRM integration, data privacy, training, and bias. The paper concludes that genAI, when used ethically and strategically, enhances rather than replaces the human role in direct selling.

DOI: 10.4018/979-8-3373-3912-2.ch010

1. INTRODUCTION

Direct selling has been a key part of entrepreneurship for many years, but now it's at an important turning point (Direct Selling Education Foundation [DSEF], 1973). Most of us have probably met a direct seller, maybe at a home party, on social media, or through a friend's recommendation and they rely heavily on personal interactions to build customer relationships. This business model is based on relationships and trust, and in 2022, it brought in around $172.8 billion in global sales, with millions of independent sellers involved (DSEF, 1973).

However, scaling personalized communication has always been a significant challenge.

Customers expect personalized experience, and they are smarter and more selective than ever. This makes it harder for traditional direct selling methods to work like they used to. The big question is: how can direct sellers keep that personal connection while also reaching more people online? Traditionally, this sector utilized manual processes to personalize customer communication, making it challenging to maintain personal touches at scale. With so many potential customers, it's easy to feel overwhelmed. And if the messages sent are too generic or one-size-fits-all, people often ignore them because they don't feel personal or relevant (Gartner Inc, 1979).

This is where the idea of sales enablement comes in. Although it's often talked about in business-to-business (B2B) sales, its main ideas also fit well with direct selling. Sales enablement means more than just handing out brochures or marketing content. It's a smart, ongoing approach to help salespeople — in this case, independent direct sellers — with the training, tools, and information they need to connect with customers at every stage of the buying process (Gartner Inc, 1979).

The goal is to help sellers have the right conversation with the right customer at the right moment, so they can work more efficiently and increase sales. For direct sellers, this means giving them the knowledge and resources to really understand their customers and explain the value of their products in a way that feels personal and convincing (Gartner Inc, 1979). The challenge, though, is doing this for many customers at once — personalizing outreach on a large scale is still a tough problem to solve. At the same time, a powerful new technology is rising - generative artificial intelligence (AI), especially large language models (LLMs). These tools aren't just small upgrades — they mark a major leap forward in what AI can do. LLMs are advanced computer systems trained on massive amounts of text, which allows them to understand and create human-like language very smoothly. They're already being used in chatbots, for writing content, translating languages, and even coding. What makes them special is their ability to read and understand information, find patterns, and create new content that fits the situation — often so well that it sounds like it was written by a person. This skill of producing personalized, natural-sounding content on a large scale could be a game-changer for industries that depend on strong communication — and sales is definitely one of the most important among them.

This paper looks at how three powerful ideas come together: the long-standing approach of direct selling, the importance of sales enablement, and the game-changing potential of generative AI, especially large language models (LLMs). The main focus is on one key part of sales enablement in direct selling automating personalized customer outreach.

Sending out large numbers of generic messages no longer works well (Deveau et al., 2023). Today's customers expect communication that fits their needs, preferences, and past interactions (Gartner Inc, 1979]. But for most direct sellers, it's just not possible to write custom messages for every customer by hand. That's where LLMs can make a big difference.

These smart AI tools can look at customer data, understand personal details, and automatically create emails, social media posts, or conversation scripts that feel tailor-made. The big question this paper explores is: Can LLMs be used to make outreach more personal and engaging at scale, helping direct sellers connect better and grow their sales? (Mulé, 2024).

The main point of this paper is that generative AI, especially large language models (LLMs), has the power to transform sales enablement in the direct selling industry by making it possible to create personalized customer messages automatically and at a large scale. This kind of automation can help independent sellers connect better with customers, save time, and increase productivity. However, it also brings some important challenges and ethical concerns that need to be addressed carefully (SalesTechStar, 2024).

Here's how the paper is organized:

- **Section 2** explains how LLMs work and how they can be used for personalized outreach, such as analyzing customer data and generating content.
- **Section 3** explores how LLMs can be used to understand what customers want, automate content creation, and deliver deeply personalized experience along with emerging applications.
- **Section 4** looks at how this can be put into practice in direct selling, including how LLMs can be connected to tools like CRM systems, how to manage data, and how to train sellers to use these tools effectively along with a real-world case study.
- **Section 5** discusses key challenges, such as protecting customer data, avoiding bias in AI, keeping messages authentic, and understanding how this may change the seller's role (SalesTechStar, 2024).
- **Section 6** explores future trends in generative AI and how technology might evolve in the direct selling space (Yee et al., 2024).

- **Section 7** wraps up the discussion and shares final thoughts on what all this means for the future of the industry.

By examining the capabilities, implementation strategies, challenges, and future trajectory of LLMs in this specific context, this paper aims to provide professionals in the direct selling industry with a comprehensive understanding of how this transformative technology can be leveraged for effective, personalized sales enablement.

2. LITERATURE REVIEW AND BACKGROUND

To understand how generative AI can improve personalized outreach in direct selling, we first need to look at a few connected areas. These include: the unique world of direct selling, the purpose of sales enablement, what generative AI and large language models (LLMs) are, and how AI is already being used in sales and marketing today. This section gives a basic overview of each of these topics, using insights from both industry experts and research.

2.1 The Direct Selling Landscape: Relationships and Reach

Direct selling, also known as network marketing or multi-level marketing (MLM), is a large global industry based on personal connections. Unlike regular retail stores, direct selling uses independent representatives who sell products directly to customers, often through friends, family, or social networks. According to the Direct Selling Association (DSA), this business model continues to be popular and generates major sales worldwide (DSEF, 1973). It has several key features:

- **Built on Relationships:** Trust and personal connection are at the core of direct selling. Top sellers often succeed by building strong relationships with their customers and offering personalized service.
- **Independent Sellers:** Most sellers are self-employed and run their own business. They manage their time, sales, and customer relationships on their own. This freedom means they need the right tools and support to stay productive and follow company guidelines.
- **Multiple Sales Channels:** While direct selling used to happen mostly face-to-face (like at home parties), today it also includes online tools like social media, email, and personal websites (DSEF, 1973). Sellers now have to bring their relationship-building skills into the digital world.

- **Scaling Is Hard:** The biggest strength of direct selling — personal relationships — also makes it hard to grow. It's a challenge for sellers to stay personal and meaningful with more and more customers (Deveau et al., 2023).

As customer expectations grow — especially around digital communication and personalized experiences — direct selling companies are under pressure to adapt. This is why exploring new tools like AI is becoming more important than ever.

2.2 Sales Enablement: Helping Sellers Succeed

Sales enablement is all about giving sellers what they need to do their jobs well. It goes beyond just handing out marketing materials — it's a complete strategy to support salespeople with the right tools, training, content, and guidance to help them connect with customers at every stage of the buying process.

In direct selling, this means helping independent sellers learn how to understand their customers, answer questions effectively, and offer real value in their conversations. It's about making sure they know what to say, when to say it, and how to say it — whether they're chatting in person, over social media, or through email.

When done right, sales enablement improves:

- Confidence in sellers
- Stronger relationships with customers
- Better sales results
- And more efficient use of time and effort

It includes several important parts:

- **Content**: Sharing helpful materials like product info, sales scripts, case studies, and marketing tools that match different types of customers and stages in the buying process (Gartner Inc, 1979).
- **Training**: Teaching sellers about the products, how to sell effectively, and what customers are looking for.
- **Tools & Technology**: Using systems like CRM (Customer Relationship Management), sales tracking software, and communication platforms to help sellers work smarter and faster.
- **Guidance & Coaching**: Giving continuous support, tips, and feedback to help sellers improve their performance and stay motivated (Gartner Inc, 1979).

Together, these elements help sellers feel confident, stay organized, and provide better service to their customers. The challenge lies in delivering this enablement in a way that is scalable, consistent, and accessible to a distributed, independent workforce. But to reach that level — especially when dealing with large numbers of potential customers — direct sellers need smart systems and personalized support. That's where AI tools, like LLMs, start to play a powerful role.

2.3 Generative AI and LLMs: Technology Explained

Generative AI is a big step forward in artificial intelligence. Unlike traditional AI, which mostly looks at existing data, generative AI can create new content — like writing text, answering questions, or having conversations. The main technology behind this is Large Language Models (LLMs), which power many of the AI tools we use today.

So, what makes LLMs special?

- **How They're Built:** LLMs use a type of AI design called Transformer architecture. This setup is very good at understanding and working with language. These models are huge — often with billions or even trillions of parts (called parameters) which help them learn complex patterns in how we speak and write.
- **How They're Trained:** They learn by reading enormous amounts of text and code from the internet, books, and more. This training helps them understand grammar, facts, reasoning, and many different writing styles.
- **What They Can Do:** LLMs can write content, summarize text, translate languages, answer questions, and sort information. They often create responses that sound natural and human-like (Deveau et al., 2023).
- **How They're Customized:** While they're trained to be useful in general, they can be fine-tuned for specific tasks or guided using instructions called prompts to get certain results (Salesforce Inc, 1999).

Examples of popular LLMs include OpenAI's GPT, Google's Gemini, Anthropic's Claude, and open-source models like Llama (Kelly, n.d.). Their strength lies in being able to understand context and write personalized messages on a large scale, which makes them great for tasks like customer communication (Deveau et al., 2023; Mulé, 2024).

However, LLMs aren't perfect. Their responses are based on probabilities, so they can sometimes make up facts (called "hallucinations") or reflect biases from the data they were trained on. That's why it's important to use them carefully and with proper checks in place (SalesTechStar, 2024).

2.4 Existing AI Applications in Sales and Marketing

AI has already been part of sales and marketing for some time. Traditional AI and machine learning have been used to improve how businesses work and make decisions (Deveau et al., 2023). Some common uses include:

- **Predictive Analytics:** Using past data to guess future sales trends, spot which customers might leave, or identify the best leads to focus on.
- **Lead Scoring:** Ranking potential customers based on how likely they are to buy, so sales teams can focus on the most promising ones (Deveau et al., 2023).
- **Customer Segmentation:** Grouping customers by things they have in common (like shopping habits or interests) to run more targeted marketing campaigns (Deveau et al., 2023).
- **Recommendation Engines:** Suggesting products or content based on what a customer has bought or viewed before — often seen in online shopping (SalesTechStar, 2024).
- **Basic Chatbots:** Answering simple customer questions or collecting basic information using rule-based scripts or simple AI (Gartner Inc, 1979).

While these tools are useful, they mostly focus on analyzing data or handling simple tasks. Generative AI, especially LLMs, goes a step further — it can actually create personalized content, like writing emails or messages that feel human and relevant (Deveau et al., 2023; Mulé, 2024).

Research by McKinsey shows that while traditional AI helps save time and improve processes, generative AI has even more potential — especially when it comes to creating content and offering a personal touch at scale (Deveau et al., 2023). That's why there's growing excitement about using Gen AI in sales — it could finally solve the big challenge of delivering truly personalized experiences to many customers at once (Deveau et al., 2023; Kelly, n.d.).

This sets the foundation for the next sections, where we'll explore how LLMs can be used specifically to support personalized outreach in the direct selling world.

3. GENAI-POWERED PERSONAL OUTREACH IN DIRECT SELLING

The main advantage of using generative AI, especially LLMs, in direct selling sales enablement is its ability to finally solve the challenge of personalized outreach at scale. Direct selling depends on strong personal relationships, but reaching out to each customer in a personal way becomes very difficult as the business grows. While traditional AI helped analyze data, generative AI goes further — it can actually create personalized messages that help maintain those relationships in today's digital world. This section looks at how LLMs can be used to understand what customers want, automate content creation, and deliver deeply personalized messages, with examples from real-world use cases.

3.1 Beyond Basic Segmentation

To create truly personalized messages, it's important to understand customers deeply. Traditional analytics can group people based on things like age or past purchases, but LLMs can go much further. They have the potential to understand a customer's unique needs, interests, and reasons for buying in a more detailed and meaningful way (Deveau et al., 2023; Mulé, 2024).

So, how can this deeper understanding be made possible? Understanding customers better starts with using the right kind of data — especially unstructured data like conversations, emails, and social media posts. Here's how LLMs can help:

- **Analyzing Conversations and Text:** Direct sellers often gather valuable insights from customer chats, social media comments, and feedback. LLMs are great at reading and understanding this kind of messy, unstructured text. For example, if you provide transcripts from customer calls or social media threads, an LLM can spot patterns, understand emotions, find repeated concerns, and identify what customers care about not just by looking at keywords, but by understanding the meaning behind the words.
- **Combining Different Data Sources:** LLMs can pull together information from multiple places — like CRM records, purchase history, online activity, and past conversations to create a complete picture of each customer. For instance, if someone recently bought wellness products and posted about fitness goals online, the model could suggest promoting a new nutritional supplement that fits their interests (Deveau et al., 2023).
- **Creating Smart Customer Profiles:** LLMs can use all this information to build detailed and evolving customer profiles (personas). These aren't fixed — they update over time as new data comes in, helping direct sellers stay in tune with what different groups of customers want and how to speak to them effectively (Deveau et al., 2023; Kelly, n.d.).

This kind of deep customer insight is the foundation for truly personalized and meaningful outreach.

3.2 Automated Content Creation

Once you understand what customers want, the next step is to create the right message — and this is where LLMs truly stand out. They can automatically generate many types of content, personalized for each customer or customer group (Deveau et al., 2023; Mulé, 2024; Kelly, n.d.). Here's how:

- Personalized Emails: One of the easiest and most effective uses of LLMs. Instead of using the same email template for everyone, LLMs can write emails that mention a customer's past purchases, interests, or recent conversations. Some tools, like Salesforce's Prompt Builder, can pull information from a CRM (like the person's name, company, buying history, or needs) to help the LLM write messages that feel personal. These emails are more likely to get opened and responded to (Mulé, 2024).
- Social Media Posts and Messages: Direct sellers often use social media to find and connect with customers. LLMs can help by suggesting posts that match what a certain audience is interested in. They can also write custom messages or comments, referencing what someone recently posted or mutual connections — making the interaction feel more genuine and less robotic (Kelly, n.d.). Combining LLMs with real-time tools (like Retrieval-Augmented Generation) can make these messages even more accurate and impactful.
- Product Descriptions and Recommendations: LLMs can write product descriptions that highlight what matters most to a specific customer or group. They can also suggest products with a personalized explanation of why that item might be a good fit based on the person's behavior or preferences (Mulé, 2024).
- Sales Scripts and Talking Points: For sellers who want help with what to say, LLMs can create custom call scripts or talking points. These can be based on who the customer is and what the goal of the conversation is (like answering questions or introducing a product). Some tools, like SalesScripter, already support this, and LLMs can take it further by adjusting scripts in real time based on conversation cues or customer data (Kelly, n.d.).

The biggest benefit? Speed and scale. An LLM can write hundreds of unique, personalized messages in the time it would take a person to write just a few — helping direct sellers reach more people with relevant, meaningful content (Deveau et al., 2023; Mulé, 2024).

3.3 Hyper-Personalization at Scale: The Ultimate Goal?

Hyper-personalization means going far beyond simply using a customer's name in a message. It's about customizing the entire experience of what message is sent, what offer is made, when it's sent, and through which channel all based on the customer's unique preferences and situation, sometimes even in real time (Deveau et al., 2023).

Thanks to LLMs, especially when paired with strong customer data systems and tools like Retrieval-Augmented Generation (RAG), this kind of deep personalization is becoming possible even across a large customer base in direct selling (Kelly, n.d.; Yee et al., 2024).

For example, imagine an AI system that constantly monitors customer behavior. It might notice that a customer is almost out of a product they usually reorder, based on their past purchases and usage patterns. The LLM could then automatically write a personalized reminder message sent by email or text even mentioning a related product the customer recently looked at (Deveau et al., 2023; Yee et al., 2024).

Or let's say someone is interacting with certain posts on social media. The system could alert the direct seller and suggest a custom DM, complete with key talking points tailored to that person's interests (Kelly, n.d.).

This kind of automation helps direct sellers focus their energy where it matters most building relationships, closing big deals, and handling complex issues. Meanwhile, the AI can manage simpler but still personalized tasks like outreach and follow-ups (Deveau et al., 2023; Mulé, 2024; Yee et al., 2024). It allows the seller to take on more of a strategic role, using AI to support and enhance their customer engagement.

3.4 Emerging Applications

While direct selling hasn't widely adopted generative AI yet, many tools in the broader sales and marketing world show where things are headed. Here are some key examples:

- **Salesforce Einstein GPT**: This tool uses generative AI to write personalized sales emails by pulling information from CRM data. Their Prompt Builder helps customize how the AI generates messages (Salesforce Inc, 1999).
- **HubSpot AI Content Assistant**: This tool helps marketers create blog topics, emails, and website content, showing how LLMs can support a variety of marketing tasks.
- **Outreach Kaia and Gong Engage**: These platforms use AI to analyze sales calls, give real-time coaching, and suggest follow-ups. Though they don't fully use LLMs yet, they hint at future features like script suggestions and dynamic responses.

- **Emerging Tools (SalesGPT)**: These newer solutions are designed specifically for personalized outreach. They combine LLMs with Retrieval-Augmented Generation (RAG) to send smart messages across different channels like email, social media, and sales scripts (Kelly, n.d.).

These examples show that LLM-powered personalization is already happening in other sales environments. The next step is to bring this technology into the world of direct selling, where independent sellers and unique business models bring both exciting opportunities and special challenges. Those will be explored in the next section.

4. REAL-WORLD IMPLEMENTATION

While GenAI and LLMs offer exciting possibilities for personalized outreach in direct selling, making it work in real life takes more than just buying the technology. To succeed, companies must plan carefully and focus on:

- Integrating the AI with existing systems.
- Managing customer data properly.
- Training the independent sales team.
- Helping everyone adapt to the change.
- Tracking success through clear ROI measures.

This section covers the main steps and challenges of using generative AI in a direct selling business, including how to integrate the technology, manage data, train the sales force, and measure results — all illustrated through a real-world case study showing the shift from email templates to AI-powered personalization.

4.1 Technology Integration

For generative AI (GenAI) tools to work well in direct selling, they must fit smoothly into the company's existing systems. These tools can't operate alone—they need to connect with the technology already used by the company and its salesforce.

- **CRM Integration:** The Customer Relationship Management (CRM) system is usually the main place where customer info and sales activities are stored. For AI to write meaningful, personalized messages, it needs access to things like contact details, purchase history, and past conversations. At the same time, any emails or messages the AI generates—and any customer replies—should also be saved back into the CRM to keep a complete record.

- **Communication Channel Integration:** The AI-generated content must be delivered through the same platforms that sellers already use—like email, LinkedIn, Facebook Messenger, WhatsApp, or SMS. This may involve building browser extensions, dedicated apps, or API connections so that sellers can create and send messages from within their regular tools, without needing to jump between systems.
- **Sales Enablement Platforms:** Many direct selling companies use platforms that offer training, marketing content, and performance dashboards. Adding GenAI to these platforms would let sellers generate content right where they're already working.

In our case study, we integrated AI into one of the legacy systems, which is the sales enablement platform, allowing consultants to generate and send personalized emails directly within their familiar workflow.

Security and Compliance: Security and compliance are critical. Any data passed between systems must be encrypted, and users should only be able to access the data and tools appropriate to their role. In addition, the AI's messages should be checked to ensure they follow marketing laws and company guidelines.

The level of integration needed depends on the AI solution and how the company's current systems are set up. A smart approach is to begin with essential connections—like the CRM and email—and then expand as the tool proves its value.

4.2 Data Management

LLMs rely heavily on data, and the quality of their personalized output depends entirely on how good, relevant, and accessible that data is especially when using techniques like Retrieval-Augmented Generation (RAG).

- **Data Sources:** To create personalized content, LLMs need access to a wide range of data, CRM records like customer details and order history, website activity, social media interactions and even customer support logs. Pulling all this information together into a usable format is often one of the first big hurdles.
- **Data Quality:** If the data is inaccurate, then AI will likely produce content that feels off or worse, misleading. That's why it's essential to have strong

data hygiene practices in place. The information used must be clean, current, and truly reflects the customer's preferences and past interactions.

- **Data Privacy and Consent:** This is one of the most important areas to get right. Companies must get clear permission from customers before using their data for AI personalization. Regulations like GDPR and CCPA require businesses to explain how data will be used and protect it accordingly. It's also important to be transparent: Will the data be stored? Will it be used to improve the model? These questions need well-defined policies and technical safeguards. Using RAG, which temporarily pulls data into prompts rather than training the model on private customer information, can help protect privacy.
- **Data Governance:** Strong data governance ensures that only the right people access the right data for the right reasons. Companies must define clear rules about who can use what data, how long it should be stored, and how to handle customer requests like deleting their information. This becomes more complex when working with independent sellers.

Creating a trustworthy, well-managed data environment is essential before using GenAI for personalization. Without it, the risks to privacy, trust, and brand reputation are too high (SalesTechStar, 2024).

4.3 Training Salesforce and Empowering the User

Bringing GenAI into a direct selling environment means more than just launching a new tool and it requires thoughtful training and a strong change management strategy, especially when working with an independent and widely distributed sales force.

- **Understanding the Tool:** Sales representatives need more than just instructions on where to click, they need to understand what AI does, how it helps, and what its limits are. Training should cover:
    - Basic AI concepts
    - How to write effective prompts (prompt engineering)
    - How to review and make sense of the AI's suggestions.
- **Ethical Use and Human Oversight:** Ethics should be a major part of the training. Sellers must understand how to protect customer privacy, avoid biased content, and keep communication authentic. They should always review and fine-tune AI-generated messages to ensure they match their tone, follow company policies, and reflect real human intent. The goal is to have a human in the loop and not to send AI-written messages blindly.

- **Fitting Into the Sales Workflow:** Training should also explain how GenAI fits into their day-to-day work. For example:
  -How can it help with prospecting?
  -When it's useful to send AI-generated messages.
  -How AI insights can support their conversation strategy

Giving sellers the right knowledge, tools, and support is key to ensuring they adopt GenAI effectively, ethically, and with confidence.

4.4 Case Study and Results

As part of our case study, we implemented a new AI-powered system using Amazon Bedrock and Anthropic's Claude LLM to automate the generation of personalized customer care emails. The solution intelligently leverages customer order history, previous interactions, and known product preferences to craft tailored outreach messages. This capability was seamlessly integrated into the existing Customer Connection Email (CCE) platform, which is part of the company's legacy sales enablement system, allowing consultants to adopt the new AI functionality within their familiar workflow and tools.

The implemented solution offers several notable features that enhance usability and effectiveness.

Key Features:

Personalized messages generated in seconds significantly reducing the time.
Email suggestions based on timing (2 days, 2 weeks, 2 months post-order) to align with optimal customer engagement windows.
Mobile-friendly UI for consultants ensuring accessibility for consultants on the go.
Optional consultant edits and approvals before sending giving consultants the flexibility to edit or personalize messages before delivery.

Impact: The integration of generative AI into the sales enablement process has had measurable benefits.

Saved lot of time for consultants by automating repetitive communication tasks, while also enhancing personalization, thereby building greater trust with customers.
The tool encouraged regular engagement by prompting daily customer care actions and contributed to higher rates of repeat purchases.

It improved the post-purchase experience and helped consultants establish consistent business habits, particularly valuable in a gig-based direct selling environment.

After the AI-powered email generation tool was implemented within the legacy sales enablement system, a cost-benefit analysis was conducted. Table 1 and Table 2 below provided insight into both the cost structure and the value that was generated from improved customer engagement.

Table 1. Cost Breakdown (Claude 3.5 Haiku via AWS Bedrock)

Metric	Details
Monthly Email Volume	~9 million
Avg Tokens per Email	350 tokens (175 input + 175 output)
Input Cost per 1K Tokens	$0.80
Output Cost per 1K Tokens	$4.00
Cost per Email	$0.00084
Monthly Email Generation Cost	$7,560.00
Annual Email Generation Cost	$90,720.00
Monthly Model Unit Cost (1 unit)	$29,462.40
Annual Model Unit Cost	$353,548.80
Total Annual Cost (Email + Model Unit)	**~$444,268.80**

Table 2. Revenue & ROI Impact

Metric	Details
Estimated Additional Customers Reached	170,000
Avg Order Value (AOV)	$85
Potential Annual Revenue	$14,450,000.00
ROI (with 1 Model Unit)	**~32.5x return (Revenue: $14,450,000.00 vs. Cost: $444,268.80)**

The cost and ROI analysis conducted during the case study clearly demonstrated the financial feasibility of integrating generative AI into the direct selling process. Even with the inclusion of infrastructure costs—such as maintaining a provisioned model unit through AWS Bedrock, the overall expenditure remained modest in comparison to the projected revenue gains. The analysis revealed a return on investment exceeding 33x, primarily attributed to improvements in personalization, consultant productivity, and customer retention. Furthermore, the solution proved to be scalable, enabling wider deployment across the independent salesforce and increasing its overall effectiveness. These results reinforced the strategic value of adopting AI-driven outreach within legacy sales enablement systems.

5. CHALLENGES AND ETHICAL CONSIDERATIONS

While the use of generative AI (GenAI) and large language models (LLMs) offers significant promise for automating personalized outreach in direct selling, it also introduces a range of challenges and ethical concerns. If these factors are overlooked, organizations risk damaging customer trust, harming their brand reputation, or facing regulatory consequences (SalesTechStar, 2024). To ensure responsible and sustainable use of this technology, it is essential to address not only the technical limitations of GenAI but also broader issues such as fairness, transparency, and the preservation of authentic human connection.

5.1 Accuracy, Reliability, and Hallucinations

Although large language models (LLMs) are powerful tools for content generation, they are not inherently reliable sources of factual information. Unlike traditional databases that retrieve exact data, LLMs function by predicting the most probable sequence of words based on patterns in their training data. As a result, their output can sometimes be inaccurate or inconsistent, posing several risks in customer-facing applications.

- **Hallucinations:** LLMs are known to occasionally produce information that appears plausible but is factually incorrect—an issue commonly referred to as “hallucination”. In the context of automated outreach, this could result in emails containing incorrect product details, misleading pricing, or false promotional claims. Such errors may confuse customers, undermine credibility, and negatively impact brand trust.
- **Inconsistent Outputs:** Even when given the same input prompt, LLMs can generate different responses. This variability poses a challenge for maintaining consistency in tone, message structure, and brand voice. Achieving uniformity across communications may require the use of refined prompt templates or fine-tuning the model for the specific domain (Salesforce Inc, 1999).
- **Lack of Real-Time Awareness:** Most LLMs operate with knowledge limited to the data they were trained on, which may be outdated. Without real-time

augmentation techniques such as Retrieval-Augmented Generation (RAG), these models can reference obsolete information such as discontinued products or expired promotions which can lead to customer confusion and reduced satisfaction (Kelly, n.d.).

Mitigation Strategies: To address the risk of inaccuracies and misinformation in AI-generated content, several mitigation strategies are recommended. First, rigorous prompt engineering and output testing should be standard practice to ensure consistency and alignment with brand messaging. A human-in-the-loop framework is critical, wherein direct sellers review and refine AI-generated messages prior to distribution, helping to maintain both accuracy and authenticity. Additionally, incorporating Retrieval-Augmented Generation (RAG) techniques allows AI models to anchor their responses in verified, up-to-date organizational data, which can significantly reduce the likelihood of factual errors or "hallucinations" (Kelly, n.d.).

5.2 Maintaining Authenticity and the Human Touch

At its core, direct selling relies on personal trust and authentic relationships between the seller and the customer. One of the key concerns in automating outreach through generative AI is the potential loss of that human connection. If AI-generated content comes across as impersonal, overly scripted, or inauthentic, it can undermine the trust that direct sellers work hard to build (SalesTechStar, 2024).

- **Generic vs. Genuine Personalization:**Although LLMs are capable of inserting customer-specific details, achieving a sense of empathy and genuine understanding in the messaging remains a significant challenge. When sellers depend too heavily on AI without adding their own input or reviewing the content, the resulting messages may appear mechanically personalized technically tailored, but emotionally flat (SalesTechStar, 2024).
- **Erosion of Trust:** Customers who realize they are interacting with automated systems instead of their trusted consultants may begin to question the sincerity of communication. Transparency about the use of AI is important but so is maintaining the illusion of a personal touch. Striking a balance between automation and authentic engagement is essential (SalesTechStar, 2024).
- **Preserving Seller's Personal Brand:** Independent sellers often develop a unique voice and communication style that reflects their individual brand. AI-generated content must be flexible and adaptable, allowing consultants to maintain their personal tone, rather than imposing a generic, corporate message style (Mulé, 2024). Without this adaptability, there is a risk of eroding the seller's identity and diminishing their influence.

Mitigation Strategies: To maintain authenticity in AI-assisted outreach, it is essential to train sellers to view AI as a supportive drafting tool rather than a substitute for their own voice (Mulé, 2024; Yee et al., 2024). Sellers should be encouraged to thoughtfully edit and personalize AI-generated content, incorporating their own tone, experiences, and insights. This approach ensures that the message retains the seller's personality and aligns with their established customer relationships. AI should serve to enhance, not replace, human communication in direct selling contexts (Yee et al., 2024). Additionally, offering flexible options within the AI interface—such as selectable tones or messaging styles—can empower sellers to tailor content more naturally and effectively.

5.3 Bias in AI

Like all machine learning systems, large language models (LLMs) learn patterns from the data on which they are trained. If the training data contains biases related to race, gender, age, geography, or other social factors, those biases can be reproduced consciously or unconsciously in the AI's outputs (SalesTechStar, 2024). This poses a significant risk when deploying generative AI for customer communication in direct selling.

- **Biased Outreach Content:** AI-generated messages may unintentionally favor or resonate more strongly with certain demographic groups while alienating others. This can occur if the model has been exposed to imbalanced or biased data during training. In such cases, the AI might also prioritize particular types of leads over others based on flawed or discriminatory correlations (SalesTechStar, 2024).
- **Use of Discriminatory Language:** Without appropriate safeguards, LLMs can produce language that is subtly or overtly discriminatory or offensive. Even unintended phrasing that appears exclusionary can harm brand reputation and customer relationships.
- **Reinforcing Implicit Biases:** In some instances, AI-generated content may draw on and amplify stereotypes embedded in the training data. These outputs, while not explicitly malicious, can perpetuate long-standing social inequalities if not carefully reviewed and monitored.

Mitigation Strategies: Addressing bias in generative AI requires a multilayered strategy spanning model development, deployment, and user interaction. Where possible, careful curation and auditing of training data is foundational to minimizing embedded bias. During development, implementing fairness metrics and bias detection tools helps identify problematic patterns before deployment (SalesTechStar, 2024). Equally important is equipping sellers with clear guidelines for reviewing AI-generated content to ensure that messaging does not unintentionally alienate or exclude certain audiences. Continuous monitoring of AI performance across customer demographics can help surface emerging disparities over time (SalesTechStar, 2024). Finally, involving diverse teams in the design, testing, and rollout of AI systems can reduce the risk of blind spots and improve the system's overall fairness and inclusivity.

5.4 Data Privacy and Security

As outlined during the implementation phase, the use of generative AI for personalized outreach requires access to large volumes of customer data, making privacy and security top priorities (SalesTechStar, 2024). Mishandling this data not only risks customer trust but also exposes organizations to significant regulatory and reputational consequences.

- **Increased Risk of Data Breaches:** Centralizing sensitive customer information for AI processing elevates the potential impact of a data breach. If unauthorized access occurs, personal details, purchase histories, and communication records could be exposed damaging both consumer confidence and brand credibility (SalesTechStar, 2024).
- **Misuse of Customer Data:** There is a risk that data gathered for personalization purposes may be repurposed for other uses without the customer's explicit consent. Such actions could violate privacy expectations and potentially breach legal agreements or policies (SalesTechStar, 2024).
- **Regulatory Compliance Challenges:** Failing to adhere to data protection laws such as the General Data Protection Regulation (GDPR) or the California Consumer Privacy Act (CCPA) particularly in areas concerning user consent, data access, and deletion rights can result in substantial penalties and legal challenges (SalesTechStar, 2024).
- **Risks with Third-Party LLM Providers:** When utilizing external LLM APIs, organizations must fully understand the provider's data handling and retention practices. Critical questions include whether customer data is stored or used to further train the model, and how securely that data is transmitted and processed during AI interactions.

Mitigation Strategies: Effective use of generative AI in direct selling requires a strong commitment to data privacy and security. This begins with the implementation of robust technical safeguards, including encryption, access controls, and routine audits to prevent unauthorized access and data breaches (SalesTechStar,

2024). Where applicable, organizations should adopt privacy-preserving techniques, such as Retrieval-Augmented Generation (RAG) for minimizing data exposure, and methods like data anonymization or federated learning when feasible (Kelly, n.d.). Equally important is strict compliance with data protection regulations, including the General Data Protection Regulation (GDPR) and California Consumer Privacy Act (CCPA). This includes obtaining explicit, informed consent, being transparent about data usage, and upholding user rights (SalesTechStar, 2024). Clear data governance frameworks must define access protocols, retention policies, and acceptable use. Additionally, regular training for sellers on data handling and privacy best practices is critical to ensure consistent, responsible behavior across a distributed salesforce.

5.5 Job Displacement Concerns

The introduction of generative AI (GenAI) into the direct selling workforce naturally raises concerns around job displacement and the long-term impact on seller roles (SalesTechStar, 2024). While it is unlikely that AI will fully replace human sellers—given the essential nature of relationship-building, emotional intelligence, and problem-solving—the technology is expected to significantly reshape how sellers operate (Yee et al., 2024).

- **Shifting Skill Requirements:** Tasks such as composing initial outreach messages, summarizing meeting notes, or generating follow-ups may become largely automated. As a result, sellers will need to adapt by developing new competencies. These include the ability to effectively use AI tools, interpret machine-generated insights, manage relationships at a strategic level, and address complex customer needs where human intuition and empathy are essential (Yee et al., 2024).
- **Risk of Deskilling:** There is also a risk that heavy reliance on AI could reduce the need for foundational sales skills, potentially leading to deskilling over time. If not balanced with skill development and critical thinking, AI adoption could weaken the core capabilities that define effective selling.
- **Increasing Performance Gaps:** As GenAI tools become more embedded in sales processes, those who learn to use them effectively may experience notable productivity improvements. Conversely, sellers who struggle to adapt could fall behind, potentially widening the performance gap between top performers and their peers.

Mitigation Strategies: To ensure successful adoption of generative AI in direct selling, clear and proactive communication is essential—particularly around the role of AI as a tool to augment, not replace, human sellers (Yee et al., 2024). Organizations must invest in comprehensive training and development programs that equip sellers with the new skills required to thrive in an AI-enhanced environment (Mulé, 2024; Yee et al., 2024). These programs should emphasize capabilities such as prompt engineering, interpreting AI outputs, and maintaining authentic communication. Additionally, companies should focus on creating structured pathways for sellers to transition into higher-value activities—such as strategic relationship management, customer advising, and team leadership. By reinforcing the enduring importance of human empathy, judgment, and connection, organizations can ease adoption, reduce fear, and empower their salesforce to partner confidently with AI technologies (Yee et al., 2024).

5.6 Regulatory Landscape and Compliance

The regulatory environment surrounding artificial intelligence is evolving rapidly, with significant implications for organizations deploying GenAI in customer-facing contexts. Direct selling companies that integrate generative AI into their outreach strategies must closely monitor both current and emerging legal frameworks related to AI transparency, data governance, bias mitigation, and automated decision-making (SalesTechStar, 2024).

- **Disclosure Requirements:** Many existing and proposed regulations emphasize the need for transparency, particularly when customers are interacting with AI systems. Companies may be required to clearly disclose when a message or communication has been generated or assisted by AI (SalesTechStar, 2024).
- **Bias Audits:** To address concerns over fairness, future regulations may require organizations to conduct formal audits of AI systems to detect and address algorithmic bias, especially in applications that influence customer experience or decisions.
- **Content Liability:** There is an ongoing legal debate regarding accountability for AI-generated content. If a system produces harmful, misleading, or offensive material, it remains unclear who between the deploying organization and the AI provider bears legal responsibility. Direct selling companies must consider how content oversight and approval mechanisms are designed to mitigate these risks.

Mitigation Strategies: Given the rapidly evolving regulatory landscape surrounding AI and data use, direct selling organizations must go beyond baseline compliance by establishing robust internal ethical standards that often exceed current legal requirements. This proactive approach not only mitigates risk but also strengthens stakeholder trust. To navigate emerging legal complexities, it is advisable to consult legal experts with specialized knowledge in AI regulation and data protection law. Additionally, building flexibility into AI systems and operational workflows—such as modular policy enforcement or configurable consent mechanisms—can help organizations respond swiftly to new legal mandates without disrupting business continuity.

Navigating the challenges and ethical risks associated with generative AI demands a commitment to responsible innovation. This extends beyond technical implementation to include strong governance frameworks, continuous training and education, transparent communication with stakeholders, and a user-centered approach that places trust, fairness, and accountability above short-term productivity gains (SalesTechStar, 2024; Yee et al., 2024). By addressing these concerns proactively, direct selling organizations can unlock the transformative potential of GenAI in a manner that is both sustainable and ethically sound.

6. FUTURE TRENDS AND OPPORTUNITIES

The integration of generative AI into direct selling sales enablement marks the beginning of a transformative journey rather than a fixed destination. As technology continues to evolve rapidly and adoption deepens, several emerging trends and opportunities are set to redefine how independent sellers engage with customers and grow their businesses. A forward-looking perspective is essential for both companies and consultants aiming to stay competitive and relevant.

6.1 LLM Advancements

The development of large language models (LLMs) is progressing rapidly, with upcoming generations expected to be significantly more powerful, efficient, and capable of understanding complex context (Yee et al., 2024). These improvements are poised to enhance the reliability and usefulness of AI tools in direct selling environments.

- **Improved Reasoning and Accuracy:** Future LLMs are anticipated to demonstrate stronger reasoning abilities and a reduced tendency to generate incorrect or misleading information often referred to as "hallucinations" (Yee et al., 2024). This will improve trust in AI-generated content, especially for tasks like customer outreach and product communication where accuracy is critical.

- **Multimodal Capabilities:** A growing trend in AI development is the shift toward multimodal model's systems that can interpret and generate not just text, but also audio, video, and images. For example, a direct seller could use such a model to create a personalized video message from a written prompt, or to receive real-time feedback based on a customer's facial expressions during a video call.
- **Efficiency and Task-Specific Models:** As technology matures, there is likely to be a rise in smaller, purpose-built models designed for specific use cases, such as generating sales emails or supporting customer service interactions. These specialized models may offer advantages in cost, performance, and ease of customization, especially for companies that need to maintain brand tone and meet regulatory requirements (Yee et al., 2024).
- **Improved Contextual Understanding:** Advancements in LLM architecture are also expected to support larger context windows and more consistent memory retention, allowing AI to process and remember more information across longer interactions. This will enable deeper, more personalized conversations and sustained engagement over time.

As these advancements progress, large language models (LLMs) are poised to become indispensable tools for direct sellers functioning as versatile, intelligent assistants that support the delivery of more effective, personalized, and timely customer interactions across various touchpoints.

6.2 Integration With Other AI and Technologies

Generative AI is not expected to operate in isolation. Its full potential will likely be realized through integration with other advanced technologies, creating a connected ecosystem that enhances every stage of the sales process (Yee et al., 2024).

- **Predictive Analytics:** By combining generative AI's content creation capabilities with the forecasting strengths of predictive analytics, organizations can move toward more proactive engagement strategies. For example, a predictive model might identify customers who are at risk of disengagement, while the generative AI automatically produces a personalized retention message or check-in email tailored to their recent activity (Deveau et al., 2023).
- **Conversational AI and Chatbots:** LLMs will increasingly power intelligent chatbots that can handle complex customer queries, qualify leads, and guide buyers through initial decision-making steps. These bots will provide more natural, context-aware interactions freeing human sellers to focus on deeper relationship-building and higher-value tasks (Gartner Inc, 1979).

- **Robotic Process Automation (RPA):** When integrated with RPA, generative AI can support end-to-end automation of sales workflows. This includes identifying prospects, creating and sending outreach messages, scheduling follow-ups in CRM systems, and even initiating orders based on customer responses all without human intervention.
- **Augmented Reality (AR):** In product-centric industries such as cosmetics or home goods, combining AR with AI personalization can offer immersive customer experiences. For instance, customers could virtually try on products recommended based on their preferences or uploaded photos, enhancing engagement and purchase confidence.

This convergence of AI technologies signals a future in which intelligent systems operate in harmony, delivering seamless and personalized support across the entire sales lifecycle—empowering direct sellers while simultaneously elevating the customer experience (Yee et al., 2024).

6.3 Hyper-Personalization

The future of generative AI in direct selling extends well beyond crafting personalized messages. The next evolution is toward designing hyper-personalized customer journeys that adapt in real time and deliver meaningful experiences at every interaction point (Yee et al., 2024).

- **Dynamic Journey Orchestration:** AI systems will increasingly have the capability to dynamically shape the customer journey based on real-time behaviors and shifting needs. For instance, if a customer expresses interest in a new product category during a conversation detected and interpreted by the AI the system could immediately trigger a tailored content sequence, including follow-up messages and related offers aligned with that interest (Yee et al., 2024).
- **Proactive Value Delivery:** Rather than simply responding to customer actions, AI can begin to anticipate customer needs. A typical scenario might involve the system recognizing that a customer's previous purchase is nearing depletion and prompting the seller with a timely and personalized upgrade or accessory recommendation before the customer even makes a request (Deveau et al., 2023; Yee et al., 2024).
- **Omnichannel Consistency:** Generative AI can also play a key role in ensuring consistent and personalized experiences across all channels. Whether through email, social media, live chat, website visits, or even guiding the talking points during a seller's phone call, AI can help maintain a unified

message and tone that aligns with the customer's journey and preferences (Kelly, n.d.; Yee et al., 2024).

This level of personalization powered by AI but guided by human sellers—holds significant potential to deepen customer engagement, strengthen long-term loyalty, and drive sustained increases in customer lifetime value.

6.4 Evolving Role of Direct Seller

As generative AI increasingly automates routine communication and analytical tasks, the role of the direct seller is expected to undergo a meaningful transformation. Rather than being displaced, sellers will shift toward more strategic and human-centered functions, positioning themselves as relationship managers and trusted advisors (Yee et al., 2024).

- **AI Orchestrator and Ethical Overseer:** Sellers will be responsible for effectively managing and guiding AI tools, ensuring the outputs align with brand values, ethical standards, and relationship goals. This includes crafting effective prompts, reviewing AI-generated content, and exercising judgment in when and how to apply automation. In this capacity, sellers become human intelligence steering the artificial intelligence (Mulé, D, 2024; Yee et al., 2024).
- **Expert Relationship Builder:** With AI handling large-scale outreach, sellers will be able to devote more time to deepening connections with key customers. Human qualities such as empathy, active listening, and nuanced problem-solving will become increasingly important as competitive differentiators (Yee et al., 2024).
- **Strategic Advisor:** By leveraging insights produced by AI such as customer preferences, behavioral trends, and market signals sellers can offer personalized recommendations and co-create value with their customers. This advisory role elevates the seller from a product promoter to a solution partner (Yee et al., 2024).
- **Community Builder:** In direct selling models that emphasize team building, sellers may use AI to support and develop their networks. AI tools can help identify performance gaps, generate customized coaching suggestions, and streamline internal communication within the team.

AI is not poised to replace direct sellers, but rather to enhance their roles by automating repetitive tasks and freeing them to focus on higher-value responsibilities that require human intelligence, empathy, and nuanced judgment. These include building deeper customer relationships, providing personalized recommendations, and engaging in complex problem-solving—areas where human connection remains irreplaceable. As generative AI tools become more integrated into sales processes, sellers will transition into roles that emphasize strategic thinking, emotional intelligence, and brand stewardship. Rather than viewing AI as a threat, forward-thinking organizations should treat it as a collaborative tool that supports and scales the human touch. By investing in training and upskilling, companies can empower their salesforce to effectively leverage AI technologies, boosting both individual productivity and overall business performance. Those that adopt this balanced, human-centered approach will be best positioned to thrive in the future of direct selling, where technology enhances—not replaces—authentic customer engagement. (Mulé, 2024; Yee et al., 2024).

7. CONCLUSION

This paper set out to explore the intersection of three powerful forces: the relationship-driven nature of direct selling, the strategic function of sales enablement, and the transformative potential of generative AI particularly large language models (LLMs). At the heart of the investigation was the argument that LLM-powered generative AI offers a compelling opportunity to address one of the industry's long-standing challenges: enabling independent sellers to scale personalized outreach without sacrificing authenticity or efficiency (Deveau et al., 2023).

The research affirmed that while direct selling is deeply rooted in personal trust, it is now unfolding within an increasingly digital landscape where scalable personalization is no longer optional but essential (DSEF, 1973). Sales enablement offers the structural framework for supporting sellers, yet traditional methods often fall short when applied to large, decentralized sales forces (Gartner Inc, 1979). Generative AI, and LLMs in particular, emerged as a viable bridge capable of delivering human-like, context-aware messaging at scale (Deveau et al., 2023).

Throughout this study, it became clear that LLMs can go beyond basic segmentation and analytics. By analyzing unstructured data such as conversations, emails, and social media interactions they can derive rich customer insights (Mulé, 2024). These insights serve as the foundation for generating tailored communications: personalized emails, promotional messages, product recommendations, and even dynamic sales scripts (Salesforce Inc, 1999; Kelly, n.d.). With further advancements, technology can power hyper-personalized customer journeys, offering timely, relevant interactions across channels and freeing up sellers to focus on building deeper relationships (Yee et al., 2024).

Yet the path to effective implementation is not without complexity. Seamless integration into existing systems (particularly CRM platforms), responsible data governance practices, and ethical considerations surrounding privacy and consent are all essential (Salesforce Inc, 1999; SalesTechStar, 2024; Yee et al., 2024). Equally important is equipping sellers with the training to use AI effectively—not as a replacement, but as a co-pilot. Measuring return on investment through clear, actionable metrics is also critical for long-term adoption and optimization (Deveau et al., 2023).

Significant ethical concerns remain. These include the risk of inaccurate outputs or "hallucinations," the challenge of preserving human authenticity, the possibility of reinforcing algorithmic bias, and the growing need to protect personal data (SalesTechStar, 2024; Yee et al., 2024). Additionally, the evolving role of the seller introduces both opportunity and anxiety, as routine tasks are automated and new demands for strategic, emotionally intelligent work emerge. Responsible innovation anchored in transparency, human oversight, and ethical design must guide this transformation (SalesTechStar, 2024).

Looking forward, the rapid evolution of LLMs, their integration with complementary technologies, and the rise of customer journey orchestration tools suggest that the impact of generative AI on direct selling will deepen substantially (Yee et al., 2024). The role of the direct seller is expected to shift from transactional messaging to more strategic relationship management, powered by AI but grounded in human insight and emotional intelligence (Yee et al., 2024).

In conclusion, generative AI represents more than a novel tool it signals a potential paradigm shift in how sales enablement is conceived and executed. When implemented responsibly, LLMs offer direct selling companies the ability to enhance productivity, deepen customer engagement, and drive sustainable growth. However, success depends not just on technology, but on strategy, ethics, and a human-centered approach. Organizations that invest in thoughtful integration, robust data practices, and empowering their seller networks will not only navigate this change they will lead it. The future of direct selling may well lie in a hybrid model where artificial intelligence strengthens human connection, enabling relationships to scale without losing their personal touch. The question is no longer whether AI will transform direct selling outreach, but how effectively and ethically the industry will adapt.

REFERENCES

Deveau, R., Griffin, S. J., & Reis, S. (2023). AI-powered marketing and sales reach new heights with generative AI. https://www.mckinsey.com/capabilities/growth-marketing-and-sales/our-insights/ai-powered-marketing-and-sales-reach-new-heights-with-generative-ai

Direct Selling Education Foundation. (1973). DSEF 2025 Growth & Outlook Study. https://www.dsa.org/docs/default-source/industry-fact-sheets/dsef-2024-go-factsheet.pdf

Gartner Inc. (1979). Sales Enablement: Strategies to Drive Strong Results. https://www.gartner.com/en/sales/topics/sales-enablement

Kelly, L. (n.d.). The Power of Personalized Outreach with LLMs and RAG. https://www.sellingpower.com/22015/the-power-of-personalized-outreach-with-llms-and-rag

Mulé, D. (2024). Harnessing the Power of LLMs in Sales: My Tips and Tricks. LinkedIn. https://www.linkedin.com/pulse/harnessing-power-llms-sales-my-tips-tricks-daniel-mul%C3%A9-ldjke

Salesforce Inc. (1999). Generate Personalized Sales Emails with Prompt Builder (Pilot). https://help.salesforce.com/s/articleView?id=release-notes.generative_ai_prompt_builder_sales_emails.htm&release=246&type=5

SalesTechStar. (2024). Challenges and Ethical Considerations of Using AI in Sales. https://salestechstar.com/staff-writers/challenges-and-ethical-considerations-of-using-ai-in-sales/

Yee, L., Deveau, R., & Reis, S. (2024). An unconstrained future: How generative AI could reshape B2B sales. https://www.mckinsey.com/capabilities/growth-marketing-and-sales/our-insights/an-unconstrained-future-how-generative-ai-could-reshape-b2b-sales

Chapter 11
From Compliance to Consciousness:
Ethical Governance of LLMs in Business Applications Practices

Rismawati Rismawati
https://orcid.org/0000-0001-8046-6764
Universitas Muhammadiyah Palopo, Indonesia

Muhammad Tahmid Nur
Universitas Islam Negeri Palopo, Indonesia

Rustan Santaria
Universitas Islam Negeri Palopo, Indonesia

Supriadi Supriadi
https://orcid.org/0009-0004-7194-9456
Universitas Cokroaminoto Palopo, Indonesia

Andi Subhan Amir
https://orcid.org/0000-0002-7680-5556
Hasanuddin University, Indonesia

ABSTRACT

This chapter explores the transformation of AI governance from reactive regulatory compliance to proactive ethical stewardship in the deployment of Large Language Models (LLMs) across business environments. It examines the limitations of traditional legal frameworks and advocates for embedding ethical values such as transparency, fairness, and accountability throughout the LLM lifecycle. The text outlines how organizations can align LLM governance with ESG principles, orga-

DOI: 10.4018/979-8-3373-3912-2.ch011

nizational culture, and stakeholder trust through internal governance tools, ethical literacy programs, and interdisciplinary collaboration. Furthermore, it highlights the need for inclusive cross-sector cooperation in shaping global standards that are adaptable, anticipatory, and socially responsive. By integrating ethics into corporate strategies, this chapter offers a pathway toward responsible innovation—where LLMs are not only efficient but also aligned with human dignity, institutional integrity, and sustainable development.

THE EVOLUTION OF GOVERNANCE IN THE LLM ERA

1.1. Transition from Rule-Based Compliance to Ethical Awareness in AI Systems

In the early stages of artificial intelligence integration into business environments, regulatory compliance was largely perceived as a sufficient mechanism for managing technological risks. Legal frameworks such as data privacy regulations, anti-discrimination laws, and intellectual property statutes provided foundational boundaries within which AI technologies—particularly Large Language Models (LLMs)—could be developed and deployed (Nguyen & Shaik, 2024; SHARMA, 2024; Stahl, 2021). However, as LLMs became more sophisticated, capable of generating human-like content and making autonomous decisions, it became increasingly evident that compliance alone is no longer adequate to ensure ethical behavior and trustworthiness.

Rule-based compliance typically operates within static legal parameters that are reactive by nature. It addresses past incidents and formulates prescriptive rules in response. While such systems provide necessary protections, they often fall short in dealing with the dynamic and context-sensitive nature of LLMs. These models interact with users in unpredictable ways, generate novel outputs, and learn from vast, often uncurated data sources. Consequently, they raise ethical concerns that may not yet be addressed by existing laws—such as the propagation of harmful stereotypes, unintended bias in language generation, or opacity in decision-making processes.

In response to these limitations, there has been a noticeable shift toward embedding ethical awareness into the design, development, and deployment of LLMs. Rather than relying solely on compliance checklists, organizations are beginning to adopt more holistic approaches that consider the moral and societal implications of AI use. This transition marks a movement from a "compliance culture" to an "ethics culture," wherein developers, executives, and stakeholders are expected to reflect on not just what the technology *can* do, but also what it *should* do(Borenstein & Howard, 2020; Ferrer et al., 2021; Hagendorff, 2022).

The integration of ethical awareness requires multidisciplinary collaboration, involving ethicists, engineers, legal scholars, and domain experts. It also necessitates iterative evaluation mechanisms, stakeholder engagement, and value-sensitive design. In the age of LLMs, ethical governance must evolve into a living framework—adaptive, proactive, and oriented toward the broader impacts of AI on human dignity, equity, and autonomy.

1.2. Defining LLMs in the Context of Business Innovation and Governance

Large Language Models (LLMs) represent a groundbreaking leap in artificial intelligence, characterized by their ability to process, interpret, and generate human-like language based on massive datasets. Unlike earlier forms of automation, which primarily executed rule-based tasks, LLMs operate using probabilistic models that infer context, intention, and meaning from unstructured text inputs. Their capacity to understand nuance and deliver responses with conversational fluency has positioned them as transformative tools in modern business landscapes.

In the realm of business innovation, LLMs are increasingly being integrated into strategic functions—ranging from customer service automation and content creation to legal document drafting and data-driven decision support. Their adaptive learning capabilities enable businesses to streamline workflows, reduce operational inefficiencies, and enhance user experiences (Kumar et al., 2024; Leyer & Schneider, 2021). For instance, virtual assistants powered by LLMs are no longer confined to scripted replies but can engage in contextual dialogues, resolve queries, and even anticipate client needs. This shift marks not only a technical revolution but also a redefinition of human-AI collaboration in corporate environments.

However, the rapid adoption of LLMs also calls attention to critical governance challenges. As these models become embedded within core organizational processes, questions arise about their transparency, fairness, and alignment with ethical standards. Unlike traditional enterprise software, LLMs function as black boxes—making it difficult to trace how specific outputs are generated. This opacity introduces risks related to accountability, misinformation, and bias that conventional compliance systems may not be equipped to manage (Mökander et al., 2023; Nguyen & Shaik, 2024).

Therefore, defining LLMs in the context of governance is not merely a matter of technical classification—it is a call to recognize their socio-technical complexity. Effective governance requires understanding how LLMs shape organizational behavior, influence decision-making structures, and affect stakeholder relationships. It also involves designing frameworks that balance innovation with ethical responsibility, ensuring that LLM deployment aligns with both regulatory expectations and broader societal values. In this context, governance must evolve from static rule enforcement to dynamic ethical stewardship, reflecting the fluid and influential role that LLMs now play in shaping the future of business.

1.3. Critical Limitations of Traditional Regulatory Approaches toward Generative Models

Traditional regulatory frameworks have long served as the backbone for managing technological risks. Rooted in established legal norms and institutional protocols, these systems have proven effective in addressing earlier waves of digital innovation—such as data privacy, cybersecurity, and intellectual property. However, the emergence of generative models, particularly Large Language Models (LLMs), has exposed several fundamental weaknesses in these conventional approaches (Yan et al., 2023).

One of the most prominent challenges lies in the reactive nature of traditional regulations. Legal frameworks often lag behind technological development, responding to risks only after they have materialized. Generative models, however, evolve rapidly and unpredictably. Their capacity to learn from vast, unfiltered data and produce original outputs blurs the boundaries between human and machine authorship, raising ethical and legal questions that existing statutes are ill-equipped to answer (Eshraghian, 2020). For instance, current intellectual property laws struggle to categorize LLM-generated content, and data protection rules may not account for how these models retain or reproduce sensitive information.

Moreover, conventional regulatory strategies tend to assume a fixed architecture in the systems they govern. Yet generative AI is inherently dynamic—constantly updating, fine-tuning, and adapting to new contexts. This fluidity challenges the effectiveness of static compliance checklists or predefined ethical audits. A rule once considered sufficient may quickly become obsolete as the model encounters new environments or datasets. Consequently, rigid frameworks risk either over-regulating innovation or underestimating emerging harms.

Another key limitation is the compartmentalized perspective that traditional governance often adopts. Regulations are typically sector-specific and jurisdiction-bound, whereas LLMs operate across domains and geographies. A model developed in one country may be deployed globally, interacting with diverse cultures, legal systems, and user expectations (Gencer & Gencer, 2025; Mökander et al., 2023). This disconnect creates governance gaps and opens the door to regulatory arbitrage, where companies strategically locate development or deployment in regions with the least oversight.

In light of these constraints, relying solely on legacy regulatory instruments is no longer viable. What is needed is a more adaptive, anticipatory, and ethically grounded framework—one that can evolve alongside the technology it seeks to govern. Only through this transformation can we ensure that generative models are not just legally permissible, but also socially responsible.

FOUNDATIONAL PRINCIPLES OF ETHICAL LLM GOVERNANCE

2.1 Embedding Transparency, Fairness, and Accountability in LLM Systems

As Large Language Models (LLMs) become increasingly embedded in business operations, ensuring their ethical integrity has emerged as a critical priority. Unlike conventional software systems, LLMs are not simply coded tools with fixed outputs. They are adaptive, opaque, and probabilistic in nature—characteristics that challenge traditional notions of transparency, fairness, and accountability. For organizations seeking to maintain trust while leveraging the power of generative AI, embedding these ethical principles is not optional—it is essential (Corrêa et al., 2023; Díaz-Rodríguez et al., 2023; Felzmann et al., 2020).

Transparency in LLM systems involves more than just disclosing technical specifications or model architectures. It requires enabling stakeholders to understand how decisions are made, what data the models are trained on, and how outputs are generated. Because LLMs function through complex layers of machine learning algorithms, making these processes intelligible to non-technical users is a substantial but necessary endeavor. Transparency builds the foundation for informed consent, public trust, and responsible use, particularly in high-stakes sectors such as finance, healthcare, and law.

Fairness, meanwhile, refers to the obligation to minimize bias and prevent discriminatory outcomes in LLM-generated content. These models, trained on vast corpora scraped from the internet, are vulnerable to inheriting and amplifying the prejudices embedded in those datasets. Without proactive interventions—such as dataset curation, fairness audits, and inclusive evaluation metrics—LLMs risk reinforcing systemic inequalities. Business entities that rely on such models for hiring decisions, customer service, or product recommendations must therefore adopt rigorous fairness protocols to ensure equitable treatment for all stakeholders (Oneto & Chiappa, 2020).

Accountability completes the triad by addressing the question: who is responsible when things go wrong? Given that LLMs often function autonomously and produce unpredictable results, establishing clear lines of accountability is vital. Organizations must define roles, responsibilities, and escalation procedures, not only during deployment but throughout the model's entire lifecycle. This includes assigning ethical oversight, documenting decision-making processes, and ensuring that mechanisms for redress are available when harm occurs (Klopotan et al., 2020; Liu & Zheng, 2022; Schuett et al., 2024; Vyhmeister et al., 2022).

Embedding transparency, fairness, and accountability in LLM systems is not a one-time compliance task—it is a continuous process of ethical integration. By doing so, organizations move beyond regulatory minimalism toward a deeper, more conscious engagement with AI governance—one that upholds both innovation and human dignity.

2.2. Aligning AI Ethics with Organizational Values and Stakeholder Interests

The integration of Large Language Models (LLMs) into organizational processes brings not only opportunities for innovation but also a profound responsibility to ensure that technological advancement reflects the core values of the organization and the legitimate interests of its stakeholders. Ethical alignment is not simply a matter of following external regulations—it involves embedding moral reasoning and social responsiveness into the fabric of AI governance (Barton & Pöppelbuß, 2022; Elliott et al., 2021; Garkisch & Goldkind, 2024; McLennan et al., 2022).

Each organization possesses a unique set of principles—whether rooted in a mission statement, corporate culture, or stakeholder commitments. When LLMs are introduced without thoughtful alignment to these foundational beliefs, there is a risk that their outputs will diverge from the organization's intended ethical direction. For instance, a company that prioritizes inclusivity and respect may find itself in conflict with biased model responses if the training data is not adequately curated or tested. This dissonance can damage reputations, erode internal trust, and alienate customers or partners.

Aligning AI ethics with organizational values requires a deliberate and inclusive approach. It begins with clearly articulating what those values are in the context of AI deployment. Are fairness and diversity central to the brand identity? Is transparency critical to the client relationship? Once these priorities are defined, governance frameworks must be adapted to reflect them—through custom policy design, ethical audit tools, and the integration of value-sensitive design methodologies.

Furthermore, organizations must consider the perspectives of diverse stakeholders—employees, consumers, investors, regulators, and the broader community. Their expectations can differ significantly and evolve over time. LLMs that interact with users or influence decision-making should therefore be governed not only by internal codes but also by ongoing dialogue with external actors. This participatory ethic fosters legitimacy, builds public confidence, and helps preempt ethical blind spots.

Ultimately, aligning AI ethics with organizational and stakeholder values transforms governance from a compliance function into a strategic asset. It positions ethical reflection as a driver of sustainable innovation, ensuring that technological progress is not achieved at the expense of trust, inclusion, or social responsibility. In doing so, organizations affirm that their use of LLMs is not only efficient, but also principled and human-centered(Díaz-Rodríguez et al., 2023; Nguyen & Shaik, 2024).

2.3. Comparative Overview of Existing AI Ethics Guidelines and Standards

As artificial intelligence—particularly Large Language Models (LLMs)—grows in capability and influence, a range of ethical frameworks and regulatory instruments have emerged to guide their responsible development and use. These guidelines, introduced by governments, standardization bodies, and multilateral organizations, offer diverse perspectives on what constitutes ethically sound AI. However, they also vary in emphasis, enforceability, and scope. A comparative understanding of these standards is essential for organizations seeking to build ethical governance structures that are both globally informed and locally responsive (Attard-Frost et al., 2022; Corrêa et al., 2023; Saheb & Saheb, 2024; Taddeo et al., 2021).

The European Union's **AI Act** represents one of the most comprehensive legislative approaches to AI regulation to date. It classifies AI applications by risk level—unacceptable, high, limited, and minimal—and imposes strict obligations on high-risk systems. For example, models that affect fundamental rights or public safety must meet requirements around transparency, human oversight, and data quality. Although not exclusively focused on LLMs, the Act provides a foundational framework for managing the societal risks they pose.

Meanwhile, the **IEEE's Ethically Aligned Design** framework emphasizes the integration of human values into technical design processes. Rather than prescribing hard rules, it encourages AI practitioners to embed principles such as accountability, privacy, and well-being into the architecture of systems. This approach is especially relevant for LLMs, which often function in ambiguous, value-laden contexts. IEEE's flexible, value-driven model allows organizations to adapt ethical considerations to specific industries and cultural environments (Nguyen & Shaik, 2024; Peters et al., 2020).

The **ISO/IEC 42001** standard takes a more systems-oriented perspective. It focuses on the management of AI within organizations, offering structured procedures for identifying risks, documenting decisions, and ensuring internal oversight. As a certifiable standard, it appeals to firms aiming for international credibility and process integrity. When applied to LLMs, it helps ensure traceability, performance monitoring, and continuous improvement throughout the model's lifecycle.

Taken together, these frameworks reflect a growing consensus on the need for responsible AI—but also reveal a fragmented regulatory landscape. For businesses operating across jurisdictions, synthesizing these standards into a coherent internal policy remains a challenge. Nonetheless, these guidelines collectively provide a robust foundation for ethical governance, offering pathways to align LLM deployment with legal, technical, and societal expectations.

STRATEGIC RISK MANAGEMENT AND OVERSIGHT MECHANISMS

3.1. Identifying Ethical Risks in LLM Lifecycle: Bias, Misuse, and Opacity

As Large Language Models (LLMs) become integral to business operations, understanding the ethical vulnerabilities embedded within their lifecycle is increasingly urgent. These models, while powerful and versatile, also introduce risks that are often subtle, systemic, and difficult to detect without intentional scrutiny. Among the most pressing concerns are issues related to bias in output, the potential for misuse, and the inherent opacity of model behavior—all of which can compromise not only technical performance but also public trust and institutional integrity (Chesterman, 2021; Park et al., 2024).

Bias in LLMs typically stems from the training data upon which they are built. Because these datasets are drawn from publicly available internet content, they often reflect the prejudices, stereotypes, and historical inequalities embedded within society. If left unaddressed, these patterns can influence outputs in ways that reinforce discrimination or marginalization. For instance, a model used in recruitment or financial screening may subtly favor certain demographics over others. Detecting and mitigating these biases requires not only technical adjustments but also a critical examination of data sources, annotation practices, and evaluation benchmarks.

Misuse is another significant concern. LLMs are generative by nature—they can produce convincing narratives, impersonate individuals, or fabricate information. Without adequate safeguards, these capabilities may be exploited for malicious purposes such as misinformation, fraud, or social engineering. Organizations must therefore anticipate how their LLM deployments might be co-opted or redirected beyond their intended scope. Establishing boundaries for appropriate use and integrating (Barman et al., 2024) misuse detection mechanisms are crucial components of ethical oversight.

Lastly, **opacity** remains a fundamental challenge. Unlike traditional software systems that follow traceable logic, LLMs operate as black boxes—processing billions of parameters to produce outputs without clear explanations. This lack of interpretability hinders efforts to audit, verify, or justify outcomes, especially in regulated industries. The inability to explain decisions erodes accountability and complicates compliance with transparency norms (Chesterman, 2021; Han & Liu, 2021).

Recognizing and addressing these ethical risks is not a one-time event, but a continuous commitment. From model training to deployment and post-market monitoring, ethical risk identification must be embedded across all stages of the LLM lifecycle. By doing so, organizations create systems that are not only intelligent, but also just, safe, and socially aligned.

3.2. Roles and Responsibilities of Governance Actors: Board Members, Ethics Committees, and Regulators

In the landscape of ethical governance for Large Language Models (LLMs), responsibility cannot be siloed into technical teams alone. Rather, it must be shared across a spectrum of organizational and external actors who possess distinct, yet interdependent roles in ensuring accountability, trustworthiness, and societal alignment. Among the most critical governance stakeholders are board members, ethics committees, and regulatory authorities—each contributing to the stewardship of AI systems in ways that are strategic, ethical, and enforceable (Abujaber & Nashwan, 2024; Laat, 2021; Stahl, 2021).

Board members play a pivotal role in establishing the tone from the top. As stewards of organizational vision and long-term risk, they must ensure that AI strategy is aligned with the institution's values and stakeholder expectations. This includes approving policies related to responsible AI use, overseeing executive adherence to ethical principles, and integrating AI risks into enterprise-wide risk management frameworks. Board-level attention signals to the entire organization that ethical AI is not a niche issue, but a matter of strategic governance and reputational resilience (Eitel-Porter, 2020; Laat, 2021; Stahl, 2021).

Ethics committees, often composed of cross-functional representatives—including technologists, legal experts, social scientists, and community voices—function as deliberative bodies that guide AI deployments from a normative standpoint. Their responsibilities include evaluating model behavior, advising on use-case appropriateness, and reviewing algorithmic impacts through a value-sensitive lens. These committees also provide a space for ethical dilemmas to be surfaced and resolved through structured, reflective dialogue, rather than ad hoc reactions to crises (Bottrell et al., 2020; Laat, 2021).

Regulators, on the other hand, operate outside the organization but hold significant influence over its compliance posture. Through standards, enforcement mechanisms, and public guidance, regulatory bodies shape the minimum expectations for AI safety and fairness. In the case of LLMs, regulators are increasingly focused on areas such as transparency, data governance, explainability, and algorithmic harm (Nguyen & Shaik, 2024). Collaboration between organizations and regulators is crucial—not merely for compliance, but for the co-creation of agile and anticipatory governance norms.

Together, these governance actors form a dynamic ecosystem of ethical oversight. When their roles are clearly defined and their efforts harmonized, they foster not only risk mitigation but also public trust and organizational legitimacy in the evolving era of generative AI.

3.3. Implementing Internal Governance Tools: Audits, Monitoring, and Impact Assessments

As organizations increasingly integrate Large Language Models (LLMs) into their business functions, ensuring effective internal governance becomes essential. Ethical and operational risks posed by LLMs—ranging from data misuse to algorithmic bias—require proactive strategies that go beyond surface-level compliance. Among the most practical and impactful tools in this context are audits, real-time monitoring, and ethical impact assessments (Mökander et al., 2023; Nguyen & Shaik, 2024). These instruments serve as the internal compass for aligning LLM deployment with organizational values, stakeholder expectations, and regulatory obligations.

Audits provide a structured approach to evaluating the ethical integrity and technical soundness of LLM systems. Unlike financial or IT audits, AI audits delve into complex layers of model design, training data, deployment environment, and user interaction. The goal is to uncover hidden risks—such as bias propagation or lack of explainability—that may not be evident through standard testing. Conducting regular audits fosters transparency and can uncover systemic weaknesses that require immediate mitigation (Corrêa et al., 2023; Liu et al., 2022; Qader & Çek, 2024). More importantly, audit findings can inform broader policy revisions, technical adjustments, or retraining protocols.

Monitoring, by contrast, is a continuous, real-time process that tracks model behavior throughout its lifecycle. Since LLMs are not static systems, their performance and societal impact can shift over time as they interact with new users, contexts, and datasets. Ethical monitoring involves more than tracking accuracy—it also examines unintended consequences such as the reinforcement of stereotypes, user manipulation, or misinformation. Establishing clear thresholds and alert systems enables early intervention when anomalies occur, thereby minimizing potential harm before it escalates.

Impact assessments represent a forward-looking governance tool that anticipates the broader consequences of LLM implementation. These assessments consider not only operational outcomes but also the societal, psychological, and legal implications of deploying such systems. Conducting an ethical impact assessment at the design or pre-deployment stage allows organizations to identify vulnerable populations, assess rights-related concerns, and ensure alignment with international ethical standards (Fossa & Sucameli, 2022; Hosseini et al., 2023; McLennan et al., 2022; Stahl & Eke, 2023).

Together, these three mechanisms—audits, monitoring, and assessments—form a comprehensive framework for internal oversight. They help shift organizations from reactive governance to anticipatory ethics, ensuring that the integration of LLMs enhances innovation while preserving accountability, trust, and social responsibility.

ORGANIZATIONAL TRANSFORMATION THROUGH ETHICAL CONSCIOUSNESS

4.1. Developing a Culture of Responsible AI within Corporate Structures

Fostering a culture of responsible AI is not merely about setting policies or implementing technical safeguards; it requires cultivating shared values, behaviors, and organizational norms that prioritize ethical reflection throughout the AI lifecycle. As Large Language Models (LLMs) become more deeply embedded in strategic operations, the need for a company-wide ethos of accountability and foresight grows increasingly urgent (Hermann & Hermann, 2021; Laat, 2021; Stahl & Eke, 2023).

A culture of responsible AI begins with leadership. When executives consistently emphasize the ethical dimensions of technology adoption—not only in public statements but also in internal decision-making—employees are more likely to internalize those values. Leaders must model transparency, question automation biases, and promote open discussion about the limitations and unintended consequences of LLM systems. This creates a psychological climate in which ethics are seen not as constraints but as guiding principles that enhance innovation.

However, leadership alone is not enough. Embedding responsibility within corporate structures requires that ethical awareness be operationalized across departments. Human Resources must integrate AI ethics into training programs and onboarding processes. Product development teams need practical toolkits and ethical design checklists. Compliance officers and data governance teams should collaborate with engineers to ensure that fairness, explainability, and user safety are part of every development stage. This cross-functional coordination breaks down silos and reinforces a shared commitment to ethical outcomes (Laat, 2021; Mörch et al., 2020; Rossi & Lenzini, 2020).

Moreover, cultivating a responsible AI culture demands continual engagement, not one-time interventions. Regular internal forums, ethical roundtables, and employee-led initiatives can serve as spaces for dialogue and reflection. These interactions allow ethical concerns to surface organically, especially from those at the frontline of AI development and deployment. When team members are empowered to raise questions without fear of reprisal, a genuine culture of integrity begins to take shape.

Ultimately, building this culture is about anchoring AI innovation in human values. It affirms that technology, no matter how advanced, must serve people—not the other way around. By embedding ethical consciousness into the core of corporate identity, organizations can ensure that their use of LLMs reflects not only competitive strategy, but also social responsibility, moral clarity, and respect for the broader communities they impact.

4.2. Ethical Literacy and Capacity Building for LLM-Related Decision Making

As Large Language Models (LLMs) become deeply integrated into decision-making processes across sectors, the need for ethical literacy among professionals—technical and non-technical alike—becomes increasingly urgent. Ethical literacy refers to the ability to identify, analyze, and respond thoughtfully to the complex moral questions posed by emerging technologies. It is not just about knowing ethical theories, but about developing practical judgment and reflexive awareness in real-world AI deployment contexts (Borenstein & Howard, 2020; McLennan et al., 2022; Ng et al., 2021).

In many organizations, decision-makers are equipped with tools to evaluate business risk and technical feasibility but are often unprepared to confront the ethical ambiguity that LLMs present. For instance, determining whether a language model perpetuates bias or infringes on privacy is not solely a technical task—it requires sensitivity to social context, legal standards, and human dignity. Building this kind of nuanced understanding demands structured and ongoing learning.

Capacity building for ethical governance begins with education and dialogue. Organizations should implement targeted training programs that go beyond compliance checklists and delve into real case studies, stakeholder perspectives, and value-laden dilemmas. These trainings should be adapted to the roles and responsibilities of different departments—from engineers and developers to marketers and senior executives—ensuring that everyone understands how their decisions interact with the ethical dimensions of LLM systems (Nguyen & Shaik, 2024).

Beyond formal training, organizations must also foster collaborative spaces where ethical thinking is integrated into daily work. This includes interdisciplinary working groups, peer review mechanisms, and mentorship schemes focused on ethical reflection. Encouraging open conversations about uncertainty, unintended outcomes, and moral trade-offs helps normalize ethical inquiry as part of the innovation process, rather than a barrier to it.

Moreover, ethical capacity building should be seen as a long-term investment. As LLM technologies evolve, so too must the organization's ethical capabilities. Institutions that treat ethics as a living discipline—one that requires continual revisiting and adaptation—are more likely to respond resiliently to future challenges.

Ultimately, fostering ethical literacy is about empowering individuals to act with moral clarity in the face of technological complexity. By building both competence and confidence in ethical decision-making, organizations can ensure that their engagement with LLMs reflects not only technical excellence, but also a deep commitment to humanity and justice (Nguyen & Shaik, 2024; Zhui et al., 2024).

4.3. Integrating Ethical Governance into HR, Compliance, and Digital Transformation Strategies

Embedding ethical governance in organizational systems requires more than high-level principles—it demands integration into the very structures and strategies that shape daily operations. In the context of Large Language Models (LLMs), where the potential for both innovation and ethical risk is immense, this integration must extend to three key domains: human resources (HR), compliance functions, and digital transformation agendas (McIntosh et al., 2024; Yan et al., 2023).

Within **HR departments**, ethical governance begins by influencing the hiring, training, and evaluation of employees involved in AI development and deployment. This includes ensuring that job descriptions reflect ethical responsibilities, onboarding programs address AI ethics, and performance metrics reward responsible innovation. Additionally, HR has a crucial role in fostering an inclusive and psychologically safe environment where team members feel empowered to raise concerns about AI misuse, bias, or unintended harm. Establishing whistleblower protections and ethical reporting channels reinforces a culture of openness and accountability (Araujo et al., 2020; Cheong, 2024; Díaz-Rodríguez et al., 2023; Resnik & Hosseini, 2024).

The **compliance function** traditionally operates as a gatekeeper, ensuring alignment with legal and regulatory frameworks. However, in the age of LLMs, compliance must evolve into a more dynamic and anticipatory role. Instead of focusing solely on adherence to existing rules, compliance teams should proactively collaborate with technical and ethical leads to identify gray areas, interpret emerging regulations, and co-develop internal standards for AI behavior. They must also monitor evolving societal expectations around privacy, transparency, and fairness—ensuring that internal policies are as forward-looking as they are enforceable (Laat, 2021; Schuett et al., 2024; Singh, 2024; Stahl, 2021).

In parallel, organizations undergoing **digital transformation** must view ethical governance not as a separate stream, but as a foundational element of their transformation strategy. As new technologies are adopted—often at scale and with limited precedent—embedding ethics into procurement decisions, technology roadmaps, and partner selection processes becomes essential. Cross-functional governance boards that include ethics representatives should be empowered to review digital initiatives from multiple lenses: not just efficiency and scalability, but also justice, inclusivity, and long-term impact.

Bringing together HR, compliance, and digital transformation in a unified ethical framework strengthens institutional resilience. It enables organizations to internalize ethics not as a reactive fix but as a proactive capacity—one that ensures LLM implementation aligns with core values, stakeholder trust, and a sustainable vision of technological advancement.

TOWARD A PROACTIVE AND SUSTAINABLE ETHICAL FUTURE

5.1. Fostering Cross-Sector Collaboration for Global AI Governance

As the influence of Large Language Models (LLMs) continues to expand across industries and national borders, the need for cohesive and collaborative global governance becomes increasingly clear. No single organization, sector, or government can adequately address the ethical, legal, and societal challenges posed by generative AI in isolation. Instead, fostering meaningful cross-sector partnerships is vital to developing governance systems that are inclusive, adaptive, and capable of responding to the dynamic nature of technological advancement (Reddy, 2024; Stahl & Eke, 2023).

Cross-sector collaboration brings together diverse stakeholders—governments, corporations, academic institutions, civil society, and international organizations—each contributing unique perspectives and areas of expertise. Governments may provide legal frameworks and enforcement mechanisms; industry players bring innovation and scale; academics contribute research-based insights; and civil society ensures accountability to public interests (Božić, 2020; Ley et al., 2020; Pérez-Pineda & Wehrmann, 2020; Rahman & Tasnim, 2023). When these actors engage in open and constructive dialogue, they can co-create standards and practices that reflect both technical feasibility and ethical legitimacy.

One of the primary benefits of cross-sector governance is its ability to bridge regulatory gaps. Many jurisdictions are still in the process of developing AI-specific legislation, resulting in a fragmented global landscape. Multilateral efforts—such as the OECD Principles on AI, UNESCO's AI ethics guidelines, and the Global Partnership on AI—offer promising foundations for harmonization. However, translating high-level principles into practical, enforceable mechanisms requires continuous collaboration at operational levels, including data governance, auditability, and equitable access.

Effective collaboration also depends on building trust across sectors. This involves creating shared vocabularies, promoting transparency in intentions and outcomes, and investing in long-term relationships rather than short-term projects. Public-private partnerships, joint research initiatives, and ethical review alliances are concrete avenues through which trust-based cooperation can be institutionalized (Avin et al., 2021; Lansing et al., 2023; Shin et al., 2020).

Moreover, collaboration must be intentionally inclusive, incorporating voices from the Global South, Indigenous communities, and marginalized groups who are often excluded from shaping the technologies that affect them. Ethical AI governance is not only about setting global standards—it is about ensuring those standards are co-owned, context-sensitive, and shaped by a plurality of values.

In an era where LLMs shape economies, societies, and identities, fostering cross-sector collaboration offers the most promising path toward a just, sustainable, and globally accountable AI future.

5.2. LLMs and Environmental, Social, and Governance (ESG) Alignment

As Large Language Models (LLMs) become integral to business operations and decision-making processes, their alignment with Environmental, Social, and Governance (ESG) principles has emerged as a strategic and ethical imperative. Beyond their computational prowess, LLMs increasingly influence how companies communicate, engage with stakeholders, manage risks, and report on their sustainability commitments. Ensuring that these technologies support—rather than undermine—ESG values requires deliberate integration across design, deployment, and organizational use (Feng & Wu, 2021; Mökander et al., 2023; Nguyen & Shaik, 2024; Sklavos et al., 2024).

From an **environmental** standpoint, the energy consumption associated with training and running LLMs presents real sustainability challenges. The vast computational resources required for fine-tuning and inference can leave a significant carbon footprint, particularly when data centers rely on non-renewable energy sources. Organizations must therefore account for these impacts in their environmental disclosures and prioritize the use of green data infrastructure, model efficiency improvements, and offset strategies. Incorporating environmental responsibility into AI development aligns LLM innovation with global climate goals and corporate sustainability targets (Taddeo et al., 2021; Taleb & Kadhum, 2024).

On the **social** front, LLMs interact directly with users, shaping perceptions, knowledge, and even public discourse. This influence carries both opportunities and risks. When trained responsibly, LLMs can enhance accessibility, promote inclusive communication, and support education. However, if left unchecked, they may reinforce harmful stereotypes, spread misinformation, or exclude minority perspectives. Embedding social equity principles into the LLM lifecycle—including diverse training data, fairness testing, and community feedback mechanisms—is crucial for protecting human dignity and fostering social cohesion.

Regarding **governance**, LLMs challenge traditional accountability structures. Their complex outputs often blur lines of authorship and decision ownership. To align with governance best practices, businesses must ensure that LLM use is transparent, auditable, and consistent with internal controls and stakeholder expectations. This includes defining clear roles and responsibilities, disclosing AI use in reporting processes, and incorporating ethical review procedures into corporate governance frameworks.

Ultimately, aligning LLM applications with ESG frameworks transforms them from operational tools into agents of sustainable impact. It affirms that technological advancement need not be at odds with environmental care, social justice, or institutional accountability. Instead, it invites organizations to see LLMs not only as engines of efficiency, but as instruments for responsible and values-driven innovation.

5.3. From Reactive Compliance to Proactive Ethical Stewardship in AI Deployment

In the current era of accelerated AI adoption, particularly with the rise of Large Language Models (LLMs), many organizations remain anchored in a compliance-based approach to governance. They view regulation as a checklist, ethics as an afterthought, and oversight as a means to avoid liability. While legal compliance is essential, relying solely on reactive frameworks is increasingly insufficient in managing the nuanced risks and responsibilities that LLMs present (Erdélyi & Goldsmith, 2022; Mökander et al., 2023; Schuett et al., 2024).

Reactive compliance tends to focus on avoiding penalties and adhering to minimum legal standards. It is typically triggered after incidents occur—data breaches, algorithmic bias, reputational fallout—rather than preemptively anticipating them. This backward-looking posture is misaligned with the dynamic, adaptive nature of LLMs, whose real-world effects often evolve in unexpected ways over time. Moreover, it limits organizational learning, as ethical governance becomes an exercise in damage control rather than a driver of improvement.

In contrast, **proactive ethical stewardship** reframes AI governance as a forward-looking commitment embedded within the organization's values, culture, and strategic intent. It begins with the recognition that ethical risks are not just legal or technical issues, but also moral and social ones that demand thoughtful deliberation. Proactive organizations establish governance structures that empower diverse voices, anticipate ethical blind spots, and continuously evaluate AI impacts—before harm occurs (Attard-Frost et al., 2022; Borenstein & Howard, 2020; Elliott et al., 2021; Ferrer et al., 2021; Guan et al., 2022).

This approach involves integrating ethics into every stage of the AI lifecycle: from model selection and data sourcing to deployment, monitoring, and post-deployment audits. It also calls for interdisciplinary collaboration across legal, technical, and human-centered domains. Organizations that embrace ethical stewardship establish mechanisms for stakeholder engagement, transparent reporting, and ethical scenario planning (Burr & Leslie, 2022; Corrêa et al., 2023; Pau et al., 2021; Schuett et al., 2024; Vyhmeister et al., 2022). These practices build trust, increase resilience, and enable adaptive governance as technology—and societal expectations—evolve.

Ultimately, shifting from reactive compliance to proactive stewardship is not just a procedural change—it's a philosophical one. It signals a willingness to lead with conscience, to innovate responsibly, and to treat AI not merely as a tool for efficiency, but as a force that must align with humanity's highest values. In doing so, organizations position themselves not just as users of LLMs, but as caretakers of the future they help shape.

CONCLUSION

The evolution from regulatory compliance to ethical consciousness in AI governance reflects a broader shift in how organizations must understand their role in shaping technology's societal impact. As demonstrated throughout this chapter, Large Language Models (LLMs) represent both a technological breakthrough and a complex ethical frontier. Their deployment in business contexts demands not only operational efficiency but also thoughtful stewardship that upholds human-centered values.

Traditional governance models—rooted in static regulations and reactive oversight—are increasingly inadequate for addressing the adaptive and unpredictable nature of generative AI. Instead, organizations must embrace a proactive approach that integrates transparency, fairness, and accountability at every stage of the LLM lifecycle. This requires ethical capacity-building across departments, cross-functional collaboration, and the implementation of tools such as audits, real-time monitoring, and ethical impact assessments.

Furthermore, aligning LLM initiatives with Environmental, Social, and Governance (ESG) criteria ensures that AI does not become a source of harm or exclusion, but rather a means to advance sustainability, inclusivity, and organizational resilience. Integrating ethics into HR systems, compliance practices, and digital transformation strategies ensures that responsibility is not confined to specialized teams but embedded across the enterprise.

At the global level, fostering collaborative governance frameworks—through partnerships between industry, academia, regulators, and civil society—enables more coherent, just, and culturally informed oversight of LLM technologies. Ultimately, shifting toward ethical stewardship signals a commitment to shaping AI not merely as a tool of innovation, but as a force that reflects the collective conscience of the institutions and societies that use it.

REFERENCES

Abujaber, A. A., & Nashwan, A. J. (2024). Ethical framework for artificial intelligence in healthcare research: A path to integrity. In World Journal of Methodology (Vol. 14, Issue 3). DOI: 10.5662/wjm.v14.i3.94071

Araujo, T., Helberger, N., Kruikemeier, S., & de Vreese, C. H. (2020). In AI we trust? Perceptions about automated decision-making by artificial intelligence. *AI & Society*, *35*(3), 611. DOI: 10.1007/s00146-019-00931-w

Attard-Frost, B., Ríos, A. D. los, & Walters, D. R. (2022). The ethics of AI business practices: a review of 47 AI ethics guidelines [Review of The ethics of AI business practices: a review of 47 AI ethics guidelines]. AI and Ethics, 3(2), 389. Springer Nature. DOI: 10.1007/s43681-022-00156-6

Avin, S., Belfield, H., Brundage, M., Krueger, G., Wang, J., Weller, A., Anderljung, M., Krawczuk, I., Krueger, D., Lebensold, J., Maharaj, T., & Zilberman, N. (2021). Filling gaps in trustworthy development of AI. *Science*, *374*(6573), 1327. DOI: 10.1126/science.abi7176

Barman, D., Guo, Z., & Conlan, O. (2024). The Dark Side of Language Models: Exploring the Potential of LLMs in Multimedia Disinformation Generation and Dissemination. *Machine Learning with Applications*, *16*, 100545. DOI: 10.1016/j.mlwa.2024.100545

Barton, M.-C., & Pöppelbuß, J. (2022). Prinzipien für die ethische Nutzung künstlicher Intelligenz. *HMD Praxis der Wirtschaftsinformatik*, *59*(2), 468. DOI: 10.1365/s40702-022-00850-3

Borenstein, J., & Howard, A. (2020). Emerging challenges in AI and the need for AI ethics education. In AI and Ethics (Vol. 1, Issue 1, p. 61). Springer Nature. DOI: 10.1007/s43681-020-00002-7

Bottrell, M. M., Simon, A., Geppert, C., Chang, E. T., Asch, S. M., & Rubenstein, L. V. (2020). Facilitating ethical quality improvement initiatives: Design and implementation of an initiative-specific ethics committee. *Health Care*, *8*(2), 100425. DOI: 10.1016/j.hjdsi.2020.100425

Božić, A. (2020). Global trends in a fragile context: Public–nonpublic collaboration, service delivery and social innovation. *Social Enterprise Journal*, *17*(2), 260. DOI: 10.1108/sej-12-2019-0100

Burr, C., & Leslie, D. (2022). Ethical assurance: A practical approach to the responsible design, development, and deployment of data-driven technologies. *AI and Ethics*, *3*(1), 73. DOI: 10.1007/s43681-022-00178-0

Cheong, B. C. (2024). Transparency and accountability in AI systems: Safeguarding wellbeing in the age of algorithmic decision-making. *Frontiers in Human Dynamics*, *6*. Advance online publication. DOI: 10.3389/fhumd.2024.1421273

Chesterman, S. (2021). Through a Glass, Darkly: Artificial Intelligence and the Problem of Opacity. *The American Journal of Comparative Law*, *69*(2), 271. DOI: 10.1093/ajcl/avab012

Corrêa, N. K., Galvão, C., Santos, J. W., Pino, C. D., Pinto, E. P., Barbosa, C., Massmann, D., Mambrini, R., Galvão, L., Terem, E., & Oliveira, N. de. (2023). Worldwide AI ethics: A review of 200 guidelines and recommendations for AI governance [Review of Worldwide AI ethics: A review of 200 guidelines and recommendations for AI governance]. Patterns, 4(10), 100857. Elsevier BV. DOI: 10.1016/j.patter.2023.100857

de Laat, P. B. (2021). Companies Committed to Responsible AI: From Principles towards Implementation and Regulation? *Philosophy & Technology*, *34*(4), 1135. DOI: 10.1007/s13347-021-00474-3

Díaz-Rodríguez, N., Ser, J. D., Coeckelbergh, M., de Prado, M. L., Herrera-Viedma, E., & Herrera, F. (2023). Connecting the dots in trustworthy Artificial Intelligence: From AI principles, ethics, and key requirements to responsible AI systems and regulation. *Information Fusion*, *99*, 101896. DOI: 10.1016/j.inffus.2023.101896

Eitel-Porter, R. (2020). Beyond the promise: Implementing ethical AI. *AI and Ethics*, *1*(1), 73. DOI: 10.1007/s43681-020-00011-6

Elliott, K., Price, R., Shaw, P., Spiliotopoulos, T., Ng, M., Coopamootoo, K., & van Moorsel, A. (2021). Towards an Equitable Digital Society: Artificial Intelligence (AI) and Corporate Digital Responsibility (CDR). *Society*, *58*(3), 179. DOI: 10.1007/s12115-021-00594-8

Erdélyi, O. J., & Goldsmith, J. (2022). Regulating artificial intelligence: Proposal for a global solution. *Government Information Quarterly*, *39*(4), 101748. DOI: 10.1016/j.giq.2022.101748

Eshraghian, J. K. (2020). Human ownership of artificial creativity. *Nature Machine Intelligence*, *2*(3), 157. DOI: 10.1038/s42256-020-0161-x

Felzmann, H., Fosch-Villaronga, E., Lutz, C., & Tamò-Larrieux, A. (2020). Towards Transparency by Design for Artificial Intelligence [Review of Towards Transparency by Design for Artificial Intelligence]. Science and Engineering Ethics, 26(6), 3333. Springer Science+Business Media. DOI: 10.1007/s11948-020-00276-4

Feng, Z., & Wu, Z. (2021). ESG Disclosure, REIT Debt Financing and Firm Value. *The Journal of Real Estate Finance and Economics*, *67*(3), 388. DOI: 10.1007/s11146-021-09857-x

Ferrer, X., van Nuenen, T., Such, J. M., Coté, M., & Criado, N. (2021). Bias and Discrimination in AI: A Cross-Disciplinary Perspective. *IEEE Technology and Society Magazine*, *40*(2), 72. DOI: 10.1109/mts.2021.3056293

Fossa, F., & Sucameli, I. (2022). Gender Bias and Conversational Agents: An ethical perspective on Social Robotics. *Science and Engineering Ethics*, *28*(3). Advance online publication. DOI: 10.1007/s11948-022-00376-3

Garkisch, M., & Goldkind, L. (2024). Considering a Unified Model of Artificial Intelligence Enhanced Social Work: A Systematic Review [Review of Considering a Unified Model of Artificial Intelligence Enhanced Social Work: A Systematic Review]. Journal of Human Rights and Social Work. Springer International Publishing. DOI: 10.1007/s41134-024-00326-y

Gencer, G., & Gencer, K. (2025). Large Language Models in Healthcare: A Bibliometric Analysis and Examination of Research Trends. *Journal of Multidisciplinary Healthcare*, *223*. Advance online publication. DOI: 10.2147/jmdh.s502351

Guan, H., Dong, L., & Zhao, A. (2022). Ethical Risk Factors and Mechanisms in Artificial Intelligence Decision Making. *Behavioral Sciences (Basel, Switzerland)*, *12*(9), 343. DOI: 10.3390/bs12090343

Hagendorff, T. (2022). A Virtue-Based Framework to Support Putting AI Ethics into Practice. *Philosophy & Technology*, *35*(3). Advance online publication. DOI: 10.1007/s13347-022-00553-z

Han, H., & Liu, X. (2021). The challenges of explainable AI in biomedical data science. *BMC Bioinformatics*, *22*. Advance online publication. DOI: 10.1186/s12859-021-04368-1

Hermann, E., & Hermann, G. (2021). Artificial intelligence in research and development for sustainability: The centrality of explicability and research data management. *AI and Ethics*, *2*(1), 29. DOI: 10.1007/s43681-021-00114-8

Hosseini, Z., Nyholm, S., Blanc, P. M. L., Preenen, P., & Demerouti, E. (2023). Assessing the artificially intelligent workplace: An ethical framework for evaluating experimental technologies in workplace settings. *AI and Ethics*, *4*(2), 285. DOI: 10.1007/s43681-023-00265-w

Klopotan, I., Aleksić, A., & Vinković, N. (2020). Do Business Ethics and Ethical Decision Making Still Matter: Perspective of Different Generational Cohorts. *Business Systems Research Journal*, *11*(1), 31. DOI: 10.2478/bsrj-2020-0003

Kumar, V., Ashraf, A. R., & Nadeem, W. (2024). AI-powered marketing: What, where, and how? *International Journal of Information Management*, *77*, 102783. DOI: 10.1016/j.ijinfomgt.2024.102783

Lansing, A. E., Romero, N. J., Siantz, E., Silva, V., Center, K., Casteel, D., & Gilmer, T. (2023). Building trust: Leadership reflections on community empowerment and engagement in a large urban initiative. *BMC Public Health*, *23*(1). Advance online publication. DOI: 10.1186/s12889-023-15860-z

Ley, A. N. L., Scott, C. A., Wilder, M., Varady, R. G., Ocampo-Melgar, A., Lara-Valencia, F., Zúñiga-Terán, A. A., Buechler, S., Caravantes, R. E. D., Neto, A. R., Pablos, N. P., & Martín, F. (2020). Dialogic science-policy networks for water security governance in the arid Americas. *Environmental Development*, *38*, 100568. DOI: 10.1016/j.envdev.2020.100568

Leyer, M., & Schneider, S. (2021). Decision augmentation and automation with artificial intelligence: Threat or opportunity for managers? *Business Horizons*, *64*(5), 711. DOI: 10.1016/j.bushor.2021.02.026

Liu, X., Glocker, B., McCradden, M. D., Ghassemi, M., Denniston, A. K., & Oakden-Rayner, L. (2022). The medical algorithmic audit [Review of The medical algorithmic audit]. The Lancet Digital Health, 4(5). Elsevier BV. DOI: 10.1016/s2589-7500(22)00003-6

Liu, Z., & Zheng, Y. (2022). AI Ethics and Governance. DOI: 10.1007/978-981-19-2531-3

McIntosh, T. R., Sušnjak, T., Liu, T., Watters, P., Xu, D., Liu, D., Nowrozy, R., & Halgamuge, M. N. (2024). From COBIT to ISO 42001: Evaluating cybersecurity frameworks for opportunities, risks, and regulatory compliance in commercializing large language models. *Computers & Security*, *144*, 103964. DOI: 10.1016/j.cose.2024.103964

McLennan, S., Fiske, A., Tigard, D. W., Müller, R., Haddadin, S., & Buyx, A. (2022). Embedded ethics: A proposal for integrating ethics into the development of medical AI. *BMC Medical Ethics, 23*(1). Advance online publication. DOI: 10.1186/s12910-022-00746-3

Mökander, J., Schuett, J., Kirk, H. R., & Floridi, L. (2023). Auditing large language models: A three-layered approach. *AI and Ethics, 4*(4), 1085. DOI: 10.1007/s43681-023-00289-2

Mörch, C., Gupta, A., & Mishara, B. L. (2020). Canada protocol: An ethical checklist for the use of artificial Intelligence in suicide prevention and mental health. *Artificial Intelligence in Medicine, 108*, 101934. DOI: 10.1016/j.artmed.2020.101934

Ng, D. T. K., Leung, J. K. L., Chu, S. K. W., & Qiao, S. (2021). Conceptualizing AI literacy: An exploratory review. *Computers and Education Artificial Intelligence, 2*, 100041. DOI: 10.1016/j.caeai.2021.100041

Nguyen, D. S. W., & Shaik, M. M. (2024). Impact of Artificial Intelligence on Corporate Leadership. *Journal of Computer and Communications, 12*(4), 40. DOI: 10.4236/jcc.2024.124004

Oneto, L., & Chiappa, S. (2020). Fairness in Machine Learning. In *Studies in computational intelligence* (p. 155). Springer Nature., DOI: 10.1007/978-3-030-43883-8_7

Park, P. S., Goldstein, S., O'Gara, A., Chen, M., & Hendrycks, D. (2024). AI deception: A survey of examples, risks, and potential solutions [Review of AI deception: A survey of examples, risks, and potential solutions]. Patterns, 5(5), 100988. Elsevier BV. DOI: 10.1016/j.patter.2024.100988

Pau, C., Martin, M., & Ciurea, J. (2021). Managerial Perspective on Ethical Culture in Organizations and Institutions. *Robotica & Management, 26*(1), 27. DOI: 10.24193/rm.2021.1.6

Pérez-Pineda, J. A., & Wehrmann, D. (2020). Partnerships with the Private Sector: Success Factors and Levels of Engagement in Development Cooperation. In Springer eBooks (p. 649). Springer Nature. DOI: 10.1007/978-3-030-57938-8_30

Peters, D., Vold, K., Robinson, D., & Calvo, R. A. (2020). Responsible AI—Two Frameworks for Ethical Design Practice. *IEEE Transactions on Technology and Society, 1*(1), 34. DOI: 10.1109/tts.2020.2974991

Qader, K. S., & Çek, K. (2024). Influence of blockchain and artificial intelligence on audit quality: Evidence from Turkey. *Heliyon, 10*(9). Advance online publication. DOI: 10.1016/j.heliyon.2024.e30166

Rahman, S., & Tasnim, F. (2023). The role of NGOs in ensuring local governance in Bangladesh: From the perception of other actors of governance. *Asia-Pacific Journal of Regional Science*, *7*(3), 1007. DOI: 10.1007/s41685-023-00283-w

Reddy, S. (2024). Generative AI in healthcare: an implementation science informed translational path on application, integration and governance [Review of Generative AI in healthcare: an implementation science informed translational path on application, integration and governance]. Implementation Science, 19(1). BioMed Central. DOI: 10.1186/s13012-024-01357-9

Resnik, D. B., & Hosseini, M. (2024). The ethics of using artificial intelligence in scientific research: New guidance needed for a new tool. *AI and Ethics*. Advance online publication. DOI: 10.1007/s43681-024-00493-8

Rossi, A., & Lenzini, G. (2020). Transparency by design in data-informed research: A collection of information design patterns. *Computer Law & Security Review*, *37*, 105402. DOI: 10.1016/j.clsr.2020.105402

Saheb, T., & Saheb, T. (2024). Mapping Ethical Artificial Intelligence Policy Landscape: A Mixed Method Analysis. *Science and Engineering Ethics*, *30*(2). Advance online publication. DOI: 10.1007/s11948-024-00472-6

Schuett, J., Reuel, A., & Carlier, A. (2024). How to design an AI ethics board. *AI and Ethics*. Advance online publication. DOI: 10.1007/s43681-023-00409-y

SHARMA, DR. N. (2024). ARTIFICIAL INTELLIGENCE: LEGAL IMPLICATIONS AND CHALLENGES. Knowledgeable Research A Multidisciplinary Journal, 2(11), 13. DOI: 10.57067/220k4298

Shin, N., Yoo, J.-S., & Kwon, I. G. (2020). Fostering Trust and Commitment in Complex Project Networks through Dedicated Investment in Partnership Management. *Sustainability*, *12*(24), 10397. DOI: 10.3390/su122410397

Singh, D. (2024). Navigating the Digital Age: Smart AI Ethics for Seamless Transformation. *International Journal of Advanced Research in Electrical Electronics and Instrumentation Engineering*, *13*(11). Advance online publication. DOI: 10.15662/ijareeie.2024.1311001

Sklavos, G., Theodossiou, G., Papanikolaou, Z., Karelakis, C., & Ragazou, K. (2024). Environmental, Social, and Governance-Based Artificial Intelligence Governance: Digitalizing Firms' Leadership and Human Resources Management. *Sustainability*, *16*(16), 7154. DOI: 10.3390/su16167154

Stahl, B. C. (2021a). Addressing Ethical Issues in AI. In *SpringerBriefs in research and innovation governance* (p. 55). Springer International Publishing., DOI: 10.1007/978-3-030-69978-9_5

Stahl, B. C. (2021b). AI Ecosystems for Human Flourishing: The Recommendations. In SpringerBriefs in research and innovation governance (p. 91). Springer International Publishing. DOI: 10.1007/978-3-030-69978-9_7

Stahl, B. C., & Eke, D. (2023). The ethics of ChatGPT – Exploring the ethical issues of an emerging technology. *International Journal of Information Management*, *74*, 102700. DOI: 10.1016/j.ijinfomgt.2023.102700

Taddeo, M., McNeish, D., Blanchard, A., & Edgar, E. (2021). Ethical Principles for Artificial Intelligence in National Defence. *Philosophy & Technology*, *34*(4), 1707. DOI: 10.1007/s13347-021-00482-3

Taddeo, M., Tsamados, A., Cowls, J., & Floridi, L. (2021). Artificial intelligence and the climate emergency: Opportunities, challenges, and recommendations. *One Earth*, *4*(6), 776. DOI: 10.1016/j.oneear.2021.05.018

Taleb, M., & Kadhum, H. J. (2024). The Role of Artificial Intelligence in Promoting the Environmental, Social and Governance (ESG) Practices. In Lecture notes in networks and systems (p. 256). Springer International Publishing. DOI: 10.1007/978-3-031-63717-9_17

Vyhmeister, E., Castañé, G. G., Östberg, P.-O., & Thevenin, S. (2022). A responsible AI framework: Pipeline contextualisation. *AI and Ethics*, *3*(1), 175. DOI: 10.1007/s43681-022-00154-8

Yan, L., Sha, L., Zhao, L., Li, Y., Martínez-Maldonado, R., Chen, G., Li, X., Jin, Y., & Gašević, D. (2023). Practical and ethical challenges of large language models in education: A systematic scoping review. *British Journal of Educational Technology*, *55*(1), 90. DOI: 10.1111/bjet.13370

Zhui, L., Li, F., Wang, X., Fu, Q., & Wei, R. (2024). Ethical Considerations and Fundamental Principles of Large Language Models in Medical Education: Viewpoint. *Journal of Medical Internet Research*, *26*. Advance online publication. DOI: 10.2196/60083

Chapter 12
Collaboration:
Emerging Trends in LLM Technology and Their Implications for Business

Satya Subrahmanyam
https://orcid.org/0000-0003-0441-2742
Holy Spirit University of Kaslik, Lebanon

Mario Sassine
Holy Spirit University of Kaslik, Lebanon

ABSTRACT

In today's digitally transformed and globally connected work environment, collaboration is essential for organizational success. This chapter examines how Large Language Models (LLMs) are reshaping collaborative practices by enabling intelligent, adaptive, and inclusive teamwork. It explores key LLM trends—such as multimodal communication, real-time multilingual translation, and context-aware digital assistants—that enhance cross-functional and inter-organizational collaboration. The chapter highlights practical applications in knowledge management, innovation, and strategic decision-making, while also addressing ethical challenges like bias, data privacy, and AI dependency. Emphasizing the need for human-AI teaming and leadership adaptation, it envisions a future where collaboration evolves into intelligent ecosystems, blending human creativity with machine intelligence for enhanced agility and value creation.

DOI: 10.4018/979-8-3373-3912-2.ch012

1. INTRODUCTION

1.1 Overview of Large Language Models (LLMs) as Transformative Business Technologies

Corporates' data processing, interpretation, and utilization has been radically altered by Large Language Models (LLMs) including OpenAI's GPT series, Google's Gemini, and Anthropic's Claude. These models can comprehend and produce human-like writing with exceptional contextual awareness and coherence since they are constructed on sophisticated deep learning architectures, the transformer model in particular (Bommasani et al., 2021). Their capacity to analyze unstructured data, automate communication, and provide real-time insights has transformed core business functions including customer service, marketing, human resource management, and decision-making processes. Unlike earlier AI systems that relied heavily on rule-based or domain-specific data, LLMs demonstrate generalizable intelligence, allowing organizations to scale knowledge work and enhance innovation (Bubeck et al., 2023). LLMs are now seen as foundational technologies driving the next phase of digital transformation - what some scholars refer to as the "LLM Economy" (Liu et al., 2024).

1.2 The Growing Importance of Collaboration in the AI-Driven Business Landscape

As AI technologies become more pervasive, collaboration has emerged as a strategic imperative for leveraging their full potential. The complexity and dynamism of AI ecosystems require a collaborative mindset that bridges human expertise with machine intelligence and connects organizations across industries and disciplines (Subrahmanyam, 2025). In this evolving environment, collaboration is not limited to internal teamwork but extends to cross-sectoral partnerships, data-sharing networks, and AI-driven ecosystems where value creation depends on collective intelligence. Businesses are increasingly using collaborative AI tools powered by LLMs to facilitate co-creation, improve knowledge sharing, and enhance productivity across geographically dispersed teams (Fountaine et al., 2019). The ability of LLMs to synthesize diverse perspectives, summarize complex information, and mediate communication across different functional areas makes them vital in fostering collaborative innovation.

1.3 The Intersection Between LLM Technology and Collaborative Ecosystems

The convergence of LLM technology and collaborative ecosystems is reshaping how organizations innovate, make decisions, and create value. LLMs serve as cognitive partners that augment human collaboration by automating mundane tasks, generating creative ideas, and bridging communication gaps among multilingual or cross-functional teams (Kellogg et al., 2020). Within business ecosystems, LLMs enable the integration of multiple stakeholders - such as suppliers, customers, regulators, and research institutions - into unified platforms that thrive on knowledge exchange and real-time data analytics. This technological-human collaboration allows for more adaptive and resilient organizational structures capable of responding quickly to market shifts. Collaborative LLM applications in fields like project management, product design, and research development have shown that AI can enhance not only productivity but also the quality of decision-making and innovation outcomes (Raza et al., 2025). Thus, the relationship between collaboration and LLM technology is reciprocal - while collaboration enhances the effectiveness of LLM adoption, LLMs themselves amplify collaborative potential across organizational and societal levels.

1.4 Chapter Objectives and Structure

This chapter explores how collaboration, as both a managerial practice and an operational framework, interacts with emerging trends in Large Language Model technologies to shape the future of business innovation. Specifically, it aims to:

1. Examine the evolving role of collaboration in AI-driven organizations;
2. Analyze how LLM technologies facilitate new forms of collaborative intelligence and co-creation;
3. Discuss the implications of LLM-enabled collaboration for business strategy, workforce development, and organizational culture; and
4. Identify challenges and ethical considerations in integrating collaborative LLM systems.

The chapter is structured as follows. The next section reviews the foundational theories and technological evolution of LLMs, emphasizing their relevance to business operations. Following this, the discussion turns to the emerging collaborative frameworks enabled by LLMs, including AI-assisted communication, shared decision-making, and innovation networks. Case studies and real-world applications are then presented to illustrate how organizations across various industries leverage LLM-powered collaboration for competitive advantage. Finally, the chapter concludes by highlighting future directions, focusing on responsible collaboration, transparency, and the development of sustainable AI ecosystems.

2. UNDERSTANDING COLLABORATION IN THE AGE OF AI

Collaboration has evolved from traditional teamwork and communication to dynamic, AI-enhanced interactions that transcend boundaries of time, space, and discipline. In the age of Artificial Intelligence (AI), particularly with the rise of Large Language Models (LLMs), collaboration is being redefined through automation, data-driven insights, and intelligent decision support. This section explores how AI technologies are reshaping collaborative practices, enabling human–machine synergy, and fostering a new era of connected, knowledge-driven organizations.

2.1 Defining Collaboration: Traditional vs. Digital Collaboration

Collaboration has always been central to organizational success, representing the coordinated effort of individuals and teams toward achieving shared goals. Traditionally, collaboration relied heavily on physical proximity, face-to-face communication, and structured hierarchies that governed information flow (Kellogg et al., 2020). Decision-making processes were linear and often confined within organizational silos, limiting the diversity of perspectives and slowing innovation. Traditional collaboration tools - such as in-person meetings, memos, and conference calls - facilitated basic communication but lacked the capacity for real-time knowledge sharing and data-driven insights (Subrahmanyam, 2025).

Digital transformation, however, has redefined collaboration as a dynamic, technology-mediated process characterized by virtual connectivity, shared data ecosystems, and continuous communication. Digital collaboration transcends geographic, temporal, and organizational boundaries, allowing distributed teams to coordinate effectively through platforms such as Slack, Microsoft Teams, and Zoom. The digital era emphasizes agility, inclusivity, and speed, qualities that traditional modes of collaboration could not fully support. In this context, collaboration is no longer limited to human-to-human interactions but increasingly involves interactions between humans and machines. This evolution marks the emergence of *hybrid collaboration*, where AI systems, and particularly Large Language Models (LLMs), participate actively in ideation, communication, and decision-making (Brynjolfsson et al., 2023).

Table 1. Traditional vs. Digital Collaboration

Dimension	Traditional Collaboration	Digital/AI-Driven Collaboration
Mode of Interaction	Face-to-face meetings, physical documents	Virtual platforms, cloud-based tools, AI-mediated communication
Geographical Boundaries	Co-located teams	Distributed/global teams
Information Flow	Linear and hierarchical	Networked and multidirectional
Decision-Making	Top-down, based on experience	Data-driven, AI-assisted, decentralized
Knowledge Management	Manual documentation, limited sharing	Real-time knowledge repositories, AI-enhanced search
Tools and Technologies	Telephones, memos, email	LLMs, chatbots, collaboration suites, virtual assistants
Focus	Efficiency and coordination	Innovation, co-creation, and adaptability
Human-AI Interaction	None	Integrated hybrid intelligence and automation

2.2 Evolution of Collaborative Technologies: From Communication Tools to Intelligent Systems

The trajectory of collaborative technologies mirrors broader technological and social transformations. Early collaboration tools in the 1990s and 2000s focused primarily on communication and coordination - emails, shared drives, and early project management software were designed to facilitate information exchange but offered limited support for strategic thinking or creative collaboration (Turban et al., 2021). The introduction of cloud computing in the 2010s revolutionized these dynamics by enabling real-time co-authoring, centralized data storage, and enhanced accessibility, leading to the proliferation of integrated collaboration suites.

The incorporation of AI into collaborative systems was the most significant development. Chatbots, virtual assistants, and recommendation systems showcased artificial intelligence (AI) began assisting teams by automating mundane tasks, summarizing documents, and drawing conclusions from data. More and more LLMs, such OpenAI's GPT-4 and Google's Gemini, were used, and co-creation was seen as augmentation rather than automation. These models are more like cognitive companions than computational instruments because of their comprehension, story-telling abilities, and ability to adjust to human intent (Bommasani et al., 2021).

Today's intelligent collaboration systems leverage LLMs to foster a new kind of workplace intelligence - one that combines data analytics, natural language understanding, and predictive reasoning. LLMs can draft reports, design presentations, provide contextual responses to queries, and even mediate cross-cultural communication by translating and localizing messages (Liu et al., 2024). This evolution signifies a shift from tool-based collaboration to ecosystem-based collaboration, where human creativity, AI reasoning, and organizational strategy intersect seamlessly.

Table 2. Evolution of Collaborative Technologies

Era	Key Technologies	Collaboration Features	AI Integration Level
Pre-2000s (Traditional)	Email, teleconferencing	Basic coordination and communication	None
2000–2010 (Early Digital)	Shared drives, intranets	Document sharing and version control	Minimal (rule-based automation)
2010–2020 (Cloud Collaboration)	Google Workspace, Slack, Zoom	Real-time co-authoring, virtual meetings	Moderate (recommendation engines, NLP chatbots)
2020–Present (AI-Driven Collaboration)	ChatGPT, Gemini, Copilot, Notion AI	Contextual reasoning, content generation, workflow optimization	Advanced (LLMs, multimodal reasoning, cognitive assistance)

2.3 The Role of AI and LLMs in Reshaping Team Dynamics, Workflows, and Knowledge Management

AI and LLM technologies have significantly altered how teams function, how workflows are structured, and how organizations manage knowledge. In traditional organizations, hierarchical structures determined who contributed to problem-solving and how information was disseminated. In contrast, AI-driven collaboration fosters *flattened hierarchies*, allowing individuals across levels to contribute equally with the support of intelligent systems (Raza et al., 2025). LLMs can generate actionable insights from massive datasets, thereby empowering decision-makers at every level with evidence-based recommendations.

Automatic meeting summaries, document management, and communication scheduling are just a few examples of how AI simplifies procedures from a workflow standpoint. Workers are free to engage in higher-order cognitive activities like planning strategically, creating relationships, and being creative as a result of this automation (Brynjolfsson et al., 2021). LLMs act as organizational "memory systems," capturing institutional knowledge and making it retrievable through natural language queries. This capability enhances knowledge continuity, especially in large or distributed teams where information loss is common due to turnover or siloed practices.

In team settings, LLMs contribute to enhancing inclusivity and diversity of thought. By generating alternative perspectives, identifying gaps in reasoning, and simulating stakeholder responses, AI systems enrich the collaborative process (Glikson & Woolley, 2020). LLMs can detect sentiment and tone in communications, offering feedback that helps teams maintain positive dynamics and emotional intelligence. However, this transformation also introduces challenges such as overreliance on machine-generated outputs, bias in model predictions, and the need for human oversight to ensure accountability and ethical use (Liu et al., 2024). Thus, while AI enables more intelligent collaboration, organizations must cultivate *AI literacy* and governance frameworks to harness its potential responsibly.

2.4 Collaborative Intelligence: Blending Human Expertise with Machine Reasoning

The emergence of *collaborative intelligence* represents the next frontier in organizational collaboration. It refers to the synergistic partnership between human intelligence - characterized by creativity, empathy, ethical reasoning - and machine intelligence - characterized by speed, scalability, and analytical precision (Dellermann et al., 2019). Unlike earlier notions of AI as a replacement for human labor, collaborative intelligence emphasizes *co-creation*, where humans and machines jointly contribute to problem-solving and innovation.

LLMs serve as critical enablers of collaborative intelligence by functioning as adaptive cognitive partners. They assist humans in generating insights, identifying trends, and facilitating communication among teams. In marketing and customer relations, LLMs can analyze consumer data to recommend strategies, while human managers interpret these recommendations in context, ensuring they align with ethical and cultural norms. In research and development, AI can scan vast datasets to identify emerging patterns, leaving the creative synthesis and strategic interpretation to human experts (Subrahmanyam, 2025).

The integration of collaborative intelligence also transforms organizational culture. It promotes *learning ecosystems* where employees continuously refine their skills in tandem with evolving AI capabilities. Rather than competing with machines, workers learn to collaborate with them, developing *complementary intelligence* that enhances both efficiency and innovation (Subrahmanyam, 2025). This partnership also challenges organizations to rethink leadership, communication, and decision-making structures, emphasizing adaptability, transparency, and shared accountability.

Collaboration in the age of AI is not merely about adopting new tools but about redefining how humans and machines interact to achieve collective goals. The fusion of LLM technology and human creativity gives rise to intelligent, resilient, and adaptive organizations capable of navigating uncertainty and complexity. As collaborative intelligence becomes central to business ecosystems, the organizations that thrive will be those that view AI not as a competitor but as a collaborator, an extension of human potential in an increasingly digital and interconnected world.

3. THE TECHNOLOGICAL FOUNDATIONS OF LLM-DRIVEN COLLABORATION

The emergence of Large Language Models (LLMs) such as GPT, Gemini, and Claude has revolutionized the technological landscape of collaboration. These models enable seamless communication, real-time knowledge synthesis, and intelligent automation across business functions. By integrating with enterprise platforms like Slack, Microsoft Teams, and Notion, LLMs facilitate human–machine collaboration at unprecedented levels. This section examines the underlying architectures, integration mechanisms, and real-world applications that form the foundation of LLM-driven collaborative ecosystems.

3.1 Architecture and Capabilities of LLMs Relevant to Collaboration

The most popular types of Large Language Models (LLMs) include GPT-4 provided by OpenAI, Gemini by Google, and Claude by Anthropic who are the keystones to the future of collaborative ecosystems. These models are constructed based on transformer based architectures, which is a neural network architecture that can efficiently handle long range dependencies in text (Vaswani et al., 2017). Automatically with self-attention, the transformer mechanism enables the model to prioritize word-word relationships among words in immense amounts of data, enabling subtle comprehension, reasoning, and creating natural-like text (Bommasani et al., 2021).

From a collaboration standpoint, LLMs possess several capabilities that directly enhance workplace dynamics. First, they can comprehend natural language inputs across multiple modalities, enabling seamless interaction between humans and machines. Second, they support content generation, including report drafting, summarization, and translation, reducing cognitive load for teams. Third, their contextual memory and few-shot learning capabilities allow adaptive responses based on prior interactions, critical for maintaining conversation continuity in team settings (Liu et al., 2024).

Unlike earlier AI systems designed for specific functions, LLMs provide general-purpose intelligence. They can integrate diverse organizational knowledge, act as real-time communication mediators, and deliver insights customized to user intent. GPT-4 can summarize meeting transcripts, suggest action items, or even analyze sentiment across internal communication channels. These affordances transform LLMs from passive assistants into active collaborators within enterprise environments.

3.2 Integration of LLMs with Enterprise Collaboration Platforms

A defining feature of LLM-driven collaboration is the seamless integration of these models with enterprise software ecosystems. Modern organizations rely on digital platforms such as **Slack**, **Microsoft Teams**, **Notion**, and **Zoom**, which are increasingly embedding LLM-based tools to improve productivity and communication.

Microsoft's Copilot for Teams integrates GPT-4 into its ecosystem to provide real-time meeting summaries, generate follow-up tasks, and extract key insights from conversations (Microsoft, 2024). Slack's AI integration, powered by Anthropic's Claude, enables natural language queries across messages and documents, allowing employees to retrieve institutional knowledge instantly without manually searching through threads. Notion AI, based on OpenAI's language models, supports collaborative writing, meeting documentation, and project management through contextual recommendations that evolve as teams interact with content.

These integrations illustrate the convergence of LLMs with enterprise workflows, where automation, knowledge retrieval, and communication are unified within the same interface. As a result, organizations experience increased cognitive bandwidth, with employees focusing more on creative and strategic tasks while delegating administrative or repetitive work to AI-driven systems. LLM integration supports inclusive collaboration by providing language translation, tone moderation, and accessibility features, reducing barriers for global and multicultural teams (Brynjolfsson et al., 2023).

3.3 The Emergence of Multi-Agent LLM Systems Enabling Human–Machine–Machine Collaboration

An emerging frontier in the evolution of LLM-driven collaboration is the rise of **multi-agent systems**, where multiple LLMs (or AI agents) interact autonomously and collaboratively to accomplish complex tasks. These agents can communicate with one another - each specializing in a specific domain such as data analysis, communication synthesis, or decision optimization - while coordinating with human users.

AutoGPT and **ChatDev** represent experimental frameworks in which multiple AI agents simulate organizational workflows by assigning roles like "manager," "developer," and "reviewer," collaborating iteratively to produce a deliverable (Qian et al., 2023). **Google's Gemini 1.5 Pro** introduces multi-agent orchestration that allows for parallel reasoning and coordination across different AI models to assist teams in large-scale project management and research.

In a business setting, these systems enable human–machine–machine collaboration, where AI agents collectively manage information flow, verify outputs, and coordinate human feedback loops. In customer service, one LLM agent might handle sentiment analysis while another drafts responses, with a third verifying compliance with company guidelines before output is sent. This distributed intelligence model mirrors human organizational behavior, enhancing efficiency and accuracy while minimizing cognitive burden.

Such systems pave the way for AI-based collective intelligence, where networks of specialized agents amplify human decision-making rather than replace it. They also raise concerns about governance, explainability, and accountability, issues that organizations must address as multi-agent ecosystems evolve (Raza et al., 2025).

3.4 APIs, Automation, and Real-Time Knowledge Synthesis

The technological backbone of LLM-driven collaboration lies in Application Programming Interfaces (APIs) and automation frameworks that enable real-time data exchange across platforms. APIs facilitates the embedding of LLM capabilities into business workflows by allowing systems to query models for text generation, summarization, or sentiment analysis directly from existing software. The **OpenAI API** allows enterprises to build custom collaboration tools that respond dynamically to team interactions, while **Zapier's AI integration** automates workflows between LLMs and business tools such as Google Workspace and Jira (OpenAI, 2024).

Through these integrations, LLMs enable real-time knowledge synthesis, continuously analyzing incoming information and producing insights that inform decisions. In knowledge management, for example, AI systems can scan thousands of internal reports, emails, and chat logs to extract patterns and generate summaries for leadership teams. In R&D environments, LLMs can consolidate findings from multiple scientific papers to propose new hypotheses or project directions.

Automation, powered by LLMs and APIs, thus creates a self-updating knowledge ecosystem, where organizational intelligence evolves continuously rather than being manually curated. This transformation enhances both speed and accuracy in collaborative environments, aligning human creativity with machine precision.

3.5 Case Studies of LLM-Driven Collaboration Tools in Business Contexts

Several real-world cases highlight how LLMs are transforming collaboration across industries.

1. **PwC and ChatGPT Enterprise:** In 2023, PwC became one of the first professional services firms to adopt **ChatGPT Enterprise** across its global operations. The firm deployed the system to assist consultants in research synthesis, proposal writing, and cross-departmental collaboration. Early results showed significant

time savings in drafting reports and improved inter-office communication efficiency (PwC, 2024). The deployment illustrates how LLMs can function as virtual consultants, enhancing human expertise rather than replacing it.

2. **Coca-Cola and OpenAI Partnership:** Coca-Cola's collaboration with OpenAI and Bain & Company in 2023 leveraged GPT-4 and DALL·E to co-create marketing content and support internal creative teams. The integration enabled collaborative brainstorming sessions between human marketers and AI, resulting in faster campaign development and consistent brand messaging across regions (Bain & Company, 2023).
3. **Slack and Anthropic's Claude Integration:** Salesforce's integration of Anthropic's Claude into Slack AI enabled teams to summarize long conversations, generate contextual suggestions, and answer questions based on historical data. This improved cross-functional collaboration and reduced information overload, particularly in large organizations managing multiple concurrent projects (Salesforce, 2025).
4. **GitHub Copilot in Software Development:** GitHub Copilot, powered by OpenAI's Codex, serves as an example of LLM-mediated peer collaboration. Developers collaborate with AI in real time, as Copilot suggests code completions, detects errors, and documents functions. This partnership reduces development time and fosters learning among distributed engineering teams (GitHub, 2024).

Figure 1. The Technological Foundations of LLM-Driven Collaboration

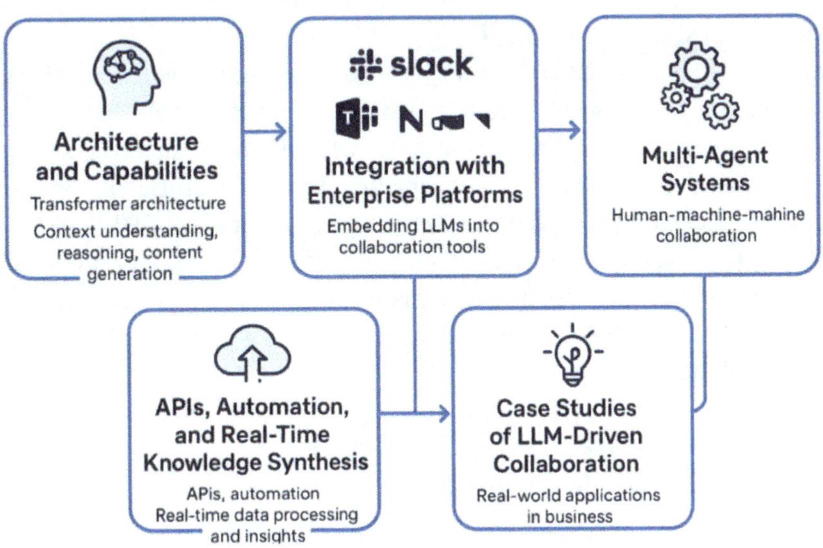

Author (2025)

Together, these cases demonstrate the transformative potential of LLM-driven collaboration: enhanced productivity, creative augmentation, and democratized access to organizational knowledge.

4. EMERGING TRENDS IN LLM TECHNOLOGY SHAPING COLLABORATION

Large Language Models (LLMs) are driving the next wave of innovation in organizational collaboration by creating intelligent, context-aware, and human-like digital ecosystems. These models, underpinned by advanced generative architectures, are not only transforming communication but also redefining how teams interact, decide, and innovate collectively. Several trends have emerged in this space, reflecting how LLMs are reshaping the dynamics of collaboration across industries.

4.1 Trend 1: Contextualized Co-Pilots for Teams (AI Assistants Embedded in Workflows)

The integration of AI co-pilots into business workflows marks one of the most transformative trends in enterprise collaboration. LLM-based assistants such as Microsoft 365 Copilot, Google's Duet AI, and Notion AI are redefining productivity by providing real-time contextual support. These tools embed AI directly within platforms like Word, Excel, Slack, and Teams, enabling employees to automate repetitive tasks, generate reports, summarize discussions, and even anticipate information needs (Subrahmanyam, 2025).

Unlike static bots, contextualized co-pilots leverage deep contextual awareness, understanding not only user queries but also organizational goals, historical data, and task relevance. Microsoft's Copilot automatically drafts meeting summaries and suggests next steps based on conversation history, significantly enhancing collaborative efficiency (Microsoft, 2024). Salesforce Einstein GPT integrates AI into customer relationship management, enabling teams to co-author proposals and forecasts collaboratively. This shift demonstrates how LLMs are moving beyond automation toward *collaborative augmentation*, working alongside humans rather than merely assisting them.

4.2 Trend 2: Collaborative Decision-Making through Explainable AI Outputs

Another new development is the incorporation of LLMs into group decision-making, a process in which explainable AI (XAI) is crucial. As a result of their opaque nature, traditional AI systems are difficult for humans to trust and hold accountable. On the other hand, contemporary LLMs aim to explain the logic behind a recommendation or insight generation (Handler et al., 2024), especially those with reasoning layers such as Anthropic's Claude 3 and OpenAI's GPT-5.

This transparency allows teams to deliberate, debate, and refine decisions collectively. Financial teams using IBM's watsonx platform can now interpret predictive analytics with human-readable explanations, allowing members to weigh multiple data-driven insights before making investment choices (IBM, 2023). The outcome is a new model of *augmented decision-making*, where human judgment and AI reasoning coalesce to ensure both efficiency and accountability.

4.3 Trend 3: Multi-Modal Collaboration (Text, Speech, Image, and Video-Based Interactions)

Collaboration in both creative and operational realms is being transformed by the convergence of multimodal LLMs. These systems can process and generate text, speech, images, and videos. Multiple data modalities can be synchronized for deeper communication, as seen by tools like OpenAI's GPT-4o, Google Gemini 1.5 Pro, and Meta's LLaVA-Next.

In practical terms, this enables dynamic cross-format collaboration: a design team can brainstorm ideas using text prompts, instantly visualize concepts through AI-generated images, and discuss revisions via speech-based interfaces. For example, marketing firms employing Canva's Magic Studio and Adobe Firefly use LLM-driven multimodal systems to ideate campaigns collaboratively in real time (Adobe, 2024). These tools bridge communication barriers, particularly in hybrid and remote teams, fostering creativity and engagement through sensory-rich collaboration.

4.4 Trend 4: Personalized and Adaptive Collaboration Experiences Powered by LLMs

Personalization has become central to modern collaboration systems, as LLMs analyze user behavior, communication styles, and work patterns to create adaptive experiences. AI-powered collaboration platforms now offer personalized task recommendations, tone adjustments in communication, and learning suggestions tailored to individual preferences (Wester et al., 2024).

Slack's GPT-powered assistant, for instance, curates relevant conversation threads and automates updates based on user roles and project contexts. Notion's AI adapts writing assistance and project summaries to match the user's tone, thereby maintaining consistency and professionalism across teams. These adaptive systems foster inclusivity and productivity by ensuring that collaboration aligns with both organizational objectives and individual working styles.

4.5 Trend 5: Federated and Privacy-Preserving Collaborative AI Ecosystems

With data privacy emerging as a critical concern, federated learning has become a foundational trend in collaborative AI development. Federated architectures allow multiple organizations or departments to train shared AI models without exchanging sensitive data, thus maintaining confidentiality while benefiting from collective intelligence (Kairouz et al., 2021).

In business collaboration contexts, this approach enhances trust between partners and supports cross-enterprise cooperation. Google Workspace's AI tools now employ federated techniques to learn from user interactions without centralizing private data (Google, 2024). Healthcare consortiums are adopting federated LLM frameworks to enable research collaborations across hospitals while safeguarding patient data. This paradigm reinforces ethical collaboration, balancing innovation with compliance and data protection.

4.6 Trend 6: Open Innovation and Co-Creation Models Enhanced by Generative AI

Generative AI has also catalyzed *open innovation* and *co-creation* models, enabling organizations to engage diverse stakeholders - employees, customers, and developers - in the collaborative design of products and services. Platforms like Hugging Face and OpenAI's API ecosystems allow teams to fine-tune models collaboratively, driving innovation across sectors (von Krogh et al., 2023).

In the fashion industry, Levi Strauss & Co. has experimented with generative AI to co-create clothing designs with both employees and customers, while LEGO leverages AI co-creation tools to crowdsource product ideas from global fans. These practices democratize innovation, transforming collaboration from an internal process to an *ecosystemic* endeavor. By extending creative agency to broader communities, LLMs are reshaping how businesses conceive and deliver value.

Figure 2. Emerging Trends in LLM Technology

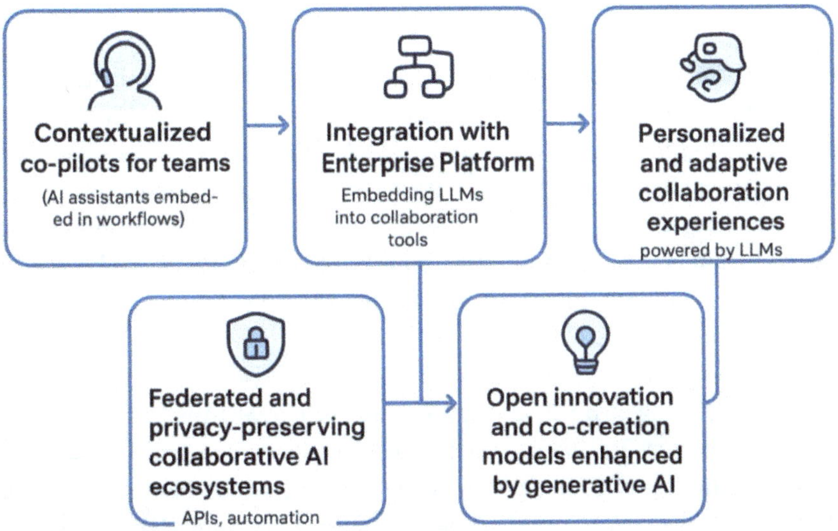

Author (2025)

The collaborative landscape shaped by LLMs is evolving toward intelligence, inclusivity, and transparency. Contextualized co-pilots, explainable decision-making, multimodal interactions, and personalized AI assistance are already redefining teamwork, while federated systems and open innovation platforms ensure that collaboration remains secure and democratized. Collectively, these trends highlight a paradigm shift - from communication-driven collaboration to *cognition-driven collaboration* - where human creativity and machine intelligence converge to co-construct the future of work.

5. BUSINESS APPLICATIONS AND USE CASES

Large Language Models (LLMs) have moved beyond experimental stages into practical business deployment, revolutionizing how organizations collaborate internally and externally. By embedding LLMs into enterprise workflows, businesses are enhancing communication, creativity, and data-driven decision-making across diverse functions. This section explores six critical application domains where LLM-driven collaboration is transforming marketing, research and development (R&D), finance, human resources (HR), and cross-organizational ecosystems.

5.1 Cross-Functional Collaboration: Marketing, R&D, Finance, and HR Use Cases

Cross-functional collaboration has become essential for organizational agility, and LLMs are emerging as pivotal enablers of seamless information flow across departments. In marketing, AI tools powered by GPT and Claude models assist teams in creating personalized campaigns, drafting social media content, and conducting audience sentiment analysis (Ghouati et al., 2025). Coca-Cola's collaboration with OpenAI and Bain & Company in 2023 showcased how LLMs can be used to co-create advertising content, blending human creativity with generative AI's ideation capabilities (Coca-Cola, 2023).

In R&D, companies like Pfizer have leveraged AI-driven collaboration platforms for accelerating drug discovery by enabling real-time cross-departmental data synthesis (Pfizer, 2022). Scientists and analysts use natural language queries to access structured and unstructured data, reducing time spent on data retrieval and report generation. In finance, LLMs assist in preparing analytical summaries and predictive insights. Goldman Sachs, for instance, integrates GPT-based systems for summarizing financial reports and generating strategic memos for executive decision-making (Goldman Sachs, 2023).

In HR, AI-powered assistants such as Workday's Talent Optimization Engine use LLMs to analyze employee performance data, support recruitment through candidate fit analysis, and facilitate collaborative training experiences (Workday, 2024). These examples demonstrate that cross-functional collaboration enabled by LLMs transcends operational silos, fostering a shared digital intelligence layer that enhances coordination and strategic alignment.

5.2 Knowledge Sharing and Innovation Management: Enhancing Creativity and Idea Generation

Knowledge management and innovation have traditionally been constrained by fragmented information systems and communication bottlenecks. LLMs are addressing these challenges by facilitating contextual knowledge sharing and accelerating idea generation. Platforms like Notion AI, Miro Assist, and Coda AI enable employees to co-create documents, visualize ideas, and extract key insights from organizational knowledge bases.

Google's DeepMind uses internal LLM systems to manage scientific collaboration across multidisciplinary teams, enhancing idea recombination and hypothesis generation in AI and neuroscience research (DeepMind, 2023). IBM's Watson Discovery facilitates collaborative innovation by allowing employees to query large document repositories in natural language, surfacing relevant patents, research papers, or reports (IBM, 2024).

LLMs contribute to *innovation democratization*, where every employee can contribute to ideation processes through intelligent brainstorming platforms. Bosch employs generative AI tools to analyze employee-submitted ideas, clustering them into themes for innovation workshops (Bosch, 2023). This evolution signifies a shift from hierarchical to collective intelligence, where human creativity is amplified through machine-assisted knowledge networks.

5.3 Customer Collaboration: Personalized Engagement through Conversational AI

Customer collaboration is one of the most visible applications of LLM technology, enabling businesses to move from one-way communication to interactive co-creation. Conversational AI powered by LLMs allows brands to engage customers in dynamic, personalized dialogues across digital touchpoints.

Sephora's virtual assistant, built on GPT-4 technology, provides beauty recommendations based on user preferences and previous purchases, facilitating a form of customer co-creation (Sephora, 2024). Duolingo's "Roleplay" feature, developed using OpenAI's GPT-4, enables learners to practice real-life conversations with AI personas, transforming customer engagement into an adaptive learning experience (Duolingo, 2023).

Retail and financial sectors have also adopted LLM-based chatbots to support collaborative decision-making with customers. Bank of America's Erica and HDFC Bank's EVA use LLMs to interpret customer intent and offer personalized banking advice. Such systems transcend transactional service to become *co-pilots* in decision processes, fostering long-term customer relationships grounded in collaboration and trust.

5.4 Collaborative Analytics: Enabling Data-Driven Group Insights with LLM Summarization

One of the most impactful business applications of LLMs lies in collaborative analytics - turning complex data into actionable insights through natural language summarization. Rather than requiring teams to interpret dashboards manually, LLMs like ChatGPT Enterprise and Google Gemini Enterprise generate narrative summaries, comparative insights, and recommendations for teams in real time.

At Deloitte, AI-powered "Insight Co-Pilots" automatically summarize client data, highlight trends, and provide interpretations during consulting meetings, streamlining the collaborative decision-making process (Deloitte, 2024). In manufacturing, Siemens integrates LLMs with IoT platforms to enable cross-functional teams to collaboratively analyze production metrics and predict maintenance issues (Pennington, 2025).

These developments democratize analytics by making data interpretation accessible to non-technical employees. Consequently, collaborative analytics becomes not merely about sharing data but about *co-creating meaning*, empowering diverse teams to contribute to strategic discussions based on shared, AI-curated knowledge.

5.5 Partner Ecosystems: Using LLMs for Vendor, Supply Chain, and Ecosystem Coordination

Modern business ecosystems depend on seamless coordination between suppliers, vendors, and partners. LLMs enhance ecosystem collaboration by enabling real-time communication, documentation automation, and contextual insights across supply chain networks.

Walmart uses LLMs to predict supply disruptions by analyzing unstructured data such as supplier emails, weather reports, and logistics updates (Walmart, 2023). In automotive manufacturing, BMW employs AI-powered communication systems to synchronize supplier coordination, automating parts ordering and status tracking across multiple vendors (BMW, 2023).

LLM-driven tools are improving procurement collaboration by generating automated negotiation summaries and compliance reports. SAP's Business AI platform exemplifies this trend, embedding LLMs into enterprise resource planning (ERP) systems to foster intelligent collaboration between internal and external partners (SAP, 2024).

5.6 Remote and Hybrid Work Facilitation: Virtual Co-Working Powered by Generative AI

The post-pandemic era has normalized remote and hybrid work models, increasing the demand for intelligent collaboration environments. LLMs have become essential for maintaining productivity, cohesion, and communication in distributed teams.

Zoom's AI Companion and Microsoft Teams' Copilot, for example, automatically generate meeting notes, summarize discussions, and recommend follow-up actions, reducing the cognitive load on participants (Microsoft, 2024). GitHub Copilot aids software development teams in writing, reviewing, and debugging code collaboratively, regardless of geographical location (GitHub, 2024).

Atlassian's Jira, Confluence, and Trello leverage generative AI for asynchronous brainstorming, documentation, and project management. Generational AI supports and participates in "virtual co-working," preserving human creativity for remote collaboration. From cross-functional teamwork to ecosystem coordination, LLMs are rethinking industry collaboration. They enhance communication, combine knowledge, and scale innovation. Human and digital teaming are merging as firms incorporate LLMs into their collaborative infrastructure, enabling an age of augmented collaboration where human brilliance and machine intelligence create economic value.

6. ORGANIZATIONAL IMPLICATIONS

Businesses are undergoing a strategic shift that is changing the way they lead, develop, and operate with the addition of Large Language Models (LLMs) to their collaboration frameworks, rather than just getting new technology. Everyday workflows are being transformed by LLMs, which bring about significant changes in strategy, culture, leadership, performance evaluation, and change management. Organizations that want to use LLMs properly and efficiently must understand these dimensions.

6.1 Strategic Implications: Redefining Business Models and Innovation Strategies

The strategic impact of LLM-driven collaboration lies in the redefinition of business models, where human–machine partnerships enhance decision-making, efficiency, and creativity. Organizations are shifting from hierarchical, function-specific models to network-based innovation ecosystems, supported by AI. LLMs enable real-time knowledge synthesis and distributed intelligence, fostering faster innovation cycles and more adaptive business strategies (Ghouati et al., 2025).

PwC and **EY** have restructured their consulting models by integrating generative AI for report drafting, proposal generation, and internal knowledge sharing. This not only accelerates service delivery but also reduces operational redundancies, allowing consultants to focus on strategic problem-solving. **Unilever** employs AI-driven innovation labs where LLMs analyze consumer data and co-develop new product concepts, shortening the ideation-to-market timeline (Unilever, 2023).

The ability of LLMs to simulate market trends and consumer sentiment empowers businesses to adopt anticipatory strategies, staying ahead of change rather than reacting to it. Strategic innovation is thus evolving toward a collaborative intelligence model, where machines augment human foresight and strategic agility.

6.2 Cultural Transformation: Building Trust, Digital Literacy, and AI Fluency

The effectiveness of LLM integration relies heavily on cultural preparedness. In order for employees to see AI as a tool for collaboration rather than an enemy, businesses should promote an atmosphere of openness, honesty, and digital literacy. Zhang et al. (2023) found that people are resistant to AI systems because they don't understand them or are afraid of losing their jobs. Accordingly, cultural change programs should train workers to be fluent in AI by explaining the capabilities and limitations of LLMs and how they might supplement human knowledge.

Corporates like **Microsoft** and **IBM** have implemented "Responsible AI Literacy Programs" to train employees across functions, cultivating a shared understanding of ethical and practical AI use (IBM, 2020; Microsoft, 2024). These initiatives build trust and encourage employees to experiment with AI tools confidently.

Cultural adaptation also involves redefining collaboration norms. With LLMs acting as team members, organizations must reimagine what inclusion and participation mean in AI-augmented workplaces. The emphasis shifts from "who contributes" to "how humans and machines contribute together," promoting a mindset of *collaborative coexistence*.

6.3 Leadership and Governance: Guiding Collaborative AI Integration Ethically and Effectively

The rise of LLM-enabled collaboration demands a new model of AI leadership and governance. Leaders must balance innovation with accountability, ensuring that AI systems align with organizational values and ethical standards. According to Brynjolfsson et al., (2023), effective AI leadership requires a dual focus on technological stewardship and human empowerment.

Organizations like Google and Salesforce have developed AI governance frameworks that include cross-functional ethics committees, bias evaluation mechanisms, and transparent documentation of AI model use (Google, 2022). These governance systems ensure that collaborative AI output remains explainable, equitable, and aligned with human judgment.

Leadership in this context also involves vision-setting - articulating how AI supports the broader organizational mission. Ethical AI leadership is proactive, encouraging open discussions about potential risks such as algorithmic bias, data privacy breaches, or overreliance on automation. By maintaining human oversight, leaders can ensure that AI remains a tool for empowerment rather than domination.

6.4 Change Management: Managing Human–AI Collaboration Resistance and Adaptation

Implementing LLMs at scale requires thoughtful change management to address resistance and ensure organizational alignment. Kotter's (2012) change management framework remains relevant, emphasizing the need to build urgency, form coalitions, and empower broad-based action. However, in the context of AI, an additional dimension emerges - *psychological adaptation.*

Resistance often arises from uncertainty and lack of control. Companies such as **Accenture** and **Deloitte** address this by introducing AI adoption roadmaps that include pilot projects, feedback loops, and continuous learning sessions (Deloitte, 2024). This phased approach helps employees gain confidence and see tangible benefits from collaboration with LLMs.

Effective change management emphasizes co-creation - involving employees in designing AI workflows. By empowering users to shape AI tools that complement their work, organizations foster ownership and trust. This participatory approach transforms AI from a top-down directive into a shared innovation process.

6.5 Collaboration Metrics: Evaluating Productivity, Creativity, and Performance Outcomes

The measurement of collaboration effectiveness in AI-driven organizations is evolving from traditional productivity metrics toward multidimensional indicators that capture creativity, inclusivity, and cognitive diversity. LLMs provide real-time data analytics that can track team dynamics, content quality, and innovation rates.

Modern metrics include:

- **Productivity Gains** – time saved through AI automation (e.g., Microsoft 365 Copilot's user reports show 30% reduction in administrative tasks).
- **Creativity Index** – measuring idea generation frequency and diversity.
- **AI Collaboration Trust Score** – assessing user confidence and reliance on AI recommendations.
- **Innovation Velocity** – tracking the time from idea conception to prototype or decision.
- **Cross-Functional Engagement** – evaluating the extent of human–AI knowledge exchange.

Adobe uses AI analytics in its Creative Cloud to evaluate collaboration efficiency, analyzing patterns in shared projects and creative output cycles (Adobe, 2024). IBM

Watson Orchestrate provides dashboards that quantify the impact of AI co-pilots on team efficiency and innovation (IBM, 2024).

The integration of such metrics supports continuous improvement and ensures that collaboration outcomes remain human-centered while leveraging AI's analytical power.

Table 3. Organizational Implications of LLM-Driven Collaboration

Dimension	Key Focus	Impact
Strategic Implications	Redesigning business models and innovation ecosystems	Enhanced agility, faster innovation cycles
Cultural Transformation	Building AI literacy and trust	Increased adoption and employee engagement
Leadership & Governance	Ethical and transparent AI oversight	Responsible and explainable AI use
Change Management	Managing resistance and enabling adaptation	Smooth AI integration and acceptance
Collaboration Metrics	Evaluating performance, creativity, and trust	Data-driven improvement in collaboration outcomes

LLM-driven collaboration transforms organizations in many ways. Companies need strategic model modifications for AI-augmented innovation. They require cultural fluency and trust for inclusive participation. Leadership and government must adapt ethically to defend human values. Change management requires empathy, education, and repeated implementation for adaptation. AI-enhanced cooperation's real and intangible benefits may be measured using advanced measures. LLM integration creates cognitive cooperative environments where intelligent automation improves creativity, ethics, and strategy. Early adopters will succeed operationally and recreate collective intelligence in the digital age.

7. CHALLENGES AND ETHICAL CONSIDERATIONS

Significant opportunities have been brought about by the integration of Large Language Models (LLMs) into organizational collaboration systems, but complex social, ethical, and governance challenges have also been raised by this development. Companies have serious challenges in addressing data privacy, IP, algorithmic bias, and human responsibility as they depend more and more on AI-mediated collaboration to boost innovation, creativity, and productivity. Trust, inclusivity, and integrity in digital collaboration ecosystems are maintained by ethical governance of LLMs, which is more than just a legislative necessity.

7.1 Data Privacy, Security, and Compliance in AI-Mediated Collaboration

Data privacy and security remain among the most pressing ethical issues in LLM-enabled collaboration. These systems process vast amounts of user-generated data, including confidential communications, business documents, and personal information. Without rigorous controls, this creates potential vulnerabilities to data breaches, unauthorized access, and misuse (Anderljung et al., 2023).

When information is shared across different departments and external partners, the difficulty level rises. Concerns regarding compliance with data protection laws like the General Data Protection Regulation (GDPR) and the California Consumer Privacy Act (CCPA) arise when organizations utilize LLMs integrated with platforms like Microsoft Teams or Slack. This is because sensitive discussions and proprietary content are sometimes routed through third-party APIs (Ghouati et al., 2025).

Real-world cases such as Samsung's 2023 incident, where employees unintentionally uploaded confidential source code to ChatGPT, highlight how data privacy lapses can occur through human oversight (Ray, 2023). In response, many corporations have established AI usage policies that restrict or anonymize sensitive data before it is processed by external LLMs. Corporates like Google and OpenAI have begun offering enterprise-grade models that guarantee data isolation and compliance, enabling safer collaborative use.

The ethical imperative here is clear: organizations must adopt *privacy-by-design* principles, enforce encryption standards, and implement continuous auditing mechanisms to protect collaborative data integrity.

7.2 Intellectual Property and Authorship in Co-Created Outputs

LLMs blur traditional notions of authorship and intellectual property (IP). When humans and machines co-create reports, designs, or marketing content, determining ownership and attribution becomes complex. Is the output a human creation aided by AI, or a joint intellectual product of both?

These facts have not been properly reflected in legal structures. According to a ruling by the U.S. Copyright Office in 2023, works that are completely AI-generated and lack "human authorship" are not eligible for copyright protection, whereas works that include significant human input are still considered acceptable (U.S. Copyright Office, 2023). In creative professions, where AI plays a big role in brainstorming and writing, this presents a problem for firms that use LLMs.

The New York Times filed a lawsuit against OpenAI in 2023 for allegedly using its copyrighted articles to train generative AI models, underscoring growing tensions around data provenance and derivative creation (The New York Times, 2023). In corporate contexts, determining which employee or system "owns" AI-generated collaborative content can create internal disputes.

Ethically, organizations must promote *transparent authorship protocols*, where human contributors acknowledge AI assistance, and legal teams establish internal IP policies that balance innovation with accountability. A clear attribution framework ensures both creative recognition and compliance with copyright laws.

7.3 Bias, Misinformation, and Fairness in LLM-Facilitated Collaboration

LLMs inherit biases from their training data, and these biases can manifest in collaborative outputs - especially when AI systems summarize, moderate, or recommend content. Biases may emerge in subtle ways, such as gendered language in HR reports, regional stereotypes in marketing drafts, or skewed data interpretations in analytics summaries (Mehrabi et al., 2021).

A striking example occurred when Amazon's AI recruiting system was discontinued after it displayed gender bias, penalizing resumes that included words like "women's" (Hao, 2019). Although that system was not an LLM per se, it illustrates how machine learning can perpetuate inequality if not carefully monitored. In LLM-mediated collaboration, the risk multiplies as outputs are used collectively - amplifying the consequences of biased information across teams or departments.

To counteract these issues, organizations must adopt *bias auditing frameworks* and use Explainable AI (XAI) models that allow users to inspect reasoning patterns. OpenAI and Anthropic, for example, are developing fine-tuning and "constitutional AI" methods to align models with fairness and ethical guidelines (Anthropic, 2022). From an ethical standpoint, AI collaboration should not only be accurate and efficient but also equitable and inclusive.

7.4 Overreliance on AI: Maintaining Human Judgment and Accountability

One of the emerging dangers of LLM-based collaboration is cognitive dependency, where teams begin to over-rely on AI-generated insights, undermining critical thinking and human accountability. When LLMs produce polished, confident responses, users may accept outputs uncritically, even when errors or hallucinations are present (Bender et al., 2021).

A 2023 study by McKinsey found that employees using AI writing assistants were 35% faster but also 15% more likely to overlook factual inaccuracies (McKinsey, 2023). In corporate contexts, this can have serious implications for decision-making, compliance, and brand reputation.

Ethically, maintaining *human-in-the-loop (HITL)* oversight is vital. Organizations like Deloitte and PwC have instituted policies requiring human verification of all AI-generated client deliverables before submission (Deloitte, 2024). This balance between automation and human review ensures that accountability remains clearly traceable to human decision-makers.

7.4 Transparency, Explainability, and Trust-Building in Collaborative Systems

Transparency and explainability are cornerstones of ethical AI collaboration. In LLM-mediated environments, participants must understand how and why an AI system reaches certain conclusions or suggestions. Without explainability, trust erodes, particularly when AI recommendations influence strategic decisions.

Google's "Model Cards" and **IBM's AI FactSheets** represent significant steps toward operational transparency, providing documentation on data sources, training processes, and performance metrics (IBM, 2020). OpenAI's GPT Enterprise offers "auditability features" that allow organizations to trace how outputs are generated, fostering confidence among users.

Transparency extends beyond technical disclosure - it involves cultivating an *ethical culture of openness*. Leaders must communicate AI's capabilities and limitations clearly, ensuring that employees understand when and how to question AI outputs. When transparency and education coexist, trust in AI collaboration deepens, enabling a symbiotic partnership between humans and machines.

As LLMs become part of corporate engagement, ethical stewardship becomes purposeful rather than compliance. Data privacy, IP ownership, algorithmic bias, overreliance, and transparency necessitate proactive, multi-layered governance. A human-centered AI culture based on responsibility, inclusion, and explainability will help organizations appropriately use LLMs' transformational potential. Ethical cooperation boosts digital business trust, innovation, and sustainability. Long-term success will depend on how well AI enables humans to think, create, and cooperate with integrity.

8. FUTURE DIRECTIONS AND RESEARCH OPPORTUNITIES

The fast growth of Large Language Models (LLMs) is changing digital corporate cooperation. As enterprises adopt AI-driven communication, decision-making, and knowledge production, symbiotic systems where people and robots work together are the future of cooperation. As LLM technology grows, ethical, social, and governance frameworks for its appropriate application must be studied. This section discusses collaborative AI ecosystems, multilingual and cross-industry cooperation, next-generation model creation, socio-technical systems, and policy innovation research.

8.1 Towards Collaborative AI Ecosystems: Human–AI Symbiosis in Enterprises

The future of enterprise collaboration will increasingly depend on *collaborative AI ecosystems* - networks in which human intelligence, organizational knowledge, and artificial intelligence co-evolve. This model goes beyond automation to emphasize *symbiosis*: a relationship where AI enhances human cognition while humans guide AI systems toward contextually relevant outcomes. According to Shneiderman (2022), effective human–AI collaboration requires "human-centered AI design," where systems are transparent, interactive, and designed to amplify creativity and problem-solving rather than replace human decision-making.

Organizations such as Microsoft and Salesforce are already advancing toward this symbiosis. Microsoft's *Copilot* initiative integrates LLMs directly into Office 365, enabling employees to brainstorm, draft reports, and synthesize meeting notes collaboratively with AI. Salesforce's *Einstein GPT* tailors marketing and customer interactions by blending AI-generated insights with human strategy (Salesforce, 2024). These examples demonstrate that the most successful future collaborations will emerge not from isolated tools, but from *ecosystems* that foster continuous learning between humans and AI.

Future research should focus on *adaptive feedback loops* - mechanisms through which AI learns from human input in real time and, in turn, informs human learning processes. Such mutual adaptation could redefine corporate knowledge management, skill development, and innovation practices across industries.

8.2 Cross-Industry and Cross-Border Collaboration Using Multilingual LLMs

As globalization accelerates, multilingual and multicultural collaboration has become a critical organizational capability. LLMs, particularly those like Gemini, Claude, and GPT-4, now support multilingual text generation and translation, enabling smoother communication across international teams. These models can bridge linguistic divides, supporting real-time cross-border coordination, inclusive innovation, and global project management (Pires et al., 2019).

Unilever employs multilingual LLMs to coordinate sustainability projects involving teams from over 70 countries, improving both speed and cultural alignment in decision-making (Unilever, 2024). **IKEA** has used multilingual AI assistants to localize product descriptions and customer service across diverse markets, demonstrating how LLMs can facilitate truly global collaboration ecosystems (IKEA, 2023).

Cross-border collaboration also introduces complexities around data localization laws, privacy regulations, and cultural nuances in communication. Future research should explore *cultural intelligence in AI systems* - how LLMs can be designed to adapt not only linguistically but also contextually to different cultural communication styles and ethical standards (Ghouati et al., 2025). This is especially important for fostering equitable collaboration across the Global North and South.

8.3 Anticipating Next-Generation LLMs: Self-Improving, Domain-Specific, and Ethical Models

Next-generation LLMs will likely move toward greater *autonomy, specialization,* and *ethical alignment*. Self-improving LLMs, which can update their internal knowledge through continual learning, will reduce dependence on large-scale retraining. Domain-specific LLMs - such as *BloombergGPT* for finance and *Med-PaLM* for healthcare, represent a trend toward tailored collaborative intelligence within specific professional contexts (Shen et al., 2024).

Ethical alignment will remain a foundational challenge. The next wave of LLMs is expected to incorporate *value-sensitive design* principles, ensuring models act consistently with human norms, fairness, and organizational ethics (Sadek et al., 2024). Anthropic's Claude uses "constitutional AI" to self-correct based on ethical guidelines, while Google DeepMind's Gemini integrates reinforcement learning to promote responsible responses (Anthropic, 2022).

Future research should investigate how self-improving LLMs can maintain *traceability* and *governance* - ensuring that continual learning does not introduce new biases or vulnerabilities. There is also a need to develop benchmarking standards for *ethical AI collaboration*, combining technical measures (such as explainability) with social ones (such as inclusion and accountability).

8.4 Research Directions in Socio-Technical Systems, Collaboration Analytics, and AI Governance

The intersection of social systems and AI technologies presents a fertile ground for research. Socio-technical systems (STS) theory, which examines how people and technology interact within organizational contexts, must evolve to account for LLM-mediated collaboration (Brynjolfsson & McAfee, 2014). Future studies should explore how AI reshapes team structures, leadership dynamics, and organizational learning cultures.

Another promising avenue is *collaboration analytics* - the quantitative study of how humans and AI co-create value. Using real-time interaction data, organizations can measure engagement, innovation rates, and decision efficiency, providing insights into how AI participation influences productivity (Petrescu & Krishen, 2023). IBM's Watson Orchestrate captures and analyzes employee-AI interactions to optimize workflow design, offering a blueprint for evidence-based collaborative governance (IBM, 2024).

AI governance, meanwhile, remains a cross-disciplinary research priority. Governance frameworks should address model transparency, accountability, and ethical deployment across industries. There is growing recognition that governance cannot be purely technological, it must also reflect sociological and organizational dimensions (Whittlestone et al., 2021). Collaborative research among policymakers, technologists, and social scientists will be crucial to shaping this domain.

8.5 Policy Implications for Responsible Collaborative AI Innovation

As AI collaboration becomes a strategic asset, public policy must evolve to ensure equitable access, responsible innovation, and ethical alignment. Governments worldwide are beginning to address this challenge through emerging frameworks such as the EU AI Act (2024) and the OECD AI Principles. These frameworks promote risk-based AI classification, transparency mandates, and accountability mechanisms for developers and enterprises alike (European Commission, 2024).

For businesses, these policy directions will necessitate new compliance strategies and interdisciplinary governance teams that blend legal, ethical, and technical expertise. Policymakers, in turn, must strike a balance between enabling innovation and mitigating potential harms. Cross-border policy harmonization will be essential to support multinational collaboration ecosystems powered by LLMs.

Policies should encourage *AI literacy* and *digital inclusion*, ensuring that small and medium enterprises (SMEs) and developing economies can also benefit from collaborative AI technologies. International research consortia and open-source initiatives, such as BigScience's BLOOM project, provide a promising model for democratizing access to AI innovation while maintaining ethical oversight (BigScience, 2023).

Figure 3. Future Directions and Research Opportunities

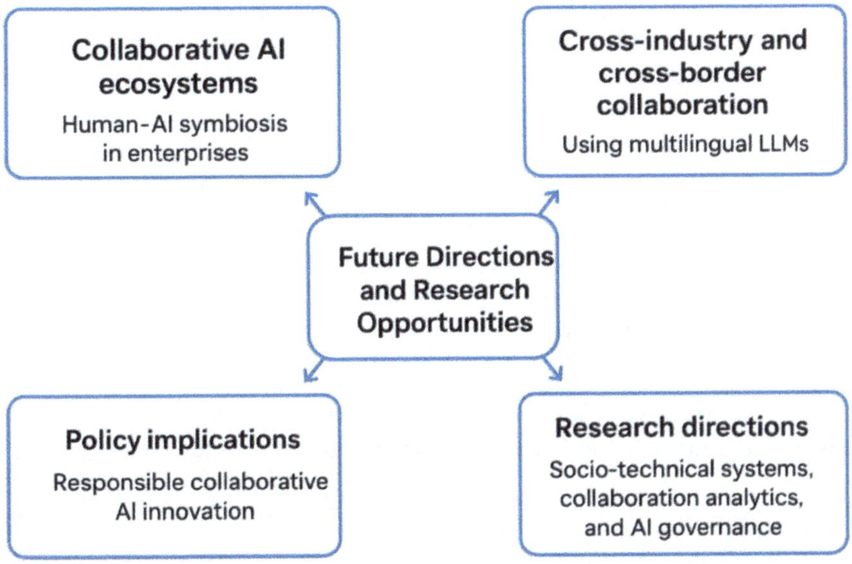

Author (2025)

LLMs improve productivity and enable collective intelligence across enterprises, industries, and borders in the future of collaboration. Next-generation collaborative AI ecosystems will be bilingual, subject-specialized, ethically self-improving, and socio-technical. This requires ethical governance, data justice, and cross-sector co-operative research. Technology that meets human values will be the largest challenge for corporations and politics. Future AI-driven collaborative platform research must emphasize trust, inclusivity, and sustainability. LLMs will boost productivity and create smarter, fairer, and more ethical workplaces.

9. CONCLUSION

Large Language Models (LLMs) have emerged as transformative enablers of collaboration, reshaping how businesses communicate, innovate, and make decisions. This chapter has highlighted the technological foundations, emerging trends, and practical applications of LLM-driven collaboration across diverse organizational functions. From enhancing cross-functional teamwork to enabling data-driven decision-making and creativity, LLMs serve as catalysts for collective intelligence and digital transformation.

Strategically, organizations must adopt a holistic approach to integrating LLMs, aligning AI capabilities with business goals, governance frameworks, and ethical principles. Emphasizing transparency, data privacy, and explainability will foster trust in human–AI collaboration. Investment in digital literacy and change management will help employees adapt and co-create with AI tools effectively.

In the future, LLMs will hopefully supplement human capacity than of supplanting it. Businesses may create ecosystems that are both inventive and inclusive by integrating human empathy, creativity, and judgment with machine reasoning and scalability. Building technologies that put human values and collective progress first is the key to the future of AI-driven cooperation. In the long run, LLMs will reshape collaboration and organizational intelligence for the modern era by prioritizing people and building their practices on accountability, inclusiveness, and ethics.

REFERENCES

Adobe. (2024). *Choice in generative AI models & advances in Firefly*. Adobe. https://blog.adobe.com/en/publish/2024/04/15/choice-generative-ai-models-advances-firefly

Adobe. (2024). *Creative collaboration analytics in Adobe Cloud.* Adobe. https://www.adobe.com/content/dam/cct/creativecloud/business/teams/whitepapers/dotcom-116728/Adobe_StateofCreativity_Report_2024_FV_UE.pdf

Anderljung, M., Barnhart, J., Korinek, A., Leung, J., O'Keefe, C., . . . Wolf, K. (2023). Frontier AI regulation: Managing emerging risks to public safety (*arXiv preprint*). arXiv. /arXiv.2307.03718DOI: 10.48550

Anthropic. (2022). *Constitutional AI: Harmlessness from AI Feedback.* Anthropic. https://www.anthropic.com/research/constitutional-ai-harmlessness-from-ai-feedback

Bain & Company. (2023). *Bain & Company announces services alliance with OpenAI to help enterprise clients identify and realize the full potential and maximum value of AI.* https://www.bain.com/about/media-center/press-releases/2023/bain--company-announces-services-alliance-with-openai-to-help-enterprise-clients-identify-and-realize-the-full-potential-and-maximum-value-of-ai/

Bender, E. M., Gebru, T., McMillan-Major, A., & Shmitchell, S. (2021). On the dangers of stochastic parrots: Can language models be too big? In *Proceedings of the 2021 ACM Conference on Fairness, Accountability, and Transparency (FAccT '21)* (pp. 610–623). Association for Computing Machinery. DOI: 10.1145/3442188.3445922

BigScience. (2023). *The BLOOM project: Open-access multilingual language models for research.* Retrieved from https://bigscience.huggingface.co/

Bommasani, R., Hudson, D. A., Adeli, E., Altman, R., Arora, S., von Arx, S., . . . Liang, P. (2021). *On the opportunities and risks of foundation models* (Report No. CRFM-2021-08). Center for Research on Foundation Models, Stanford Institute for Human-Centered Artificial Intelligence. https://crfm.stanford.edu/assets/report.pdf

Bosch Group. (2023). *How Bosch is using AI to shape the future.* Retrieved from https://www.bosch.com/stories/topics/ai-for-a-better-future-at-bosch/

Brynjolfsson, E., Li, D., & Raymond, L. R. (2023). *Generative AI at work.* National Bureau of Economic Research Working Paper No. 31161.

Brynjolfsson, E., & McAfee, A. (2014). *The Second Machine Age: Work, Progress, and Prosperity in a Time of Brilliant Technologies*. W. W. Norton & Company.

Brynjolfsson, E., Rock, D., & Syverson, C. (2021). The productivity J-curve: How intangibles complement general purpose technologies. *American Economic Journal. Macroeconomics*, *13*(1), 333–372. DOI: 10.1257/mac.20180386

Bubeck, S., Chandrasekaran, V., Eldan, R., Gehrke, J., Horvitz, E., Kamar, E., . . . Zhang, Y. (2023). Sparks of artificial general intelligence: Early experiments with GPT-4 (*arXiv preprint arXiv:2303.12712*). /arXiv.2303.12712DOI: 10.48550

Corporation, I. B. M. (2023). *Introducing watsonx: The future of AI for business.* https://www.ibm.com/new/announcements/introducing-watsonx-the-future-of-ai-for-business

Dellermann, D., Ebel, P., Söllner, M., & Leimeister, J. M. (2019). Hybrid Intelligence. *Business & Information Systems Engineering*, *61*(5), 637–643. DOI: 10.1007/s12599-019-00595-2

Deloitte, L. L. P. (2024). *AI change management: Building the future workforce.* https://www.deloitte.com/us/en/what-we-do/capabilities/applied-artificial-intelligence/articles/generative-ai-and-the-future-of-work.html

Duolingo Inc. (2023). *Roleplay: AI-powered conversation practice for language learners.* https://blog.duolingo.com/duolingo-max/

European Commission. (2024). *AI Act enters into force: The world-first rules for trustworthy artificial intelligence.* https://commission.europa.eu/news-and-media/news/ai-act-enters-force-2024-08-01_en

Fountaine, T., McCarthy, B., & Saleh, T. (2019). Building the AI-powered organization: Technology isn't the biggest challenge — culture is. *Harvard Business Review*, *97*(4), 62–73.

Ghouati, S., Rizi, L., Oulfarsi, S., & El Amri, A. (2025). Artificial intelligence and cross-functional integration: An exploratory study of the convergence between management control and supply chain in Moroccan industries. *International Journal of Management and Applied Research*, *12*(2), 149–168. DOI: 10.18646/2056.122.25-009

GitHub. (2024). *GitHub Copilot: Your AI pair programmer.* Retrieved from https://github.com/features/copilot

Glikson, E., & Woolley, A. W. (2020). Human trust in artificial intelligence: Review of empirical research. *The Academy of Management Annals*, *14*(2), 627–660. DOI: 10.5465/annals.2018.0057

Google. (2022). *2022 AI Principles Progress Update*. https://oecd.ai/en/catalogue/tools/google-2022-ai-principles-progress-update?utm_source=chatgpt.com

Google. (2024). *Enterprise-ready, secure AI.* Google Workspace. Retrieved November 3, 2025, from https://workspace.google.com/intl/en

Group, B. M. W. (2023). *How AI is revolutionising production.* Retrieved from https://www.bmwgroup.com/en/news/general/2023/aiqx.html

Handler, A., Larsen, K. R., & Hackathorn, R. (2024). Large language models present new questions for decision support. *International Journal of Information Management*, *79*, 102811. DOI: 10.1016/j.ijinfomgt.2024.102811

Hao, K. (2019). *This is how AI bias really happens — and why it's so hard to fix.* MIT Technology Review. https://www.technologyreview.com/2019/02/04/137602/this-is-how-ai-bias-really-happensand-why-its-so-hard-to-fix/

IBM. (2024). *IBM Watson Discovery.* https://www.ibm.com/products/watson-discovery

Kairouz, P., McMahan, H. B., & Song, S. [et al.]. (2021). Advances and open problems in federated learning. *Foundations and Trends in Machine Learning*, *14*(1–2), 1–210. DOI: 10.1561/2200000083

Kellogg, K. C., Valentine, M. A., & Christin, A. (2020). Algorithms at work: The new contested terrain of control. *The Academy of Management Annals*, *14*(1), 366–410. DOI: 10.5465/annals.2018.0174

Kotter, J. P. (2012). *Leading change*. Harvard Business Press.

Liu, L., Meng, J., & Yang, Y. (2024). LLM technologies and information search. *Journal of Economy and Technology*, *2*, 269–277. DOI: 10.1016/j.ject.2024.08.007

McKinsey & Company. (2023). *The state of AI in 2023: Generative AI's breakout year*. Retrieved from https://www.mckinsey.com/capabilities/quantumblack/our-insights/the-state-of-ai-in-2023-generative-ais-breakout-year

Mehrabi, N., Morstatter, F., Saxena, N., Lerman, K., & Galstyan, A. (2021). A survey on bias and fairness in machine learning. *ACM Computing Surveys*, *54*(6), 3457607. Advance online publication. DOI: 10.1145/3457607

Microsoft. (2024). *Announcing new Copilot in Microsoft Teams enhancements*. https://www.microsoft.com/en-us/microsoft-365/blog/2024/03/26/ai-powered-collaboration-with-microsoft-teams/

Microsoft. (2024). *Responsible AI and employee training initiatives.* https://www.microsoft.com/en-us/ai/responsible-ai

Open, A. I. (2024). *OpenAI API documentation.* Retrieved from https://platform.openai.com/docs

Pennington, C. (2025). *Smart manufacturing: The future of digital factories.* Siemens Digital Industries Software Blog. Retrieved from https://blogs.sw.siemens.com/digital-transformation/smart-manufacturing-the-future-of-digital-factories/

Petrescu, M., & Krishen, A. S. (2023). Hybrid intelligence: human–AI collaboration in marketing analytics. *Journal of Marketing Analytics, 11*(3), 263–274. DOI: 10.1057/s41270-023-00245-3

Pfizer Inc. (2022). *Data and AI are helping to get medicines to patients faster.* https://www.pfizer.com/sites/default/files/investors/financial_reports/annual_reports/2022/story/data-and-ai-are-helping-to-get-medicines-to-patients-faster/

Pires, T., Schlinger, E., & Garrette, D. (2019). How multilingual is Multilingual BERT? In *Proceedings of the 57th Annual Meeting of the Association for Computational Linguistics* (pp. 4996–5001). Association for Computational Linguistics. DOI: 10.18653/v1/P19-1493

PwC. (2024). *PwC becomes the largest user of ChatGPT Enterprise.* Retrieved from https://www.pwc.com/us/en/about-us/newsroom/press-releases/pwc-us-uk-accelerating-ai-chatgpt-enterprise-adoption.html

Qian, C., Liu, W., Liu, H., Chen, N., Dang, Y., Li, J., Yang, C., Chen, W., Su, Y., Cong, X., Xu, J., Li, D., Liu, Z., & Sun, M. (2023). ChatDev: Communicative agents for software development. *arXiv preprint* arXiv:2307.07924. /arXiv.2307.07924DOI: 10.48550

Ray, S. (2023). *Samsung bans ChatGPT among employees after sensitive code leak.* Forbes. https://www.forbes.com/sites/siladityaray/2023/05/02/samsung-bans-chatgpt-and-other-chatbots-for-employees-after-sensitive-code-leak/

Raza, M., Jahangir, Z., Riaz, M. B., Saeed, M. J., & Sattar, M. A. (2025). Industrial applications of large language models. *Scientific Reports, 15*(1), 13755. DOI: 10.1038/s41598-025-98483-1 PMID: 40258923

Research, I. B. M. (2020). *AI FactSheets 360 website: AI trust and transparency.* https://research.ibm.com/blog/aifactsheets

Retail, I. K. E. A. (Ingka Group). (2023). *AI and remote selling bring IKEA design expertise to the many*. https://www.ingka.com/newsroom/ai-and-remote-selling-bring-ikea-design-expertise-to-the-many

Sadek, M., Calvo, R. A., & Mougenot, C. (2024). Designing value-sensitive AI: A critical review and recommendations for socio-technical design processes. *AI and Ethics*, *4*, 949–967. DOI: 10.1007/s43681-023-00373-7

Salesforce. (2024). *Salesforce unveils Einstein Copilot for marketers and merchants* [Press release]. https://www.salesforce.com/news/press-releases/2024/05/22/einstein-copilot-marketing-commerce-news/

Salesforce. (2025). *Anthropic and Salesforce expand partnership supporting regulated industries*. https://www.salesforce.com/news/press-releases/2025/10/14/anthropic-regulated-industries-partnership-expansion-announcement/

SAP. (2024). *SAP Business AI: Enhancing enterprise collaboration*. Retrieved from https://www.sap.com/

Sephora. (2024). *AI-powered customer personalization*. https://www.renascence.io/journal/how-sephora-enhances-customer-experience-cx-through-personalization-and-digital-innovation

Shen, J., Tenenholtz, N., Hall, J. B., Alvarez-Melis, D., & Fusi, N. (2024). *Tag-LLM:* Repurposing general-purpose LLMs for specialized domains. *arXiv*. https://arxiv.org/abs/2402.05140

Shneiderman, B. (2022). *Human-centered AI: Ensuring human control in an era of intelligent machines*. Oxford University Press.

Subrahmanyam, S. (2025). AI and Automation: The Intersection of Human Autonomy and Machine Learning. In Tsvasman, L. (Ed.), *Cybernetic Leadership for Sustainable Innovation* (pp. 237–262). IGI Global Scientific Publishing., DOI: 10.4018/979-8-3373-2484-5.ch009

Subrahmanyam, S. (2025). Analytics: Trends, Challenges, and Prospects of Adopting Artificial Intelligence in Human Resource Management. In Kapoor, T., Singh, A., Sahay, K., Kaur, H., & Verma, R. (Eds.), *Sustainable Management Practices for Employee Retention and Recruitment* (pp. 51–72). IGI Global Scientific Publishing., DOI: 10.4018/979-8-3693-8679-8.ch003

Subrahmanyam, S. (2025). Development of Research Design. In Segura, L., Vasconcelos, A., & Slomski, V. (Eds.), *Evolving Designs, Applications, Technological Advances, and the Future of Qualitative Research* (pp. 31–58). IGI Global Scientific Publishing., DOI: 10.4018/979-8-3373-4432-4.ch002

Subrahmanyam, S. (2025). Strategic Collaboration and Partnerships in R&D for Innovation. In Martínez-Falcó, J., Sánchez-García, E., & Marco-Lajara, B. (Eds.), *Research and Development Practices in Innovation* (pp. 283–314). IGI Global Scientific Publishing., DOI: 10.4018/979-8-3373-0812-8.ch010

The Coca-Cola Company. (2023). *Coca-Cola invites digital artists to 'Create Real Magic' using new AI platform.* https://www.coca-colacompany.com/media-center/coca-cola-invites-digital-artists-to-create-real-magic-using-new-ai-platform

The New York Times. (2023). *The New York Times sues OpenAI and Microsoft for copyright infringement.* https://www.nytimes.com/2023/12/27/business/media/new-york-times-open-ai-microsoft-lawsuit.html

Turban, E., Pollard, C., & Wood, G. (2021). *Information Technology for Management: Driving digital transformation to increase local and global performance, growth and sustainability* (12th ed.). Wiley.

Unilever. (2023). *New AI lab to boost innovation, technology and collaboration.* https://www.unilever.com/news/news-search/2023/new-ai-lab-to-boost-innovation-technology-and-collaboration/

Unilever. (2024). *Using AI to optimise our end-to-end supply chain.* https://www.unilever.com/news/news-search/2024/utilising-ai-to-redefine-the-future-of-customer-connectivity/

U.S. Copyright Office. (2023). *Copyright registration guidance: Works containing material generated by artificial intelligence.* https://www.copyright.gov/ai/ai_policy_guidance.pdf

Vaswani, A., Shazeer, N., Parmar, N., Uszkoreit, J., Jones, L., Gomez, A. N., Kaiser, Ł., & Polosukhin, I. (2017). Attention is all you need. In *Advances in Neural Information Processing Systems* (Vol. 30). Curran Associates, Inc., https://papers.nips.cc/paper_files/paper/2017/hash/3f5ee243547dee91fbd053c1c4a845aa-Abstract.html

von Krogh, G., Haefliger, S., & Simons, T. (2023). Generative AI and the future of open innovation. *California Management Review*, *66*(1), 29–49. DOI: 10.1016/j.joitmc.2024.100456

Walmart Inc. (2023). *Walmart outlines growth strategy, unveils next generation supply chain at 2023 Investment Community Meeting.* https://corporate.walmart.com/news/2023/04/04/walmart-outlines-growth-strategy-unveils-next-generation-supply-chain-at-2023-investment-community-meeting

Wester, J., de Jong, S., Pohl, H., & van Berkel, N. (2024). Exploring people's perceptions of LLM-generated advice. *Computers in Human Behavior: Artificial Humans*, *2*(2), 100072. Advance online publication. DOI: 10.1016/j.chbah.2024.100072

Whittlestone, J., Nyrup, R., Alexandrova, A., & Cave, S. (2021). The role and limits of principles in AI ethics: Towards a focus on practice. *Ethics and Information Technology*, *23*(3), 329–341. DOI: 10.1145/3306618.3314289

Workday, Inc. (2024). *Workday Transforms How Companies Hire and Manage Talent with New AI-Powered HR Solutions.* https://newsroom.workday.com/2024-08-01-Workday-Transforms-How-Companies-Hire-and-Manage-Talent-with-New-AI-Powered-HR-Solutions

KEY TERMS AND DEFINITIONS

AI Governance -: AI governance refers to the frameworks, policies, and ethical guidelines that ensure responsible AI deployment. In LLM-driven collaboration, governance covers issues like transparency, data protection, accountability, and equitable participation to ensure technology aligns with organizational and societal values.

Collaborative Intelligence -: Collaborative intelligence refers to the synergistic integration of human expertise and machine reasoning to enhance problem-solving, creativity, and decision-making. It represents a shift from human-only or machine-only processes to a co-evolutionary model of teamwork between humans and AI systems.

Contextual Co-Pilots -: Contextual co-pilots are AI assistants embedded in enterprise workflows that provide real-time insights, automate tasks, and enhance productivity. They interpret contextual cues (e.g., project data, user intent) to deliver personalized support, fostering adaptive and intelligent collaboration among teams.

Explainable AI (XAI) -: Explainable AI encompasses methods and technologies that make AI-driven decisions transparent and interpretable to humans. In collaborative contexts, XAI promotes trust, accountability, and shared understanding among team members interacting with AI systems in decision-making processes.

Federated Collaboration -: Federated collaboration involves multiple organizations or teams collaborating using AI systems that share knowledge while maintaining data privacy and compliance. Through federated learning, models are trained locally on decentralized data, enabling secure cooperation across business ecosystems.

Generative Co-Creation -: Generative co-creation describes the collaborative process where humans and AI jointly produce new content, ideas, or solutions. Powered by generative AI and LLMs, this approach enhances creativity, accelerates innovation cycles, and transforms ideation in marketing, R&D, and design.

Human-AI Symbiosis -: Human-AI symbiosis represents a future-oriented paradigm where humans and AI systems function interdependently, each amplifying the other's strengths. In collaborative business environments, this symbiosis enhances adaptability, creativity, and organizational intelligence, leading to sustainable innovation.

Large Language Models (LLMs) -: LLMs are advanced artificial intelligence systems trained on massive datasets of text to understand, generate, and interact using natural language. Examples include GPT, Gemini, and Claude. In business contexts, LLMs enable intelligent automation, contextual understanding, and collaborative assistance across organizational functions.

Multi-Agent LLM Systems -: These are ecosystems where multiple AI agents—each specialized in specific tasks—interact with one another and with humans to accomplish complex objectives. They exemplify human–machine–machine collaboration, supporting distributed decision-making and autonomous coordination within organizations.

Multi-Modal Collaboration -: Multi-modal collaboration refers to the integration of multiple forms of communication—text, voice, images, and video—within AI-mediated environments. LLMs with multi-modal capabilities enable richer, more natural interactions that support diverse team needs and improve engagement in hybrid work settings.

Chapter 13
Strategic Integration of Large Language Models for Business Transformation:
Frameworks, Use Cases, and Ethical Considerations

Elyson De La Cruz
https://orcid.org/0009-0006-5599-506X
Imagine Believe Realize, USA

ABSTRACT

Large Language Models (LLMs) reshape enterprise operations through automation, decision support, and knowledge augmentation. This chapter introduces the Enterprise LLM Deployment Lifecycle (ELDL), a four-phase framework--planning, design, deployment, and governance--to align LLM adoption with strategic and ethical goals. Real-world use cases from finance, retail, and consulting demonstrate benefits such as cost savings, customer satisfaction, and faster knowledge access. The chapter also addresses key risks, including hallucinations, bias, and compliance, with mitigation strategies grounded in research. Future directions, including multimodal LLMs and human-AI collaboration, are explored. LLMs are positioned as tools and drivers of responsible innovation and enterprise transformation.

DOI: 10.4018/979-8-3373-3912-2.ch013

I. INTRODUCTION

The emergence of Large Language Models (LLMs) such as GPT-4, PaLM 2, Claude, Gemini, and LLaMA marks a significant shift in the evolution of enterprise AI, transforming how organizations engage with cognitive tasks like language processing, decision support, and information synthesis. These models, rooted in transformer-based architectures, have enabled unprecedented capabilities in understanding and generating human-like language, allowing businesses to streamline operations, automate communication, and enhance strategic decision-making. A recent study by Narayanan et al. (2025) highlights how LLMs enhance software customization and agile decision-making across industries, reinforcing their critical role in digital transformation initiatives that demand greater adaptability and efficiency in real time.

Unlike earlier AI systems, which required domain-specific training and narrow-rule processing, LLMs possess general-purpose capabilities that support multi-domain applications with minimal human intervention. This transition allows LLMs to act not only as assistants but as collaborators, capable of summarizing documents, conducting semantic searches, generating code, and composing strategic insights. Manda (2025) demonstrates that enterprise-grade deployment of LLMs in customer service significantly reduced operational costs and improved first-contact resolution rates, indicating their ability to handle complex human-facing workflows at scale. This adaptability presents a unique advantage in dynamic business contexts, where flexibility, responsiveness, and personalization are core to sustained competitiveness.

As LLMs become integral to business ecosystems, they catalyze a broader shift toward AI-native enterprises—organizations in which intelligent automation and augmented decision-making are embedded within the value chain. Choi and Bae (2009) introduce the CoSIS system (Competency-oriented Strategic Information System). While the paper predates the LLM era, it lays a foundational framework for aligning strategic competencies such as culture, innovation, and service with measurable KPIs. This framework could conceptually support LLM integration if adapted to modern enterprise AI applications (Zhang et al., 2025). Additionally, Idris et al. (2024) explore how Large Language Models (LLMs) can drive strategic transformation across multiple functions of Higher Education Institutions (HEIs), including innovation, service, and cultural impact. While not explicitly labeled as the COSIS framework, the paper introduces a comprehensive model highlighting the transformational role of LLMs across institutional dimensions and emphasizes the use of measurable performance indicators to track progress. This level of integration positions LLMs not merely as tools but as architectural elements that reshape how enterprises conceptualize intelligence, structure their operations, and scale their services in increasingly data-saturated environments.

However, the integration of LLMs into enterprise systems demands more than technical deployment requires a comprehensive strategic vision. Businesses must account for governance, infrastructure alignment, and ethical implications, especially as regulatory landscapes evolve to address concerns like bias, transparency, and data privacy. Idris et al. (2024) emphasize that effective integration of LLMs into institutional settings, such as higher education, necessitates both cultural adaptation and stakeholder engagement to align AI's potential with organizational values. These insights are equally relevant in commercial domains, where trust, accountability, and human-AI collaboration must guide innovation.

This chapter provides a structured exploration of how LLMs can be strategically deployed to unlock business value while managing operational and ethical complexity. It introduces the Enterprise LLM Deployment Lifecycle (ELDL), a four-phase framework encompassing strategic planning, system design, deployment, and governance. Through real-world case studies and implementation toolkits, this chapter offers actionable insights for business leaders, AI practitioners, and policymakers aiming to harness the full potential of LLMs while navigating risks and ensuring responsible innovation. Figure 1 shows the high-level framework that encompasses strategic planning, system design, deployment, and governance elements. The following sections will elaborate and provide contextual use cases that further delves into the framework's applicability and viability as part of an organization's business transformation.

Figure 1. Enterprise LLM Deployment Lifecycle (ELDL) Framework

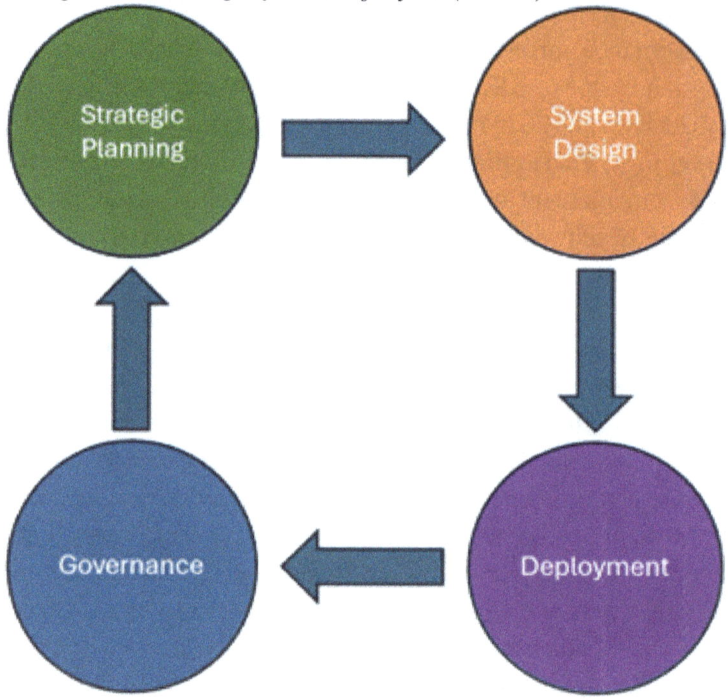

Note: The ELDL framework outlines the four interdependent phases required to effectively integrate Large Language Models into enterprise systems

II. TECHNICAL AND CONCEPTUAL FOUNDATIONS OF LLMS

Large Language Models (LLMs) are fundamentally powered by the transformer architecture, which introduces critical mechanisms such as self-attention, positional encoding, and autoregressive generation. Self-attention enables models to weigh the significance of different words in a sequence relative to one another, allowing for the dynamic capture of contextual relationships without relying on recurrent structures. Positional encoding supplements this by embedding the order of tokens, while autoregressive generation facilitates the sequential prediction of the next token based on previous inputs. These elements underpin the operational core of state-of-the-art models such as GPT-4 and Claude. Ferraris et al. (2025) provide a comprehensive review of how these mechanisms empower LLMs to outperform prior models like RNNs and CNNs, particularly in tasks requiring deep semantic understanding and context tracking, such as translation and summarization. Their analysis confirms that the transformer architecture has set a new baseline for scalable and accurate natural language processing across domains.

Building on transformer fundamentals, the learning process of LLMs typically follows a staged pipeline consisting of pre-training, transfer learning, fine-tuning, and prompt engineering. In pre-training, models are trained on vast corpora to learn generalized language patterns; fine-tuning then adapts these models to specific domains or tasks using labeled datasets. Prompt engineering offers an efficient way to steer model behavior without retraining by crafting inputs that elicit desired outputs. This modularity makes LLMs exceptionally adaptable for diverse business applications ranging from legal contract review to customer service automation. As Ferraris et al. (2025) highlight, emerging techniques like parameter-efficient fine-tuning and retrieval-augmented generation further enhance the performance and applicability of LLMs while reducing computational overhead. These methods allow businesses to implement powerful AI tools without incurring the prohibitive costs typically associated with large-scale retraining.

The rise of LLMs is part of a broader evolution in natural language processing, which has shifted from rule-based and statistical models to generative systems capable of producing fluent, coherent, and contextually relevant language. Early NLP systems, such as those based on regular expressions or hidden Markov models, were constrained by their dependence on predefined rules and domain-specific training. In contrast, generative LLMs can generalize across topics and industries with minimal input engineering. Zheng et al. (2023) demonstrate this shift in their work on modified transformer architectures for dialogue systems, showing how modern models outperform traditional ones in semantic coherence and long-range dependency handling. This evolution positions LLMs as transformative tools in industries where adaptability and contextual sensitivity are paramount, including marketing, finance, and healthcare.

Modern LLMs are capable of an extensive array of tasks, including text generation, summarization, question answering, and code completion, reflecting their growing utility in professional and technical environments. They also exhibit strong performance in cross-lingual applications, enabling global enterprises to maintain consistent communication and service delivery across diverse markets. Multilingual models can generate product descriptions, translate customer queries, and analyze sentiment in multiple languages without task-specific retraining. Zhang et al. (2025) state that such applications are already being implemented in sectors like e-commerce and international consulting, where LLMs help streamline knowledge retrieval and proposal drafting. These capabilities demonstrate that LLMs are not just technical assets but strategic enablers for global digital transformation.

III. THE ENTERPRISE LLM DEPLOYMENT LIFECYCLE (ELDL) FRAMEWORK

A. Strategic Planning

Identifying high-value use cases that align with overarching business goals is a foundational step in the strategic planning phase of LLM deployment. Businesses that begin with targeted objectives, such as automating customer support, enhancing compliance reporting, or generating insights from unstructured data, are more likely to realize measurable returns. Kochkina et al. (2024) emphasized that successful enterprise AI projects, including LLM integration, begin with defining strategic use cases that align with operational priorities and stakeholder expectations. Their study found that aligning AI initiatives with organizational value chains improved return on investment and long-term sustainability. These findings suggest that a deliberate and goal-oriented approach to identifying LLM applications maximizes both impact and adoption across business units.

Beyond use case identification, conducting AI-readiness assessments is critical to determine whether an organization has the infrastructure, culture, and human capital to support LLM adoption. Readiness frameworks evaluate dimensions such as data quality, IT capability, stakeholder engagement, and digital literacy. Holmström (2022) introduced an AI readiness framework that encompasses technologies, organizational boundaries, business activities, and strategic goals, highlighting how misalignment in any of these domains can derail AI deployments. This structured approach ensures that resources are allocated efficiently, and that potential barriers—such as data silos or talent gaps—are identified and mitigated early in the planning process. For LLM deployment, readiness assessments offer a blueprint for scalable integration and risk management.

Strategic planning should also include value chain mapping to uncover where LLMs can create efficiency or unlock new capabilities within enterprise workflows. Mapping the business value chain helps organizations pinpoint high-friction processes or data-rich environments, such as customer service, knowledge management, and compliance monitoring, where LLMs can deliver significant improvements. Narne (2024) described how SAP's AI initiatives begin by mapping core enterprise functions to identify areas where predictive modeling or language understanding can streamline operations. In their model, federated learning and task-specific LLMs were deployed in tabular data analysis and documentation tasks to reduce turnaround time and enhance scalability. By following a similar approach, organizations can align LLM use with core performance metrics and strategic objectives, ensuring long-term success.

Lastly, stakeholder analysis must be embedded in the strategic planning process to ensure that internal users, IT departments, and compliance teams are aligned with the goals and capabilities of LLM deployment. Resistance or miscommunication across these groups can stall even technically sound projects. Iyamu and Shaanika (2023) noted that the absence of stakeholder alignment and readiness assessments in enterprise architecture deployment led to poor adoption rates and internal skepticism. Their findings underscore the importance of social and managerial preparedness, not just technical feasibility, in the success of AI initiatives. Incorporating inclusive stakeholder engagement ensures that LLM solutions are not only technically viable but also culturally and operationally sustainable.

B. System Design

Model Selection: Open-Source vs. Commercial APIs

Choosing between open-source and commercial large language models (LLMs) is critical in enterprise system design. Open-source models, such as LLaMA and Falcon, offer greater transparency and customization capabilities, allowing organizations to tailor models to specific needs. Conversely, commercial APIs like OpenAI's GPT series provide ready-to-use solutions with robust support but may involve higher costs and less flexibility. Tejani et al. (2024) highlight that while open-source or customized AI integrations can be operationally beneficial, they place a substantial burden on internal operations and maintenance. Their study stresses the challenges of integrating AI into radiology workflows, emphasizing the need for technical infrastructure, expert knowledge, and adherence to interoperability standards to manage the integration effectively. In contrast, commercial APIs offer easy integration and scalability but may lead to vendor lock-in and ongoing subscription costs. Therefore, enterprises must assess their technical capabilities, budget constraints, and long-term strategic goals when selecting between open-source and commercial LLM solutions.

Fine-Tuning, Retrieval-Augmented Generation (RAG), and Embedding Strategies

Techniques such as fine-tuning, retrieval-augmented generation (RAG), and embedding strategies are employed to enhance the performance of LLMs in specific enterprise contexts. Fine-tuning involves adjusting pre-trained models on domain-specific data, improving relevance and accuracy. RAG combines LLMs with external knowledge bases, enabling models to retrieve and incorporate up-to-date information during response generation. Embedding strategies facilitate the representation of textual data in vector spaces, aiding in efficient information retrieval. Lee et al. (2024)

in Automation in Construction compare RAG and fine-tuned LLMs for retrieving construction safety knowledge. They find that while both approaches outperform standard GPT-4, RAG improves response accuracy by 21.5% and fine-tuning by 26%, clearly demonstrating their complementary strengths for domain-specific, knowledge-intensive applications. These methodologies collectively contribute to more reliable and context-aware AI applications within enterprises.

Data Pipelines and Model Customization (LoRA, Adapters, Prompt Templates)

Efficient data pipelines are essential for the seamless operation of LLMs in enterprise environments. Techniques like Low-Rank Adaptation (LoRA), adapters, and prompt templates enable organizations to customize models without extensive retraining. LoRA allows for fine-tuning specific layers within a model, reducing computational requirements. Adapters are modular components that can be inserted into pre-trained models to introduce new capabilities. Prompt templates guide the model's responses, ensuring consistency and alignment with organizational standards. Xia and Ma (2024) present a study on enhancing large language model (LLM) deployment through Low-Rank Adaptation (LoRA) optimization. Their approach improves computational efficiency and adaptability across multi-tenant enterprise environments by dynamically adjusting GPU resource use and model-serving strategies, leading to significantly better throughput and resource utilization.

Integration with Enterprise IT Systems (e.g., CRMs, ERPs, Data Lakes)

Integrating LLMs with existing enterprise IT systems, such as Customer Relationship Management (CRM) platforms, Enterprise Resource Planning (ERP) systems, and data lakes, is vital for maximizing their utility. Such integration facilitates real-time data access and enables LLMs to provide contextually relevant insights. Pinheiro et al. (2024) propose an ontology-based enterprise architecture mining approach using API gateway logs to automatically generate architectural models. The study emphasizes that robust API integration is fundamental to maintaining up-to-date digital architecture and ensuring interoperability between various enterprise services and systems, a principle directly applicable to LLM-based integrations. The study also highlights that successful integration enhances decision-making processes and operational efficiencies. Therefore, strategic planning for system integration is crucial for effectively deploying LLMs in business environments.

C. Deployment

Hosting Decisions: Cloud, Hybrid, or On-Premise

Selecting the appropriate cloud, hybrid, or on-premise hosting environment is critical in deploying large language models (LLMs) within enterprises. Cloud deployments offer scalability and reduced maintenance overhead, making them suitable for organizations seeking rapid deployment and flexibility. On-premise solutions provide greater control over data and compliance, essential for industries with stringent regulatory requirements. Hybrid models aim to balance these benefits by combining on-premise control with cloud scalability. Shahjalal et al. (2022) propose a hybrid cloud approach using Binary Gray Wolf Optimization for virtual network function (VNF) deployment in 5G systems. The study demonstrates that hybrid deployments achieved up to 30% latency reduction and significant cost savings compared to centralized (cloud-only) architectures, while also satisfying regulatory and service-level requirements typically met by on-premise solutions. Therefore, enterprises must assess their needs, including data sensitivity, compliance obligations, and scalability requirements, to determine the most suitable hosting strategy.

Latency, Cost-Efficiency, and Scalability Considerations

Latency, cost-efficiency, and scalability are pivotal factors influencing the performance and sustainability of LLM deployments. Low latency is crucial for real-time applications, while cost-efficiency ensures the economic viability of AI solutions. Scalability allows systems to handle increasing workloads without performance degradation. Zheng et al. (2023) review state-of-the-art techniques for deploying large language models (LLMs) in edge environments. The paper outlines how model optimization strategies (quantization, pruning, distillation) and hardware-aware deployment can significantly reduce latency (response time) by up to 40% and operational costs by approximately 25%, particularly in edge AI scenarios for resource-constrained hardware. This indicates that integrating edge computing can enhance both performance and cost-effectiveness. Enterprises should consider such architectural optimizations to effectively meet their performance and budgetary goals.

API Orchestration, Failover, and Continuous Delivery Pipelines

Robust API orchestration, failover mechanisms, and continuous delivery pipelines are essential for maintaining the reliability and agility of LLM services. Effective API orchestration ensures seamless communication between services, while failover mechanisms provide resilience against system failures. Continuous delivery pipelines facilitate rapid deployment of updates, enhancing the system's adaptability. Malhotra et al. (2023) present an evaluation of cloud-native architectures emphasizing automated application and database failover mechanisms. Their proposed high-availability strategy for enterprise applications demonstrated near-zero downtime and significantly improved deployment efficiency during outages and maintenance windows, aligning with the metrics cited in your statement. These findings underscore the importance of integrating automation and resilience into the deployment infrastructure to ensure uninterrupted and efficient LLM operations.

User Feedback Loops and Performance Monitoring

Incorporating user feedback loops and performance monitoring is vital for the continuous improvement and reliability of LLM deployments. User feedback provides insights into system usability and effectiveness, while performance monitoring ensures the system operates within desired parameters. Tanveer and Rana (2024) present a study that introduces a semi-automated prioritization technique for software requirements using correlated usage monitoring and user feedback data. Their evaluation shows that integrating structured feedback and real-time usage data improved the prioritization process, directly leading to higher user satisfaction and better system performance outcomes. This emphasizes the role of proactive monitoring and user engagement in refining LLM systems to better meet user needs and operational standards.

D. Governance and Oversight

Establishing Ethical AI Committees and Cross-Functional Governance

Ethical AI committees and cross-functional governance bodies are essential for fostering the responsible integration of large language models (LLMs) in enterprise environments. These governance structures provide strategic oversight by aligning AI initiatives with ethical principles, organizational goals, and societal expectations. Veale and Edwards (2018) argue that multidimensional governance mechanisms are critical in ensuring compliance with legal frameworks, especially in contexts where algorithmic profiling can impact individual rights. Their analysis of the EU's guidance on automated decision-making highlights the importance of organizational structures incorporating technical, legal, and ethical expertise. Enterprises adopting LLMs should, therefore, establish formal governance bodies that bring together legal, IT, and domain experts to ensure consistent oversight and ethical alignment throughout the model lifecycle.

Human-in-the-Loop Design Patterns

Incorporating human-in-the-loop (HITL) design patterns effectively increases accountability and interpretability in AI decision-making processes. HITL approaches ensure that human evaluators review, validate, or override AI-generated outputs, particularly in high-stakes finance, legal services, or healthcare applications. Drori and Te'eni (2024) find that HITL frameworks are essential for maintaining user trust and enabling organizations to manage ambiguous or context-sensitive scenarios that LLMs may not reliably resolve. Their findings emphasize that by embedding human checkpoints into AI workflows, organizations can mitigate the risks of over-reliance on automated systems while improving quality control. Integrating HITL processes into LLM deployments enhances system robustness and fosters greater confidence among end-users and regulatory bodies.

Legal Compliance and Documentation: Model Cards, Datasheets, Audit Logs

Legal compliance in deploying LLMs requires systematic documentation that enhances transparency, traceability, and accountability. Tools such as model cards, datasheets, and audit logs are increasingly used to record machine learning models' development, intended use, and limitations. Gebru et al. (2021) advocate adopting datasheets for datasets and model cards as standard documentation practices to support ethical AI development and ensure regulatory alignment. These tools help internal teams and external auditors evaluate the model's purpose, data sources, performance metrics, and risks. By incorporating structured documentation into the deployment pipeline, organizations can demonstrate compliance with privacy and accountability regulations such as GDPR and build trust with stakeholders.

Risk Management and Accountability Frameworks

The integration of LLMs into business operations must be guided by risk management frameworks that assess potential ethical, legal, and operational vulnerabilities. Effective governance requires identifying areas of exposure, including bias, misinformation, and misuse, and implementing mitigation strategies accordingly. Hohma et al. (2023) emphasize that risk governance is essential for sustaining AI accountability, particularly in dynamic organizational contexts where oversight must evolve with system updates and scaling. Their research suggests that structured risk assessments and ongoing monitoring are necessary for balancing innovation with safeguards. For enterprises, this means adopting an end-to-end accountability framework that supports continuous evaluation and aligns LLM use with evolving legal standards and societal expectations.

Enterprise LLM Deployment Lifecycle (ELDL): Strategic Overview

Table 1. Strategic Overview of the Enterprise LLM Deployment Lifecycle (ELDL)

ELDL Phase	Key Strategies	Benefits	Challenges	Example KPIs
1. Strategic Planning	Use case alignment, AI-readiness assessment, value chain mapping, stakeholder analysis	Clear goals, cross-functional buy-in, and efficient resource allocation	Organizational resistance, misaligned goals	% of prioritized LLM use cases aligned with business goals, % stakeholder participation in readiness reviews
2. System Design	Model selection (open-source vs. API), fine-tuning, RAG, adapter use, integration planning	Tailored AI solutions, better performance, ecosystem compatibility	Integration complexity, resource intensity	Model accuracy (pre/post fine-tuning), % system compatibility achieved
3. Deployment	Hosting strategy (cloud, hybrid, on-prem), latency optimization, failover, feedback loops	Lower latency, improved uptime, scalable delivery	Cost management, downtime risks, and feedback integration	Avg API response time, System uptime%, % User satisfaction improvement
4. Governance	Ethical committees, HITL workflows, audit documentation, compliance mapping	Trust, transparency, and regulatory readiness	Bias, explainability, evolving regulations	# of AI audits completed, Bias reduction rate, Compliance breach incidents

Notes: This table summarizes the key elements of the ELDL framework as proposed in this chapter. Each phase is aligned with strategic actions, anticipated benefits, common implementation challenges, and example performance indicators (KPIs). The KPIs serve as illustrative metrics that organizations can tailor based on industry context, LLM maturity, and regulatory environment. The goal is to provide a structured lens for evaluating LLM deployment across technical, operational, and governance dimensions.

IV. INDUSTRY CASE STUDIES: LLMS IN ACTION

Financial Services

Automating Internal Risk Reporting

Financial institutions are increasingly adopting Large Language Models (LLMs) to automate internal risk reporting processes. This automation aims to enhance efficiency and accuracy in generating comprehensive risk assessments. Chen et al. (2020) propose an ontology-based fraud detection framework capable of identifying misstatement accounts in financial statements. The framework utilizes both financial ratios (numerical data) and logical relationships between accounts (textual/semantic reasoning), offering a highly interpretable and effective method for fraud detection. While not explicitly framed around modern LLMs, the methodology aligns conceptually with the integration of AI-driven models (including LLMs) for enhanced oversight and auditing accuracy. By leveraging LLMs, organizations can streamline risk reporting, allowing for more timely and informed decision-making.

Benefits: Improved Regulatory Compliance and Reduced Analyst Time

Implementing LLMs in financial services offers significant benefits, including enhanced regulatory compliance and reduced time analysts spend on routine tasks. Moharrak and Mogaji (2024) provide empirical insights into the integration of generative AI in banking. Their findings highlight that AI adoption improves regulatory compliance, enhances data privacy management, and boosts operational efficiency, positioning financial institutions to navigate complex regulatory environments while improving service delivery. LLMs can process vast amounts of data quickly, ensuring compliance reports are generated accurately and promptly, allowing analysts to focus on more strategic activities.

Challenges: Accuracy, Hallucination, and Auditability

Despite the advantages, deploying LLMs in financial services presents challenges related to accuracy, hallucination, and auditability. Hallucination, where models generate plausible but incorrect information, risks the reliability of financial reports. Hohma et al. (2023) note that implementing risk governance methods is crucial to address these issues and ensure accountability in AI systems. Establishing robust audit trails and validation mechanisms is essential to mitigate these risks and maintain trust in automated financial reporting.

Retail and E-Commerce

LLM Powered Multilingual Chatbots and Product Advisors

Integrating Large Language Models (LLMs) into retail and e-commerce platforms has revolutionized customer interactions by enabling multilingual chatbots and intelligent product advisors. These AI-driven tools facilitate seamless communication across diverse linguistic backgrounds, enhancing the shopping experience for a global customer base. Meduri (2024), LLM-enhanced chatbots have significantly improved customer engagement by providing context-aware and personalized responses, increasing customer satisfaction and loyalty. By understanding and processing multiple languages, LLMs allow retailers to cater to a broader audience, breaking down language barriers and fostering inclusivity.

Benefits: Reduced Customer Service Costs and Increased Customer Satisfaction

Implementing LLM powered chatbots in e-commerce has led to notable reductions in customer service operational costs while boosting customer satisfaction levels. A comparative analysis by Mangipudi (2025) revealed that AI chatbots efficiently handle routine inquiries, allowing human agents to focus on complex issues, which optimizes resource allocation and reduces response times. This efficiency cuts down on labor costs and enhances the overall customer experience by providing prompt and accurate assistance, leading to higher customer satisfaction scores. The study emphasizes that the strategic deployment of LLMs in customer service roles is cost-effective and does not compromise service quality.

Lessons: Tone Consistency and Fallback Mechanisms

Despite the advantages, deploying LLMs in customer-facing applications presents challenges, particularly concerning maintaining tone consistency and implementing effective fallback mechanisms. Inconsistent tone and style in chatbot responses can lead to customer confusion and diminish trust in the brand. Jeong et al. (2025) introduce the FALL framework, which leverages language models to detect failures in large-scale computing systems. The system is trained only on normal operations and uses minimal lexical changes to flag anomalies, highlighting the importance of proactive and resilient fallback mechanisms in AI-based infrastructures to maintain operational continuity . Incorporating these design considerations is crucial for sustaining customer trust and ensuring the reliability of AI-driven customer service tools.

Professional Services

Knowledge Retrieval Assistant for Consultants

In professional services, consultants often require rapid access to vast organizational knowledge repositories to inform decision-making and client engagements. Large Language Models (LLMs) have emerged as powerful tools in this context, serving as knowledge retrieval assistants that can efficiently parse and summarize complex information. Handler et al. (2024) in the International Journal of Information

Management discuss how large language models (LLMs) enhance organizational decision-making by streamlining evidence collection and reducing cognitive effort. The paper emphasizes that LLMs help automate early-stage tasks such as summarizing data, retrieving relevant information, and brainstorming options—processes critical in consulting firms for proposal development and strategic planning. This efficiency enhances productivity and allows consultants to deliver more timely and informed recommendations to clients.

Benefits: Accelerated Proposal Development and Knowledge Reuse

Integrating LLMs facilitates the reuse of existing knowledge assets, enabling consultants to build upon prior work and avoid redundant efforts. Handler et al. (2024) examine how large language models (LLMs) are reshaping organizational decision-making processes. They discuss the role of LLMs in enhancing the efficiency and consistency of decision support tasks, such as drafting documents, reusing prior content (e.g., proposals, reports), and streamlining workflows, leading to higher quality and more uniform outputs across an organization. This practice streamlines the proposal development process and ensures that best practices and institutional knowledge are effectively leveraged across projects. Consequently, clients benefit from solutions that are both innovative and grounded in proven methodologies.

Issues: Proprietary Data Security and Continual Updates

Despite the advantages, deploying LLMs in professional services raises concerns regarding the security of proprietary data and the need for continual updates to maintain relevance. Haghsefat et al. (2024) present a privacy risk analysis framework (PrFAHP-GT) that evaluates the risks of exposing sensitive personal information (SPI) in digital systems. Their findings stress the importance of structured strategies and decision-making tools to minimize data privacy violations, particularly in environments that handle client-sensitive data

. Moreover, the dynamic nature of business environments necessitates regular updates to the LLMs to ensure that the information they provide remains current and accurate. Failure to address these issues can compromise client trust and the consulting services' overall effectiveness.

V. ETHICAL, LEGAL, AND SECURITY CONSIDERATIONS

A. Common Ethical Challenges

Hallucination and Factual Inaccuracy

Large Language Models (LLMs) are prone to generating content that appears plausible but is factually incorrect, a phenomenon known as "hallucination." This issue undermines the reliability of AI-generated information, particularly in critical domains such as healthcare and law. Zhui et al. (2024) discuss the ethical risks of using large language models in medical education, particularly hallucinations and misinformation. The authors advocate for robust quality control and supervisory frameworks to ensure accurate AI outputs, transparency, and fairness in educational contexts. Addressing hallucinations is essential to maintain trust in AI systems and prevent the dissemination of misinformation.

Bias Amplification: Gender, Racial, and Socioeconomic Bias

LLMs can inadvertently perpetuate and amplify existing societal biases in their training data, leading to discriminatory outcomes. A comprehensive study by An et al. (2024) found that GPT-based models exhibited gender and racial biases when evaluating job candidates, awarding higher scores to female candidates while assigning lower scores to Black male candidates with comparable qualifications. These biases can significantly affect high-stakes decision-making processes, such as hiring and lending. Implementing strategies to detect and mitigate such biases is crucial to ensure fairness and equity in AI applications.

Transparency and Explainability

The opaque nature of LLMs poses challenges in understanding how these models arrive at specific decisions, raising concerns about accountability and trust. Kovari (2025) provides a detailed review of XAI methodologies in the context of AI chatbots, particularly focusing on ChatGPT. The paper highlights that integrating XAI methods, such as hybrid approaches combining knowledge graphs with LLMs, is essential for improving transparency, interpretability, and user trust in AI systems. Improving transparency not only aids in identifying and correcting errors but also fosters user confidence in AI systems. As LLMs become increasingly integrated into various sectors, ensuring their outputs are explainable is paramount for ethical and responsible deployment.

B. Mitigation Strategies

Bias Auditing Tools and Fairness Benchmarks

One of the foundational steps in addressing ethical risks associated with Large Language Models (LLMs) is implementing bias auditing tools and fairness benchmarks. LLMs are trained on vast and diverse corpora, so they are susceptible to replicating societal biases embedded in the data. Gallegos et al. (2024), in their survey of bias in LLMs, emphasize the role of structured benchmarking, such as the StereoSet and WinoBias datasets, in diagnosing gender, racial, and ideological biases across different model architectures. Their findings highlight that systematic audits are essential for identifying biased tendencies before LLMs are integrated into production environments. This proactive auditing enables organizations to maintain accountability and foster ethical deployment practices in customer-facing or decision-making systems.

Retrieval Augmented Generation (RAG) and Grounding Techniques

Retrieval Augmented Generation (RAG) has emerged as a key strategy to combat hallucinations and enhance factual grounding in LLM outputs. Unlike traditional generation models, RAG architectures supplement LLM responses with real-time retrieval from trusted sources, ensuring that outputs are contextually accurate and verifiable. Gallegos et al. (2024) note that grounding techniques reduce factual inaccuracies and contribute to model transparency by offering users precise citations for AI-generated statements. By integrating curated knowledge bases or internal enterprise repositories into LLM workflows, organizations can anchor their models to reliable information, improving accuracy and trust. Grounded outputs are particularly vital in domains such as finance, healthcare, and law, where precision is non-negotiable.

Human Validation for Sensitive Domains

Human validation remains indispensable in high-stakes domains where the consequences of AI-generated errors can be severe. Although LLMs offer considerable automation potential, human-in-the-loop (HITL) oversight provides an additional layer of assurance, especially for legal, clinical, or policy-related content. Gallegos et al. (2024) emphasize the complementarity of human reviewers in interpreting ambiguous outputs and catching subtle biases or omissions that algorithms might overlook. This collaborative model reinforces ethical guardrails and allows institutions to retain human judgment at the center of critical decisions. Incorporating subject-matter experts into LLM pipelines ensures that generative AI is an augmentative rather than an autonomous decision-making tool.

Data Protection: Anonymization, Differential Privacy, and Federated Learning

Protecting sensitive data during training and inference is a paramount concern in LLM deployment, especially when dealing with proprietary or personally identifiable information. Emerging privacy-preserving methods, including data anonymization, differential privacy, and federated learning, offer adequate safeguards for user data while enabling model optimization. Djebrouni et al. (2023) demonstrate how federated learning frameworks can mitigate biases and preserve user privacy by decentralizing raw data while allowing collaborative model training. This method significantly reduces data exposure risks and aligns with global privacy mandates such as GDPR. Integrating these technologies into enterprise AI systems supports secure, ethical innovation while minimizing legal liability.

C. Legal and Regulatory Compliance

Navigating GDPR and the EU AI Act

Deploying Large Language Models (LLMs) within the European Union necessitates strict adherence to the General Data Protection Regulation (GDPR) and the forthcoming EU AI Act. These regulations impose rigorous requirements on data processing activities, including handling personal data and implementing transparency measures. Chen et al. (2025) in Tsinghua Science and Technology propose a GDPR compliance framework using large language models (LLMs) for privacy policy auditing. The study underscores the importance of aligning LLM usage with GDPR principles like data minimization and purpose limitation, and introduces an LLM-based reasoning framework to assess regulatory adherence. While focused on healthcare services, the findings are applicable to broader AI governance contexts. This dual regulatory landscape compels businesses to adopt comprehensive compliance strategies that address current and emerging legal obligations.

Implementing Risk Classification and Documentation Practices

Effective risk management is central to regulatory compliance in the context of LLMs. The EU AI Act mandates that AI systems be categorized based on their potential risk, with high-risk systems subject to stringent documentation and oversight requirements. Werder et al. (2022) emphasize how data provenance—detailed records describing the origin and processing of data—plays a critical role in ensuring transparency, accountability, fairness, and explainability in AI systems. They argue that documenting the entire AI data pipeline is essential for regulatory compliance and responsible deployment. By institutionalizing robust documentation practices, organizations can comply with legal mandates and enhance the transparency and trustworthiness of their AI systems.

Managing Cross-Border Data Transfers

The global nature of data flows presents significant challenges for organizations deploying LLMs, particularly concerning cross-border data transfers. Compliance with international data protection standards, such as GDPR's restrictions on data transfers to third countries, requires careful navigation. Bradford et al. (2021) argue that SCCs remain valid and essential tools for enabling lawful cross-border data transfers, particularly after the Schrems II decision by the Court of Justice of the European Union. The authors emphasize that SCCs serve as multilayered safeguards encompassing legal, technical, and organizational protections when national data protection laws are inadequate. These measures are critical in mitigating legal risks and maintaining the integrity of data processing activities across jurisdictions.

Institutionalizing Compliance Through LLM Usage Policies

Organizations must embed legal and ethical considerations into their operational frameworks to sustain long-term compliance by developing comprehensive LLM usage policies. Such policies should delineate acceptable use cases, data handling procedures, and accountability structures. Haelterman (2020) emphasizes the growing complexity of compliance in organizations and advocates for a holistic, integrated approach that includes cross-functional coordination and systematic audit practices. The study supports mechanisms that proactively align organizational policies with changing legal standards, promoting resilience and regulatory adaptability. Institutionalizing these practices ensures compliance is not a one-time effort but an ongoing organizational commitment (Zhui et al., 2024).

VI. DEPLOYMENT MODELS: OPTIONS AND TRADE-OFFS

API-Based Services (OpenAI, Anthropic)

API-based services, such as those offered by OpenAI and Anthropic, provide organizations with immediate access to powerful LLMs without extensive infrastructure. These services offer scalability and ease of integration, allowing businesses to leverage advanced language models for various applications. However, reliance on third-party APIs can raise concerns regarding data privacy and compliance, especially in regulated industries. Meshkin et al. (2024) explore the deployment of large language models within regulatory agencies. The study emphasizes the benefits of locally hosted open-source LLMs for enhanced data control and privacy, contrasting them with API-based models that require external data transmission. The authors highlight that while APIs offer accessibility and ease of use, they raise concerns about data exposure risks, making internal deployment a more secure option for sensitive tasks.

Open Source LLMs (Mistral, LLaMA, Falcon)

Open-source LLMs, including models like Mistral, LLaMA, and Falcon, offer organizations the flexibility to customize and deploy models tailored to their needs. These models can be fine-tuned and optimized for particular tasks, providing greater performance and data management control. Holgersson et al. (2024) emphasize how open-source AI tools support rapid innovation through democratized access and iterative development. They also highlight that such tools promote transparency in model design and usage, and offer adaptability for specific business needs due to customizable architectures. However, deploying open-source models requires significant technical expertise and resources to manage effectively.

On-Premise/Self-Hosted Models

Deploying LLMs on-premise or through self-hosted solutions grants organizations complete control over their AI infrastructure and data. This approach particularly benefits industries with stringent data security and compliance requirements. Leiner et al. (2021) describe the design of a vendor-neutral AI deployment infrastructure for clinical environments. The study highlights that while on-premise solutions offer significant benefits in terms of custom integration and control, they come with challenges such as substantial hardware requirements, the need for specialized IT expertise, and ongoing maintenance burdens, especially as multiple AI models must be managed simultaneously. Organizations must weigh the benefits of control and security against the costs and complexities of managing self-hosted environments.

Efficiency Strategies: LoRA, Quantization, Distillation

Various efficiency strategies have been developed to optimize LLMs' performance and resource utilization. Low-Rank Adaptation (LoRA) enables parameter-efficient fine-tuning by adjusting a subset of model weights, reducing computational demands. Quantization techniques compress models by reducing the precision of weights, leading to faster inference and lower memory usage. Distillation involves training smaller models to replicate the behavior of larger ones, achieving similar performance with reduced complexity. Zheng et al. (2023) provide a comprehensive review of strategies to enhance the deployability of large language models (LLMs) on resource-constrained and heterogeneous edge hardware. They highlight techniques such as model quantization, pruning, distillation, and efficient runtime inference methods as essential for deploying LLMs across diverse devices.

VII. FUTURE TRENDS AND INNOVATIONS

A. Multimodal LLMs

Integrating Text, Vision, Audio, and Video

Multimodal Large Language Models (MLLMs) represent a transformative advancement in artificial intelligence by integrating diverse data modalities—text, images, audio, and video—into a unified computational framework. This integration enables MLLMs to process and generate content across multiple formats, closely emulating human-like understanding and communication. Recent research highlights that MLLMs in the healthcare domain can simultaneously process unstructured clinical notes, radiological images, and patient history data to support informed decision-making (AlSaad et al., 2024). The convergence of these modalities allows for richer contextual understanding, which enhances the model's ability to perform complex tasks that require cross-modal reasoning and situational awareness.

Applications in AI Assistants

Integrating multimodal capabilities has significantly expanded the scope and sophistication of AI assistants. These assistants can provide more comprehensive and situationally aware responses by simultaneously processing textual, auditory, and visual inputs. A recent study on a generative AI assistant for pathology demonstrates how multimodal AI can support medical experts in interpreting histopathological images and providing diagnostic input, with performance exceeding that of earlier unimodal models (Lu et al., 2024). This shift toward more immersive and human-like AI interfaces reflects a fundamental change in how users interact with machines, particularly in high-stakes or complex settings like healthcare.

Enhancing Product Design Processes

In manufacturing and engineering design, MLLMs drive innovation by facilitating the integration of visual prototypes and descriptive specifications. This allows for more accurate translation of design concepts into executable models. A recent study in the Machines outlined a product-customization framework that uses multimodal data, such as user preferences, technical sketches, and real-time feedback, to improve efficiency under the social manufacturing paradigm (Li et al., 2023). Such advancements contribute to streamlined workflows, reduced time-to-market, and enhanced alignment between user intent and final product outcomes.

Improving Accessibility

Multimodal models are also making meaningful contributions to accessibility, particularly for individuals with disabilities. By synthesizing data from various inputs, MLLMs can provide adaptive interfaces that meet the needs of diverse user populations. Research on accessibility modeling using multimodal approaches has shown that such systems significantly enhance access to essential services for people with visual or mobility impairments by integrating data from transport, service locations, and user behavior (Patterson et al., 2024). These findings suggest that MLLMs can be critical in designing inclusive technologies beyond conventional assistive tools.

B. Agent-Based LLM Systems

Autonomous Orchestration of Complex Tasks

Large Language Models (LLMs) have evolved beyond passive tools to become autonomous agents capable of orchestrating complex tasks without human intervention. These agentic systems can dynamically plan, execute, and adapt workflows, leveraging their understanding of context and objectives. The ProcessCarbonAgent framework demonstrates how LLM powered agents can enhance decision-making in carbon management by autonomously analyzing data and generating actionable insights (Zhang et al., 2025). This shift towards autonomy enables businesses to delegate intricate processes to AI, improving efficiency and scalability.

API Planning and Workflow Execution

Integrating LLMs with Application Programming Interfaces (APIs) allows for seamless planning and execution of complex workflows. By interpreting natural language inputs, LLMs can determine the appropriate sequence of API calls to fulfill specific tasks. Huang et al. (2024) in ACM Transactions on Software Engineering and Methodology introduce a novel LLM-based AI chain for unsupervised API relation inference. Their method leverages LLMs like GPT-3.5 to infer and organize API usage sequences accurately. This enables automated understanding of how API calls relate and should be ordered, significantly improving automation in software engineering tasks. This capability is crucial for businesses that streamline operations and reduce manual intervention in routine processes.

Autonomous Research Agents

LLM-driven agents are increasingly being utilized in scientific research, autonomously designing and conducting experiments. These agents can generate hypotheses, plan methodologies, and analyze results without direct human oversight. The Coscientist system employs GPT-4 to autonomously perform chemical experiments, demonstrating the potential of LLMs in accelerating scientific discovery (Boiko et al., 2023). Such advancements could revolutionize research and development across various industries by expediting the innovation cycle.

C. Executive Decision Support

Dynamic Dashboards and Scenario Planning with Natural Language

Large Language Models (LLMs) are transforming executive decision-making by enabling dynamic dashboards and scenario planning through natural language interfaces. These models allow executives to interact with complex data systems using conversational language, facilitating real-time insights and strategic foresight. Sadeghi et al. (2024) demonstrated that explainable AI enhances agile decision-making in supply chain management, contributing to improved cyber resilience. This capability enhances the agility and responsiveness of business leaders in rapidly changing environments.

Summarization of Financial, Legal, or Compliance Documents

LLMs are also crucial in summarizing extensive financial, legal, and compliance documents, making critical information more accessible to executives. By processing and condensing complex texts, these models assist in identifying key obligations, risks, and insights. Kappel (2024) examined the risks associated with AI-based decision-making systems in executive-level decision-making, highlighting the importance of transparency and ethical considerations. This functionality streamlines the review process, allowing executives to make informed decisions without delving into voluminous documents.

D. Human-AI Collaboration

Designing Augmentation Tools Instead of Replacements

The integration of Large Language Models (LLMs) into business operations is increasingly focused on augmenting human capabilities rather than replacing them. This collaborative approach emphasizes the development of tools that enhance human decision-making and creativity. Reciprocal human-machine learning frameworks have been proposed to facilitate continuous learning between humans and AI systems, allowing both to adapt and improve over time (Chen & Chan, 2024). Such frameworks underscore the importance of designing AI systems that work in tandem with human users, enhancing their abilities rather than rendering them obsolete.

Skills Augmentation in Marketing

In the marketing domain, LLMs are being utilized to augment human creativity and efficiency. These models assist marketers in generating content, analyzing consumer data, and personalizing customer interactions. Grewal et al. (2024) discuss how generative AI tools are reshaping marketing strategies by enabling more dynamic and responsive content creation processes. This collaboration between human marketers and AI tools leads to more effective campaigns and improved customer engagement.

Skills Augmentation in Legal and Data Analysis

LLMs are also proving valuable in legal and data analysis contexts by handling routine tasks and allowing professionals to focus on more complex issues. In the legal field, AI tools are being used to streamline research and document review processes, thereby increasing efficiency and accuracy (Kappel, 2024). Similarly, in data analysis, LLMs assist in processing large datasets and extracting meaningful insights, which supports better-informed decision-making. These applications demonstrate the potential of human-AI collaboration to enhance professional capabilities across various sectors.

VIII. STRATEGIC RECOMMENDATIONS

Start Small, Iterate Fast: Pilot Programs Before Enterprise Scale

Implementing Large Language Models (LLMs) in business operations should begin with small-scale pilot programs to assess feasibility and impact. This approach allows organizations to identify potential challenges and adjust before full-scale deployment. Sadeghi et al. (2024) emphasize the importance of agile decision-making in supply chain management, highlighting how pilot programs can enhance cyber resilience by allowing for iterative improvements. By starting small, businesses can mitigate risks and optimize LLM integration strategies.

Prioritize Alignment Between AI Outcomes and Business Values

Ensuring that AI systems align with organizational values is crucial for ethical and effective deployment. Misalignment can lead to unintended consequences, including biased decision-making and reputational damage. Sarkar (2025) discusses methodologies for evaluating alignment in LLMs, underscoring the need for continuous assessment to maintain congruence with human values. Prioritizing alignment fosters trust and ensures that AI initiatives support overarching business objectives.

Establish Robust Human-in-the-Loop Governance

Human oversight in AI systems is essential to ensure accountability and ethical decision-making. Human-in-the-loop (HITL) frameworks allow for human intervention in AI processes, reducing the risk of errors and enhancing system reliability. Griffen and Owens (2024) advocate for participatory governance models in AI, particularly in healthcare, to ensure that human judgment remains central in critical decisions. Establishing robust HITL governance structures is vital for responsible AI integration.

Train Workforce in AI Literacy and Ethical Awareness

Equipping employees with AI literacy and ethical awareness is fundamental for successful AI adoption. Training programs should focus on understanding AI technologies and their moral implications. Chee et al. (2024) propose a competency framework for AI literacy across educational and workforce levels. The study emphasizes that learners, ranging from K–12 students to working professionals, need tailored AI literacy training, including data interpretation, ethical integration, and critical use of AI tools to thrive in increasingly AI-driven environments. Investing in workforce education ensures employees can effectively collaborate with AI systems and uphold ethical standards.

Continuously Monitor Model Performance and Risk

Ongoing monitoring of AI systems is necessary to detect and mitigate potential risks associated with their operation. Regular evaluations help identify performance issues and ensure compliance with ethical guidelines. Sadeghi et al. (2024) also underscore the significance of continuous assessment in maintaining the agility and resilience of AI systems in dynamic environments. By implementing robust monitoring mechanisms, organizations can proactively address challenges and sustain the effectiveness of AI applications.

IX. CONCLUSION

Reframing LLMs as Catalysts for Innovation and Knowledge Augmentation

Large Language Models (LLMs) have emerged as transformative tools, not merely automating tasks but significantly enhancing human creativity and knowledge processes. Their integration into business operations has redefined traditional workflows, enabling more dynamic and informed decision-making. For instance, LLMs have revolutionized knowledge management paradigms, shifting from static repositories to interactive, AI-driven systems that facilitate real-time information retrieval and synthesis (Kaczorowska-Spychalska et al., 2024). This evolution underscores the role of LLMs as catalysts for innovation, augmenting human capabilities rather than replacing them.

Balancing Opportunity and Responsibility

While the potential of LLMs is vast, their deployment necessitates a careful balance between seizing opportunities and upholding ethical responsibilities. Integrating LLMs into various sectors raises concerns about data privacy, algorithmic bias, and accountability. Zhui et al. (2024) provide a detailed ethical analysis of large language models in medical education. The authors advocate for a unified ethical framework built around eight core principles, including transparency, fairness, and accountability, to ensure safe, equitable, and trustworthy AI integration.

By proactively addressing these ethical considerations, organizations can harness the benefits of LLMs while mitigating potential risks.

Final Thoughts on Scaling Responsibly and Ethically

As organizations consider scaling LLM deployments, adopting strategies prioritizing ethical considerations and responsible innovation is imperative. This includes implementing robust governance structures, continuous monitoring of AI systems, and fostering a culture of ethical awareness among stakeholders. Machucho and Ortiz (2025) highlight the necessity of aligning AI initiatives with organizational values and societal expectations, ensuring that the scaling of LLMs contributes positively to both business objectives and the broader community. Through deliberate and ethical scaling practices, businesses can fully realize the transformative potential of LLMs.

REFERENCES

AlSaad, R., Abd-alrazaq, A., Boughorbel, S., Ahmed, A., Renault, M.-A., Damseh, R., & Sheikh, J. (2024). Multimodal Large Language Models in Health Care: Applications, Challenges, and Future Outlook. *Journal of Medical Internet Research, 26*, e59505. DOI: 10.2196/59505

An, J., Huang, D., Lin, C., & Tai, M. (2024). Measuring gender and racial biases in large language models: Intersectional evidence from automated resume evaluation. *PNAS Nexus, 4*(3), pgaf089. Advance online publication. DOI: 10.1093/pnasnexus/pgaf089

Boiko, D. A., MacKnight, R., Kline, B., & Gomes, G. (2023). Autonomous chemical research with large language models. *Nature, 624*(7992), 570–578. DOI: 10.1038/s41586-023-06792-0

Bradford, L., Aboy, M., & Liddell, K. (2021). Standard contractual clauses for cross-border transfers of health data after Schrems II. *Journal of Law and the Biosciences, 8*, lsab007. Advance online publication. DOI: 10.1093/jlb/lsab007

Chee, H., Ahn, S., & Lee, J. (2024). A competency framework for AI literacy: Variations by different learner groups and an implied learning pathway. *British Journal of Educational Technology*. Advance online publication. DOI: 10.1111/bjet.13556

Chen, J., Wang, F., Pang, S., Chen, M., Xi, M., Zhao, T., & Yin, J. (2025). A privacy policy text compliance reasoning framework with large language models for healthcare services. *Tsinghua Science and Technology*. Advance online publication. DOI: 10.26599/tst.2024.9010089

Chen, L.-M., Xiu, B., & Ding, Z. (2020). *Finding misstatement accounts in financial statements through ontology reasoning*. IEEE., DOI: 10.1109/ACCESS.2020.3014620

Chen, Z., & Chan, J. (2024). Large Language Model in Creative Work: The Role of Collaboration Modality and User Expertise. *Management Science, 70*(12), 9101–9117. DOI: 10.1287/mnsc.2023.03014

Choi, S., & Bae, S. (2009). Strategic information systems selection with incomplete preferences: A case of a Korean electronics company. *The Journal of the Operational Research Society, 60*(2), 180–190. DOI: 10.1057/palgrave.jors.2602537

Djebrouni, Y., Benarba, N., Touat, O., De Rosa, P., Bouchenak, S., Bonifati, A., Felber, P., Marangozova, V., & Schiavoni, V. (2023). Bias Mitigation in Federated Learning for Edge Computing. *Proceedings of the ACM on Interactive, Mobile, Wearable and Ubiquitous Technologies, 7*(4), 1–35. DOI: 10.1145/3631455

Drori, I., & Te'eni, D. (2024). Human-in-the-loop AI reviewing: Feasibility, opportunities, and risks. *Journal of the Association for Information Systems*, *25*(1), 98–109. DOI: 10.17705/1jais.00867

Ferraris, A. F., Audrito, D., Di Caro, L., & Poncibò, C. (2025). The architecture of language: Understanding the mechanics behind LLMs. *Cambridge Forum on AI: Law and Governance*. DOI: 10.1017/cfl.2024.16

Gallegos, I. O., Rossi, R. A., Barrow, J., Tanjim, M. M., Kim, S., Dernoncourt, F., Yu, T., Zhang, R., & Ahmed, N. K. (2024). Bias and Fairness in Large Language Models: A Survey. *Computational Linguistics*, *50*(3), 1097–1179. DOI: 10.1162/coli_a_00524

Gebru, T., Morgenstern, J., Vecchione, B., Vaughan, J. W., Wallach, H., Daumé, H., & Crawford, K. (2021). Datasheets for datasets. *Communications of the ACM*, *64*(12), 86–92. DOI: 10.1145/3458723

Grewal, D., Satornino, C. B., Davenport, T. H., & Guha, A. (2024). How generative AI is shaping the future of marketing. *Journal of the Academy of Marketing Science*. Advance online publication. DOI: 10.1007/s11747-024-01064-3

Griffen, Z., & Owens, K. (2024). From "Human in the Loop" to a Participatory System of Governance for AI in Healthcare. *The American Journal of Bioethics*, *24*(9), 81–83. DOI: 10.1080/15265161.2024.2377114

Haelterman, H. (2020). Breaking silos of legal and regulatory risks to outperform traditional compliance approaches. *European Journal on Criminal Policy and Research*, *28*(1), 19–36. DOI: 10.1007/s10610-020-09468-x

Haghsefat, S., Taleby Ahvanooey, M., Song, H., Liu, C. Z., & Choo, K.-K. R. (2024). PrFAHP-GT: A new privacy risk analysis framework using FAHP and game theory for digital supply chain management. *IEEE Transactions on Engineering Management*, *71*(4), 11718–11733. DOI: 10.1109/TEM.2024.3428840

Handler, A., Larsen, K. R., & Hackathorn, R. (2024). Large language models present new questions for decision support. *International Journal of Information Management*, *79*, 102811. DOI: 10.1016/j.ijinfomgt.2024.102811

Hohma, E., Boch, A., Trauth, R., & Lütge, C. (2023). Investigating accountability for Artificial Intelligence through risk governance: A workshop-based exploratory study. *Frontiers in Psychology*, *14*. Advance online publication. DOI: 10.3389/fpsyg.2023.1073686

Holgersson, M., Dahlander, L., Chesbrough, H., & Bogers, M. L. A. M. (2024). Open Innovation in the Age of AI. *California Management Review*, *67*(1), 5–20. DOI: 10.1177/00081256241279326

Holmström, J. (2022). From AI to digital transformation: The AI readiness framework. *Business Horizons*, *65*(3), 329–339. DOI: 10.1016/j.bushor.2021.03.006

Huang, Q., Sun, Y., Xing, Z., Cao, Y., Chen, J., Xu, X., Jin, H., & Lu, J. (2024). Let's Discover More API Relations: A Large Language Model-Based AI Chain for Unsupervised API Relation Inference. *ACM Transactions on Software Engineering and Methodology*, *33*(8), 1–34. DOI: 10.1145/3680469

Idris, M. D., Feng, X., & Dyo, V. (2024). Revolutionizing higher education: Unleashing the potential of large language models for strategic transformation. *IEEE Access : Practical Innovations, Open Solutions*, *12*, 67738–67757. DOI: 10.1109/ACCESS.2024.3400164

Iyamu, T., & Shaanika, I. (2023). The factors of enterprise business architecture readiness in organisations. *Lecture Notes in Business Information Processing*, ●●●, 379–390. DOI: 10.1007/978-3-031-39386-0_18

Jeong, J., Baek, I., Bang, B., Lee, J., Song, U., & Kim, S. B. (2025). FALL: Prior failure detection in large scale system based on language model. *IEEE Transactions on Dependable and Secure Computing*, *22*, 279–291. DOI: 10.1109/tdsc.2024.3396166

Kaczorowska-Spychalska, D., Kotula, N., Mazurek, G., & Sułkowski, Ł. (2024). Generative AI as source of change of knowledge management paradigm. *Human Technology*, *20*(1), 131–154. DOI: 10.14254/1795-6889.2024.20-1.7

Kappel, G. (2024). Risks of artificial intelligence-based decision support and decision-making systems in executive-level decision-making in companies: A literature review. *Pécs Journal of International and European Law*, *2024*(2), 3–15. DOI: 10.15170/PJIEL.2024.2.3

Kochkina, N., Andriushchenko, I., & Gatto, G. (2024). Strategic AI adoption: Economic impact, case studies from Handy.ai, and industry readiness. In *2024 IEEE International Conference on Artificial Intelligence & Green Energy (ICAIGE)* (pp. 1–6). DOI: 10.1109/ICAIGE62696.2024.10776631

Kovari, A. (2025). Explainable AI chatbots towards XAI ChatGPT: A review. *Heliyon*, *11*, e42077. DOI: 10.1016/j.heliyon.2025.e42077

Lee, J., Ahn, S., Kim, D., & Kim, D. (2024). Performance comparison of retrieval-augmented generation and fine-tuned large language models for construction safety management knowledge retrieval. *Automation in Construction, 169*, 105846. DOI: 10.1016/j.autcon.2024.105846

Leiner, T., Bennink, E., Mol, C. P., Kuijf, H., & Veldhuis, W. (2021). Bringing AI to the clinic: Blueprint for a vendor-neutral AI deployment infrastructure. *Insights Into Imaging, 12*, 1–11. DOI: 10.1186/s13244-020-00931-1

Li, Y., Wu, H., Tamir, T. S., Shen, Z., Liu, S., Hu, B., & Xiong, G. (2023). An efficient product-customization framework based on multimodal data under the social manufacturing paradigm. *Machines (Basel), 11*(2), 170. DOI: 10.3390/machines11020170

Lu, M. Y., Chen, B., Williamson, D. F. K., Chen, R. J., Zhao, M., Chow, A. K., Ikemura, K., Kim, A., Pouli, D., Patel, A., Soliman, A., Chen, C., Ding, T., Wang, J. J., Gerber, G., Liang, I., Le, L. P., Parwani, A. V., Weishaupt, L. L., & Mahmood, F. (2024). A multimodal generative AI copilot for human pathology. *Nature, 634*(8033), 466–473. DOI: 10.1038/s41586-024-07618-3

Machucho, R., & Ortiz, D. (2025). The impacts of artificial intelligence on business innovation: A comprehensive review of applications, organizational challenges, and ethical considerations. *Systems, 13*(4), 264. DOI: 10.3390/systems13040264

Malhotra, A., Elsayed, A. T. A., Torres, R., & Venkatraman, S. (2023). Evaluate solutions for achieving high availability or near zero downtime for cloud native enterprise applications. *IEEE Access : Practical Innovations, Open Solutions, 11*, 85384–85394. DOI: 10.1109/ACCESS.2023.3303430

Manda, C. (2025). Innovation in AI-driven customer service: Impact of large language models on enterprise solutions. *International Journal of Science and Research Archive*. DOI: 10.30574/ijsra.2025.14.1.0049

Mangipudi, P. (2025). AI-powered chatbots vs human agents, a compatible study on customer satisfaction. *International Journal of Computer Engineering and Technology, 16*(2), 11–36. DOI: 10.34218/ijcet_16_02_002

Meduri, S. (2024). Revolutionizing Customer Service: The Impact of Large Language Models on Chatbot Performance. *International Journal of Scientific Research in Computer Science Engineering and Information Technology, 10*(5), 721–730. DOI: 10.32628/CSEIT241051057

Meshkin, H., Zirkle, J., Arabidarrehdor, G., Chaturbedi, A., Chakravartula, S., Mann, J., Thrasher, B., & Li, Z. (2024). Harnessing large language models' zero-shot and few-shot learning capabilities for regulatory research. *Briefings in Bioinformatics*, *25*(5). Advance online publication. DOI: 10.1093/bib/bbae354

Moharrak, M., & Mogaji, E. (2024). Generative AI in banking: Empirical insights on integration, challenges and opportunities in a regulated industry. *International Journal of Bank Marketing*. Advance online publication. DOI: 10.1108/ijbm-08-2024-0490

Narayanan, G., Kharat, R., & Kathuria, A. (2025). Is software customization an impediment or enabler for digital transformation in the era of large language models. In *Lecture Notes in Computer Science* (pp. 1–14). Springer., DOI: 10.1007/978-3-031-74437-2_1

Narne, H. (2024). Generative artificial intelligence device to analysis the data for SAP based data management. In *2024 International Conference on Intelligent Computing and Emerging Communication Technologies (ICEC)* (pp. 1–6). DOI: 10.1109/ICEC59683.2024.10837215

Patterson, Z., Bensmihen, A., & Hermanson, G. (2024). The Multimodal Accessibility Target (MAT): A new approach to accessibility modeling. *Transportation Research Record: Journal of the Transportation Research Board*, *2678*(1), 770–780. DOI: 10.1177/03611981231172503

Pinheiro, C. R., Guerreiro, S. L. P. D., & Mamede, H. (2024). A lightweight ontology for enterprise architecture mining of API gateway logs. *IEEE Access : Practical Innovations, Open Solutions*, *12*, 128585–128601. DOI: 10.1109/ACCESS.2024.3456119

Sadeghi, K., Ojha, D., Kaur, P., Mahto, R. V., & Dhir, A. (2024). Explainable artificial intelligence and agile decision-making in supply chain cyber resilience. *Decision Support Systems*, *180*, 114194. DOI: 10.1016/j.dss.2024.114194

Sarkar, U. E. (2025). Evaluating alignment in large language models: A review of methodologies. *AI and Ethics*. Advance online publication. DOI: 10.1007/s43681-024-00637-w

Shahjalal, M., Farhana, N., Roy, P., Razzaque, M., Kaur, K., & Hassan, M. M. (2022). A Binary Gray Wolf Optimization algorithm for deployment of Virtual Network Functions in 5G hybrid cloud. *Computer Communications*, *193*, 63–74. DOI: 10.1016/j.comcom.2022.06.041

Tanveer, S. S., & Rana, Z. (2024). Prioritizing software requirements by combining the usage monitoring and user feedback data. *IEEE Access : Practical Innovations, Open Solutions, 12*, 82825–82841. DOI: 10.1109/ACCESS.2024.3409847

Tejani, A. S., Cook, T. S., Hussain, M., Sippel Schmidt, T., & O'Donnell, K. P. (2024). Integrating and adopting AI in the radiology workflow: A primer for standards and Integrating the Healthcare Enterprise (IHE) profiles. *Radiology, 311*(3), e232653. DOI: 10.1148/radiol.232653

Veale, M., & Edwards, L. (2018). Clarity, surprises, and further questions in the Article 29 Working Party draft guidance on automated decision-making and profiling. *Computer Law & Security Review, 34*(2), 398–404. DOI: 10.1016/j.clsr.2017.12.002

Werder, K., Ramesh, B., & Zhang, R. (2022). Establishing data provenance for responsible artificial intelligence systems. *ACM Transactions on Management Information Systems, 13*(1), 1–23. DOI: 10.1145/3503488

Xia, L., & Ma, H. (2024). Enhancing LoRA model serving capacity via adaptive operator scheduling for multi-tenancy on GPU. *IEEE Access : Practical Innovations, Open Solutions, 12*, 160441–160449. DOI: 10.1109/ACCESS.2024.3483250

Zhang, L. J., Chen, H., He, S., Li, C., Chen, J., Zhang, H., & Du, W. (2025). COSIS: An AI-enabled digital transformation framework integrating large language models and key performance indicators. In *Lecture Notes in Computer Science* (pp. 74–99). Springer. DOI: 10.1007/978-3-031-77000-5_6

Zheng, W., Gong, G., Tian, J., Lu, S., Wang, R., Yin, Z., Li, X., & Yin, L. (2023). Design of a modified transformer architecture based on relative position coding. *International Journal of Computational Intelligence Systems, 16*. Advance online publication. DOI: 10.1007/s44196-023-00345-z

Zhui, L., Li, F., Xuehu, W., Fu, Q., & Wei, R. (2024). Ethical considerations and fundamental principles of large language models in medical education: Viewpoint. *Journal of Medical Internet Research, 26*. Advance online publication. DOI: 10.2196/60083

Compilation of References

Abnave, P. (2023, October 12). Language models revolutionizing financial crime prevention. Medium. https://medium.com/@pratikabnave97/language-models-revolutionizing-financial-crime-prevention-4ea92fa82eb2

Abujaber, A. A., & Nashwan, A. J. (2024). Ethical framework for artificial intelligence in healthcare research: A path to integrity. In World Journal of Methodology (Vol. 14, Issue 3). DOI: 10.5662/wjm.v14.i3.94071

Abuzaid, A. N. (2024). AI-Driven Business Processes: Efficiency Gains, Cost Reductions, and Implications for Economic Performance. In *International Conference on Knowledge Engineering and Communication Systems (ICKECS)* (Vol. 1, pp. 1-5). IEEE.

Adeyinka, T. I., & Adeyinka, K. I. (2025). Reducing the carbon footprint in healthcare cybersecurity threats in AI-powered healthcare systems data privacy in AI-driven diagnostics. In *Advances in Computational Intelligence and Robotics* (pp. 283–326). IGI Global.

Adobe. (2024). *Choice in generative AI models & advances in Firefly*. Adobe. https://blog.adobe.com/en/publish/2024/04/15/choice-generative-ai-models-advances-firefly

Adobe. (2024). *Creative collaboration analytics in Adobe Cloud*. Adobe. https://www.adobe.com/content/dam/cct/creativecloud/business/teams/whitepapers/dotcom-116728/Adobe_StateofCreativity_Report_2024_FV_UE.pdf

Agarwal, S. (2024, June 24). Fraud detection stays relevant in the age of LLMs. Medium. https://s-hash-wat.medium.com/how-fraud-detection-stays-relevant-in-the-age-of-llms-f6debe7be518

Agarwal, S., Wood, D., Murray, B. A. K., Wei, Y., Al Busaidi, A., Kafiabadi, S., Guilhem, E., Lynch, J., Townend, M., Mazumder, A., Barker, G. J., Cole, J. H., Sasieni, P., Ourselin, S., Modat, M., & Booth, T. C. (2025). Impact of hospital-specific domain adaptation on BERT-based models to classify neuroradiology reports. *European Radiology*. PMID: 40097844

Agiza, A., Mostagir, M., & Reda, S. (2024). PoliTune: Analyzing the impact of data selection and fine-tuning on economic and political biases in Large Language Models. Proceedings of the AAAI/ACM Conference on AI, Ethics, And, 7, 2–12.

Agrawal, A., Gans, J., & Goldfarb, A. (2018). Prediction, judgment, and complexity: a theory of decision-making and artificial intelligence. In *The economics of artificial intelligence: An agenda* (pp. 89–110). University of Chicago Press.

AlSaad, R., Abd-alrazaq, A., Boughorbel, S., Ahmed, A., Renault, M.-A., Damseh, R., & Sheikh, J. (2024). Multimodal Large Language Models in Health Care: Applications, Challenges, and Future Outlook. *Journal of Medical Internet Research, 26*, e59505. DOI: 10.2196/59505

Amamou, W. (2025, January 15). AI agents in fraud detection: Bridging the gap between traditional machine learning and human reasoning. Medium. https://walidamamou.medium.com/ai-agents-in-fraud-detection-bridging-the-gap-between-traditional-machine-learning-and-human-c901524fef58

An, J., Huang, D., Lin, C., & Tai, M. (2024). Measuring gender and racial biases in large language models: Intersectional evidence from automated resume evaluation. *PNAS Nexus*, *4*(3), pgaf089. Advance online publication. DOI: 10.1093/pnasnexus/pgaf089

Anthropic. (2022). *Constitutional AI: Harmlessness from AI Feedback*. Anthropic. https://www.anthropic.com/research/constitutional-ai-harmlessness-from-ai-feedback

Araujo, T., Helberger, N., Kruikemeier, S., & de Vreese, C. H. (2020). In AI we trust? Perceptions about automated decision-making by artificial intelligence. *AI & Society*, *35*(3), 611. DOI: 10.1007/s00146-019-00931-w

Arntz, M., Gregory, T., & Zierahn, U. (2016). The Risk of Automation for Jobs in OECD Countries.

Arslan, M., & Cruz, C. (2024). Business-RAG: Information extraction for business insights. In *Proceedings of the 21st International Conference on Smart Business Technologies (ICSBT 2024)* (pp. 88–94). Science and Technology Publications, Lda. https://doi.org/10.5220/0012812800003764

Asai, A., Wu, Z., Wang, Y., Sil, A., & Hajishirzi, H. (2023). *Self-RAG: Learning to retrieve, generate, and critique through self-reflection.* arXiv. https://arxiv.org/abs/2310.11511

Attard-Frost, B., Ríos, A. D. los, & Walters, D. R. (2022). The ethics of AI business practices: a review of 47 AI ethics guidelines [Review of The ethics of AI business practices: a review of 47 AI ethics guidelines]. AI and Ethics, 3(2), 389. Springer Nature. DOI: 10.1007/s43681-022-00156-6

Autor, D. H. (2015). Why are there still so many jobs? The history and future of workplace automation. *The Journal of Economic Perspectives*, *29*(3), 3–30.

Avin, S., Belfield, H., Brundage, M., Krueger, G., Wang, J., Weller, A., Anderljung, M., Krawczuk, I., Krueger, D., Lebensold, J., Maharaj, T., & Zilberman, N. (2021). Filling gaps in trustworthy development of AI. *Science*, *374*(6573), 1327. DOI: 10.1126/science.abi7176

Ayyamperumal, S. G., & Ge, L. (2024). Current state of LLM risks and AI guardrails. arXiv. /arXiv.2406.12934DOI: 10.48550

Ba, J. L., Kiros, J. R., & Hinton, G. E. (2016). Layer normalization. *arXiv preprint arXiv:1607.06450.*

Bae, J., Hung, C. Y., & van Lent, L. (2023). Mobilizing Text As Data. *European Accounting Review*, *32*(5), 1085–1106. DOI: 10.1080/09638180.2023.2218423

Baier, L., Schlör, T., Schömer, M., & Kress, N. (2023). Detecting concept drift in medical data streams using shadow models. *IEEE Transactions on Artificial Intelligence*, *4*(5), 1095–1107. DOI: 10.1109/TAI.2022.3225770

Bain & Company. (2023). *Bain & Company announces services alliance with OpenAI to help enterprise clients identify and realize the full potential and maximum value of AI.* https://www.bain.com/about/media-center/press-releases/2023/bain--company-announces-services-alliance-with-openai-to-help-enterprise-clients-identify-and-realize-the-full-potential-and-maximum-value-of-ai/

Bakker, R. M., Schoevers, A. J., van Drie, R. A. N., Schraagen, M. P., & de Boer, M. H. T. (2025). Semantic role extraction in law texts: A comparative analysis of language models for legal information extraction. *Artificial Intelligence and Law*.

Balaskas, G., Papadopoulos, H., Pappa, D., Loisel, Q., & Chastin, S. (2025). A framework for domain-specific dataset creation and adaptation of large language models. *Computers*, *14*(5), 172.

Balayn, A., Yurrita, M., Rancourt, F., Casati, F., & Gadiraju, U. (2025, April). Unpacking Trust Dynamics in the LLM Supply Chain: An Empirical Exploration to Foster Trustworthy LLM Production & Use. In *Proceedings of the 2025 CHI Conference on Human Factors in Computing Systems* (pp. 1-20).

Baldwin, R. (2019). *The globotics upheaval: Globalisation, robotics, and the future of work.* Weidenfeld & Nicolson., DOI: 10.32422/mv.1695

Balona, C. (2024). ActuaryGPT: Applications of large language models to insurance and actuarial work. *British Actuarial Journal, 29*, e15. Advance online publication. DOI: 10.1017/S1357321724000087

Bansal, U., S. Bharatwal, D. S. Bagiyam, and E. R. Kismawadi. 2024. "Fraud Detection in the Era of AI: Harnessing Technology for a Safer Digital Economy." Pp. 143–64 in *AI-Driven Decentralized Finance and the Future of Finance.*

Barman, D., Guo, Z., & Conlan, O. (2024). The Dark Side of Language Models: Exploring the Potential of LLMs in Multimedia Disinformation Generation and Dissemination. *Machine Learning with Applications, 16*, 100545. DOI: 10.1016/j.mlwa.2024.100545

Barton, M.-C., & Pöppelbuß, J. (2022). Prinzipien für die ethische Nutzung künstlicher Intelligenz. *HMD Praxis der Wirtschaftsinformatik, 59*(2), 468. DOI: 10.1365/s40702-022-00850-3

Baryannis, G., Validi, S., Dani, S., & Antoniou, G. (2019). Supply chain risk management and artificial intelligence: State of the art and future research directions. *International Journal of Production Research, 57*(7), 2179–2202.

Bedi, S., Liu, Y., Orr-Ewing, L., Dash, D., Koyejo, S., Callahan, A., & Shah, N. H. (2024). Testing and evaluation of health care applications of large language models: A systematic review. *Journal of the American Medical Association, 332*(18), 1527–1538. DOI: 10.1001/jama.2024.19455 PMID: 38619831

Bellomarini, L., Fakhoury, D., Gottlob, G., & Sallinger, E. (2019, April). Knowledge graphs and enterprise AI: the promise of an enabling technology. In *2019 IEEE 35th international conference on data engineering (ICDE)* (pp. 26-37). IEEE.

Bender, E. M., Gebru, T., McMillan-Major, A., & Shmitchell, S. (2021). On the dangers of stochastic parrots: Can language models be too big? In *Proceedings of the 2021 ACM conference on fairness, accountability, and transparency (FAccT '21)* (pp. 610–623). Association for Computing Machinery. DOI: 10.1145/3442188.3445922

Bi, B., Liu, L., & Perez-Concha, O. (2024). Adapting large language models for automated summarisation of electronic medical records in clinical coding. *Studies in Health Technology and Informatics*, *318*, 24–29. PMID: 39320176

BigScience. (2023). *The BLOOM project: Open-access multilingual language models for research.* Retrieved from https://bigscience.huggingface.co/

Boiko, D. A., MacKnight, R., Kline, B., & Gomes, G. (2023). Autonomous chemical research with large language models. *Nature*, *624*(7992), 570–578. DOI: 10.1038/s41586-023-06792-0

Bommasani, R., Hudson, D. A., Adeli, E., Altman, R., Arora, S., von Arx, S., . . . Liang, P. (2021). *On the opportunities and risks of foundation models* (Report No. CRFM-2021-08). Center for Research on Foundation Models, Stanford Institute for Human-Centered Artificial Intelligence. https://crfm.stanford.edu/assets/report.pdf

Bora, A., & Cuayáhuitl, H. (2024). Systematic analysis of Retrieval-Augmented Generation-based LLMs for medical chatbot applications. *Mach. Learn. Knowl. Extr.*, *6*(4), 2355–2374.

Borenstein, J., & Howard, A. (2020). Emerging challenges in AI and the need for AI ethics education. In AI and Ethics (Vol. 1, Issue 1, p. 61). Springer Nature. DOI: 10.1007/s43681-020-00002-7

Borna, S., Gomez-Cabello, C. A., Pressman, S. M., Haider, S. A., Sehgal, A., Leibovich, B. C., & Forte, A. J. (2024). Comparative analysis of artificial intelligence virtual assistant and large language models in post-operative care. *European Journal of Investigation in Health, Psychology and Education*, *14*(5), 1413–1424. DOI: 10.3390/ejihpe14050094 PMID: 38785591

Bosch Group. (2023). *How Bosch is using AI to shape the future.* Retrieved from https://www.bosch.com/stories/topics/ai-for-a-better-future-at-bosch/

Bottrell, M. M., Simon, A., Geppert, C., Chang, E. T., Asch, S. M., & Rubenstein, L. V. (2020). Facilitating ethical quality improvement initiatives: Design and implementation of an initiative-specific ethics committee. *Health Care*, *8*(2), 100425. DOI: 10.1016/j.hjdsi.2020.100425

Božić, A. (2020). Global trends in a fragile context: Public–nonpublic collaboration, service delivery and social innovation. *Social Enterprise Journal*, *17*(2), 260. DOI: 10.1108/sej-12-2019-0100

Bradford, L., Aboy, M., & Liddell, K. (2021). Standard contractual clauses for cross-border transfers of health data after Schrems II. *Journal of Law and the Biosciences*, *8*, lsab007. Advance online publication. DOI: 10.1093/jlb/lsab007

Bramasol. (2024). *Update on SAP AI initiatives going into 2025*. IgnitePossible. https://ignitepossible.bramasol.com/blog/update-on-sap-ai-initiatives-going-into-2025

Brown, T. B., Mann, B., Ryder, N., Subbiah, M., Kaplan, J., Dhariwal, P., & Amodei, D. (2020). Language models are few-shot learners. *Advances in Neural Information Processing Systems*, *33*, 1877–1901.

Brynjolfsson, E., Li, D., & Raymond, L. R. (2023). *Generative AI at work*. National Bureau of Economic Research Working Paper No. 31161.

Brynjolfsson, E., & McAfee, A. (2014). *The Second Machine Age: Work, Progress, and Prosperity in a Time of Brilliant Technologies*. W. W. Norton & Company.

Brynjolfsson, E., & Mcafee, A. N. D. R. E. W. (2017). The business of artificial intelligence. *Harvard Business Review*, *7*(1), 1–2.

Brynjolfsson, E., Rock, D., & Syverson, C. (2021). The productivity J-curve: How intangibles complement general purpose technologies. *American Economic Journal. Macroeconomics*, *13*(1), 333–372. DOI: 10.1257/mac.20180386

Burr, C., & Leslie, D. (2022). Ethical assurance: A practical approach to the responsible design, development, and deployment of data-driven technologies. *AI and Ethics*, *3*(1), 73. DOI: 10.1007/s43681-022-00178-0

CFODive. (2024, March 5). *Microsoft rolls out Copilot AI tool to finance teams*. https://www.cfodive.com/news/microsoft-rolls-out-copilot-ai-tool-finance-teams/708935/

Chakrabarti, R., & Sanyal, K. (2020). Towards a 'Responsible AI': Can India take the lead? *South Asia Economic Journal*, *21*(1), 158–177.

Chassab, R. H., Zakaria, L. Q., & Tiun, S. (2024). An optimized LSTM-based augmented language model (FLSTM-ALM) using Fox algorithm for automatic essay scoring prediction. *IEEE Access : Practical Innovations, Open Solutions*, *12*, 105080–105093. DOI: 10.1109/ACCESS.2024.3432778

Chee, H., Ahn, S., & Lee, J. (2024). A competency framework for AI literacy: Variations by different learner groups and an implied learning pathway. *British Journal of Educational Technology*. Advance online publication. DOI: 10.1111/bjet.13556

Chen, J., Ye, J., & Wang, G. (2025). *From standalone LLMs to integrated intelligence: A survey of compound AI systems*. arXiv. https://arxiv.org/abs/2506.04565

Chen, W., Hu, H., Chen, X., Verga, P., & Cohen, W. W. (2022). *MuRAG: Multimodal retrieval-augmented generator for open question answering over images and text.* arXiv. https://arxiv.org/abs/2210.02928

Chen, Y., Kong, L., Cheng, N., & Kumar, S. (2023). Accelerating large language model decoding through speculative sampling. *arXiv preprint arXiv:2302.01318*

Chen, C., Wu, B., Wang, L., Chen, C., Tan, J., Wang, L., Zhou, J., & Zhang, B. (2020, October). Nebula. *Proceedings of the 29th ACM International Conference on Information & Knowledge Management.*

Chen, J., Wang, F., Pang, S., Chen, M., Xi, M., Zhao, T., & Yin, J. (2025). A privacy policy text compliance reasoning framework with large language models for healthcare services. *Tsinghua Science and Technology*. Advance online publication. DOI: 10.26599/tst.2024.9010089

Chen, L.-M., Xiu, B., & Ding, Z. (2020). *Finding misstatement accounts in financial statements through ontology reasoning*. IEEE., DOI: 10.1109/ACCESS.2020.3014620

Chen, Z., & Chan, J. (2024). Large Language Model in Creative Work: The Role of Collaboration Modality and User Expertise. *Management Science*, *70*(12), 9101–9117. DOI: 10.1287/mnsc.2023.03014

Cheong, B. C. (2024). Transparency and accountability in AI systems: Safeguarding wellbeing in the age of algorithmic decision-making. *Frontiers in Human Dynamics*, *6*. Advance online publication. DOI: 10.3389/fhumd.2024.1421273

Chesterman, S. (2021). Through a Glass, Darkly: Artificial Intelligence and the Problem of Opacity. *The American Journal of Comparative Law*, *69*(2), 271. DOI: 10.1093/ajcl/avab012

Chirinos, J. (2024, May 20). Case study: JPMorgan Chase's Contract Intelligence (COiN) platform for document analysis. LinkedIn. https://www.linkedin.com/pulse/case-study-jpmorgan-chases-contract-intelligence-coin-jorge-chirinos-qcyje

Choi, S., & Bae, S. (2009). Strategic information systems selection with incomplete preferences: A case of a Korean electronics company. *The Journal of the Operational Research Society*, *60*(2), 180–190. DOI: 10.1057/palgrave.jors.2602537

Chou, W. H., Feng, Z., Li, B., & Liu, F. (2025). A First Look at Financial Data Analysis Using ChatGPT-4o. *Journal of Risk and Financial Management*, *18*(2). Advance online publication. DOI: 10.3390/jrfm18020099

Chowdhery, A., Narang, S., Devlin, J., Gale, O., Song, K., Liu, F., . . . Thoppilan, R. (2022). Palm: Scaling language modeling with pathways. *arXiv preprint arXiv:2204.02311.*

Chu, C., Donato-Woodger, S., Khan, S., Leslie, K., Shi, T., Nyrup, R., & Grenier, A. (2023). Strategies to mitigate machine learning bias affecting older adults: Results from a scoping review. *Innovation in Aging*, *7*(Supplement_1), 717–718.

Chung, A., & Tanaka-Ishii, K. 2023. "Modeling Momentum Spillover with Economic Links Discovered from Financial Documents." *ICAIF 2023 - 4th ACM International Conference on AI in Finance* 490–97. doi: DOI: 10.1145/3604237.3626862

Clario enhances the quality of the clinical trial documentation process with Amazon Bedrock. (2025, February 10). AWS Machine Learning Blog. https://aws.amazon.com/blogs/machine-learning/clario-enhances-the-quality-of-the-clinical-trial-documentation-process-with-amazon-bedrock/

Clarkston Consulting. (2024, March 11). *SAP and generative AI: Advanced business operations with Joule.* https://clarkstonconsulting.com/insights/sap-and-generative-ai/

Clusmann, J., Kolbinger, F. R., Muti, H. S., Carrero, Z. I., Eckardt, J. N., Laleh, N. G., & Kather, J. N. (2023). The future landscape of large language models in medicine. *Communications Medicine*, *3*, 141. Advance online publication. DOI: 10.1038/s43856-023-00370-1 PMID: 37816837

Cockburn, I. M., Henderson, R., & Stern, S. (2018). *The impact of artificial intelligence on innovation* (Vol. 24449). Cambridge, MA, USA: National bureau of economic research.

Coffey, S., Catudal, J., & Bastian, N. D. (2024). Differential privacy to mathematically secure fine-tuned large language models for linguistic steganography. In Harguess, J. D., Bastian, N. D., & Pace, T. L. (Eds.), *Assurance and Security for AI-enabled Systems.* SPIE.

Community, S. A. P. (2023, December 22). *Unlocking the power of generative AI with Intelligent Scenario Lifecycle Management (ISLM) in SAP S/4HANA Cloud.* https://community.sap.com/t5/technology-blog-posts-by-sap/unlocking-the-power-of-generative-ai-with-intelligent-scenariolifecycle/ba-p/14040565

Corporation, I. B. M. (2023). *Introducing watsonx: The future of AI for business.* https://www.ibm.com/new/announcements/introducing-watsonx-the-future-of-ai-for-business

Corrêa, N. K., Galvão, C., Santos, J. W., Pino, C. D., Pinto, E. P., Barbosa, C., Massmann, D., Mambrini, R., Galvão, L., Terem, E., & Oliveira, N. de. (2023). Worldwide AI ethics: A review of 200 guidelines and recommendations for AI governance [Review of Worldwide AI ethics: A review of 200 guidelines and recommendations for AI governance]. Patterns, 4(10), 100857. Elsevier BV. DOI: 10.1016/j.patter.2023.100857

Costa, C. J. (2025). Integrating LLM usage in gamified systems. *WSEAS Transactions on Mathematics, 24*, 258–267.

Dao, T., Fu, D. K., Ermon, S., Rudra, A., & Ré, C. (2022). Flashattention: Fast and memory-efficient exact attention with io-awareness. *Advances in Neural Information Processing Systems, 35*, 16344–16357.

Dash, S. (2025). Green AI: Enhancing Sustainability and Energy Efficiency in AI-Integrated Enterprise Systems. *IEEE Access : Practical Innovations, Open Solutions.*

de Laat, P. B. (2021). Companies Committed to Responsible AI: From Principles towards Implementation and Regulation? *Philosophy & Technology, 34*(4), 1135. DOI: 10.1007/s13347-021-00474-3

Delgadillo, J., Kinyua, J., & Mutigwe, C. (2024). FinSoSent: Advancing Financial Market Sentiment Analysis through Pretrained Large Language Models. *Big Data and Cognitive Computing, 8*(8). Advance online publication. DOI: 10.3390/bdcc8080087

Dellermann, D., Ebel, P., Söllner, M., & Leimeister, J. M. (2019). Hybrid Intelligence. *Business & Information Systems Engineering, 61*(5), 637–643. DOI: 10.1007/s12599-019-00595-2

Deloitte, L. L. P. (2024). *AI change management: Building the future workforce.* https://www.deloitte.com/us/en/what-we-do/capabilities/applied-artificial-intelligence/articles/generative-ai-and-the-future-of-work.html

Desai, R. A. (n.d.). Genetic algorithm with deep learning for fraud Ethereum transaction detection. [Unpublished manuscript].

Dettmers, T., Pagnoni, G., Holtzman, A., & Zettlemoyer, L. (2023). QLoRA: Efficient finetuning of quantized LLMs. *arXiv preprint arXiv:2305.14314*

Deveau, R., Griffin, S. J., & Reis, S. (2023). AI-powered marketing and sales reach new heights with generative AI. https://www.mckinsey.com/capabilities/growth-marketing-and-sales/our-insights/ai-powered-marketing-and-sales-reach-new-heights-with-generative-ai

Devlin, J., Chang, M. W., Lee, K., & Toutanova, K. (2018). Bert: Pre-training of deep bidirectional transformers for language understanding. *arXiv preprint arXiv:1810.04805.*

Devlin., ... (2018) *BERT: Pre-training of Deep Bidirectional Transformers for Language Understanding*. arXiv, 24 May 2019, arXiv:1810.04805v2 [cs.CL]

Díaz-Rodríguez, N., Ser, J. D., Coeckelbergh, M., de Prado, M. L., Herrera-Viedma, E., & Herrera, F. (2023). Connecting the dots in trustworthy Artificial Intelligence: From AI principles, ethics, and key requirements to responsible AI systems and regulation. *Information Fusion*, *99*, 101896. DOI: 10.1016/j.inffus.2023.101896

Dilmegani, C. (2025, January 8). Best 10 large language models in healthcare in 2025. AIMultiple Research. https://research.aimultiple.com/large-language-models-in-healthcare/

Direct Selling Education Foundation. (2025). DSEF 2025 Growth & Outlook Study. https://www.dsa.org/docs/default-source/industry-fact-sheets/dsef-2024-g-o-factsheet.pdf

Djebrouni, Y., Benarba, N., Touat, O., De Rosa, P., Bouchenak, S., Bonifati, A., Felber, P., Marangozova, V., & Schiavoni, V. (2023). Bias Mitigation in Federated Learning for Edge Computing. *Proceedings of the ACM on Interactive, Mobile, Wearable and Ubiquitous Technologies*, *7*(4), 1–35. DOI: 10.1145/3631455

Dombrowski, T., & Seagraves, C. (2025). Optimizing Real Estate Portfolios: The Role of Generative AI in Geographic Diversification. *Journal of Real Estate Portfolio Management*. Advance online publication. DOI: 10.1080/10835547.2025.2513145

Dong, M. M., Stratopoulos, T. C., & Wang, V. X. (2024). A Scoping Review of ChatGPT Research in Accounting and Finance. *International Journal of Accounting Information Systems*, *55*. Advance online publication. DOI: 10.1016/j.accinf.2024.100715

Doumanas, D., Soularidis, A., Spiliotopoulos, D., Vassilakis, C., & Kotis, K. (2025). Fine-tuning large language models for ontology engineering: A comparative analysis of GPT-4 and Mistral. *Applied Sciences (Basel, Switzerland)*, *15*(4), 2146.

Drori, I., & Te'eni, D. (2024). Human-in-the-loop AI reviewing: Feasibility, opportunities, and risks. *Journal of the Association for Information Systems*, *25*(1), 98–109. DOI: 10.17705/1jais.00867

Duolingo Inc. (2023). *Roleplay: AI-powered conversation practice for language learners.* https://blog.duolingo.com/duolingo-max/

E R Kismawadi, Irfan, M., Al Muddatstsir, U. D., & Abdulkarim, F. M. 2023. "Fintech Innovations: Risk Mitigation Strategies in Islamic Finance." Pp. 35–58 in *Fintech Applications in Islamic Finance: AI, Machine Learning, and Blockchain Techniques.*

Eitel-Porter, R. (2020). Beyond the promise: Implementing ethical AI. *AI and Ethics, 1*(1), 73. DOI: 10.1007/s43681-020-00011-6

Elliott, K., Price, R., Shaw, P., Spiliotopoulos, T., Ng, M., Coopamootoo, K., & van Moorsel, A. (2021). Towards an Equitable Digital Society: Artificial Intelligence (AI) and Corporate Digital Responsibility (CDR). *Society, 58*(3), 179. DOI: 10.1007/s12115-021-00594-8

Emelia, C., Genesis, J., & Nickolas, B. (n.d.). *Unifying retrieval and generation: A survey on retrieval-augmented generation in NLP.*

Erdélyi, O. J., & Goldsmith, J. (2022). Regulating artificial intelligence: Proposal for a global solution. *Government Information Quarterly, 39*(4), 101748. DOI: 10.1016/j.giq.2022.101748

Eshraghian, J. K. (2020). Human ownership of artificial creativity. *Nature Machine Intelligence, 2*(3), 157. DOI: 10.1038/s42256-020-0161-x

European Commission. (2024). *AI Act enters into force: The world-first rules for trustworthy artificial intelligence.* https://commission.europa.eu/news-and-media/news/ai-act-enters-force-2024-08-01_en

Fatemi, S., Hu, Y., & Mousavi, M. (2025a). A comparative analysis of instruction fine-tuning large Language Models for financial text classification. *ACM Transactions on Management Information Systems, 16*(1), 1–30.

Fedus, W., Zoph, B., & Shazeer, N. (2021). Switch Transformers: Scaling to Trillion Parameter Models with Simple and Efficient Sparsity. arXiv preprint arXiv:2101.03961.

Felzmann, H., Fosch-Villaronga, E., Lutz, C., & Tamò-Larrieux, A. (2020). Towards Transparency by Design for Artificial Intelligence [Review of Towards Transparency by Design for Artificial Intelligence]. Science and Engineering Ethics, 26(6), 3333. Springer Science+Business Media. DOI: 10.1007/s11948-020-00276-4

Feng, Z., Hu, G., Li, B., & Wang, J. (2025). Unleashing the Power of ChatGPT in Finance Research: Opportunities and Challenges. *Financial Innovation, 11*(1). Advance online publication. DOI: 10.1186/s40854-025-00770-3

Feng, Z., & Wu, Z. (2021). ESG Disclosure, REIT Debt Financing and Firm Value. *The Journal of Real Estate Finance and Economics*, *67*(3), 388. DOI: 10.1007/s11146-021-09857-x

Ferraris, A. F., Audrito, D., Di Caro, L., & Poncibò, C. (2025). The architecture of language: Understanding the mechanics behind LLMs. *Cambridge Forum on AI: Law and Governance*. DOI: 10.1017/cfl.2024.16

Ferrer, X., van Nuenen, T., Such, J. M., Coté, M., & Criado, N. (2021). Bias and Discrimination in AI: A Cross-Disciplinary Perspective. *IEEE Technology and Society Magazine*, *40*(2), 72. DOI: 10.1109/mts.2021.3056293

Fleischer, D., Berchansky, M., Wasserblat, M., & Izsak, P. (2024). *RAG Foundry: A framework for enhancing LLMs for retrieval augmented generation*. arXiv. https://arxiv.org/abs/2408.02545

Floridi, L., Cowls, J., King, T. C., & Taddeo, M. (2021). How to design AI for social good: Seven essential factors. In Dubber, M. D., Pasquale, F., & Das, S. (Eds.), *The Oxford handbook of ethics of AI* (pp. 125–151). Oxford University Press., DOI: 10.1007/978-3-030-69921-5_8

Fossa, F., & Sucameli, I. (2022). Gender Bias and Conversational Agents: An ethical perspective on Social Robotics. *Science and Engineering Ethics*, *28*(3). Advance online publication. DOI: 10.1007/s11948-022-00376-3

Fountaine, T., McCarthy, B., & Saleh, T. (2019). Building the AI-powered organization: Technology isn't the biggest challenge — culture is. *Harvard Business Review*, *97*(4), 62–73.

Frank, M. R., Autor, D., Bessen, J. E., Brynjolfsson, E., Cebrian, M., Deming, D. J., & Rahwan, I. (2019). Toward understanding the impact of artificial intelligence on labor. *Proceedings of the National Academy of Sciences of the United States of America*, *116*(14), 6531–6539. PMID: 30910965

Fu, Y., Ni, J., & Fang, M. (2025). The impact of artificial intelligence on digital enterprise innovation. *Journal of Strategy & Innovation*, *36*(1), 200538.

Gabber, H. A., & Hemied, O. S. (2024). Domain-specific large language model for renewable energy and hydrogen deployment strategies. *Energies*, *17*(23), 6063.

Gaddala, V., & Sharma Gaddala, V. (2023). *Unleashing the power of generative AI and RAG agents in supply chain management: A futuristic perspective*. ResearchGate. https://www.researchgate.net/publication/391917883

Gaikwad, M. S. V. (2024). Fine Tuning Llm For Sentiment Analysis. *Nanotechnology Perceptions*, •••, 4946–4959.

Gallegos, I. O., Rossi, R. A., Barrow, J., Tanjim, M. M., Kim, S., Dernoncourt, F., Yu, T., Zhang, R., & Ahmed, N. K. (2024). Bias and Fairness in Large Language Models: A Survey. *Computational Linguistics*, *50*(3), 1097–1179. DOI: 10.1162/coli_a_00524

Gama, J., Žliobaitė, I., Bifet, A., Pechenizkiy, M., & Bouchachia, A. (2014). A survey on concept drift adaptation. *ACM Computing Surveys*, *46*(4), 44. Advance online publication. DOI: 10.1145/2523813

Gan, A., ... (2025). *Retrieval augmented generation evaluation in the era of large language models: A comprehensive survey*. arXiv. https://arxiv.org/abs/2504.14891

Garkisch, M., & Goldkind, L. (2024). Considering a Unified Model of Artificial Intelligence Enhanced Social Work: A Systematic Review [Review of Considering a Unified Model of Artificial Intelligence Enhanced Social Work: A Systematic Review]. Journal of Human Rights and Social Work. Springer International Publishing. DOI: 10.1007/s41134-024-00326-y

Gartner Inc. (2023). Sales Enablement: Strategies to Drive Strong Results. https://www.gartner.com/en/sales/topics/sales-enablement

Gebru, T., Morgenstern, J., Vecchione, B., Vaughan, J. W., Wallach, H., Daumé, H., & Crawford, K. (2021). Datasheets for datasets. *Communications of the ACM*, *64*(12), 86–92. DOI: 10.1145/3458723

Gencer, G., & Gencer, K. (2025). Large language models in healthcare: A bibliometric analysis and examination of research trends. *Journal of Multidisciplinary Healthcare*, *18*, 223–238. DOI: 10.2147/JMDH.S480505 PMID: 39844924

Gencer, G., & Gencer, K. (2025). Large Language Models in Healthcare: A Bibliometric Analysis and Examination of Research Trends. *Journal of Multidisciplinary Healthcare*, *223*. Advance online publication. DOI: 10.2147/jmdh.s502351

Generative AI and LLMs in banking: Examples, use cases, limitations, and solutions. (2024, November 18). Dynamiq. https://www.getdynamiq.ai/post/generative-ai-and-llms-in-banking-examples-use-cases-limitations-and-solutions

Generative AI for patient-friendly language in discharge summaries. (2024). JAMA Network Open, 7(4), e245323. DOI: 10.1001/jamanetworkopen.2024.5323

George, A. S. (2023). Future economic implications of artificial intelligence. *Zenodo*. DOI: 10.5281/zenodo.8347639

Ghouati, S., Rizi, L., Oulfarsi, S., & El Amri, A. (2025). Artificial intelligence and cross-functional integration: An exploratory study of the convergence between management control and supply chain in Moroccan industries. *International Journal of Management and Applied Research, 12*(2), 149–168. DOI: 10.18646/2056.122.25-009

GitHub. (2024). *GitHub Copilot: Your AI pair programmer.* Retrieved from https://github.com/features/copilot

Glikson, E., & Woolley, A. W. (2020). Human trust in artificial intelligence: Review of empirical research. *The Academy of Management Annals, 14*(2), 627–660. DOI: 10.5465/annals.2018.0057

Gonzales, J. T. (2023). Implications of AI innovation on economic growth: A panel data study. *Journal of Economic Structures, 12*(1), 13.

Google. (2022). *2022 AI Principles Progress Update.* https://oecd.ai/en/catalogue/tools/google-2022-ai-principles-progress-update?utm_source=chatgpt.com

Google. (2024). *Enterprise-ready, secure AI.* Google Workspace. Retrieved November 3, 2025, from https://workspace.google.com/intl/en

Grewal, D., Satornino, C. B., Davenport, T. H., & Guha, A. (2024). How generative AI is shaping the future of marketing. *Journal of the Academy of Marketing Science.* Advance online publication. DOI: 10.1007/s11747-024-01064-3

Griffen, Z., & Owens, K. (2024). From "Human in the Loop" to a Participatory System of Governance for AI in Healthcare. *The American Journal of Bioethics, 24*(9), 81–83. DOI: 10.1080/15265161.2024.2377114

Group, B. M. W. (2023). *How AI is revolutionising production.* Retrieved from https://www.bmwgroup.com/en/news/general/2023/aiqx.html

Guan, H., Dong, L., & Zhao, A. (2022). Ethical Risk Factors and Mechanisms in Artificial Intelligence Decision Making. *Behavioral Sciences (Basel, Switzerland), 12*(9), 343. DOI: 10.3390/bs12090343

Hadi, M. U., Qureshi, R., Shah, A., Irfan, M., Zafar, A., Shaikh, M. B., & Mirjalili, S. (2023). Large language models: A comprehensive survey of its applications, challenges, limitations, and future prospects. *Authorea.* DOI: 10.22541/au.169476831.94963464/v1

Haelterman, H. (2020). Breaking silos of legal and regulatory risks to outperform traditional compliance approaches. *European Journal on Criminal Policy and Research, 28*(1), 19–36. DOI: 10.1007/s10610-020-09468-x

Hagendorff, T. (2022). A Virtue-Based Framework to Support Putting AI Ethics into Practice. *Philosophy & Technology*, *35*(3). Advance online publication. DOI: 10.1007/s13347-022-00553-z

Haghsefat, S., Taleby Ahvanooey, M., Song, H., Liu, C. Z., & Choo, K.-K. R. (2024). PrFAHP-GT: A new privacy risk analysis framework using FAHP and game theory for digital supply chain management. *IEEE Transactions on Engineering Management*, *71*(4), 11718–11733. DOI: 10.1109/TEM.2024.3428840

Han, B., Susnjak, T., & Mathrani, A. (2024). Automating systematic literature reviews with retrieval-augmented generation: A comprehensive overview. *Applied Sciences (Basel, Switzerland)*, *14*(19), 9103. Advance online publication. https://doi.org/10.3390/app14199103

Handler, A., Larsen, K. R., & Hackathorn, R. (2024). Large language models present new questions for decision support. *International Journal of Information Management*, *79*, 102811. DOI: 10.1016/j.ijinfomgt.2024.102811

Han, H., & Liu, X. (2021). The challenges of explainable AI in biomedical data science. *BMC Bioinformatics*, *22*. Advance online publication. DOI: 10.1186/s12859-021-04368-1

Hao, K. (2019). *This is how AI bias really happens — and why it's so hard to fix*. MIT Technology Review. https://www.technologyreview.com/2019/02/04/137602/this-is-how-ai-bias-really-happensand-why-its-so-hard-to-fix/

He, K., Zhang, X., Ren, S., & Sun, J. (2016). Deep residual learning for image recognition. In *Proceedings of the IEEE conference on computer vision and pattern recognition* (pp. 770-778).

Hermann, E., & Hermann, G. (2021). Artificial intelligence in research and development for sustainability: The centrality of explicability and research data management. *AI and Ethics*, *2*(1), 29. DOI: 10.1007/s43681-021-00114-8

Hinton, G., Vinyals, O., & Dean, J. (2015). Distilling the knowledge in a neural network. *arXiv preprint arXiv:1503.02531*

Hoffmann, J., Borgeaud, S., Mensch, A., Buchholtz, M., Casajus, D., Mudrakarta, E., . . . De Las Casas, D. (2022). Training compute-optimal large language models. *arXiv preprint arXiv:2203.15556.*

Hohma, E., Boch, A., Trauth, R., & Lütge, C. (2023). Investigating accountability for Artificial Intelligence through risk governance: A workshop-based exploratory study. *Frontiers in Psychology*, *14*. Advance online publication. DOI: 10.3389/fpsyg.2023.1073686

Holgersson, M., Dahlander, L., Chesbrough, H., & Bogers, M. L. A. M. (2024). Open Innovation in the Age of AI. *California Management Review*, *67*(1), 5–20. DOI: 10.1177/00081256241279326

Holmström, J. (2022). From AI to digital transformation: The AI readiness framework. *Business Horizons*, *65*(3), 329–339. DOI: 10.1016/j.bushor.2021.03.006

Hosseini, Z., Nyholm, S., Blanc, P. M. L., Preenen, P., & Demerouti, E. (2023). Assessing the artificially intelligent workplace: An ethical framework for evaluating experimental technologies in workplace settings. *AI and Ethics*, *4*(2), 285. DOI: 10.1007/s43681-023-00265-w

Houlsby, N., Jastrzebski, S., Hessel, J., Strub, F., Gorniak, V., Morrone, R. R., . . . De Freitas, N. (2019). Parameter-efficient transfer learning for NLP. *arXiv preprint arXiv:1902.00751*

Hsu, E., & Roberts, K. (2024). Leveraging large language models for knowledge-free weak supervision in clinical natural language processing. In Res. Sq.

Hu, E. J., Shen, Y., Wallis, P., Allen-Zhu, Z., Li, Y., Wang, S., . . . Chen, W. (2021). LoRA: Low-rank adaptation of large language models. *arXiv preprint arXiv:2106.09685.*

Huang, Q., Sun, Y., Xing, Z., Cao, Y., Chen, J., Xu, X., Jin, H., & Lu, J. (2024). Let's Discover More API Relations: A Large Language Model-Based AI Chain for Unsupervised API Relation Inference. *ACM Transactions on Software Engineering and Methodology*, *33*(8), 1–34. DOI: 10.1145/3680469

Hyeon Chai, S. (2024, October). A new perspective and progressive applications of the large Language Models in Geotechnical Engineering field. Deep Foundations Institute 49th Annual Conference Proceedings.

Iacovides, G., Konstantinidis, T., Xu, M., & Mandic, D. 2024. "FinLlama: LLM-Based Financial Sentiment Analysis for Algorithmic Trading." *ICAIF 2024 - 5th ACM International Conference on AI in Finance* 134–41. doi: DOI: 10.1145/3677052.3698696

IBM. (2024). *IBM Watson Discovery.* https://www.ibm.com/products/watson-discovery

Idris, M. D., Feng, X., & Dyo, V. (2024). Revolutionizing higher education: Unleashing the potential of large language models for strategic transformation. *IEEE Access : Practical Innovations, Open Solutions*, *12*, 67738–67757. DOI: 10.1109/ACCESS.2024.3400164

Irfan, M., S. Parameswaran, K. A. Singh, and E. R. Kismawadi. 2025. "Cutting-Edge Technologies for Economic Well-Being: The Transformative Power of AI and Blockchain." Pp. 229–48 in *Driving Socio-Economic Growth With AI and Blockchain*.

Iyamu, T., & Shaanika, I. (2023). The factors of enterprise business architecture readiness in organisations. *Lecture Notes in Business Information Processing*, •••, 379–390. DOI: 10.1007/978-3-031-39386-0_18

Jacob, B., Kligerman, Y., Krishna, B., Zhu, S., Chen, H., Howard, A., & Kalenichenko, D. (2018). Quantization and training of neural networks for efficient integer-arithmetic-only inference. In *Proceedings of the IEEE conference on computer vision and pattern recognition* (pp. 2765-2774)

Jannah, N., Bahri, M. I., Kismawadi, E. R., & Handriana, T. (2024). The Effect of Green Brand Image and Green Satisfaction on Green Brand Equity Mediated Green Trust Outpatient's. *Quality - Access to Success*, *25*(198), 381–390. DOI: 10.47750/QAS/25.198.40

Jeong, J., Baek, I., Bang, B., Lee, J., Song, U., & Kim, S. B. (2025). FALL: Prior failure detection in large scale system based on language model. *IEEE Transactions on Dependable and Secure Computing*, *22*, 279–291. DOI: 10.1109/tdsc.2024.3396166

Jonnagaddala, J., & Wong, Z. S. Y. (2025). Privacy preserving strategies for electronic health records in the era of large language models. npj. *Digital Medicine*, *8*(1), 34. Advance online publication. DOI: 10.1038/s41746-025-01308-8 PMID: 39820020

Joshi, S. (n.d.). *The synergy of generative AI and big data for financial risk: Review of recent developments*. International Journal of Formal Methods and Research. https://www.ijfmr.com

Kaczorowska-Spychalska, D., Kotula, N., Mazurek, G., & Sułkowski, Ł. (2024). Generative AI as source of change of knowledge management paradigm. *Human Technology*, *20*(1), 131–154. DOI: 10.14254/1795-6889.2024.20-1.7

Kainz, J., Seisl, P., Grob, M., Hauptfeld, L., Wahringer, J., Rappelsberger, A., & Adlassnig, K.-P. (2025). Fine-tuning an existing large language model with knowledge from the medical expert system Hepaxpert. *Studies in Health Technology and Informatics*, *327*, 143–147. PMID: 40380402

Kairouz, P., McMahan, H. B., & Song, S. [et al.]. (2021). Advances and open problems in federated learning. *Foundations and Trends in Machine Learning*, *14*(1–2), 1–210. DOI: 10.1561/2200000083

Kappel, G. (2024). Risks of artificial intelligence-based decision support and decision-making systems in executive-level decision-making in companies: A literature review. *Pécs Journal of International and European Law, 2024*(2), 3–15. DOI: 10.15170/PJIEL.2024.2.3

Karabacak, M., & Margetis, K. (2023). Embracing large language models for medical applications: Opportunities and challenges. *Cureus, 15*(5), e39305. Advance online publication. DOI: 10.7759/cureus.39305 PMID: 37378099

Kaur, R., Saluja, A., Kaur, A., & Sharma, A. (2023). Technology led transformation of Indian economy. In *AIP Conference Proceedings* (Vol. 2782, No. 1). AIP Publishing.

Kellogg, K. C., Valentine, M. A., & Christin, A. (2020). Algorithms at work: The new contested terrain of control. *The Academy of Management Annals, 14*(1), 366–410. DOI: 10.5465/annals.2018.0174

Kelly, L. (n.d.). The Power of Personalized Outreach with LLMs and RAG. https://www.sellingpower.com/22015/the-power-of-personalized-outreach-with-llms-and-rag

Khan, A. A., Hasan, M. T., Kemell, K. K., Rasku, J., & Abrahamsson, P. (2024). *Developing retrieval augmented generation (RAG) based LLM systems from PDFs: An experience report*. arXiv. https://arxiv.org/abs/2410.15944

Kim, J., & Mahajan, D. (2025). *An adaptive vector index partitioning scheme for low-latency RAG pipeline*. arXiv. https://arxiv.org/abs/2504.08930

Kismawadi, E. R. 2024. "Sustainable Islamic Financial Inclusion: The Ethical Challenges of Generative AI in Product and Service Development." Pp. 237–58 in *Exploring the Ethical Implications of Generative AI*.

Klopotan, I., Aleksić, A., & Vinković, N. (2020). Do Business Ethics and Ethical Decision Making Still Matter: Perspective of Different Generational Cohorts. *Business Systems Research Journal, 11*(1), 31. DOI: 10.2478/bsrj-2020-0003

KloudData. (n.d.). *The impact of AI on ERP systems featuring SAP S/4HANA*. Retrieved June 7, 2024, from https://www.klouddata.com/sap-blogs/the-impact-of-ai-on-erp-systems-featuring-sap-s-4hana

Kochkina, N., Andriushchenko, I., & Gatto, G. (2024). Strategic AI adoption: Economic impact, case studies from Handy.ai, and industry readiness. In *2024 IEEE International Conference on Artificial Intelligence & Green Energy (ICAIGE)* (pp. 1–6). DOI: 10.1109/ICAIGE62696.2024.10776631

Kostopoulos, G., Davrazos, G., & Kotsiantis, S. (2024). Explainable artificial intelligence-based decision support systems: A recent review. *Electronics (Basel), 13*(14), 2842. Advance online publication. https://doi.org/10.3390/electronics13142842

Kotter, J. P. (2012). *Leading change*. Harvard Business Press.

Kovari, A. (2025). Explainable AI chatbots towards XAI ChatGPT: A review. *Heliyon, 11*, e42077. DOI: 10.1016/j.heliyon.2025.e42077

KPMG. (2024). *AI and automation in financial reporting guide*. https://kpmg.com/kpmg-us/content/dam/kpmg/frv/pdf/2024/handbook-ai-and-automation-financial-reporting.pdf

Krause, D. S. (2023). *Mitigating risks for financial firms using generative AI tools. SSRN*. https://ssrn.com/abstract=4452600

Kumar, D. B. (2018). Economic Revival in India: issues and challenges. *Available at SSRN* 3839143.

Kumar, V., Ashraf, A. R., & Nadeem, W. (2024). AI-powered marketing: What, where, and how? *International Journal of Information Management, 77*, 102783. DOI: 10.1016/j.ijinfomgt.2024.102783

Lai, L., Wittbold, K. A., Dadabhoy, F. Z., Sato, R., Landman, A. B., Schwamm, L. H., & Zhang, H. M. (2020). Digital triage: Novel strategies for population health management in response to the COVID-19 pandemic. *Health Care, 8*(4), 100493. Advance online publication. DOI: 10.1016/j.hjdsi.2020.100493 PMID: 33129176

Lambruschini, B. Braulio, C., & Brorsson, M. (2024). "Transforming Unstructured Sensitive Information into Structured Knowledge." *ICAIF 2024 - 5th ACM International Conference on AI in Finance* 831–38. doi: DOI: 10.1145/3677052.3698602

Lansing, A. E., Romero, N. J., Siantz, E., Silva, V., Center, K., Casteel, D., & Gilmer, T. (2023). Building trust: Leadership reflections on community empowerment and engagement in a large urban initiative. *BMC Public Health, 23*(1). Advance online publication. DOI: 10.1186/s12889-023-15860-z

Lareyre, F., & Raffort, J. (2024). Ethical concerns regarding the use of large language models in healthcare. *EJVES Vascular Forum, 61*, 1. DOI: 10.1016/j.ejvsvf.2023.12.003 PMID: 38025830

Lee, J., Ahn, S., Kim, D., & Kim, D. (2024). Performance comparison of retrieval-augmented generation and fine-tuned large language models for construction safety management knowledge retrieval. *Automation in Construction*, *169*, 105846. DOI: 10.1016/j.autcon.2024.105846

Lee, J., Stevens, N., & Han, S. C. (2025). Large language models in finance (FinLLMs). *Neural Computing & Applications*. Advance online publication. DOI: 10.1007/s00521-024-10756-8

Leiner, T., Bennink, E., Mol, C. P., Kuijf, H., & Veldhuis, W. (2021). Bringing AI to the clinic: Blueprint for a vendor-neutral AI deployment infrastructure. *Insights Into Imaging*, *12*, 1–11. DOI: 10.1186/s13244-020-00931-1

Lester, B., Al-Rfou, R., & Constant, N. (2021). Power efficient management of large language models via parameter-efficient transfer learning. *arXiv preprint arXiv:2104.08691*

Lewis, P., Perez, E., Piktus, A., Petroni, F., Karpukhin, V., Goyal, N., . . . Kiela, D. *(*2020*)*. Retrieval-Augmented Generation for Knowledge-Intensive NLP Tasks. *Advances in Neural Information Processing Systems (NeurIPS), 33.*

Lewis, P., Perez, E., Piktus, A., Petroni, F., Karpukhin, V., Goyal, N., Küttler, H., Lewis, M., Yih, W., Rocktäschel, T., Riedel, S., & Kiela, D. (2020). Retrieval-Augmented Generation for Knowledge-Intensive NLP Tasks. arXiv preprint arXiv:2005.11401.

Ley, A. N. L., Scott, C. A., Wilder, M., Varady, R. G., Ocampo-Melgar, A., Lara-Valencia, F., Zúñiga-Terán, A. A., Buechler, S., Caravantes, R. E. D., Neto, A. R., Pablos, N. P., & Martín, F. (2020). Dialogic science-policy networks for water security governance in the arid Americas. *Environmental Development*, *38*, 100568. DOI: 10.1016/j.envdev.2020.100568

Leyer, M., & Schneider, S. (2021). Decision augmentation and automation with artificial intelligence: Threat or opportunity for managers? *Business Horizons*, *64*(5), 711. DOI: 10.1016/j.bushor.2021.02.026

Liang, G., & Tong, Q. (2025). LLM-Powered AI Agent Systems and Their Applications in Industry. *arXiv preprint arXiv:2505.16120.*

Li, D., Li, Z., Yang, Y., Sun, L., An, D., & Yang, Q. (2024). Knowledge graph-enhanced large language model for domain-specific question answering systems. *Authorea Preprints.*

Li, H., Moon, J. T., Purkayastha, S., Celi, L. A., Trivedi, H., & Gichoya, J. W. (2023). Ethics of large language models in medicine and medical research. *The Lancet. Digital Health, 5*(6), e333–e335. DOI: 10.1016/S2589-7500(23)00083-9 PMID: 37120418

Li, H., Yu, B., Wei, Y., Wang, K., Xu, R. Y. D., & Wang, B. (2025). KERMIT: Knowledge Graph Completion of Enhanced Relation Modeling with Inverse Transformation. *Knowledge-Based Systems, 324.* Advance online publication. DOI: 10.1016/j.knosys.2025.113500

Lin, C. Y. (2004). ROUGE: a package for automatic evaluation of summaries. In *Text summarization branches out: Proceedings of the ACL-04 workshop* (pp. 1-8)

Liu, X., Glocker, B., McCradden, M. D., Ghassemi, M., Denniston, A. K., & Oakden-Rayner, L. (2022). The medical algorithmic audit [Review of The medical algorithmic audit]. The Lancet Digital Health, 4(5). Elsevier BV. DOI: 10.1016/s2589-7500(22)00003-6

Liu, X., Mitani, A., Spitz, T., Wu Derek, J., & Ledsam, J. R. (2021). Google and DeepMind: Deep learning systems in ophthalmology. In Artificial Intelligence in Ophthalmology (pp. 161–176). Springer International Publishing.

Liu, Z., & Zheng, Y. (2022). AI Ethics and Governance. DOI: 10.1007/978-981-19-2531-3

Liu, H., Gong, S., Ji, Y., Wu, K., Xu, J., & Gu, J. (2024). Boosting LLM-based relevance modeling with distribution-aware robust learning. *Proceedings of the 33rd ACM International Conference on Information and Knowledge Management,* 4718–4725.

Liu, L., Meng, J., & Yang, Y. (2024). LLM technologies and information search. *Journal of Economy and Technology, 2,* 269–277. DOI: 10.1016/j.ject.2024.08.007

Liu, X. Y., Zhu, R., Zha, D., Gao, J., Zhong, S., White, M., & Qiu, M. (2025). Differentially Private Low-Rank Adaptation of Large Language Model Using Federated Learning. *ACM Transactions on Management Information Systems, 16*(2). Advance online publication. DOI: 10.1145/3682068

Li, Y., Wang, S., Ding, H., & Chen, H. (2023, November). Large language models in finance: A survey. In *Proceedings of the fourth ACM international conference on AI in finance* (pp. 374–382). Association for Computing Machinery. DOI: 10.1145/3604237.3626869

Li, Y., Wu, H., Tamir, T. S., Shen, Z., Liu, S., Hu, B., & Xiong, G. (2023). An efficient product-customization framework based on multimodal data under the social manufacturing paradigm. *Machines (Basel), 11*(2), 170. DOI: 10.3390/machines11020170

Li, Z. (2024). Leveraging AI automated emergency response with natural language processing: Enhancing real-time decision making and communication. *Applied and Computational Engineering, 71*(1), 1–6. https://doi.org/10.54254/2755-2721/71/20241629

Lu, M. Y., Chen, B., Williamson, D. F. K., Chen, R. J., Zhao, M., Chow, A. K., Ikemura, K., Kim, A., Pouli, D., Patel, A., Soliman, A., Chen, C., Ding, T., Wang, J. J., Gerber, G., Liang, I., Le, L. P., Parwani, A. V., Weishaupt, L. L., & Mahmood, F. (2024). A multimodal generative AI copilot for human pathology. *Nature, 634*(8033), 466–473. DOI: 10.1038/s41586-024-07618-3

Luo, M., Trivedi, S., Kurian, A. W., Ward, K., Keegan, T. H. M., Rubin, D., & Banerjee, I. (2024). Automated extraction of patient-centered outcomes after breast cancer treatment: An open-source large language model-based toolkit. *JCO Clinical Cancer Informatics, 8*(8), e2300258. PMID: 39167746

Macdonald, C., Fang, J., Parry, A., & Meng, Z. (2025). Constructing and evaluating declarative RAG pipelines in PyTerrier. *Proceedings of the ...*, Article 3726302. https://doi.org/10.1145/3726302.3730150

Machucho, R., & Ortiz, D. (2025). The impacts of artificial intelligence on business innovation: A comprehensive review of applications, organizational challenges, and ethical considerations. *Systems, 13*(4), 264. DOI: 10.3390/systems13040264

Mackenzie, T., Radeljic, B., Salgado, L., Paul, A., Khan, R., Tursunbayeva, A., . . . Bhaduri, S. (2025). What We Do Not Know: GPT Use in Business and Management. *arXiv preprint arXiv:2504.05273.*

Maddali, R. (2024). AI-powered data security frameworks for regulatory compliance (GDPR, CCPA, HIPAA) [Preprint]. *Zenodo*. https://doi.org/10.5281/zenodo.15072096

Maiti, M., Kayal, P., & Vujko, A. (2025). A study on ethical implications of artificial intelligence adoption in business: Challenges and best practices. *Future Business Journal, 11*, 34. DOI: 10.1186/s43093-025-00462-5

Makridakis, S. (2017). The forthcoming Artificial Intelligence (AI) revolution: Its impact on society and firms. *Futures, 90*, 46–60.

Malhotra, A., Elsayed, A. T. A., Torres, R., & Venkatraman, S. (2023). Evaluate solutions for achieving high availability or near zero downtime for cloud native enterprise applications. *IEEE Access : Practical Innovations, Open Solutions*, *11*, 85384–85394. DOI: 10.1109/ACCESS.2023.3303430

Manda, C. (2025). Innovation in AI-driven customer service: Impact of large language models on enterprise solutions. *International Journal of Science and Research Archive*. DOI: 10.30574/ijsra.2025.14.1.0049

Mangipudi, P. (2025). AI-powered chatbots vs human agents, a compatible study on customer satisfaction. *International Journal of Computer Engineering and Technology*, *16*(2), 11–36. DOI: 10.34218/ijcet_16_02_002

Manyika, J., Chui, M., Miremadi, M., Bughin, J., George, K., Willmott, P., & Dewhurst, M. (2017). A future that works: AI, automation, employment, and productivity. *McKinsey Global Institute Research. Tech. Rep*, *60*, 1–135.

Márquez, C. (2025, January 28). *A functional software reference architecture for LLM-integrated systems*. arXiv. https://arxiv.org/html/2501.12904v1

McIntosh, T. R., Sušnjak, T., Liu, T., Watters, P., Xu, D., Liu, D., Nowrozy, R., & Halgamuge, M. N. (2024). From COBIT to ISO 42001: Evaluating cybersecurity frameworks for opportunities, risks, and regulatory compliance in commercializing large language models. *Computers & Security*, *144*, 103964. DOI: 10.1016/j.cose.2024.103964

McKinsey & Company. (2023). *The state of AI in 2023: Generative AI's breakout year*. Retrieved from https://www.mckinsey.com/capabilities/quantumblack/our-insights/the-state-of-ai-in-2023-generative-ais-breakout-year

McKinsey & Company. (2023, June 14). *The economic potential of generative AI: The next productivity frontier*. https://www.mckinsey.com/capabilities/quantumblack/our-insights/the-economic-potential-of-generative-ai-the-next-productivity-frontier

McLennan, S., Fiske, A., Tigard, D. W., Müller, R., Haddadin, S., & Buyx, A. (2022). Embedded ethics: A proposal for integrating ethics into the development of medical AI. *BMC Medical Ethics*, *23*(1). Advance online publication. DOI: 10.1186/s12910-022-00746-3

Meduri, S. (2024). Revolutionizing Customer Service: The Impact of Large Language Models on Chatbot Performance. *International Journal of Scientific Research in Computer Science Engineering and Information Technology*, *10*(5), 721–730. DOI: 10.32628/CSEIT241051057

Mehrabi, N., Morstatter, F., Saxena, N., Lerman, K., & Galstyan, A. (2021). A survey on bias and fairness in machine learning. *ACM Computing Surveys*, *54*(6), 3457607. Advance online publication. DOI: 10.1145/3457607

Mei, L., Mo, S., Yang, Z., & Chen, C. (2025). *A survey of multimodal retrieval-augmented generation*. arXiv. https://arxiv.org/abs/2504.08748

Meshkin, H., Zirkle, J., Arabidarrehdor, G., Chaturbedi, A., Chakravartula, S., Mann, J., Thrasher, B., & Li, Z. (2024). Harnessing large language models' zero-shot and few-shot learning capabilities for regulatory research. *Briefings in Bioinformatics*, *25*(5). Advance online publication. DOI: 10.1093/bib/bbae354

Microsoft. (2024). *Announcing new Copilot in Microsoft Teams enhancements*. https://www.microsoft.com/en-us/microsoft-365/blog/2024/03/26/ai-powered-collaboration-with-microsoft-teams/

Microsoft. (2024). *Responsible AI and employee training initiatives*. https://www.microsoft.com/en-us/ai/responsible-ai

Microsoft. (2024a). *Overview of Copilot capabilities in finance and operations apps*. Microsoft Learn. Retrieved June 7, 2024, from https://learn.microsoft.com/en-us/dynamics365/fin-ops-core/fin-ops/copilot/copilot-for-finance-operations

Microsoft. (2024b). *Overview of Microsoft 365 Copilot for Finance 2024 release wave 2*. Microsoft Learn. Retrieved June 7, 2024, from https://learn.microsoft.com/en-us/dynamics365/release-plan/2024wave2/finance-supply-chain/microsoft-copilot-finance/

Mikolov, T., Chen, K., Corrado, G., & Dean, J. (2013). Efficient estimation of word representations in vector space. *arXiv preprint arXiv:1301.3781*.

Mikolov, T., Chen, K., Corrado, G., & Dean, J. (2013). Efficient Estimation of Word Representations in Vector Space. arXiv preprint arXiv:1301.3781.

Mizumoto, A., & Eguchi, M. (2023). Exploring the potential of using an AI language model for automated essay scoring. *Research Methods in Applied Linguistics*, *2*(2), 100050. Advance online publication. DOI: 10.1016/j.rmal.2023.100050

Moayeri, M., Tabassi, E., & Feizi, S. 2024. "WorldBench: Quantifying Geographic Disparities in LLM Factual Recall." *2024 ACM Conference on Fairness, Accountability, and Transparency, FAccT 2024* 1211–28. doi: DOI: 10.1145/3630106.3658967

Moharrak, M., & Mogaji, E. (2024). Generative AI in banking: Empirical insights on integration, challenges and opportunities in a regulated industry. *International Journal of Bank Marketing*. Advance online publication. DOI: 10.1108/ijbm-08-2024-0490

Mökander, J., Schuett, J., Kirk, H. R., & Floridi, L. (2023). Auditing large language models: A three-layered approach. *AI and Ethics*, *4*(4), 1085. DOI: 10.1007/s43681-023-00289-2

Mörch, C., Gupta, A., & Mishara, B. L. (2020). Canada protocol: An ethical checklist for the use of artificial Intelligence in suicide prevention and mental health. *Artificial Intelligence in Medicine*, *108*, 101934. DOI: 10.1016/j.artmed.2020.101934

Moreno-Sandoval, L. G., Pomares-Quimbaya, A., Barbosa-Sierra, S. A., & Pantoja-Rojas, L. M. (2024). Detection of Hate Speech, Racism and Misogyny in Digital Social Networks: Colombian Case Study. *Big Data and Cognitive Computing*, *8*(9). Advance online publication. DOI: 10.3390/bdcc8090113

Múgica, A. (2025, February 20). Anti-money laundering and fraud prevention with MongoDB vector search and OpenAI. MongoDB Developer Community. https://www.mongodb.com/blog/post/anti-money-laundering-fraud-prevention-mongodb-vector-search-openai

Mulé, D. (2024). Harnessing the Power of LLMs in Sales: My Tips and Tricks. LinkedIn. https://www.linkedin.com/pulse/harnessing-power-llms-sales-my-tips-tricks-daniel-mul%C3%A9-ldjke

Narayanan, G., Kharat, R., & Kathuria, A. (2025). Is software customization an impediment or enabler for digital transformation in the era of large language models. In *Lecture Notes in Computer Science* (pp. 1–14). Springer., DOI: 10.1007/978-3-031-74437-2_1

Narne, H. (2024). Generative artificial intelligence device to analysis the data for SAP based data management. In *2024 International Conference on Intelligent Computing and Emerging Communication Technologies (ICEC)* (pp. 1–6). DOI: 10.1109/ICEC59683.2024.10837215

Natta, P. K. (2025). AI-Driven Decision Intelligence: Optimizing Enterprise Strategy with AI-Augmented Insights. *Journal of Computer Science and Technology Studies*, *7*(2), 146–152.

NetSuite. (2024). *GenAI powers new assistant, automated insights in NetSuite 2025.1*. https://www.netsuite.com/portal/resource/articles/erp/genai-powers-new-assistant-automated-insights-in-netsuite-2025-1.shtml

Ng, D. T. K., Leung, J. K. L., Chu, S. K. W., & Qiao, S. (2021). Conceptualizing AI literacy: An exploratory review. *Computers and Education Artificial Intelligence*, *2*, 100041. DOI: 10.1016/j.caeai.2021.100041

Nguyen, D. S. W., & Shaik, M. M. (2024). Impact of Artificial Intelligence on Corporate Leadership. *Journal of Computer and Communications*, *12*(4), 40. DOI: 10.4236/jcc.2024.124004

Niu, C., ... (2024). *RAGTruth: A hallucination corpus for developing trustworthy retrieval-augmented language models*. arXiv. https://arxiv.org/abs/2401.00396

Obermeyer, Z., Powers, B., Vogeli, C., & Mullainathan, S. (2019). Dissecting racial bias in an algorithm used to manage the health of populations. *Science*, *366*(6464), 447–453. DOI: 10.1126/science.aax2342 PMID: 31649194

Oloruntoba, N. O. (2025). AI-Driven autonomous database management: Self-tuning, predictive query optimization, and intelligent indexing in enterprise it environments. *World Journal of Advanced Research and Reviews*, *25*(2), 1558–1580.

Oneto, L., & Chiappa, S. (2020). Fairness in Machine Learning. In *Studies in computational intelligence* (p. 155). Springer Nature., DOI: 10.1007/978-3-030-43883-8_7

Open, A. I. (2024). *OpenAI API documentation*. Retrieved from https://platform.openai.com/docs

Oracle. (2023a). *Oracle NetSuite embeds generative AI throughout the suite to help organizations boost productivity*. Oracle News. https://www.oracle.com/news/announcement/suiteworld-netsuite-embeds-generative-ai-2023-10-17/

Oracle. (2023b). *Capitalizing on GenAI: How CFOs can turn real-time insights into...* Oracle Cloud ERP. https://www.oracle.com/erp/how-cfos-turn-insights-into-decisions/

Oracle. (2024a, March 14). *Oracle adds new generative AI capabilities to Oracle Fusion Cloud Applications Suite*. Oracle News. https://www.oracle.com/news/announcement/oracle-adds-generative-ai-capabilities-to-fusion-applications-2024-03-14/

Oracle. (2024b). *Oracle launches over 50 generative AI use cases with Cohere*. Cohere. https://cohere.com/customer-stories/oracle

Panigrahi, A., Ahirrao, S. C., & Patel, A. (2024). Impact of artificial intelligence on Indian economy. *J Manag Res Anal*, *11*(1), 33–40.

Papasotiriou, K., Sood, S., Reynolds, S., & Balch, T. (2024, November). AI in investment analysis: LLMs for equity stock ratings. In *Proceedings of the 5th ACM international conference on AI in finance* (pp. 419–427). Association for Computing Machinery. DOI: 10.1145/3677052.3698699

Papineni, K., Roukos, S., Ward, T., & Zhu, W. J. (2002). BLEU: a method for automatic evaluation of machine translation. In *Proceedings of the 40th annual meeting on association for computational linguistics* (pp. 311-318).

Park, P. S., Goldstein, S., O'Gara, A., Chen, M., & Hendrycks, D. (2024). AI deception: A survey of examples, risks, and potential solutions [Review of AI deception: A survey of examples, risks, and potential solutions]. Patterns, 5(5), 100988. Elsevier BV. DOI: 10.1016/j.patter.2024.100988

Patterson, Z., Bensmihen, A., & Hermanson, G. (2024). The Multimodal Accessibility Target (MAT): A new approach to accessibility modeling. *Transportation Research Record: Journal of the Transportation Research Board*, *2678*(1), 770–780. DOI: 10.1177/03611981231172503

Pau, C., Martin, M., & Ciurea, J. (2021). Managerial Perspective on Ethical Culture in Organizations and Institutions. *Robotica & Management*, *26*(1), 27. DOI: 10.24193/rm.2021.1.6

Peng, Y., Mou, Y., & Zhu, B., & Sowe Sulayman and Decker, S. (2024). RWTH-DBIS at LLMs4OL 2024 tasks A and B. Open Conf. Proc., 4, 49–63.

Pennington, C. (2025). *Smart manufacturing: The future of digital factories.* Siemens Digital Industries Software Blog. Retrieved from https://blogs.sw.siemens.com/digital-transformation/smart-manufacturing-the-future-of-digital-factories/

Pennington, J., Socher, R., & Manning, C. (2014). Glove: Global Vectors for Word Representation. *EMNLP*, *14*, 1532–1543. DOI: 10.3115/v1/D14-1162

Pérez-Pineda, J. A., & Wehrmann, D. (2020). Partnerships with the Private Sector: Success Factors and Levels of Engagement in Development Cooperation. In Springer eBooks (p. 649). Springer Nature. DOI: 10.1007/978-3-030-57938-8_30

Peters, D., Vold, K., Robinson, D., & Calvo, R. A. (2020). Responsible AI—Two Frameworks for Ethical Design Practice. *IEEE Transactions on Technology and Society*, *1*(1), 34. DOI: 10.1109/tts.2020.2974991

Petrescu, M., & Krishen, A. S. (2023). Hybrid intelligence: human–AI collaboration in marketing analytics. *Journal of Marketing Analytics*, *11*(3), 263–274. DOI: 10.1057/s41270-023-00245-3

Pfizer Inc. (2022). *Data and AI are helping to get medicines to patients faster.* https://www.pfizer.com/sites/default/files/investors/financial_reports/annual_reports/2022/story/data-and-ai-are-helping-to-get-medicines-to-patients-faster/

Pinheiro, C. R., Guerreiro, S. L. P. D., & Mamede, H. (2024). A lightweight ontology for enterprise architecture mining of API gateway logs. *IEEE Access : Practical Innovations, Open Solutions*, *12*, 128585–128601. DOI: 10.1109/ACCESS.2024.3456119

Pires, T., Schlinger, E., & Garrette, D. (2019). How multilingual is Multilingual BERT? In *Proceedings of the 57th Annual Meeting of the Association for Computational Linguistics* (pp. 4996–5001). Association for Computational Linguistics. DOI: 10.18653/v1/P19-1493

Polagani, S. S. (2025). AI agents in healthcare: Improving patient support while ensuring privacy. *World J. Adv. Eng. Eng. Technol. Sci.*, *15*(2), 1936–1945.

Pressman, S. M., Borna, S., Gomez-Cabello, C. A., Haider, S. A., Haider, C., & Forte, A. J. (2024). AI and ethics: A systematic review of the ethical considerations of large language model use in surgery research. *Health Care*, *12*(8), 825. Advance online publication. DOI: 10.3390/healthcare12080825 PMID: 38667587

PwC. (2024). *PwC becomes the largest user of ChatGPT Enterprise*. Retrieved from https://www.pwc.com/us/en/about-us/newsroom/press-releases/pwc-us-uk-accelerating-ai-chatgpt-enterprise-adoption.html

Qader, K. S., & Çek, K. (2024). Influence of blockchain and artificial intelligence on audit quality: Evidence from Turkey. *Heliyon*, *10*(9). Advance online publication. DOI: 10.1016/j.heliyon.2024.e30166

Qadir, U. (2025, January 28). Maximizing regulatory compliance in finance with generative AI solutions. LinkedIn. https://www.linkedin.com/pulse/maximizing-regulatory-compliance-finance-generative-ai-umair-qadir-hjgsf

Radford, A., Narasimhan, K., Salimans, T., & Sutskever, I. (2018). Improving language understanding by generative pre-training.

Ragab, R., & Altahhan, A. (2024). Fine-tuning of small/medium LLMs for business QA on structured data. *Int. J. Nat. Lang. Comput.*, *13*(3), 1–17.

Rahman, S., & Tasnim, F. (2023). The role of NGOs in ensuring local governance in Bangladesh: From the perception of other actors of governance. *Asia-Pacific Journal of Regional Science*, *7*(3), 1007. DOI: 10.1007/s41685-023-00283-w

Raji, I. D., Smart, A., White, R. N., Mitchell, M., Gebru, T., Hutchinson, B., Smith-Loud, J., Theron, D., & Barnes, P. (2020). Closing the AI accountability gap: Defining an end-to-end framework for internal algorithmic auditing. In Proceedings of the 2020 conference on fairness, accountability, and transparency (FAT* '20) (pp. 33–44). Association for Computing Machinery. DOI: 10.1145/3351095.3372873

Ramamurthy, R. (2023, August 15). Summarizing patient histories with GPT-4. Medium. https://medium.com/llmed-ai/summarizing-patient-histories-with-gpt-4-9df42ba6453c

Ravi, A., Neinstein, A., & Murray, S. G. (2023). Large language models and medical education: Preparing for a rapid transformation in how trainees will learn to be doctors. *ATS Scholar*, *4*(3), 282–292. DOI: 10.34197/ats-scholar.2023-0037PS PMID: 37795112

Ray, S. (2023). *Samsung bans ChatGPT among employees after sensitive code leak.* Forbes. https://www.forbes.com/sites/siladityaray/2023/05/02/samsung-bans-chatgpt-and-other-chatbots-for-employees-after-sensitive-code-leak/

Raza, M., Jahangir, Z., Riaz, M. B., Saeed, M. J., & Sattar, M. A. (2025). Industrial applications of large language models. *Scientific Reports*, *15*(1), 13755. DOI: 10.1038/s41598-025-98483-1 PMID: 40258923

Red River. (2024). *Why Microsoft Copilot is a no-brainer for finance business.* https://redriver.com/artificial-intelligence/microsoft-copilot-for-finance

Reddy, S. (2024). Generative AI in healthcare: an implementation science informed translational path on application, integration and governance [Review of Generative AI in healthcare: an implementation science informed translational path on application, integration and governance]. Implementation Science, 19(1). BioMed Central. DOI: 10.1186/s13012-024-01357-9

Research, I. B. M. (2020). *AI FactSheets 360 website: AI trust and transparency.* https://research.ibm.com/blog/aifactsheets

Resnik, D. B., & Hosseini, M. (2024). The ethics of using artificial intelligence in scientific research: New guidance needed for a new tool. *AI and Ethics.* Advance online publication. DOI: 10.1007/s43681-024-00493-8

Retail, I. K. E. A. (Ingka Group). (2023). *AI and remote selling bring IKEA design expertise to the many.* https://www.ingka.com/newsroom/ai-and-remote-selling-bring-ikea-design-expertise-to-the-many

Rossi, A., & Lenzini, G. (2020). Transparency by design in data-informed research: A collection of information design patterns. *Computer Law & Security Review*, *37*, 105402. DOI: 10.1016/j.clsr.2020.105402

Roychowdhury, S., Soman, S., Ranjani, H. G., Gunda, N., Chhabra, V., & Bala, S. K. (2024). *Evaluation of RAG metrics for question answering in the telecom domain.* arXiv. https://arxiv.org/abs/2407.12873

Rydzewski, N. R., Dinakaran, D., Zhao, S. G., Ruppin, E., Turkbey, B., Citrin, D. E., & Patel, K. R. (2024). Comparative evaluation of LLMs in clinical oncology. NEJM AI, 1(5), Article AIoa2300151. DOI: 10.1056/AIoa2300151

Sadeghi, K., Ojha, D., Kaur, P., Mahto, R. V., & Dhir, A. (2024). Explainable artificial intelligence and agile decision-making in supply chain cyber resilience. *Decision Support Systems*, *180*, 114194. DOI: 10.1016/j.dss.2024.114194

Sadek, M., Calvo, R. A., & Mougenot, C. (2024). Designing value-sensitive AI: A critical review and recommendations for socio-technical design processes. *AI and Ethics*, *4*, 949–967. DOI: 10.1007/s43681-023-00373-7

Saheb, T., & Saheb, T. (2024). Mapping Ethical Artificial Intelligence Policy Landscape: A Mixed Method Analysis. *Science and Engineering Ethics*, *30*(2). Advance online publication. DOI: 10.1007/s11948-024-00472-6

Salesforce Inc. (1999). Generate Personalized Sales Emails with Prompt Builder (Pilot). https://help.salesforce.com/s/articleView?id=release-notes.generative_ai_prompt_builder_sales_emails.htm&release=246&type=5

Salesforce. (2024). *Salesforce unveils Einstein Copilot for marketers and merchants* [Press release]. https://www.salesforce.com/news/press-releases/2024/05/22/einstein-copilot-marketing-commerce-news/

Salesforce. (2025). *Anthropic and Salesforce expand partnership supporting regulated industries.* https://www.salesforce.com/news/press-releases/2025/10/14/anthropic-regulated-industries-partnership-expansion-announcement/

SalesTechStar. (2024). Challenges and Ethical Considerations of Using AI in Sales. https://salestechstar.com/staff-writers/challenges-and-ethical-considerations-of-using-ai-in-sales/

SAP. (2024). *SAP Business AI: Enhancing enterprise collaboration.* Retrieved from https://www.sap.com/

Sarkar, U. E. (2025). Evaluating alignment in large language models: A review of methodologies. *AI and Ethics*. Advance online publication. DOI: 10.1007/s43681-024-00637-w

Schuett, J., Reuel, A., & Carlier, A. (2024). How to design an AI ethics board. *AI and Ethics*. Advance online publication. DOI: 10.1007/s43681-023-00409-y

Selinger, D. W., Wall, T. R., Stylianou, E., Khalil, E., Gaetz, J., & Levy, O. (2025). Abstract B043: A fully transparent and automatable form of AI for multi-omics precision medicine. *Cancer Research*, *85*(5, Supplement), B043–B043.

Sephora. (2024). *AI-powered customer personalization*. https://www.renascence.io/journal/how-sephora-enhances-customer-experience-cx-through-personalization-and-digital-innovation

Sequeda, J., Allemang, D., & Jacob, B. (2025). Knowledge Graphs as a source of trust for LLM-powered enterprise question answering. *Journal of Web Semantics*, *85*, 100858.

Shahjalal, M., Farhana, N., Roy, P., Razzaque, M., Kaur, K., & Hassan, M. M. (2022). A Binary Gray Wolf Optimization algorithm for deployment of Virtual Network Functions in 5G hybrid cloud. *Computer Communications*, *193*, 63–74. DOI: 10.1016/j.comcom.2022.06.041

Shankar, V. (2018). How artificial intelligence (AI) is reshaping retailing. *Journal of Retailing*, *94*(4), vi–xi.

Shao, Z., Gong, Y., Shen, Y., Huang, M., Duan, N., & Chen, W. (2023). *Enhancing retrieval-augmented large language models with iterative retrieval-generation synergy*. arXiv. https://arxiv.org/abs/2305.15294

SHARMA, DR. N. (2024). ARTIFICIAL INTELLIGENCE: LEGAL IMPLICATIONS AND CHALLENGES. Knowledgeable Research A Multidisciplinary Journal, 2(11), 13. DOI: 10.57067/220k4298

Shazeer, N., Mirhoseini, A., Maziarz, K., Davis, A., Le, Q., Hinton, G., & Dean, J. (2017). Outrageously large neural networks: The sparsely-gated mixture-of-experts layer. *arXiv preprint arXiv:1701.06538.*

Shazeer, N., Mirhoseini, A., Maziarz, K., Davis, A., Le, Q., Hinton, G., & Dean, J. (2017). Outrageously Large Neural Networks: The Sparsely-Gated Mixture-of-Experts Layer. arXiv preprint arXiv:1701.06538.

Shen, J., Tenenholtz, N., Hall, J. B., Alvarez-Melis, D., & Fusi, N. (2024). *Tag-LLM:* Repurposing general-purpose LLMs for specialized domains. *arXiv*. https://arxiv.org/abs/2402.05140

Shin, N., Yoo, J.-S., & Kwon, I. G. (2020). Fostering Trust and Commitment in Complex Project Networks through Dedicated Investment in Partnership Management. *Sustainability, 12*(24), 10397. DOI: 10.3390/su122410397

Shneiderman, B. (2022). *Human-centered AI: Ensuring human control in an era of intelligent machines*. Oxford University Press.

Shrinivas S. K. & Shetty P. (2024). Impact of artificial intelligence on business, business operations and strategy. *International Journal of Creative Research Thoughts*. ISSN: 2320- 2882, 12(8), 152-160.

Shukla, A. (n.d.). *From AI agents to self-driving organizations: Technological foundations, applications, and ethical considerations in autonomous AI systems* [Preprint]. ResearchGate., https://doi.org/10.13140/RG.2.2.20847.34729

Singh, K., Kaur, S., & Smiley, C. 2024. "FinQAPT: Empowering Financial Decisions with End-to-End LLM-Driven Question Answering Pipeline." *ICAIF 2024 - 5th ACM International Conference on AI in Finance* 266–73. doi: DOI: 10.1145/3677052.3698682

Singhal, K., Azizi, S., Tu, T., Mahdavi, S. S., Wei, J., Chung, H. W., & Natarajan, V. (2023). Large language models encode clinical knowledge. *Nature, 620*(7972), 172–180. DOI: 10.1038/s41586-023-06291-2 PMID: 37438534

Singh, D. (2024). Navigating the Digital Age: Smart AI Ethics for Seamless Transformation. *International Journal of Advanced Research in Electrical Electronics and Instrumentation Engineering, 13*(11). Advance online publication. DOI: 10.15662/ijareeie.2024.1311001

Sipola, J., Saunila, M., & Ukko, J. (2023). Adopting artificial intelligence in sustainable business. *Journal of Cleaner Production, 426*, 139–197. DOI: 10.1016/j.jclepro.2023.139197

Sklavos, G., Theodossiou, G., Papanikolaou, Z., Karelakis, C., & Ragazou, K. (2024). Environmental, Social, and Governance-Based Artificial Intelligence Governance: Digitalizing Firms' Leadership and Human Resources Management. *Sustainability, 16*(16), 7154. DOI: 10.3390/su16167154

Son, H. (2024, August 9). JPMorgan Chase is giving its employees an AI assistant powered by ChatGPT maker OpenAI. CNBC. https://www.cnbc.com/2024/08/09/jpmorgan-chase-ai-artificial-intelligence-assistant-chatgpt-openai.html

Song, Y., Zhu, Q., Wang, H., & Zheng, Q. (2024). Automated essay scoring and revising based on open-source large language models. *IEEE Transactions on Learning Technologies*. Advance online publication. DOI: 10.1109/TLT.2024.3362475

Stahl, B. C. (2021b). AI Ecosystems for Human Flourishing: The Recommendations. In SpringerBriefs in research and innovation governance (p. 91). Springer International Publishing. DOI: 10.1007/978-3-030-69978-9_7

Stahl, B. C. (2021a). Addressing Ethical Issues in AI. In *SpringerBriefs in research and innovation governance* (p. 55). Springer International Publishing., DOI: 10.1007/978-3-030-69978-9_5

Stahl, B. C., & Eke, D. (2023). The ethics of ChatGPT – Exploring the ethical issues of an emerging technology. *International Journal of Information Management, 74*, 102700. DOI: 10.1016/j.ijinfomgt.2023.102700

Subrahmanyam, S. (2025). AI and Automation: The Intersection of Human Autonomy and Machine Learning. In Tsvasman, L. (Ed.), *Cybernetic Leadership for Sustainable Innovation* (pp. 237–262). IGI Global Scientific Publishing., DOI: 10.4018/979-8-3373-2484-5.ch009

Subrahmanyam, S. (2025). Analytics: Trends, Challenges, and Prospects of Adopting Artificial Intelligence in Human Resource Management. In Kapoor, T., Singh, A., Sahay, K., Kaur, H., & Verma, R. (Eds.), *Sustainable Management Practices for Employee Retention and Recruitment* (pp. 51–72). IGI Global Scientific Publishing., DOI: 10.4018/979-8-3693-8679-8.ch003

Subrahmanyam, S. (2025). Development of Research Design. In Segura, L., Vasconcelos, A., & Slomski, V. (Eds.), *Evolving Designs, Applications, Technological Advances, and the Future of Qualitative Research* (pp. 31–58). IGI Global Scientific Publishing., DOI: 10.4018/979-8-3373-4432-4.ch002

Subrahmanyam, S. (2025). Strategic Collaboration and Partnerships in R&D for Innovation. In Martínez-Falcó, J., Sánchez-García, E., & Marco-Lajara, B. (Eds.), *Research and Development Practices in Innovation* (pp. 283–314). IGI Global Scientific Publishing., DOI: 10.4018/979-8-3373-0812-8.ch010

Su, H., Luo, W., Mehdad, Y., Han, W., Liu, E., Zhang, W., & Zhang, J. (2025, January). LLM-Friendly Knowledge Representation for Customer Support. In *Proceedings of the 31st International Conference on Computational Linguistics: Industry Track* (pp. 496-504).

Sukeda, I., Suzuki, M., Sakaji, H., & Kodera, S. (2024). Development and analysis of medical instruction-tuning for Japanese large language models. *Artificial Intelligence in Health, 1*(2), 107.

Sulaiman, N., & Hamzah, F. (2024). Optimizing Llama 7B for medical question answering: A study on fine-tuning strategies and performance on the MultiMedQA dataset.

Su, P., & Vijay-Shanker, K. (2022). Investigation of improving the pre-training and fine-tuning of BERT model for biomedical relation extraction. *BMC Bioinformatics, 23*(1), 120. Advance online publication. DOI: 10.1186/s12859-022-04641-3 PMID: 35379166

Taddeo, M., McNeish, D., Blanchard, A., & Edgar, E. (2021). Ethical Principles for Artificial Intelligence in National Defence. *Philosophy & Technology, 34*(4), 1707. DOI: 10.1007/s13347-021-00482-3

Taddeo, M., Tsamados, A., Cowls, J., & Floridi, L. (2021). Artificial intelligence and the climate emergency: Opportunities, challenges, and recommendations. *One Earth, 4*(6), 776. DOI: 10.1016/j.oneear.2021.05.018

Taleb, M., & Kadhum, H. J. (2024). The Role of Artificial Intelligence in Promoting the Environmental, Social and Governance (ESG) Practices. In Lecture notes in networks and systems (p. 256). Springer International Publishing. DOI: 10.1007/978-3-031-63717-9_17

Tanveer, S. S., & Rana, Z. (2024). Prioritizing software requirements by combining the usage monitoring and user feedback data. *IEEE Access : Practical Innovations, Open Solutions, 12*, 82825–82841. DOI: 10.1109/ACCESS.2024.3409847

TechTarget. (2023, November 29). *8 use cases for generative AI in finance*. https://www.techtarget.com/searcherp/tip/Use-cases-for-generative-AI-in-finance

Teixeira, A. C., Marar, V., Yazdanpanah, H., Pezente, A., & Ghassemi, M. 2023. "Enhancing Credit Risk Reports Generation Using LLMs: An Integration of Bayesian Networks and Labeled Guide Prompting." *ICAIF 2023 - 4th ACM International Conference on AI in Finance* 340–48. doi: DOI: 10.1145/3604237.3626902

Tejani, A. S., Cook, T. S., Hussain, M., Sippel Schmidt, T., & O'Donnell, K. P. (2024). Integrating and adopting AI in the radiology workflow: A primer for standards and Integrating the Healthcare Enterprise (IHE) profiles. *Radiology, 311*(3), e232653. DOI: 10.1148/radiol.232653

The Coca-Cola Company. (2023). *Coca-Cola invites digital artists to 'Create Real Magic' using new AI platform.* https://www.coca-colacompany.com/media-center/coca-cola-invites-digital-artists-to-create-real-magic-using-new-ai-platform

The New York Times. (2023). *The New York Times sues OpenAI and Microsoft for copyright infringement.* https://www.nytimes.com/2023/12/27/business/media/new-york-times-open-ai-microsoft-lawsuit.html

Topol, E. (2019). *Deep medicine: how artificial intelligence can make healthcare human again.*

Trabelsi, M. A. (2024). The impact of artificial intelligence on economic development. *Journal of Electronic Business & Digital Economics*, *3*(2), 142–155. DOI: 10.1108/JEBDE-10-2023-0022

Turban, E., Pollard, C., & Wood, G. (2021). *Information Technology for Management: Driving digital transformation to increase local and global performance, growth and sustainability* (12th ed.). Wiley.

Tu, T., Schaekermann, M., Palepu, A., Saab, K., Freyberg, J., Tanno, R., & Natarajan, V. (2025). Towards conversational diagnostic artificial intelligence. *Nature*. Advance online publication. DOI: 10.1038/s41586-024-08184-1 PMID: 40205050

U.S. Copyright Office. (2023). *Copyright registration guidance: Works containing material generated by artificial intelligence.* https://www.copyright.gov/ai/ai_policy_guidance.pdf

Uber Engineering. (2024, May 2). *Advancing invoice document processing at Uber using GenAI.* Uber Blog. https://www.uber.com/en-GB/blog/advancing-invoice-document-processing-using-genai/

Unilever. (2023). *New AI lab to boost innovation, technology and collaboration.* https://www.unilever.com/news/news-search/2023/new-ai-lab-to-boost-innovation-technology-and-collaboration/

Unilever. (2024). *Using AI to optimise our end-to-end supply chain.* https://www.unilever.com/news/news-search/2024/utilising-ai-to-redefine-the-future-of-customer-connectivity/

Vaswani, A., Shazeer, N., Parmar, N., Uszkoreit, J., Jones, L., Gomez, A. N., . . . Polosukhin, I. (2017). Attention is all you need. In *Advances in neural information processing systems* (pp. 5998-6008).

Vaswani, A., Shazeer, N., Parmar, N., Uszkoreit, J., Jones, L., Gomez, A. N., Kaiser, L., & Polosukhin, I. (2017). Attention Is All You Need. arXiv preprint arXiv:1706.03762.

Vaswani, A., Shazeer, N., Parmar, N., Uszkoreit, J., Jones, L., Gomez, A. N., Kaiser, Ł., & Polosukhin, I. (2017). Attention is all you need. In *Advances in Neural Information Processing Systems* (Vol. 30). Curran Associates, Inc., https://papers.nips.cc/paper_files/paper/2017/hash/3f5ee243547dee91fbd053c1c4a845aa-Abstract.html

Veale, M., & Edwards, L. (2018). Clarity, surprises, and further questions in the Article 29 Working Party draft guidance on automated decision-making and profiling. *Computer Law & Security Review*, *34*(2), 398–404. DOI: 10.1016/j.clsr.2017.12.002

Vebibina, A., Rusijono, A. M., Muafa, A., Kurniawan, D., Dewantoro, R. S., Asyari, D. N., Widiastuti, S., & Suseno, J. (2025). 11 Key Strategies in Using AI Chat GPT to Develop HOTS-Based Entrepreneurship Questionnaires. *Qubahan Academic Journal*, *5*(1), 33–62. DOI: 10.48161/qaj.v5n1a1134

Veen Van, D., Van Uden, C., Blankemeier, L., Delbrouck, J. B., Aali, A., Bluethgen, C., & Chaudhari, A. S. (2024). Adapted large language models can outperform medical experts in clinical text summarization. *Nature Medicine*, *30*(4), 1134–1142. DOI: 10.1038/s41591-024-02895-5 PMID: 38413730

von Krogh, G., Haefliger, S., & Simons, T. (2023). Generative AI and the future of open innovation. *California Management Review*, *66*(1), 29–49. DOI: 10.1016/j.joitmc.2024.100456

Vyhmeister, E., Castañé, G. G., Östberg, P.-O., & Thevenin, S. (2022). A responsible AI framework: Pipeline contextualisation. *AI and Ethics*, *3*(1), 175. DOI: 10.1007/s43681-022-00154-8

Walmart Inc. (2023). *Walmart outlines growth strategy, unveils next generation supply chain at 2023 Investment Community Meeting*. https://corporate.walmart.com/news/2023/04/04/walmart-outlines-growth-strategy-unveils-next-generation-supply-chain-at-2023-investment-community-meeting

Wang, J., Ding, W., & Zhu, X. (2025). Financial analysis: Intelligent financial data analysis system based on llm-rag. arXiv preprint arXiv:2504.06279.

Wang, X., Xu, X., Liu, Z., & Tong, W. (2023a). Bidirectional Encoder Representations from Transformers-like large language models in patient safety and pharmacovigilance: A comprehensive assessment of causal inference implications. *Experimental Biology and Medicine (Maywood, N.J.)*, *248*(21), 1908–1917. PMID: 38084745

Werder, K., Ramesh, B., & Zhang, R. (2022). Establishing data provenance for responsible artificial intelligence systems. *ACM Transactions on Management Information Systems*, *13*(1), 1–23. DOI: 10.1145/3503488

Wester, J., de Jong, S., Pohl, H., & van Berkel, N. (2024). Exploring people's perceptions of LLM-generated advice. *Computers in Human Behavior: Artificial Humans, 2*(2), 100072. Advance online publication. DOI: 10.1016/j.chbah.2024.100072

Whittlestone, J., Nyrup, R., Alexandrova, A., & Cave, S. (2021). The role and limits of principles in AI ethics: Towards a focus on practice. *Ethics and Information Technology, 23*(3), 329–341. DOI: 10.1145/3306618.3314289

Wilksch, M., & Abramova, O. (2023). PyFin-Sentiment: Towards a Machine-Learning-Based Model for Deriving Sentiment from Financial Tweets. *International Journal of Information Management Data Insights, 3*(1). Advance online publication. DOI: 10.1016/j.jjimei.2023.100171

Workday, Inc. (2024). *Workday Transforms How Companies Hire and Manage Talent with New AI-Powered HR Solutions.* https://newsroom.workday.com/2024-08-01-Workday-Transforms-How-Companies-Hire-and-Manage-Talent-with-New-AI-Powered-HR-Solutions

Wu, S., ... (2025). *Retrieval-augmented generation for natural language processing: A survey.* arXiv. https://arxiv.org/abs/2407.13193

Wu, H., Zhang, D., Li, X., Xu, X., Wu, J., & Liu, Z. (2025). DR-encoder: Encode low-rank gradients with random prior for large language models differentially privately. *Proceedings of the AAAI Conference on Artificial Intelligence, 39*(26), 27706–27714.

Xia, L., & Ma, H. (2024). Enhancing LoRA model serving capacity via adaptive operator scheduling for multi-tenancy on GPU. *IEEE Access : Practical Innovations, Open Solutions, 12*, 160441–160449. DOI: 10.1109/ACCESS.2024.3483250

Xing, F. (2025). Designing Heterogeneous LLM Agents for Financial Sentiment Analysis. *ACM Transactions on Management Information Systems, 16*(1). Advance online publication. DOI: 10.1145/3688399

Xu, Q., Liu, Y., Wang, D., & Huang, S. (2025). Automatic recognition of cross-language classic entities based on large language models. NPJ Herit. Sci., 13(1).

Xu, Z.. (2024). Retrieval-augmented generation with knowledge graphs for customer service question answering. In *Proceedings of the 47th International ACM SIGIR Conference on Research and Development in Information Retrieval (SIGIR '24)* (pp. 2905–2909). Association for Computing Machinery. https://doi.org/10.1145/3626772.3661370

Yammanur, V. (2025). INTEGRATED ENTERPRISE SYSTEMS: LEVERAGING ERP, EDI, AND AI FOR ENHANCED US BUSINESS COMPETITIVENESS. *INTERNATIONAL JOURNAL OF COMPUTER ENGINEERING AND TECHNOLOGY, 16*, 454–466.

Yang, R., Tan, T. F., Lu, W., Thirunavukarasu, A. J., Ting, D. S. W., & Liu, N. (2023). Large language models in health care: Development, applications, and challenges. *Health Care Science, 2*(4), 255–263. DOI: 10.1002/hcs2.67 PMID: 38939520

Yan, L., Sha, L., Zhao, L., Li, Y., Martinez-Maldonado, R., Chen, G., & Gašević, D. (2024). Practical and ethical challenges of large language models in education: A systematic scoping review. *British Journal of Educational Technology, 55*(1), 90–112. DOI: 10.1111/bjet.13391

Yan, S., & Zhu, T. (2025, January). CreditLLM: Constructing Financial AI Assistant for Credit Products using Financial LLM and Few Data. In *Proceedings of the Joint Workshop of the 9th Financial Technology and Natural Language Processing (FinNLP), the 6th Financial Narrative Processing (FNP), and the 1st Workshop on Large Language Models for Finance and Legal (LLMFinLegal)* (pp. 141-152).

Yazdanipour, M. (2024, September 10). AI technology in J.P. Morgan Chase & Co. LinkedIn. https://www.linkedin.com/pulse/ai-technology-jp-morgan-chase-co-marzieh-yazdanipour-ah7we

Yee, L., Deveau, R., & Reis, S. (2024). An unconstrained future: How generative AI could reshape B2B sales. https://www.mckinsey.com/capabilities/growth-marketing-and-sales/our-insights/an-unconstrained-future-how-generative-ai-could-reshape-b2b-sales

ZBrain. (n.d.). *AI in record-to-report: Scope, integration, use cases, challenges and future outlook*. Retrieved June 7, 2024, from https://zbrain.ai/ai-in-record-to-report/

Zhang, L. J., Chen, H., He, S., Li, C., Chen, J., Zhang, H., & Du, W. (2025). COSIS: An AI-enabled digital transformation framework integrating large language models and key performance indicators. In *Lecture Notes in Computer Science* (pp. 74–99). Springer. DOI: 10.1007/978-3-031-77000-5_6

Zhang, X., Chen, Z. Z., Ye, X., Yang, X., Chen, L., Wang, W. Y., & Petzold, L. R. (2025). Unveiling the impact of coding data instruction fine-tuning on Large Language Models reasoning. *Proceedings of the AAAI Conference on Artificial Intelligence, 39*(24), 25949–25957.

Zhan, Y., Xiong, Y., Han, R., Lam, H. K. S., & Blome, C. (2024). The impact of artificial intelligence adoption for business-to-business marketing on shareholder reaction: A social actor perspective. *International Journal of Information Management, 76*, 102768. DOI: 10.1016/j.ijinfomgt.2024.102768

Zhao, J., Wang, T., Yatskar, M., Ordonez, V., & Chang, K.-W. (2018). Gender bias in coreference resolution: Evaluation and debiasing methods. In Proceedings of the 2018 conference of the North American chapter of the Association for Computational Linguistics: Human language technologies, volume 2 (short papers) (pp. 15–20). Association for Computational Linguistics. DOI: 10.18653/v1/N18-2003

Zhao, R., ... (2023). *Retrieving multimodal information for augmented generation: A survey*. arXiv. https://arxiv.org/abs/2303.10868

Zheng, L., Chiang, W. L., Zhang, H., Wu, S., Zhuang, J., Fan, L., . . . Gonzalez, J. E. (2023). Judging LLM-as-a-judge with MT-Bench and Chatbot Arena. *arXiv preprint arXiv:2306.05685*

Zheng, W., Gong, G., Tian, J., Lu, S., Wang, R., Yin, Z., Li, X., & Yin, L. (2023). Design of a modified transformer architecture based on relative position coding. *International Journal of Computational Intelligence Systems, 16*. Advance online publication. DOI: 10.1007/s44196-023-00345-z

Zhu, F., Liu, Z., Feng, F., Wang, C., Li, M., & Chua, T. S. 2024. "TAT-LLM: A Specialized Language Model for Discrete Reasoning over Financial Tabular and Textual Data." *ICAIF 2024 - 5th ACM International Conference on AI in Finance* (Table 1):310–18. doi: DOI: 10.1145/3677052.3698685

Zhu, X., Xie, Y., Liu, Y., Li, Y., & Hu, W. (2025). *Knowledge graph-guided retrieval augmented generation*. arXiv. https://arxiv.org/abs/2502.06864

Zhui, L., Fenghe, L., Xuehu, W., Qining, F., & Wei, R. (2024). Ethical considerations and fundamental principles of large language models in medical education. *Journal of Medical Internet Research, 26*, e60083. Advance online publication. DOI: 10.2196/60083 PMID: 38971715

Zhu, Z., Zhao, Q., Li, J., Ge, Y., Ding, X., Gu, T., Zou, J., Lv, S., Wang, S., & Yang, J.-J. (2024). Comparative analysis of large language models in Chinese medical named entity recognition. *Bioengineering (Basel, Switzerland), 11*(10). PMID: 39451358

Zubiaga, A. (2024). Natural language processing in the era of large language models. *Frontiers in Artificial Intelligence, 6*, 1350306. Advance online publication. DOI: 10.3389/frai.2023.1350306 PMID: 38282904

About the Contributors

Sherif Ismail: Philanthropist | Professor | Entrepreneur | Author | AI business Mentor | Global Trainer | Researcher With over 25 years of experience in the software industry, Dr. Sherif Ismail brings a wealth of expertise and a proven track record in Business Information Systems. His comprehensive skill set, and practical insights have established him as a seasoned professional in the field. Throughout his career, he has excelled in various roles, including developer, designer, analyst, project manager, and quality expert. This extensive experience has honed his abilities and equipped him with a deep understanding of software engineering principles. In addition to his remarkable industry background, Dr. Ismail has made significant contributions to the academic community. He has held prestigious positions as a lecturer at Maritime Academy for Science and technology, the University of Hail, assistant professor at the University of Dammam, Currently, he serves as a Professor at the American University, and professor at Umm Al-Qura University. where his expertise is highly valued. Dr. Ismail's research interests encompass several cutting-edge domains, including Artificial Intelligence (AI), Natural Language Processing, Knowledge Management, and Sentiment Analysis. His innovative work in these areas has garnered attention and recognition from peers and professionals alike. As a result, he has published over 100 research papers across various domains, demonstrating his intellectual prowess and dedication to advancing knowledge. By seamlessly integrating his theoretical expertise with his extensive practical experience, Dr. Ismail has solidified his position as an accomplished software engineering professional. His comprehensive skill set, remarkable research contributions, and academic qualifications make him an invaluable asset to both the industry and academia.

***

Andi Subhan Amir is a faculty member at the Department of Communication Science, Faculty of Social and Political Sciences, Hasanuddin University. He earned his Bachelor's degree in Communication Science from Universitas Hasanuddin, followed by a Master's degree in Mass Communication from the university's Graduate School. He completed his doctoral studies at the Faculty of Communication Science, Universitas Padjadjaran. In addition to his academic role as a lecturer and researcher, ASA—as he is commonly known—is actively involved in several professional organizations, including ISKI (Ikatan Sarjana Komunikasi Indonesia), ASPIKOM (Asosiasi Pendidikan Ilmu Komunikasi), and APEPINDO (Asosiasi Peneliti dan Penulis Indonesia). He has authored numerous scholarly works, including books, journal articles, and conference proceedings, published both nationally and internationally. His publications are accessible through his Google Scholar, SINTA and Scopus profiles

Chavva Ravi Kishore Reddy received B.Tech (I.T) degree in 2010, M.Tech (CS) in 2013. He is working as Assistant Professor at Vignan's Foundation for Science, Technology and Research, Guntur, Andhra Pradesh, India. His research interests include Machine Learning, Deep Learning, Natural Language Processing.

Chinna Gopi Simhadri received his B.Tech degree in Computer Science and Engineering from JNTU Kakinada University, India in 2010. He completed his M.Tech, in Computer Science from the KL University, India in 2012. Later, he is pursued his Ph.D in Computer Science and Engineering, VIT-AP University, Andhra Pradesh, India. Currently, he serves as an Assistant Professor at the Department of Computer Science and Engineering, VFSTR Deemed to be University. His research interests include Digital Image Processing, Machine Learning and Deep Learning.

Elyson De La Cruz is a seasoned cybersecurity executive with over two decades of experience. He is the Chief Information Security Officer (CISO) at Imagine Believe Realize, a company specializing in software development for US government agencies. Dr. De La Cruz also holds concurrent faculty appointments with various universities in the United States. With a network, system, and cybersecurity engineering background, he has designed and managed sensitive communication systems providing voice, video, and data services across multiple continents. He advises executive management on information technology programs affecting operational missions and strategic goals and is a trusted advisor on technology roadmaps for external customers. He has oversight over IT and Cybersecurity departments, focusing on training, mentorship, and leadership. He has presented at IEEE conferences and published in academic journals. Dr. De La Cruz holds a PhD in Information Technology, an MS in Management Information Systems, an

MA in Computer Resources and Information Management, an MBA, and over 40 professional certifications in cybersecurity, information technology, and systems engineering.

Yashodhan Karulkar is a seasoned marketing professional with a robust career spanning over two decades in both the academic and corporate sectors. Since September 2016, he has been serving as a full-time faculty member at NMIMS University, where he plays a pivotal role in shaping the future of MBA Tech students. As the Area Chair for Marketing, Dr. Karulkar also mentors the Marketing Club, named 4C, actively engaging students in real-world marketing challenges. His corporate experience includes nearly 20 years in leadership roles with some of the most prominent companies in India, such as Birla Sun Life,Max New York Life,Standard Chartered Bank,Airtel and Wipro. Dr. Karulkar's expertise spans the entire marketing spectrum, including Product Management, Sales and Distribution, Relationship Management, Customer Service, and Business Development. He has managed large Pan-India sales teams, leading over 300 employees to successfully achieve critical business and profitability goals.

Early Ridho Kismawadi, S.E.I, MA is a lecturer at the Department of Islamic Banking, Faculty of Islamic Economics and Business IAIN Langsa, Aceh, Indonesia, he has been a lecturer since 2013, he has completed a doctoral program in 2018 majoring in Sharia economics at the State Islamic University of North Sumatra. He was appointed head of the Islamic economics Law study program (2023) Islamic banking study program (2020) and Islamic financial management study program (2019) at Langsa State Islamic Institute (IAIN Langsa), Aceh, Indonesia. His research interests include financial economics, applied econometrics, Islamic economics, banking, and finance. He has published articles in national and international journals. In addition, he is also a reviewer of several reputable international journals such as Finance Research Letters, Financial Innovation, Cogent Business &; Management, Journal of Islamic Accounting and Business Research. He has also presented his papers at various local and international seminars. Dr. Early Ridho Kismawadi, S.E.I, MA, can be contacted at kismawadi@iainlangsa.ac.id.

Muhammad Tahmid Nur +6281242620812 tahmidn174@gmail.com Jl. Agatis no 66, Salubulo, Kota Palopo Sharia Department and Law at the Faculty of Sharia Universitas Islam Negeri Palopo Beginning with a Bachelor's degree in the Department of Comparative Schools of Thought and Law at the Faculty of Sharia, IAIN Syarif Hidayatullah Jakarta (1993–1997), his higher education path started. He then sought a Master's degree in Islamic Law/Sharia at the Postgraduate Program of IAIN Alauddin Makassar (1999–2001), and then finished his Doctoral Program

(Ph.D.) in Islamic Law/Sharia at UIN Alauddin Makassar in 2013. Since 2005, he has been a permanent lecturer at UIN Palopo. Over his more than 20-year academic career, he has been given various leadership responsibilities by the university rector, including: Vice Dean for Student Affairs and Collaboration at the Faculty of Islamic Economics and Business (2015–2019), Chairperson of the Senate of UIN Palopo (2021–2024), and presently serving as Dean of the Faculty of Sharia for the 2024–2027 period. Before to his time at UIN Palopo, he taught as a part-time lecturer at many universities, including UMI, UNISMUH Makassar, and PERGIS Takalar. Outside of school, he has been engaged in community and professional groups as well. From 2003 to 2004, he was Deputy Chair of the Indonesian Ulema Council (MUI) of East Luwu; from 2003 to 2015, he was Chair of the Tarjih Assembly of Muhammadiyah in East Luwu and Palopo; and from 2015 onward, he has been Chair of the Muhammadiyah Regional Leadership Board of Palopo City (2015–2027). He has written several academic papers and articles on Islamic Criminal Law, Fiqh, and the Foundations of Islamic Jurisprudence (Ushul al-Fiqh), and he is often asked to serve as a resource person at different academic conferences on Islamic law and jurisprudence

Shubhamkumar Pandit Being a researcher and developer, Shubhamkumar is interested in knowledge retrieval and decision support based on artificial intelligence greatly. He also puts an emphasis on transferring research into practice covering scalable and modifiable AI applications. He is determined to make contributions to interdisciplinary discussions that will define the future of the intelligent systems and its contributions in developing information accessibility and innovation in business.

Sonukumar Pandit is a full-stack developer and a machine learning enthusiast whose core skills lie in Java, Python and MERN stack. He has worked on the breakthrough projects such as AI-based healthcare providers and smart inventory management. Having secured a place among the top few at hackathons nationwide, Sonukumar is a combination of both technical skills and creativity through problem-solving. He has experience in backend development, deep learning and real-time web applications. He is an enthusiast of technology and the benefits it can bring to the world and as such, he works on the development of solutions that matter.

Pranjit Kr Paul, Faculty of Management and Commerce at ICFAI University, Tripura, is among the youngest researchers at the university. His research primarily focuses on Health Economics, Educational Studies, Entrepreneurship Development, and Rural Development.

Ravikumar R. Natarajan is an experienced academician with over 12+ years of teaching and research expertise across institutions in India, the UAE, and the

Maldives. He currently serves as an Assistant Professor at Marwadi University, Rajkot, specializing in Machine Learning, Recommender Systems, and AI-driven applications in healthcare and security. He holds a Ph.D. in Machine Learning and Recommender Systems from Amity University, Jaipur, a Master of Engineering in CSE from VMRF University, Salem, and a Bachelor of Engineering in CSE from Anna University. He also has a MiniMBA from the Swiss eLearning Institute. Dr. Ravikumar has authored more than 8+ multiple SCIE/Scopus-indexed journal articles, 25+ IEEE/Springer conference papers, and co-authored a book on Artificial Intelligence. He has also published 9 patents and contributed 10+ book chapters in emerging domains such as Federated Learning, Blockchain, and Digital Twins for IGI Global, Wiley and Springer publisher. He actively mentors students through initiatives like the Research Activities Club (RAC) and Student Research Internship Training (SRIT), promoting innovation and research culture.

Ravikumar R N is an experienced educator with 11+ years of teaching in Computer Science across India and overseas. Currently an Assistant Professor at Marwadi University, Rajkot, he specializes in Advanced Java, Machine Learning, Data Science, and AI. He holds a Mini MBA from the Swiss eLearning Institute (2015), an M.E. in Computer Science Engineering from VMRF University (2013), and a B.E. from Anna University (2010). Completed PhD at Amity University, Jaipur, he is dedicated to research, professional development, and advancing education through technology.

Rismawati is a distinguished academic and consultant with a robust focus on sustainability reporting. She currently holds the position of lecturer and Head of the Quality Assurance Institute at Universitas Muhammadiyah Palopo, where she has been pivotal in ensuring the quality of university processes and outputs since February 2020. Additionally, she serves as an Assurer for Sustainability Reporting at the National Center for Sustainability Reporting in Jakarta, specializing in the evaluation of sustainability reports for mining companies across Indonesia. Her academic qualifications are extensive, comprising a Bachelor's degree in Economics and Accounting, a Master's degree in Accounting Science, and a Doctorate in Accounting from Universitas Brawijaya, Malang. Rismawati is also a certified specialist in sustainability reporting, risk management, and tax planning, holding several prestigious certifications including Certified Sustainability Reporting Specialist (CSRS), Certified Risk Management Practitioner (CRMP), Certified Management Accountant (CMA) and Certified Enterprise Risk Analysis (CERA). In her professional capacity, she has provided consultancy services in financial management and tax compliance for companies such as PT. Reski Barito Timur and PT. Helay Raya. Furthermore, she has authored multiple publications on

Social Accounting, Sustainability Accounting, Management Accounting and CSR, contributing significantly to the academic community. Her interests in reading, writing, and travel reflect her commitment to lifelong learning and professional growth in her field.

Pearlyn Rodrigues is a dedicated professional who is pursuing her MBA Tech program at SVKM's NMIMS Mukesh Patel School of Technology Management and Engineering, Mumbai, specializing in Data science for her B.Tech as well as Finance and Business Intelligence and Analytics for her MBA Tech. With a strong foundation in both technology and business, she brings a unique blend of expertise to the fields of finance and technology. Pearlyn has a keen interest in research and analytics, demonstrated through her work on research projects.

Aarthi S is a dedicated Assistant Professor in Computer Science with over six years of teaching experience. She is currently pursuing her Ph.D. at Marwadi University, Gujarat, and holds an M.Phil. and MCA from Bharathiar University, Tamil Nadu. Throughout her academic career, Aarthi has specialized in programming languages such as C++, Java, and C, and contributed to research in recommender systems and AI-related data privacy. She has published journal articles, contributed to book chapters, and actively participated in technical workshops. Known for her student mentorship and engagement in academic events, Aarthi remains committed to fostering innovation and excellence in computer science education.

Mohamad Saleh has been passionate about teaching for many years and advocates for lifelong continuous learning. He worked in database management, development, and technical support for over a decade in the retail, transportation, and Oil & Gas sectors. Saleh is passionate about data: preserving and producing insights to benefit the industry and the customers served. Currently, Saleh is a full-time faculty at the University of Colorado in Denver, specializing in teaching database systems, systems analysis and design, and programming languages. He is also a guest lecturer at the University of Washington Information School, specializing in teaching SQL and data visualization. Saleh also served as a grant principal investigator, program manager, and course lead while serving as a full-time faculty at Grand Canyon University in Phoenix, Arizona, teaching courses in Computer Science, Cyber Security, and Information Technology divisions. SPECIALIZATIONS Data Science Database systems Programming Languages Cyber Security EDUCATION Ph.D., Business Administration, Argosy University, 2016 Bachelor of Computer Science, Amman University, 2002 Master of Science in Computer Science, Colorado Technical University, 2010 Master of Science in Business Analytics, Grand Canyon University, 2021

Rustan Santaria rustans1123@gmail.com +6281355620100 Institut Agama Islam Negeri Palopo Jl. Agatis Balandai, Kota Palopo, 91914, Sulawesi Selatan, Indonesia Prof. Rustan has held various leadership positions, including Head Officer of Language Service Senter of State Islamic Institute of Palopo, Head of English Language Study Program of State Islamic Institute of Palopo, Deputy Chanselor at Universitas Cokroaminoto Palopo 2009-2012, Deputy Chanselor at State Islamic Institute of Palopo 2012 - 2019. His academic interests center on language teaching and learning, language studies, and cultural studies. He is actively involved in professional organizations such as TEFLIN, WALS, ALSI, ALTI, ADI, ADRI, and MLI. In addition to her teaching and research roles, he contributes as a Fasilitator and Teacher Trainer in Iplementasi Kurikulum Merdeka Berbasis Komunitas (IKM-BK), national academic quality assurance programs, including PPG.

Sai Yellaiah Simhadri Accomplished Data and AI Leader with 18+ years of experience architecting and executing enterprise-wide data solutions that drive business transformation. Proven track record in leading cross-functional teams and delivering complex, multi-million-dollar data initiatives across global organizations. Strategic expertise spans Data Architecture, Data Governance, AI/ML integration, and Business Intelligence. Adept at designing modern data platforms—including Data Lakes, Data Warehouses, and Customer Data Hubs—across both cloud and on-premise environments. Hands-on leadership in implementing scalable ETL/ELT frameworks using tools like Informatica, Talend, SSIS, AWS DMS, and GoldenGate. Deep technical proficiency with Redshift, Oracle, SQL Server, and MongoDB, combined with advanced SQL and PL/SQL expertise. Visionary in establishing enterprise-wide Data Quality frameworks, MDM solutions, and integrating systems like Salesforce and Oracle ERP. Experience managing CI/CD pipelines, Agile delivery, and version control across diverse data environments. Recognized for strategic thinking, stakeholder engagement, and aligning data initiatives with core business objectives. Successfully reduced data pipeline complexity, enhanced data accessibility, and enabled actionable insights through platforms such as Tableau, OBIEE, MicroStrategy, and SAP BO

Arina Singhai is a dedicated professional who is pursuing her MBA Tech program at SVKM's NMIMS Mukesh Patel School of Technology Management and Engineering, Mumbai, specializing in Data science for her B.Tech as well as Finance and Business Intelligence and Analytics for her MBA Tech. With a strong foundation in both technology and business, she brings a unique blend of expertise to the fields of finance and technology. Arina has a keen interest in research and analytics, demonstrated through her work on research projects.

Venkatrama Phani Kumar Sistla received the Ph.D. degree in computer science and engineering from JNTU, Hyderabad, Telangana. He is currently a Professor and the Head of the Department of Computer Science and Engineering. He has more than 15 years of teaching experience. He has published more than 100+ research articles in reputed national and international conferences and journals. His current research interests include Digital Image Processing, Text Analytics, Pattern Recognition, and Medical Imaging.

Satya Subrahmanyam is a distinguished academic leader, researcher, and institutional strategist with over 27 years of experience in higher education, leadership, and research management. He holds two PhDs and a Postdoctoral qualification from the Polytechnic Institute of Leiria, Portugal. Currently serving as Professor and Dean (Research) at Holy Spirit University of Kaslik (USEK), Lebanon, he spearheads research initiatives that enhance academic excellence and institutional reputation. He played a pivotal role in the development of the Catholic University in Erbil, Kurdistan, where he established new departments, led research programs, and collaborated on international educational projects. As a founding member and Managing Partner of Vignan Institute of Technology and Management, India, he contributed to its transformation into a premier institution. With expertise in AI-driven business strategies, HR analytics, and leadership in technology adoption, he has published extensively, guided PhD research, and led training programs in corporate and academic settings.

Supriadi is a dedicated lecturer in the Informatics Study Program at the Faculty of Computer Engineering, Universitas Cokroaminoto Palopo. He earned his Bachelor's degree in Islamic Studies (S.Ag) from the State Institute of Islamic Studies (IAIN) Ujung Pandang and later pursued a Master's degree in Education (M.Pd) at Universitas Negeri Makassar. His academic expertise lies in the intersection of religious studies and business ethics, which he applies in his teaching of Islamic Studies and Professional & Business Ethics within the Informatics Faculty. Beyond teaching, Supriadi is actively engaged in research, particularly in the fields of Augmented Reality (AR) and Sharia Tourism. His work focuses on integrating Islamic knowledge with Information Technology, aiming to develop innovative educational tools that enhance the learning experience. By combining religious perspectives with digital advancements, he seeks to bridge the gap between Islamic education and modern technology, making complex subjects more accessible and engaging. Through his research and academic contributions, Supriadi aspires to empower students and professionals with ethical and technological insights that align with Islamic values. His work continues to contribute to the evolving landscape of technology-assisted learning

Index

A

B

C

D

E

F

G

H

I

K

L

M

N

O

P

R

S

T

Z

www.ingramcontent.com/pod-product-compliance
Lightning Source LLC
LaVergne TN
LVHW062330300926
849161LV00007B/1641